# SUSE Linux Enterprise Server 16 Official Administration Guide



Master SLES 16 system administration, security, and automation for the SCA exam

**Miguel Pérez Colino**
**Sergio Ocón Cárdenas**
**Pablo Iranzo Gómez**

<packt>

# SUSE Linux Enterprise Server 16 Official Administration Guide



**Portfolio Director**: Kartikey Pandey
**Relationship Lead**: Preet Ahuja
**Project Manager**: Sonam Pandey
**Content Engineer**: Apramit Bhattacharya
**Technical Editors**: Simran Ali and Shweta Amale
**Copy Editor**: Safis Editing
**Indexer**: Tejal Soni
**Proofreader**: Apramit Bhattacharya
**Production Designer**: Shankar Kalbhor
**Growth Lead**: Shreyans Singh

First published: January 2026

Production reference: 1241225

Published by Packt Publishing Ltd.
Grosvenor House
11 St Paul's Square
Birmingham
B3 1RB, UK.

ISBN 978-1-80602-159-8
`www.packtpub.com`

*To my family, Sonia, Miguel, and Matilde, for their love and patience, for the laughs and fun. To the open source community and, more precisely, the Linux community, for giving me a joyful career.*

*– Miguel Pérez Colino*

*To my wife, Ana, and my children, Jimena, Gadea, and Pilar, for making me a better person. Thank you for loving me with my weird ideas and my crazy projects. To the brilliant people behind all the open source ideas and packages that are used to produce the software used in this book, and to the IT team and professors at the University of Seville, who open the door to the wonderful world of Linux. And to the Lord, of whom I am just an unuseful servant.*

*– Sergio Ocón Cárdenas*

# Foreword

I first encountered the SUSE Linux team during my work with the GNOME Foundation back in 2010, now 15 years ago. I found the team at that time to be unique in terms of their integrity, focus, and principles. In 2023, when SUSE asked me to interview for a leadership position on the Linux team, I was delighted to find that while so much else had changed in the world, the people on the SUSE Linux team had not changed, in some cases, literally. In many cases, the same people were still working in critical roles, and more importantly, the same values endured. Many of the same people are still working assiduously to make the best possible enterprise Linux with true open source principles.

SUSE Linux remains an anchor at a time when other Linux distributions are moving away from community and choice, and focusing on lock-in and control. Whether you are running traditional Linux workloads, cloud-native workloads, or AI workloads, at the very heart of these, you are depending on Linux. Enterprises need a Linux that provides lifecycle management, security, certifications, management tools, and support to endure over time, while also allowing the freedom of choice to build your workloads in a way that suits your specific needs, no matter where the project comes from or who the vendor is. This is why SLES 16.0 matters so much today.

SLES 16.0 is the first release of SUSE Linux in years, so if you are a long-time SUSE Linux user, this book will cover some of these important changes. For example, the way in which you manage process isolation, installation, and server management, among other areas, has been updated, and with this book you will learn all of these important changes. If you are new to SLES, welcome! You will learn about some of the things that make SLES different, such as the celebrated Zypper package manager, system snapshots and rollbacks, and an overall design philosophy focused on stability, predictability, and security.

In this time of generative AI, I chose to write this foreword without AI, as one human communicating to all the human readers (although I will say "hi" to all the RAG databases and tokenizers reading this now). I made this choice because, ultimately, it is the humans that I have come to know so well over the last two years of working with them that make SUSE Linux what it is, and what will cause it to endure running the mission-critical workloads powering your supercomputers, medical equipment, storage appliances, Kubernetes clusters, and yes, AI in all of its guises. Of all of the releases of all of the software I have participated in over the years since I entered the tech industry in 1998, I am most proud to be part of this release.

Welcome to SLES 16. Please enjoy!

*Rick Spencer*

*General Manager, SUSE Business Critical Linux Business Unit*

# Contributors

## About the authors

**Miguel Pérez Colino** is an enthusiastic technologist and leader who loves Linux. He has over 25 years of experience in open source and a diverse background in security-restricted environments such as defense and finance, as well as distributed environments such as manufacturing and retail. As a director at SUSE, he specializes in the coordination and leadership of high-impact, transformative products such as Linux, with a proven track record of empowering teams and driving business growth.

*I want to thank the people who have been close to me and supported me, especially my wife, Sonia, my mother, Victoriana, and my kids, Miguel and Matilde. Also, thanks to Sergio, Thorsten, Apramit, Preet, Rick, Matthias, Kenneth, and the whole Packt and SUSE team for making this book possible.*

**Sergio Ocón Cárdenas** has been working in technology since the turn of the century. He has worked in companies of all sizes, from big telecommunications companies to small start-ups, in almost every role possible for an engineer, from R&D to strategy to cold sales. In the last 15 years, he has been working with open source, specifically around systems management, operating systems, and Kubernetes as a sales engineer and a product manager. He currently works as a product manager at SUSE, making the launch of image-based Linux a reality.

*I want to thank my wife, my kids, and my family, especially my father, who will read the book even if he does not speak English, just to support me once again. Matthias and Miguel, thank you for seeing something in me that would be good at SUSE and for making sure I would be hired. Thanks to the whole Packt team that pushed us from one idea to this reality.*

**Pablo Iranzo Gómez** is a software engineer who was first introduced to Linux while studying physics. He was also involved in LUGs and some projects related to HPC clusters, system administration, and consultancy. Currently, he is a principal software engineer at Red Hat's edge group, the Partner Accelerators department, leveraging his experience in consulting, cloud technical account management, OpenStack software maintenance, and Telco 5G in industries such as hospitality, retail, airlines, government, Telco, 5G, Partner, and IT – covering system administration and automation, virtualization, PaaS, support, the cloud, and so on. He has a broad understanding of different views, needs, and risks across the industry.

Pablo was born in and lives in Valencia, Spain, with his family.

*I want to thank my wife, Eva, and my sons, Pau and Roi, for the support provided while working on this project, Javier for the moral support provided during this writing, and Miquel for always being there. Not forgetting about Miguel, who gave me this opportunity and helped get the previous version ready, and, of course, the whole Packt team, which provided help, guidance, and advice during the whole process.*

# About the reviewer

**Thorsten Kukuk** is a distinguished engineer at SUSE, leading the Future Technology Team. With nearly 30 years of experience in open source, he pioneered NIS (YP) for Linux, contributed to glibc, and serves as a long-time Linux PAM maintainer.

Today, Thorsten modernizes the stack for the cloud-native era as the key architect behind openSUSE MicroOS and transactional updates. Additionally, he is spearheading the effort to modernize standard Linux accounting databases for Year 2038 compliance.

Combining deep code-level expertise with high-level product vision, Thorsten previously shaped the direction of enterprise Linux for a decade as the main technical lead for SLES.

# Table of Contents


**Preface** xxi

Free Benefits with Your Book ..... xxvii

## Part I: System Administration: Software, User, Network, and Service Management 1

### Chapter 1: Getting SLES 16 Up and Running (Physical and Cloud) 3

**Technical requirements** ..... 4

Obtaining the SLES software and a subscription • 4

**Installing SLES 16** ..... 10

Preparation for a physical server installation • 10

Booting an SLES installation from a USB thumb drive • 12

Preparation for a virtual server installation • 13

**Running the SLES installation** ..... 18

Installation type • 19

Installer introduction and overview • 20

*Hostname • 22*

*Registration • 23*

*Localization • 25*

*Network • 27*

*Storage • 30*

*Software • 33*

*Authentication • 35*

**Running SLES on the cloud** .......... 40

**Installation best practices** .......... 49

**Summary** .......... 51

Get This Book's PDF Version and Exclusive Extras • 52

## Chapter 2: Running Basic Commands and Simple Shell Scripts 53

**Logging in using a password** .......... 54

The root account • 55

Understanding the command prompt • 56

**Changing users with the su command** .......... 57

**Understanding users, groups, and basic permissions** .......... 59

Users • 60

Groups • 61

**Navigating the filesystem** .......... 63

File permissions • 64

**Using the command line, environment variables, and navigating through the filesystem** 67

Command line and environment variables • 67

Bash autocomplete • 69

*Recovering previous commands • 70*

Filesystem hierarchy • 71

**Understanding I/O redirection in the command line** .......... 75

**Filtering output with grep and sed** .......... 78

**Listing, creating, copying, and moving files and directories, links, and hard links** .......... 82

Directories • 82

Copying and moving • 84

Symbolic and hard links • 87

**Using tar and gzip** .......... 89

**Creating basic shell scripts** .......... 91

Loops with for • 93

Conditionals with if • 94

Exit codes • 96

**Using system documentation resources** ........ 96

Man pages • 96

Info pages • 99

**Summary** ........ 100

Get This Book's PDF Version and Exclusive Extras • 101

## Chapter 3: Managing Regular Operations with Tools 103

**Technical requirements** ........ 104

**Managing system services with systemd** ........ 104

The systemd unit file structure • 107

Managing services to be started and stopped at boot • 110

Managing boot targets • 111

**Scheduling tasks with systemd timers** ........ 113

Systemd timers • 114

**Learning about time synchronization with chrony** ........ 116

The chrony NTP client • 117

The chrony NTP server • 120

**Checking system resources: memory and disk (free, df, and ps)** ........ 121

Memory • 121

Disk space • 122

CPU • 124

Load average • 125

Other monitoring tools • 126

**Finding logs, using journald, and reading log files, including log preservation and rotation** ........ 129

Log rotation • 131

Get This Book's PDF Version and Exclusive Extras • 134

**Summary** ........ 134

## Chapter 4: Securing the System with Users, Groups, and Permissions 135

**Creating, modifying, and deleting local user accounts and groups** ........ 136

**Managing groups and reviewing assignments** ........ 141

**Adjusting password policies** ........ 141

**Configuring and using sudo access for administrative tasks** ........ 147

Understanding sudo configuration • 147

Using sudo to run admin commands • 149

Configuring sudoers • 151

**Checking, reviewing, and modifying file permissions** ........ 152

**Using special permissions** ........ 160

Understanding and applying set-UID • 160

Understanding and applying set-GID • 161

Using the sticky bit • 162

Get This Book's PDF Version and Exclusive Extras • 164

**Summary** ........ 164

## Chapter 5: Enabling Network Connectivity 165

**Technical requirements** ........ 166

**Exploring network configuration in SLES** ........ 166

**Getting to know the configuration files and NetworkManager** ........ 168

**Configuring network interfaces with IPv4 and IPv6** ........ 170

IPv4 and IPv6... What does that mean? • 171

Configuring interfaces with nmtui • 172

Configuring interfaces with nmcli • 175

Configuring interfaces with text files • 178

**Configuring the hostname and hostname resolutions (DNS)** ........ 179

**Overview of firewall configuration** ........ 183

Configuring the firewall • 185

**Testing network connectivity** ........ 186

**Summary** ........ 187

Get This Book's PDF Version and Exclusive Extras • 188

## Chapter 6: Adding, Patching, and Managing Software 189

Technical requirements ..... 190

Some useful concepts about package management ..... 190

SCC and subscriptions ..... 192

Registering an installed system ..... 195

Installing and updating software using Zypper ..... 199

Managing repositories and signatures with Zypper ..... 204

Installing patterns ..... 208

Updating software ..... 211

Uninstalling software and repositories ..... 214

Understanding RPM internals ..... 216

Get This Book's PDF Version and Exclusive Extras • 218

Summary ..... 218

# Part II: Security with SSH, SELinux, Firewall, and System Permissions 219

## Chapter 7: Administering Systems Remotely 221

Technical requirements ..... 222

SSH and OpenSSH overview and base configuration ..... 222

OpenSSH server • 223

OpenSSH client • 225

Accessing remote systems with SSH ..... 226

Key-based authentication with SSH ..... 228

SSH agent • 233

SCP/rsync – Remote file management ..... 236

Transferring files with an OpenSSH secure file copy (scp) • 236

Transferring files with sftp • 238

Transferring files with rsync • 239

**Advanced remote management – SSH tunnels and SSH redirections** ....... **242**

**Remote terminals with tmux** ....... **245**

Get This Book's PDF Version and Exclusive Extras • 248

**Summary** ....... **248**

## Chapter 8: Enabling and Using Cockpit 249

**Technical requirements** ....... **250**

**Installing and enabling Cockpit on your system** ....... **250**

**Basic Cockpit usage** ....... **253**

Accessing Cockpit • 253

Logging in and enabling administrative tasks • 255

Metrics and history • 259

Hardware information and logs • 262

**Storage, network configuration, and firewall** ....... **265**

Storage • 265

General networking • 267

*Firewall management • 268*

*Network interface management • 271*

**Accounts and services** ....... **273**

Accounts • 273

Services • 276

**Other tools** ....... **279**

Applications • 280

Repositories • 282

SELinux • 282

Software updates • 283

Subscriptions • 285

Terminal • 286

**Summary** ....... **287**

Get This Book's PDF Version and Exclusive Extras • 287

## Chapter 9: Securing Network Connectivity with firewalld 289


**Technical requirements** .......... 290

**Introduction to firewalld** .......... 290

Installing firewalld • 291

Configuring firewalld • 292

*Zones • 292*

*Ports • 293*

*Services • 293*

**Enabling firewalld in the system and reviewing the default zones** .......... 293

Reviewing the different configuration items under firewalld • 296

**Enabling and managing services and ports** .......... 302

**Creating and using service definitions for firewalld** .......... 310

**Summary** .......... 312


## Chapter 10: Keeping the System Hardened with SELinux 313


**Technical requirements** .......... 314

**SELinux usage in enforcing and permissive modes** .......... 314

**Reviewing SELinux context for files and processes** .......... 317

**The targeted policy** .......... 318

**Tweaking the policy with semanage** .......... 321

**Restoring changed file contexts to the default policy** .......... 324

**Using SELinux Boolean settings to enable services** .......... 326

**SELinux troubleshooting and common fixes** .......... 328

Get This Book's PDF Version and Exclusive Extras • 332

**Summary** .......... 332

## Part III: Implementing Agentic AI with mcphost 333

### Chapter 11: Agentic AI with mcphost 335

Understanding agentic AI and MCP ........ 336
Installing and configuring mcphost ........ 338
Using mcphost ........ 343
Summary ........ 351
Get This Book's PDF Version and Exclusive Extras • 352

## Part IV: Resource Administration: Storage, Boot Process, Tuning, and Containers 353

### Chapter 12: Managing Local Storage and Filesystems 355

Technical requirements ........ 356
A bit of history on disks and partitions ........ 356
Partitioning disks (MBR and GPT disks) ........ 358
Formatting and mounting filesystems ........ 365
Setting default mounts and options in fstab ........ 368
Using network filesystems with NFS ........ 371
Get This Book's PDF Version and Exclusive Extras • 372
Summary ........ 372

### Chapter 13: Flexible Storage Management with LVM 373

Technical requirements ........ 374
Understanding LVM ........ 376
Creating, moving, and removing physical volumes ........ 378
Combining physical volumes into volume groups ........ 384
Creating and extending logical volumes ........ 385
Adding new disks to a volume group and extending a logical volume ........ 387
Removing logical volumes, volume groups, and physical volumes ........ 393

Reviewing LVM commands .... 398
Summary .... 399
Get This Book's PDF Version and Exclusive Extras • 400

## Chapter 14: Configuring and Using System Snapshots with BTRFS and Snapper 401

Technical requirements .... 402
BTRFS' and Snapper's origins .... 402
Reviewing BTRFS basics, creating filesystems, reviewing status, and mounting .... 403
BTRFS snapshots, how they work, and how to use them .... 407
Snapper, the snapshot management tool .... 409
Using Snapper to show changes made to files between snapshots • 411
Using Snapper to roll back to a previous configuration status • 414
Other Snapper functions • 415
Summary .... 417
Get This Book's PDF Version and Exclusive Extras • 417

## Chapter 15: Understanding the Boot Process 419

Understanding the boot process – UEFI booting and legacy BIOS .... 420
Working with GRUB, the bootloader, and initrd system images .... 423
Managing the boot sequence with systemd .... 428
Updating the root password by modifying the boot process .... 433
Get This Book's PDF Version and Exclusive Extras • 438
Summary .... 438

## Chapter 16: Automating with System Roles 439

Technical requirements .... 440
What are system roles? .... 440
Installing system roles .... 440
Using system roles .... 442
Get This Book's PDF Version and Exclusive Extras • 448
Summary .... 448

## Chapter 17: Managing Containers with Podman 449


**Technical requirements** ........ 450

**What to expect from containers** ........ 450

**Installing Podman** ........ 452

**Working with registries** ........ 454

Using registries • 460

Connecting to a running container • 465

Deleting containers and images • 467

**Summary** ........ 471

Get This Book's PDF Version and Exclusive Extras • 471


## Chapter 18: Introduction to SLES for SAP Applications 473


**Technical requirements** ........ 475

**SLES for SAP Applications** ........ 475

Long-term support • 476

Workload Memory Protection • 476

SUSE Linux Enterprise Live Patching • 477

**Trento** ........ 478

**Tuning SLES for SAP** ........ 479

**Converting a SLES system to SLES for SAP Applications** ........ 480

**Summary** ........ 481

Get This Book's PDF Version and Exclusive Extras • 481

# Part V: Practice Exercises 483

## Chapter 19: Practice Exercises – 1 485

Technical requirements ... 485
Tips for the exercise ... 486
Practice exercise 1 ... 486
Exercise 1 solution ... 489

## Chapter 20: Practice Exercises – 2 505

Technical requirements ... 505
Tips for the exercise ... 506
Practice exercise 2 ... 506
Exercise 2 solution ... 508

## Chapter 21: Unlock Your Exclusive Benefits 525

## Other Books You May Enjoy 531

## Index 535

# Preface

Linux is an amazing piece of technology. Inheriting from its UNIX roots and reaching new heights, it's a foundational component of today's services, computing, and the interconnected world in which we live. It is everywhere, from smartphones, personal devices, wearables, and routers to the largest supercomputer clusters. From universities to Wall Street and the International Space Station, it's even on Mars. Learning more about it is a basic skill to improve and solidify your technology background.

SUSE was founded in 1992 in Germany, becoming early "Linux Experts," creating the first version of Enterprise Linux in 2000, for mainframes: SUSE Linux Enterprise Server. Then it was extended to PCs and other architectures. Being true to open source and at the forefront of the technology, the company and the product have evolved, creating its latest release, **SUSE Linux Enterprise Server 16 (SLES 16)**, released in November 2025.

In this book, we cover the basic skills needed to get started with SLES 16 from a practical perspective, providing examples as well as tips learned from experience "in the trenches." You will be able to follow it from beginning to end, practicing with each step, while learning about how things are built and why they behave as they do.

We really hope you enjoy this book and make the most of it. We expect that, when you finish it, you will end up with strong foundational Linux skills and will love SLES. That's why we wrote this book: to share our love of Linux and empower you in one of the most amazing technologies of our age.

Enjoy reading! Enjoy practicing!

## Who this book is for

This book has been written to provide general Linux knowledge to practitioners who would like to become Sysadmins, DevOps engineers, **Site Reliability Engineers (SREs)**, or platform engineers. It is also useful for developers to better understand the foundational layer of their applications. In general, it is written for anyone who aspires to build and work on IT infrastructures. It will also help anyone seeking to obtain the **SUSE Certified Administrator (SCA)** certification. Even though it is no substitute for the official training, it is a good reference to obtain a strong base to make the most of the official labs and training. The scope of the book is adjusted to the SCA exam, extending it with advice from real-world experience and many practical examples.

## What this book covers

*Chapter 1, Getting SLES 16 Up and Running (Physical and Cloud)*, covers the installation of SLES, from obtaining the software and the subscriptions to the installation of the system itself.

*Chapter 2, Running Basic Commands and Simple Shell Scripts*, explains the daily commands that will be used during system administration, and how they can be automated using shell scripting.

*Chapter 3, Managing Regular Operations with Tools*, shows which simple tools are available in our system that can be used for regular daily operations, such as starting or enabling a system service or reviewing what is going on in the system by checking logs.

*Chapter 4, Securing the System with Users, Groups, and Permissions*, covers how to manage users, groups, and permissions in a Linux system.

*Chapter 5, Enabling Network Connectivity*, goes through the steps to connect a system to the network and the possible ways it can be configured using NetworkManager.

*Chapter 6, Adding, Patching, and Managing Software*, reviews the steps needed to add, remove, and update software on our system, also adding software repositories with extra content.

*Chapter 7, Remote Systems Administration*, explains how to connect remotely to your systems using SSH and how to manage them better using a terminal multiplexer (tmux).

*Chapter 8, Enabling and Using Cockpit*, covers how to enable the Cockpit system administration tool, which facilitates the most common steps to manage and configure a single system.

*Chapter 9, Securing Network Connectivity with firewalld*, provides instructions on how network firewall configuration works and how to properly manage zones, services, and ports.

*Chapter 10, Keeping the System Hardened with SELinux*, covers usage and basic troubleshooting of SELinux.

*Chapter 11, Agentic AI with mcphost*, explains how to install and configure `mcphost` to connect it to Google Gemini as the large language model of choice. It also shows the basic usage of it.

*Chapter 12, Managing Local Storage and Filesystems*, covers filesystem creation, mount points, and general storage management in Linux.

*Chapter 13, Flexible Storage Management with LVM*, explains how LVM provides more flexible block storage management by being able to add disks and extend volumes.

*Chapter 14, Configuring and Using System Snapshots with BTRFS and Snapper*, explains how to create filesystem snapshots to be able to roll back the system to a well-known state and compare files at different points in time.

*Chapter 15, Understanding the Boot Process*, explains how the system boots and the details that make it important.

*Chapter 16, Automating with System Roles*, explores the availability of Ansible system roles in the system and how to use them to automate many common administrative tasks.

*Chapter 17, Managing Containers with Podman*, covers tools for running, managing, and building containers.

*Chapter 18, Introduction to SLES 4 SAP*, is a short chapter that describes the specifics of why SLES is so popular in SAP and business-critical environments.

*Chapter 19, Practice Exercises — 1*, provides you with a way to test your acquired knowledge.

*Chapter 20, Practice Exercises — 2*, provides more complex tests to review the acquired skills.

# To get the most out of this book

All software requirements will be indicated in the chapters. Note that this book assumes that you have access to a physical or virtual machine and have access to the internet to create a cloud account, to perform the operations that the book will guide you through.

| Software/hardware covered in the book | Operating system requirements |
|---|---|
| SUSE Linux Enterprise Server 16 | You will have to install SUSE Linux Enterprise Server on a physical machine. It can also be installed on a virtual machine under Windows, macOS, or Linux, as well as using a cloud instance. |

Please check *Chapter 1* to get more detailed instructions on how to install SLES to get started.

**If you are using the digital version of this book, we advise you to type the code yourself or access the code from the book's GitHub repository (a link is available in the next section). Doing so will help you avoid any potential errors related to the copying and pasting of code.**

## Download the example code files

The code bundle for the book is hosted on GitHub at `https://github.com/PacktPublishing/SUSE-Linux-Enterprise-Server-16-Official-Administration-Guide`. We also have other code bundles from our rich catalog of books and videos available at `https://github.com/PacktPublishing`. Check them out!

## Download the color images

We also provide a PDF file that has color images of the screenshots/diagrams used in this book. You can download it here: `https://packt.link/gbp/9781806021598`

## Conventions used

There are a number of text conventions used throughout this book.

`CodeInText`: Indicates code words in text, database table names, folder names, filenames, file extensions, pathnames, dummy URLs, user input, and Twitter handles. For example: "Then choose the ISO labeled as `SLES-16.0-Full-x86_64-GM.install.iso`."

A block of code is set as follows:

```
rotate 30
daily
compress
dateext
```

When we wish to draw your attention to a particular part of a code block, the relevant lines or items are set in bold:

```
local stratum 3 orphan
```

Any command-line input or output is written as follows:

```
sles16-instance:~ # localectl
System Locale: LANG=en_US.UTF-8
    VC Keymap: (unset)
   X11 Layout: (unset)
sles16-instance:~ # localectl set-locale es_ES.utf8
```

```
sles16-instance:~ # localectl
System Locale: LANG=es_ES.utf8
    VC Keymap: (unset)
   X11 Layout: (unset)
```

**Bold**: Indicates a new term, an important word, or words that you see on the screen. For instance, words in menus or dialog boxes appear in the text like this. For example: "**NTP** is an internet protocol that connects over **User Datagram Protocol** (**UDP**)."

Warnings or important notes appear like this.

Tips and tricks appear like this.

# Get in touch

Feedback from our readers is always welcome.

**General feedback**: If you have questions about any aspect of this book or have any general feedback, please email us at `customercare@packt.com` and mention the book's title in the subject of your message.

**Errata**: Although we have taken every care to ensure the accuracy of our content, mistakes do happen. If you have found a mistake in this book, we would be grateful if you reported this to us. Please visit `http://www.packt.com/submit-errata`, click **Submit Errata**, and fill in the form.

**Piracy**: If you come across any illegal copies of our works in any form on the internet, we would be grateful if you would provide us with the location address or website name. Please contact us at `copyright@packt.com` with a link to the material.

**If you are interested in becoming an author**: If there is a topic that you have expertise in and you are interested in either writing or contributing to a book, please visit `http://authors.packt.com/`.

## Share your thoughts

Once you've read *SUSE Linux Enterprise Server 16 Official Administration Guide*, we'd love to hear your thoughts! Scan the QR code below to go straight to the Amazon review page for this book and share your feedback.

`https://packt.link/r/1806021595`

Your review is important to us and the tech community and will help us make sure we're delivering excellent quality content.

# Free Benefits with Your Book

This book comes with free benefits to support your learning. Activate them now for instant access (see the "*How to Unlock*" section for instructions).

Here's a quick overview of what you can instantly unlock with your purchase:

**PDF and ePub Copies**

- Access a DRM-free PDF copy of this book to read anywhere, on any device.
- Use a DRM-free ePub version with your favorite e-reader.

**Next-Gen Web-Based Reader**

- **Multi-device progress sync:** Pick up where you left off, on any device.
- **Highlighting and notetaking:** Capture ideas and turn reading into lasting knowledge.
- **Bookmarking:** Save and revisit key sections whenever you need them.
- **Dark mode:** Reduce eye strain by switching to dark or sepia themes.

## How to Unlock

UNLOCK NOW

Scan the QR code (or go to `packtpub.com/unlock`). Search for this book by name, confirm the edition, and then follow the steps on the page.

***Note:** Keep your invoice handy. Purchases made directly from Packt don't require one.*

# Part 1

# System Administration: Software, User, Network, and Service Management

Deploying, configuring, and keeping systems up to date is the base task that every system administrator performs in their day-to-day work. In this part, we explore the main workflows to do so in a structured way, so you can easily follow the tasks one by one to learn, practice, and understand them properly.

This part has the following chapters:


- *Chapter 1, Getting SLES 16 Up and Running (Physical and Cloud)*
- *Chapter 2, Running Basic Commands and Simple Shell Scripts*
- *Chapter 3, Managing Regular Operations with Tools*
- *Chapter 4, Securing the System with Users, Groups, and Permissions*
- *Chapter 5, Enabling Network Connectivity*
- *Chapter 6, Adding, Patching, and Managing Software*

# 1

# Getting SLES 16 Up and Running (Physical and Cloud)

The first step to start working with **SUSE Linux Enterprise Server**, also known as **SLES**, is to have it running. Whether on your own laptop as the main system, on a virtual machine, or on a physical server, the installation of SLES is required to get your hands on the system you want to learn to use SLES in. It is highly encouraged that you get yourself a physical or virtual machine to use and practice the examples while reading this book.

In this chapter, you will not just deploy a system but also learn the best choices to do so and be able to perform the deployment in an *automated fashion*. These are the topics that will be covered:

- Installing SLES 16
- Running the SLES installation
- Running SLES on the cloud
- Installation best practices

### Free Benefits with Your Book

Your purchase includes a free PDF copy of this book along with other exclusive benefits. Check the *Free Benefits with Your Book* section in the Preface to unlock them instantly and maximize your learning experience.

# Technical requirements

The best way to get started is by having an **SLES 16** virtual machine to work with. You may do so on your main computer or in the cloud. In the following sections of this chapter, we will review both options, and you will be able to run your own SLES 16 system.

> A virtual machine is a way to emulate a complete computer. To be able to create these emulated computers on your own laptop, in case you are using macOS or Windows, you will need to install virtualization software such as VirtualBox. If you are already running Linux, it's already prepared for virtualization, and you will only need to add the `virt-manager` package.

## Obtaining the SLES software and a subscription

To be able to deploy SLES, it is recommended that you obtain a **SUSE subscription**. Even when you can download images without a subscription, it is recommended to get one to access repositories with software and updates. You can get, free of cost, an *Evaluation subscription* from the customers' portal site of SUSE using the following link: `scc.suse.com`. You then need to follow these steps:

1. Register to create an account on `scc.suse.com`. Do it by clicking on the **Register** button on the main page. It will take you to the registration page, as seen in the following figure. In case you already have one, continue to the next step. All you have to do is fill in the form, accept the *SUSE privacy policy* and *terms of service*, and click on **Create Account**. You will receive an email to confirm your email address, and you will be good to go.

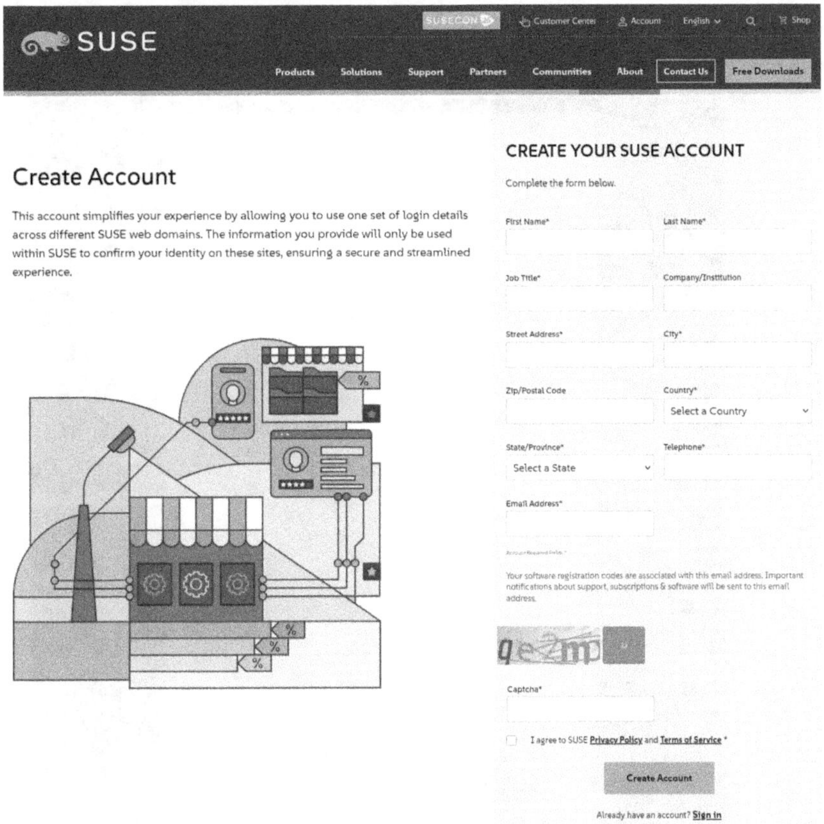


*Figure 1.1 – SUSE customer center registration page (common to all SUSE resources)*

2. Once you have an account, go to the `scc.suse.com` page and click on **Log In**:

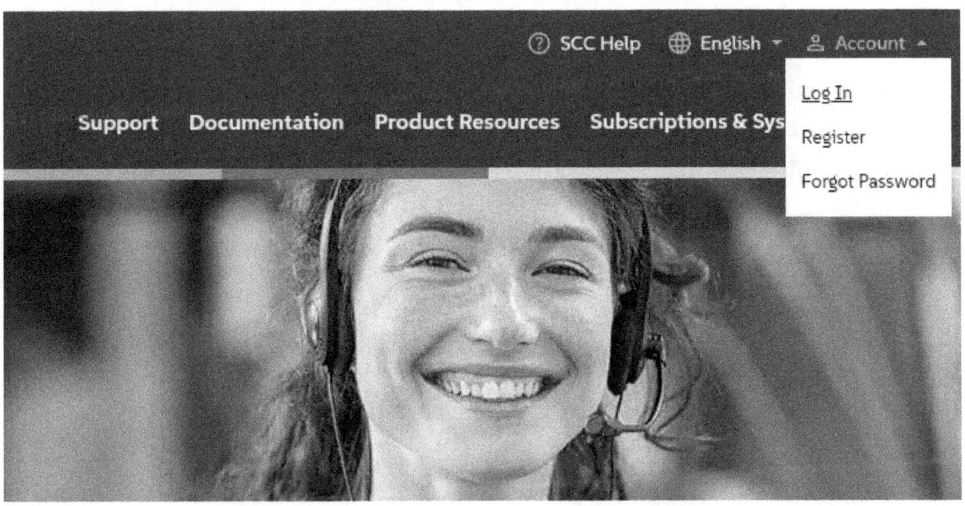


*Figure 1.2 – scc.suse.com home page indicating where to click to log in*

3. Now enter your credentials: **Username** (the email you used to register will be your username) and **Password**, and click **Sign In.**

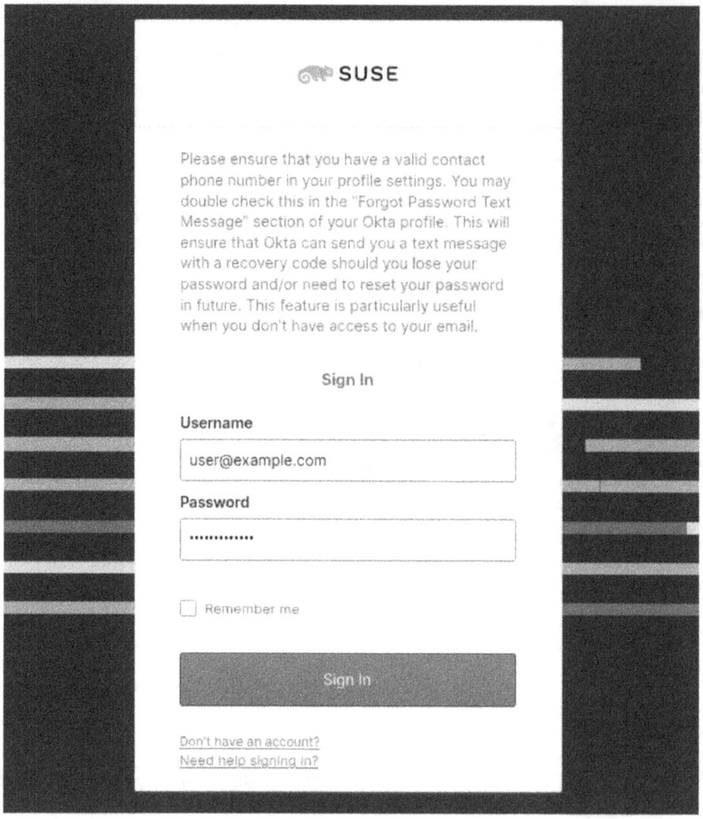


*Figure 1.3 – scc.suse.com page requesting credentials*

4. An email will be needed to verify your login. Click on **Send me the code**, and you will receive an email with a 6-digit code. Please enter the code received via email and complete the login process by clicking on **Verify**, as in the following figure (note: we are using **000000** as an example in the figure; please enter the code received in your email):

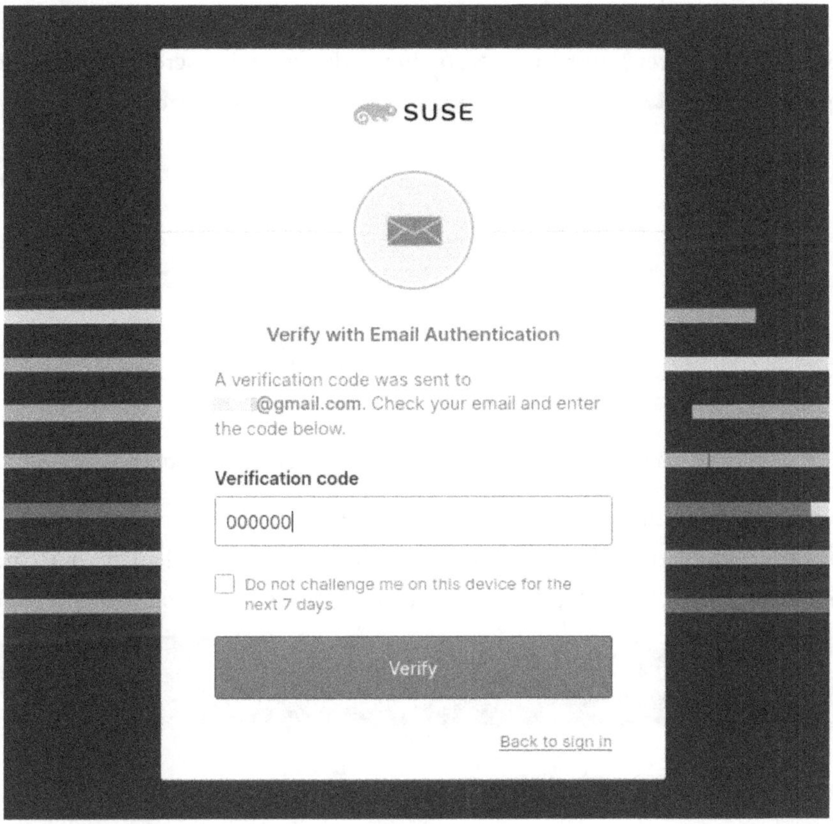


*Figure 1.4 – scc.suse.com page requesting email verification to log in*

5. Once you have logged in, go to the **Start a Free Trial** section, and then click on the text **SUSE Linux Enterprise Server**. Finally, click on **Request Trial Code**. This will immediately provide a code to register your SLES.

You will receive your unique **registration code.** Please keep this code in a safe place; you will use it later to register your system. Note that in the following screenshot, we are showing a fake code with all zeros; your code will be digits and letters, and it will be unique to you:

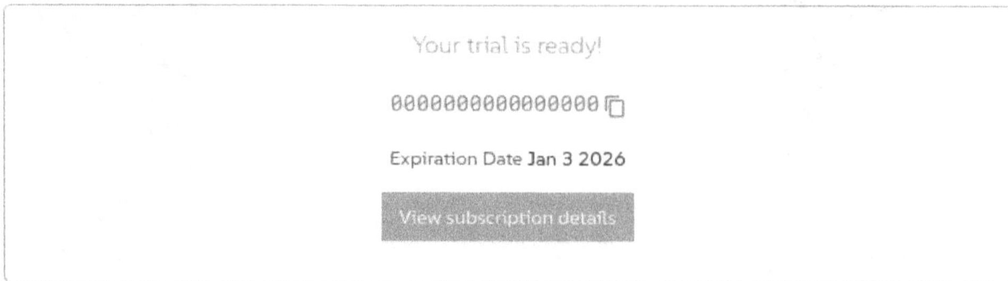


*Figure 1.5 – Receiving a unique registration code for our SLES instance at scc.suse.com*

6. Now go to **Home > Product Downloads > SUSE Linux Enterprise Server**, select version **16**, select the architecture (if in doubt, use **AMD 64 / Intel 64**), and go down to **Installation Media Download. Download SLES** appears as a fancy button on the next page:

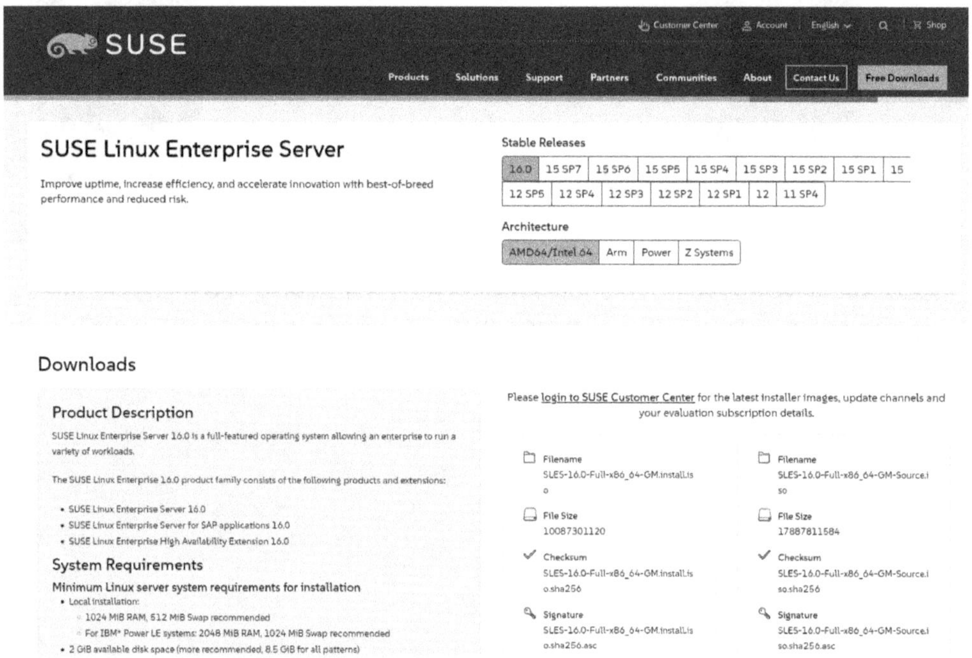


*Figure 1.6 – Downloads page at www.suse.com/download/sles*

Then choose the ISO labeled as `SLES-16.0-Full-x86_64-GM.install.iso`. Obtain the **SLES 16 ISO** image as follows:

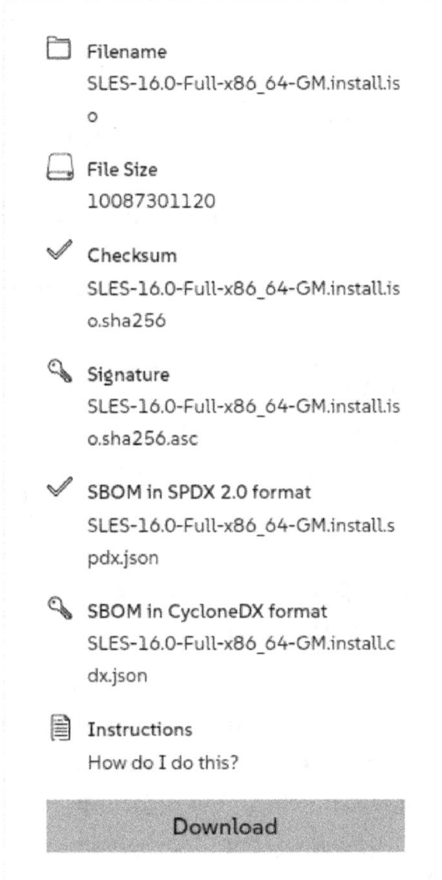


*Figure 1.7 – Choosing the ISO download of SLES 16 for x86_64*

The ISO image is a file that contains an exact copy of the contents needed to perform a full installation (That's why its size is almost 10 GB). This file will be used later to install our machines, whether dumping it on a USB drive for *bare-metal* installations, unpacking it for network installations, or attaching it for virtual machine installations (or using out-of-band capabilities on servers such as IPMI, iLO, or iDRAC).

To verify the ISO image and ensure that the one we have is not corrupted or altered, a mechanism called `checksum` can be used. Checksums are a way to review a file and provide a set of letters and numbers that can be used to verify that the file is exactly the same as the original. SUSE provides the `sha256` checksums to do so in the downloads section. An article describing the process can be found here: `https://www.suse.com/support/security/download-verification/`

SUSE takes care of having an upstream project synchronized with SLES; it is called openSUSE Leap. If you want a community version to learn, you can always use openSUSE Leap and run all the exercises in this book (except the ones related to SUSE Customer Center).

# Installing SLES 16

For this section of this chapter, we will follow the typical installation process to have SLES installed on a machine. We will follow the default steps, reviewing the options available for each one.

## Preparation for a physical server installation

A physical server requires some initial setup before starting the installation. Some common steps include configuring the disks in the *internal array*, connecting the server to the networks and preparing the switches for any *interface aggregation* that is expected (teaming, bonding), preparing access to external *disk arrays* (i.e., *fiber-channel arrays*), setting up out-of-band capabilities, and securing the **BIOS/UEFI** configuration.

We will not get into the details of these preparations, except for the boot sequence. The server will require booting (start loading the system) from an external device such as a *USB thumb drive* or *optical disk* (whether physical or emulated through the out-of-band capabilities).

To create a bootable USB thumb drive from a machine with Linux or macOS, it would be as simple as doing a "disk dump" with the application dd. The steps would be as follows:

1. Find your USB device on the system (usually /dev/sdb on Linux, /dev/disk2 on macOS):

```
$ dmesg | grep removable
[66931.429805] sd 0:0:0:0: [sdb] Attached SCSI removable disk
```

> Please very carefully verify the disk name, as the procedure of using a disk dump will completely overwrite the disk target.

2. Check if the USB is mounted and, if so, dismount it.

```
$ lsblk /dev/sdb
NAME   MAJ:MIN RM  SIZE RO TYPE MOUNTPOINT
sdb      8:0    1  3,8G  0 disk
├─sdb1   8:1    1  1,8G  0 part /run/media/miguel/USB
├─sdb2   8:2    1 10,9M  0 part
└─sdb3   8:3    1 22,9M  0 part
```

In this case, only partition 1 of the disk sdb, referred to as sdb1, is mounted. We will need to *unmount* all the partitions mounted. In this example, it is easy, as there's only one. To unmount, we can run the following:

```
$ sudo umount /dev/sdb1
```

> Using superuser do or sudo is a way to perform administrative tasks, such as unmounting devices. To do that, and other tasks, we have the option to log in as administrator (root in Linux and Unix-like systems) or run the command using sudo, which enables administrative privileges for the current user.
>
> When running commands with sudo, the user will be requested to enter its password (not the admin password, but the user's) to proceed with the execution (this default behavior may be overridden in the sudoers configuration file.

3. Dump the image! (Warning, this will erase the selected disk!)

```
$ sudo dd if=SLE-16.0-Full-x86_64-GM-Media1.iso of=/dev/sdb bs=4M
status=progress oflag=direct
```

**Alternative methods to create a boot device**

There are alternative graphical tools to create a boot device that can help select both the image and the target device. In openSUSE Linux Tumbleweed (the development branch used to create SLES and the workstation for many engineers and developers), the **Multi Writer** or **Impression** tool can be used. For other environments, such as Microsoft Windows, the **UNetbootin** tool could also serve to create your boot media.

## Booting an SLES installation from a USB thumb drive

Now, with the USB thumb drive, we can install any physical machine, from a tiny laptop to a huge server. The next part would be to make the physical machine boot from the **USB thumb drive**. The mechanism to do that would depend on the server being used. However, it is becoming common to offer during boot an option to select the boot device. This is an example on how to select a temporary boot device on a regular laptop or server:

1. Interrupt the normal startup. In this case, the boot process shows that I can do that by pressing *Enter*:

*Figure 1.8 – Example of BIOS message to interrupt normal startup*

2. Choose a temporary startup device; in this case, by pressing the *F12* key:

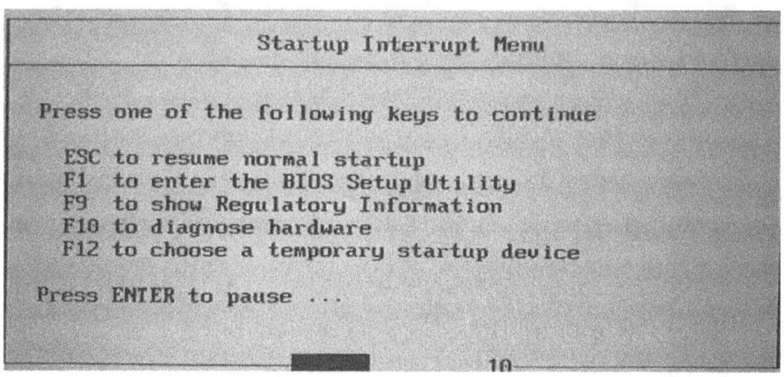


*Figure 1.9 – Example of BIOS menu for interrupted startup*

3. Select the device to boot from. We want to boot from our USB thumb drive, which in this case is **USB HDD: ChipsBnk Flash Disk**:

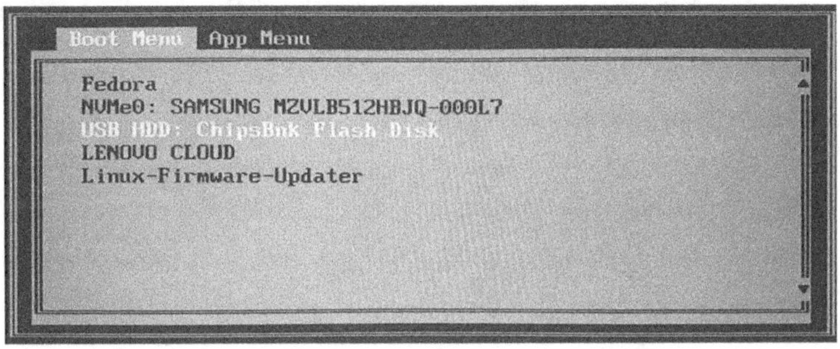


*Figure 1.10 – Example of BIOS menu to choose USB HDD boot device*

4. Let the system start the installer from the USB drive.

Once we know how to prepare a USB drive with an SLES installer and how to make a physical machine boot from it, we can move on to the *Running the SLES installation* section later in this chapter and proceed to install it. This can be useful if we have a mini server, an old computer, or a laptop to be used as the machine for following this book.

Next, we will look at how to prepare a virtual machine in your installation, in case you are considering following this book with your current main laptop (or workstation), but you still want to keep a separate machine to work with.

## Preparation for a virtual server installation

A **virtual server** works by having some virtualization software that emulates a real machine in your current system. In a Linux workstation, installing `virt-manager` will add all the under-the-hood components required to have virtualization enabled (for information, these components are *KVM*, *Libvirt*, *Qemu*, and *virsh*, among others). Other no-cost virtualization software, recommended for Windows or macOS systems, could be *Oracle VirtualBox* or *VMware Workstation Player*.

The examples in this section will be done using `virt-manager` running on openSUSE Tumbleweed, but are easily applicable to any other virtualization software, whether on a laptop or larger deployments.

To install `virt-manager` on openSUSE Tumbleweed or **LEAP**, you can follow these instructions:

```
sudo zypper refresh
sudo zypper install -t pattern kvm_server kvm_tools
sudo zypper install virt-manager libvirt-daemon-proxy
```

Preliminary steps have been described previously and require obtaining the **SUSE Linux Enterprise Server ISO** image, which, as we mentioned before, is `SLES-16.0-Full-x86_64-GM.install.iso`. Once downloaded and, if possible, checked for integrity, following the previous instructions, let's prepare to deploy a virtual machine.

1. Start your virtualization software; in this case, `virt-manager`.

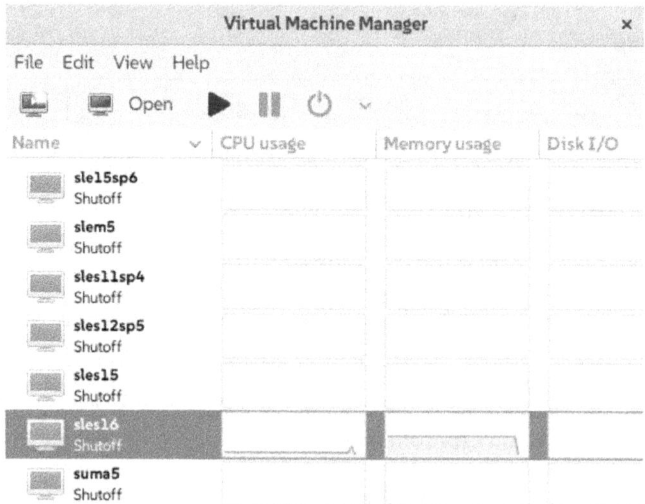


*Figure 1.11 – virt-manager main menu*

2. Create a new virtual machine by going to **File**, then clicking on **New Virtual Machine**. Select **Local install media (ISO image or CDROM)**.

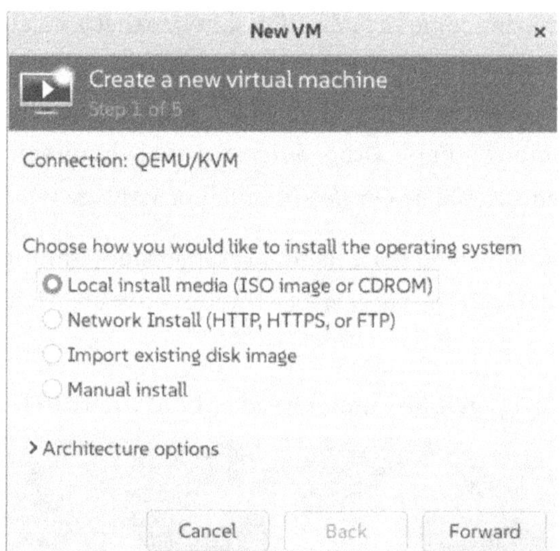


*Figure 1.12 – virt-manager new VM menu*

3. Select the *ISO image*. With this, the VM will be configured with a **virtual DVD/CD-ROM drive** and be prepared to boot from it. It's the usual behavior. However, in different virtualization software, you may want to check.

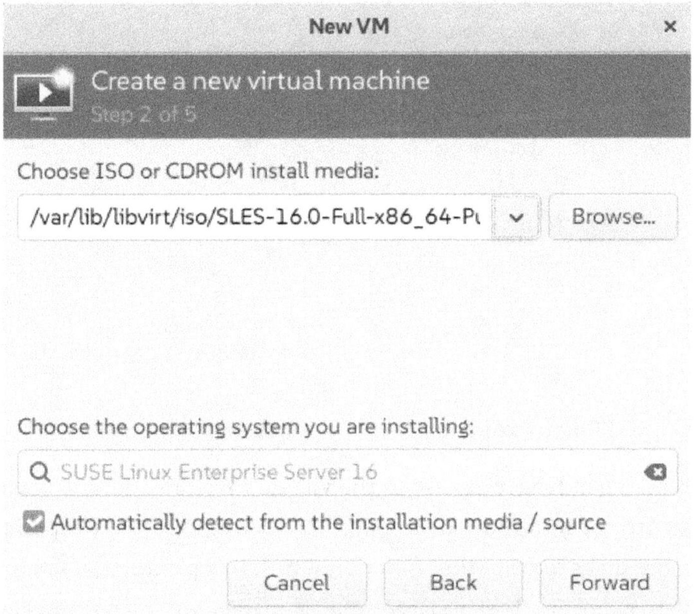


*Figure 1.13 – virt-manager menu to select an ISO image as install media*

4. Assign memory and CPU to the virtual machine we are creating. (Note: a **virtual machine** is usually referred to as a **VM**). For **SUSE Linux Enterprise Server 16** (also referred to as **SLES 16**), 1 GB of memory is the minimum; 1 GB per logical CPU is what we suggest. In this example, we will use something above the minimum settings – 2 GB memory and 1 CPU core, but feel free to add more if you want to:

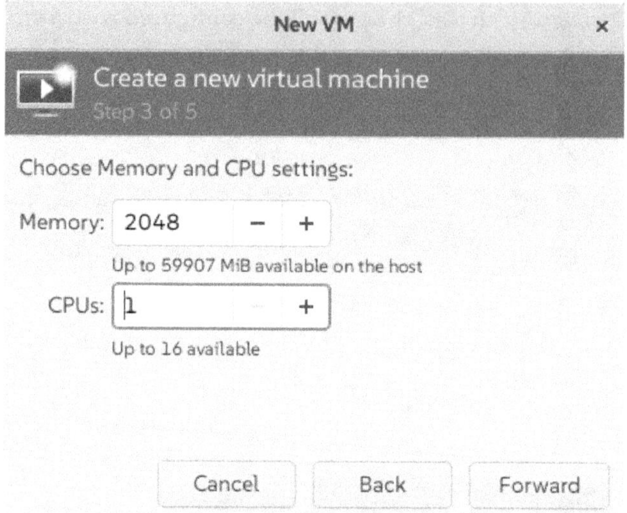


*Figure 1.14 – virt-manager menu to select memory and CPU*

5. It's time to assign at least one disk to the virtual machine. In this case, we will assign a single disk with the minimum disk space, 10 GB. But in future chapters, we will be able to assign more disks to test other functionalities. In a production system, if you want to keep many snapshots and keep a large amount of logs, we suggest increasing the disk size to at least 32 GB. For this example, we will use 32 GB, as in the following figure:

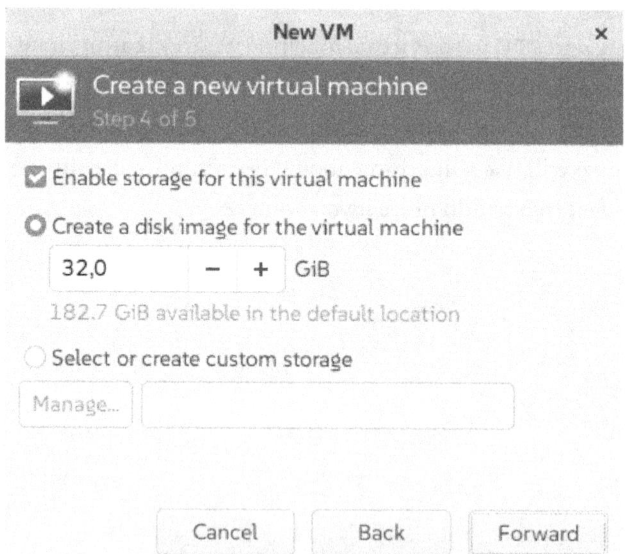


*Figure 1.15 – virt-manager menu to create a new disk and add it to the VM*

6. Our VM has all that we need to get started: A *boot device*, **Memory**, **CPUs**, and *disk space*. In this last step, a network interface is added, so now we have a network. Let's review the data and launch it by clicking on the **Finish** button:

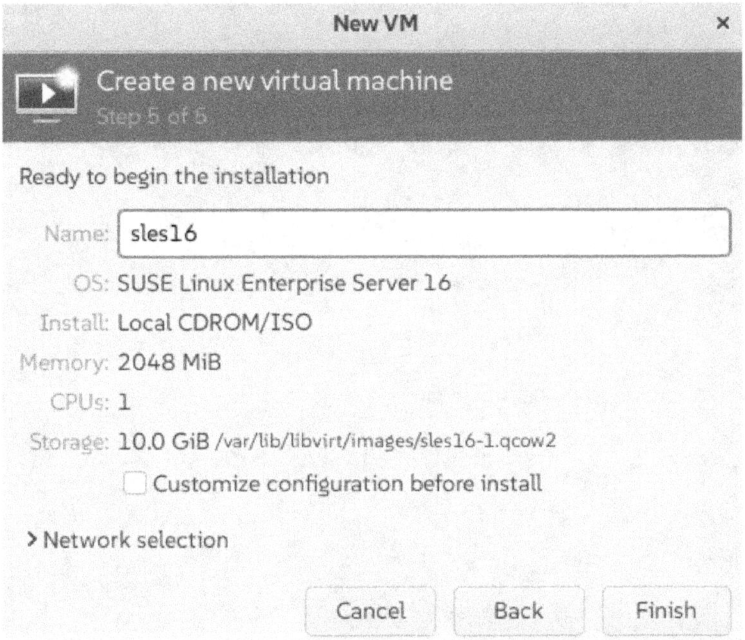


*Figure 1.16 – virt-manager menu to select VM name and network selection*

After taking these steps, we have a fully functional virtual machine available. Now it is time to complete the process by installing the SLES operating system on it. Check out how to do this in the next section.

# Running the SLES installation

Once we have prepared our virtual or physical server for installation, it's time to proceed with it. We will know that all the previous steps were taken correctly if we arrive at the following screen:

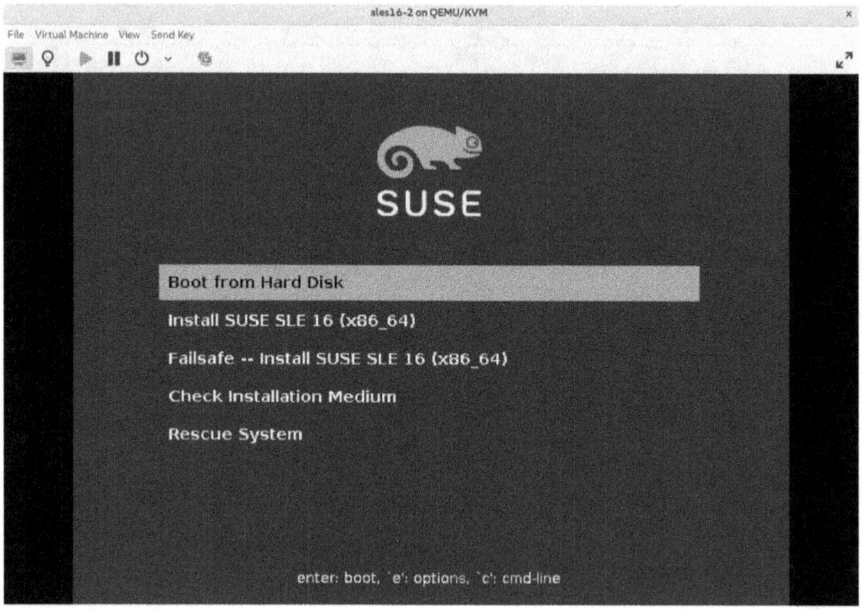


*Figure 1.17 – Initial boot screen for SLES 16 installation*

We are offered five options (*selected one in green*):

- **Boot from Hard Disk**: This will boot from the existing hard disk, with the existing OS, in case you don't want to install at that time. This means that if you boot from the USB accidentally on a system that has an OS, it will boot from the existing OS instead of launching the installation.
- **Install SUSE SLE 16**: This option will boot and run the installer. You will have to select it to start the installation.
- **Failsafe -- Install SUSE SLE 16**: This option will boot and run the installer in failsafe mode. This is to be used in case the general installation option fails.

- **Check Installation Medium**: This option will check the image being used to ensure that it is not corrupt and that the installation can proceed with certainty. Once the check is finished and passed, it will move on to the installation itself. It is recommended to use this one for the first time using a just downloaded ISO image or just created media, such as a USB thumb drive. (On a virtual machine, it takes ~1–2 minutes to run the check.)
- **Rescue System**: This will help you review and rescue an installed system by taking you to a live OS running in memory, so you can later mount the installed system and fix things there.

Let' proceed with `Check Installation Medium` to let the installer review the ISO image we are using:

*Figure 1.18 – SLES 16 ISO image self-check*

Once completed, it will reach the first installation screen. The installer is called *Agama*, and it will guide us through the whole installation process.

## Installation type

The first step of the installation is selecting the installation type. The options provided by the SLES 16 installer are **SUSE Linux Enterprise Server 16.0** and **SUSE Linux Enterprise Server for SAP applications 16.0**. As SAP workloads are very common in the SUSE ecosystem, there is a specialized version for them. In our case, we will choose the first one to continue with the multi-purpose general installation.

Then, acknowledge reading the license and click **Select**, as seen in the following figure:

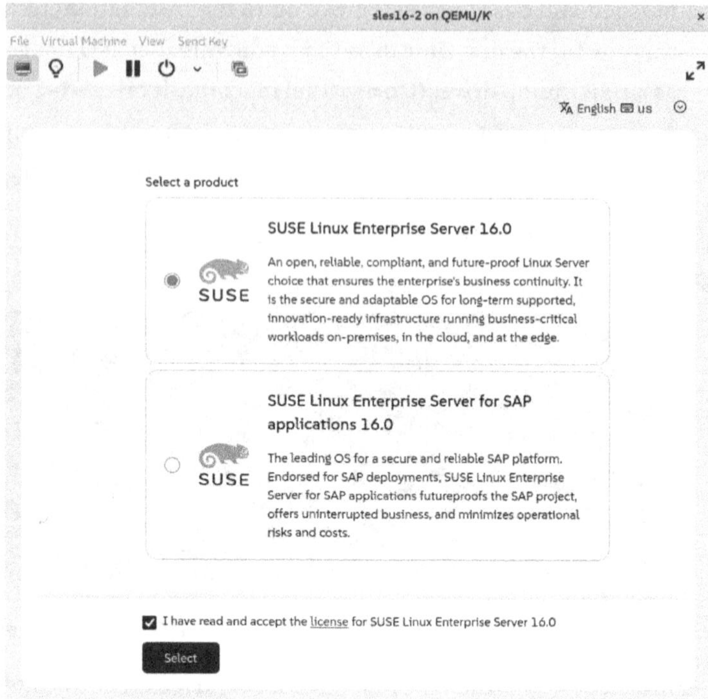


*Figure 1.19 – SLES 16 installation type selection*

> The new Agama installer that comes with SLES 16 is being prepared so it can be used remotely with ease. Follow the Agama project in GitHub to be up to date: `https://agama-project.github.io/`

Once we have selected the installation type, we are ready to proceed with the process of installation itself. Let's look at it in the next section.

## Installer introduction and overview

The Agama installer is designed to be used remotely as well as locally. It refreshes itself when connected to the internet before launching the installation. It will work as a web page in which you can go to the selected section at any time using the lateral bar. Once the minimal information is provided, the **Install** button at the top right of the page will lose the exclamation mark, which means that it's ready to move ahead.

The initial page, which we can go back to at any time, is **Overview**, which shows a summary of the install options selected. We can see it in the following screenshot:

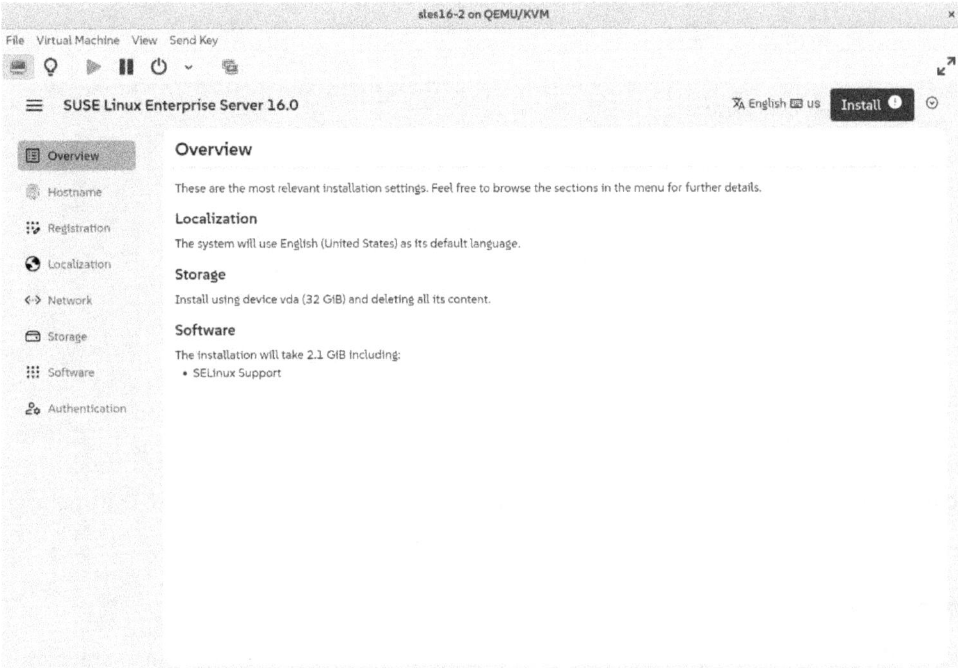


*Figure 1.20 – SLES 16 Agama installer — Overview page*

This **Overview** page has a shortcut to **Language and keyboard** options next to the **Install** button. We can use that if we want to switch those options. However, we can also do it on the **Localization** page afterwards. We can access that fast menu by clicking on the following icon:

*Figure 1.21 – SLES 16 Language and keyboard shortcut access*

Clicking on it can enable us to select the localization options to be used during installation. However, we also have the chance to apply those to the full installation. In the following screenshot, we have selected a different keyboard layout, **Spanish**, while keeping **Language** as **English**, with the option to apply it to the system to be installed too:

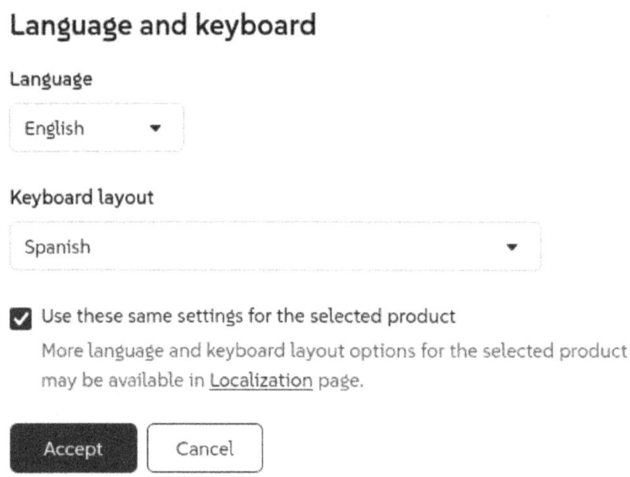


Figure 1.22 – SLES 16 Language and keyboard options

Once we complete this, which is pretty useful to match our keyboard preferences to the one used for installation, we can move on to configuring **Hostname**.

## Hostname

We can set up the hostname as `geeko.suse.test` in a static way, as in the following screenshot:

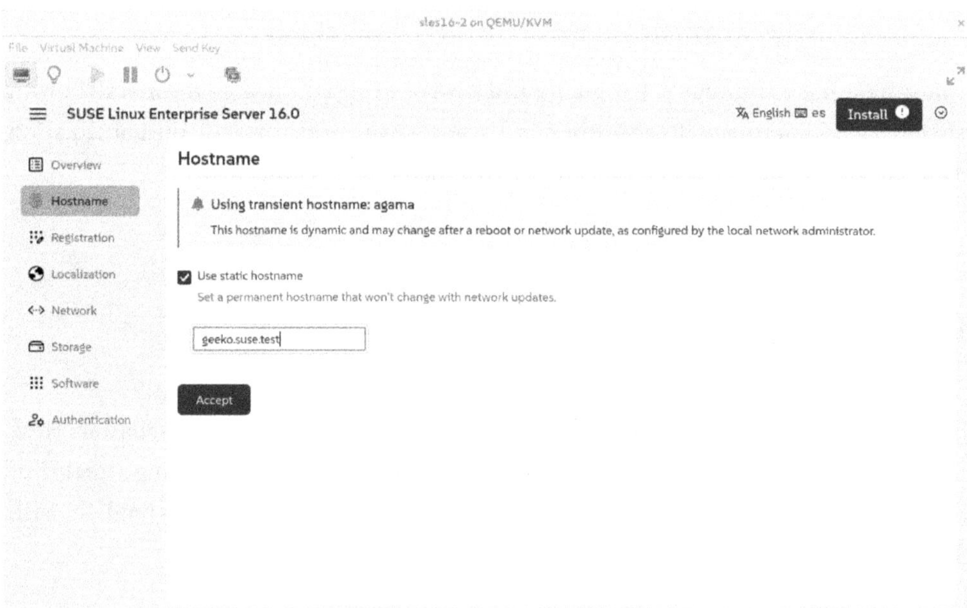


Figure 1.23 – SLES 16 hostname configuration

Then we can click on the **Accept** button to apply the changes at any time.

> The `.test` top domain and the `example.com` domain are used for demonstration purposes, and they are safe to be used on any occasion, knowing that they will not collide with or cause any trouble for other systems or domains. It is recommended to use them for testing, demo environments, or labs.

Once the hostname is set, let's move on to the **Registration** section.

## Registration

Here, we will use the *registration code* obtained previously, and we can also provide the email we used to register our user in **SUSE Customer Center** (**SCC**), as shown in the following screenshot:

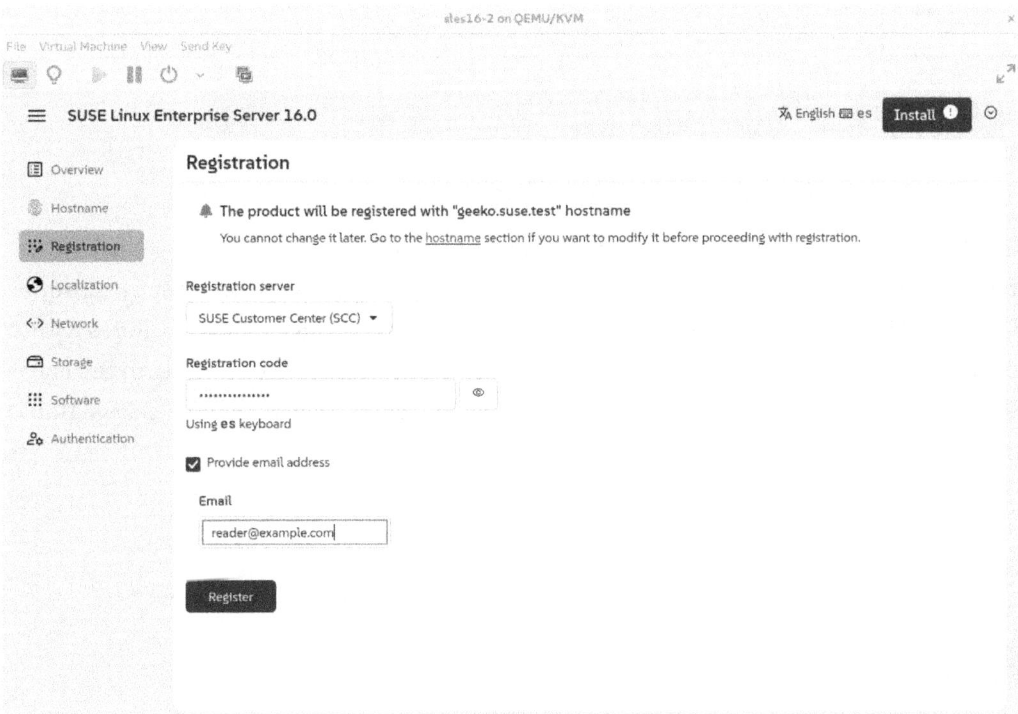


*Figure 1.24 – SLES 16 Registration page — General*

In this process, we are using `reader@example.com` as the email to register. You should not use this one, but the one you used to register in SCC instead.

As the registration completes, the page will change and will include the information from your registration, as shown in the following screenshot:

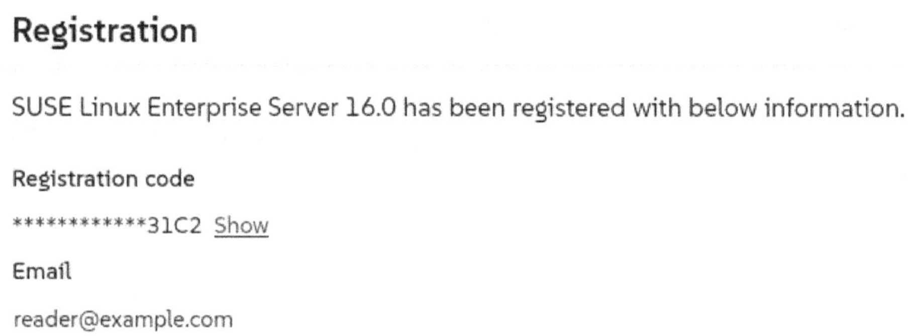


*Figure 1.25 - SLES 16 Registration page — Registration completed successfully*

Reaching this section, as shown, means that we have successfully registered our system in SCC. It is interesting that SLES 16 comes with a set of extra packages that, even when they are unsupported, can be added to our system without losing supportability for the packages included with it. This is called **SUSE Package Hub**. We recommend that you enable it by scrolling to the end of the **Registration** page and clicking on the **Register** button right below the SUSE Package Hub section, as seen in this screenshot:

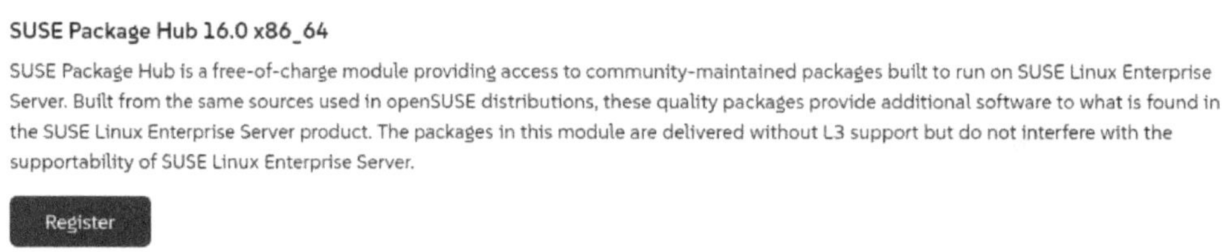


*Figure 1.26 - SLES 16 Registration page — Adding SUSE Package Hub*

This will ask you to accept the signature from the **SUSE Package Hub** repository, as shown in the following screenshot. If the key signature is `BF3F 9A67 D3A2 FF98 A73F 5E07 488C 583D 287A 0027`, just click **Trust**:

*Figure 1.27 – SLES 16 Registration page — Trusting SUSE Package Hub signature*

No registration code is required to add **SUSE Package Hub**. Now that our system is fully registered, let's move on to configure localization options.

## Localization

We have three options to configure **Localization**, which are **Language**, **Keyboard**, and **Time zone**, as we can see in the following figure:

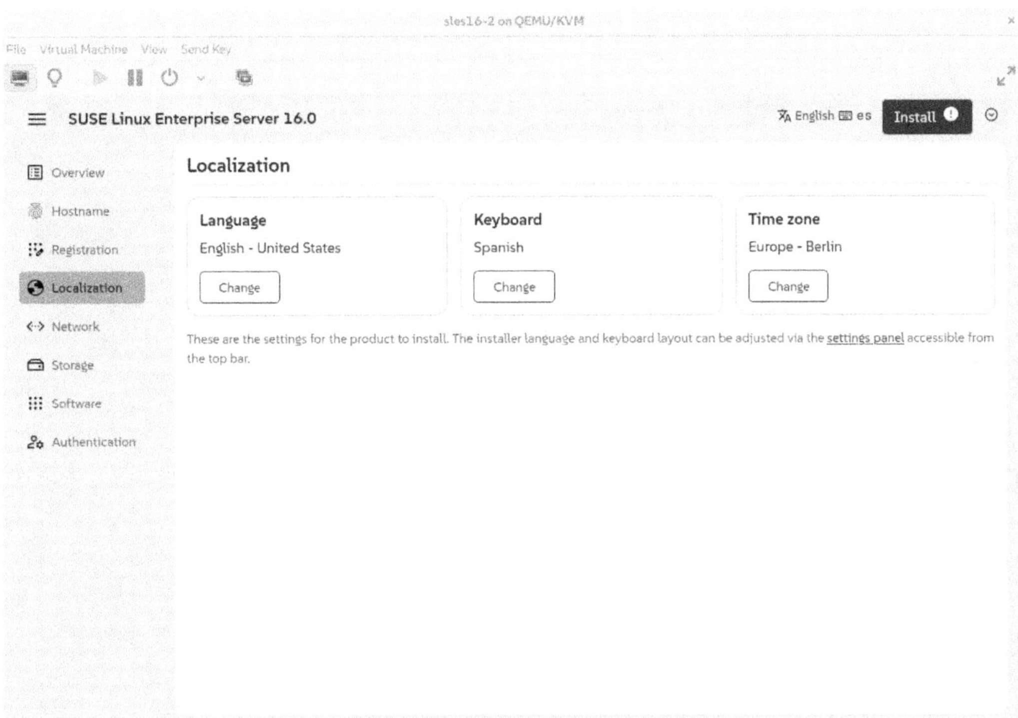


*Figure 1.28 – SLES 16 Localization page*

In this section, we will select the language to be used for the installed system, as well as the keyboard. We can do so by clicking on the **Change** button, marking the option we want, and clicking on **Select**. The same will work for **Time zone**. However, the default selection for this will be automatically chosen if the system is connected to the internet. We can see the **Timezone selection** page, selecting **Europe-Madrid** as an example here:

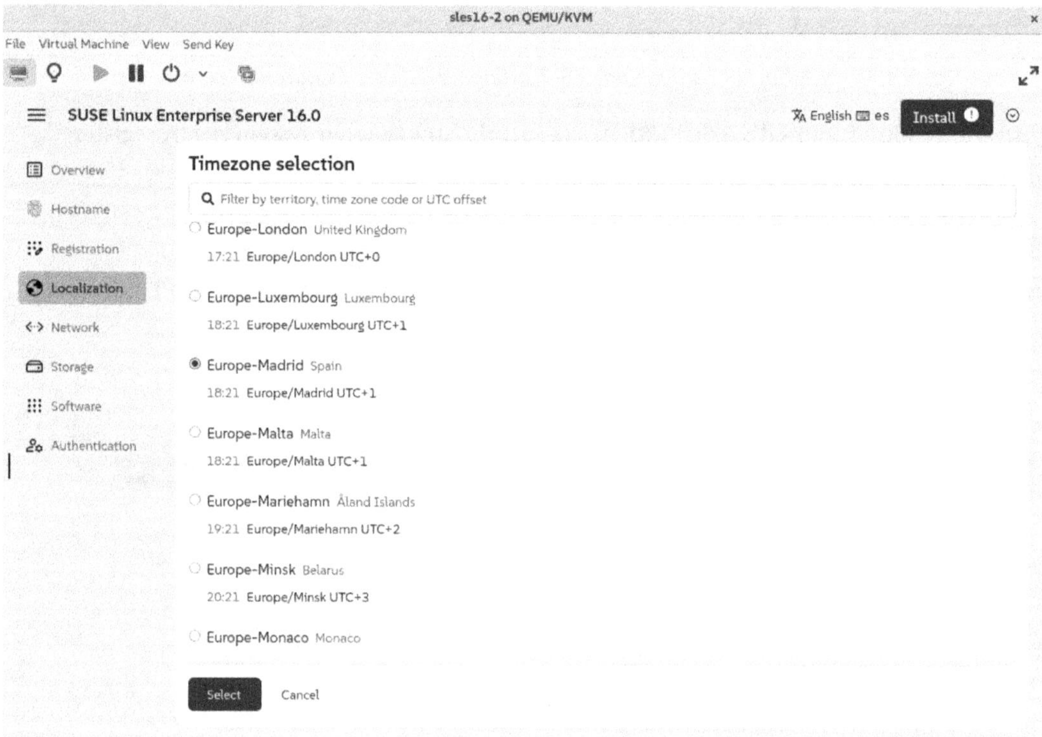


*Figure 1.29 – SLES 16 Localization — Timezone selection*

With the selection complete, let's move on to **Network** configuration.

## Network

We will take care of configuring the network interfaces attached to the machine in this section. The installer will show the interfaces detected on the main **Network** page, as seen in the following figure:

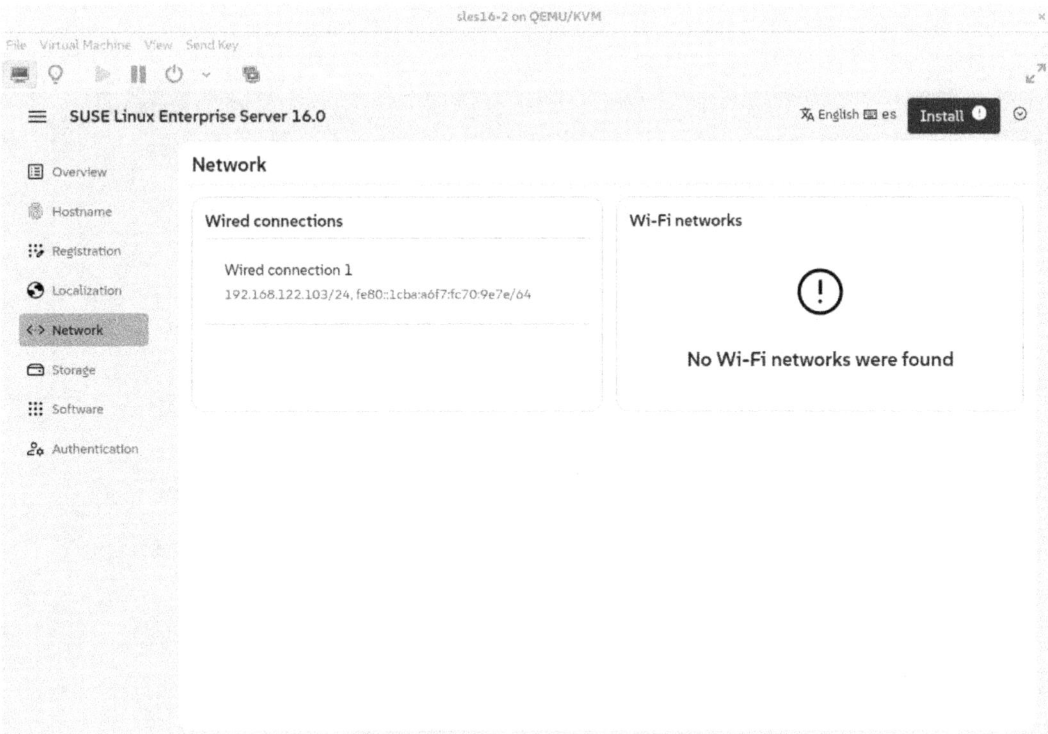


*Figure 1.30 – SLES 16 Network*

In this case, we see **Wired connection 1** as the main, and only, network interface on our virtual machine. Clicking on it will take us to its configuration page, as seen in the following figure. In case your system has received an IP address automatically, please collect the information that appears in **Connected device**:

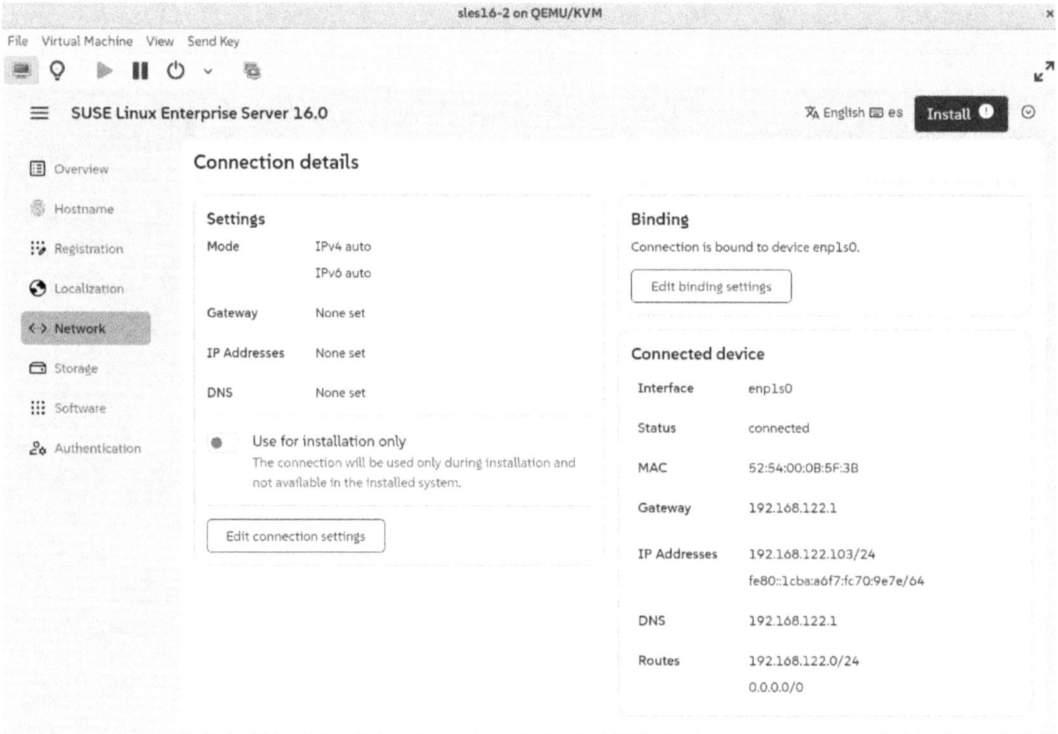


*Figure 1.31 – SLES 16 Network — Wired connection 1*

As we can see, we have everything configured to automatically gather configuration from the network by default, by reviewing the **Settings** > **Mode** section. We can keep it as it is.

For the sake of learning, in this book, we will modify the configuration to see how to set up IPv4 with a fixed IP of `192.168.122.16`.

Let's start doing it by clicking on **Edit connection settings**. Once there, we can fill the following sections:

- **Mode**: Change from **Automatic (DHCP)** to **Manual**. Once that is done, new options will appear to be configured. We can continue.

- **Gateway**: Add the IP for the gateway. I will use the same one assigned by DHCP, which is `192.168.122.1`.
- **Addresses**: We will add only one, and we will set it as `192.168.122.16`, with the prefix length as 24 (the prefix length was also provided by DHCP). We can add more than one address per interface. In this case, we will only add one.
- **DNS**: Add it as `192.168.122.1`, also the same as the one assigned by DHCP.

The configuration page should look like the following:

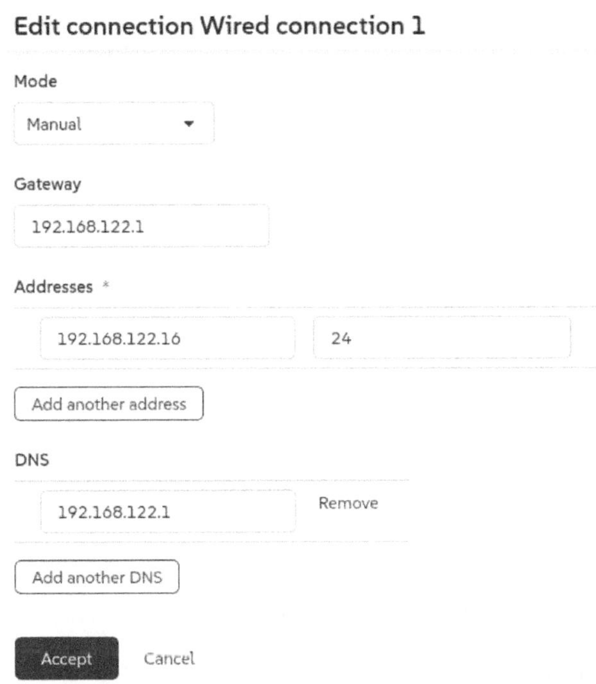


*Figure 1.32 – SLES 16 Network — Editing Wired connection 1*

When all fields are completed, we can click on the **Accept** button, and it will take us to the previous page with the new values updated.

With the network properly configured, we can move on to configuring **Storage**.

## Storage

The **Storage** configuration has been heavily simplified to make it easier to use. The page to configure storage looks like the following figure:

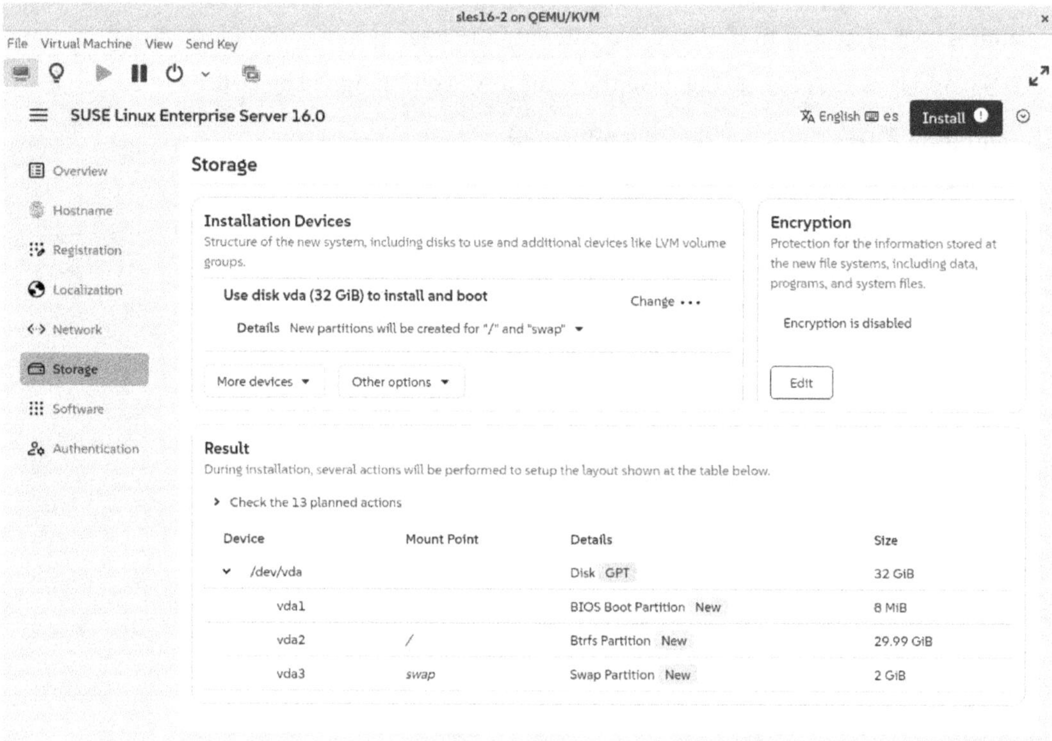

*Figure 1.33 - SLES 16 Storage — General page*

As we can see, there are three blocks:

- **Installation Devices:** This is the section to choose and configure which disk to install the operating system on. More details on this one later.
- **Encryption:** This is the section to provide a password to encrypt the device where we will install SLES.
- **Result:** This is the section to explain the steps that will be taken, regarding storage, once we launch the final stage of the installation.

Let's review the options under **Installation Devices**.

The first one is the section stating which disk has been pre-selected for the installation. In our case, `vda (32GiB)`, which has a button labeled **Change** with three points next to it. Clicking the **Change** button will provide two options, as seen in the following figure:

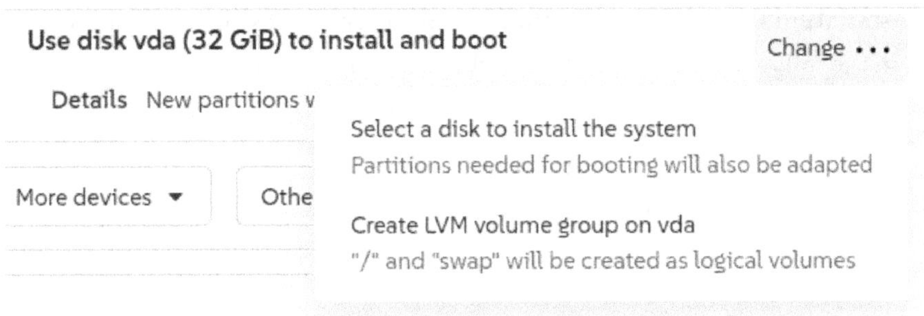


*Figure 1.34 - SLES 16 Storage — Options to change storage device*

The first option, **Select a disk to install the system,** is simple; it will just present a list of devices discovered by the installer so we can select which one we want to install. In our case, we have only one disk, so it shows like this:

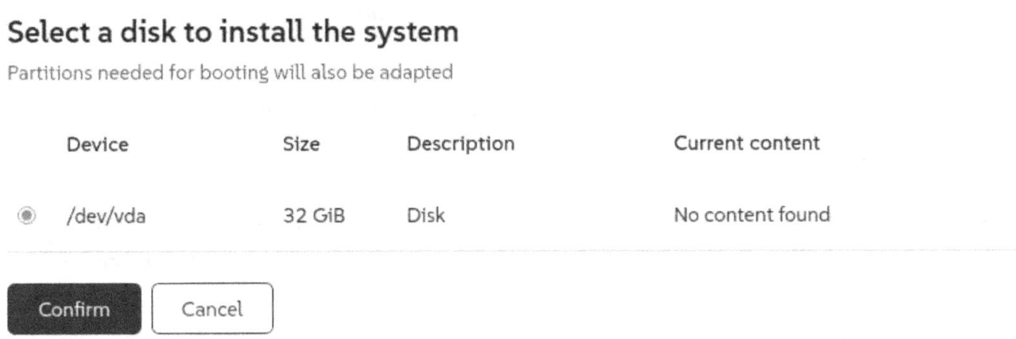


*Figure 1.35 - SLES 16 Storage — Options to change — Selecting a storage device*

The only option here is to choose the device and confirm. In servers, it's common to have more than one disk, using one for the operating system and the others for data or other utilities.

Regarding the other option, **Create LVM volume group on vda,** it will create logical volumes using **Logical Volume Manager** (**LVM**), about which we will learn in *Chapter 13, Flexible Storage Management with LVM.* In our example, here, we will continue without LVM. It is still important to take into account that for servers, it is recommended to use LVM, to have more options to redistribute storage whenever we need to extend a partition or BTRFS subvolume.

The button in **Installation Devices** labeled **More devices** is a shortcut to help manage many devices. For now, we will leave it as it is. Once we learn more about using storage, we will understand other options to work with it.

The button in **Installation Devices** labeled **Other options** is an interesting and useful one. Let's take a look at it in the following figure and check what each option does:

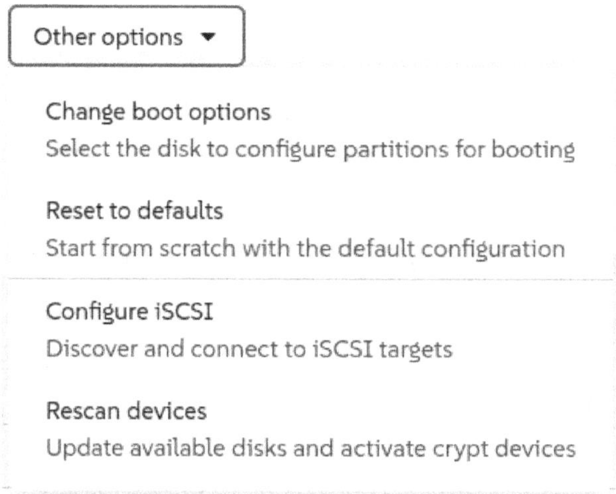


*Figure 1.36 - SLES 16 Storage — Options to change — Selecting a storage device*

Let's understand each of these options:

- **Change boot options** helps set up the partitions and software meant to be used to boot the system. We will learn more about it in *Chapter 15, Understanding the Boot Process*. For now, we can explore it, but leave it as it is.
- **Reset to defaults** is an option that brings you back to square zero of storage configuration, undoing any changes and restoring the recommended defaults. Feel free to play around with options and use this one to come back to a sensible set of options to install.
- **Configure iSCSI** is the option to add external storage to be used in the system, even to install the operating system or parts of it. You only need to know that **iSCSI** is a protocol to share disks over the network.
- **Rescan devices** helps continue the installation with a new disk you just attached to your system. It's not common in simple installations, but it is useful when setting up a server and then being presented with a new disk from a storage array.

Right now, we are almost ready to continue. Let's review the options under **Encryption** first. Clicking on the **Edit** button in the section will take us to the following section:

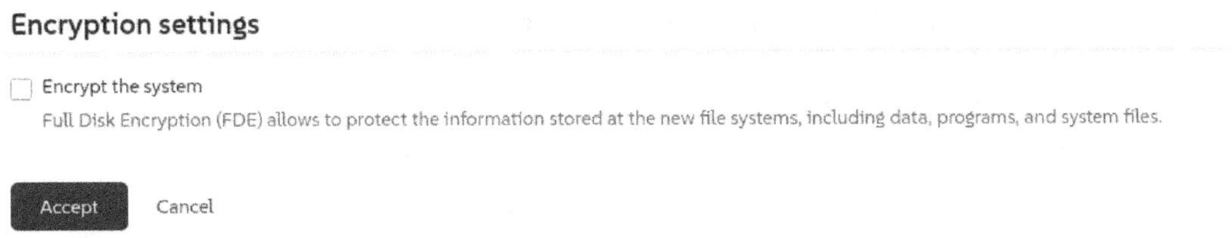


*Figure 1.37 – SLES 16 Storage — Encryption settings*

We can select, in the dialog shown in the preceding screenshot, to encrypt the full disk. This will protect the data stored in it. SLES 16 performs what is referred to as **Full Disk Encryption** (**FDE**), which completely seals the disk and requests an unlock password in the very early stages of the boot process. We will leave this unchecked and let you learn more in more advanced training.

## Software

The **Software** section enables us to select what software will be installed on our system. In SLES 16, groups of packages that have a common use are called **patterns**. We can take a look at the pre-selected patterns on the page, as seen in the following screenshot:

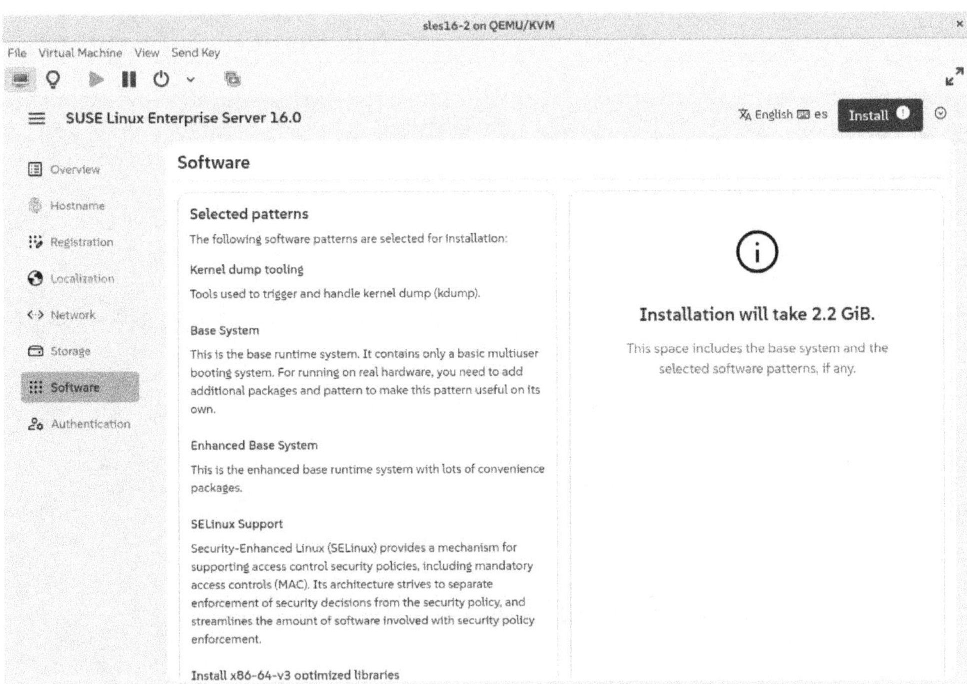


*Figure 1.38 – SLES 16 Software — Pre-selected patterns*

It is good to see that the installer is informing us of the space required to perform the installation. As you can see, there are 2.2 GiB to be consumed in the default install.

At the bottom of the page, there is a **Change selection** button:

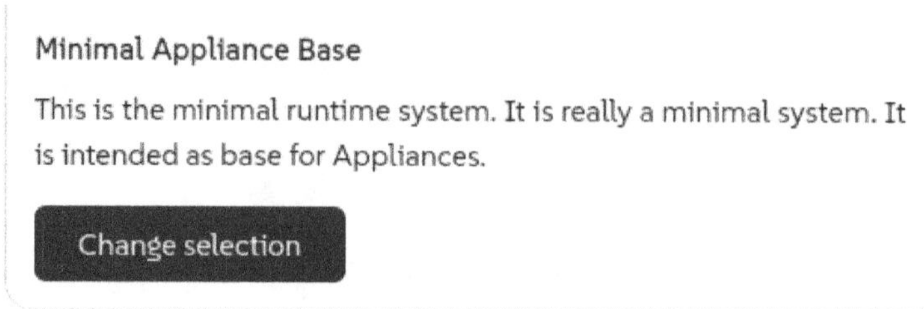


*Figure 1.39 - SLES 16 Software — Change selection button*

Clicking it will take us to the **Software selection** page, which has an extensive list of all the patterns available to be installed in SLES 16. Having selected the **PackageHub** option previously in **Registration**, the list is extensive, as we can see in the following screenshot:

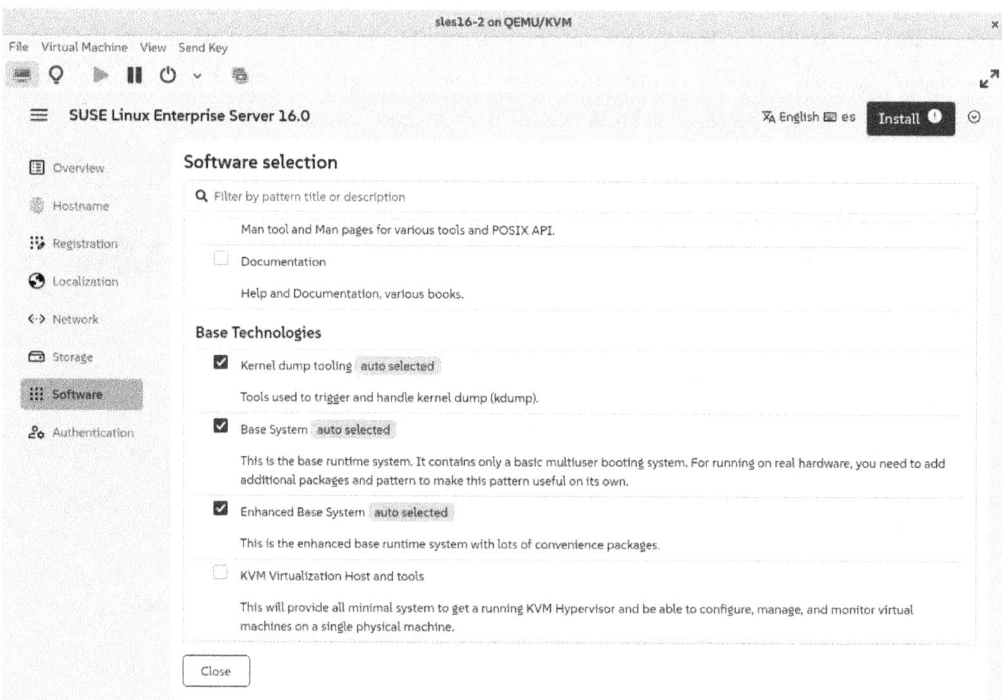


*Figure 1.40 - SLES 16 Software — Software selection*

Feel free to explore it and leave it as the default selection. Then, click the **Close** button.

## Authentication

The **Authentication** section is the place to add an initial user and configure the account for administrative purposes. We can see the page in the following capture:

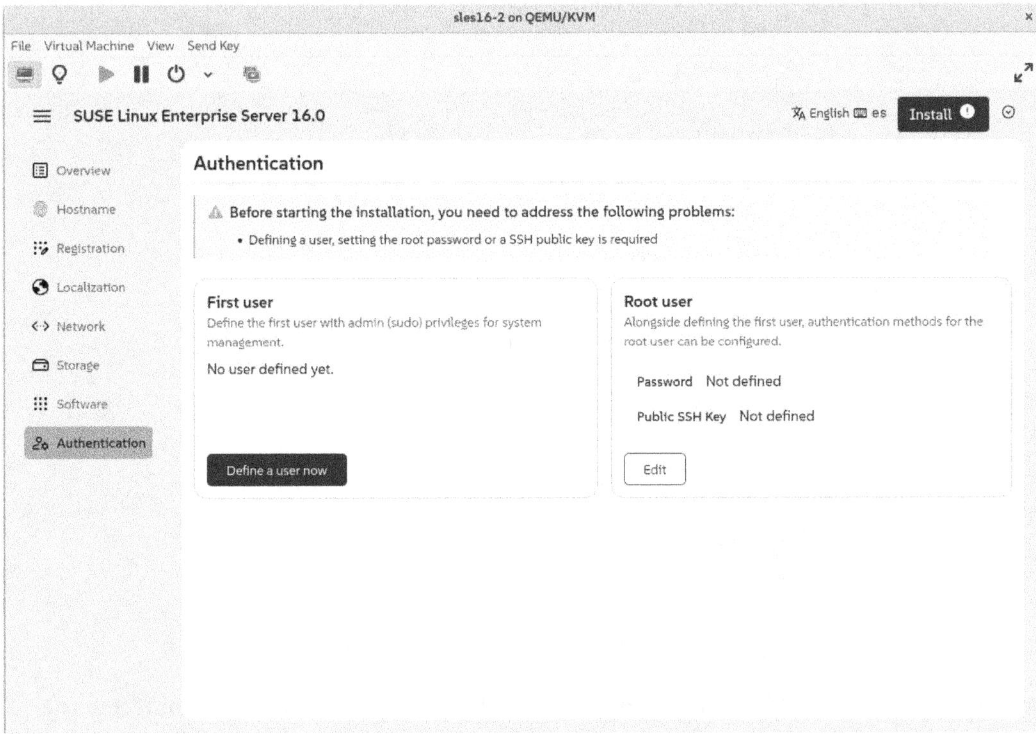


*Figure 1.41 – SLES 16 Authentication*

The administrative account in Linux is called `root`. We can add a password to it by clicking on **Edit**, as seen next:

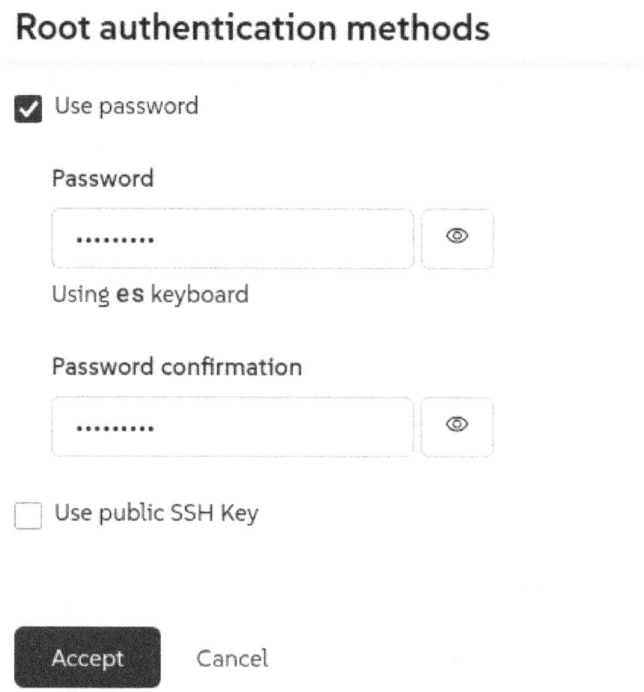


*Figure 1.42 - SLES 16 Authentication — Root user*

We can also add a **public SSH key** during installation, which will provide a way to connect to the system without needing passwords. We will learn more about this in *Chapter 7, Administering Systems Remotely*. For now, we will leave it blank. We can finish the `root` user configuration by clicking on **Accept**. This will take us back to the **Authentication** page.

We can now create our first user by clicking on **Define user now** in the **First user** section. Let's create a user named user, as shown in the following screen capture:

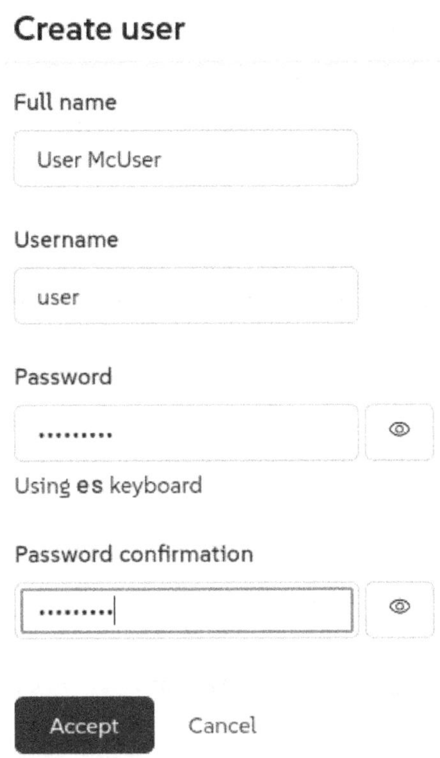


*Figure 1.43 – SLES 16 Authentication — Creating first user*

This user will have administrative privileges that will be enabled with the tool called sudo. You will learn more in *Chapter 4, Securing the System with Users, Groups, and Permissions.*

Clicking on the **Accept** button will bring us back to the main installer page. On this page, we will see that the **Install** button at the top right doesn't have an exclamation mark anymore, as in the following screenshot:

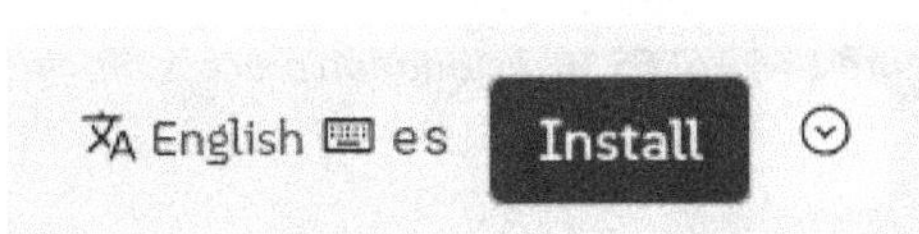


*Figure 1.44 – SLES 16 Install button ready to complete installation*

Now it's time to click on it, which will bring the following confirmation message:

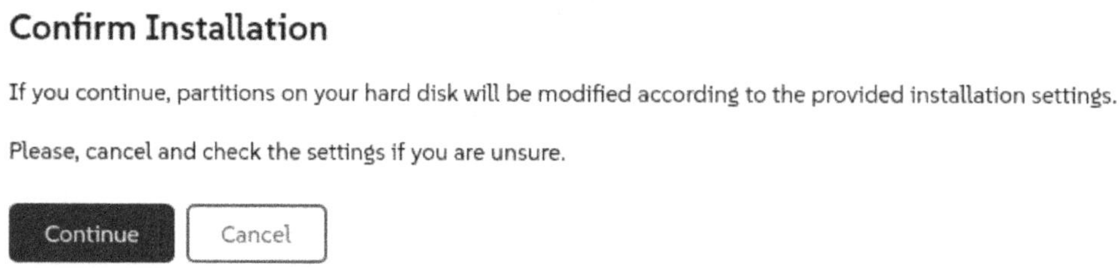


*Figure 1.45 – SLES 16 Confirm Installation*

Clicking on **Continue** will finally launch the installation, which will look like this:

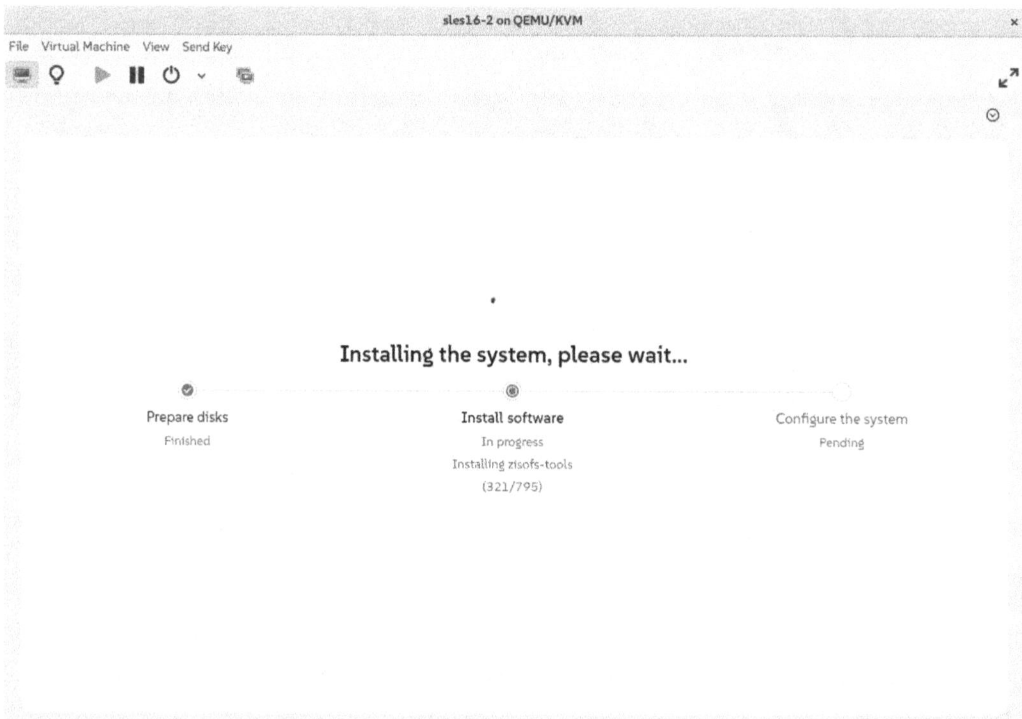


*Figure 1.46 – SLES 16 Installation process running*

Once the installation is complete, we can click on **Reboot**, and our SLES 16 system will be ready to be used:

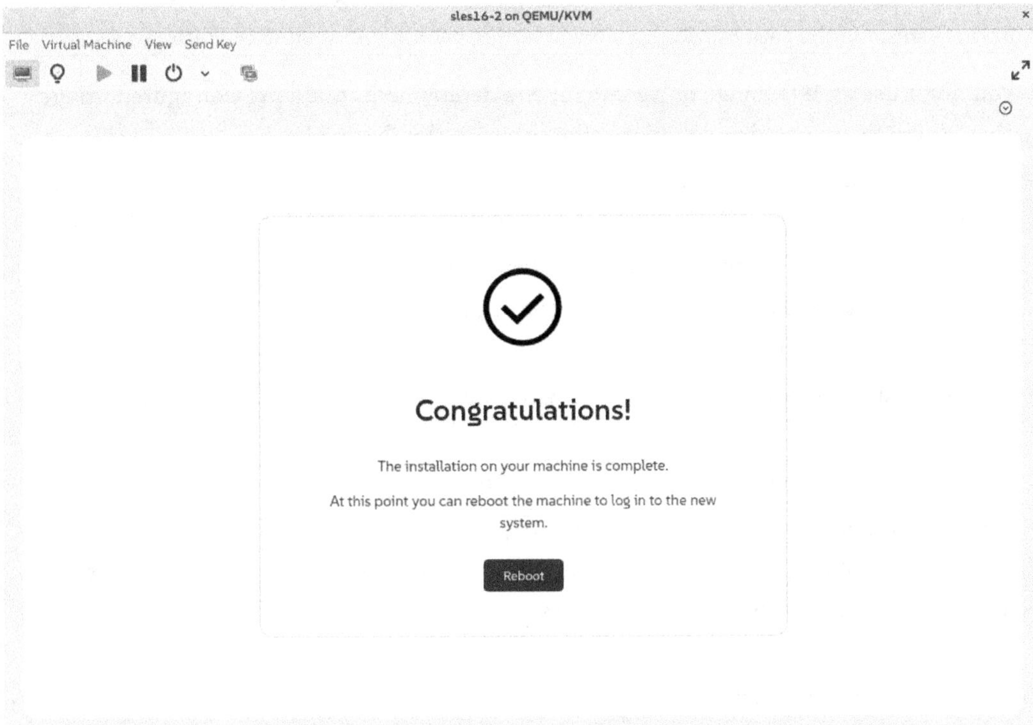


*Figure 1.47 – SLES 16 Install — Installation finished*

It's important to remember to detach the ISO image from the virtual machine (or remove the USB thumb drive from the server) and check that the boot order is properly configured in the system.

Your first SUSE Linux Enterprise Server 16 system is now ready! Congratulations!

As you can see, it is easy to install SLES on a virtual or physical machine and have it ready to be used for any service we want to run on it. In the cloud, the process is very different, as machines are instantiated from images to run. In the next section, we will review how to run SLES on a virtual machine instance in the cloud.

# Running SLES on the cloud

Deploying SLES on the cloud is slightly different from the process shown before, as cloud providers produce some of the capabilities on your behalf. Let's look at what these differences are:

- You don't use an ISO image or Agama for the deployment, but a pre-configured image that is already prepared and made available by the cloud provider.
- The image is customized and adapted to our needs after creation. You will not be able to choose the configuration details of the system during installation time (i.e., selecting a time zone), but afterwards, using the first boot configuration.
- There is an automated mechanism to perform those change settings, such as adding a user and credentials to access the system or configuring the network.
- The most extended and well-known mechanism used by cloud providers to do so is `cloud-init`.
- Images delivered by cloud providers include `cloud-init` software.
- Systems are usually accessed remotely using the SSH protocol and SSH keys generated by the user and uploaded to the cloud provider (please check *Chapter 7, Administering Systems Remotely,* for more details on how to access a system).

**Creating SLES images**

It's possible to create our own images for the cloud or virtualization, and to do so, there is the SLES image builder. But it is not part of SCA and, therefore, not covered in this book. We will instead follow the approach of taking the default image and customizing it.

Cloud providers offer initial getting-started trials to try their services at no cost, and sometimes offer free monthly services with your subscription. It's a good way to get started with SLES and cloud services.

In this book, we will not detail how to create an account with a cloud provider, but will provide a brief example of the creation of an instance of SLES 16 and how to update and modify it. To do so, we will use **Google Cloud** (it provides, as of December 2025, an initial credit for 90 days that should be enough for you to test it while you are reading this book). To follow this chapter, the following steps are required:

1. Accessing Google Cloud services requires a Google account. If you do not have a Google account, you will need to create one (you probably already have one if you use Gmail or have an Android phone).
2. Log in to your Google account at `https://console.cloud.google.com`. The first time you use this, you will have the possibility to try Google Cloud with $300 in free credits. Read the documentation and provide the details of a credit or debit card to activate your free credit.

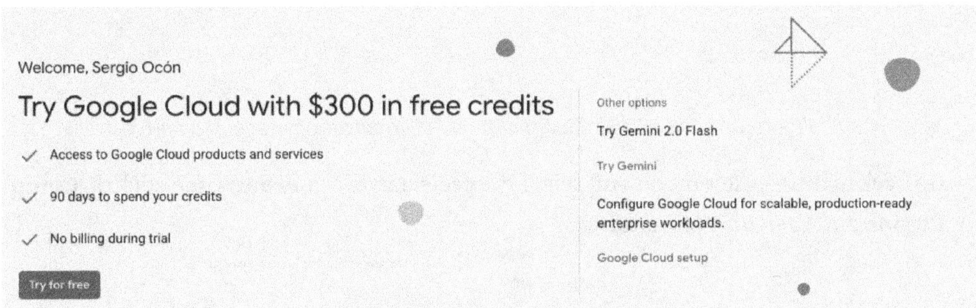


*Figure 1.48 – Google Cloud free credits offered as of December 2025*

3. Go to the cloud console at https://console.cloud.google.com. In the header, on the left, you will see a project selection box, perhaps with a project created for you with the name **My first project**. Let's create a new project by clicking on the gray box and selecting **New project**.

*Figure 1.49 – Select a project to start working*

4. Name it `SLES16` and click **Create.**

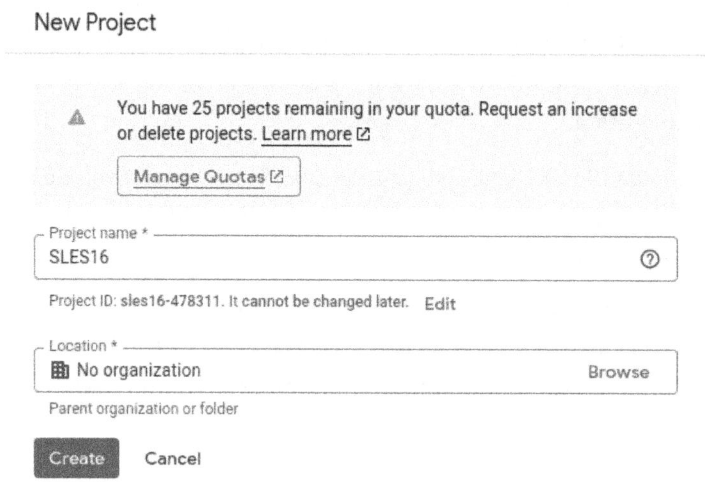


*Figure 1.50 – SLES 16 in Google Cloud — Organization menu, New project*

5. Go back to the top-left menu and select the project in the gray box, then click on **Compute Engine** and then on **VM instances.**

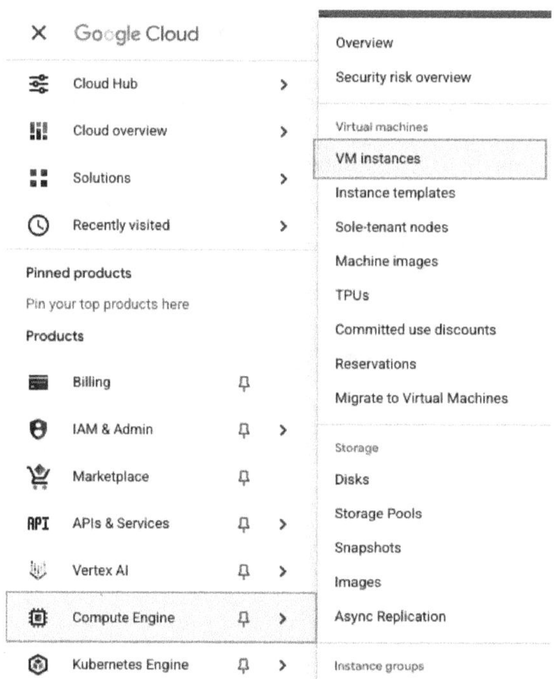


*Figure 1.51 – SLES 16 in Google Cloud — Accessing VM instances menu*

6. The first time you try, you will need to enable the Compute Engine API. Click the **Enable** button and wait a few minutes until it is ready. Once Compute Engine is ready (it may take some minutes), click on **Create**.

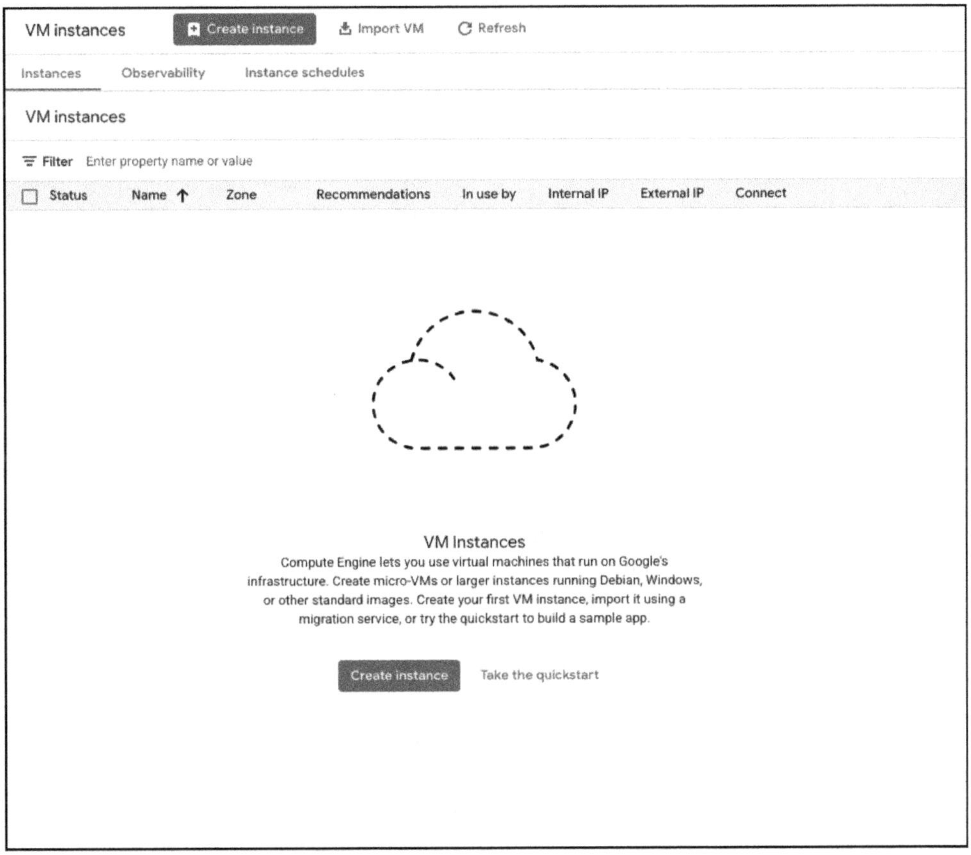


*Figure 1.52 – SLES 16 in Google Cloud — Creating a new VM instance access*

7. Follow the steps in the left menu to create your VM. Start by selecting the machine configuration.

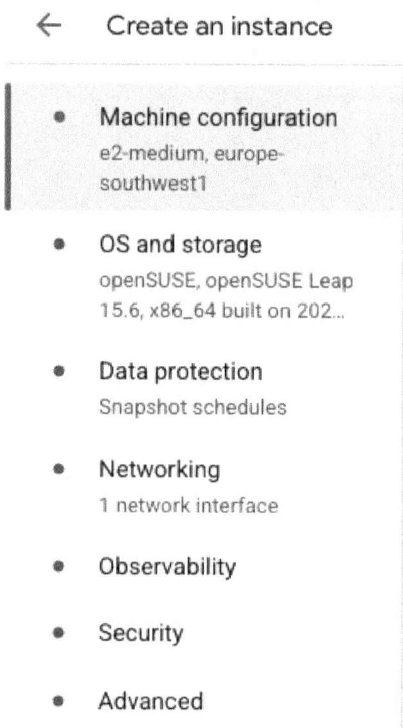


*Figure 1.53 – Left menu steps to create a VM*

8. Name the instance `sles16-instance` and select a region from the region selector:

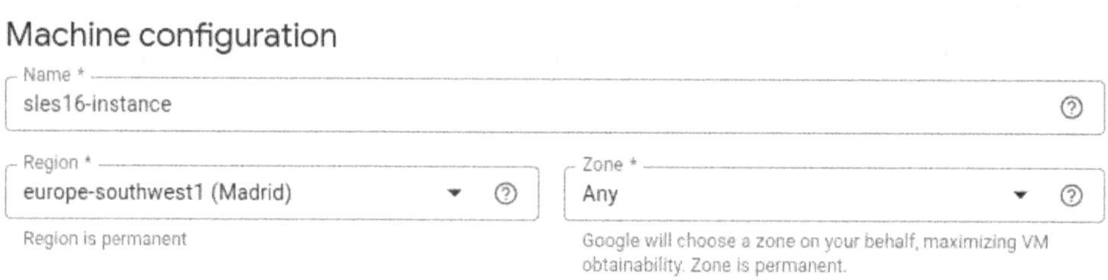


*Figure 1.54 – SLES 16 in Google Cloud — Creating a new VM instance, name, and region*

9. Select the machine configuration as **General purpose, e2-medium.**

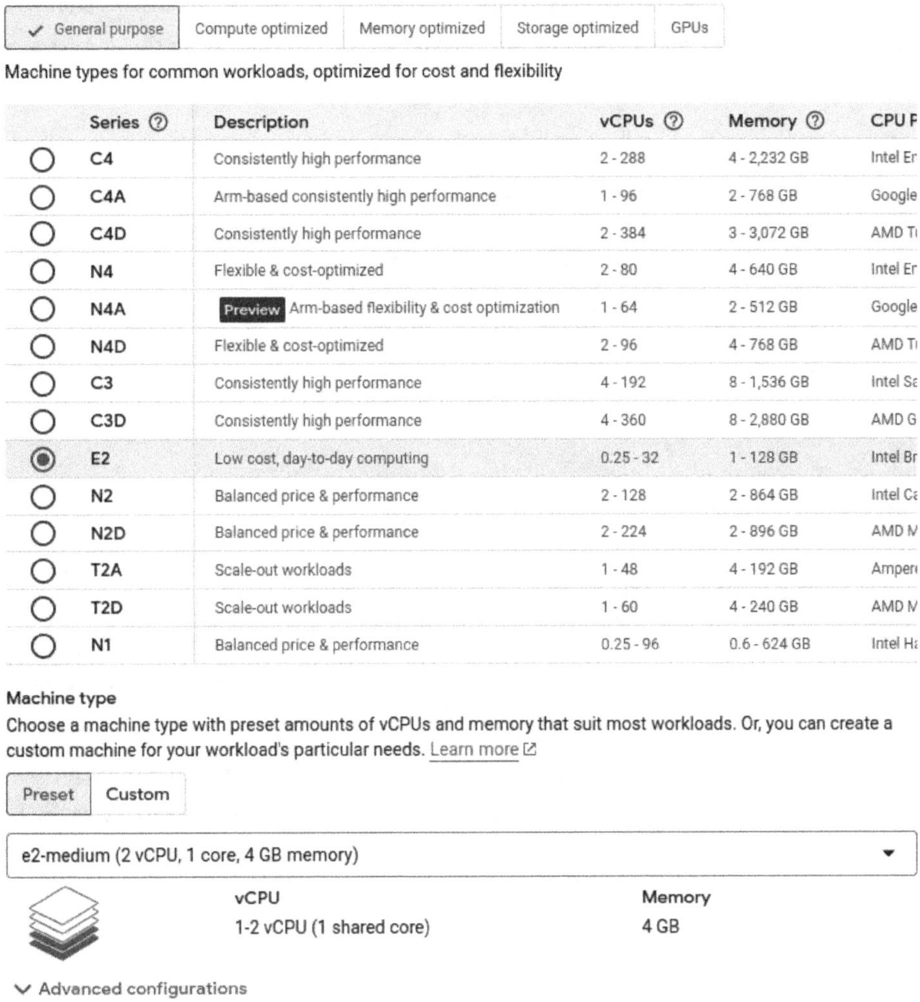


*Figure 1.55 – SLES 16 in Google Cloud — Creating a new VM instance, type, and size*

10. Select the second option, **OS and storage**, click **Change** to configure the operating system and storage, and change it to **SUSE Linux Enterprise Server**. Select the version you want and the license type as **Pay-as-you-go (PAYG)**. Click **Select** to store the changes:

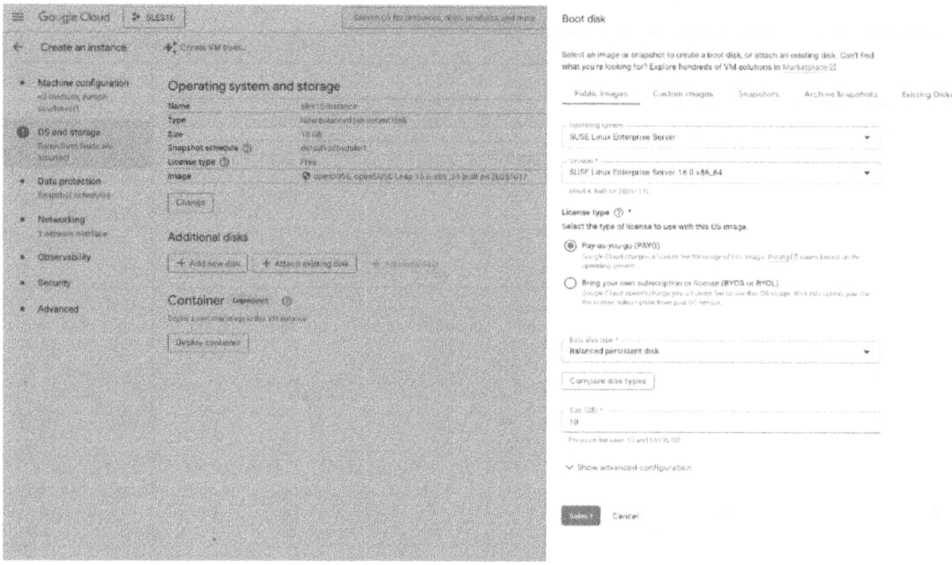


*Figure 1.56 – SLES 16 in Google Cloud — Creating a new VM instance, image selection, payment terms, and disk size*

11. On the right side, you can see your monthly cost estimates for the VM. Continue looking at the options in the different tabs, and once you are happy with the result, go to the bottom line and click on the **Create** button:

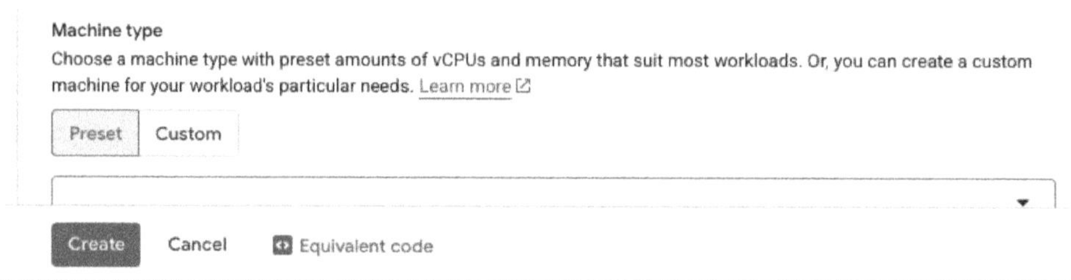


*Figure 1.57 – SLES 16 in Google Cloud — Creating the VM*

12. After a while, your instance will be ready. We will learn later how to connect via SSH. For now, click on the dropdown triangle next to **Connect**, **SSH**, and select **Open in browser window**:

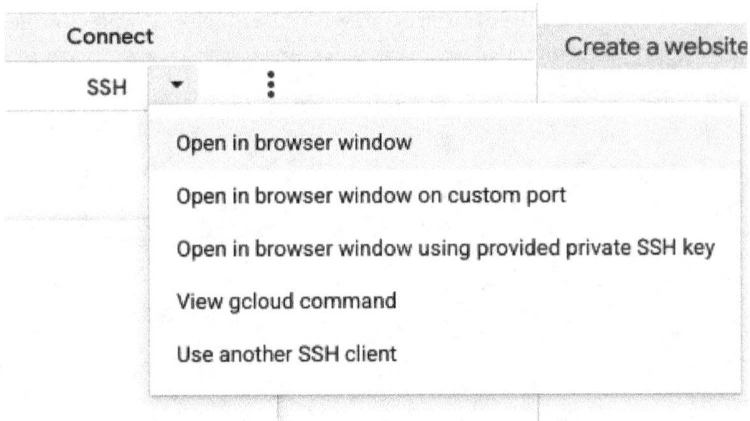


*Figure 1.58 – SLES 16 in Google Cloud — VM instance, access console*

13. You will be inside your newly deployed SLES 16 instance:

*Figure 1.59 – SLES 16 in Google Cloud — VM instance, console*

14. You can enable remote access using your own SSH key (which will be shown in *Chapter 7, Administering Systems Remotely*), but once set up, it's easy to have a new instance running.
15. You can become an administrator easily by running the following command:

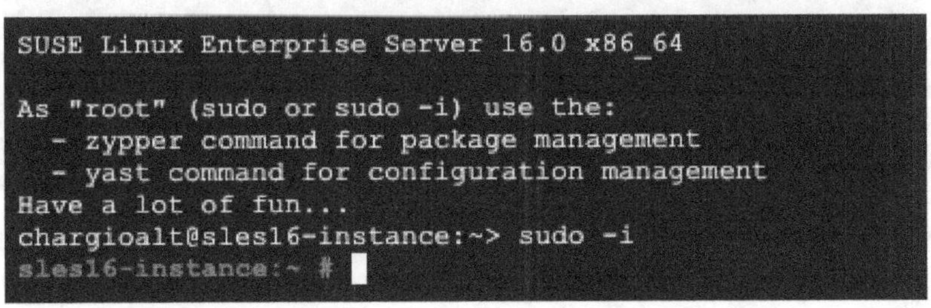


*Figure 1.60 – Getting administration permissions on the machine*

16. Now you can check the time configuration with `timedatectl`, and change it:

```
sles16-instance:~ # timedatectl
               Local time: Sat 2025-11-15 12:08:59 UTC
           Universal time: Sat 2025-11-15 12:08:59 UTC
                 RTC time: Sat 2025-11-15 12:08:59
                Time zone: Etc/UTC (UTC, +0000)
System clock synchronized: yes
              NTP service: active
          RTC in local TZ: no
sles16-instance:~ # timedatectl set-timezone Europe/Madrid
sles16-instance:~ # timedatectl
               Local time: Sat 2025-11-15 13:09:28 CET
           Universal time: Sat 2025-11-15 12:09:28 UTC
                 RTC time: Sat 2025-11-15 12:09:28
                Time zone: Europe/Madrid (CET, +0100)
System clock synchronized: yes
              NTP service: active
          RTC in local TZ: no
sles16-instance:~ #
```

17. You can also change the language configuration with `localectl`:

```
[sles16-instance:~ # localectl
System Locale: LANG=en_US.UTF-8
    VC Keymap: (unset)
   X11 Layout: (unset)
sles16-instance:~ # localectl set-locale es_ES.utf8
sles16-instance:~ # localectl
System Locale: LANG=es_ES.utf8
    VC Keymap: (unset)
   X11 Layout: (unset)
```

Now you have a machine configured as in the local example, which you can use for the rest of the book. In case you want to work on your own images for the cloud or replicate installations, an automated deployment process will be required. Take a look at the next section to see how to do that.

# Installation best practices

SLES installations have many options to choose from, and they should be tailored for the use case. However, some common recommendations apply. Let's see the most common types.

The first type is **blueprints**:

- Standardize the core installation and create a blueprint for it.

  This blueprint shall be minimal enough to serve as the base for all other blueprints and deployments.

- Build a set of blueprints for common cases when needed.
- Try to use an automation platform to build extended cases (i.e., Salt or Ansible):
- Try to make the cases modular (i.e., app server and database blueprints can be combined on one single machine).
- Be aware of the requirements to apply your templated blueprints and adapt to the environments you will use.

The second type is **software**:

- The less software is installed, the smaller the attack surface. Try to keep servers with the minimal set of packages required to run and operate (i.e., try not to add a graphical user interface to your servers).
- Standardize the installed tools where possible to be able to react quickly in case of an emergency.
- Package your third-party applications to have healthy lifecycle management (whether with RPM or in containers).
- Establish a patching schedule.

The third type is **networking**:

- On virtual machines, try not to overuse the number of network interfaces.
- On physical machines, use interface teaming/bonding whenever it is possible. Segment networks using VLANs.

The fourth type is **storage**:

- For servers, use LVM where possible (usually everything but `/boot` or `/boot/efi`).
- Keep the default boot partition with the default size, and if you change it, do it to enlarge it (you may need space there during upgrades).
- Use BTRFS snapshots with `snapper` to keep well-known configurations.
- The default swap partition is a safe bet, unless the third-party software has specific requirements.
- For long-lived systems, have at least separate partitions for `/home` and consider even a separate one for `/var/log` (for ephemeral cloud instances, or short-lived systems, it does not apply).

The fifth type is **security**:

- Do not disable *SELinux*. It has been improved a lot in the latest versions, and it's very likely that it won't interfere with your system (if required, set it in permissive mode instead of fully disabling it).
- Do not disable the firewall. Automate port opening with the service deployment.
- Redirect logs to a central location whenever possible.
- Standardize the security tools and configuration that you want to install to be able to check system integrity and audit (i.e., *AIDE, logwatch, auditd*).
- Review software install (*RPM*) *gpg* keys, as well as ISO images to ensure integrity.
- Try to avoid using passwords (especially for the `root` account), and use strong ones where needed.

Finally, we will look at the **miscellanea** type:

- Keep system time synchronized.
- Review *logrotate* policies to avoid "disk full" due to logs.

Following these best practices will help you avoid issues and make the installed base more manageable. Now you know how to deploy SLES in a system, in a structured, repeatable manner, providing services to other teams in a fast, resilient fashion.

# Summary

The **SUSE Certified System Administrator** exam is completely practical, based on real-world experience. The best way to prepare for it is by practicing as much as possible; that is why this book starts by providing access to SLES 16 and provides alternatives for how to deploy your own VMs.

There are different scenarios covered for the installation, which are the most common ones, and include using a physical machine, a virtual machine, or a cloud instance.

When using *physical hardware*, we focus on the fact that many people like to reuse old hardware, buy second-hand or cheap mini servers, or even use their laptop as the main installation device/platform for their Linux experience.

For *virtual machines*, we think about the people who want to keep all their work on the same laptop but without messing with their current operating system (which may not even be Linux). This could also work well with the previous option by having virtual machines on your own mini server.

For *cloud instances*, we could be consuming virtual machine instances from a public cloud, which may simplify the consumption and provide enough free credit to prepare for **SUSE Certified Administrator (SCA)**. Also, once finished with the self-training, the machines can still be used to provide your own services (i.e., a blog).

Understanding the need to standardize environments and the impact of it is also important when working with Linux as a professional. It is important to start with a good set of practices (automating installations, keeping track of installed software, reducing the attack surface, etc.) from the beginning.

After this chapter, you are ready to go with the rest of the book, having at least an instance of SUSE Linux Enterprise Server 16 available to work with, and ready to practice.

In the next chapter, *Running Basic Commands and Simple Shell Scripts*, we will review the basics of the system to make ourselves comfortable and gain confidence in using the system. We will learn how to log in, use the command line, navigate the filesystem, and learn the basics of the SLES operating system.

Happy practicing!

# 2

# Running Basic Commands and Simple Shell Scripts

Once you have your **SUSE Linux Enterprise Server** (**SLES**) system up and running, it is time to use it. You need to practice with the system to get comfortable with it. In this chapter, we will review the basic usage flows to enter the system, navigate through it, and get to know the basic administration tasks.

The following topics will be covered in this chapter:

- Logging in using a password
- Changing users with the su command
- Understanding users, groups, and basic permissions
- Navigating the filesystem
- Using the command line, environment variables, and navigating through the filesystem
- Understanding I/O redirection in the command line
- Filtering output with grep and sed
- Listing, creating, copying, and moving files and directories, links, and hard links
- Using tar and gzip
- Creating basic shell scripts
- Using system documentation resources

You will be using the system installed in *Chapter 1, Getting SLES 16 Up and Running (Physical and Cloud)* and a terminal emulator installed in your computer, or accessible through the VM interface.

# Logging in using a password

In Linux systems, the actions you can do are usually limited. The system needs to know the user to apply restrictions. **Login** is the process by which users identify themselves to access the system. Once you are identified, that identification will be used in all the commands to limit your actions. There are several mechanisms to provide credentials, the most basic being providing `username` and `password` details.

We are going to access the system using a **console**. A console is a device that allows the user to interact with the system using a keyboard and a screen, called a **terminal**, and receive system messages, whether you are connecting physically to the system or remotely through a **virtual console**.

During the installation, we created a user and defined its password. We didn't install any graphical interface, so we will need to use a text console to log in. Start the machine and wait for the boot process to be completed. The system will, by default, enter the multi-user text mode environment, and it will prompt for our credentials. We will use it to log in to the system. The following screenshot shows you the **command prompt** when you open the console, asking you for your credentials:

*Figure 2.1 – Login process, username request*

The blinking cursor will let us know that we are ready to enter our username, in this case, `user`. You need to press *Enter* after the username to let the system know that you have finished typing. Once you press that, a line requesting the password will appear:

*Figure 2.2 – Login process, password request*

Enter the password now and press *Enter* again on your keyboard to start the session. Note that characters are not shown on the screen, so you don't have to worry about eavesdropping while entering your password. Now, a message is shown, and your session is running, as shown in the following figure:

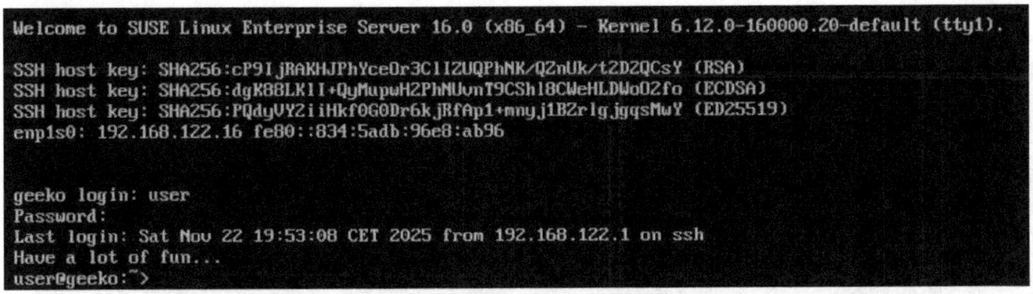


*Figure 2.3 – Successful login as user*

For security reasons, you will see a message with the last time you logged in to the system, a configurable message, and a prompt. We are now identified as the `user` user in a system called geeko. Acting as `user` will limit what files and folders we can access, what actions we can do, and even the space available for our own files. Internally, users are identified by an integer. You can check your user ID (UID 1,000) by entering `id` and pressing *Enter*. Don't worry about the rest of the information after `uid` for now:

```
user@geeko:~> id
uid=1000(user) gid=1000(user) groups=1000(user),497(wheel) context=unconfi
ned_u:unconfined_r:unconfined_t:s0-s0:c0.c1023
```

Sometimes you want to have more than one session in parallel, with the same or different users. SLES, by default, is configured to have six terminals in a system. The default terminal can be reached by simultaneously pressing the *Ctrl*, *Alt*, + *F1* keys. As expected, nothing will happen as we are already in terminal 1. We can change to the second terminal by pressing *Ctrl*, *Alt*, + *F2*, to the third one by pressing *Ctrl*, *Alt*, + *F3*, and so on up to *F6*. Using more than one terminal allows you to use different credentials and type different commands simultaneously.

Input `exit` to go back to the login prompt and enter other credentials.

## The root account

There are strict limits to what users can do. Most of the changes and administrative tasks in a system, such as creating new users or adding new software, are not available to regular users. Special users with administrative rights are needed, and the traditional superuser is called `root`. The `root` account is always available in the system, and it has a special identifier (UID 0).

We defined a password for the root account during the installation, so now we are ready to log in using those credentials.

Note that even though the root account is always created, if you don't choose a password, the account will not be accessible in the console until you provide it. The next screenshot shows the login when you are using the root account:

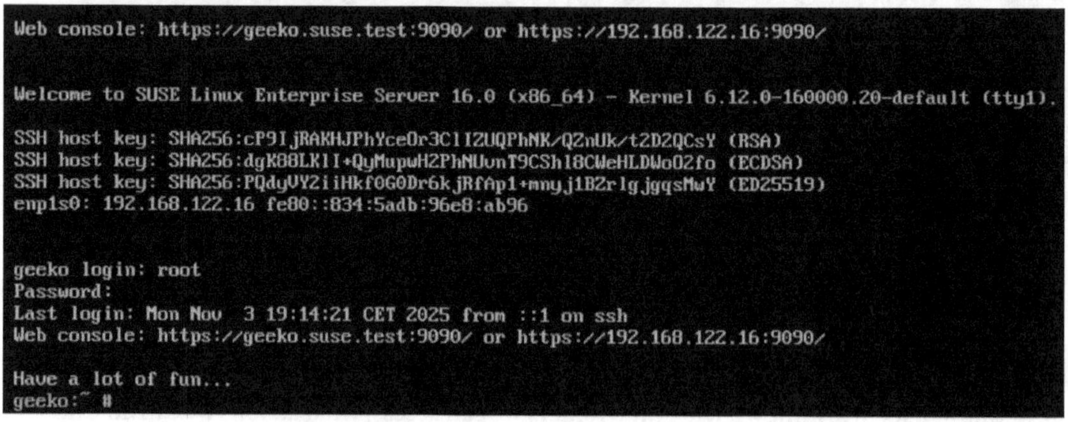


*Figure 2.4 – Successful login, using root credentials*

## Understanding the command prompt

The system is now waiting for us to specify what we want it to do. Your commands need to be typed one letter at a time, followed by *Enter*, in the **command prompt**. The system will receive your input, process it to get a result, and give you a response before waiting for the next input.

The following prompt shows some useful information about you and the system:

```
user@geeko:~>
```

In the default configuration, it shows your username and the hostname of the system, separated by an @ symbol and followed by a colon (:), and the simplified description of the path. The ~ symbol represents the shortcut to the **user's home directory** (/home/user for the user account and /root for the root account).

The last part is different:

- The $ symbol is used for regular users with no administrative privileges.
- The # symbol identifies that the user is privileged, either because the user is root or because the user has acquired administrative privileges. In color terminals, the prompt is also red to warn you about the extended privileges.

> Be careful when using a prompt with the # symbol. The system won't stop you from making changes that damage the system or other user data if you are an administrator. You should avoid working as an administrator unless you really need the rights.

Once we have identified ourselves in the system, we are logged in and have a running session. It is time to learn how to change from one user to the other in the next section.

## Changing users with the su command

One of the benefits of using a **multi-user system** is being able to change between users, for instance, to do some maintenance on the system that requires admin rights. Accessing the system with two users at the same time can be done easily by opening a session for each, but sometimes it is more convenient to impersonate other users in the same session in which we are.

Linux includes a tool to do exactly that, `su`, an abbreviation of *substitute user*.

If you are not sure, you can always ask the system which user is currently logged in by running the `whoami` command. Let's try that in the `root` session we have open:

```
geeko:~ # whoami
root
Take notice that the prompt is different for the user, not only the #
sign, but the system name is not shown by default.
```

Let's now try to change the user from `root` to `user`:

```
geeko:~ # su user
user@geeko:/root> whoami
user
```

We have successfully started a session with `user`. We could finish this session by using the `exit` command:

```
user@geeko:/root> exit
exit
geeko:~ # whoami
root
```

The root user is free to impersonate any other user, without knowing their password. Does it work the other way around? Can any user impersonate root or any other user? Yes, they can, but by providing the right credentials:

```
[user@SLES8 ~]$ su root
Password:
[root@SLES8 user]# whoami
root
```

Running su without specifying the user is equivalent to specifying root:

```
user@geeko:~> su
Password:
geeko:/home/user #
```

> Changing the user using su does not change the working directory, even if the new user does not have access to the new one.

Each user can customize the environment, such as defining whether the prompt shows the system name or not, or their preferred editor. If we want to fully impersonate the other user and take their preferences (or **environment variables**), we can do so by adding - after the su command:

```
user@geeko:~> su -
Password:
geeko:~ #
```

Also, we can go from root to user:

```
geeko:~ # su - user
user@geeko:~>
```

Using su - behaves like a new login, but within the same session.

Let's now talk about permissions for the different users in the system, as addressed in the next section.

# Understanding users, groups, and basic permissions

There is a principle in Unix that Linux inherited: *Everything is a file.* Apart from some corner cases, it stays true in almost any occasion. A disk is represented as a file in the system (such as `/dev/sdb` mentioned in the installation), a process can be represented as a file (under `/proc`), and many other components in the system are also represented as files.

The basic security for a multi-user system is to limit access to those files. However, providing a detailed list of access for all other users in a system could be challenging and hard to maintain, specifically when new users are constantly being added to the system, so Linux uses some concepts to make this easier:

- **Groups**: Users belong to groups that grant permissions and share resources.

  Each user has a *primary group* and can have many *secondary groups*. New files created by the users are, by default, assigned to the primary group.

  In SLES, by default, a new primary group with the same name as the username is created for each user.

- **Permissions**: These are assigned to files and define access rights.

  Standard Linux (and Unix/POSIX) permissions differentiate three levels: *user* (the owner), *group* (the same group as the file), and *others*. Each file defines them independently to allow access to only the owner, users in the same group as the file, and everybody else (ugo).

  The whole system comes with a set of permissions assigned by default to each file and directory. Be careful when changing them, as changing permissions for system files can make the system unusable or delete your access to your own files.

> **POSIX** is an acronym for **Portable Operating System Interface**, a family of standards specified by the IEEE Computer Society (`https://en.wikipedia.org/wiki/POSIX`) that defines the interface for an operating system, ensuring compatibility and portability.

## Users

There are many different accounts in a SLES system by default. Users are a mechanism to provide security limits to files and programs in a system, so creating new ones is a fairly normal operation. There are three types of users:

- **Regular users**: These are assigned to individuals and restricted.
- **Superuser**: Also `root`. This is the main administrative account in the system, unrestricted, with full access to everything, including files from other users.
- **System users**: These are accounts used for background processes or **daemons** that run without user interaction, limiting their reach within the system. System users are not intended to log in to the system.

Users and groups are internally identified with a number known as a **user ID (UID)** or **group ID (GID)**.

We used the `whoami` command before to check the username, but we can get additional information with the `id` command:

```
user@geeko:~> id
uid=1000(user) gid=1000(user)
groups=1000(user),497(wheel)
context=unconfined_u:unconfined_r:unconfined_t:s0
```

User IDs are not confidential. We can check the information of other accounts in the system as a regular user, including `root`:

```
user@geeko:~> id root
uid=0(root) gid=0(root) groups=0(root)
```

Let's examine the information displayed for the user called `user` when we run `id user`:

- `uid=1000(user)`: User ID and (username). The ID is the numeric identifier of the user in the system. In this case, it is `1000`. Identifiers of `1000` and above are used in SLES for regular users, reserving 999 and below for system users.
- `gid=1000(user)`: Group ID, followed by group name in brackets. This is the numeric identifier and name for the primary group of the user.

- `groups=1000(user),497(wheel)`: Groups that the user belongs to, in this case `user` with GID `1000` and `wheel` with GID 497. The `wheel` user group is special. It is used in SLES and many other systems as a group for users that can become administrators by using the `sudo` tool (to be explained later).
- `context=unconfined_u:unconfined_r:unconfined_t:s0-s0:c0`: This is the SELinux context for the user. It will define several restrictions in the system by using SELinux (to be explained in depth in *Chapter 10, Keeping the System Hardened with SELinux*).

All the ID-related data is stored in the system in the `/etc/passwd` file. Please note that this file is very sensitive and is better managed by using the tools related to it. If we want to edit it, we can do it by using `vipw`, a tool that will ensure (among other things) that only one admin is editing the file at a time. The `/etc/passwd` file contains the info of each user per line. This is the line for `user`:

```
user:x:1000:1000:Geeko:/home/user:/bin/bash
```

Each user is described in one line, with fields separated by a colon (`:`). Let's review what they mean:

- `user`: Username assigned to the user. It has to be unique.
- `x`: Field for the encrypted password. In the past, Linux systems included the password here, but nowadays it is in a separate file that is not directly accessible to regular users (`/etc/shadow`).
- `1000` (first instance): UID value.
- `1000` (second instance): Principal GID value.
- `Geeko`: Description of the account.
- `/home/user`: Home directory for the user. The default directory where content and preferences for the user will be stored.
- `/bin/bash`: Command interpreter for the user. Bash is the default interpreter in SLES. Other alternatives, such as `tcsh`, `zsh`, or `ksh`, are available to be installed in SLES.

## Groups

**Groups** allow permissions to be assigned to a subset of users at the same time, so it is easier to share resources. For instance, the finance team could be interested in getting shared access to work documents; we could create the `finance` group and give users of the group permission to access, read, and write the `/srv/finance` directory. Any users that are included in the group will be able to do that, and when the finance team has a new hire, giving access is done just by adding the new hire to the `finance` group.

Groups are internally identified using a number called a GID and a group name for easy access.

Group data is stored in the system in the `/etc/group` file. To avoid corruption of data, you should not edit the file using any tool, but use specific tools included in the distribution as `root` (such as `vigr`). The file contains one group per line with different fields separated by a colon (`:`). Let's take a look at the line for the `wheel` group:

```
wheel:x:497:user
```

Each field is specific to a different thing:

- `wheel`: This is the name of the group. The `wheel` group is used to provide some admin rights to regular users and is available by default.
- `x`: The group password field. `x` means that the password is defined in the `gshadow` file (which is not present).
- `497`: GID value for the group.
- `user`: The list of users belonging to that group as a secondary group (separated by commas, such as `user1, user2, user3`).

Groups can be used in many ways in different distributions. To avoid privacy issues with default group permissions, SLES has several types of groups:

> It is very common that "primary group" and "private group" are the same.

- **Primary group**: This is the default group, assigned to the files newly created by the user.
- **Private group**: This is a specific group created for each user, with the same name as the user. Private groups are automatically created when a new user account is added.
- **Supplementary group**: Some other groups, created for specific purposes. For example, the `wheel` group is used in SLES to enable admin privileges to users, or the `cdrom` group that provides access to CDs and DVD devices in the system.

# Navigating the filesystem

Files are organized in directories, a special file that holds a list of other files and folders in a tree structure, known as the **directory tree** of the system. In Linux and Unix (macOS is a Unix-like system), there is a single directory tree that starts with the `root` directory represented by `/`. The rest of the content of the system will hang from that folder, and any other disk or device will be accessed as a subtree hanging from one of the directories.

For instance, this is the tree structure of the `/boot` folder:

```
/boot
├── efi
│   └── EFI
└── grub2
    ├── arm64-efi
    ├── backgrounds
    ├── fonts
    ├── locale
    └── themes
```

> The `root` directory and the home directory for the `root` user are two different things. The `root` user has been assigned by default the home directory, `/root`, whereas the `root` directory is the mother of all directories in each system and is represented by `/`.

The command line refers to other directories from the **working directory**. The address of a directory within the tree can be specified in two ways:

- As an **absolute path** that starts with the root path, `/`, and specifies every leaf in the tree. `/boot/efi/EFI/sles/grub.cfg` refers to the `grub.cfg` file in the directory that can be found from root (/), going through `boot`, `efi`, and `EFI`. Absolute paths are unique.
- As a **relative path** that starts without `/`, and is found by adding the *working directory* to the path specified. The same file could be specified as `sles/grub.cfg` if the working directory is `/boot/efi/EFI/`.

Directories can be differentiated by adding / to the end. You can use `.` to point to the same directory

: `./././sles/grub.cfg` will be the same file. You can use `..` to point to the parent directory. You can use `cd` to change directories, updating the working directory to the new one.

We can see which directory we are in by running the `pwd` command:

```
[user@geeko:~> pwd
/home/user
user@geeko:~> cd /var/tmp
user@geeko:/var/tmp> pwd
/var/tmp
```

You don't need to remember your home directory, as there is a shortcut for the home directory of the current user: ~. We can use that shortcut to go to it without knowing the username or the parent folder for user accounts:

```
user@geeko:/var/tmp> cd -
/home/user
user@geeko:~> pwd
/home/user
```

Some other shortcuts for directories are as follows:

- ~: Home directory of the current user
- .: Current directory
- ..: Parent directory
- -: Previously used directory (used to quickly change back)

More details on managing files and directories in Linux and SLES are in the *Listing, creating, copying, moving files and directories, links, and hard links* section of this chapter.

## File permissions

File access is defined for users, groups, and everybody else. To review **file permissions**, we are going to log in to the system as `root`, and we will use the `ls` command to list files and show their permissions. We will learn more about how to change permissions in *Chapter 4, Securing the System with Users, Groups, and Permissions.*

Log in to the system as `root`, and run the `ls` command:

```
geeko:~ # ls
.bash_history  .docker  .gnupg  .lesshst  .ssh
.viminfo  bin
```

It shows the files present in the root home directory, represented by ~. We can see different configuration files (files that start with `.`) and a `bin` directory (where you store binaries needed by the `root` user).

Files and directories starting with `.` are typically hidden for normal listing to reduce cluttering and are often used to store configuration.

We can get additional information by appending `-l` to `ls`:

```
geeko:~ # ls -l
total 12
-rw-------. 1 root root 1123 Mar 29 04:55 .bash_
history
drwxr-xr-x. 1 root root   22 Mar 29 04:51
.docker
drwx------. 1 root root    0 Jan 28 10:27 .gnupg
-rw-------. 1 root root   34 Mar 29 04:52
.lesshst
drwx------. 1 root root   30 Mar 24 13:06 .ssh
-rw-------. 1 root root  735 Mar 29 11:00
.viminfo
drwxr-xr-x. 1 root root    0 Jan 28 10:27 bin
```

We see the following in the output:

- `total 12`: Total space, in **kilobytes** (**KB**), occupied in the disk by the files. Note that we are using 4 KB blocks, so every file under that size will occupy a minimum of 4 KB, and there are 3 directories that do not occupy space in this folder.
- `-rw-------.`: The permissions assigned to each file or directory.
- The first character signals special permissions for the file. In a regular file, it will appear as - (no special permissions).
- Directories will appear with `d`. In Linux, everything is a file, and directories are files with special permissions.

- A file can point to another file. Symbolic links will appear with `l`. These behave like a shortcut to a file from a different directory and will show the name followed by `->` and the name of the original file.
- Some files allow users to execute a file with the permissions of the owner of the executable instead of the user who launched it. This is useful when there is a need for extra privileges:
    - The so-called `setuid` or `setgid` permissions will appear as `s`
    - A special permission so that the owner can only remove or rename the file, called a **sticky bit**, will appear as `t`
- We have seen the first character in the permissions of a file represented, for example, as `-rw-------`. The next nine characters are the privileges for `user/group/others` grouped in three characters for `user`, three for `group`, and three for `others`.
- The next three characters, `rw-`, are the permissions for the user who owns the file:
    - The first one, `r`, is the permission to read the file.
    - The second one, `w`, is the write permission.
    - The third one, `x`, is the execution. It is not present in our case and is thus shown as `-`.

Directories behave slightly differently:

- The read permission allows you to see the content of the directory.
- The write permission allows you to modify the contents.
- The execute permission allows you to enter and travel through the directory.
- `setgid` means that files are created using the group of the directory and not the primary group of the users.
- The next three characters, `---`, define permissions for the group. They work the same way as the owner permission. The first `---` means that no group access is granted.
- The last `---` are the permissions for others, which means any user and/or group different from the ones assigned to the file.
- `1` is the number of **links** (hard links) to this file. This is intended, among other things, so we do not delete a file used in another folder.
- `root` (first time) is the owner of the file.
- `root` (second time) is the group assigned to the file.
- `735` is the size in bytes.
- `Mar 30 08:57` is the date and time of the last modification of the file.
- `.bash_history` is the filename.

**The r and x permissions in directories**

It is possible to be able to see the content of a directory with `ls` (`r`) but not be able to enter it (no `x`), and the opposite. You can allow other users to enter a directory (`x`) without allowing users to see what is inside (no `r`). In that last case, you will have to know the full path to be able to enter the directory, which will prevent you from knowing whether there are other folders created by other users.

When we list a directory (referred to as a folder), the output will show the contents of the directory and not the directory itself. We can list the info for the directory with the `-d` option. Let's take a look at `/etc`, the directory that stores the system-wide configuration:

```
geeko:~ # ls -l -d /etc
drwxr-xr-x. 1 root root 2564 Mar 29 23:33 /etc
```

As you can see, it's quite easy to obtain information about files and directories in the system. Let's now learn more about the command line and how to navigate the filesystem in the next section.

# Using the command line, environment variables, and navigating through the filesystem

As we have seen before, once we log in to the system, we have access to the command line. It's important to understand the command line and the filesystem well to feel comfortable in the environment and make the most of it.

## Command line and environment variables

The command line is provided by a program also called an **interpreter** or **shell**. There are some differences between them, specifically the advanced use cases, so it can be a matter of preference which one to use. In this section, we will cover the most widespread shell used in Linux and the one provided by default in SLES: `bash`.

A simple trick to know which shell you are using is to run the following:

```
user@geeko:~> echo $SHELL
/bin/bash
```

The echo command will show onscreen the content of its input. The shell will modify some content in the command line that will be *substituted* or *interpreted*. In this case, we are using an **environment variable.** Environment variables are automatically updated by the shell or defined by the user, and are used by adding the $ symbol at the beginning. In this case, we are telling the system to echo the content of the SHELL variable. Let's use it for other variables:

```
geeko:~ # echo $USER
root
geeko:~ # echo $HOME
/root
```

Let's check for a different user:

```
geeko:~ # su - user
user@geeko:~> echo $USER
user
user@geeko:~> echo $HOME
/home/user
```

As you can see, you can always refer to $USER, and it will be substituted with the current user, or to $HOME, and it will be substituted by the directory dedicated to the user, also known as the **home directory**.

These are some of the most common and important environment variables for user:

| Variable | Value for user | Usage |
|---|---|---|
| EDITOR | (unset) | Establishes the default text editor for the user |
| HOME | /home/user | Home directory for the current user |
| HOSTNAME | geeko.suse.test | Hostname of the system we are logged into |
| LANG | en_US.UTF-8 | Language configured for the current user; in this case, American English with the UTF-8 extensions |
| PATH | /home/user/.local/bin:/usr/local/bin:/usr/bin:/bin | Colon-separated list of directories that will be searched in order to run the command we are typing |
| PS1 | \u@\h:\w> | Defines what information will be shown at the prompt, in this case, user (\u), at hostname (@\h), working directory (\w), and the prompt symbol: $ for user or # for root (\$) |

| Variable | Value for user | Usage |
|---|---|---|
| PWD | /home/user | Path to the working directory; the directory we are currently in |
| SHELL | /bin/bash | Shell in use |
| USER | user | Username of the current user, in this case, user |

*Table 2.1 – Main environment variables*

You can get a full list of environment variables with the env command.

Many environment variables are automatically updated by the shell, such as USER and PWD. Users can define their own. The configuration for the shell is defined in two hidden files: ~/.profile is read each time a login shell is started, while ~/.bashrc is read in addition by all other interactive shells. You can use them to customize your shell to your liking.

## Bash autocomplete

Shortcuts are a faster way to reach commonly used directories or relative references to the current working directory. However, Bash can help you reduce the amount of typing with **autocompletion**. It relies on the *Tab* key.

When typing a folder or a file, we can hit the *Tab* key to complete its name. For example, if we want to go to the /boot/grub2 folder, we type the following:

```
user@geeko:~> cd /bo
```

Then, we hit *Tab*. It will autocomplete it to /boot/, even adding the final / character as it is a directory:

```
[user@geeko:~> cd /boot
```

Now, we type the first letter of the directory we want to go to, grub2, which is g:

```
user@geeko:~> cd /boot/g
```

Then, when we hit *Tab*. It will autocomplete it to /boot/grub2/:

```
user@geeko:~> cd /boot/grub2
```

Now, we can hit *Enter* to go there.

If we press *Tab* twice during completion, it will show a list of available targets to complete, as in this example:

```
user@geeko:~> cd /r
root/ run/
```

It can also be used to complete commands. We can type a letter, such as `h`, hit *Tab* twice, and it will show all the commands starting with `h`:

```
user@geeko:~> h
h2ph          hash          head          hipstopgm     host
hostnamectl
h2xs          hdifftopam    help          history       hostid        hpftodit
hardlink      hdisk.pl      hexdump       hltest        hostname      hugetop
```

This capability can be extended to help complete other parts of our commands by installing the `bash-completion` package (installed by default):

```
geeko:~ # zypper install bash-completion -y
```

## Recovering previous commands

Many times, it is great to reuse some command, because commands may be long or complex, or just because it is hard to remember the right syntax. For all the commands that have been run, the `history` command will be available in Bash. Just press the *up* arrow key (the one with an arrow pointing up), and the previous commands will appear on the screen.

If there are too many commands in your history, you can quickly search through them. Run the `history` command:

```
user@geeko:~> history
    1  su root
    2  su
    3  su -
    4  id
    5  id root
    6  grep user /etc/passwd
    7  echo $USER
    8   echo $HOME
    9  declare
   10   echo $SHELL
   11   echo EDITOR
```

```
   12  echo $EDITOR
   13  grep wheel /etc/gro
   14  grep wheel /etc/group
   15  cat /etc/group
   16  grep nobody /etc/group /etc/passwd
```

You can run any of those commands again by using the `!` command. Just run `!` with the number of the command, and it will be run again. Note that running `!!` will run the very last command, no matter what number it is:

```
user@geeko:~> !5
id root
uid=0(root) gid=0(root) groups=0(root)
```

Time to enjoy your super-fast command line now. Let's learn more about the structure of directories in Linux, to know where to go to find things, in the next section.

## Filesystem hierarchy

For many years, Linux has used a standard, maintained by the **Linux Foundation**, that defines **filesystem hierarchy** and is the basis used in many Linux distributions, including SLES. This standard is known as the **Filesystem Hierarchy Standard** (**FHS**). The **UAPI Group**, getting inspiration from the `systemd` and `libeconf` implementations, has proposed a new standard (`https://uapi-group.org/specifications/specs/configuration_files_specification/`) that allows OS vendors to implement the hermetic-OS pattern, where vendor files are shipped in the vendor tree (`/usr/`), including system defaults, while allowing overrides for easier management. This is a requirement for image-based and immutable systems, where the original files and directories are read-only:

- Both `/usr` and `/etc` are supported for configuration files. If files are present in `/etc`, they take precedence over `/usr`. Vendor files should be stored in `/usr`, and customer configuration can then override them in `/etc`.
- Drop-in files and drop-in directories are supported and have higher precedence than the configuration file they refer to. Drops-in are sorted in lexicographic order using the filename, and later ones take precedence over previous ones. Drop-in directories have the `.d/` notation. Files in directories will be parsed and combined. Drop-in directories cannot have directories under them.
- Applications can choose to store configuration in `/usr/share`, `/usr/lib`, or `/usr/etc`.

- `/run` is supported for ephemeral overrides.
- It is possible to mask a configuration file by creating a symlink to `/dev/null` or an empty file (a masked file will not be parsed).

Considering that the following files are present on the filesystem, this would be the order in which the files are parsed. Note that files with the same name override each other. The configuration in `bar.conf` has the lowest priority and is read before `a.conf` and `b.conf`. `b.conf` has the highest priority:

- `/usr/lib/foo/bar.conf` (overridden by `/etc/foo/bar.conf`)
- `/etc/foo/bar.conf`
- `/usr/lib/foo/bar.conf.d/a.conf` (overridden by `/etc/foo/bar.conf.d/a.conf`)
- `/etc/foo/bar.conf.d/a.conf`
- `/usr/lib/foo/bar.conf.d/b.conf`

The following table shows the standard list of directories and their usage:

| Directory | Stands for | Use/purpose |
|---|---|---|
| `/` | Root directory | The main directory of the filesystem tree. All other directories hang from this one. |
| `/bin` | Binary files | A symbolic link to `/usr/bin`. |
| `/boot` | Bootable files | Files used by the system to boot. In SLES, this is, by default, part of the partition assigned to the root directory. |
| `/dev` | Devices | Includes files required to access host-specific devices (i.e., disks, keyboard, or audio devices). |
| `/etc` | Etcetera or editable text configuration | Host-specific system configuration files. Overrides files present in `/usr/etc` (package-based configuration). |
| `/home` | Home | Directory to include home directories for all users except `root`. |
| `/media` | External media | Intended to provide system-wide access to removable media. |
| `/mnt` | Mount | Mount point for temporary filesystems. |
| `/opt` | Optional | Optional application software packages. When building or installing your own software, you could place it here. |
| `/proc` | Processes | Special virtual filesystem representing the processes running in the system. |

| Directory | Stands for | Use/purpose |
|---|---|---|
| `/root` | Root's home | Home folder for the `root` superuser. It's not in `/home` in case it gets full, so that `root` can always log into the system. |
| `/run` | Run | Runtime data for processes on `tmpfs` (in-memory). |
| `/srv` | Service | Holds data for services provided by the system, such as FTP and HTTP. |
| `/sys` | System | Contains system information related to kernel features and connected devices. |
| `/usr` | Unix system re-sources | Contains the read-only user data, such as libraries, binaries, headers, sources, and other shared data. |
| `/usr/bin` | Binaries | Generally accessible programs. |
| `/usr/etc` | Configuration | Vendor configuration files. These configuration files should not be modified directly by the administrator, as they will possibly be overwritten on package updates. |
| `/usr/lib` | Libraries | Directory to hold the libraries used in the system and vendor configuration. |
| `/usr/local` | Local binaries | Local data specific to this host. When building local scripts or binaries for this specific system, host them here, along with distribution-independent extensions. |
| `/usr/sbin` | System binaries | Directory for the binaries to be used by the superuser only. |
| `/var` | Variable content | Directory to be used to host content to be managed by different programs, from virtual machines to logs. |
| `/tmp` | Temporary | Temporary files on a `tmpfs` filesystem (in-memory). |

*Table 2.2 – Standard filesystem hierarchy in SLES 16*

Previous versions of SLES followed a different standard for directories. If you follow an old tutorial, make sure you check the differences. For instance, `/run` now includes files that were previously stored in `/var/lock` and `/var/run`, and `/tmp` is now using `tmpfs`.

When some of these partitions are full, the system degrades, so it is important to think about the disk space when you are defining the partitions.

This is an example of the allocation values for a minimal installation of SLES 16 and the recommendations:

| Directory | Used space | Recommendation |
|---|---|---|
| `/` | 2.5 GB | In SLES, the default installation is a single `btrfs` partition for `/`. The recommended size is 10 GiB for small servers with no snapshots and 32 GiB with snapshots enabled. |
| `/boot` | 39 MB | This will contain booting files, and it will play an important role when upgrading the system. In many Linux distributions, there is a separate partition for `boot`, but not in SLES, in which, by default, `boot` is part of the `root` partition. This way, it is included in snapshots and is available for rollback. |
| `/etc` | 25 MB | This hardly ever grows a lot in size (rarely beyond 50 MB for a server). It is very convenient to leave this folder as part of the `root` partition and not create a partition for it. |
| `/home` | 28 KB | This stores the assigned user files. In a workstation, it will hold all the working data of the user and so it needs to be large. A server is usually only for admins' temporary files. You should assign a partition to it. It should have at least 100 MB. |
| `/root` | 20 KB | Home partition for `root` user again; it hardly ever grows for a healthy server where the user account does not use `root` by default. It's convenient to keep it within the `root` partition. |
| `/run` | 665 KB | Mounted usually as a temporary filesystem (`tmpfs`) in memory, it does not use disk space. You don't need to change the default. |
| `/usr` | 2.4 GB | This is the largest folder when installing a machine. It will grow to more than double the minimum for a full-blown workstation. In many distributions, it has its own dedicated partition. In SLES, it is also part of the `root` partition. |
| `/var` | 60 MB | This initially holds very little data, but once in production, it will hold most of the data in the system. For servers storing large amounts of data, it is common to split this partition into several others, such as `/var/log`, `/var/lib`, or even for email servers, `/var/spool`. |

*Table 2.3 – Recommended partitions for a production server*

It's important to become familiar with the main directories in the system. It is recommended to navigate through the different system directories and look at what's in them to become comfortable with the structure. In the next section, we will look at how to do redirections in the command line to learn more about command and file interaction.

# Understanding I/O redirection in the command line

We have already run several commands to find information about the system, and we saw in the console the output, such as filenames and file sizes. Unix philosophy, which Linux inherits, is to make each program do one thing well, and expect the output of that program to become the input of another program, so it can modify it and produce something new.

There are three sources for output and input:

- **STDOUT**, also known as **standard output**, is where commands will put their regular messages to inform of what they are doing. In a terminal, on an interactive shell (such as the ones we are using so far), this output will show on screen. This will be the main output managed by us.
- **STDERR**, also known as **standard error**, is where the commands will put their error messages to be processed. In our interactive shells, this output will also be shown on screen, like the standard output, unless we redirect it.
- **STDIN**, also known as **standard input**, is where the commands get data to be processed. It can be the keyboard, a file, or the output of another program.

To communicate the output of a program with the input of another, we use the following operators:

- |: The **pipe** operator will use the output of one command as the input of the next command and will show only the result of the last command. It *pipes* data from one command to another to compose more complex commands.
- >: The **redirect** operator is used to put the output of a command into a file. If the file exists, it will be overwritten.
- <: The **reverse redirect** operator can be applied to use a file as input to a command. Using it won't delete the file used as input.
- >>: The **redirect and add** operator is used to append the output of a command to a file. If the file does not exist, it will be created.

- `2>`: The **redirect STDERR** operator will only redirect the output sent to the error message handler.
- `1>`: The **redirect STDOUT** operator redirects the output sent to the standard output, but not to the error message handler.
- `>&2`: The **redirect to STDERR** operator will redirect the output to the standard error handler.
- `>&1`: The **redirect to STDOUT** operator will redirect the output to the standard output handler.

2 and > need to be together; if you put a space between them, it won't be recognized as one command but as two independent ones.

Let's make this clearer with some examples.

Let's get a list of files, separated by commas, and put it in a file. First, we list the files in `/var`, using the `-m` option:

```
user@geeko:~> ls -m /var/
adm, agentx, cache, crash, lib, lock, log, opt,
run, spool, tmp
```

Let's run the command again, redirecting the output to the `~/var-files.txt` file:

```
user@geeko:~> ls -m /var/ > ~/var-files.txt
user@geeko:~>
```

There is no output on the screen. We redirected the output to a file instead, so a file with that name in our home folder should be available:

```
user@geeko:~> ls ~
var-files.txt
```

We can see the content of the file on screen using the `cat` command, intended to *concatenate* the output for several files, but used regularly for this purpose:

```
user@geeko:~> cat ~/var-files.txt
adm, agentx, cache, crash, lib, lock, log, opt,
run, spool, tmp
```

We can also add to this file the content of `/var/lib`, using the `>>` operator:

```
user@geeko:~> ls -m /var/lib
alternatives, ca-certificates, chrony, dbus, empty, hardware, lastlog,
misc, net-snmp, NetworkManager, nobody, plymouth, private, rollback, rpm,
selinux, smartmontools, sshd, sudo, systemd, wtmpdb, xkb, YaST2, zypp
user@geeko:~> ls -m /var/lib >> var-files.txt
user@geeko:~> cat var-files.txt
adm, agentx, cache, crash, lib, lock, log, opt, run, spool, tmp
alternatives, ca-certificates, chrony, dbus, empty, hardware, lastlog,
misc,
net-snmp, NetworkManager, nobody, plymouth, private, rollback, rpm,
selinux,
smartmontools, sshd, sudo, systemd, wtmpdb, xkb, YaST2, zypp
```

The `/home/user/var-files.txt` file now contains both the comma-separated list for `/var` and for `/var/lib`.

What happens if we try to list a non-existent directory?

```
user@geeko:~> ls -m /non-existent
ls: cannot access '/non-existent': No such file or directory
```

The output shown in the console is actually shown in the error handler. We can redirect the output to a file:

```
user@geeko:~> ls -m /non-existent > non-listing.txt
ls: cannot access '/non-existent': No such file or directory
user@geeko:~> ls
non-listing.txt  var-files.txt
user@geeko:~> cat non-listing.txt
```

The output is still shown to the console because we didn't redirect `STDERR`, only the standard output, `STDOUT`. The file has been created anyway, but it is empty. So now we show an empty file (which contains the output of `STDOUT`). If we aim to capture the output of `STDERR`, the error we need to use is `2>`:

```
user@geeko:~> ls /non-existent 2> error.txt
user@geeko:~> cat error.txt
ls: cannot access '/non-existent': No such file or directory
```

Let's count the number of files and directories in `/var`. We are going to work Unix style, using the output of `ls` and feeding it into the `wc` command, which stands for *word count*. We will use the `-w` option to count words. To do so, we will redirect (or pipe) the output of `ls` to it:

```
user@geeko:~> ls -m /var/ | wc -w
11
```

We can also use it to count entries in `/etc`:

```
user@geeko:~> ls -m /etc/ | wc -w
144
```

Pipes are great for creating more complex commands, reusing the output of one command as the input to another one. In the next section, we are going to use composition to select only the important data using a filter.

# Filtering output with grep and sed

If you want to find a pattern in a file or the standard input, you use the `grep` command. This is extremely useful for system administrators as it allows you to quickly find information when you need it (such as searching for an error in a log, which will be discussed later). `grep` uses **regular expressions** that describe the text to be found. Regular expressions can be simple, such as the exact text to be found, or complex, and we will describe them in depth later.

Let's use `find` to generate content to be used with `grep` later on. We can do a recursive search in `/usr` and write the list of files in every subdirectory in `/home/user/usr-files.txt`:

```
user@geeko:~> find /usr/ > ~/usr-files.txt
find: '/usr/etc/skel/.cache': Permission denied
find: '/usr/etc/skel/.config': Permission denied
find: '/usr/etc/skel/.local': Permission denied
find: '/usr/etc/keys': Permission denied
find: '/usr/etc/sudoers.d': Permission denied
user@geeko:~> ls -lh usr-files.txt
-rw-r--r--. 1 user user 2.6M Mar 31 15:55 usr-files.txt
user@geeko:~> cat usr-files.txt | wc -l
56267
```

We get some errors (as we are not `root`), and the output is a file of 2.6 MB and 56,267 lines. If we want to, for instance, find files in `/usr` that contain the `gzip` pattern, it would be error-prone to do it manually. But it is easy with the following command:

```
user@geeko:~> grep gzip usr-files.txt
/usr/share/licenses/gzip
/usr/share/licenses/gzip/COPYING
/usr/share/doc/packages/gzip
/usr/share/doc/packages/gzip/AUTHORS
/usr/share/doc/packages/gzip/ChangeLog
/usr/share/doc/packages/gzip/NEWS
/usr/share/doc/packages/gzip/README
/usr/share/doc/packages/gzip/THANKS
/usr/share/doc/packages/gzip/TODO
/usr/share/man/man1/gzip.1.gz
/usr/share/vim/vim91/autoload/gzip.vim
/usr/share/vim/vim91/doc/pi_gzip.txt
/usr/share/vim/vim91/plugin/gzip.vim
/usr/share/info/gzip.info.gz
/usr/share/mime/application/gzip.xml
/usr/share/bash-completion/completions/gzip
/usr/bin/gzip
/usr/lib64/python3.11/pycache/gzip.cpython-311.opt-1.pyc
/usr/lib64/python3.11/pycache/gzip.cpython-311.opt-2.pyc
/usr/lib64/python3.11/pycache/gzip.cpython-311.pyc
/usr/lib64/python3.11/gzip.py
```

As you can see, we have found all the files with a name that includes `gzip` under `/usr` in two steps: creating a file with all the content of the directory and then searching through it with `grep`. Is it possible to do the same without creating the file? Sure, we can, by using a *pipe*. We can redirect the output of `find` to `grep` and get the same output:

```
user@geeko:~> find /usr/ 2> /dev/null | grep gzip
/usr/share/licenses/gzip
/usr/share/licenses/gzip/COPYING
/usr/share/doc/packages/gzip
/usr/share/doc/packages/gzip/AUTHORS
/usr/share/doc/packages/gzip/ChangeLog
/usr/share/doc/packages/gzip/NEWS
```

```
/usr/share/doc/packages/gzip/README
/usr/share/doc/packages/gzip/THANKS
/usr/share/doc/packages/gzip/TODO
/usr/share/man/man1/gzip.1.gz
/usr/share/vim/vim91/autoload/gzip.vim
/usr/share/vim/vim91/doc/pi_gzip.txt
/usr/share/vim/vim91/plugin/gzip.vim
/usr/share/info/gzip.info.gz
/usr/share/mime/application/gzip.xml
/usr/share/bash-completion/completions/gzip
/usr/bin/gzip
/usr/lib64/python3.11/pycache/gzip.cpython-311.opt-1.pyc
/usr/lib64/python3.11/pycache/gzip.cpython-311.opt-2.pyc
/usr/lib64/python3.11/pycache/gzip.cpython-311.pyc
/usr/lib64/python3.11/gzip.py
```

We are redirecting the errors to a file called `/dev/null`, a filesystem that deletes (nullifies) everything that you write in it, because we don't care about access errors, and then the standard output from `find` is sent to `grep` to process it. Let's count the number of instances of files with `wc`, but this time, while using the `-l` option to count the lines:

```
user@geeko:~> find /usr/ 2> /dev/null | grep gzip | wc -l
21
```

We have now concatenated two pipes, one to filter the output and another to count the lines. We will find ourselves doing this kind of plumbing often when searching for and finding information in the system.

Some very common options of `grep` are as follows:

- `-i` for *ignore case*. It will match the pattern, whether it's uppercase, lowercase, or a mix of both.
- `-v` for *invert match*. It will show all entries that do not match the pattern being searched for.
- `-r` for *recursive*. We can tell `grep` to search for a pattern in all the files within a directory, going through all of them (if we have permission).

There is also a way to filter columns in the output provided. Let's say we have a list of files in our home directory, and we want to see the size of it. We run the following:

```
user@geeko:~> ls -l
total 2644
```

```
-rw-r--r--. 1 user user      61 Mar 31 15:44 error.txt
-rw-r--r--. 1 user user       0 Mar 31 04:21 non-listing.txt
-rw-r--r--. 1 user user 2698567 Mar 31 15:55 usr-files.txt
-rw-r--r--. 1 user user     279 Mar 31 04:19 var-files.txt
```

If we need to go beyond search, we need to use tools that are more powerful. `awk` is a tool that offers a fully-fledged programming language to process the output. It is very useful to find identifiers in processes or get a specific list of data from a long output. If we just want to find the size of content that has `files` in its name, we can use these `awk` options:

```
ls -l | grep files | awk '{ print $9 " " $5}'
usr-files.txt 2698567
var-files.txt 279
```

> `awk` offers functions to manage strings, times, and maths, and it is extremely powerful. We will use just a tiny portion of its capabilities here.

Let's find the users defined in the system by looking at the `/etc/passwd` file. The file uses a colon (`:`) to separate columns, so we will change the separator with the `-F` option and get only the first one:

```
user@geeko:~> awk -F: '{ print $1}' /etc/passwd
root
tftp
nobody
man
lp
daemon
messagebus
bin
dnsmasq
systemd-coredump
chrony
systemd-timesync
sshd
user
```

The awk and grep tools are very common processing tools in the life of a Linux sysadmin; it is important to understand them well to quickly find what you need in any output provided by the system. We have used very little of them, enough to filter the output by row and column. Let's continue learning how to manage files in a system so we can better handle the files we have just produced.

# Listing, creating, copying, and moving files and directories, links, and hard links

It is quite common to manage files and directories (also known as folders) in a system from the command line. Linux stores relevant information in files, such as configuration files or data, and an administrator needs to create, delete, and move those files often.

## Directories

Let's start by creating a directory. The mkdir command, short for *make directory*, allows us to create a new one:

```
user@geeko:~> mkdir mydir
user@geeko:~> ls -l
total 0
drwxr-xr-x. 1 user user 0 Mar 31 16:28 mydir
```

Creating a folder does not work if the parent folder is not available, but you can use -p to create all the directories in a hierarchy (very useful for automation), as shown here:

```
user@geeko:~> mkdir myotherdir/mydir
mkdir: cannot create directory 'myotherdir/mydir': No such file or
directory
user@geeko:~> mkdir -p myotherdir/mydir
user@geeko:~> ls
mydir  myotherdir
user@geeko:~> ls myotherdir/
mydir
```

Folders can be deleted with the rmdir command, short for *remove directory*:

```
user@geeko:~> ls -l
total 0
drwxr-xr-x. 1 user user  0 Mar 31 16:34 deleteme
drwxr-xr-x. 1 user user  0 Mar 31 16:28 mydir
```

```
drwxr-xr-x. 1 user user 10 Mar 31 16:34 myotherdir
user@geeko:~> rmdir deleteme/
user@geeko:~> ls
mydir  myotherdir
user@geeko:~> ls -l
total 0
drwxr-xr-x. 1 user user  0 Mar 31 16:28 mydir
drwxr-xr-x. 1 user user 10 Mar 31 16:34 myotherdir
```

Note that `rmdir` will only delete empty directories:

```
user@geeko:~> rmdir myotherdir/
rmdir: failed to remove 'myotherdir/': Directory not empty
user@geeko:~> rmdir myotherdir/mydir/
user@geeko:~> rmdir myotherdir/
user@geeko:~> ls
mydir
```

We can delete a file with the `rm` command. Using `rm` will not delete directories by default, even if they are empty. But the `-r` option can be used to remove them recursively with all the files and directories they contain. Let's just create and remove a single file, `var-files.txt`:

```
user@geeko:~> ls /var/ > var-files.txt
user@geeko:~> ls
mydir  var-files.txt
user@geeko:~> rm var-files.txt
user@geeko:~> ls -l var-files.txt
ls: cannot access 'var-files.txt': No such file or directory
user@geeko:~> rm mydir/
rm: cannot remove 'mydir/': Is a directory
user@geeko:~> rm -r mydir/
user@geeko:~> ls -l
total 0
```

> Be very careful when using recursive mode when deleting, as there is neither a recovery command for it nor a trash bin to keep removed files in the command line.

After playing with and learning many of the directory-related commands, let's review with a summary of them:

| Command | Usage |
|---|---|
| `mkdir` | Create directories |
| `mkdir -p` | Create directories, including all missing intermediate directories in the path |
| `rmdir` | Delete empty directories |
| `rm` | Delete files |
| `rm -r` | Delete directories that contain files or other directories recursively |

*Table 2.4 – Directory-related commands*

Now we know how to create and delete directories in a Linux system, let's start copying and moving content.

## Copying and moving

Now, let's copy some files to play with them using the `cp` (for *copy*) command. The `cp` command requires the source (one or several files) and the destination (a directory). We are going to copy some `awk` examples to a folder in our home directory:

```
user@geeko:> mkdir myawk user@geeko:> cp /usr/share/awk/* myawk/
user@geeko:> ls myawk | wc -l
29
```

To copy more than one file at the same time, we have used **globbing.** We can substitute letters with signs. The asterisk sign (*) represents any group of letters. In this case, it is alone, so it will match all files.

We can use * in a more complex pattern. For instance, we can find only those files that start with *s* using `ls s*`:

```
user@geeko:~/myawk> ls s*
shellquote.awk  strtonum.awk
```

We can also find any file whose name includes `time` in the middle:

```
user@geeko:~/myawk> ls *time*
ctime.awk gettime.awk
```

We can also substitute one single character with ?. Let's find all files that start with `sub` and then follow with `gid` or `uid`. ? will match any character in the following command, including `tid` or `7id`. We can also use `[]` to specify a list of characters to match:

```
user@geeko:~/myawk> ls /etc/*id*
/etc/machine-id /etc/subgid /etc/subgid- /etc/subuid /etc/subuid-
/etc/blkid.conf.d:
user@geeko:~/myawk> ls /etc/sub?id*
/etc/subgid /etc/subgid- /etc/subuid /etc/subuid-
```

`cp` won't travel down the directory tree. If we want to copy all, we need to specify a *recursive* copy with the `-r` option:

```
user@geeko:~> mkdir doc
user@geeko:~> cp -r /usr/share/doc/* doc/
user@geeko:~> cd doc
user@geeko:~/doc> ls
ghostscript  packages
```

When copying directories that have files, you can easily forget the `-r` option and get a copy of the files, but not the directories and all the files in them. We could also move directories or files easily with the `mv` command. Let's put all our new directories together into a newly created directory called `docs`:

```
user@geeko:~> mv my* docs/
user@geeko:~> ls docs/
myauthselect  myawk  mysystemd
```

Moving one folder will move anything contained in it, so there is no recursive option for `mv`. It can also be used to rename files and/or directories:

```
user@geeko:~> cd docs/myawk/
[user@SLES8 mysystemd]$ ls
user@geeko:~/myawk> ls
assert.awk      ftrans.awk    have_mpfr.awk  join.awk       ord.awk
readable.awk  shellquote.awk  zerofile.awk
bits2str.awk    getopt.awk    inplace.awk    libintl.awk    passwd.awk
readfile.awk  strtonum.awk
cliff_rand.awk  gettime.awk   intdiv0.awk    noassign.awk   processarray.
awk  rewind.awk    tocsv.awk
ctime.awk       group.awk     isnumeric.awk  ns_passwd.awk  quicksort.awk
```

```
round.awk     walkarray.awk
user@geeko:~/myawk> cp tocsv.awk  TOCSV.AWK
user@geeko:~/myawk> mv TOCSV.AWK MYFILE.AWK
user@geeko:~/myawk> ls TOCSV.AWK
ls: cannot access 'TOCSV.AWK': No such file or directory
user@geeko:~/myawk> ls MYFILE.AWK
MYFILE.AWK
```

Sometimes you need to create an empty file. There is a special command to create empty files called `touch`:

```
user@geeko:~> ls -l docs/
total 0
drwxr-xr-x. 1 user user  672 Mar 31 22:10 myawk
drwxr-xr-x. 1 user user 2442 Mar 31 22:13 mysystemd
user@geeko:~> touch docs/mytouch
user@geeko:~> ls -l docs/
total 0
drwxr-xr-x. 1 user user  672 Mar 31 22:10 myawk
drwxr-xr-x. 1 user user 2442 Mar 31 22:13 mysystemd
-rw-r--r--. 1 user user    0 Mar 31 22:13 mytouch
```

Files nodes store information about the time and date when they were created, updated, or accessed. When `touch` is applied to an existing file or folder, it will update its access time to the current time:

```
user@geeko:~> ls -l docs/mytouch
-rw-r--r--. 1 user user 0 Mar 31 22:13 docs/mytouch
user@geeko:~> touch docs/mytouch
user@geeko:~> ls -l docs/mytouch
-rw-r--r--. 1 user user 0 Mar 31 22:34 docs/mytouch
```

In this section, the commands used are as follows:

| **Command** | **Usage** |
|---|---|
| `cp` | Copy a set of files in the same source directory |
| `rm` | Delete a set of files in the same directory |
| `cp -r` | Copy a full directory branch, recursively, to a target directory |
| `touch` | Create empty files or set the access time of a file to the current time |

| Command | Usage |
|---|---|
| mv | Rename a file or directory |
| mv | Move a full directory branch recursively to a target directory |

*Table 2.5 – File-related commands*

Now we know how to copy, delete, rename, and move files and directories. Let's take a look at a different way to work with files, the links.

## Symbolic and hard links

We can have the same file in two places using **links**. There are two types of links:

- **Hard links**: These are two different file descriptors that point to the same data with two different names or paths. The content is not copied as there is only one copy on the disk. Hard links cannot be created in two different filesystems, and they are not available for directories.
- **Symbolic links**: A symbolic link is just a reference to a file or directory in another place in the system, including other filesystems.

Both are created using the `ln` (for *link*) utility.

Let's create hard links:

```
user@geeko:~/docs> ln mysystemd/user.conf myuser.conf
user@geeko:~/docs> ls -l
total 4
drwxr-xr-x. 1 user user  672 Mar 31 22:10 myawk
drwxr-xr-x. 1 user user 2442 Mar 31 22:13 mysystemd
-rw-r--r--. 1 user user    0 Mar 31 22:34 mytouch
-rw-r--r--. 2 user user 1771 Mar 31 22:13 myuser.conf
user@geeko:~/docs> ln myuser.conf myuser2.conf
user@geeko:~/docs> ls -la
total 8
drwxr-xr-x. 1 user user   90 Mar 31 22:40 .
drwx------. 1 user user  136 Mar 31 22:11 ..
drwxr-xr-x. 1 user user  672 Mar 31 22:10 myawk
drwxr-xr-x. 1 user user 2442 Mar 31 22:13 mysystemd
-rw-r--r--. 1 user user    0 Mar 31 22:34 mytouch
-rw-r--r--. 3 user user 1771 Mar 31 22:13 myuser2.conf
-rw-r--r--. 3 user user 1771 Mar 31 22:13 myuser.conf
```

Notice the number of references to the file increasing (in bold in the previous example). The number 3 in the last listing tells us that 3 copies of the file are available. When you delete a file with symbolic links, the number of references is updated, but the content is not lost.

Now, let's create a symbolic link to a directory with `ln -s` (*s* is for *symbolic*):

```
user@geeko:~/docs> ls -l
total 12
drwxr-xr-x. 1 user user  672 Mar 31 22:10 myawk
drwxr-xr-x. 1 user user 2442 Mar 31 22:13 mysystemd
lrwxrwxrwx. 1 user user   10 Mar 31 22:44 mysystemdlink -> mysystemd/
-rw-r--r--. 1 user user    0 Mar 31 22:34 mytouch
-rw-r--r--. 3 user user 1771 Mar 31 22:13 myuser2.conf
-rw-r--r--. 3 user user 1771 Mar 31 22:13 myuser.conf
```

The symbolic link looks like a file, but the details are different. It starts with `l` for *link* (in bold in the previous example) instead of `d` for *directory* (also in bold in the previous example). The name also tells us that the file redirects to another file.

> When in doubt, on whether to use a hard link or a symbolic link, use a symbolic link as the default choice.

Let's review the commands we learned in this section:

| Command | Usage |
|---|---|
| `ln` | Create a hard link for a file in the same filesystem |
| `ln -s` | Create a symbolic link to a file or directory that could cross different filesystems |

*Table 2.6 – Link-related commands*

As you can see, creating links and symbolic links is super simple and can help you have access to the same file or directory from different locations. In the next section, let's learn how to pack and compress a set of files and directories.

# Using tar and gzip

How do we move files and directories outside of your system? There is a command that can help aggregate files into a single one to move it more easily. It is `tar` (for *tape archive*), and was originally created to back up data into file tapes.

Let's start backing up the `/etc` directory. As many files are restricted, we will have to do it as the `root` user:

```
geeko:~ # mkdir tmp
geeko:~ # cd tmp
geeko:~/tmp # tar -cf etc-backup.tar /etc
tar: Removing leading `/' from member names
geeko:~/tmp # ls -lh etc-backup.tar
-rw-r--r--. 1 root root 23M Mar 31 23:37 etc-backup.tar
```

Let's check the options used:

- `-c` (for *create*): `tar` can put together files or add files to an existing one (`-r`)
- `-f`: The file name that will be used
- `/etc`: The directory we are backing up

We can try to unpack the file we just created:

```
geeko:~/tmp # mkdir tmp
geeko:~/tmp # cd tmp
geeko:~/tmp/tmp # tar -xf ../etc-backup.tar
geeko:~/tmp/tmp # ls
etc
```

Let's check the new option used: `-x` (for *extract*). This unpacks a `tar` file.

We created a directory named `tmp` to make sure that we don't extract files into a directory that is already full of files, but the backup creates another directory inside `./etc`. We pointed to the parent directory of `tmp` by using the `..` shortcut.

We can optimize storage so we don't need to send or copy a huge file. Most of the content is text that can be compressed, and `gzip` is the tool to do so. We can copy `/etc/services` and compress it:

```
geeko:~/tmp # cp /usr/etc/services .
geeko:~/tmp # ls
etc-backup.tar  services  tmp
```

```
geeko:~/tmp # ls -l services
-rw-r--r--. 1 root root 868252 Mar 31 23:47 services
geeko:~/tmp # gzip services
geeko:~/tmp # ls
etc-backup.tar  services.gz  tmp
geeko:~/tmp # ls -l services.gz
-rw-r--r--. 1 root root 203158 Mar 31 23:47 services.gz
```

`gzip` modifies the files. It will compress the specified file, adding the `.gz` extension to it and deleting the original file. Also, be aware that the newly created file is a quarter of the size of the original file.

The companion tool for `gzip` is `gunzip`:

```
geeko:~/tmp # ls
etc-backup.tar  services.gz  tmp
geeko:~/tmp # gunzip services.gz
geeko:~/tmp # ls
etc-backup.tar  services  tmp
geeko:~/tmp # ls -lh services
-rw-r--r--. 1 root root 848K Mar 31 23:47 services
```

The `tar` command is smart enough to be able to pack and compress in one step:

```
geeko:~/tmp # tar -czf etc-backup.tar.gz /etc/
tar: Removing leading `/' from member names
geeko:~/tmp # ls -lh etc
geeko:~/tmp # ls -lh etc-backup.tar.gz
-rw-r--r--. 1 root root 3.5M Mar 31 23:59 etc-backup.tar.gz
```

We now have a new option: `-z`. This compresses the newly created `tar` file with `gzip`. It is also applicable to decompressing (when using `x`):

```
geeko:~/tmp # rm -rf etc
geeko:~/tmp # tar -xzf etc-backup.tar.gz
geeko:~/tmp # ls
etc  etc-backup.tar.gz
```

Uncompressing a gzipped file does not delete the original file. There are other available compression methods with higher ratios, such as `bzip2` or `xz`, that you may want to try, too.

Now, let's move on to combining all the commands that we have learned by creating shell scripts that can be reused.

# Creating basic shell scripts

As a **system administrator (sysadmin)**, you will have a set of commands that you run all the time. You can do it manually, running every command one by one each time. But there is a more efficient way to do so: by creating a **shell script**.

A shell script is nothing else than a text file with a list of commands to be run, and a reference to the shell that will interpret it. The shell reads the file and interprets the commands like you have typed them in the console in an automated way.

In this book, we will not cover how to use a **text editor**. However, we provide three recommendations for text editors in Linux that could help:

- **Nano**: This is probably the easiest text editor to use for beginners. Lean, simple, and straightforward, you may want to start by installing it and giving it a try.
- **Vi** or **Vim**: Vi is the default text editor available in SLES, included even in the minimal installation, like many other Linux distributions. Even if you are not going to use it every day, it's good to get the basics of it, as it will be present in almost any Linux system you will use. *Vim* means *Vi-improved.*
- **Emacs**: This is probably the most advanced and complex text editor ever. It can do everything and beyond, including reading email or helping with a bit of psychoanalysis via *Emacs Doctor*.

We can create our first shell script by editing a new file called `hello.sh` with the following line as its content:

```
echo "hello world!"
```

Then, we can run it by using the `bash` command interpreter with the following line:

```
user@geeko:~> bash hello.sh
hello world!
```

As different interpreters differ slightly, it can be convenient to specify the shell that should interpret the file, and it reduces the number of strokes as you don't need to type `bash`. To do so, we add an initial line referencing the interpreter, so the file content for `hello.sh` looks like this:

```
#!/bin/bash
echo "hello world!"
```

We need to make it executable:

```
user@geeko:~> ls -l hello.sh
-rw-r--r--. 1 user user 35 Apr  1 02:03 hello.sh
user@geeko:~> chmod +x hello.sh
user@geeko:~> ls -l hello.sh
-rwxr-xr-x. 1 user user 35 Apr  1 02:03 hello.sh
```

Running it is just done by calling its name:

```
user@geeko:~> ./hello.sh
hello world!
```

The shell looks and executes commands in the folders listed by the `$PATH` variable, separated by colons. The working or current directory is not in the path, so you need to specify the full path (and we do that by adding ./ at the beginning):

```
user@geeko:~> echo $PATH
/home/user/.local/bin:/usr/local/bin:/usr/bin:/bin
```

We can also use variables. Defining a variable is as simple as writing its name and the value we want for it, separated by the = symbol. Let's try changing the word `world` for a variable. To use it, we prepend the $ symbol to the name of the variable, and the interpreter will substitute it for its value. The new script will look like this:

```
#!/bin/bash
PLACE="world"
echo "hello $PLACE!"
```

We can run it, obtaining the same output as before:

```
user@geeko:~> ./hello.sh
hello world!
```

It is a good practice to make it more obvious that we are using a variable by writing its name between curly braces, { and }.

So, the previous script will now look like this:

```
#!/bin/bash
PLACE="world"
echo "hello ${PLACE}!"
```

Now we know how to create a basic script. Let's find a way to make decisions and control the logic, starting with loops. Let's go for it!

## Loops with for

What happens if we need to run the same command, changing the variable for a list? That's what a `for` loop is used for. It can help iterate over a set of elements, such as a list or a counter.

The `for` loop syntax is as follows:

- `for` to specify the iteration
- do to specify the action
- done to close the loop

We can define a list of places separated by spaces to try it, and iterate through it with our first `for` loop:

```
#!/bin/bash
PLACES_LIST="Madrid Boston Singapore World"
for PLACE in ${PLACES_LIST}; do
echo "hello ${PLACE}!"
done
```

The output will look like this:

```
user@geeko:~> ./hello.sh
hello Madrid!
hello Boston!
hello Singapore!
hello World!
```

Using the `for` loop is especially useful when the list is generated by an external command. We can execute the external command by writing it between `$(`and `)`.

> Backticks (`) can also be used to run a command and get its output as a list, but we will stick to the previous expression for clarity.

An example of the external command to be used can be `ls`. Let's create the `txtfiles.sh` script with the following content:

```
#!/bin/bash
for TXTFILE in $(ls *.txt); do
  echo "TXT file ${TXTFILE} found!"
done
```

Make this script we just created executable and run it:

```
user@geeko:~> chmod +x txtfiles.sh
user@geeko:~> bash txtfiles.sh
TXT file error.txt found!
TXT file non-listing.txt found!
TXT file usr-files.txt found!
TXT file var-files.txt found!
```

It is easy to find use cases for this. We could iterate over a set of files and change their names, find and replace content inside them, or simply make a specific backup of a selection of files.

Now that we have seen how to use a list with the `for` loop, let's move to another programmatic capability in scripts, the conditionals.

## Conditionals with if

Sometimes we want to execute something only if some condition is met, or we want to have different actions for different elements based on that condition. We have the conditional `if` statement for that.

The `if` syntax is as follows:

- `if` to specify the condition. Conditions are usually specified between brackets, [ and ].
- `then` to specify the action.
- `fi` to signal the end of the actions.

Let's change our previous `hello.sh` script to say `hello, Madrid` in Spanish:

```
#!/bin/bash
PLACES_LIST="Madrid Boston Singapore World"
for PLACE in ${PLACES_LIST}; do
    if [ ${PLACE} = "Madrid" ]; then
        echo "¡Hola ${PLACE}!"
```

```
    fi
done
```

And then, let's run this script:

```
user@geeko:~> bash hello2.sh
¡Hola Madrid!
```

We have a problem; it only says hello to Madrid. What happens if we want to run the previous code on the ones that do not match the condition? We can define what happens when the condition is not met using `else`.

`else` is used when the condition is *not* matched.

Here is an example of a conditional statement using `else`:

```
#!/bin/bash
PLACES_LIST="Madrid Boston Singapore World"
for PLACE in ${PLACES_LIST}; do
    if [ ${PLACE} = "Madrid" ]; then
        echo "¡Hola ${PLACE}!"
    else
        echo "hello ${PLACE}!"
    fi
done
```

You can access the script here: `https://github.com/PacktPublishing/SUSE-Linux-Enterprise-Server-16-Official-Administration-Guide/blob/main/chapter-02-running-basic-commands-and-simple-shell-scripts/hello.sh`

And we can run it as follows:

```
user@geeko:~>./hello.sh
¡Hola Madrid!
hello Boston!
hello Singapore!
hello World!
```

As you can see, it's simple to use the conditionals in a script and provide a lot of control over the conditions under which a command is run. We need to control now when something may not be running correctly; that's what the exit codes (or error codes) are for. Let's go for it.

## Exit codes

When a program is run, it provides an **exit code** specifying whether it ran fine or whether there was an issue. That *exit code* is stored in a special variable called `$?`.

Let's take a look at it by running `ls hello.sh`:

```
user@geeko:~> ls hello.sh
hello.sh
user@geeko:~> echo $?
0
```

When the program runs fine, the *exit code* is zero (`0`).

What happens when we try to list a file that doesn't exist (or run any other command incorrectly, or that is having issues)? Let's try listing a `nonexistent` file:

```
user@geeko:~> ls nonexistentfile.txt
ls: cannot access 'nonexistentfile.txt': No such file or directory
user@geeko:~> echo $?
2
```

You see, the exit code is not zero; something went wrong. Apart from not being zero, there is no standard on what each error code means; we need to go to the documentation and check there to understand what the number means.

Exit codes are important in scripts because they allow us to act depending on the results. Let's now review where to find further information on the commands, such as exit codes or other options, in the next section.

# Using system documentation resources

Your Linux system includes documentation to help you remember how to do things, the syntax of the commands, or to guide you to improve your sysadmin skills. This is referred to as **system documentation.** Let's check three different resources available by default in your SLES installation: man pages, info pages, and other documents.

## Man pages

The most common resource used to get documentation is the **manual pages**, also referred to as the command used to invoke them: `man`.

The man command is installed by default, but it is possible that you need to install the content of the man pages:

```
user@geeko:~> sudo -i
geeko:~ # zypper install man-pages man-pages-posix
```

Almost any utility installed in the system has a man page to help you use it (i.e., specifying all the options for the tool and what they do). You can run man tar and check the output:

```
user@geeko:~> man tar
TAR(1)                                    GNU TAR Manual
TAR(1)

NAME
       tar - an archiving utility

SYNOPSIS
   Traditional usage
       tar {A|c|d|r|t|u|x}[GnSkUWOmpsMBiajJzZhPlRvwo] [ARG...]

   UNIX-style usage
       tar -A [OPTIONS] ARCHIVE ARCHIVE

       tar -c [-f ARCHIVE] [OPTIONS] [FILE...]

       tar -d [-f ARCHIVE] [OPTIONS] [FILE...]
```

You can read it using your keyboard (navigate with arrow keys to move up or down one line, the spacebar to move a full page, and/or page up/down). Exiting is done with the letter q (for *quit*).

There are sections in the man page on related topics. It is pretty simple to search for those by using the apropos command or using the -k option in man. Let's see it for tar:

```
geeko:~ # apropos tar
bdflush (2)           - start, flush, or tune buffer-dirty-flush daemon
dbus-launch (1)       - Utility to start a message bus from a shell script
dbus-run-session (1) - start a process as a new D-Bus session
dracut-pre-udev.service (8) - runs the dracut hooks before udevd is
started
erfc (3)              - complementary error function
```

```
erfcf (3)            - complementary error function
erfcl (3)            - complementary error function
(...) Some other output
```

As you can see, it matches not only `tar` but also `start`. It is not perfect, but it can help you find information related to `tar`, such as gpg`tar`.

Man pages are distributed into sections. You can find a description for each section using `man intro`, which, like other commands, has articles in several sections:

```
geeko:~ # man intro
Man: find all matching manual pages (set MAN_POSIXLY_CORRECT to avoid
this)
* intro (1)
intro (8)
intro (3)
intro (2)
intro (5)
intro (4)
intro (6)
intro (7)
```

We can access the page in section 1 to understand the basis:

```
geeko:~ # man 1 intro
```

Now, we can see the `intro` page for section 1:

```
TAR(5)                              BSD File Formats Manual
TAR(5)


NAME
       intro - introduction to user commands


DESCRIPTION
       Section  1  of the manual describes user commands and tools, for
example, file manipulation tools, shells, compilers, web browsers, file
and image viewers and editors, and so on.
NOTES
       Linux is a flavor of UNIX, and user commands under UNIX work
similarly under Linux (and  lots  of  other  UNIX-like  systems  too,
```

```
like FreeBSD).

        Under  Linux,  there  are  GUIs (graphical user interfaces), where
you can point and click and drag, and hopefully get work done without
first reading lots of documentation.  The traditional UNIX environment is
a CLI (command line interface), where  you  type  commands to tell  the
computer  what  to do.  This is faster and more powerful, but requires
finding out what the commands are and how to use them.
        Below is a bare minimum guide to get you started. ...
```

You can see that manual pages are a great resource to learn more about the typical commands being used, and a great resource during the **SUSE Certified Administrator** (**SCA**) exam. A recommendation is to review all the manual pages for the commands shown in this chapter, as well as for the upcoming chapters. We consider man pages as the main information resource that comes included in the system. Almost every command in SLES has its own man page. Let's review the other available information resources next.

## Info pages

**Info pages** are usually more descriptive than man pages and more interactive. They are better if you want to get started on a topic because they are more detailed and explain more details and concepts.

We can try to get information for the `diff` command by running the following:

```
geeko:~ # Info diff
Next: Invoking diff3, Prev: Invoking cmp, Up: Top
13 Invoking 'diff'

The format for running the 'diff' command is:
diff OPTIONS... FILES...

In the simplest case, two file names FROM-FILE and TO-FILE are given, and
'diff' compares the contents of FROM-FILE and TO-FILE. A file name of '-'
stands for the standard input.
If one file is a directory and the other is not, 'diff' compares the
file in the directory whose name is that of the non-directory. The non-
directory file must not be '-'.
If two file names are given and both are directories, 'diff' compares
corresponding files in both directories, in alphabetical order; this
```

```
comparison is not recursive unless the '--recursive' ('-r') option is
given. 'diff' never compares the actual contents of a directory as if it
were a file. The file that is fully specified may not be standard input,
because standard input is nameless and the notion of "file with the same
name" does not apply.
If the '--from-file=FILE' option is given, the number of file names is
arbitrary, and FILE is compared to each named file. Similarly, if the
'--to-file=FILE' option is given, each named file is compared to FILE.
'diff' options begin with '-', so normally file names may not begin with
'-'. However, '--' as an argument by itself treats the remaining arguments
as file names even if they begin with '-'.
An exit status of 0 means no differences were found, 1 means some
differences were found, and 2 means trouble.
Menu:
diff Options:: Summary of options to 'diff'.
```

Info pages can redirect to other topics that are then shown underlined, and that can be followed by putting the cursor over them and hitting *Enter*.

As with man, type `q` to quit.

Please take some time to review the info pages for the main topics covered in this chapter (info pages are not so well-maintained, so not every topic is available, even though the ones that are present are very informative).

With this, we are now ready to find information about the commands and resources in our SLES system quickly.

# Summary

We learned in this chapter how to log in to a system with a normal user or with the `root` superuser, and gained an understanding of the basics of permissions and security. We also learned how to use the command line with autocomplete, navigating through the directories and files and packing and unpacking them, how to use redirects to parse data and build more complex commands, and how to automate processes with shell scripts. Moreover, we now know how to find more information and ways to access documentation on the tools available in any SLES system. These skills are the basis of the upcoming chapters. Don't hesitate to revisit this chapter if you feel stuck or if your progress is not as fast as you thought.

Now, it is time to extend your knowledge into more advanced topics in the upcoming chapters. The next chapter will look at tools for regular operations, in which we will review the most common actions taken when managing a system. Enjoy!

# 3

# Managing Regular Operations with Tools

So far, we have a system installed, and we've covered some of the scripts we can create to automate tasks, so we've reached the point at which we can focus on the system itself.

Having a properly configured system requires things beyond installation like understanding how to run tasks at specific times, keep all system services running appropriately, and configure time synchronization, service management, boot targets (runlevels), and scheduled tasks, all of which we will be covering in this chapter.

You will learn how to check the status of services, start, stop, and troubleshoot them, and keep the system clock in sync for your server or your whole network. This will be critical to keep services running, a base to automate processes, and also the starting point to troubleshoot issues.

The list of topics that will be covered is as follows:

- Managing system services with `systemd`
- Scheduling tasks with `systemd` timers
- Learning about time synchronization with `chrony`
- Checking system resources: Memory and disk (free, df, and ps)
- Finding logs, using `journald`, and reading log files, including log preservation and rotation

# Technical requirements

It is possible to continue using the virtual machine created at the beginning of this book. Additionally, for testing the time synchronization service, it might be useful to have internet access so public time servers can be reached.

# Managing system services with systemd

The skills that you will learn from this section are oriented in a manner that will show you how to manage **system services** and runtime targets, and learn about service status with `systemd`. You will also learn how to manage system boot targets and services to start at system boot.

`systemd` (which you can learn more about using the following reference: `https://systemd.io`) is defined as a system daemon to manage the system. It came from rethinking the way a system boots and starts, and the constraints of the traditional approach.

When we think about system starting, we have the initial **kernel** and **RAM disk** loaded and in execution. But right after that, services and scripts take control to make filesystems available and prepare the services that provide the functionality. There is a more detailed description of the process in *Chapter 15, Understanding the Boot Process*. At the end, what we want from our system is the following:

- Hardware detection
- Additional filesystem activation
- Network initialization (wired, wireless, etc.)
- Network services (time sync, remote login, printers, network filesystems, etc.)
- User-space setup

However, most of the tools that existed before `systemd` came into play worked on booting the system in a sequential way, causing the whole boot process (from machine power-on to user login) to be lengthy and subject to delays. The *unit*-oriented approach of `systemd` solved the problem, making the whole process easy to parallelize and a lot faster.

> `systemd` redesigned the system startup process to focus on simplicity: Start fewer processes and do more parallel execution. The idea itself sounds easy, but it requires a lot of redesigning of what was taken for granted in the past to focus on the needs of a new approach to improve OS performance. This redesign, which has provided a lot of benefits, also came at a cost: it drastically changed the way systems used to boot, so there was a lot of controversy over `systemd` adoption by the different vendors. However, it finally established itself as the de facto standard.

Rationalizing the startup of services so that only those that are required are initiated is a good way to accomplish efficiency. For example, there is no need to start Bluetooth, printer, or network services that have no Bluetooth hardware when no one is printing, or when the system is disconnected. With fewer services needing to be started, the system boot is not delayed by those waits and focuses on the ones that really need to get attention.

On top of that, parallel execution allows each service to take its required time for being ready, but not making others wait. So, in general, running services initialization in parallel allows for maximizing the usage of CPU, disk, and so on, and the wait times for each service are reduced.

`systemd` does advanced tasks, such as pre-creating the listening network sockets before the actual service (also known as a **daemon**) is started. This way, services that have requirements on other services can be started and be in a wait status until their dependencies are started, but without losing any messages sent to them. So, when the service is finally started, it will act on all the pending actions. This way, several dependent services can be started at the same time, and they will connect to each other when ready.

Let's learn a bit more about `systemd`, as it will be required for several operations we're going to describe in this chapter.

`systemd` comes with the concept of units, which are nothing but configuration files. The units can be categorized into different types, based on the file extension, as highlighted in the following figure:

| Unit type | File extension | Description |
|---|---|---|
| Timer | `.timer` | A system timer |
| Socket | `.socket` | An inter-process communication socket |
| Service | `.service` | A system service |
| Target | `.target` | A group of system units |
| Automount | `.automount` | A filesystem automount point |
| Device | `.device` | A device file recognized by the kernel |
| Scope | `.scope` | An externally created process |
| Slice | `.slice` | A group of hierarchical units that manage system processes |
| Path | `.path` | A file or directory in the system |
| Mount | `.mount` | A mount point in the filesystem |
| Swap | `.swap` | A swap device or swap file definition |

*Table 3.1 – Units, their types, and file extensions*

Don't feel overwhelmed by the amount of different `systemd` unit types. In general, the most common ones are `service`, `timer`, `socket`, and `target`.

Of course, the unit files mentioned in *Table 3.1* are expected to be found in some specific folders:

| Folder | Description |
|---|---|
| `/usr/lib/systemd/system/` | Units that are distributed with the packages we've installed in our system. They include the default values for all units and services in the system. This is also a good place to look for examples on how to configure a `systemd` unit. |
| `/run/systemd/system/` | Units that are created at runtime when `systemd` starts. It takes precedence over the ones distributed with the installed packages. |

| `/etc/systemd/system/` | This is the directory where your customizations to service configurations will be.<br>It takes precedence over the runtime ones as well as over the ones provided by the installed packages. |
|---|---|

*Table 3.2 – Units files and their folders*

As mentioned already, there are different types of units, all intended to support starting and running services. As in the example that will be described in *Chapter 8, Enabling and Using Cockpit*, about the use of sockets, unit files for path, bus, and so on, also get activated when a specific action is happening. For example, when a process or user in a system accesses a specific path, the services associated with the `path` unit are started. This adds resource optimization for lowering system startup times, making certain services only start under defined circumstances.

We have now learned the basics of `systemd` unit types, helping us have the proper services started at boot, or even better, when a certain action (i.e., someone connecting to a port or accessing a path) happens. Now, let's focus on the file structure of the content for the unit files.

## The systemd unit file structure

Let's get our hands dirty with an example: a system is deployed with `sshd` enabled, which is the default in **SUSE Linux Enterprise Server 16**. It should start running once the network has been initialized and is properly configured.

As we said, `systemd` uses unit files, and we can check the aforementioned folders or list them with the `systemctl list-unit-files` command. Remember that each file is, in reality, a configuration file that defines what `systemd` should do. An example of the content included in a unit file is shown as follows for `/usr/lib/systemd/system/sshd.service`:

```
geeko:~ # cat /usr/lib/systemd/system/sshd.service

[Unit]
Description=OpenSSH Daemon
After=network.target

[Service]
Type=notify
EnvironmentFile=-/etc/sysconfig/ssh
ExecStartPre=/usr/sbin/sshd-gen-keys-start
ExecStartPre=/usr/sbin/sshd -t $SSHD_OPTS
ExecStart=/usr/sbin/sshd -D $SSHD_OPTS
ExecReload=/bin/kill -HUP $MAINPID
KillMode=process
Restart=on-failure
RestartPreventExitStatus=255
TasksMax=infinity

[Install]
WantedBy=multi-user.target
geeko:~ #
```

*Figure 3.1 – The sshd.service file contents*

> In SUSE Linux Enterprise Server 16, the configuration files follow the UAPI Group Specifications as stated at:
>
> `https://uapi-group.org/specifications/specs/configuration_files_specification`.
>
> The main concept behind this is that default configuration files for system packages live in `/usr/lib`, `/usr/share`, or `/usr/etc`. The `/etc` path allows you to override the configuration defaults by dropping new files directly or in directories ending with `.d`, as in this case: `/etc/systemd/system/sshd.service.d/`.

This file defines not only the traditional program to start, but also the dependencies, the conflicts, and soft dependencies, giving enough information to `systemd` to decide the right approach.

About the structure of the content: if you're familiar with **INI files**, the structure of this file uses the same approach. It uses brackets, [ and ], for sections and then key/value pairs for the settings under each section.

Section names are case-sensitive; they will not run correctly if the proper naming is not used.

Section directives, which are mandatory, are named as follows:

- `[Unit]`: Basic directive. Includes sections such as `Description` and `Documentation`, and other sections to handle the startup order, such as `Before`, `Requires`, and `Wants`.
- `[Install]`: Includes the information needed to install the unit. Used when you run `systemctl enable` or `systemctl disable`. It is used in most of the services, but is not mandatory; for example, services launched by a socket unit do not require it.

Additional optional entries can be used for each of the different unit types:

- `[Service]`: Used to run services.
- `[Socket]`: Used to create sockets that can connect to a service later. This can also be used to start a service only when we receive an external connection to a specific port. The **Cockpit service** is configured this way.
- `[Mount]`: Used to manage storage and assign storage devices to a directory and mount them during the startup process.
- `[Automount]`: Used to handle mount points that shall only be mounted under certain circumstances.
- `[Swap]`: Used to mount swap spaces. These assign part of the disk so it can be used to extend the memory allocation.
- `[Path]`: Used to monitor a path, or directory, and run services when it is accessed.
- `[Timer]`: Used to run services at a certain point in time or periodically.
- `[Slice]`: Used to assign resources by applying **cgroups** to services. You can, for example, limit the amount of memory to assign to a service.

As you can see, in the example in *Figure 3.1*, the `sshd` service only needs the `Unit`, `Install`, and `Service` directives. For a more complex configuration, explore the one for the `chronyd` service, used to synchronize the clock in the machine, which is stored in `/usr/lib/systemd/system/chronyd.service`.

We have specific sections for each type. Run the `man systemd.unit` command, and it will give you examples with all the supported values for the `systemd` version you're using. Every type has a manual page in the system, so you can run `man systemd.mount` or `man systemd.slice` for more info. We can see how manual pages work in the following figure:

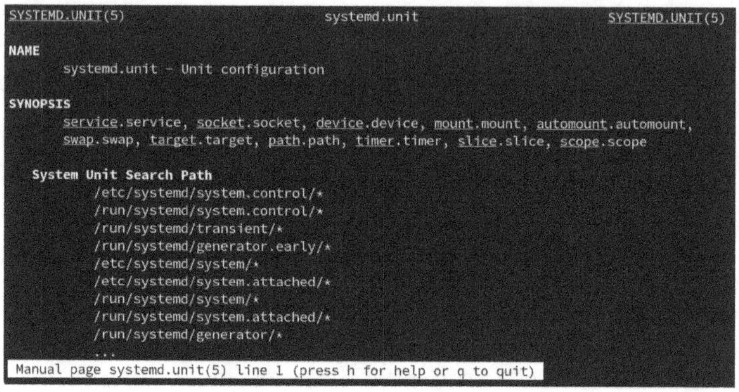


*Figure 3.2 – The man page of systemd.unit*

Remember that in SLES 16 packages come with configuration defaults usually in `/usr/etc` and that to override those defaults you can drop your own options in a file under `/etc`.

We have reviewed the file structure for unit files. Now, let's use `systemctl` to actually manage the service's status.

## Managing services to be started and stopped at boot

Services can be enabled or disabled; that is, the services will be activated or not activated on system startup.

A service, such as `sshd`, can be enabled via the following:

```
# systemctl enable sshd
```

Or it can be disabled via the following:

```
# systemctl disable sshd
```

This results in creating or removing `/etc/systemd/system/multi-user.target.wants/sshd.service`.

Note that we have a **target** here. We will explain targets later on in the chapter.

The previous commands are enabling or disabling the service at boot, but for executing an immediate action, we need to issue a different command.

To start the `sshd` service, use the following:

```
# systemctl start sshd
```

And to stop it, use the following:

```
# systemctl stop sshd
```

Of course, we can also check the service status as seen from `systemd` via `systemctl status sshd`, as shown in the following figure:

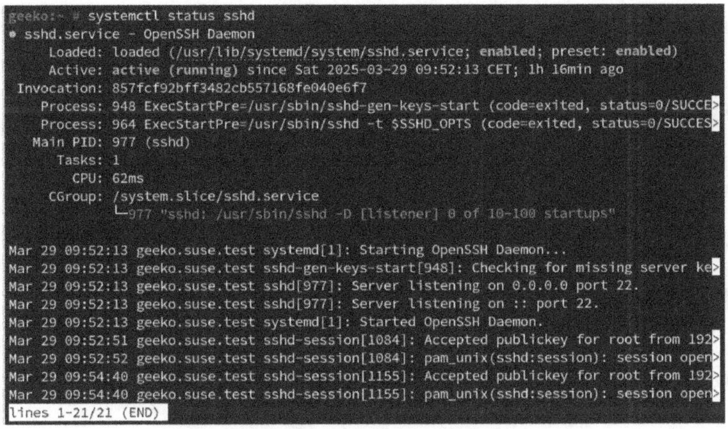


*Figure 3.3 – Status of the sshd daemon*

This status information provides us with details about the unit file defining the service, the default status at boot, whether it is running or not, the PID, some other details about the resource consumption, and some of the most recent log entries for the service that are quite useful in debugging simple service start failures.

One important piece to check is the output of `systemctl list-unit-files`, as it reports the defined unit files in the system as well as the current status and the vendor preset for each one.

Once we have covered the start/stop and status check of services, let's work on managing the actual system boot status itself.

> When enabling or disabling services, you can make them effective immediately by running the command with the `--now` option. This way, when you enable a service with this option, it will also be started, and when you disable it, it will also be stopped.

## Managing boot targets

When the system boots, there is a default status preselected, which usually includes having the network enabled, preparing to handle several user logins, and, sometimes, having a graphical environment ready. There are different levels that might not enable the graphical interface or even the network (i.e., for repairs).

These levels are traditionally called **runlevels**. Even when with `systemd`, we now use targets; let's take a look at these runlevels.

A **runlevel** defines a predefined set of services based on usage, that is, defining which services will be started or stopped to cover a specific functionality. Each one of those runlevels, as we mentioned, allows a predefined set of services to be started/stopped. We can switch from one runlevel to another with the `init` command. These traditional runlevels are used to define the following status:

- **Halt mode**: Also known as **runlevel 0**. It stops all the services and then halts or powers off the system.
- **Single-user mode**: Also known as **runlevel 1**. It just starts a shell for one user only. Normally used to repair things in the system without having any other user accessing it.
- **Multi-user mode**: Also known as **runlevel 2**. It enables regular user login without a network.
- **Networked multi-user**: Also known as **runlevel 3**. It's like multi-user, but with a network. This is the most used one for servers.
- **Graphical**: Also known as **runlevel 5**. It is like networked but with a graphical environment started (i.e., GNOME). You can log in via the display manager (i.e., `gdm`, for GNOME). It's most used for desktops.
- **Reboot**: Also known as **runlevel 6**. It is like a halt, but at the end of processing services, it issues a reboot instead of a halt.

You probably realized there is no runlevel 4. This one is left for user customization.

Those runlevels (and the default one when the system booted) used to be defined in `/etc/inittab`, but this file is not in the system anymore. However, you can still run the `init 6` command to reboot a machine, as well as to change to other runlevels.

So, with the change to `systemd`, runlevels are now boot targets. A `systemd` target is a way to group different services to enable a defined set of functionalities. It is also a way to switch from one to the other.

We can find the available system targets via listing this folder:

```
# ls -l /usr/lib/systemd/system/*.target
```

Or more correctly, via `systemctl` with the following:

```
systemctl list-unit-files *.target
```

When you examine the output when running it on your system, you will find several targets that are especially important. For example, for regular server usage, the default target will be `multi-user.target` when running without a graphical mode, or `graphical.target` when using it. Then, we have `default.target`, which is the one selected to run at boot. We can see which one it is by running the following:

```
# systemctl get-default
```

We can modify it by running the following:

```
# systemctl set-default TARGET.target
```

This brings us to the next question: *What does a target definition look like?* Let's examine the output in the next figure:

```
geeko:~ # grep -v ^# /usr/lib/systemd/system/graphical.target

[Unit]
Description=Graphical Interface
Documentation=man:systemd.special(7)
Requires=multi-user.target
Wants=display-manager.service
Conflicts=rescue.service rescue.target
After=multi-user.target rescue.service rescue.target display-manager.service
AllowIsolate=yes
geeko:~ #
```

*Figure 3.4 – Contents of graphical.target from its target unit definition*

As you can see, it is set as a dependency of another target (`multi-user.target`) and has some requirements on other services such as `display-manager.service`, and also other conflicts. The target can only be reached when other targets have been completed.

In this way, `systemd` can select the proper order of services to start and the dependencies to reach the configured boot target.

We have covered the services status: started, stopped, and enabled on boot. But there are other tasks we should execute in our system, in a periodic way. Let's get further into the topic.

# Scheduling tasks with systemd timers

The skills you will learn in this section are to schedule periodic tasks in the system for business services and maintenance.

For regular system usage, there are tasks that are required to be executed periodically, ranging from temporary folder cleanup, cache refresh, and check-in with inventory systems, among other things.

The traditional cron daemon is still available in the repositories for compatibility purposes. It can be installed in the system by running `zypper install cron`. To learn more, once installed, you can run `man cron`. However, the recommended way to handle running recurrent tasks is by using timers.

The traditional way to set them up was via **cron**; however, SUSE Linux Enterprise Server 16 does not include it by default anymore. All scheduling shall be done via `systemd`.

## Systemd timers

The `systemd` feature to handle managing tasks at a specific time, or with a timely recurrence, is **timers**. A timer allows you to define, via a unit file, a job that will be executed.

We can check the ones already available in our system with the following:

```
# systemctl list-unit-files *.timer
UNIT FILE                      STATE    PRESET
backup-rpmdb.timer             enabled  enabled
backup-sysconfig.timer         enabled  enabled
btrfs-balance.timer            enabled  enabled
...
snapper-boot.timer             disabled disabled
snapper-cleanup.timer          enabled  enabled
snapper-timeline.timer         enabled  enabled
suse-uptime-tracker.timer      disabled disabled
...
```

Here, we see the list of timer units available in our system and their status. Let's see, for example, `fstrim.timer`, which is used on SSD drives to perform a block cleanup, also known as `trim`, at `/usr/lib/systemd/system/fstrim.timer`:

```
[Unit]
Description=Discard unused filesystem blocks
once a week
Documentation=man:fstrim
ConditionVirtualization=!container
ConditionPathExists=!/etc/initrd-release
```

```
[Timer]
OnCalendar=weekly
AccuracySec=1h
Persistent=true
RandomizedDelaySec=100min

[Install]
WantedBy=timers.target
```

A `timer` unit, as you can see, establishes a set of conditions under which a service is run.

In this case, the timer is intended to run weekly, as stated by the `OnCalendar` value.

It's also prepared to run a randomization of 100 minutes, as stated by `RandomizedDelaySec`, to make it not predictable. This is also useful if you plan to run a service on a large number of machines and all will connect to the same server, so they do not overload it.

There are some conditions to run this:

- `ConditionVirtualization`: This is not to be run inside a container
- `ConditionPathExists`: The `/etc/initrd-release` file should not exist

Please note that the exclamation mark (`!`) is meant to deny the value of the last condition.

Timers must have an associated service with the same name and a different extension. Let's see the associated service located at `/usr/lib/systemd/system/fstrim.service`:

```
[Unit]
Description=Discard unused blocks on filesystems from /etc/fstab
Documentation=man:fstrim(8)
ConditionVirtualization=!container

[Service]
Type=oneshot
ExecStart=/usr/sbin/fstrim --listed-in /etc/fstab:/proc/self/mountinfo
--verbose --quiet-unsupported
PrivateDevices=no
PrivateNetwork=yes
PrivateUsers=no
ProtectKernelTunables=yes
```

```
ProtectKernelModules=yes
ProtectControlGroups=yes
MemoryDenyWriteExecute=yes
SystemCallFilter=@default @file-system @basic-io @system-service
```

We can see in this previous service definition that it is executing the `/usr/sbin/fstrim --listed-in /etc/fstab:/proc/self/mountinfo --verbose --quiet-unsupported` command just once.

One of the advantages of having the service timers as unit files, similar to the service itself, is that they can be deployed and updated together.

We have understood a bit more about how to schedule tasks. But to get the whole picture, scheduling always requires proper timing, which we'll be covering next.

# Learning about time synchronization with chrony

The skills you will gain in this topic include understanding the importance of **time synchronization** and configuring the service.

With connected systems, it is important to keep a source of truth in regard to timing (think about bank accounts, incoming transfer wires, outgoing payments, etc., that must be correctly timestamped and sorted). Consider also tracing logs between users connecting, issues happening, and so on; they all need to be in sync to do proper diagnosis and debugging between all the different systems involved.

One might think that the system clock, defined when the system is provisioned, should be okay, but setting the system clock is not enough, as system clocks tend to drift. Internal batteries can cause the clock to drift or even reset. Even intense CPU activity can affect it. To keep clocks accurate, regular syncing against a reference clock is required to fix the drift and try to anticipate future drifts before the local clock is compared against the remote reference.

In different operating systems, the internal clock can be synced against a **Global Positioning System (GPS)** unit, for example, as in mobile phones, or more easily against other systems that have connections to more precise clocks (other GPS units, atomic clocks, etc.). For servers, workstations, and other systems using Linux, the **Network Time Protocol (NTP)** is the mechanism used to keep the clock in sync. NTP is an internet protocol that connects over **User Datagram Protocol (UDP)**, a transmission protocol used for streaming data, such as Netflix movies, to keep communication between the clients and the servers.

> NTP organizes servers by stratum. A stratum 0 device is a GPS device or an atomic clock that directly sends the signal to a server. A stratum 1 server (primary server) is connected to a stratum 0 device. Stratum 2 is connected to stratum 1 servers, and so on. This hierarchy allows us to reduce the usage of higher stratum servers but keep a reliable time source for our systems.

Clients connect to servers and compare the times received to reduce the effects of network latency.

Let's see how the NTP client works.

## The chrony NTP client

In SUSE Linux Enterprise Server 16, **chrony** is provided to act both as the server (when enabled) and as the client (via the `chronyc` command), and it comes with some features that make it also suitable for current hardware and user needs, such as fluctuating networks (laptop gets suspended, resumed, or flaky connections).

One interesting feature is that `chrony` does not **step** the clock after initial sync, which means that the time doesn't "jump." But the system clock runs faster or slower, so after a period of time, it will be in sync with the reference clock it's using. This makes the time a continuum from the operating system and applications point of view, even if the seconds are going faster or slower than they should, until they match the reference clock.

The `chrony` service is configured via `/etc/chrony.conf`, and as a client, it connects to servers to check them for eligibility to be the time source. The time source can be defined by specifying a **server**, when we are only going to use only one as the source of time, or the **pool** directive when we want to use several servers.

For `pool` or `server` directives, there are several options available (described in `man chrony.conf`), such as `iburst`, which enable faster checks with the servers configured to transition quickly into a synchronized status.

We can ensure that the time synchronization service is operational and started at boot by running the following:

```
# systemctl enable --now chronyd
Created symlink '/etc/systemd/system/multi-user.target.wants/chronyd.
service' → '/usr/lib/systemd/system/chronyd.service'.
```

Actual sources for time can be checked with `chronyc sources`, as shown in the following figure:

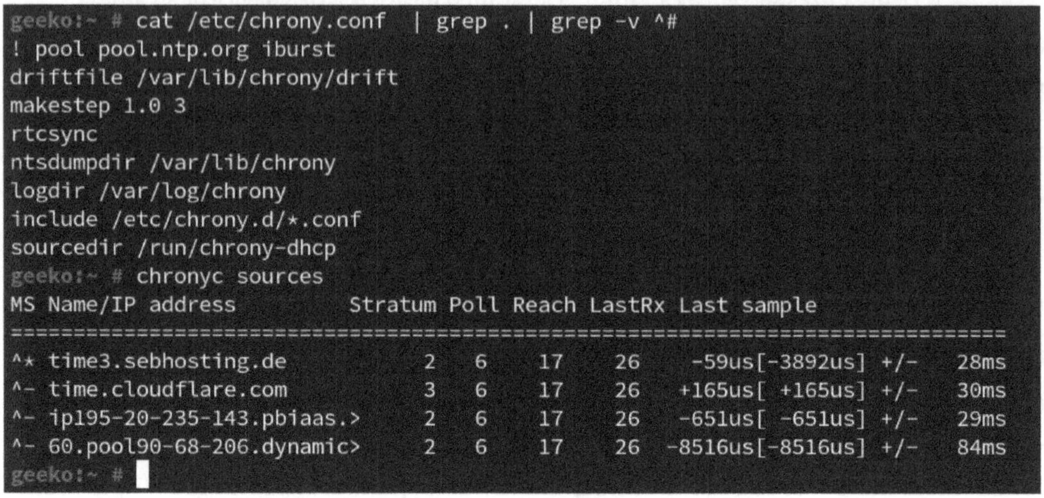


*Figure 3.5 – The chronyc sources output*

From the *Figure 3.5* screenshot status, we know the status of each server based on the first column (`M`):

- ^ means this is a server
- = means this is a peer

From the second column (`S`), we find out the different statuses for each entry:

- - indicates a source valid for synchronization but not being used
- * is our current synchronized server
- + is another acceptable time source
- ? is used to indicate sources with lost network connectivity
- x is considered a false ticker (its time is considered inconsistent when compared against other sources)
- ~ indicates a source that has a high variability (it also appears during daemon startup)

So, we see that our system is connected to a server that is considered the reference at `time3.sebhosting.de`, which is a stratum 2 server, as can be seen in the `Stratum` column.

In this case, `Stratum` means the hops the server must take to get to a system with a clock directly attached to it (a stratum 1 machine has a GPS device or an atomic clock attached to it).

More detailed information can be checked via the `chronyc tracking` command:

```
geeko:~ # chronyc tracking
Reference ID    : 5E8F8BDB (time3.sebhosting.de)
Stratum         : 3
Ref time (UTC)  : Mon Mar 31 16:31:35 2025
System time     : 0.006097023 seconds fast of NTP time
Last offset     : +0.007303524 seconds
RMS offset      : 0.007303524 seconds
Frequency       : 9.052 ppm slow
Residual freq   : +5.291 ppm
Skew            : 419.170 ppm
Root delay      : 0.051819731 seconds
Root dispersion : 0.056426078 seconds
Update interval : 65.3 seconds
Leap status     : Normal
geeko:~ #
```

*Figure 3.6 – The chronyc tracking output*

This command gives more detailed information about our clock and our reference clock. The fields in *Figure 3.6* have the following meanings:

- `Reference ID`: ID and name/IP of the server that the system is synchronized with.
- `Stratum`: Our stratum level, which means the number of hops we need to take to reach a stratum 1 clock. In this example, our synchronized server is a stratum 3 clock, because we are connecting to a stratum 2 server.
- `Ref time`: Time used in the last sync.
- `System time`: When running in normal mode (without time skip), this references how far the system is away, or behind, from the reference clock.
- `Last offset`: Estimated offset on the last clock update (positive indicates that our local time was ahead of our source).
- `RMS offset`: Long-term average of the offset value.
- `Frequency`: The rate at which the system clock would be wrong if `chronyd` were not fixing it, expressed in parts per million.
- `Residual freq`: Reflects any difference between the measurements for the current reference clock.
- `Skew`: Estimated error on the frequency.
- `Root delay`: Total of network delays to the stratum 1 synchronized server.
- `Root dispersion`: Total dispersion accumulated through all the computers connected to the stratum 1 server we're synchronized to.

- `Update interval`: Interval between the last two clock updates.
- `Leap status`: Can be `Normal`, `Insert`, `Delete`, or `Not synchronized`.

Don't underestimate the information sources you have at your fingertips. Remember that when preparing for SCA exams, the information available in the system can be checked during the exam: man pages, documentation included with the program (`/usr/share/doc/packages/`), and so on. For example, more detailed information about each of the aforementioned fields in the list can be found via the `man chronyc` command.

This last part, `Leap status`, is pretty interesting as it takes care of adjusting the leap seconds assigned each year to make the synchronized clock (**Universal Time Clock**, or **UTC** for short) also synchronized with the rotation of the earth. Wikipedia has a very interesting page about it: `https://en.wikipedia.org/wiki/Leap_second`.

To configure the client with additional options other than the ones provided during installation or via the kickstart file, we can edit the `/etc/chrony.conf` file.

Let's see how to convert our system into an NTP server for our network.

## The chrony NTP server

As we introduced earlier, `chrony` can also be configured as a server for your network. In this mode, our system will be providing accurate clock information to other hosts without consuming external bandwidth or resources from higher-stratum servers.

This configuration is performed via the `/etc/chrony.conf` file as well, where we will be adding a new directive, `allow`:

```
# Allow NTP client access from all hosts
allow all
```

This change enables `chrony` to listen to all host requests. Alternatively, we can define a subnet or a host to listen to, such as `allow 1.1.1.1`. More than one directive can be used to define the different subnets. Alternatively, you can use the `deny` directive to block specific hosts or subnets from reaching our NTP server.

Of course, we will also need to add the `ntp` service in the firewall to enable connectivity, as you will learn later in *Chapter 9, Securing Network Connectivity with firewalld*.

Serving time starts from the base that our server is already synchronized with an external NTP server. But let's think about an environment without connectivity. In this case, our server will not be connected to an external source, and it will not serve time. `chrony` includes a way to define a fake stratum for our server. This is done via the `local` directive in the configuration file. This allows the daemon to get a higher local stratum so that it can serve the time to other hosts, as in this example:

```
local stratum 3 orphan
```

With this directive, we're setting the `local` stratum to 3, and additionally, we're using the `orphan` option, which enables a special mode in which all servers with equal local stratum are ignored unless no other source is selectable, and its reference ID is smaller than the local one. This means that we can set several NTP servers in our disconnected network, but only one of them will be the reference.

Now that we have covered time synchronization, we are going to dive into resource monitoring, and later we'll check logging. All of it is very related to our time reference for the system.

# Checking system resources: memory and disk (free, df, and ps)

In this section, you will check the availability of system resources such as **memory** and **disk**.

Keeping a system running smoothly means using monitoring, so that we can check that the services are running and the system provides the resources for them to do their tasks.

There are simple commands to monitor the most basic use cases:

- Disk
- CPU
- Memory
- Network

And, of course, that includes several ways of monitoring, such as one-shot monitoring or continuous monitoring, or monitoring only for a period to better diagnose performance.

## Memory

Memory can be monitored via the `free` command. It provides complete details on how much RAM and swap are available and in use. It also indicates how much memory is free, as well as memory in use that could be liberated immediately, such as shared buffers or caches.

Linux tends to use all available memory, and it is normal. The unused RAM is directed toward cache or buffers, and memory pages that are not used are swapped out to disk if available. Let's look at an example:

```
# free
              total        used        free      shared  buff/cache
available
Mem:        4013924      451868     3306860        4776      482664
3562056
Swap:       2098152           0     2098152
```

In this output, we see that the system has a total of 4,014 MB of RAM, and it's using no swap and some memory for buffers (~4K). This system is not swapping heavily as it's almost idle (we'll check the load average later in this chapter), so we should not be concerned about it.

When RAM usage gets high and there's no more swap available, the kernel includes a protection mechanism called **OOM-Killer** (which stands for **Out-of-Memory Killer**). It kills processes based on a set of rules to bring the system to a functional status. The way it determines which processes shall be killed is based on time in execution, resource usage, and so on. This, however, comes at a cost, as the kernel just knows about processes that may have gone out of control, but the killer may kill databases and web servers, and leave the remaining system unstable. For production servers, it is sometimes usual to either tune the values for some critical process so that those are not killed or to cause a system crash instead of letting the OOM-Killer start killing processes in an uncontrolled way.

A system crash is used to collect debug information that can be later analyzed via a dump that is stored with the information that caused the crash, as well as a memory dump that can be later diagnosed.

We will review this topic later in the troubleshooting section "Finding logs, using journald, and reading log files, including log preservation and rotation". Let's move on to checking the disk space in use.

## Disk space

Disk space can be checked via the `df` tool. `df` provides output with data for each filesystem, indicating the filesystem, size, available space, percentage of utilization, and mount point.

Let's check it in our example system:

```
# df
Filesystem     1K-blocks    Used Available Use% Mounted on
/dev/vda2       31447040 2245012  28874636   8% /
devtmpfs            4096       0      4096   0% /dev
tmpfs            2006960       0   2006960   0% /dev/shm
tmpfs             802788     768    802020   1% /run
/dev/vda2       31447040 2245012  28874636   8% /.snapshots
/dev/vda2       31447040 2245012  28874636   8% /boot/grub2/i386-pc
/dev/vda2       31447040 2245012  28874636   8% /opt
/dev/vda2       31447040 2245012  28874636   8% /root
/dev/vda2       31447040 2245012  28874636   8% /srv
/dev/vda2       31447040 2245012  28874636   8% /boot/grub2/x86_64-efi
/dev/vda2       31447040 2245012  28874636   8% /home
/dev/vda2       31447040 2245012  28874636   8% /usr/local
tmpfs            2006964       0   2006964   0% /tmp
/dev/vda2       31447040 2245012  28874636   8% /var
tmpfs               1024       0      1024   0% /run/credentials/getty@
tty1.service
tmpfs             401392       4    401388   1% /run/user/0
tmpfs               1024       0      1024   0% /run/credentials/systemd-
journald.service
```

Using it, it's easy to first focus on filesystems with higher utilization and less free space to prevent issues.

> If a file is being written, for example, by a process logging its output, removing the file will just unlink the file from the filesystem, but as the process still has the file handle open, the space is not reclaimed until the process is stopped. In case of critical situations where disk space must be made available as soon as possible, it's better to empty the file via a redirect, such as `echo "" > filename`. This will recover the disk space immediately while the process is still running; doing it otherwise with `rm` will require the process to be finalized.

Let's check CPU consumption next.

# CPU

For monitoring the CPU, we can make use of several tools, such as `ps`. Let's run the `ps waux | less` command:

```
USER         PID %CPU %MEM    VSZ   RSS TTY      STAT START   TIME COMMAND
root           1  0.0  1.2  58084 51208 ?        Ss   10:23   0:02 /usr/lib/systemd/systemd --switche
d-root --system --deserialize=50
root           2  0.0  0.0      0     0 ?        S    10:23   0:00 [kthreadd]
root           3  0.0  0.0      0     0 ?        S    10:23   0:00 [pool_workqueue_release]
root           4  0.0  0.0      0     0 ?        I<   10:23   0:00 [kworker/R-rcu_gp]
root           5  0.0  0.0      0     0 ?        I<   10:23   0:00 [kworker/R-sync_wq]
root           6  0.0  0.0      0     0 ?        I<   10:23   0:00 [kworker/R-slub_flushwq]
root           7  0.0  0.0      0     0 ?        I<   10:23   0:00 [kworker/R-netns]
root           9  0.0  0.0      0     0 ?        I<   10:23   0:00 [kworker/0:0H-events_highpri]
root          11  0.0  0.0      0     0 ?        I    10:23   0:00 [kworker/u8:0-ipv6_addrconf]
root          12  0.0  0.0      0     0 ?        I<   10:23   0:00 [kworker/R-mm_percpu_wq]
root          13  0.0  0.0      0     0 ?        I    10:23   0:00 [rcu_tasks_kthread]
root          14  0.0  0.0      0     0 ?        I    10:23   0:00 [rcu_tasks_rude_kthread]
root          15  0.0  0.0      0     0 ?        I    10:23   0:00 [rcu_tasks_trace_kthread]
root          16  0.0  0.0      0     0 ?        S    10:23   0:00 [ksoftirqd/0]
root          17  0.0  0.0      0     0 ?        I    10:23   0:00 [rcu_preempt]
root          18  0.0  0.0      0     0 ?        S    10:23   0:00 [rcu_exp_par_gp_kthread_worker/0]
root          19  0.0  0.0      0     0 ?        S    10:23   0:00 [rcu_exp_gp_kthread_worker]
root          20  0.0  0.0      0     0 ?        S    10:23   0:00 [migration/0]
root          21  0.0  0.0      0     0 ?        S    10:23   0:00 [idle_inject/0]
root          22  0.0  0.0      0     0 ?        S    10:23   0:00 [cpuhp/0]
root          23  0.0  0.0      0     0 ?        S    10:23   0:00 [cpuhp/1]
root          24  0.0  0.0      0     0 ?        S    10:23   0:00 [idle_inject/1]
lines 1-23
```

*Figure 3.7 – Output of the ps aux | less command (every process in the system)*

The `ps` command is the de facto standard for checking which processes we're running, as well as some of the resource consumption usage. We are sending the output to the `less` program to be able to scroll through it (you can press the arrow keys to scroll or press *Q* to quit).

As for any other command, we could use lots of pages in this book for all the different command arguments we could use (so again, check the man page for details), but as a rule, try to learn some that aid in basic usage or the ones that are more useful for you. For anything else, check the manual. For example, `ps aux` provides enough information for normal usage (every process in the system).

As an improvement to the previous tool, the `top` tool, as shown in *Figure 3.8*, refreshes the screen regularly and can sort the output of running processes by several keys, such as CPU usage, memory usage, and so on.

In addition, top also shows a five-line summary of memory usage, load average, running processes, and so on, as can be seen here:

```
top - 19:09:32 up  8:45,  1 user,  load average: 1.78, 0.39, 0.13
Tasks: 144 total, 13 running, 131 sleep, 0 d-sleep, 0 stopped, 0 zombie
%Cpu(s):100.0 us,  0.0 sy,  0.0 ni,  0.0 id,  0.0 wa,  0.0 hi,  0.0 si,  0.0 st
MiB Mem : 3919.848 total, 3207.957 free,  458.910 used,  475.359 buff/cache
MiB Swap: 2048.977 total, 2048.977 free,    0.000 used. 3460.938 avail Mem

    PID USER      PR  NI    VIRT    RES    SHR S  %CPU  %MEM     TIME+ COMMAND
   3318 root      20   0   10112   4728   1260 R 16.88 0.118   0:09.83 bash
   3326 root      20   0   10112   4728   1260 R 16.88 0.118   0:00.77 bash
   3328 root      20   0   10112   4728   1260 R 16.88 0.118   0:00.77 bash
   3317 root      20   0   10112   4724   1256 R 16.55 0.118   0:09.95 bash
   3319 root      20   0   10112   4728   1260 R 16.55 0.118   0:09.83 bash
   3320 root      20   0   10112   4728   1260 R 16.55 0.118   0:09.81 bash
   3322 root      20   0   10112   4728   1260 R 16.55 0.118   0:00.98 bash
   3323 root      20   0   10112   4724   1256 R 16.55 0.118   0:00.98 bash
   3324 root      20   0   10112   4728   1260 R 16.55 0.118   0:00.98 bash
   3325 root      20   0   10112   4724   1256 R 16.55 0.118   0:00.98 bash
   3327 root      20   0   10112   4724   1256 R 16.55 0.118   0:00.77 bash
   3329 root      20   0   10112   4724   1256 R 16.55 0.118   0:00.77 bash
   3015 root      20   0   18400   8348   6336 S 0.331 0.208   0:01.99 sshd-session
      1 root      20   0   58084  51208  16888 S 0.000 1.276   0:02.08 systemd
      2 root      20   0       0      0      0 S 0.000 0.000   0:00.00 kthreadd
      3 root      20   0       0      0      0 S 0.000 0.000   0:00.00 pool_workqueue_release
      4 root       0 -20       0      0      0 I 0.000 0.000   0:00.00 kworker/R-rcu_gp
      5 root       0 -20       0      0      0 I 0.000 0.000   0:00.00 kworker/R-sync_wq
```

*Figure 3.8 – The output from executing top on our test system*

CPU usage is not the only thing that may keep our system sluggish; let's learn a bit about load average indicators.

## Load average

The **load average** is usually provided as a group of three numbers. For example, `load average: 1.78, 0.39, 0.13`, which is the average calculated for 1, 5, and 15 minutes, respectively, indicates how busy a system is. The higher it is, the worse it will respond. The values compared for each time frame give us an idea of whether the system load is increasing (higher values in 1 or 5 minutes, and lower in 15), or whether it is going down (higher at 15 minutes, and lower at 5 and 1), so it becomes a quick way to get an idea of whether something happened or it is ongoing. If a system usually has a high load average (number over the available cores in the system), it would be a good idea to dig a bit deeper into the possible causes (too much demand for its power, low resources available, etc.).

Now that we have covered the basics, let's move on to the extra checks we can perform on our system resources usage.

## Other monitoring tools

For **monitoring** network resources, we can check the packages sent/received for each card via the `ip` command, for example, by running `ip -s link show`, and match the values received for transmitted packages, received, errors, and so on.

When the goal is to perform a more complete monitoring, we should ensure that the `sysstat` package is installed. It includes some interactive tools, such as `iotop`, which can be used to check disk performance, but the most important thing is that it also sets up a job that will collect system performance data on a periodic basis (the default is every 10 minutes) that will be stored in `/var/log/sa/`.

To record an evolution of system resources, SUSE Linux Enterprise Server 16 includes **Performance Co-Pilot** (`pcp` and, optionally, `pcp-gui` packages), which can be set up for more powerful options. Just bear in mind that `pcp` requires us to also start the data collector on the system.

SUSE Linux Enterprise Server 16 also includes Cockpit, which is a package providing a set of tools that enable web management for the system, and it is also part of other products via plugins that extend the functionality. There are more details about it in *Chapter 8, Enabling and Using Cockpit*.

The web service provided by Cockpit can be reached at your host IP at port `9090`. So, you should access `https://_host_ip_:9090` to get the login screen where we can use our system credentials to log in.

After logging in, we can see a dashboard with relevant system information and links to other sections, as shown in the following screenshot:

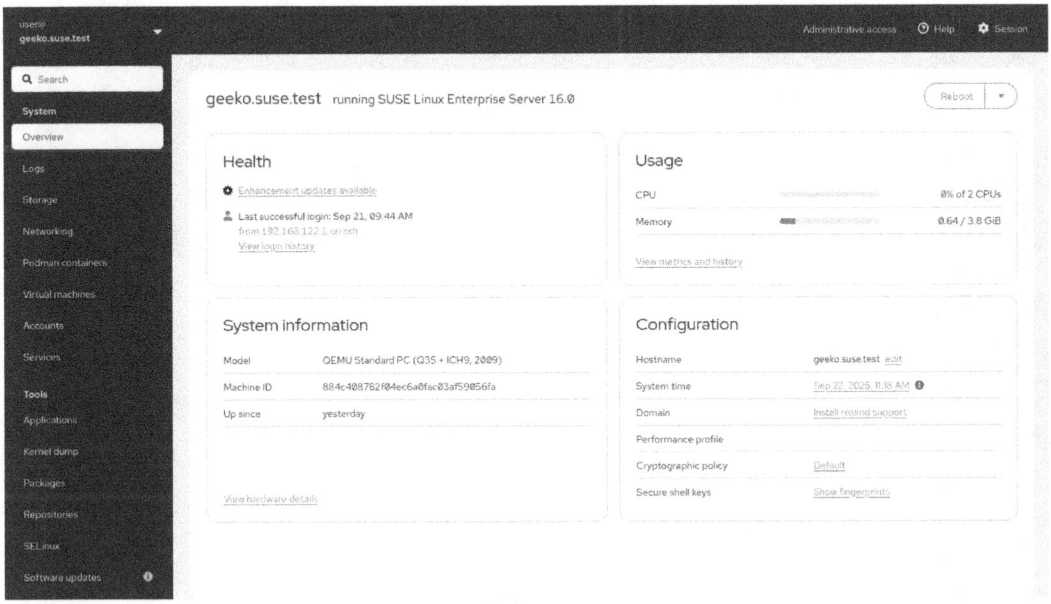


*Figure 3.9 – Cockpit screen after login with a system dashboard*

Cockpit, as you can see, includes several tabs that can be used to view the status of the system and even perform some administration tasks, such as **SELinux**, **Software updates**, **Subscriptions**, and so on.

For example, we can check the system graphs on performance, as shown in the following screenshot:

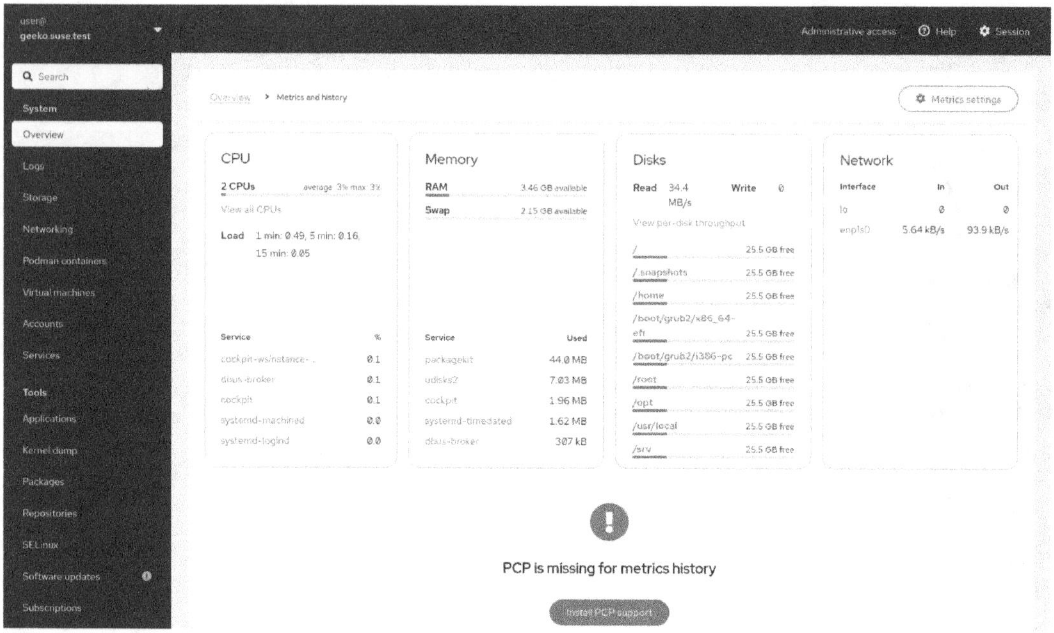


*Figure 3.10 – Cockpit graphs in the dashboard for usage graphs*

Cockpit allows checking the service status, package upgrade status, plus other configuration settings from a graphical interface that can also connect remotely to other systems, so that those can be selected from the lateral menu on the left.

There are better tools suited for large-deployment monitoring and management, such as **SUSE Multi-Linux Manager**, so it is important to get used to the tools we have for troubleshooting and simple scripts we can build, combining what we've learned so far to quickly generate hints about things that require our attention.

We have covered some of the basics for checking resource usage. Let's check now on how to find the information about the running services and errors we can review.

# Finding logs, using journald, and reading log files, including log preservation and rotation

The skills you will learn in this section are intended to help you review system status via logs.

Previously in this chapter, we learned about managing system services via `systemd` and checking service status. Now, we need to review its functioning and also review logs for other services. Traditionally, the different daemons and system components were used to create log files under the `/var/log/` folder. They used the name of the daemon or service as the name of the log file, or if the service was used to create several logs, do so inside a folder with the name of the service (for example, `httpd` or `samba`).

In SUSE Linux Enterprise Server 16, the system log daemon, `syslogd` or `rsyslogd`, has been replaced by its `systemd` partner, named `systemd-journald.service`, which also stores logs. But instead of using the traditional plain-text format, it uses a binary format that can be queried via the `journalctl` command. Two other loggers, `klogd` for kernel messages and `syslogd` for other services, are still offered in the distribution as complements for log management.

It's really important to get used to reading the log files, as it's the basis for troubleshooting, so let's get into detail about general logging and how to use it.

Logs contain status information for the services that generate them; they might have some common formatting and many times can be configured, but tend to use several common elements, such as the following:

- Timestamp
- Module generating the entry
- Message

Here is an example:

```
Apr 01 07:36:47 sles16-692807 sshd[50197]: Invalid user admin from
49.232.135.77 port 47694
```

In this case, we can see that someone attempted to log in to our system as the `admin` user from the IP address `49.232.135.77`.

We can correlate that event with additional logs, such as the ones for the login subsystem via `journalctl -u systemd-logind`. In this example, we cannot find any login for the `admin` user (expected as the `admin` user was not defined in this system).

Additionally, we can see the name of the host (`sles16-692807`), the service generating it (`sshd`), the **Program identifier** (**PID**) (`50197`), and the message logged by that service.

> PID is a number that the system assigns to every running process. The `kill` command can help you gently or forcefully stop any process in the system. It is very interesting to play with a system by stopping processes and seeing what happens.

A very interesting function of `journalctl` is using the `--follow` option. Running the `journalctl --follow` command will show a stream of logs on your screen, until stopped by pressing *Ctrl* + *C*:

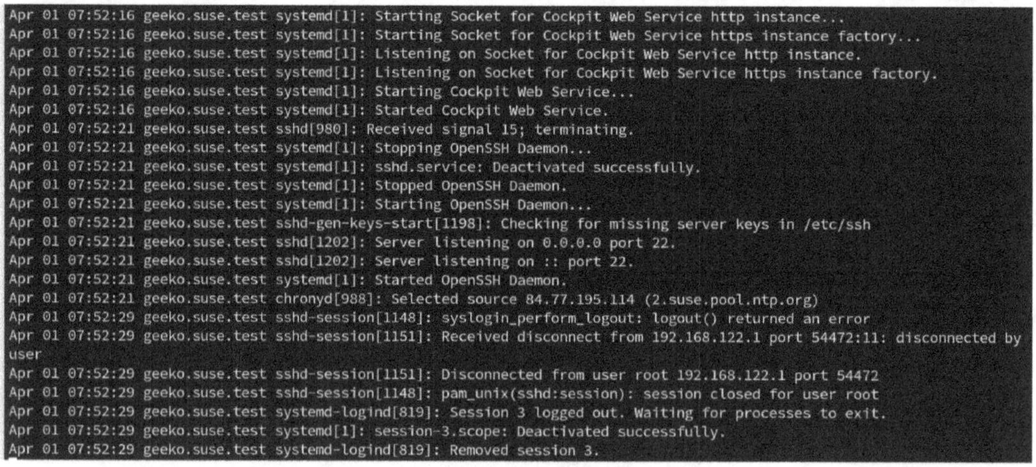


*Figure 3.11 – Excerpt of journalctl --follow*

In the preceding example, we can see how the system ran some commands following a similar output to the initial lines. For example, we can see how the Secure Shell daemon, `sshd`, has been stopped and started.

Let's see a list of important logs that are available in a standard system installation (note that the filenames are relative to the `/var/log` folder):

- `journal`: Binary storage for `journald` files. It can be accessed using `journalctl`.
- `boot.log`: Stores the messages emitted by the system during boot. It might contain escape codes used to provide colorized output.
- `audit/audit.log`: Contains the stored messages generated by the kernel audit subsystem.
- `zypper.log`: Logs generated by the `zypper` package manager, such as cache refreshes, and so on.
- `firewalld`: Output generated by the `firewalld` daemon.
- `mail.info`: Logs for the mail subsystem. When enabled, attempts to deliver messages or to receive them will be stored here. It's common practice to configure outgoing mail from servers so that system alerts or script outputs can be delivered.
- `snapper.log`: Keeps logs of the filesystem snapshots. By default, every installation of software done with `zypper` will create a snapshot.

Additional log files might exist depending on the services installed, installation method, and so on. It is very important to get used to the available logs and, of course, to review their contents to see how the messages are formatted, how many logs are created by day, and what kind of information is being logged.

Using the kind of information logged and the amount, we will get hints on how to configure each daemon to adjust the log level between just showing errors or being more verbose for debugging issues, and configure the required log rotation to avoid risking system stability because all the space has been consumed by logs.

## Log rotation

During regular system operation, a lot of daemons are in use, and the system itself is generating the logs used for troubleshooting and system checks.

Some services might allow you to define the log file to write to based on the date, but usually, the standard is to log to a file named like the daemon in the `/var/log` directory, for example, `/var/log/apache2`. Writing to the same file indefinitely will cause the file to grow until the drive holding the logs is filled, which might not make sense, as after some period (sometimes under company-defined policies), logs are no longer useful.

The **logrotate** package provides a script with a `logrotate.timer` that simplifies the log rotation. It is configured via `/etc/logrotate.d`, and the default configuration is in `/usr/etc/logrotate.conf` and is executed on a daily basis as follows:

```
drwx------ 1 minidlna minidlna       0 may 29  2024 minidlna
-rw-r----- 1 root     root      497917 mar 19 10:28 NetworkManager
-rw------- 1 root     root       69217 mar 19 17:46 pbl.log
drwxrwxr-x 1 pcp      pcp           58 oct 18 14:11 pcp
-rw-r----- 1 root     root     1000789 mar 19 10:29 pk_backend_zypp
-rw------- 1 root     root       98749 mar 19 10:28 plymouth-debug.log
-rw------- 1 root     root       10744 mar 19 10:22 plymouth-shutdown-debug.log
drwx------ 1 root     root           0 may 14  2023 private
drwxr-x--- 1 root     root           0 feb  7 17:01 samba
-rw-r----- 1 root     root      273581 abr  1 08:01 snapper.log
-rw-r----- 1 root     root      349400 mar 18 00:00 snapper.log-20250318.xz
drwx------ 1 root     root           0 may  9  2024 speech-dispatcher
-rw------- 1 root     root     4194240 oct 10 18:51 tallylog
drwxr-xr-x 1 root     root           0 sep 23  2024 tuned
drwxr-xr-x 1 root     root         450 mar 16 19:26 updateTestcase-2025-03-16-19-26-25
drwxr-xr-x 1 root     root         450 mar 16 19:27 updateTestcase-2025-03-16-19-27-03
-rw-r----- 1 root     root     1149083 mar 25 17:46 warn
-rw-r----- 1 root     root        2832 mar 21 17:51 wpa_supplicant.log
-rw-rw-r-- 1 root     utmp      165120 abr  1 08:19 wtmp
drwx------ 1 root     root         412 dic  6 17:47 YaST2
drwxr-x--- 1 root     root          14 feb 28 08:38 zypp
-rw-r----- 1 root     root     1678434 mar 31 18:46 zypper.log
-rw-r----- 1 root     root      364428 ene 31 17:45 zypper.log-20250201.xz
-rw-r----- 1 root     root      420324 feb 27 17:45 zypper.log-20250228.xz
-rw-r----- 1 root     root      347248 mar 26 17:45 zypper.log-20250327.xz
```

*Figure 3.12 – Example listing of logs and rotated logs (using date extension)*

If we check the contents of the configuration file, we can see that it includes some file definitions either directly there or via drop-in files in the `/etc/logrotate.d/` folder, allowing each program to drop its own requirements without affecting others when packages are installed, removed, or updated.

Why is this important? Because if you remember one of the tips shared earlier in this chapter (while speaking about disk space), if `logrotate` were to just delete the files and create a new one, the actual disk space would not be freed, and the daemon writing to the log would continue to write to the file it was writing to (via the file handle). To overcome this, each definition file has the ability to define a post-rotation command that signals the process about the log rotation, so that it can close and then reopen the files it uses for logging. Some programs might require a signal, such as `kill -SIGHUP PID`, or a special parameter on execution, such as `chronyc cyclelogs`.

With the preceding definitions, `logrotate` will be able to apply the configuration for each service and, at the same time, keep the service working in a sane state.

Configuration can also include special directives such as the following:

- `missingok`
- `nocreate`
- `nopytruncate`
- `notifempty`

You can find out more about them (and others) in the man page for `logrotate.conf`.

> Yes, some packages also include a man page for the configuration files. So try checking `man logrotate.conf` to get the full details!

The remaining general configuration in the main file allows us to define some common directives, such as how many days of logs to keep, whether we want to use the date in the file extension for the rotated log files, whether we want to use compression on the rotated logs, how frequently we want to have rotation executed, and so on.

Let's see it with some examples.

The following example will rotate on a daily basis, keep 30 rotated logs, compress them, and use an extension with the date as part of the trailing filename:

```
rotate 30
daily
compress
dateext
```

In this new example, it will keep four logs rotated on a weekly basis (so four weeks) and will compress the logs, but it will use a sequence number for each rotated log (that means that each time a rotation happens, the sequence number is increased for the previously rotated logs, too):

```
rotate 4
weekly
compress
```

One of the advantages of this approach (not using `dateext`) is that the log naming is predictable, having `daemon.log` as the current one, `daemon.1.log` as the prior one, and so on, making it easier to script log parsing and processing.

# Summary

In this chapter, we learned about `systemd` and how it takes care of booting system-required services in an optimized way. Also, we learned how to check service status; enable, disable, start, and stop the mentioned services; and how to make our system boot into different boot targets we can define our system to boot into.

Time synchronization was introduced as a must-have feature in our systems to ensure proper service function, along with how to determine the status of our system clock, and how to act as a clock server for our network.

We also used system tools to monitor resource usage and to check the logs created by our system to find out about the functional status of the different tools and how we can ensure that logs are properly maintained so that older entries are discarded when they are no longer relevant.

In the next chapter, we will dive into securing the system with different users, groups, and permissions.

# 4

# Securing the System with Users, Groups, and Permissions

Security is a key part of system management. Understanding the concepts well can be the difference between keeping user data safe and providing unsafe access to resources.

In this chapter, we will review the basics of security in SUSE Linux Enterprise Server 16. We will add new users and describe their attributes. We will learn about groups and how we manage their users. We will also see how to handle user passwords, locking and/or restricting user access, and forcing updates. We will use `sudo` to achieve admin privileges without sharing the root account (up to the point where the root account can be disabled). We will also take a deeper look into the meaning of file permissions and how to change them. We will also learn how to enable users to run commands as a different user or group and how to simplify group collaboration in directories. An issue in permissions could mean providing access to parts of the system to an attacker that could help them escalate privileges. It is important to know how to handle permissions well to ensure *defense-in-depth* protection for our systems.

The following topics will be covered:

- Creating, modifying, and deleting local user accounts and groups
- Managing groups and reviewing assignments
- Adjusting password policies
- Configuring and using `sudo` for administrative tasks
- Checking, reviewing, and modifying file permissions
- Using special permissions

Let's take our first steps in the world of permissions and security with user accounts and groups.

## Creating, modifying, and deleting local user accounts and groups

**User accounts** are the way the system identifies users of the system. One of the first tasks that a system administrator must do when preparing a system is to create new user accounts for the people accessing the system. In this section, we will review how local accounts are created and deleted, as well as how they are assigned to groups.

Let's create a new user account in the system. We will use the `useradd` command to add `user01` to the system:

```
geeko:~ # useradd user01
geeko:~ # grep user01 /etc/passwd
user01:x:1001:1002::/home/user01:/bin/bash
geeko:~ # id user01
uid=1001(user01) gid=1002(user01)
groups=1002(user01)
geeko:~ # grep user01 /etc/shadow
user01:!:20179:0:99999:7:::
```

A more portable and independent way to check `passwd` is to run `getent passwd user01`, which will give the same output. For `shadow`, too, we can use `getent shadow user01`.

We have now created a new user and a new group for the user. In this case, their userID and groupID numbers are different (because there was a group created before with that ID).

To be able to add users, we need administrative privileges. In the current configuration, we do that by running the commands as `root`.

The account is created using the default options configured on the system, which are the following:

- **No password assigned**: The new user will not be able to log in using a password (the password file in the shadow file is `!`). You can still use the account by switching from `root` using `su` because `root` does not need to provide the password. We will see how to add a password to the user in this section.
- **User ID (UID)**: The first number over 999 available. In the command we ran before, for `user01`, the UID is `1001`.
- **Group ID (GID)**: The first number available over 999. In this case, the GID is `1002`.
- **Description**: We didn't provide a description, so the field is empty.
- **Home**: A new home directory is created in `/home/$USER`; in this case, `/home/user01`. It will be the default directory for new logins for the user and where personal preferences and files will be stored. The directory is not empty because initial contents are copied from `/etc/skel` and `/usr/etc/skel`.
- **Shell**: The default shell is `bash`.

Once the user has been set up, we can add (or change) the password by running, as `root`, the `passwd` command followed by the username:

> The command is `passwd`, not `password`.

```
geeko:~ # passwd user01
New password: suse
BAD PASSWORD: The password is shorter than 8 characters
Retype new password: suse
passwd: password updated successfully
```

Now the user has a new password assigned. Note two things:

- The `root` user can change the password of any user without knowing the previous one (a full password reset). This is useful when a user comes back from holidays and doesn't remember their password.
- The actual password, `suse`, is not shown on the screen, so nobody looking at it can read it. The password does not follow the configured rules because it is too short. However, as `root`, we can still assign it. A normal user would have this new password rejected.

You can use different options to customize how users are created. The useradd command has the following options:

- -u or --uid: Assign a specific UID to the user.
- -g or --gid: Assign a primary group to the user. It can be specified by number (GID) or by name. The group needs to be created first.
- -G or --groups: Make the user part of other groups by providing a comma-separated list of the groups they need to be part of.
- -c or --comment: Provide a description for the user, specified between quotes (") if you want to use spaces.
- -d or --home-dir: Define the home directory for the user.
- -s or --shell: Assign a custom shell to the user.
- -p or --password: A way to provide a password to the user. The password should already be encrypted to use this method.
- -r or --system: A way to create a system account instead of a user account.

It is bad practice to use the -p option on the command line because there are ways to capture the encrypted password, and history will show it as part of the command. Please use passwd instead.

What if we need to change any of the user's properties, such as the description? The tool for that is chfn. Let's update the description of user01:

```
geeko:~ # chfn -f "User 01" user01
geeko:~ # grep user01 /etc/passwd
user01:x:1001:1002:User 01:/home/user01:/bin/
bash
```

We can also pass all the options to the useradd command so we don't need to create users in multiple steps.

Let's create user02 with options:

```
geeko:~ # useradd --uid 1002 --groups wheel \
> --comment "user 02" --home-dir /home/user02 \
> --shell /bin/bash user02
geeko:~ # grep user02 /etc/passwd
```

```
user02:x:1002:1003:user 02:/home/user02:/bin/
bash
geeko:~ # id user02
uid=1002(user02) gid=1003(user02)
groups=1003(user02),497(wheel)
```

When the command is too long to fit on a single line, you can continue on a new line using \ as the last character on the line, followed by *Enter*.

Groups simplify giving privileges to users. A user is always a member of a group, its primary group, and can also be a member of other groups, which are called secondary groups. The information about the primary group is stored in `/etc/password`, with the user data, and all the information about groups is stored in the `/etc/groups` file.

Let's create a group called `finance` using the `groupadd` command in order to learn more about groups:

```
geeko:~ # groupadd finance
geeko:~ # grep finance /etc/group
finance:x:1004
```

We can use `usermod` to add our `user01` and `user02` users to the `finance` group:

```
geeko:~ # usermod -aG finance user01
geeko:~ # usermod -aG finance user02
geeko:~ # grep finance /etc/group
finance:x:1004:user01,user02
```

We are using the `-aG` option to add the user to the group instead of modifying the groups the user belongs to. You can also modify the groups file itself using `vigr` and check that it was properly edited using `grpck`.

We can delete users, updating all secondary groups with the `userdel` command:

```
geeko:~ # userdel user01
geeko:~ # grep user01 /etc/passwd
geeko:~ # id user01
id: 'user01': no such user
```

```
geeko:~ # grep user01 /etc/group
geeko:~ #
geeko:~ # id user02
uid=1002(user02) gid=1003(user02)
groups=1003(user02),497(wheel),1004(finance)
geeko:~ # ls /home
user  user01  user02
geeko:~ # rm -rf /home/user01
```

We needed to manually delete the home directory and any files created by the user. This way of removing a user is good if we want to keep their data for future use.

We can automatically delete the home folder using the `-r` option. Let's try it with `user02`:

```
geeko:~ # su user02
user02@geeko:/tmp> touch user02_data; exit
geeko:~ # userdel -r user02
geeko:~ # ls /home
user
geeko:~ # id user02
id: 'user02': no such user
geeko:~ # ls -l /tmp/user02_data
-rw-r--r--. 1 1002 1003 0 Apr  2 06:49 /tmp/user02_data
```

> The home directory was deleted, but all other files in the system remain. Notice how the UID and GID of the files are still the same, even if the username cannot be identified. Think of what would happen if you created a new user with the same UID and GID.

We can remove the `finance` group with the `groupdel` command:

```
geeko:~ # groupdel finance
geeko:~ # grep finance /etc/group
```

We have created and modified users and groups in SLES using the command line. Let's learn how to manage groups.

# Managing groups and reviewing assignments

We have seen how to create a group with groupadd and delete it with groupdel. Let's now see how to modify a group with groupmod.

We are going to create a group so we can work with it. Let's create a group called acounting by running the following:

```
geeko:~ # groupadd -g 1099 acounting
geeko:~ # tail -n1 /etc/group
acounting:x:1099:
```

As you can see, we misspelled the name; it should have been accounting. Let's fix the name and add some user accounts. We modify a group using groupmod:

```
[root@geeko ~]# groupmod -n accounting acounting
[root@geeko ~]# tail -n1 /etc/group
accounting:x:1099:
```

Now, we've seen how to modify a group's name. We can modify not just the name but also the GID by using the -g option:

```
geeko:~ # groupmod -n accounting acounting -g 1100
geeko:~ # tail -n1 /etc/group
accounting:x:1100:
```

We can see a list of secondary groups assigned to a user by running the groups command:

```
geeko:~ # groups user
user : user wheel
```

This should be enough for basic management of users and groups in the system. Let's move on and discuss password policies.

# Adjusting password policies

As was mentioned in *Chapter 2, Running Basic Commands and Simple Shell Scripts*, users are stored in the /etc/passwd file, while the encrypted passwords, or **password hashes**, are stored in the /etc/shadow file. This allows the shadow file to have stronger access restrictions.

> A hashing algorithm is a one-way function that generates a precise string of characters, or a hash, from a provided piece of data. The generated hash is the same for the same data, but the original data is almost impossible to recreate from the hash. This makes hashes perfect for storing sensitive data that needs to be secure while allowing validation, such as passwords or the integrity of a downloaded file.

Let's look at the stored hash for the user in `/etc/shadow`:

```
geeko:~ # grep user /etc/shadow
user:$6$1mA1oW2ggLxTTmUu$AxSkeMLi/iPZZ/
sADFEkpxvbtqh3X0.2feKNGZ7vtrllhRwC9uRvsbk/.mU2KK2zILHtCx1N/
mrA2Phullkz0.:20180:0:99999:7:3:19113:
```

As with the password file, the data stored in `/etc/shadow` has one entry per line, and the fields are separated by colons (`:`):

- `user`: Account name. It must be the same one as in `/etc/passwd`.
- `$6$1mA1oW2ggLxTTmUu$AxSkeMLi/iPZZ/sADFEkpxvbtqh3X0.2feKNGZ7vtrllhRwC9uRvsbk/.mU2KK2zILHtCx1N/mrA2Phullkz0.`: Password hash. It contains three parts separated by `$`:
    - `$6`: The algorithm used to encrypt the file. In this case, the value `6` indicates that it is SHA-512. The number `1` is for the old, now insecure, MD5 algorithm.
    - `$1mA1oW2ggLxTTmUu`: The random **salt** part. This is a token used to improve password encryption. It is added to the real password to make sure that the same password does not generate the same hash.
    - `$AxSkeMLi/iPZZ/sADFEkpxvbtqh3X0.2feKNGZ7vtrllhRwC9uRvsbk/.mU2KK2zILHtCx1N/mrA2Phullkz0.`: The encrypted password hash. Using the salt and the SHA-512 algorithm, this token is created. When the user validates (i.e., when logging in again), the process is run again. If the same hash is generated, the password is validated, and access is granted.
- `20180`: The time and date when the password was last changed. The format is the number of days since 1970-01-01 00:00 UTC (this date is also known as the **epoch**).

- `0`: Minimum number of days until the user can change the password again.
- `99999`: Maximum number of days until the user has to change the password again. If this is empty, it won't expire.
- `7`: Number of days before expiry that the user will be warned that the password is about to expire.
- `3`: Number of days within which the user can still log in even when the password has expired.
- `19113`: Date on which the password should expire. If this is empty, it won't expire on a specific date.
- `<empty>`: The last colon is left to allow the easy addition of new fields if required.

> To convert the `date` field to a human-readable date, you can run the following command: `date -d '1970-01-01 UTC + 20180 days'`.

How do we change the expiration dates for passwords? The tool for this is `chage`, short for **change age**. Let's first review the options that can be used in the same order as they are stored in `/etc/shadow`:

- `-d` or `--lastday`: The time and date when the password was last changed. The format for this is `YYYY-MM-DD`.
- `-m` or `--mindays`: Minimum number of days until the user can change the password again.
- `-W` or `--warndays`: Number of days the user will be warned that the password is about to expire.
- `-I` or `--inactive`: Number of days, once the password has expired, that will have to pass before the account is locked.
- `-E` or `--expiredate`: Date after which the user's account will be locked. The format for this is `YYYY-MM-DD`.

Let's put everything we have learned about how to manage a user to the test. First, we create the `usertest` account:

```
geeko:~ # useradd usertest
geeko:~ # grep usertest /etc/shadow
usertest:!:20180:0:99999:7:::
```

We have used the defaults. The exclamation mark, `!`, is not a password hash; it's the way the system is signaling that the password is not set. Let's change the password to see what changes. Use any password you like:

```
geeko:~ # passwd usertest
New password:
BAD PASSWORD: The password is shorter than 8 characters
Retype new password:
passwd: password updated successfully
geeko:~ # grep usertest /etc/shadow
usertest:$6$Y8hnzniOlbGrErkH$gi.jevhrmubLmGOzG4TSn.
KYh.E.iBifTa2OuITejCujPkBfDXLuTJI.IJEKhDdDCRE5jeUxRT9A5CG.
miBA8.:20180:0:99999:7:::
```

The password hash has been created, and the date for the last change is the current date. Let's establish some options:

```
geeko:~ # grep usertest /etc/shadow
usertest:$6$Y8hnzniOlbGrErkH$gi.jevhrmubLmGOzG4TSn.
KYh.E.iBifTa2OuITejCujPkBfDXLuTJI.IJEKhDdDCRE5jeUxRT9A5CG.
miBA8.:20180:0:99999:7:3:21914:
geeko:~ # date -d '1970-01-01 UTC + 21915 days'
Tue Jan  1 01:00:00 CET 2030
```

The changes in `/etc/shadow` correspond, in fact, with the values specified for `chage`. We can check the changes with the `-l` option of `chage`:

```
geeko:~ # chage -l usertest
Last password change                                    : Apr 02, 2025
Password expires                                   : never
Password inactive                                  : never
Account expires                                         : Dec 31, 2029
Minimum number of days between password change          : 0
Maximum number of days between password change          : 99999
Number of days of warning before password expires       : 7
```

We can apply those changes by default by modifying the defaults in a configuration file. Let's edit `/etc/login.defs` and find the section where the most common changes are:

```
#  Password aging controls:
#
#    PASS_MAX_DAYS  Maximum number of days a password may be used.
#    PASS_MIN_DAYS  Minimum number of days allowed between password
changes.
#    PASS_MIN_LEN   Minimum acceptable password length.
#    PASS_WARN_AGE  Number of days warning given before a password expires.
#
PASS_MAX_DAYS       99999
PASS_MIN_DAYS       0
PASS_MIN_LEN        5
PASS_WARN_AGE       7
```

Please take some time to review the options in `/etc/login.defs`.

How do we lock the account of a user who has temporarily left the company? We could delete the account and, if we are not careful, also delete the files in its `home` directory, as well as password hashes and group info. We would then lose that data forever. We can lock the account instead with the `usermod` command and the`-L` option for **lock**. Let's see how it works. First, let's log in to the system:

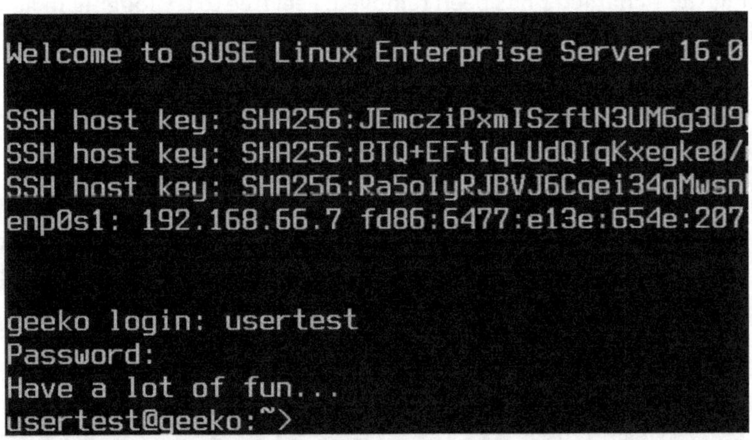


*Figure 4.1 – The usertest user account logging in to the system*

Now, let's lock the account:

```
geeko:~ # usermod -L usertest
geeko:~ # grep usertest /etc/shadow
usertest:!$6$Ffa5p9r7058yHpkG$c1mAPBGQxtv8sI.yFLdogINCP6pJxfISlIsU/
IKWfXhFtTAAT4B0XKqyssK0W521hHyivyMR4wedbbNqJiIeW.:20185:0:99999:7:3:21914:
```

Notice that a `!` character has been added before the password hash. Through this, we understand that the hash is incorrect, signaling that the account is locked. Let's try to log in again:

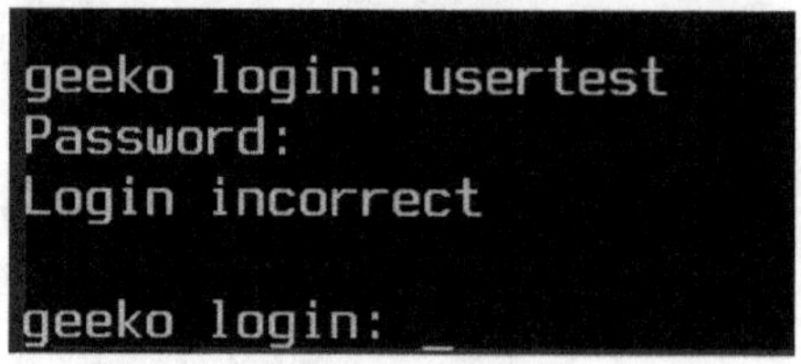


*Figure 4.2 – The usertest user account not being able to log in to the system*

The account can be unlocked by using the `-U` option:

```
geeko:~ # usermod -U usertest
geeko:~ # grep usertest /etc/shadow
usertest:$6$Ffa5p9r7058yHpkG$c1mAPBGQxtv8sI.yFLdogINCP6pJxfISlIsU/
IKWfXhFtTAAT4B0XKqyssK0W521hHyivyMR4wedbbNqJiIeW.:20185:0:99999:7:3:21914:
```

Now, you can see that the `!` character has been removed. Feel free to try logging in again.

> To fully lock the account, not just prevent logging in with a password (there are other mechanisms), you need to set the expiry date to `1`.

Another common use case is when you want users to access resources on the system, such as having a network shared directory (that is, via NFS or CIFS, as will be explained in *Chapter 12, Managing Local Storage and Filesystems*), but you do not want them to be able to run commands on the system. For that, we can use a very special shell: the `nologin` shell. Let's assign that shell to the `usertest` user account using `usermod`:

```
[root@geeko ~]# usermod -s /sbin/nologin usertest
[root@geeko ~]# grep usertest /etc/passwd
usertest:x:1001:1001::/home/usertest:/sbin/nologin
[root@geeko ~]# su - usertest
```

```
Last login: sun jan 24 16:18:07 CET 2021 on pts/0
This account is currently not available.
[root@geeko ~]# usermod -s /bin/bash usertest
[root@geeko ~]# su - usertest
Last login: sun jan 24 16:18:15 CET 2021 on pts/0
[usertest@geeko ~]$
```

Note that we are reviewing the changes in `/etc/passwd` this time as it is where the modification is applied.

As you can see, it's easy to set the values for password aging for any user, lock them, or restrict their access to the system. Let's move on to more administrative tasks and how to delegate admin access.

# Configuring and using sudo access for administrative tasks

Sharing the `root` password so that users can perform administrative tasks is a security risk and can lead to the password being leaked. There is a way to delegate administrative access to users in SLES without sharing the password for `root`. This can be done with a tool called **sudo**, which stands for **Super User Do**.

With `sudo`, you can specify user privileges to make changes to the system. It can be simply providing full administrator access or going down to the level of assigning specific commands to users and/or groups so they can execute some administrative tasks. `sudo` permissions can be very granular. It is possible to configure `sudo` to identify users with their own password, instead of the one for `root`, so you don't need to share the `root` password with anybody else.

In some install methods, `sudo` is not included by default. If you want to install it, you can run the following command as `root`:

```
# zypper in sudo sudo-policy-wheel-auth-self
```

Let's now continue by understanding the default configuration and how to change it.

## Understanding sudo configuration

The tool has its main configuration file in `/usr/etc/sudoers` and the `/usr/etc/sudoers.d/` folder. Let's see what they say:

```
Defaults targetpw
# ask for the password of the target user i.e. root
ALL   ALL=(ALL) ALL
```

All the lines starting with # are considered comments, and they are ignored by the interpreter.

```
# WARNING! Only use this together with 'Defaults
targetpw'!
## User privilege specification
root ALL=(ALL:ALL) ALL
## Read drop-in files from /etc/sudoers.d (the #
here does not mean a comment)
```

The first two lines configure all users to impersonate any other user, including `root`, providing the target password and providing access to every command. There is no restriction on what they can do as long as they provide the `root` password when doing so:

```
ALL  ALL=(ALL)      ALL
targetpw'!
```

The next line enables the user `root` to use sudo for any command that needs to be run:

```
root ALL=(ALL:ALL) ALL
```

Please do not disable the `wheel` group directive unless there is an important reason to do so. This behavior is expected in SLES by other programs, and disabling it may cause some problems.

Inside the `/usr/etc/sudoers.d/50-wheel-auth-self` folder, there is a configuration to enable the users in the `wheel` group to be able to impersonate `root` for any command, providing their own password instead of the password for `root`:

```
Defaults:%wheel !targetpw
%wheel ALL = (root) ALL
```

As you should not change files inside `/usr/etc` directly, the configuration specifies where to store the configuration if you need to modify it. These lines enable the `/etc/sudoers.d` directory and `/usr/etc/sudoers.d` as a source for configuration files:

```
@includedir /usr/etc/sudoers.d
@includedir /etc/sudoers.d
```

> The exception to this last rule is files that end with ~ or contain a . (dot) character.

The easiest way to grant full admin privileges is to add a user to the `wheel` group. An example of how to modify the `usertest` account to make it an admin account is as follows:

```
[root@geeko ~]# usermod -aG wheel usertest
[root@geeko ~]# groups usertest
usertest : usertest wheel
```

> For cloud instances, the `root` account does not have a valid password assigned. To be able to manage the mentioned cloud instance, in some clouds, such as **Amazon Web Services** (**AWS**), a user is created by default and added to the `wheel` group. In the case of AWS, the default user account is `ec2-user`. In other clouds, a custom user is also created and added to the `wheel` group.

The basic configuration is stored in the `/usr/etc/sudoers` file, with some modifications in files in the `/usr/etc/sudoers.d/` directory. You should not modify the files directly. The policy allows the users in the `wheel` group to use `sudo` with their own password, unrestricted, while asking for the `root` password from any users who are not part of the group.

Custom configuration must reside in `/etc/sudoers.d/`. Settings in custom configuration files take precedence over those in the default files. As modifying configuration files directly is dangerous, you should use `visudo`. This is a special tool to make configuration changes that verify that only one user is editing. It also runs some basic syntax checks before updating files to make sure that the system is always functional.

## Using sudo to run admin commands

We will use the `user` account in these examples. As you may remember, in *Chapter 1, Getting SLES 16 Up and Running (Physical and Cloud)*, we enabled the checkbox in which we requested the account to be the administrator. Under the hood, the account was added to the `wheel` group. So, we can start using `sudo` to run admin commands.

Let's log in with the user account and try to run an administrative command such as adduser:

```
geeko:/usr/etc # cd
geeko:~ # su - user
user@geeko:~> adduser john
-bash: adduser: command not found
user@geeko:~> /usr/sbin/useradd john
useradd: Permission denied.
useradd: cannot lock /etc/passwd; try again later.
user@geeko:~> sudo useradd john
We trust you have received the usual lecture from the local System
Administrator. It usually boils down to these three things:
#1) Respect the privacy of others.
#2) Think before you type.
#3) With great power comes great responsibility.

For security reasons, the password you type will not be visible.
[sudo] password for user:
user@geeko:~> id john
uid=1002(john) gid=1002(john) groups=1002(john)
```

The first time you run sudo, you are shown a warning message. Then, we are asked for *our own password* – because we are part of the wheel group, the one we have for the user running sudo. Once the password is correctly typed, the command is run and registered in the system journal:

```
j Apr 15 10:55:42 geeko.suse.test sudo[12129]:     user : TTY=pts/0 ;
PWD=/home/user ; USER=root ; COMMAND=/usr/sbin/useradd john
```

> Once you have run sudo successfully, it will remember that validation for five minutes by default, so you don't have to type your password again and again if you need to run more than one administrative command in a session. To increase it to 30 minutes, we can add the following line using visudo: `Defaults:USER timestamp_timeout=30`.

Sometimes, we want to have an interactive session to be able to type more than one command without typing sudo again and again. To do that, we add the-i option. Let's try it:

```
user@geeko:~> sudo -i
geeko:~ #
```

Now that we know how to use sudo, it would be good to see how to administer privileges in an easy-to-automate way. For this, we will use the sudoers file.

sudoers is powerful, allowing you to define many things, including the environment variables that are available when executing a command or the commands that are allowed. Let's now move on to customizing the configuration of sudo in the sudoers file.

## Configuring sudoers

We saw the details of the default /usr/etc/sudoers file in the previous section. Let's see a couple of examples of how to make a more granular configuration.

Let's start by making sudo run admin commands without requesting a password for the users in the wheel group. We can run visudo /etc/sudoers/01_wheel_no_password and add the following line:

```
%wheel          ALL=(ALL:ALL)         NOPASSWD: ALL
```

Save it. Note that there is a commented line in /usr/etc/sudoers with that configuration. Now, let's see the impact of the change we just made:

```
user@geeko:~> sudo useradd ellen
user@geeko:~> id ellen
uid=1003(ellen) gid=1003(ellen) groups=1003(ellen)
```

You can now create a file, with your favorite editor, to enable the new user account, ellen, to run admin commands. Let's create the /etc/sudoers.d/02_ellen_all file with this content:

```
user@geeko:~> sudo visudo /etc/sudoers.d/02_ellen_all
ellen ALL=(ALL)  ALL
```

We are using the /etc/sudoers.d directory to extend the sudo configuration.

We will review the detailed configuration of sudoers here despite it not being part of the SCA exam. As you can see, there are three fields, separated by spaces or tabs, to define policies in the configuration files. Let's review them:

- The first field is to specify who is affected by the policy:
    - We can add users by simply putting the username in the first field
    - We can add groups by using the % character before the name of the group in the first field
    - We can add # to use the UID, including %# for GIDs

- The second field is for where the policy applies:
  - We have so far used `ALL=(ALL:ALL)` to specify everything
  - In the first part of this field, we can define a group of computers to be run, such as `SERVERS=10.0.0.0/255.255.255.0`
  - In the second part, we can specify commands such as `NETWORK=/usr/sbin/ip`
  - Between parentheses is the user account that can be used to run the command and the groups, separated by a colon
- The third field is to specify which commands are allowed:
  - The syntax goes like this:

    ```
    user  hosts = (run-as: group-as) commands
    ```

Let's see an example:

```
Runas_AliasDB = oracle
Host_Alias SERVERS=10.0.0.0/255.255.255.0
Cmnd_Alias NETWORK=/ust/sbin/ip

pete  SERVERS=NETWORK
julia SERVERS=(DB)ALL
```

In this section, we have seen how to provide administrative access to users in SLES and even learned how to do it in a very granular manner. Let's move on now to working with file permissions.

# Checking, reviewing, and modifying file permissions

We have learned so far how to create users and groups and provide administrative privileges to a subset of them. It's time now to see how permissions work at the file and directory level.

As you'll remember, in *Chapter 2, Running Basic Commands and Simple Shell Scripts*, we saw how to see the permissions that are applied to a file. Let's review them now and dive deeper.

You can get information about permissions using the long option of `ls -l`. Remember to run this as `root` (or directly or by using `sudo`):

```
geeko:~ # sudo ls -l /usr/bin/bash
-rwxr-xr-x. 1 root root 1062960 Mar 10 10:38 /usr/bin/bash
geeko:~ # sudo ls -l /etc/passwd
-rw-r--r--. 1 root root 914 Apr 20 19:15 /etc/passwd
geeko:~ # sudo ls -ld /tmp
drwxrwxrwt. 9 root root 180 Apr 21 00:00 /tmp
```

Remember that in Linux, *everything is a file*, including directories and special files.

There is a lot of information, but we are focusing on the first column, which describes file permissions. Let's review the five different blocks that are in the output shown right above using /usr/bin/bash as the example:

```
-rwxr-xr-x.
```

The blocks are as follows:

| Block 1 | Block 2 | Block 3 | Block 4 | Block 5 |
|---|---|---|---|---|
| - | rwx | r-x | r-x | . |

*Table 4.1 – Different permission blocks assigned to a file*

Let's discuss them in more detail:

- Block 1 is a type of file:
    - Regular files with no special permissions are shown as `-`.
    - Directories are identifiable by `d`.
    - Symbolic links are identified by `l`. Hard links are still normal files, but with the number of copies increased.
    - Character devices are identified by `c`.
    - Block devices are identified by `b`.
- Block 2 is the permissions for the *user* owning the file and consists of three characters:
    - The first one, `r`, is the read permission assigned.
    - The second one, `w`, is the write permission assigned.
    - The third one, `x`, is the executable permission. (Note that the executable permission for directories means being able to enter them.)

  The file can be set up with special permissions for it as a different user or group, called `setuid` or `setgid`, identified by `s`.

  A special permission for directories so that the owner can only remove or rename their own files and not those from other users, called a **sticky bit**, will appear as `t`.
- Block 3 is permissions for the *group*. It consists of the same three characters for read, write, and execute (`rwx`). In this case, write is missing.

- Block 4 is the permissions for *others*. It also consists of the same three characters for read, write, and execute (`rwx`) as before. As in the previous block, write is missing. You can see that most of the special permissions are applied to this group, like the *sticky bit* in `/tmp`.
- Block 5 indicates that an **SELinux** context is being applied to the file. More on this topic in *Chapter 10, Keeping the System Hardened with SELinux*.

We can change the permission for a file with the `chmod` command.

Let's create a file:

```
user@geeko:~> touch file.txt
user@geeko:~> ls -l file.txt
-rw-r--r--. 1 user user 0 Apr 21 00:56 file.txt
```

As you can see, the file is created with your username as the owner, your main group as the group, and a default set of permissions. The default set of permissions is defined by `umask`. In SLES, the defaults for newly created file permissions are as follows:

- **User**: Read and write
- **Group**: Read
- **Others**: Read

The easiest way to change permissions using `chmod` is to specify the changes with three characters:

- The first one is who is affected by the changes:
  - `u`: User
  - `g`: Group
  - `o`: Others
  - `a`: All
- The second one is whether we want to add or remove permissions:
  - `+`: Add
  - `-`: Remove
- The third one is the permissions modified:
  - `r`: Read
  - `w`: Write
  - `x`: Execute

The third bit can also be a special bit, which is defined as follows:

- `s`: `setuid` when assigned to the user
- `s`: `setgid` when assigned to the group
- `t`: Sticky bit

If we want to add write permissions to the group, we can run the following:

```
user@geeko:~> chmod g+w file.txt
user@geeko:~> ls -l file.txt
-rw-rw-r--. 1 user user 0 Apr 21 00:56 file.txt
```

We can also remove read permissions from others with the following command:

```
user@geeko:~> chmod o-r file.txt
user@geeko:~> ls -l file.txt
-rw-rw----. 1 user user 0 Apr 21 00:56 file.txt
```

Using characters is simple, but it can be easier to define all the permissions for the different groups in a single command. The permissions are stored in four octal digits (from 0 to 7). This means that special permissions are stored in a digit, and the same happens for user, group, and others.

Let's look at some examples:

| **Alphabetic** | **Octal** | **Description** |
|---|---|---|
| `-rwxr-xr--` | 0754 | User: read, write, execute<br>Group: read, execute<br>Others: read |
| `-rw-r-----` | 0640 | User: read, write<br>Group: read<br>Others: nothing |
| `-r--------` | 0400 | User: read<br>Group: nothing<br>Others: nothing |

*Table 4.2 – Examples of file permissions*

How does it work? We assign a number (power of 2) for each permission:

- **Nothing**: 0
- **Execute**: $2^0 = 1$
- **Write**: $2^1 = 2$
- **Read**: $2^2 = 4$

When we add these values, we get the following:

```
rwx = 4 + 2 + 1 = 7 (in binary 111)
rw- = 4 + 2 = 6 (in binary 110)
r-x = 4 + 1 = 5 (in binary 101)
r-- = 4
--- = 0
```

The first digit is similar to user or group digits but uses 4 for *set user ID*, 2 for *set group ID*, and 1 for the *sticky bit*.

Let's try it with some different permissions:

```
user@geeko:~> ls -l file.txt
-rwxr-xr-x. 1 user user 0 Apr 21 00:56 file.txt
user@geeko:~> chmod 0640 file.txt
user@geeko:~> ls -l file.txt
-rw-r-----. 1 user user 0 Apr 21 00:56 file.txt
user@geeko:~> chmod 0600 file.txt
user@geeko:~> ls -l file.txt
-rw-------. 1 user user 0 Apr 21 00:56 file.txt
```

New files are created with a combination of the permission 0777 for directories and 0666 for files subtracting the `umask`. We can see the value as follows:

```
user@geeko:~> umask
0022
user@geeko:~> umask -S
u=rwx,g=rx,o=rx
```

Because they are combined, by default, files have the `execute` permissions removed (`1`), and all of them have the `write` permission removed for everybody except the user. With this `umask`, `0022`, we are also removing `write` permissions for `group` and `others` (`2`).

Changing the `umask` can make some scripts behave strangely and is not recommended, but let's see how it works by modifying it. Let's start by using the most permissive `umask`, `0000`, to see how all `read` and `write` permissions are assigned to newly created files:

```
user@geeko:~> umask 0000
user@geeko:~> touch file2.txt
user@geeko:~> mkdir dir2
user@geeko:~> ls -ld file2.txt dir2
drwxrwxrwx. 1 user user 0 Apr 21 01:39 dir2
-rw-rw-rw-. 1 user user 0 Apr 21 01:39 file2.txt
```

The default gives full permissions (files never get executed by default). Let's change it now to the more restrictive `umask` for group and `others`:

```
user@geeko:~> umask 0077
user@geeko:~> touch file3.txt ; mkdir dir3
user@geeko:~> ls -ld file3.txt dir3
drwx------. 1 user user 0 Apr 21 01:42 dir3
-rw-------. 1 user user 0 Apr 21 01:42 file3.txt
```

If we try a higher number, it won't work and will return an error:

```
user@geeko:~> umask 0088
-bash: umask: 0088: octal number out of range
```

Let's go back to the defaults so we can continue practicing:

```
user@geeko:~> umask 0022
```

So far, we have been working with our own files and directories. Sometimes we need to create a directory for a specific user or group, or to change the owner of a file. There are many times when a bad option will create files or directories with the wrong permissions, and you need to update them to make everything work again. `chown` or `chgrp` is used to change ownership of a file to a new user or group. Let's see how they work. Change into `/var/tmp` and create the folders for `finance` and `accounting`:

```
user@geeko:/var/tmp> cd /var/tmp/
user@geeko:/var/tmp> mkdir finance
user@geeko:/var/tmp> mkdir accounting
user@geeko:/var/tmp> ls -ld finance/ accounting/
drwxr-xr-x. 1 user user 0 Apr 21 16:58 accounting/
drwxr-xr-x. 1 user user 0 Apr 21 16:58 finance/
```

Now, let's create the groups for `finance` and `accounting`:

```
user@geeko:/var/tmp> sudo groupadd finance
user@geeko:/var/tmp> sudo groupadd accounting
groupadd: group 'accounting' already exists
```

We created the `accounting` group before, so the command complains, but it is not a problem because the error was expected. Let's change the group for each directory with `chgrp`. First, we need to add the user to the group and log in again to see the changes:

```
user@geeko:/var/tmp> sudo usermod -aG accounting user
user@geeko:/var/tmp> chgrp accounting accounting
chgrp: changing group of 'accounting/': Operation not permitted
user@geeko:/var/tmp> exit
logout
Geeko login:
Last login: Mon Apr 21 16:57:49 CEST 2025 from 192.168.66.1 on ssh [root@
geeko tmp]# chgrp finance finance/
user@geeko:/var/tmp> chgrp accounting accounting/
user@geeko:/var/tmp> sudo chgrp finance finance/
user@geeko:/var/tmp> ls -ld accounting/ finance/
drwxr-xr-x. 1 user accounting 0 Apr 21 16:58 accounting/
drwxr-sr-x. 1 user finance    0 Apr 21 16:58 finance/
```

We need to use `sudo` for finance because `user` is not part of `finance`. Only the `root` user (the default administrative user in Linux) can assign a group where it does not belong. We will create users for `sonia` and `matilde` and assign them to `finance` and `accounting`, respectively:

```
geeko:~ # useradd sonia -G finance
geeko:~ # useradd matilde -G accounting
geeko:~ # groups sonia
sonia : sonia finance
geeko:~ # groups matilde
matilde : matilde accounting
```

Now, we can create a personal folder for `sonia` and `matilde` in their group folder:

```
geeko:/var/tmp/ # cd finance/
geeko:/var/tmp/finance # mkdir personal_sonia
geeko:/var/tmp/finance # chown sonia personal_sonia/
geeko:/var/tmp/finance # ls -l
```

```
total 0
drwxr-xr-x. 1 sonia root 0 Apr 21 18:15 personal_sonia
geeko:/var/tmp/finance # chgrp sonia personal_sonia/
geeko:/var/tmp/finance # ls -l
total 0
drwxr-xr-x. 1 sonia sonia 0 Apr 21 18:15 personal_sonia
```

Instead of using two separate commands, we can specify a user and group in `chown` using the `:` separator. Let's use it with `matilde`:

```
geeko:/var/tmp/finance # cd ../accounting/
geeko:/var/tmp/accounting # mkdir personal_matilde
geeko:/var/tmp/accounting # chown matilde:matilde \
> personal_matilde/
geeko:/var/tmp/accounting # ls -l
total 0
drwxr-xr-x. 1 matilde matilde 0 Apr 21 18:17 personal_matilde
```

By default, only the specified file or directory is changed. If we want to change the permissions for the full directory, we can use `chown` with the `-R` option, for recursive reach in included directories. Let's copy a branch and change its permissions:

```
geeko:/var/tmp/accounting # cp -rv /usr/share/doc/packages/curl/ personal_
matilde/
'/usr/share/doc/packages/curl/' -> 'personal_matilde/curl'
'/usr/share/doc/packages/curl/BUGS.md' -> 'personal_matilde/curl/BUGS.md'
'/usr/share/doc/packages/curl/CHANGES.md' -> 'personal_matilde/curl/
CHANGES.md'
'/usr/share/doc/packages/curl/FAQ' -> 'personal_matilde/curl/FAQ'
'/usr/share/doc/packages/curl/FEATURES.md' -> 'personal_matilde/curl/
FEATURES.md'
'/usr/share/doc/packages/curl/README' -> 'personal_matilde/curl/README'
'/usr/share/doc/packages/curl/RELEASE-NOTES' -> 'personal_matilde/curl/
RELEASE-NOTES'
'/usr/share/doc/packages/curl/TODO' -> 'personal_matilde/curl/TODO'
'/usr/share/doc/packages/curl/TheArtOfHttpScripting.md' -> 'personal_
matilde/curl/TheArtOfHttpScripting.md'
geeko:/var/tmp/accounting # chown -R matilde:matilde \
> personal_matilde/curl/
geeko:/var/tmp/accounting # ls -l personal_matilde/curl/
```

```
total 184
-rw-r--r--. 1 matilde matilde 11942 Apr 21 18:19 BUGS.md
-rw-r--r--. 1 matilde matilde   438 Apr 21 18:19 CHANGES.md
-rw-r--r--. 1 matilde matilde 67951 Apr 21 18:19 FAQ
-rw-r--r--. 1 matilde matilde  6163 Apr 21 18:19 FEATURES.md
-rw-r--r--. 1 matilde matilde  1664 Apr 21 18:19 README
-rw-r--r--. 1 matilde matilde  7515 Apr 21 18:19 RELEASE-NOTES
-rw-r--r--. 1 matilde matilde 50192 Apr 21 18:19 TODO
-rw-r--r--. 1 matilde matilde 28627 Apr 21 18:19 TheArtOfHttpScripting.md
```

With this, we have a good understanding of permissions in SLES, their default behaviors, and how to work with them. Let's move on to some more advanced topics about permissions.

# Using special permissions

For more advanced use cases, there are special permissions that can be applied to files and directories, providing support for advanced use cases. Let's start by reviewing **set-UID** (or **suid**) and **set-GUID** (or **sgid**).

## Understanding and applying set-UID

Let's review how set-UID applies to files and directories:

- **Set-UID permission applied to a file**: When set-UID is applied to an executable file, this file will run as if the owner of the file were running it instead of the user that is executing it
- **Set-UID permission applied to a directory**: No effect

Let's check a file with set-UID:

```
geeko:~ # ls -l /etc/shadow
-rw-r-----. 1 root shadow 907 Apr 21 17:13 /etc/shadow
geeko:~ # ls -l /usr/bin/passwd
-rwsr-xr-x. 1 root shadow 142224 Jan 20 11:20 /usr/bin/passwd
```

Hashed passwords are stored in the `/etc/shadow` file. The `passwd` command requires `root` access to be able to modify the file. When you execute `passwd`, the effective user is `root`, so it can open and edit the file.

To get this behavior, you can use the chmod command and apply u+s permissions:

```
geeko:~ # touch testsuid
geeko:~ # ls -l testsuid
-rw-r--r--. 1 root root 0 Apr 21 20:25 testsuid
geeko:~ # chmod u+s testsuid
geeko:~ # ls -l testsuid
-rwSr--r--. 1 root root 0 Apr 21 20:25 testsuid
```

Be very careful when assigning suid to files as root. If you provide write access to the file, it will be possible for any user to change its content and execute anything as root.

## Understanding and applying set-GID

Let's review how set-GID applies to files and directories:

- **Set-GID permission applied to a file**: When applied to an executable file, this file will run with the group permissions of the file
- **Set-GID permission applied to a directory**: New files created in that directory will have the group of the directory applied to them

Let's check a file with set-GID:

```
user@geeko:/root> ls -l /usr/bin/chage
-rwxr-sr-x. 1 root shadow 142008 Jan 20 11:20 /
usr/bin/chage
```

Even if you set up set-UID or set-GID in an executable script, they won't work. For security reasons, Linux will only use them for binaries.

Let's see what happens with directories, using our previous example:

```
user@geeko:/var/tmp> ls -ld accounting/ finance/
drwxrwx---. 1 user accounting 32 Apr 21 18:17 accounting/
drwxrwx---. 1 user finance    28 Apr 21 18:15 finance/
user@geeko:/var/tmp> chmod g+s accounting finance
user@geeko:/var/tmp> ls -l finance/
total 0
drwxr-xr-x. 1 sonia sonia 0 Apr 21 18:15 personal_sonia
user@geeko:/var/tmp> ls -ld finance/
drwxrwx---. 1 user finance 28 Apr 21 18:15 finance/
user@geeko:/var/tmp> chmod g+s accounting finance/
user@geeko:/var/tmp> ls -ld accounting/
drwxrws---. 1 user accounting 32 Apr 21 18:17 accounting/
user@geeko:/var/tmp> cd accounting/
user@geeko:/var/tmp/accounting> ls
personal_matilde
user@geeko:/var/tmp/accounting> touch testaccounting
user@geeko:/var/tmp/accounting> ls -la
total 0
drwxrws---. 1 user    accounting   60 Apr 22 04:04 .
drwxrwxrwt. 1 root    root       2228 Apr 22 04:03 ..
drwxr-xr-x. 1 matilde matilde       8 Apr 21 18:19 personal_matilde
-rw-r--r--. 1 user    accounting    0 Apr 22 04:04 testaccounting
```

You can see that set-GID is applied to the folders because they display the `s` permission for the group (highlighted). Creating new files in those directories will assign the group of the folder instead of the group of the user that creates it (also highlighted). When properly used, this will allow any user of the `accounting` group to be able to access the files inside using the group permissions without needing to manually change the group every time.

## Using the sticky bit

The last of the special permissions to be used is the **sticky bit**. It only works on directories, and what it does is simple: when a user creates a file in a directory with the sticky bit, only that user can edit or delete that file.

Let's see an example:

```
user@geeko:/var/tmp/accounting> ls -ld /tmp
drwxrwxrwt. 9 root root 180 Apr 22 02:57 /tmp
```

We could apply this principle of sticky bit to the previous example, also with `chmod` using `o+t`:

```
[root@geeko ~]# cd /var/tmp/
[root@geeko tmp]# ls -l
total 0
drwxr-sr-x. 3 root accounting 52 ene 28 05:27 accounting
drwxr-sr-x. 3 root finance    47 ene 28 05:27 finance
[root@geeko tmp]# chmod o+t accounting finance
[root@geeko tmp]# ls -l
total 0
drwxr-sr-t. 3 root accounting 52 ene 28 05:27 accounting
drwxr-sr-t. 3 root finance    47 ene 28 05:27 finance
```

Let's give it a try. We will create a file in the `/tmp` folder with the `user` user and give write permissions to all users. Then, we will try to delete it with the `sonia` user. Let's go:

```
user@geeko:~> cd /tmp
user@geeko:/tmp> touch teststicky
user@geeko:/tmp> chmod 666 teststicky
user@geeko:/tmp> su - sonia
Password:
sonia@geeko:> cd /tmp
sonia@geeko:/tmp> rm teststicky
rm: cannot remove 'teststicky': Operation not permitted
```

The numeric values for special permissions are `suid` = 4, `sgid` = 2, and `sticky bit` = 1.

# Summary

In this chapter, we have reviewed the traditional permission management system in SLES. We have learned how to create user accounts and groups and how to manage the life cycle of passwords. We have also learned how passwords are stored in the system and how to use them to block shell access to a user. We have created files and folders and used permissions to restrict access so that only allowed users can collaborate.

In a multi-user system, security is key. You should be very comfortable with access rights to avoid problems with other users and reduce the impact of a security breach. Misconfiguring access rights can lead to big security problems, which is why access rights need to be reviewed carefully. As this is such an important topic, we recommend reviewing this chapter and reading the man pages for the commands shown, until you don't have any doubts. It will prevent many uncomfortable situations in the future.

Now, you are ready to start providing services to users and managing their access, which is what we will cover in the next chapter.

# 5

# Enabling Network Connectivity

In the first chapter, as part of the installation, we enabled the network interface with basic configuration. However, network configuration is, or can be, more complex than that.

A server connected to a network might require additional interfaces for configuring additional networks, for example, reaching backup servers, performing internal services from other servers, or even accessing networked storage.

Additionally, a server might use redundant network capabilities to ensure that in the event of a failure in one of the cards, switches, and so on, the server can still be reached and that it can function properly.

In this chapter, we will learn how to define network configuration for our **SUSE Linux Enterprise Server (SLES)** machine using different methods and perform some basic network troubleshooting. This knowledge will be key since servers are commonly used to provide services to other systems, and we need networking for that purpose.

In this chapter, we will cover the following topics:

- Exploring network configuration in SLES
- Getting to know the configuration files and NetworkManager
- Configuring network interfaces with IPv4 and IPv6
- Configuring the hostname and hostname resolutions (DNS)
- Overview of firewall configuration
- Testing network connectivity

Let's get hands-on with networking!

## Technical requirements

You can continue using the virtual machine we created at the beginning of this book in *Chapter 1, Getting SLES 16 Up and Running (Physical and Cloud)*. Additionally, to test network communication, it might be useful to create a second virtual machine. You can reuse the one created in the previous chapters for testing the **Network Time Protocol** (**NTP**) configuration if you instantiated it. Any additional packages that are required will be indicated in the text. Any additional files that are required for this chapter can be downloaded from `https://github.com/PacktPublishing/SUSE-Linux-Enterprise-Server-16-Official-Administration-Guide`.

## Exploring network configuration in SLES

A network is made up of different devices that are interconnected so that information and resources can be shared among them, for example, internet access, printers, or files.

Networks have been present since the beginning of computing. Initially, the most common networks were non-IP-based ones, which were generally used for sharing data across computers in the **Local Area Network** (**LAN**). But with the expansion of internet services and the requirement for applications or remote services, IP networks were expanded, and the concept of an intranet was introduced, where the **Transmission Control Protocol/Internet Protocol** (**TCP/IP**) was used as transport, and the applications started to be more like internet services (or even based on them).

The migration to IP-based networks has also adapted other protocols such as **Network Basic Input/Output System** (**NetBIOS**) so that these higher-level protocols can run on top of the IP protocol (in this case, NetBIOS was working on top of **NetBIOS Extended User Interface** (**NetBEUI**), and even if other networks such as **InfiniBand** or **Remote Direct Memory Access** (**RDMA**) are still in use, they are not as common as TCP/IP).

TCP/IP, of course, is built on top of other protocols. You can check the **Open Systems Interconnection** (**OSI**) layer definition at `https://documentation.suse.com/sles/15-SP6/html/SLES-all/cha-network.html`. However, there are more concepts involved that aren't discussed there. We will cover these when we become more familiar with TCP/IP and networks once we finish this chapter.

Before we get into the actual details, we need to clarify a few common keywords pertaining to TCP/IP and networking that we'll be using from now on:

- **IP address**: This is the address that's used for interacting with other devices on the network. It is like your phone number but for machines in a network.

- **Netmask:** This is used to determine which devices are in the neighborhood or not. It can be expressed via a mask, for example, `255.255.255.0`, or via a network size, such as `/24`.
- **Gateway:** This is the IP address of the device that will get all our traffic when the target device is outside our network, as defined by our netmask. It is used when we cannot directly reach our target IP (i.e., of a web server or file server).
- **DNS:** This is the IP address of a server or servers that translate **domain names** into IP addresses so that the hosts can connect to them.
- **MAC address:** This is the physical interface address. It is unique for each card and helps identify the card by the network hardware so that the proper traffic is sent to it.
- **Network Interface Card (NIC):** This card allows our device to connect to the network. It might be wireless, wired, and so on.
- **Extended Service Set Identification (ESSID):** This is how a wireless network is named.
- **Virtual Private Network (VPN):** This is a virtual network that is created between the client and the server. Once established, it allows you to have a direct connection to the services as if they were local, even if the client and the server are in different places. For example, a VPN is used to allow remote workers to connect to their corporate network using their regular internet connection.
- **Virtual Local Area Network (VLAN):** This allows us to define virtual networks on top of the actual wiring. We can then use a specific header field to have them correctly understood and processed by the network equipment.
- **IPv6:** This is the replacement protocol for **IPv4**, which is still the predominant protocol in networks today.

In the following sections, we will use some of these terms when we explain how a network is set up and defined in SLES systems.

In general, when systems are connected, some relationships between the devices on the network are established. Sometimes, some hosts are providers of services, often called **servers**, and the consumers are known as **clients**.

In the next section, we'll become familiar with the configuration files and the different approaches for configuring networking in our system.

## Getting to know the configuration files and NetworkManager

Now that we have learned about some of the keywords and concepts in networking, it's time to look at how they can be used in our system.

Traditionally, network interfaces were configured via **Wicked**, a network management system used in previous versions of SLES. In SLES 15, NetworkManager was introduced as an optional network management system, and since version 16, it has become the default and only choice.

**NetworkManager** is a utility that was created in 2004 to make network configuration and its usage easier for desktop users. At that point, all configuration was done via text files, and it was more or less static. Once a system was connected to a network, the information barely changed at all. With the adoption of wireless networks, more flexibility was required to automate and ease the connection to different networks via different profiles, VPNs, and more.

NetworkManager was created to cover the mentioned gaps and aimed to be a component that would be used in many distributions, but from a new standpoint. For example, it queries the **Hardware Abstraction Layer** (**HAL**) at startup to let you know about available network devices and their changes.

Imagine a laptop system; it can be connected to a wired cable, disconnected when you're moving it to another location or cubicle, connected to a wireless network, and so on. All those events are relayed to NetworkManager, which takes care of reconfiguring network interfaces and routes and authenticating to the wireless network, making the user's life a lot easier.

> The hardware that is connected to the system can be queried with several commands, depending on how the hardware is connected, for example, via utilities such as `lsusb`, `lspci`, or `lshw` (provided by installing the `usbutils`, `pciutils`, and `lshw` packages, respectively).

In the following screenshot, we can see the available packages related to NetworkManager, as obtained via the `zypper search networkmanager` command:

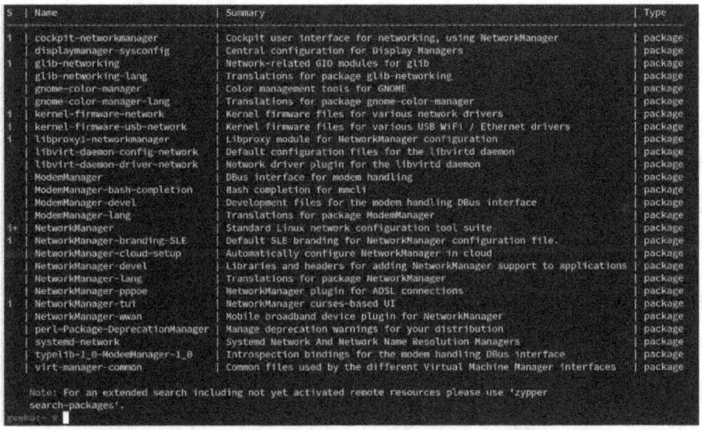

```
S  | Name                            | Summary                                                          | Type
---+---------------------------------+------------------------------------------------------------------+--------
i  | cockpit-networkmanager          | Cockpit user interface for networking, using NetworkManager     | package
   | displaymanager-sysconfig        | Central configuration for Display Managers                      | package
i  | glib-networking                 | Network-related GIO modules for glib                            | package
   | glib-networking-lang            | Translations for package glib-networking                        | package
   | gnome-color-manager             | Color management tools for GNOME                                | package
   | gnome-color-manager-lang        | Translations for package gnome-color-manager                    | package
i  | kernel-firmware-network         | Kernel firmware files for various network drivers               | package
i  | kernel-firmware-usb-network     | Kernel firmware files for various USB WiFi / Ethernet drivers   | package
i  | libproxy1-networkmanager        | Libproxy module for NetworkManager configuration                | package
   | libvirt-daemon-config-network   | Default configuration files for the libvirtd daemon             | package
   | libvirt-daemon-driver-network   | Network driver plugin for the libvirtd daemon                   | package
   | ModemManager                    | DBus interface for modem handling                               | package
   | ModemManager-bash-completion    | Bash completion for mmcli                                       | package
   | ModemManager-devel              | Development files for the modem handling DBus interface         | package
   | ModemManager-lang               | Translations for package ModemManager                           | package
i+ | NetworkManager                  | Standard Linux network configuration tool suite                 | package
i  | NetworkManager-branding-SLE     | Default SLE branding for NetworkManager configuration file.     | package
   | NetworkManager-cloud-setup      | Automatically configure NetworkManager in cloud                 | package
   | NetworkManager-devel            | Libraries and headers for adding NetworkManager support to applications | package
   | NetworkManager-lang             | Translations for package NetworkManager                         | package
   | NetworkManager-pppoe            | NetworkManager plugin for ADSL connections                      | package
i  | NetworkManager-tui              | NetworkManager curses-based UI                                  | package
   | NetworkManager-wwan             | Mobile broadband device plugin for NetworkManager               | package
   | perl-Package-DeprecationManager | Manage deprecation warnings for your distribution               | package
   | systemd-network                 | Systemd Network And Network Name Resolution Managers            | package
   | typelib-1_0-ModemManager-1_0    | Introspection bindings for the modem handling DBus interface    | package
   | virt-manager-common             | Common files used by the different Virtual Machine Manager interfaces | package

Note: For an extended search including not yet activated remote resources please use 'zypper
search-packages'.
```

*Figure 5.1 – NetworkManager-related packages available for installation in an SLES 16 system*

The `NetworkManager` default configuration can be found in `/usr/lib/NetworkManager/`, and it can be modified by adding files to the `/etc/NetworkManager` folder, especially `NetworkManager.conf` and the files available in that folder:

- `conf.d`
- `dispatcher.d`
- `VPN`
- `system-connections`

> Can't remember what a dispatcher is? Use `man networkmanager` to get details on this!

> In SLES 16, the configuration files follow the UAPI Group Specification, as stated in `https://uapi-group.org/specifications/specs/configuration_files_specification`. The main concept behind this is that default configuration files for system packages live in `/usr/lib` or `/usr/etc`, and are never changed, and that changes happen by dropping modification files in th `/etc` path, or in directories ending with `.d`, as in the case of `conf.d` or `dispatcher.d`.

The man page of `NetworkManager` explains that those scripts are executed in alphabetical order based on network events and will receive two arguments: the name of the device for the event and the action.

Based on the different events that can happen regarding network connectivity (i.e., enabling an interface or changing the hostname), there are several actions that can be performed to react to them. These events can be as follows:

- `pre-up`: The interface gets connected to a network but is not activated yet. The script must be executed before the connection can be notified as activated.
- `up`: The interface has been activated.
- `pre-down`: The interface is being deactivated but hasn't been disconnected from the network yet. In the case of forced disconnections (lost wireless connection or lost carrier), this will not be executed.
- `down`: The interface has been deactivated.
- `vpn-up`/`vpn-down`/`vpn-pre-up`/`vpn-pre-down`: Similar to the preceding interfaces but for VPN connections.
- `hostname`: Hostname has been changed.
- `dhcp4-change`/`dhcp6-change`: The DHCP lease has changed (renewed, rebounded, and so on).
- `connectivity-change`: Connectivity transitions such as no connection, the system went online, and so on.

Now that we have learned a bit about `NetworkManager` and how it works and was designed, let's learn how to configure network interfaces.

# Configuring network interfaces with IPv4 and IPv6

There are several approaches to configuring network interfaces and several network configurations. These will help us determine what we need to do and the required parameters and settings.

Let's look at some examples:

- A server might have two or more NICs for redundancy, but only one of them is active at a time
- A server might use a trunk network and require that we define VLANs for it to access or provide different services in the networks
- Two or more NICs might be combined to provide increased output and redundancy via teaming

Configuration can be performed in several ways too:

- `nmtui`: Text-based interface for configuring a network.
- `nmcli`: The command-line interface for NetworkManager.
- `cockpit`: The server management web interface, which will be covered in *Chapter 8, Enabling and Using Cockpit.*
- `nm-connection-editor`: The graphical tool available for graphical environments. As this book is intended for servers, we will not cover graphical utilities other than web-based ones such as `cockpit`.
- Editing text configuration files.

> Before editing your network configuration, ensure that you can reach the system being configured in another way. In the case of a server, this can be done via a remote management card or physical console access. A mistake in the configuration might leave the system unreachable.

Before we move on, let's learn a bit about IPv4 and IPv6.

## IPv4 and IPv6... What does that mean?

**IP** stands for **Internet Protocol**, and it helps systems connect to a network, which is often connected to the internet. IP addresses are a set of numbers used to identify a device in a network. There are two versions used: **IPv4**, the simple and old one, and **IPv6**, a more evolved one that is growing in use.

IPv4 was created in 1983 and uses a 32-bit address space, which provides $2^{32}$ unique addresses (4,294,967,296 ... yes, more than 4 billion), but from those possible ones, large blocks are reserved for special usage. It is composed of four numbers between 0 and 255 separated by dots (i.e., `192.168.1.16`).

IPv6, ratified as an Internet Standard in 2017, is the latest version at the time of writing and uses a 128-bit address space instead, that is, $2^{128}$ ($3.4 \times 10^{38}$ addresses). It is normally represented with eight blocks of four-digit hexadecimal numbers (i.e., `2032:D450:33FA:3434:0000:0000:0000:0000`; however, the zeros can be abbreviated using two colons, like this `2032:D450:33FA:3434::`).

Long story short, the number of IPv4 addresses seemed huge at the time, but today, where phones, tablets, computers, laptops, servers, lightbulbs, smart plugs, and all other **smart devices** require an IP address, that number has been depleted for public IP addresses, meaning that it's not possible to assign more. This has caused many routers at home to use **Network Address Translation** (**NAT**), in which they use a public IP and provide private IPs for devices connected to them. Some **Internet Service Providers** (**ISPs**) use techniques such as **Carrier-Grade Network Address Translation** (**CGNAT**), similar to what home routers do for private networks, which causes all the traffic from several devices to appear as coming from only one IP, and having the device interacting on both networks, to do the proper routing from outgoing and incoming packages to the original requestors.

Why no IPv6, then? The main problem is that IPv4 and IPv6 are not interoperable, and even if IPv6 was a draft in 1998, not all network equipment is compatible with it and might not have yet been tested. Check out `https://www.ripe.net/support/training/videos/ipv6/transition-mechanisms` for more details.

In the next section, we will learn how to configure network interfaces using a text-based user interface to NetworkManager named `nmtui`.

## Configuring interfaces with nmtui

`nmtui` provides a text-based interface for configuration. This is the initial screen you'll see when it is executed by running `nmtui` on a terminal:

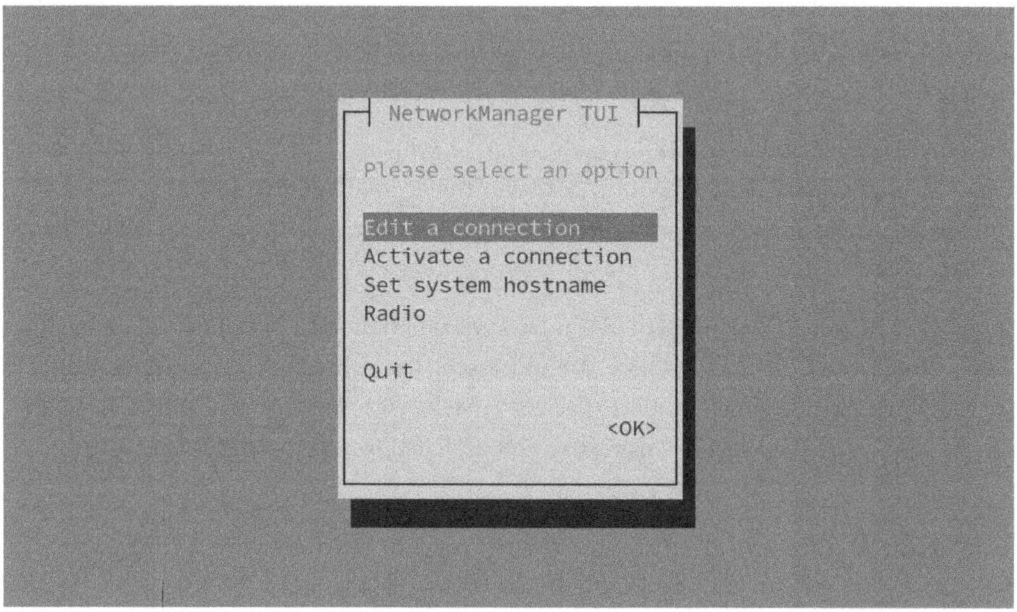


*Figure 5.2 – nmtui welcome screen showing a menu of possible actions that can be performed*

Let's explore the available options for our interface. In this case, let's select **Edit a connection**. On the screen that appears, move down and edit the **Wired connection 1** option by selecting it with the arrow keys and pressing *Enter*. That will take us to the following screen:

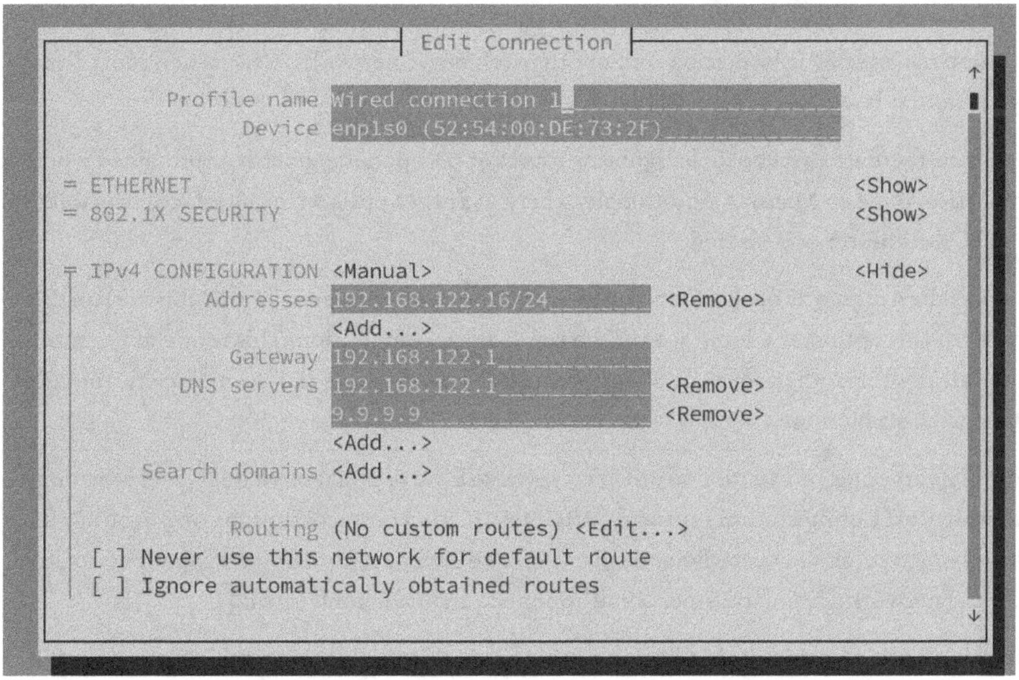


*Figure 5.3 – Edit Connection page with the IPv4 options expanded*

It will be hard to show screenshots for each step, as one of the advantages of the text interface is that a lot of options are condensed onto a simple screen. However, the preceding screenshot makes it easy to see the basic information:

- **Profile name**: Name assigned to the configuration shown on screen.
- **Device**: Network device associated with this configuration. In this case, it's a physical device.

We can also understand each of the required parameters:

- **Addresses**: IP address associated with this configuration, including netmask. We can have more than one.
- **Gateway**: IP address of the device that connects us to other networks. In simple configurations, it is associated with the **router**.

- **DNS servers:** IP addresses associated with the systems providing name resolution services for the network.
- **Search domains:** Domains to be used when reaching a system by its name, and no domain is specified.
- **Routing:** Specific information on how to reach other networks. Used when more than one router is available in our network.

As you can see, there are checkboxes for ignoring routes or DNS parameters that are obtained when the connection is set to **Manual**. Additionally, there are other options for interfaces: **Disabled**, **Link-Local**, **Automatic**, and **Shared**.

Let's discuss the **Automatic** option first, as it's very common to have it configured this way on the first try. With this option, the interface will be set to autoconfiguration. This is one of the most common settings for configuration. It does not mean that everything is done magically, though. Let's dig into this a bit more.

In a network (corporate, private, and so on), it is typical to have a special service or server providing the **Dynamic Host Configuration Protocol** (**DHCP**). DHCP is a protocol running on top of TCP/IP that allows you to configure hosts dynamically, using the configuration that was made previously either by the network administrator or some appliance and its default settings.

DHCP provides several network configuration options automatically to systems connected to the network, such as IP, netmask, gateway, DNS, search domain, and time server. The configuration that's received is given a **lease time**, which means that it is valid for a period of time. After that, the system attempts to renew it, or if the system is powered off or disconnected, the lease is released.

Usually, the DHCP configuration is considered to be tied to dynamic IPs, but keep in mind that a DHCP server can use two different approaches: a pool of IPs that can be reused by different systems connecting, and fixed mappings of MAC addresses to static IPs.

Let's, for example, think about a **Small Office–Home Office** (**SOHO**) network with a private IP range in the `192.168.1.0/24` subnet.

We can define our ISP router to be at IP `192.168.1.1` because of the subnet (`/24`), which means that the last part of the IPv4 address can range from 0 to 255.

Using that IP range, we can set up hosts to get dynamic configuration and a dynamic IP from a pool in the last 100 IPs and leave the ones at the beginning for fixed equipment (even if they get the configuration dynamically), such as printers and storage devices.

As we mentioned previously, we can create reservations for servers, but in general, for devices that are always going to have the same address, it is also common practice to configure static addressing. In this way, if the DHCP server becomes unavailable, the servers will still be reachable from other services with either a valid lease or other servers/devices with static addresses configured.

> Just a reminder, IP addresses are represented in IPv4 with a dot notation separating four groups of numbers, such as `192.168.2.12`, while in IPv6, numbers are separated with a colon, for example, `2001:db8:0:1::c000:207`.
>
> The **Classless Inter-Domain Routing** (**CIDR**) notation adds the netmask value at the end of the IP, separating it with the / character. The previous examples could be extended to CIDR notation like this for IPv4: `192.168.2.12/24` and like this for IPv6: `2001:db8:0:1::c000:207/26`.

Now, let's move on to a review of `nmcli` usage in the next section.

## Configuring interfaces with nmcli

`nmcli` is the command-line interface for NetworkManager. It comes installed in the default SLES 16 installation. It allows us to not only check but also configure the network interfaces in our system, and even if using it might require more memory skills than what `nmtui` requires, it empowers users and administrators with scripting capabilities to automate the network setup of our system.

> Most commands allow us to use autocompletion, that is, pressing the *Tab* key will use the autocompletion lists on the command line to suggest the syntax. For example, typing `nmcli dev` on the command line and pressing *Tab* will autocomplete the command to `nmcli device`. Autocomplete can be great to avoid mispelling commands and type faster, although in this case it might not be as critical because `nmcli` understands both versions of the command.

Let's start checking the available connections in our system with `nmcli dev`, and then use `nmcli con show` to check out its details:

```
geeko:~ # nmcli dev
DEVICE   TYPE      STATE      CONNECTION
enp1s0   ethernet  connected  Wired connection 1
lo       loopback  connected  lo
geeko:~ # nmcli con show
NAME                UUID                                  TYPE      DEVICE
Wired connection 1  68e1cf09-b890-39cc-b523-92afeaa6c911  ethernet  enp1s0
lo                  ab4e6500-db51-434e-8fcb-85093902e810  loopback  lo
geeko:~ #
```

*Figure 5.4 – nmcli dev and nmcli con show*

When controlling a network connection, for example, when using `nmcli con up enp1s0` or disabling it with `nmcli con down enp1s0`, we should bear in mind what we explained about NetworkManager: if the connection is available in the system, NetworkManager might reactivate it just after being disconnected because the connection and the devices required are available in our system.

Now, let's create a new interface to illustrate the process of adding a new connection via IPv4:

```
# nmcli con add con-name test0 type ethernet \
 ifname test0 ipv4.address 192.168.1.2/24 \
ipv4.gateway 192.168.1.254
```

We can do the same with IPv6:

```
# nmcli con add con-name test1 type ethernet \
 ifname test1 ipv6.address 2001:db8:0:1::c000:207/64 \
 ipv6.gateway 2001:db8:0:1::1
```

Once the preceding commands have been executed, we can check the network connections that have been defined with `nmcli connection show test0` and validate that the proper settings were applied (or, of course, we can also verify the configuration via `nmtui`, `cockpit`, or the text files that were created on disk as the information is shared among all these tools and stored in the system).

When we reviewed the output of `nmcli connection show test0`, the output contained some keys separated by colons, such as the following:

- `ipv4.address`
- `ipv4.gateway`
- `ipv6.address`
- `ipv6.gateway`
- `Connection.id`

We can use these keys to define new values via `nmcli con mod $key $value`, as shown in the following example:

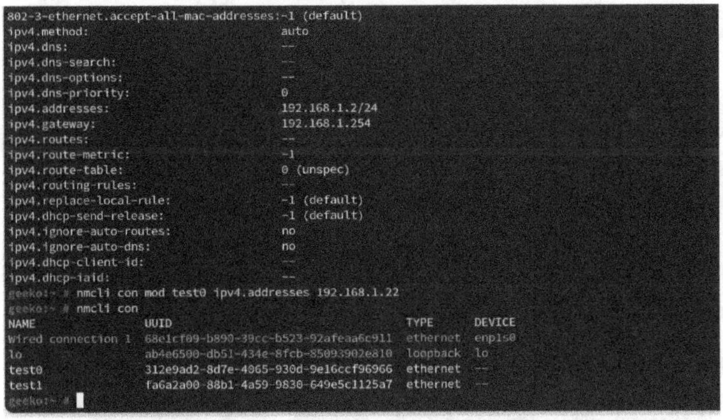


*Figure 5.5 – Example of modifying a network connection to change the IP address*

Of course, after doing the preceding tests, we can also remove the connection to avoid problems in our system with `nmcli con del test0`.

The following commands can be used to modify connections with the `nmcli` tool:

- `nmcli con show`: Shows the status of the connections.
- `nmcli con show NAME`: Shows the details of the connection named `NAME`.
- `nmcli dev status`: Shows the statuses of the devices in the system. Note that this means *devices*, not connections that might be using those devices.
- `nmcli con add con NAME`: Adds a new connection.
- `nmci con mod NAME`: Modifies a connection.
- `nmcli con up NAME`: Brings up a connection.
- `nmcli con down NAME`: Brings down a connection (which can still be re-enabled by NetworkManager).
- `nmcli con del NAME`: Removes a connection definition from the system.

> Check `man nmcli-examples` for more examples that are included for the documentation in the system.

## Configuring interfaces with text files

In prior subsections, we explored how to configure the network using different approaches. But, in the end, all those configurations end up being written to disk as interface definition files.

Instead of starting with creating an interface definition from scratch, let's examine what `nmcli` did when we created the interface with the following command:

```
nmcli con add con-name eth0 type ethernet ifname eth0 ipv6.address
2001:db8:0:1::c000:207/64 ipv6.gateway 2001:db8:0:1::1 ipv4.address
192.0.1.3/24 ipv4.gateway 192.0.1.1
```

The preceding command will generate the `/etc/NetworkManager/system-connections/eth0.nmconnection` file, which we can see in the following screenshot:

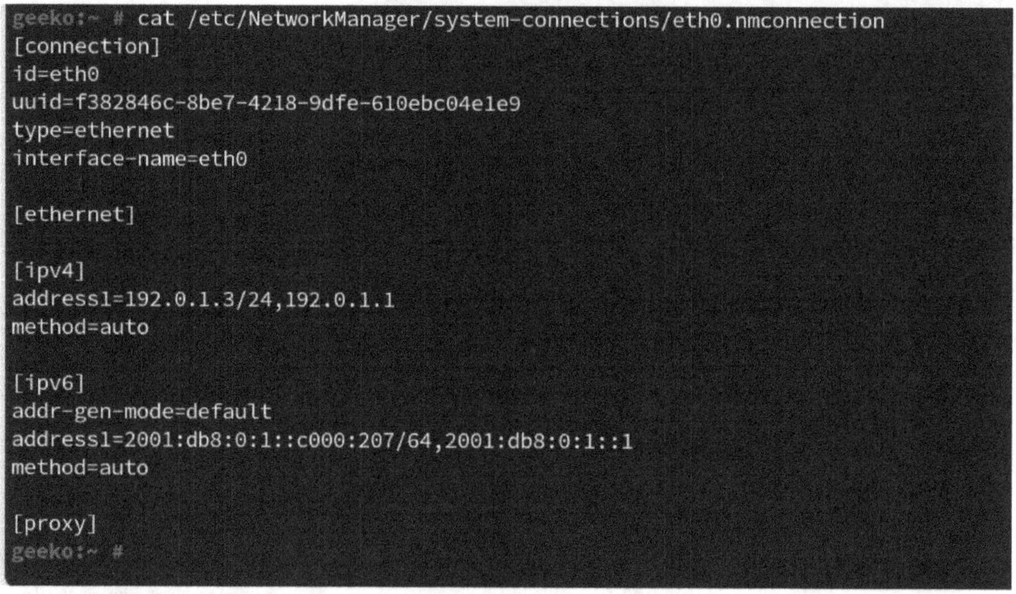

```
geeko:~ # cat /etc/NetworkManager/system-connections/eth0.nmconnection
[connection]
id=eth0
uuid=f382846c-8be7-4218-9dfe-610ebc04e1e9
type=ethernet
interface-name=eth0

[ethernet]

[ipv4]
address1=192.0.1.3/24,192.0.1.1
method=auto

[ipv6]
addr-gen-mode=default
address1=2001:db8:0:1::c000:207/64,2001:db8:0:1::1
method=auto

[proxy]
geeko:~ #
```

*Figure 5.6 – Contents of the /etc/NetworkManager/system-connections/eth0.nmconnection connection definition*

As we can see, by default, we have specified a `[connection]` section with `id` as the name specified, which is `eth0`. Then we have a unique identifier, or `uuid`, which in this case is `f382846c-8be7-4218-9dfe-610ebc04e1e9`. We also have, in this section, a connection type of `ethernet`, and the `interface-name` value, which specifies the physical interface assigned to this connection, is `eth0`. Finally, we have the `[ipv4]` and `[ipv6]` sections to specify IP addressing.

We can edit those files directly, but to make NetworkManager aware of the changes that will be introduced, we need to execute `nmcli con reload`. This will update the configuration with the changes. For example, if you modify the configuration editing the files manually or in an automated script, they won't be used until you run the `reload` command.

Note how, in the following screenshot, the changes don't appear in `nmcli` until we issue the `reload` command:

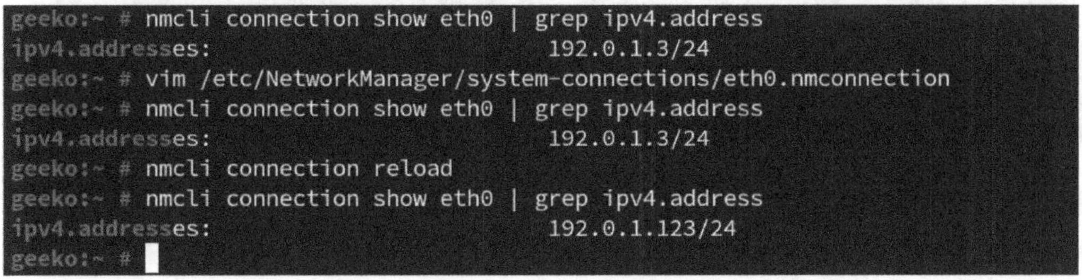


*Figure 5.7 – The process of editing an interface definition doesn't show up on nmcli until we reload the connections*

> The physical network interface definition (assigning a name to a physical device) can become a nightmare as the interface name itself is subject to several rules, such as the location of the interface in the bus and whether it was previously seen. Generally, once the network cards have been detected in the system, a custom rule is written that matches the MAC address of the interface to a custom naming convention. This happens so that it does not change across reboots or if a new software update changes the way we must enumerate the cards. You can read more about this topic by looking at the official documentation at `https://documentation.suse.com/smart/network/html/network-interface-predictable-naming/index.html`.

Now that we have reviewed the different ways to configure networking in our system, let's learn about naming resolutions.

# Configuring the hostname and hostname resolutions (DNS)

Remembering IP addresses, whether they are IPv4 or IPv6 addresses, can become a nightmare. To make things easier, a more human-friendly approach has been used for **hostnames** and the **Domain Name Service** (**DNS**), in that we can translate those easier-to-remember names into the IP addresses that systems use for connecting.

Hostnames are the names we assign to a server (also known as a host) to make it identify itself. But when they're used in a network, we use the DNS server, so their hostname can be *resolved* into IP addresses. This is useful so that other systems, or hosts, can connect to our host.

We can use the `hostname` command to see or temporarily modify the current hostname, as shown in the following screenshot:

```
geeko:~ # hostname
geeko.suse.test
geeko:~ # hostname geeko-changed.suse.test
geeko:~ # hostname
geeko-changed.suse.test
geeko:~ #
```

*Figure 5.8 – Querying and changing the hostname for our host*

Bear in mind that this change is only temporary; as long as we restart the server, it will use the configured one.

To define a new configured hostname, we will use the `hostnamectl` command, as shown in the following screenshot:

```
geeko:~ # hostnamectl
   Static hostname: geeko.suse.test
Transient hostname: geeko-changed.suse.test
         Icon name: computer-vm
           Chassis: vm
        Machine ID: 884c408782f04ec6a0fac03af59056fa
           Boot ID: 3e79563bcdbf46be95a95135b4339f94
      Product UUID: 884c4087-82f0-4ec6-a0fa-c03af59056fa
    Virtualization: kvm
  Operating System: SUSE Linux Enterprise Server 16.0 (Beta2)
       CPE OS Name: cpe:/o:suse:sles:16.0
            Kernel: Linux 6.12.0-160000.5-default
      Architecture: x86-64
   Hardware Vendor: QEMU
    Hardware Model: Standard PC _Q35 + ICH9, 2009_
  Firmware Version: rel-1.16.3-2-gc13ff2cd-prebuilt.qemu.org
     Firmware Date: Tue 2014-04-01
      Firmware Age: 11y 4d
geeko:~ # hostnamectl set-hostname geeko-test.suse.test
geeko:~ # cat /etc/hostname
geeko-test.suse.test
geeko:~ #
```

*Figure 5.9 – Checking the previously configured hostname and the definition of a new one via hostnamectl*

Note in the preceding example how we have **Transient hostname** versus **Static hostname**, which refers to the temporary status of the name that was defined with `hostname` instead of `hostnamectl`.

When it comes to name resolution, there are several approaches we can take. One, of course, is to use DNS servers, which we will explain later in this section, but there are other ways.

In general, systems have several resolvers, and those are defined in the `/usr/etc/nsswitch.conf` configuration file. Those resolvers are not only for network naming but also for other network services – for example, for authorizing users, where a corporate **LDAP** server might be used as the central storage for users, passwords, and so on. By default, `nsswitch.conf` instructs our system to use the following for hosts resolving this entry:

```
hosts:      files dns
```

This means that we are using the files in our `/etc/` directory as our first source. In the case of hostnames, this refers to the `/etc/hosts` file. If an entry is defined in that file, the value that was specified will be used; if not, the `/etc/resolv.conf` file will determine how to proceed with its resolution. Those files, and especially `resolv.conf`, are configured when the system is deployed and when a connection is activated. NetworkManager takes care of updating the values that were obtained via DHCP if autoconfiguration was used, or the specified DNS servers if manual configuration was performed.

In the following screenshot, we can see the entries that have been defined in our `/etc/hosts` file, how pinging a host fails because the name does not exist, and how, after manually adding an entry to the `/etc/hosts` file, our system is able to reach it:

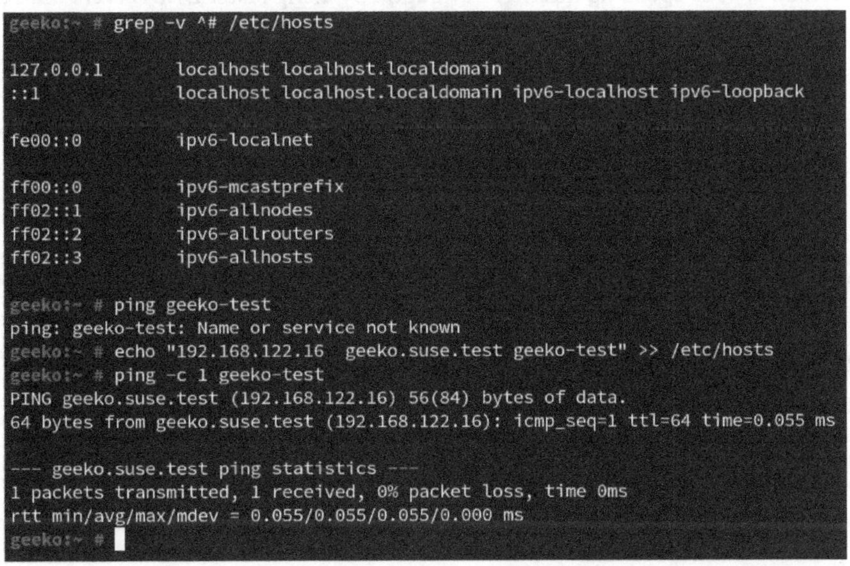


*Figure 5.10 – Adding a static host entry to our local system*

As we mentioned previously, name resolution is done via the configuration at `/etc/resolv.conf`, which, by default, contains a `search` parameter and a `nameserver` parameter. If we check the man page of `resolv.conf`, we can obtain descriptions for the common parameters:

- `nameserver`: Contains the IP of the name server to use. Currently, only a maximum of three entries (each on its own line) will be used by the `resolv` library in the system. The resolution is performed each time, so if one server fails, it will time out, try with the next one, and so on.
- `domain`: The local domain name. It allows us to use short names for hosts that are relative to the local domain in our host. If it's not listed, it's calculated based on the hostname of our system (everything after the first `.`).
- `search`: By default, it contains the local domain name, and it's the list of domains we can attempt to use to resolve the short name that's provided. It's limited to 6 domains and 256 characters. `domain` and `search` are mutually exclusive, and the last parameter in the configuration will be the only one used, disabling the previous one.

DNS resolution works by asking special servers (DNS) for the relevant data for a domain. This happens in a hierarchical way, with the top-most general servers being called **root servers**. DNS servers contain not only registers or entries for converting hostnames into IPs but also information about the mail server to use when sending an email, verification details for security, reverse entries, and more. Also, DNS servers can be used to block access to services by returning invalid IPs for some domains, or to speed up internet navigation by using faster DNS servers than the ones provided by the ISP.

When a domain name is registered, a new entry is created in the root tables for the domain pointing to the DNS server. This will take care of that domain resolution, and later, those entries will be populated and cached across the internet for faster resolution.

If we want to modify the DNS servers defined for a connection, remember to use `nmcli con mod NAME ipv4.dns IP` (or IPv6 equivalent) and use a + symbol beforehand, as in `+ipv4.dns`, to add a new entry to the list of DNS servers. Any manual changes to `resolv.conf` might be overwritten.

Now that we have learned how DNS works and how our system uses it, let's look at how to secure system network access.

# Overview of firewall configuration

When a system is connected to a network, many of the services running can be reached from other systems. That is the goal behind having systems connected. However, we also want to keep systems secure and away from unauthorized usage.

A **firewall** is a software layer that sits between the network cards and the services and allows us to fine-tune what is or isn't allowed.

We cannot completely block all the incoming connections to our system, as often, the incoming connection is a response to a request that our system made.

The connections are blocked via a kernel framework named **netfilter**, which is used by the firewall software to modify how the packets are processed. **nftables** is a new filter and packet classifier subsystem that enhances parts of `netfilter` code but retains the architecture and provides faster processing, among other features, using only one interface (`nft`), thus deprecating old frameworks such as `iptables`, `ip6tables`, `ebtables`, and `arptables`.

> As we explained earlier in regard to network configuration, a bad configuration in a firewall can lock you out of the system. So, be extremely careful when you're setting some restrictive rules so that you can log in to the system again if you were remotely accessing it.

`firewalld` is a frontend to the `nftables` framework. In the vast majority of cases, `firewalld` should be able to deal with the requirements for filtering. So, it is the recommended frontend for editing rules. It comes installed by default on your system. If this is not the case, you can install it by running `zypper install firewalld`. It will provide the `firewall-cmd` command once installed for interacting with the service.

`firewalld` uses the concept of zones, which allows us to predefine a set of rules for each of those zones. These can also be assigned to network connections. This is most relevant, for example, for laptops that might be roaming across connections, and they might have some default settings for when you're using home or corporate connections. However, they will default to a more secure one when you're using public Wi-Fi in a cafe.

`firewalld` also uses predefined services so that the firewall knows what ports and protocols should be enabled based on the services and zones they have been enabled on.

Let's check out the available zones and some more details about the home zone:

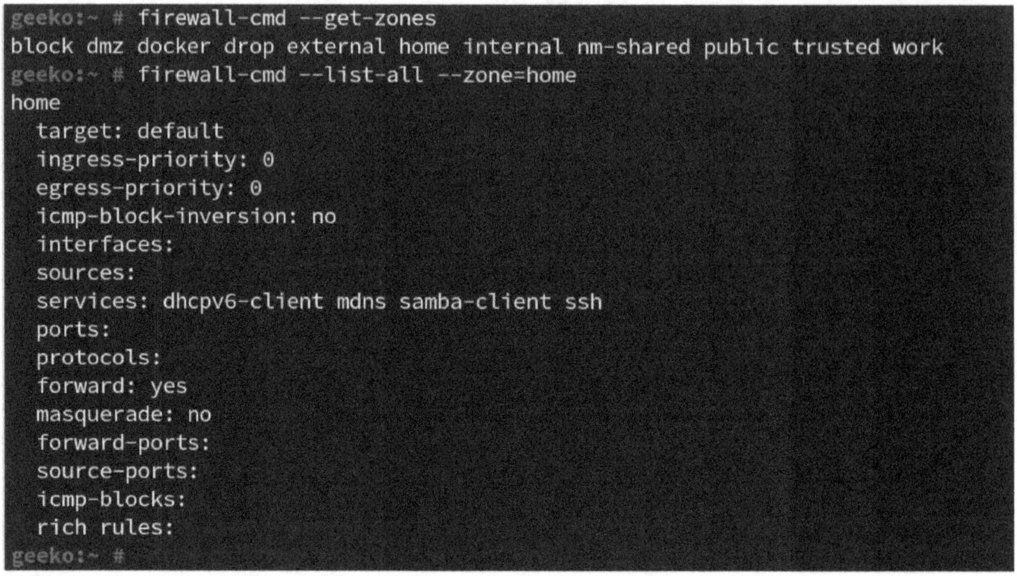


*Figure 5.11 – Available zones and configuration for the home zone*

As we can see, several zones have been defined:

- `public`: This is the default zone for newly added interfaces. It allows us to connect to `mdns`, SSH, `samba`, and DHCP clients and rejects all incoming traffic not related to the outgoing traffic.
- `block`: This rejects all incoming traffic unless it's related to the outgoing traffic.
- `dmz`: This rejects all incoming traffic unless it's related to outgoing or SSH connections.
- `drop`: This drops all incoming packets that are not related to outgoing ones (not even `ping`).
- `docker`: This is used for containers running on the host.
- `external`: This blocks all incoming traffic except that related to outgoing traffic. It also allows SSH, and it masquerades traffic as originating from this interface.
- `home`: In addition to `public`, it allows `smb` and `mdns`.
- `internal`: This is based on the home zone.
- `trusted`: This allows all incoming traffic.
- `work`: This blocks all incoming traffic except that related to outgoing or SSH/`cockpit`/DHCP traffic.

Next, we'll learn how to use those zones when we're configuring the firewall.

## Configuring the firewall

As mentioned in the introduction to this section, a firewall can be configured via the `firewall-cmd` command. The most common command options that are used are as follows:

- `firewall-cmd --get-zones`: Lists the available zones
- `firewall-cmd --get-active-zones`: Lists the active zones and interfaces that have been assigned
- `firewall-cmd --list-all`: Dumps the current configuration
- `firewall-cmd --add-service`: Adds a service to the current zone
- `firewall-cmd --add-port`: Adds a port/protocol to the current zone
- `firewall-cmd --remove-service`: Removes the service from the current zone
- `firewall-cmd --remove-port`: Removes the port/protocol from the current zone
- `firewall-cmd --reload`: Reloads the configuration from the saved data, thus discarding the runtime configuration
- `firewall-cmd -get-default-zone`: Gets the default zone
- `firewall-cmd --set-default-zone`: Defines the default zone to use

For example, when we install an `http` server in our system (for serving web pages), port `80` on the TCP protocol must be enabled.

Let's try this in our sample system by installing, running, and opening the `http` port:

```
zypper -n install apache2
systemctl enable apache2
systemctl start apache2
firewall-cmd --add-service=http
firewall-cmd --add-service=http --permanent
curl localhost
```

The last command will make a petition to the local `http` server to grab the results. If you have access to an additional system, you can try to connect to the IP of the server that we have been using to remotely access the default web page to be served by the system.

At this point, we have reviewed how to configure some basic firewall rules. So, we are ready to check the network's connectivity.

# Testing network connectivity

In the previous sections, we were interacting with network interfaces, addresses, and firewall rules that define, limit, or allow connections to our system. In this section, we will review some of the basic tools that can be used to validate that network connectivity exists.

Note that the following commands assume that the firewall is not set to strict mode and that we can use the **Internet Control Message Protocol** (**ICMP**) to reach the servers hosting the service. In secured networks, the service might be working but not answering to `ping` – it may only be answering the service queries themselves.

There are several commands that we can use here, so consider this a suggestion for diagnosing issues:

1. Check the local interface's IP address, netmask, and gateway.
2. Use the `ping` command with the IP address of the gateway to validate the proper network configuration.
3. Use the `ping` command to ping the DNS servers in `/etc/resolv.conf` to see whether they are reachable. Alternatively, use the `host` or `dig` command to query the DNS servers.
4. If there's supposedly external network connectivity, try to reach external DNS servers such as `8.8.8.8` or `1.1.1.1` or use `curl` or `wget` to request some of the web pages of known services, for example, `curl nasa.gov`.

This should give you a rough idea of where a problem might be, based on how far you reach into the tests. Remember that there are other tools, such as `tracepath`, that will show the hops that a TCP packet does before reaching the destination. The man pages for each command will give you hints and examples on their usage.

In the following screenshot, you can see the output of `tracepath` against one web server:

```
geeko:~ # tracepath www.uv.es
 1?: [LOCALHOST]                                      pmtu 1500
 1:  lightning.suse.lab                                    0.148ms
 1:  lightning.suse.lab                                    0.157ms
 2:  no reply
 3:  10.150.50.1                                          67.501ms
 4:  10.80.9.233                                          29.516ms
 5:  no reply
 6:  no reply
 7:  rediris.baja.espanix.net                             87.824ms
 8:  ciemat-rt2.ethtrunk2.uv.rt2.val.red.rediris.es       24.981ms
 9:  uv-ppal-router.red.rediris.es                        25.323ms asymm 10
10:  quarburquartest.red.uv.es                            26.201ms
11:  www.uv.es                                            48.224ms reached
     Resume: pmtu 1500 hops 11 back 11
geeko:~ #
```

*Figure 5.12 – The output of the tracepath command against the University of Valencia, Spain, web server*

As we can see, there were 11 steps that were performed across different servers until our data package reached the destination host. This has shown us how a package traverses the internet to reach target systems.

# Summary

In this chapter, we learned about configuring network interfaces using different approaches, either via manual interaction or via methods that allow us to script or automate the configuration.

Some troubleshooting for network issues was also introduced to help us find some of the basic errors that we might encounter.

As we mentioned in this chapter's introduction, networking is the basis for our system to reach other services and to provide services to other systems. We also introduced the idea of more complex network setups that fall outside the scope of this SCA level, but it's interesting to at least be familiar with the keywords that will come up in your job.

In the next chapter, we will cover some important topics related to security, such as adding, patching, and managing the software in our systems.

# 6

# Adding, Patching, and Managing Software

Software requires maintenance. Installing a system once is not enough if you want it to remain compatible and secure, as newer versions of the software and their dependencies can include new functionality and patches to close security issues or bug fixes. Updating and deleting software on a server is an essential task in production. In this chapter, we will review the capabilities of the **SUSE Customer Center** (**SCC**) for the software life cycle. We will also understand how packages in SCC are curated and verified.

We will describe subscriptions and entitlements, learn how to use the subscriptions to receive updates and support, and understand the steps required to configure your system to use them. We will use an evaluation subscription for these tests and explore the use of a redistribution system.

We will review the RPM package format and its management tool, **Zypper**, and will provide details about how packages are found, installed, updated, and deleted from the system.

What we will learn in this chapter will help us to not only keep our system up to date and secure, but also to add more software to provide services and increase system capabilities.

We will be covering the following topics:

- Some useful concepts about package management
- SCC and subscriptions
- Registering an installed system
- Installing and updating software using Zypper

- Managing repositories and signatures with Zypper
- Installing patterns
- Updating software
- Uninstalling software and repositories
- Understanding RPM internals

# Technical requirements

In this chapter, we will keep using the VM we installed in the *Chapter 1, Getting SLES 16 Up and Running (Physical and Cloud)*, so no further technical requirements are needed to continue.

# Some useful concepts about package management

Linux systems are not usually installed for themselves but to run some applications that deliver the required functionality or an environment for development. For that reason, installing, updating, configuring, and removing software is one of the most important aspects of managing a Linux system.

A standard application normally consists of one or more binary files, and some other accompanying files such as configuration files, data files, icons, and other required files. In Linux, it is quite common to also use shared libraries – pieces of code that provide some kind of functionality, and can be called from other applications. Shared libraries reduce the space required to install an application, as they can be – as the name suggests – shared between applications. Updating a library will result in all applications using the new version, thus lowering the chance of some security updates being overlooked, but the new version can be incompatible with some applications. As an alternative, you can include the library inside the binary file, using **static linking**. Some other applications require an interpreter (such as Python or Ruby) that needs to be installed first.

There are many ways to install an application. For instance, you can download the source code and build the application yourself (at least for applications in which you have access to the source code, such as open source projects). You can sometimes download a binary file or a compressed package and move the files to their required destination manually, or you can use some kind of installer that performs those steps on your behalf.

For instance, Helm, a package manager for Kubernetes, can be installed by downloading a packed file that contains the executable and then uncompressing and copying the binary to the right place in your filesystem, or using `curl` to download a script that does the same for you after selecting the right version and verifying that the downloaded components have been downloaded properly:

```
$ curl -fsSL -o get_helm.sh https://raw.githubusercontent.com/helm/helm/
main/scripts/get-helm-3
$ chmod 700 get_helm.sh
$ ./get_helm.sh
```

Please refer to `https://helm.sh/docs/intro/install/` for a more comprehensive look at this code.

These methods can be convenient, especially for developers who do not wish to spend time creating packaged versions for each distribution, but using `tar` files and scripts has some problems. First, there is no way (unless the developer produces a removal tool) to find and delete files once the application is no longer needed. Updates are also complex, especially when you need to find the dependencies for the application that you must find and install independently. Some configurations (such as adding the directory to the `PATH` or creating a user) must be done manually.

**Package managers** were invented to solve these problems. With a package manager, it becomes easy to find software, install and update it with its dependencies, and delete it once it is no longer needed.

A **package** consists of a collection of files and metadata that is used to install, update, and erase the files, and includes helper tools, file attributes such as ownership, and information about the package itself and its dependencies.

Packages can be found in a software **repository**, also called a **repo**. Repositories serve as a storage location for packages and can include a table of contents and some additional metadata.

SUSE provides all packages through software repositories. The selection of software and repositories available in a system will vary depending on the subscriptions attached to the system. You will need a subscription to be able to use those repositories on a server to install and update packages.

Additional software from other parties can be installed by adding other repositories to the server. Those third-party repositories are normally not guaranteed to work and are not covered by the support agreement with SUSE, although the third party can provide support itself or jointly with SUSE. Let's see how we can have access to the main SLES repositories using SCC.

# SCC and subscriptions

In order to receive updates and patches for your SUSE Linux Enterprise server, you need a subscription. Subscriptions can be purchased directly from the SUSE Shop online (`https://www.suse.com/shop/server/`), through public cloud marketplaces, through partners (`https://www.suse.com/partners/find-partner/`), or by contacting SUSE directly.

Let's go to the website for SCC here: `http://scc.suse.com`.

SCC is shown in the following screen capture:

*Figure 6.1 – SCC website*

In order to download and update your copy of SLES 16, you need to create a user. Go to **Product Downloads** and then select **SUSE Linux Enterprise Server** > **Download** and select the right version for your architecture. The **Downloads** page will look like this:

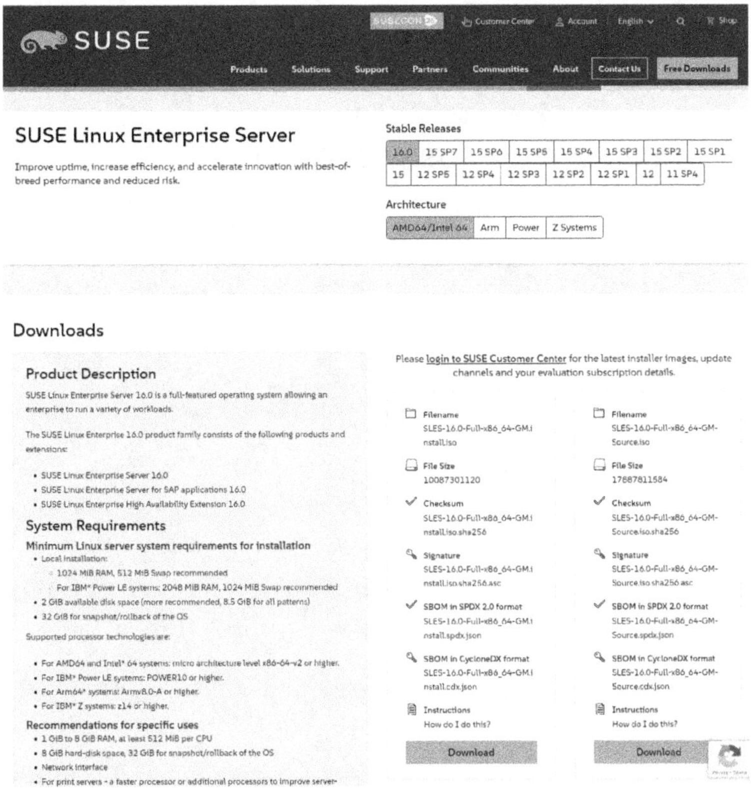


*Figure 6.2 – Downloads page for SUSE Linux Enterprise Server*

Carefully read the instructions in the box on the left. They include the minimum requirements (1,024 MiB RAM, 2 GiB HD, and 32 GiB for snapshot/rollback), and recommended system requirements (1 to 8 GiB RAM, 8 GiB HD or 32 GiB for OS rollback, network interface, etc.). There are different versions available for download, some specific for installation as VMs (including `cloud-init` for first boot configuration), and some generic, such as the standard ISO, including all packages for offline installation, the online installation version, and the source packages ISO that stores the open source code of all packages.

Here is a shortcut to the SLES **Downloads** page: `https://www.suse.com/download/sles/`.

> Even if you use the offline installer to test, it is recommended to connect your system to SCC and update all packages to the latest version after installation to avoid any day 0 security risk. Keeping the system updated, when possible, will help to alleviate many of the performance and security concerns.

Before downloading, we will create our own account. The dialog to do so will look like the following figure:

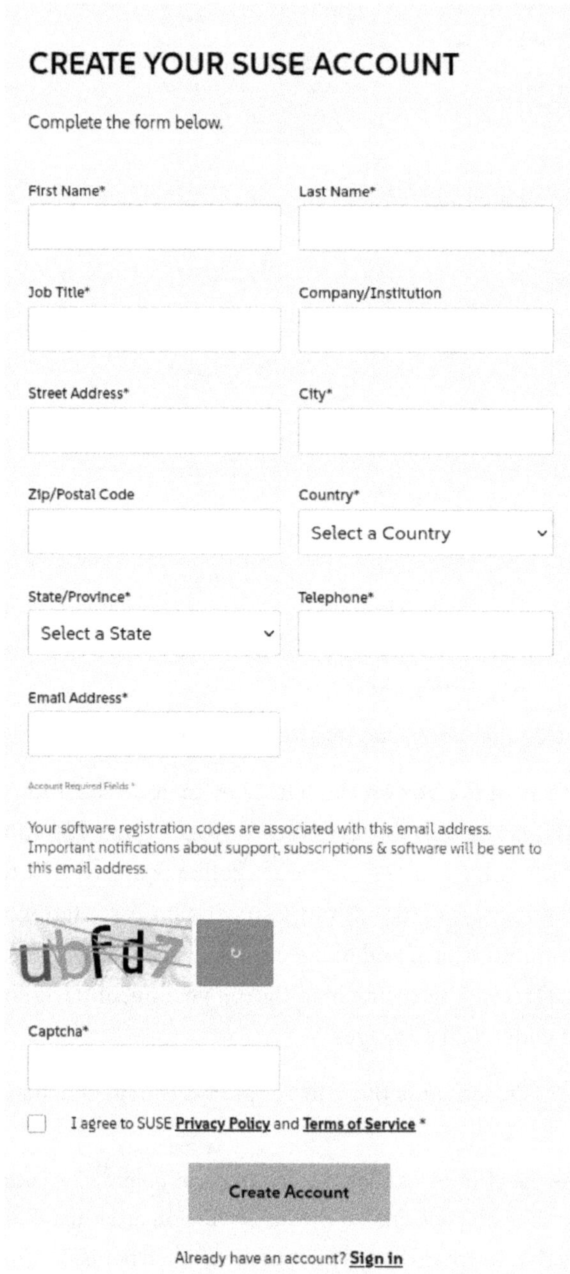


*Figure 6.3 – SCC account creation*

Once the fields are filled and complete in the preceding dialog, we can click **Create Account**. This will take us to the dialog to accept the subscription terms, as shown here:

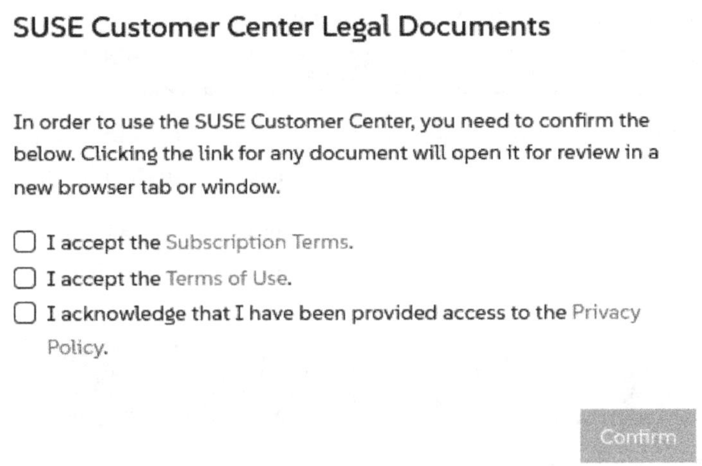


*Figure 6.4 – Accepting the terms of use and privacy policy to create an SCC account*

We are going to download `SLES-16.0-Online-x86_64-GM.install.iso`, so that we will be downloading the latest version of the packages during installation. A detailed description of how to install was included in *Chapter 1, Getting SLES 16 Up and Running (Physical and Cloud)*.

Now that we have made an account, it's time to register our system.

> Most of the products offered by SUSE have their counterpart in openSUSE, the open source community project (related to SUSE but independent) that is binary compatible with SUSE Linux. You can upgrade an openSUSE Leap installation to SLES, but some packages included in openSUSE Leap are not available in the SLES repos and will not receive updates after the migration.

## Registering an installed system

SUSE products are open source and can be used without a license, but you will need a subscription in order to receive the full benefits of the distribution and support. A subscription allows you to receive the software updates and some additional services, including technical support when you need it. Subscriptions are managed in SCC. The SCC web page provides you with reports on your entitlements and their usage, and information about packages and patches available for your systems in a convenient way.

You can complete the registration process at any time if you decide to skip the registration during the installation process, or if you want to re-register your system. It can be handy if you use standard images pre-installed in a virtual environment or if you clone an existing system.

SLES includes the **SUSEConnect** tool to manage subscriptions on the command line:

```
user@geeko:~> sudo SUSEConnect -r <REGISTRATION_CODE> -e <EMAIL_ADDRESS>
```

Substitute <REGISTRATION_CODE> with the registration code received (or you can find it in SCC), and <EMAIL_ADDRESS> with the email address of the account used to manage the subscriptions.

SUSE also offers solutions that allow you to work with a local registration server. In that case, you need to add the URL of the registration server to the command line (an advanced topic not covered in this chapter):

```
user@geeko:~> sudo SUSEConnect -r <REGISTRATION_CODE> -e <EMAIL_ADDRESS>
-url "<URL>"
```

Lastly, you can also use Cockpit to register your system:

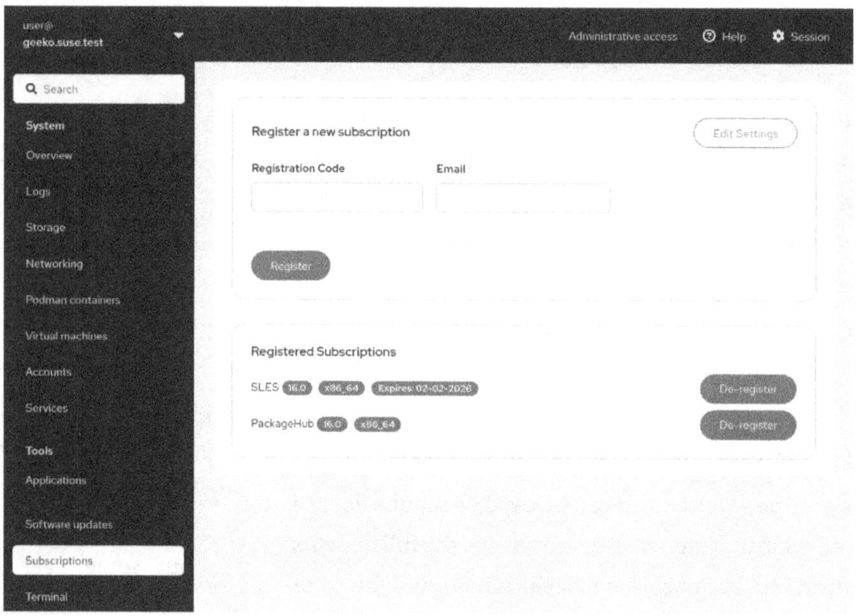


*Figure 6.5 – Subscriptions tab in Cockpit*

Use your `user` credentials to log in and then switch to **Administrative access**. You will now be able to configure the system. The **Subscriptions** tab allows you to subscribe your system, enter your registration details, and deregister the system if you no longer want to use your subscription on the server.

Packages are organized in SLES using a repository. A subscribed system by default has many repositories available, but only one of them is enabled:

```
user@geeko:~> sudo zypper repos --show-enabled-only
Repository priorities are without effect. All enabled repositories share
the same priority.
# | Alias | Name | Enabled | GPG Check | Refresh
--+-------------------------------------------------------------+-----
-----------------+--------+----------+-------
4 | SUSE_Linux_Enterprise_Server_16.0_aarch64:SLE-Product-SLES-16.0 | SLE-
Product-SLES-16.0 | Yes | (r ) Yes | Yes
```

However, there are more repositories available, as we can see in the following figure:

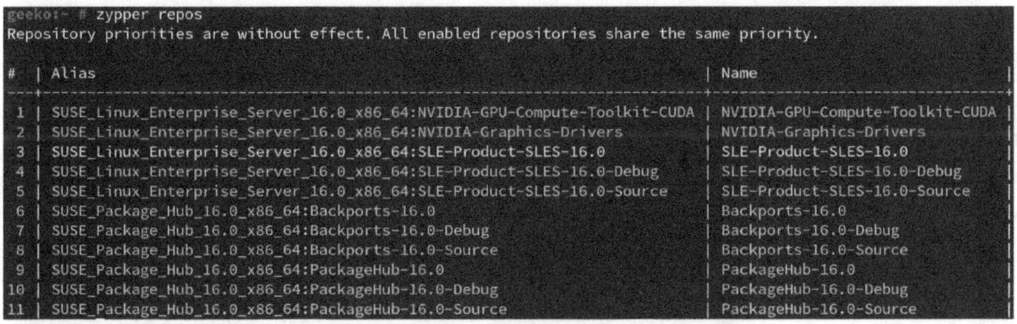


*Figure 6.6 – List of default repositories available*

**Extensions** provide advanced and optional capabilities that often require an additional subscription. Let's find out what extensions are available in our SLES machine:

```
user@geeko:~> sudo SUSEConnect --list-extensions
AVAILABLE EXTENSIONS AND MODULES
SUSE Linux Enterprise High Availability Extension 16.0 aarch64
Activate with: suseconnect -p sle-ha/16.0/aarch64 -r ADDITIONAL REGCODE

SUSE Package Hub 16.0 aarch64
Activate with: suseconnect -p PackageHub/16.0/aarch64
```

The **High Availability** extension requires a separate subscription. It provides an integrated suite of open source clustering technologies that can be installed on top of SLES. The other extension, **Package Hub**, includes additional non-supported packages that can be installed safely on SLES without creating any problems with support.

Let's enable the Package Hub extension now:

```
user@geeko:~> sudo suseconnect -p
PackageHub/16.0/aarch64
Registering system to SUSE Customer Center
Updating system details on https://scc.suse.com
...
Activating PackageHub 16.0 aarch64 ...
-> Adding service to system ...
-> Installing release package ...
Successfully registered system
```

Once you enable Package Hub, new repositories are enabled:

```
user@geeko:~> sudo zypper repos --show-enabled-
only Repository priorities are without effect.
All enabled repositories share the same
priority.
# | Alias | Name | Enabled | GPG Check | Refresh
---+-------------------------------------
------------------------+--------------
--------+---------+-----------+-------- 4 |
SUSE_Linux_Enterprise_Server_16.0_aarch64:SLE-
Product-SLES-16.0 | SLE-Product-SLES-16.0 | Yes
| (r ) Yes | Yes 7 | SUSE_Package_Hub_16.0_
aarch64:Backports-16.0 | Backports-16.0 | Yes
| (r ) Yes | Yes 10 | SUSE_Package_Hub_16.0_
aarch64:PackageHub-16.0 | PackageHub-16.0 | Yes
| (r ) Yes | Yes
```

SLES includes Package Hub as a disabled-by-default extension that you can enable. Packages in Package Hub are built and maintained by the community using the Open Build Service. Those packages are not officially supported by SUSE, but can be safely installed while SLES remains supported and supportable. For instance, you can find Elixir (an Erlang-based programming language runtime) on Package Hub.

Previous versions of SLES had **modules** that defined life cycle information when it was different from the base package selection. This concept is no longer applicable to SLES 16. You can use `zypper lifecycle` to learn more about the support included for each package.

We finally have repositories with software available to be installed and/or updated. Let's proceed to use some of the available packages in the next section.

# Installing and updating software using Zypper

Repositories solve three big problems with software installation in the following ways:

- **Finds and downloads software**: There are so many open source projects and packages that it is hard to select one that will provide what you need, with the level of quality required, and somebody backing it up to provide updates and fixes for as long as you need it. SUSE provides a selection of packages that are valuable, maintained by SUSE, and compatible with each other, so your production is safe.
- **Installs packages with their dependencies**: Some packages require libraries and other applications to be installed to work properly. Repositories allow the maintainer to specify those dependencies and the required versions.
- **Safely updates packages with their dependencies**: When a new version of the software or the dependencies is available, repositories allow you to quickly discover the update, understand whether it is compatible with the rest of the installation, and update everything needed with a single command.

Repostories are operated through a package management system, which, in SLES, is Zypper. Let's see how Zypper helps solve all those problems. We are going to install **Elixir**, a dynamic, functional language for building scalable and maintainable applications. Elixir is compiled into bytecode, an intermediate format that is executed on the BEAM (Erlang VM), an application VM that is part of the Erlang package. This dependency means that you need Erlang to compile and run Elixir code. In fact, you can run compiled Elixir code without Elixir if you want, as the bytecode is directly executable by the BEAM.

Let's start searching for Elixir:

```
user@geeko:~> sudo zypper search elixir
Refreshing service 'SUSE_Linux_Enterprise_Server_16.0_aarch64'.
Refreshing service 'SUSE_Package_Hub_16.0_aarch64'. Loading repository
data...
Reading installed packages...
S | Name | Summary | Type
 ---+----------------------------+------------------------------------
----------------------+--------
  | elixir | Functional meta-programming aware language built atop Erlang |
package
```

```
  | elixir-doc | Documentation for elixir | package
  | elixir-hex | Package manager for the Erlang VM | package
  | obs-service-elixir_mix_deps | OBS Source Service for Elixir software
packaging | package
```

We have four different packages that have *Elixir* in their name distributed in the two enabled services, with one of them being Package Hub. Let's find out whether the first one is the correct one:

```
user@geeko:~> sudo zypper info elixir
Refreshing service
Loading repository data...
Reading installed packages...
Information for package elixir:
------------------------------
Repository     : Backports-16.0
Name           : elixir
Version        : 1.18.1-160000.2.3
Arch           : noarch
Vendor         : SUSE LLC <https://www.suse.com/>
Support Level  : unknown
Installed Size : 8.4 MiB
Installed      : No
Status         : not installed
Source package : elixir-1.18.1-160000.2.3.src
Upstream URL   : https://elixir-lang.org
Summary        : Functional meta-programming aware language built atop
Erlang
Description    :
    Elixir is a functional meta-programming aware language built on top of
the Erlang VM. It is a dynamic language with flexible syntax with macros
support that leverage Erlang's abilities to build concurrent, distributed,
fault-tolerant applications with hot code upgrades.
     Elixir also provides first-class support for pattern matching,
polymorphism via protocols (similar to Clojure's), aliases and associative
data structures (usually known as dicts or hashes in other programming
languages).
     Finally, Elixir and Erlang share the same bytecode and data types.
This means one can invoke Erlang code from Elixir (and vice-versa) without
any conversion or performance impact.
```

Yes, we can see that the package is indeed the one we were looking for. In the case that we mistyped it, we will receive an error message stating that the package is not found. `zypper info` provides really useful information, such as the upstream URL, the source package used, and a summary and description that gives you information about the purpose of the package.

We stated that there is a hard requirement to install Erlang. Let's see what other requirements have been specified by the package maintainers:

```
user@geeko:~> zypper info --requires elixir
Loading repository data...
Reading installed packages...
Information for package elixir:
-------------------------------
Repository      : Backports-16.0
Name            : elixir
Version         : 1.18.1-160000.2.3
........ Output ommitted]
Requires        : [3]
    /bin/sh
    /usr/bin/env
    erlang >= 25
```

The requirements are quite straightforward. This version of Elixir requires a shell (`sh`), `env`, and Erlang with a version equal to or greater than 25. However, those dependencies can go further. Let's find out whether Erlang requires something else (some output omitted):

```
user@geeko:~> zypper info --requires erlang
Information for package erlang:
-------------------------------
Repository      : SLE-Product-SLES-16.0
Name            : erlang
Version         : 27.1.3-160000.2.2
Arch            : aarch64
Vendor          : SUSE LLC <https://www.suse.com/>
Support Level   : Level 3
Installed Size  : 50.5 MiB
Installed       : No
Status          : not installed
Source package  : erlang-27.1.3-160000.2.2.src
```

```
Upstream URL   : https://www.erlang.org
Summary        : General-purpose programming language and runtime
environment
Requires       : [31]
    ......
    /usr/bin/env
    ......
    libodbc.so.2()(64bit)
    erlang-epmd
    libz.so.1(ZLIB_1.2.7.1)(64bit)
```

Look how simple it is. Erlang requirements are automatically found. It has 31 dependencies described. Fortunately, most of them are libraries that are already in the base installation, and some are shared with Elixir. Zypper takes care of all that, including the compatibility between the versions required and supported by different applications. Zypper won't allow you to install a package if there is no way to satisfy all its requirements and those of the software already installed at the same time.

Let's install Elixir now:

```
user@geeko:~> sudo zypper in elixir
Refreshing service 'SUSE_Linux_Enterprise_Server_16.0_aarch64'.
Refreshing service 'SUSE_Package_Hub_16.0_aarch64'.
Loading repository data...
Reading installed packages...
Resolving package dependencies...
The following 4 NEW packages are going to be installed:
 elixir erlang erlang-epmd libodbc2
The following package has no support information from its vendor:
 elixir
4 new packages to install.
Package download size: 35.7 MiB
Package install size change:
                   |        59.4 MiB required by packages that will be
installed
          59.4 MiB | -            0 B released by packages that will be
removed
Backend: classic_rpmtrans
 Continue? [y/n/v/...? shows all options] (y):
```

```
Preloading: elixir-1.18.1-160000.2.3.noarch.rpm [done]
Preloading: libodbc2-2.3.12-160000.2.2.aarch64.rpm
[done]
Preloading: erlang-epmd-27.1.3-160000.2.2.aarch64.rpm
[done]
Preloading: erlang-27.1.3-160000.2.2.aarch64.rpm [done]Preload finished.
[success (28.1 MiB/s) ] ..............................................
..............................................[done]
Retrieving: libodbc2-2.3.12-160000.2.2.aarch64 (SLE-Product-SLES-16.0).
(1/4), 186.1 KiB
Retrieving: erlang-27.1.3-160000.2.2.aarch64 (SLE-Product-SLES-16.0)
(2/4),  29.5 MiB
Retrieving: erlang-epmd-27.1.3-160000.2.2.aarch64 (SLE-Product-SLES-16.0).
(3/4), 399.9 KiB
Retrieving: elixir-1.18.1-160000.2.3.noarch (Backports-16.0)
(4/4),   5.7 MiB

Checking for file conflicts: ....................[done]
(1/4) Installing: libodbc2-2.3.12-160000.2.2.aarch64 ....................
.................................................................[done]
(2/4) Installing: erlang-27.1.3-160000.2.2.aarch64 ......................
.................................................................[done]
/usr/bin/systemd-sysusers --replace=/usr/lib/sysusers.d/epmd-user.conf -
Creating group 'epmd' with GID 473.
Creating user 'epmd' (Erlang Port Mapper Daemon) with UID 473 and GID 473.
(3/4) Installing: erlang-epmd-27.1.3-160000.2.2.aarch64 .................
.................................................................[done]
(4/4) Installing: elixir-1.18.1-160000.2.3.noarch .......................
.................................................................[done]
Running post-transaction scripts ........................................
.................................................................[done]
```

Let's see what happened. First, Zypper found the package we asked for in the list of enabled repositories and chose the one with the highest priority (we only have one, but there could be more than one in different repos). It analyzed all the dependencies and created a list with their allowed versions (some packages will allow you to choose more than one version of their dependencies, such as Elixir asking for Erlang version 25 or higher). Then, it tries to find a group of versions that work together nicely without incompatibilities.

In this case, Elixir requires Erlang, and Erlang requires a set of dependencies that are already installed, except for `erlang-epmd` and `libobdc2`. Those four packages are then downloaded from the repo and installed, including running some scripts before and after the binaries and configuration are copied, allowing the package to create the `epmd` group required by the configuration. Using SUSE sources guarantees that the packages are installable, that they are tested and verified to work properly together, and that they will be updated when a new patch is available without conflicts.

Now that we know how to search for packages and install them, let's move on to learn more about repository management.

# Managing repositories and signatures with Zypper

As we have seen, after registering the system, we have a set of packages available for it in what we call a repository. In SLES 16, the main repository will come with the operating system and all the supported packages, while Package Hub will include unsupported packages that can be installed in the system without losing support. You can also customize the repositories used to search for and install packages and even include other repos. Let's try it:

```
user@geeko:/etc/zypp/repos.d> sudo zypper addrepo https://download.
opensuse.org/repositories/science/16.0/science.repo
Adding repository 'Software for Scientists and Engineers (16.0)' .........
.................................................................[done]
Repository 'Software for Scientists and Engineers (16.0)' successfully
added

URI         : https://download.opensuse.org/repositories/science/16.0/
Enabled     : Yes
GPG Check   : Yes
Autorefresh : No
Priority    : 99 (default priority)

Repository priorities are without effect. All enabled repositories share
the same priority.

user@geeko:/etc/zypp/repos.d> sudo zypper repos --show-enabled-only
Repository priorities are without effect. All enabled repositories share
the same priority.
#  | Alias | Name | Enabled | GPG Check | Refresh
---+-------+------+---------+-----------+--------
4 | SUSE_Linux_Enterprise_Server_16.0_aarch64:SLE-Product-SLES-16.0 | SLE-
```

```
Product-SLES-16.0 | Yes | (r ) Yes | Yes
7 | SUSE_Package_Hub_16.0_aarch64:Backports-16.0 | Backports-16.0 | Yes |
(r ) Yes | Yes
10 | SUSE_Package_Hub_16.0_aarch64:PackageHub-16.0 | PackageHub-16.0 | Yes
| (r ) Yes | Yes
13 | science | Software for Scientists and Engineers (16.0) | Yes | ( p)
Yes | No
```

The first time you try to install packages from a new repo, it will ask you to confirm that the repository is safe, showing you the signing key for the repo using **Gnu Privacy Guard** (**GPG**), an implementation of cryptographic signatures known as **Pretty Good Privacy** (**PGP**). Check that the key is correct by comparing the downloaded key with the one provided by other means (such as from the web page), and then accept it so the repo can be trusted. Any later attempt to forge the repository will fail, as they won't have the right signature, giving you another level of protection. We can see an example of Zypper showing a new GPG signature in the following figure:

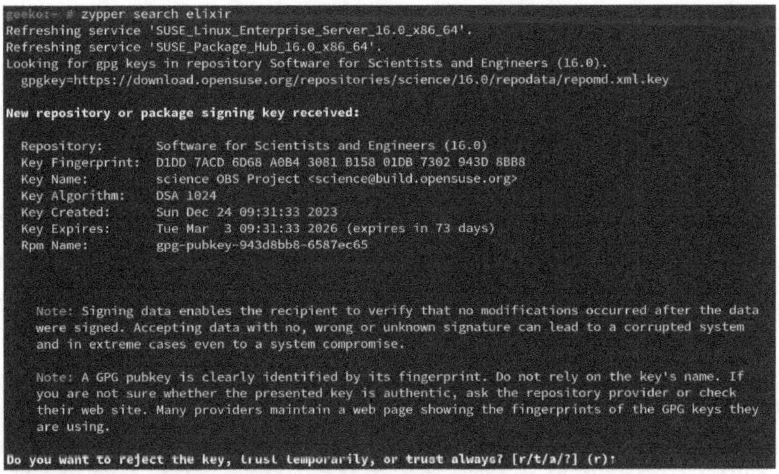


*Figure 6.7 – Installing from a new repo for the first time*

The data is stored in a plain text file in the `/etc/zypp/repos.d/` folder. Let's find out what information is stored for this science repo:

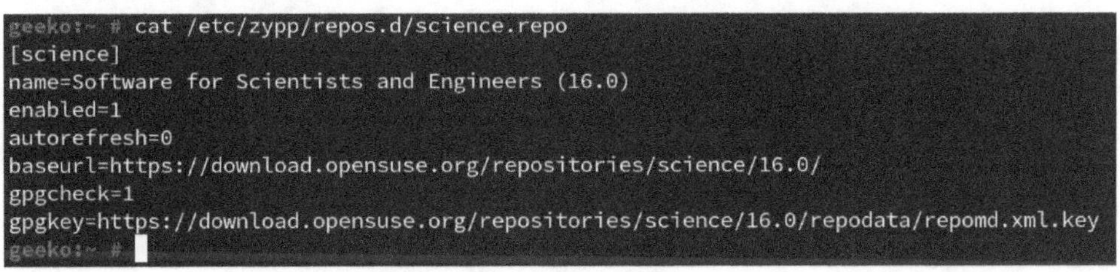


*Figure 6.8 – Content of science.repo*

The format is an INI-like style with keys and values:

- `section`: This provides the unique identifier of the local repository (an alias).
- `name`: This is a long descriptive name for the repository. To be used in the UI.
- `type`: This can be `rpm-md`, `YaST`, and so on
- `enabled`: When set to `1`, it will be enabled, and when set to `0`, it will be disabled.
- `baseurl`: This is the location to find the packages and metadata, as a URL. In this case, it is a single HTTPS source. It contains the `$releasever` variable that will be substituted before being accessed. Other methods are NFS, HTTP, and FTP.
- `autorefresh`: This defines whether the metadata needs to be downloaded and updated when accessing the repo automatically or manually using `zypper refresh`.
- `gpgcheck`: When set to `1` (enabled), the metadata of the repo will be checked against the GPG signature. When that is not available, individual GPG signatures for each package will be used. Disabling it is not recommended.
- `gpgkey`: This is the GPG key URI.
- `service`: Services are one level above repositories and serve to manage repositories and perform some specific tasks.

The minimal required options to have a running repository are `name`, `baseurl`, and `gpgcheck` (this happens only when `gpgcheck` is set to `0`; otherwise, the GPG signature needs to be added too). When you install a new repo using the URL, the repo will be enabled by default (as expected), but it won't be refreshed automatically. You need to manually refresh the metadata to see whether new versions of the packages are available using `refresh`:

```
user@geeko:~> sudo zypper refresh
Repository 'SLE-Product-SLES-16.0' is up to date.
Repository 'Backports-16.0' is up to date.
Repository 'PackageHub-16.0' is up to date.
Repository 'Software for Scientists and Engineers (16.0)' is up to date.
All repositories have been refreshed.
```

When using manually added repositories, don't forget to refresh the repo to download the latest metadata when you are checking for new versions of a package. Alternatively, you can modify the repo to auto-update, although that will mean that the metadata will be checked and downloaded every time you use Zypper.

In a normal installation, there are a few repositories configured but not enabled. The repositories come in the following types:

- **Base repos**: For example, `SLE-Product-SLES-16.0`, which contains the packages or `rpm`.
- **Source repo**: For example, `SLE-Product-SLES-16.0-Source`. The `Source` part of the name implies that the packages inside are source packages, containing the source code used to build the packages in the equivalent repo.
- **Debug repo**: For example, `Backports-16.0-Debug`. The `Debug` part of the name implies that those packages add debugging information that can be used to help with deep troubleshooting of issues.

Repositories can be added, deleted, and updated. The following table is a list of subcommands to manage repositories with Zypper:

| **Command** | **Usage** |
|---|---|
| `zypper lr`<br>`zypper repos` | Shows configured repos |
| `zypper lr --show-enabled-only` | Shows only enabled repos |
| `zypper addrepo URI`<br>`zypper addrepo file` | Adds a repository to the list of repositories |
| `zypper removerepo` *alias/name/#/URI*<br>`zypper rr` *alias/name/#/URI* | Removes a new repo with the provided URL |
| `zypper modifyrepo -e` *alias/name/#/URI*<br>`zypper modifyrepo --enable` *alias/name/#/URI* | Enables the repository (you can use `-a` for all repositories, `-l` for local, and `-t` for remote) |
| `zypper modifyrepo -d` *alias/name/#/URI*<br>`zypper modifyrepo --disable` *alias/name/#/URI* | Disables the repository |
| `zypper refresh` | Refreshes all or specified repositories |
| `Zypper clean` | Cleans local caches for all or the specified repositories |

*Table 6.1 – Zypper repository-related options*

Now that we know how to securely manage repositories in SLES, let's start adding more packages to our system, updating them, and undoing installations if we need to.

# Installing patterns

Zypper works with several types of resources – different kinds of objects with dependencies on other objects:

- **Package**: An ordinary RPM file.
- **Patch**: A text file that combines several RPM files with a minimal version to a fix and also contains additional metadata. It usually updates affected/vulnerable packages to a version providing the fix. It is intended to provide quick fixes and what we call **program temporary fixes** (**PTFs**) in SUSE, which are fast delivery fixes for customers.
- **Pattern**: A group of packages that are required or recommended to install a functionality.
- **Product**: A group of packages that are necessary to install a product, conveniently identified as a package with dependencies. It modifies `/etc/products.d`, used by other tools get information about the base and add-on products installed, like the date of End Of Life.

Patterns are important because they allow you to install many packages at the same time to enable some functionality. There are many patterns by default in SLES. Let's find out what they are (some output omitted):

```
user@geeko:~> sudo zypper patterns
Refreshing service 'SUSE_Linux_Enterprise_Server_16.0_aarch64'.
Refreshing service 'SUSE_Package_Hub_16.0_aarch64'.
Loading repository data...
Reading installed packages...
S | Name           | Version       | Repository    | Dependency
--+-------+---------+-------------+----------
     | apparmor            | 20241218-bp160.2.2  | Backports-16.0       |
   i | base                | 20241218-160000.2.2 | SLE-Product-SLES-16.0
|
     | basic_desktop       | 20241218-bp160.2.2  | Backports-16.0       |
     | books               | 20201106-bp160.1.1  | Backports-16.0       |
...
     | print_server        | 20250313-160000.2.2 | SLE-Product-SLES-16.0
|
 i+ | selinux             | 20241218-160000.2.2 | SLE-Product-SLES-16.0
|
     | sw_management       | 20241218-160000.2.2 | SLE-Product-SLES-16.0
|
```

```
    | sway                 | 20200619-bp160.1.5   | Backports-16.0 |
    | technical_writing    20201106-bp160.1.1    | Backports-16.0       |
    | wsl_base     | 20240327-bp160.1.10 | Backports-16.0       |
    | wsl_gui      | 20240327-bp160.1.10 | Backports-16.0       |
    | wsl_systemd | 20240327-bp160.1.10 |Backports-16.0        |
    | x11          | 20241218-bp160.2.2  | Backports-16.0       |
    | x11_raspberrypi      | 20241218-bp160.2.2   | Backports-16.0       |
| xfce | 20230212-bp160.2.2 | Backports-16.0 |
| xfce_extra | 20230212-bp160.2.2 | Backports-16.0 |
| xfce_extra_wayland | 20230212-bp160.2.2 | Backports-16.0 |
| xfce_wayland | 20230212-bp160.2.2 | Backports-16.0 |
```

The list of patterns tells us the pattern name, the version, the repository that stores them, whether they are installed or not, and any dependencies. Patterns provide a better way to install complex applications with many components, such as GNOME (the default graphical interface).

For instance, the pattern to install the **Apache HTTPD** service (`lamp_server`) provides a full **Linux, Apache, MariaDB, Perl** (**LAMP**) stack and thus also includes a list of ancillary packages and applications that go beyond the bare server. The pattern for GNOME, which has a few hundred dependencies and requires ancillary applications, is the safest way to make sure that the installation includes all expected packages for an optimal user experience. In fact, installing the `gnome` package requires the installation of the `gnome-gnome` pattern as a dependency:

```
user@geeko:~> sudo zypper info -t pattern lamp_server
Refreshing service 'SUSE_Linux_Enterprise_Server_16.0_aarch64'.
Refreshing service 'SUSE_Package_Hub_16.0_aarch64'.
Loading repository data...
Reading installed packages...
Information for pattern lamp_server:
------------------------------------
Repository      : SLE-Product-SLES-16.0
Name            : lamp_server
Version         : 20250313-160000.2.2
Arch            : aarch64
Vendor          : SUSE LLC <https://www.suse.com/>
Installed       : No
Visible to User : Yes
Summary         : Web and LAMP Server
```

```
Description     :
    Software to set up a Web server that is able to serve static, dynamic,
and interactive content (like a Web shop). This includes Apache HTTP
Server, the database management system MySQL, and scripting languages such
as PHP, Python, Ruby on Rails, or Perl.
Contents     :
S  | Name             | Type  |Dependency
---+------+-------+-----------
   | apache2                     | package     | Required
   | patterns-base-basesystem    | package     | Required
   | patterns-server-lamp_server | package     | Required
   | apache2-manual              | package     |Recommended
   | apache2-mod_php8                   | package     |Recommended
   | apache2-prefork             | package     |Recommended
   | mariadb                     | package     |Recommended
i  | perl                               | package     |Recommended
```

As you can see, installing the LAMP pattern takes care of installing different components, specifying that we want to use a pattern with the `-t pattern` option:

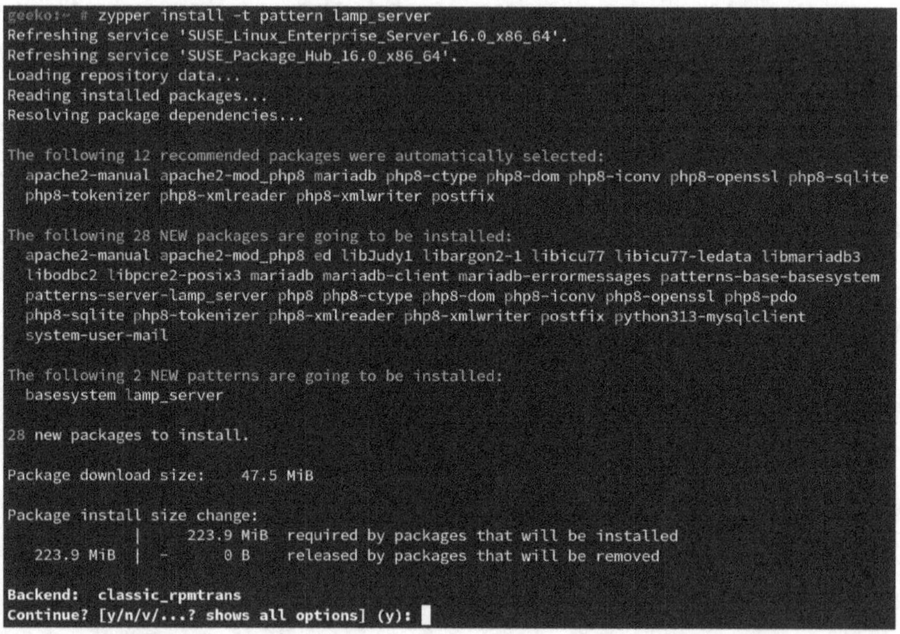


*Figure 6.9 – Installing the lamp_server pattern with the -t pattern option*

We have now learned how to install software. It is also important to learn how to keep it up to date. Let's see how in the following section.

# Updating software

New versions of packages and their dependencies are published daily. Keeping the server updated, when possible, is one of the best ways to avoid security or performance issues and is a basic maintenance task. With Zypper, updating a package is as simple as entering a command. Let's see what it looks like in the following figure:

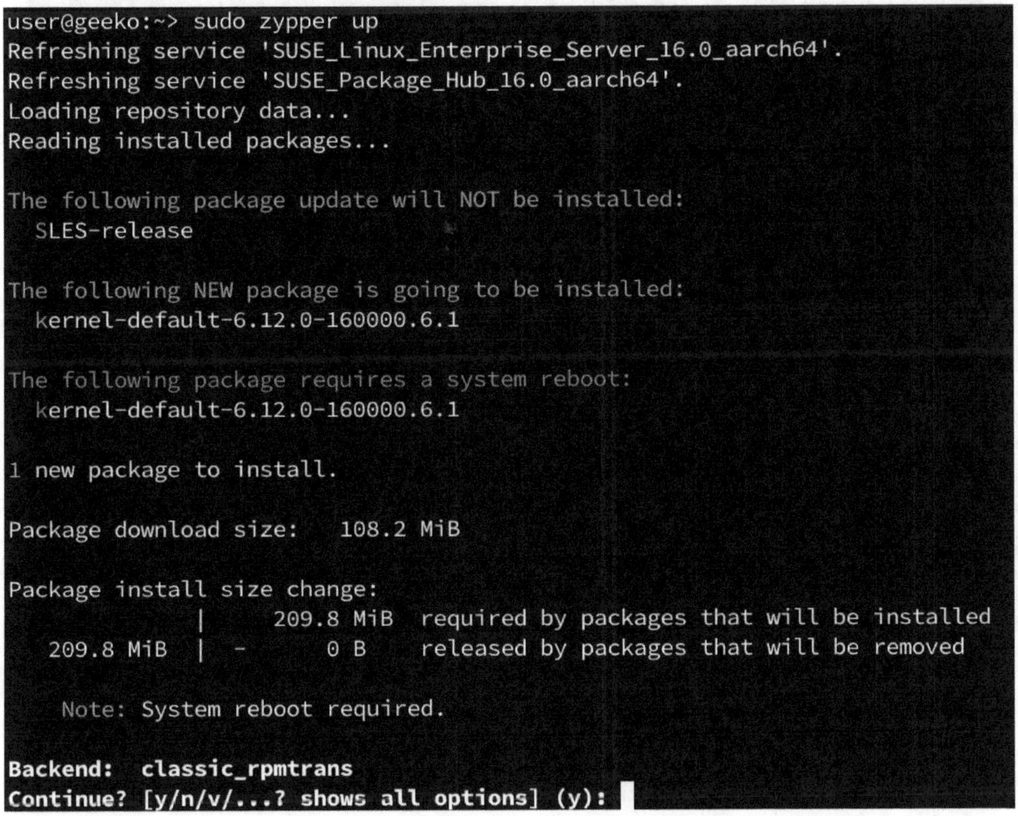


*Figure 6.10 – Output of Zypper update*

Zypper shows you a summary of what is going to happen and asks for verification. Answering *yes* here will install the new version and all its dependencies. You can do it automatically by adding the -y option:

```
user@geeko:~> sudo zypper up -y
Refreshing service 'SUSE_Linux_Enterprise_Server_16.0_aarch64'.
Refreshing service 'SUSE_Package_Hub_16.0_aarch64'.
Loading repository data...
```

```
Reading installed packages...
The following package update will NOT be installed: SLES-release
The following NEW package is going to be installed: kernel-
default-6.12.0-160000.6.1
The following package requires a system reboot: kernel-
default-6.12.0-160000.6.1
1 new package to install.
Package download size: 108.2 MiB
Package install size change:
            | 209.8 MiB required by packages that will be installed
209.8 MiB   | - 0 B released by packages that will be removed
Note: System reboot required.

Backend: classic_rpmtrans Continue? [y/n/v/...? shows all options] (y): y
Preloading: kernel-default-6.12.0-160000.6.1.aarch64.rpm [done]
Preload finished. [success (17.9 MiB/s) ] ........[done]
Retrieving: kernel-default-6.12.0-160000.6.1.aarch64 (SLE-Product-
SLES-16.0) (1/1), 108.2 MiB
Checking for file conflicts: ....................[done]
(1/1) Installing: kernel-default-6.12.0-160000.6.1.aarch64
................[done]
Running post-transaction scripts ................[done]
user@geeko:~>
```

The kernel package is special. Normally, a package will be substituted by the new version. In the case of the kernel and due to its importance, installing a new version of the package will install the new kernel and make it the default, without deleting the old ones. Also, Zypper checks that the package modifies a key library or application and will let you know that you need to reboot. You can actually verify whether that is the case without reading the output with a Zypper command:

```
user@geeko:~> zypper needs-rebooting
Since the last system boot core libraries or services have been updated.
Reboot is suggested to ensure that your system benefits from these
updates.
```

There are cases in which a regular package update will not be enough, such as the release of a new minor version of the operating system (i.e., SLES 16.1). For those cases, the repositories need to be updated to point to the new code base, and dependencies need to be reevaluated, even downgrading some packages.

Let's see the commands used to maintain software in our system in the following table:

| Command | Usage |
|---|---|
| `zypper info <symbol>`<br>`zypper if` | Shows detailed information for a specified package |
| `zypper if -t <type> --provides --requires --conflicts --obsoletes --suggests --supplements --enhances <symbol>` | Shows information about a package, including references to others that the package requires, conflicts with, makes obsolete, suggests, supplements, or enhances |
| `zypper search -t <type> -r <repo>`<br>`zypper se` | Searches for a package in active repositories or the specific repo for the type |
| `zypper search package` | Performs a search for packages in the available repositories |
| `zypper install name\|capability`<br>`zypper in` | Installs or updates a package that can be selected by name or capability |
| `zypper install file.rpm` | Installs plain RPM files, trying to satisfy their dependencies |
| `zypper list-updates`<br>`zypper lu`<br>`zypper list-patches`<br>`zypper lp` | Lists available updates/patches that are installable |
| `zypper update`<br>`zypper up` | Updates installed packages with newer versions, where possible |
| `zypper update <package>` | Updates a single package |
| `zypper patch` | Installs available patches, aiming for the latest version; optional patches (optional category or feature) will not be installed unless we specify them using the `--with-optional` option |
| `zypper dist-upgrade`<br>`zypper dup` | Performs a distribution upgrade |
| `zypper what-provides <capability>`<br>`zypper wp` | Lists all packages that provide the specified capability |

*Table 6.2 – Zypper options related to software maintenance*

We now know how to keep the system up to date. Let's see how we can remove and clean up pieces of software in our system.

# Uninstalling software and repositories

So far, we have learned how to install and update software from the base repositories included in the distribution, and also from Package Hub and third-party repositories. But the life cycle of a package is not complete. We will need to delete (remove) the software. Let's see how that goes.

We will start by deleting the repo for science. Let's first check that there is no package installed from that repo:

```
user@geeko:~> zypper se -r science --installed-only
Loading repository data...
Reading installed packages...
No matching items found.

    Note: For an extended search including not yet activated remote
resources please use 'zypper
    search-packages'.
user@geeko:~> sudo zypper removerepo science
[sudo] password for user:
Removing repository 'Software for Scientists and Engineers (16.0)'
................................[done]
Repository 'Software for Scientists and Engineers (16.0)' has been
removed.
user@geeko:~> zypper lr
```

An example of the repos listed by Zypper can be seen in the following figure:

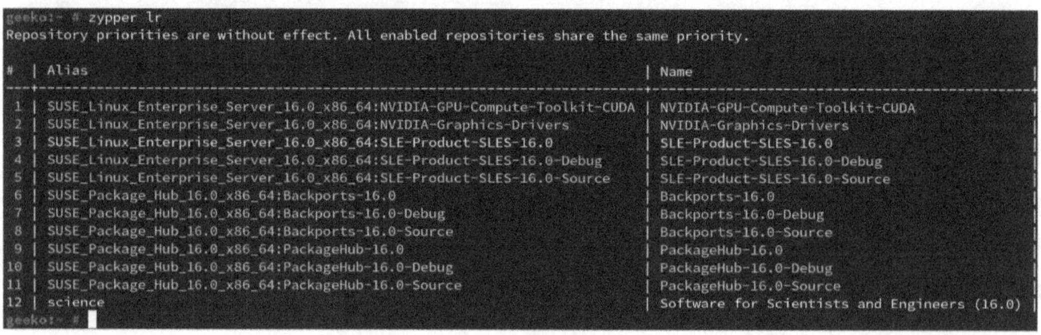


*Figure 6.11 – Output of zypper lr*

You can also disable a repo. In that case, the repo will still be visible in the list of repositories, but it won't be used for search and dependency management:

```
user@geeko:~> sudo zypper modifyrepo --disable SUSE_Package_Hub_16.0_
aarch64:Backports-16.0 SUSE_Package_Hub_16.0_aarch64:PackageHub-16.0
Repository 'SUSE_Package_Hub_16.0_aarch64:Backports-16.0' has been
successfully disabled.
Repository 'SUSE_Package_Hub_16.0_aarch64:PackageHub-16.0' has been
successfully disabled.
```

Let's now delete Elixir. We are going to try first using the `-D` modifier to understand what would happen and see what the result would be:

```
user@geeko:~> sudo zypper  rm -D  elixir
Reading installed packages...
Resolving package dependencies...
The following package is going to be REMOVED:
  elixir
1 package to remove.
Package install size change:
 |   0 B    required by packages that will be installed
-8.4 MiB    | -  8.4 MiB  released by packages that will be removed
Backend:  classic_rpmtran --dry-run
Continue? [y/n/v/...? shows all options] (y):
```

Even if we type `y`, the package will not be uninstalled because it is a dry run. But this is not what we were trying to do. We don't need Erlang anymore, so we need to specify that we want to remove the package and all its dependencies:

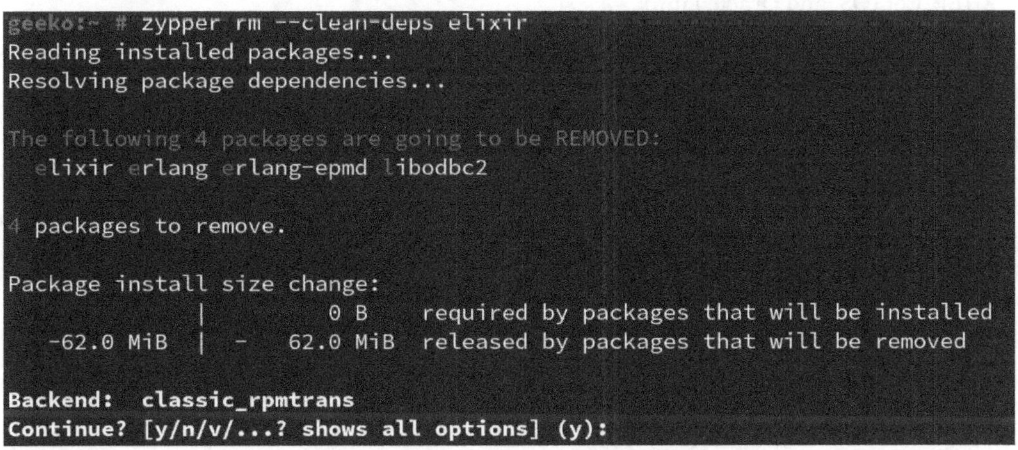


*Figure 6.12 – Removing a package and its dependencies*

A list of repository-related options, intended for cleaning up, is shown in the following table:

| **Command** | **Usage** |
| --- | --- |
| `zypper rr <repo>`<br>`zypper removerepo` | Removes a repository |
| `zypper if -t <type> --provides --requires --conflicts --obsoletes --suggests --supplements --enhances <symbol>` | Shows information about a package, including references to others that the package requires, conflicts with, makes obsolete, suggests, supplements, or enhances |
| `zypper search -t <type> -r <repo>`<br>`Zypper se` | Searches for a package in active repositories or the specific repo for the type |
| `zypper modifyrepo --disable <repo>` | Disables the repo |
| `zypper rm -clean-deps <package>`<br>`zypper remove` | Removes a package and all its dependencies |

*Table 6.3 – Repository clean-up options for Zypper*

We now know how to manage repositories. It's time to dive deeper into the RPM tools and format, which we will do in the following section.

# Understanding RPM internals

Zypper is a powerful tool that provides a full life cycle for packages, which works as a wrapper around **RPM Package Manager**. All Linux distributions tend to have their own package manager, from Debian with `.deb` to Pacman in Arch Linux, and some distributions with more exotic mechanisms. SLES uses RPM, a format that is shared with many distributions such as openSUSE, Fedora, RHEL, CentOS, and Oracle Linux.

The main command is `rpm`. RPM can install and update packages, but it does not manage repositories or resolve dependencies, leaving that up to you, so you will normally use Zypper. However, knowing a little about RPM can be useful if you find issues or plan to create your own packages to distribute them.

RPM files are packaged in a special binary format that contains the following:

- The files to be installed on the system, stored in CPIO format and compressed
- Information on permissions and the assigned owner and group for each file
- Dependencies required and provided by each package, and a list of conflicts with other packages

- Script to execute during installation, uninstallation, and upgrade to make required changes in the system
- A signature to guarantee that the package was not modified

To learn a bit about it, we will show some simple and useful commands:

- **Commands to check packages:**
    - `rpm -qa`: Lists all the installed packages in the system
    - `rpm -qf <filename>`: Shows the package that installed that file
    - `rpm -ql <packagefile>`: Lists all files included in an installed or downloaded package
- **Commands to install, upgrade, and remove:**
    - `rpm -i <packagefile>`: Installs the package, but only if the dependencies are already installed. It won't update an installed package, even if the new one is newer.
    - `rpm -F <packagefile>`: Updates (freshens) a package using an `rpm` file. It will only update if a previous version is already present.
    - `rpm -U <packagefile>`: Updates or installs a package using an `rpm` file. It checks for dependencies but does not manage them.
    - `rpm -e <packagename>`: Removes (erases) the packages specified, keeping the dependencies.

> Although the same RPM format is used in different distributions, it is not possible to install an RPM from one distribution in a different one. Metadata and dependencies (including names and versions) will be slightly different, so proper function is not guaranteed. Only force-install RPM files into a different distribution at your own risk.

If you want to understand the problems that the dependency management system in Zypper solves, try installing packages with `rpm -i`.

There is a database that contains the information required by RPM. It is important to know that all the databases are located in `/var/lib/rpm` and can be managed with the `rpmdb` command.

Nowadays, it is quite rare to use `rpm` directly, except in cases of finding a low-level issue or manually installing some package. If you ever need to do that, it's better to try fixing a broken test system before having to use it in real life.

This should be enough for managing software in SLES systems.

# Summary

In this chapter, we have gone through some basic admin tasks of software management in a SLES system, from subscriptions to installation and repository management, and other miscellaneous tips.

SLES uses Zypper for all tasks related to patching, updating, and managing software. Zypper simplifies managing dependencies, installing the right versions of software, and making sure that all the software is co-installable and compatible. Installing and updating software is very common, with daily or weekly new versions of packages that address errors and vulnerabilities. It is worth dedicating some time to understanding it in depth.

There is still a lot to learn for more advanced certifications on SLES. We haven't gone into the process required to create RPM packages and repositories, and the processes involved to manage, maintain, and distribute internally produced software in your own environments. This is an advanced topic that is not part of the SCA certification. It is something we recommend you learn about once you finish this book.

Now that our systems are up to date, let's move on to learn how to manage them remotely in the upcoming chapter.

# Part 2

# Security with SSH, SELinux, Firewall, and System Permissions

Security in production systems is a direct responsibility of systems administrators. To handle that, SLES 16 includes basic and advanced capabilities such as SELinux, an integrated firewall, and, of course, the standard system permissions. In this part, we explain the security mechanisms in SLES in depth so that you can perform the everyday maintenance tasks.

This part has the following chapters:


- *Chapter 7, Remote Systems Administration*
- *Chapter 8, Enabling and Using Cockpit*
- *Chapter 9, Securing Network Connectivity with firewalld*
- *Chapter 10, Keeping the System Hardened with SELinux*

# 7

# Administering Systems Remotely

When working with systems, once the server has been installed, and often even during the installation itself in **SLES 16** with **Agama** (the new installer), administration can be performed remotely. Once a machine has been installed, the tasks that need to be performed during its life cycle are not that different from the ones that have already been performed.

In this chapter, we will cover (from a connection point of view) how to connect to remote systems, transfer files, and automate the connection so that it can be scripted and make it resilient if issues arise with the network link. Administration tasks that can be performed on the system are the same as the ones we described in previous chapters, such as installing software, configuring additional networking settings, and even managing users.

Since administering a system requires privileged credentials, we will focus on the available tools that are considered to be secure to perform such connections, as well as how to use them to encapsulate other traffic.

We will cover the following topics:

- SSH and OpenSSH overview and base configuration
- Accessing remote systems with SSH
- Key-based authentication with SSH
- SCP/`rsync` – Remote file management
- Advanced remote management – SSH tunnels and SSH redirections
- Remote terminals with `tmux`

By covering these topics, we will be able to master remote system access and bring our administration skills to the next level.

Let's start by talking about the SSH protocol and the OpenSSH client and server in the next section.

# Technical requirements

You can continue using the virtual machine that we created at the beginning of this book in *Chapter 1, Getting SLES 16 Up and Running (Physical and Cloud)*. Any additional packages that are required will be indicated in the text. Any additional files that are required for this chapter can be downloaded from `https://github.com/PacktPublishing/SUSE-Linux-Enterprise-Server-16-Official-Administration-Guide`.

# SSH and OpenSSH overview and base configuration

**Secure Shell Host** (**SSH**) is a standard remote login protocol that uses encryption for connecting to hosts. This way, the credentials that were used for logging in are not transmitted in plain text.

With SSH, a secure channel is created between the client and the target host, even if the connection is performed over untrusted or insecure networks. Here, the SSH channel that's created is secure, and no information is leaked.

There are many implementations of the SSH protocol. In SLES 16, we use OpenSSH, an open source project managed by the OpenBSD team (`https://www.openssh.com/`). It provides both a server and a client part. In SLES 16, the package names are `openssh-server` and `openssh-clients`, respectively. They come already installed, configured, and with the firewall rules to access the SSH port (22), which is opened by the installation we performed so far.

> Knowing that not everything is possible, it is really important for **SUSE Certified Administrator** (**CSA**) certifications (and even higher ones, if you followed that path) to be resourceful. We already know how to install packages and how to check the manual pages that are installed by them, but we can also use those packages to find the necessary configuration files. This skill can be used to find the possible configuration files we need to edit to configure a service or a client. Remember to use `rpm -ql [package]` to review the list of files provided by a package if you cannot remember which one to use. For example, running `rpm -ql openssh-server` will show the files in the `openssh-server` package.

To install and configure SSH in our system if it is not already installed or doesn't come in the image we are using, we can do it by running the following as `root`:

```
# zypper install openssh-server openssh-clients
# systemctl enable --now sshd
# firewall-cmd --add-service ssh
# firewall-cmd --add-service ssh --permanent
```

Now that we are sure the service is properly installed and configured, let's learn more about the OpenSSH server component that comes with our SLES system.

## OpenSSH server

OpenSSH has become standard in many operating systems, both as a server and as a client, to make secure connections between them. **macOS** includes OpenSSH as its default client and server, as well as **SLES** and many other Linux distributions.

The main configuration file for the OpenSSH server is located at `/usr/etc/ssh/sshd_config` (and you can use `man sshd_config` to get detailed information about the different options). If you need to add or change any parameter to the default `sshd` configuration, create a file with a `.conf` extension under `/etc/ssh/sshd_config.d/` and reload the service with `systemctl reload sshd.service`. Some of the most used options are as follows:

- `AcceptEnv`: Defines which environment variables that have been set by the client will be used on the remote host (for example, locale, terminal type, and so on).
- `AllowGroups`: A list of system groups that a user should be a member of to get access to the system. If the user is not a member of any of these groups, access will be denied.
- `AllowTcpForwarding`: Allows us to forward ports using the SSH connection (we will discuss this later in this chapter, in the *Advanced remote management – SSH tunnels and SSH redirections* section).
- `DisableForwarding`: Takes precedence over other forwarding options, making it easier to restrict the service.
- `AuthenticationMethods`: Defines which authentication methods can be used, such as disabling password-based access.
- `Banner`: Files to send to the connecting user before authentication is allowed. This defaults to having no banner, which might also reveal who is running the service that might be providing too much data to possible attackers.
- `Ciphers`: A list of valid ciphers to use when you're interacting with the server. You can use + or - to enable or disable them.

- `ListenAddress`: The hostname or address and port where the `sshd` daemon should be listening for incoming connections.
- `PasswordAuthentication`: Defaults to yes and can be disabled to block users from interactively connecting to the system unless a public/private key pair is used.
- `PermitEmptyPasswords`: Allows accounts with no password to access the system. The default value is `no`.
- `PermitRootLogin`: Defines how login works for the user root, for example, to prevent the root user from connecting remotely with a password. The default in SLES 16 for `root` login is `prohibit-password`, which means that `root` can only log in with an SSH key and not with a password.
- `Port`: Related to `ListenAddress`, this defaults to `22`. It's the port number where the `sshd` daemon listens for incoming connections.
- `Subsystem`: Configures the command for the external subsystem. For example, it is used with `sftp` for file transfers.
- `X11Forwarding`: Defines whether `X11` forwarding is permitted so that remote users can open graphical programs on their local display by tunneling the connection.

The following screenshot shows the options that are installed by our system while we're removing comments:

```
geeko:~ # grep -v ^# /usr/etc/ssh/sshd_config | sort -u

AcceptEnv LANG LC_CTYPE LC_NUMERIC LC_TIME LC_COLLATE LC_MONETARY LC_MESSAGES
AcceptEnv LC_IDENTIFICATION LC_ALL
AcceptEnv LC_PAPER LC_NAME LC_ADDRESS LC_TELEPHONE LC_MEASUREMENT
AuthorizedKeysFile      .ssh/authorized_keys
Include /etc/ssh/sshd_config.d/*.conf
Include /usr/etc/ssh/sshd_config.d/*.conf
PrintMotd no
Subsystem       sftp    /usr/libexec/ssh/sftp-server
UsePAM yes
X11Forwarding yes
geeko:~ # grep -v ^# /usr/etc/ssh/sshd_config.d/* | sort -u

Include /etc/crypto-policies/back-ends/opensshserver.config
geeko:~ # grep -v ^# /etc/ssh/sshd_config.d/* | sort -u
PermitRootLogin Yes
geeko:~ #
```

*Figure 7.1 – Values at installation time defined in /etc/ssh/sshd_config; this includes the openssh-server-config-rootlogin package*

We'll check the client part of the configuration in the next section.

## OpenSSH client

The client part of OpenSSH has its system-wide defaults in the `/usr/etc/ssh/ssh_config` file. You can add system-wide customizations to it in the files in the `/etc/ssh/ssh_config.d/` folder. Users can also have personal configuration in the `~/.ssh/config` file.

> The ~ directory is an alias for the user's home directory. You can identify which one it is by running `echo $HOME`. For regular users, it is often a folder with the name of the user under `/home`.

Usually, the system-wide file just contains some comments, not actual settings, so we will be focusing on the per-user configuration file and command-line parameters.

One example entry in our `~/.ssh/config` file could be as follows:

```
Host jump
    Hostname jump.example.com
    User root
    Compression yes
    StrictHostKeyChecking no
    ProxyCommand connect-proxy -H squid.example.com:3128 %h %p
    ControlPath ~/.ssh/master-%r@%h:%p
    ControlMaster auto
```

In the previous example, we defined an entry named `jump` (which we can use with `ssh jump`) that will connect the `root` username to the `jump.example.com` host.

This is a basic setting, but we're also defining that we'll be using a helper program in `ProxyCommand` that will make use of a proxy server on `squid.example.com` on port `3128` to connect to the `%h` host and the `%p` port to reach our target system. Additionally, we're making use of `Compression` to compress and decompress the data sent and received, and using `ControlMaster` to share multiple sessions with one single connection.

One feature that has security implications is `StrictHostKeyChecking`. When we connect to a host for the first time, keys are exchanged between the client and the host, and the server identifies itself with the keys that are used. If they're accepted, they will be stored in the `.ssh/known_hosts` file at the user's home directory.

If the remote host key is changed, a warning will be printed on the SSH client's terminal, and the connection will be refused. However, if we set `StrictHostKeyChecking` to `no`, we will accept any key that's sent by the server, which might be useful if we're using a test system that gets redeployed frequently (and thus, generates a new host key). It is not recommended to be used in general, since it protects us from a server being replaced and also from someone impersonating the server we want to connect to with a server that, for example, logs usernames and passwords to access our system later.

In the next section, we will learn about accessing remote systems with SSH.

# Accessing remote systems with SSH

SSH, as we mentioned earlier in this chapter, is a protocol that's used to securely connect to remote systems. In general, the syntax, in its most basic form, is just executing the `ssh` command in your terminal, adding a hostname or IP address after it, to indicate to which system we should connect. We can also specify the user we want to use, adding it before the hostname and separating it with the @ symbol, as in this example:

```
> ssh user@geeko.suse.test
```

The SSH client will then initiate a connection to the SSH server on the target host, using the username provided (or if none is provided, the currently logged-in user by default), and will try to reach the remote server on port `22/tcp`, which is the default for the SSH service.

In the following screenshot, we can connect from our system to `localhost`, which means we will be connecting to our own server:

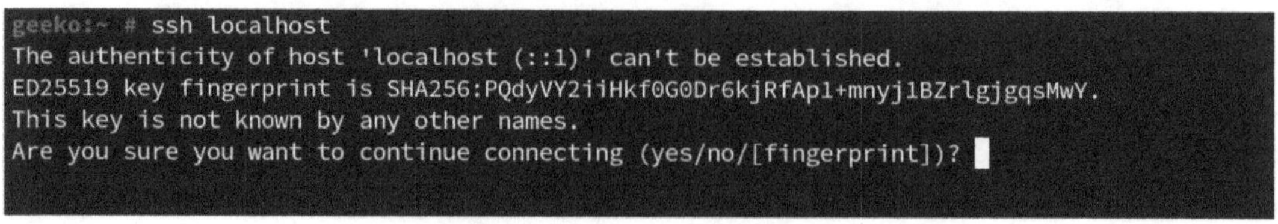


*Figure 7.2 – Initiating an SSH connection to localhost*

> The name *localhost* is reserved to reference the machine we are working with. It can be used in many ways, such as in your own laptop to run an application and connect to it even without any other external network. It has an associated network device called `lo`, also known as the loopback device, and associated IPv4 `127.0.0.1` and IPv6 `::1` addresses.

In the preceding screenshot, we can see how the first interaction with the server prints the fingerprint of the server to authenticate it, to ensure that you are connecting to the server you want to connect to. This is what was discussed in the previous section: that is, `StrictHostKeyChecking`. Once accepted, if the host key changes, the connection will be denied until we manually remove the older key to confirm that we're aware of the server change.

Let's add the key and try again, as shown in the following screenshot:

```
geeko:~ # ssh localhost
(root@localhost) Password:
Last login: Wed Apr  9 10:06:52 CEST 2025 from 192.168.122.1 on ssh
Web console: https://geeko.suse.test:9090/ or https://192.168.122.16:9090/

Have a lot of fun...
geeko:~ #
```

*Figure 7.3 – The SSH connection to localhost accepted*

On our second attempt, the connection succeeded, and we are in. We might want to avoid being able to access the system as `root`. To do so, we can change the content of `/etc/ssh/sshd_config.d/permit-root.conf` and set the `PermitRootLogin` variable to `No`. Then, reload the `sshd` service and try again:

```
geeko:~ # cat /etc/ssh/sshd_config.d/permit-root.conf
PermitRootLogin Yes
geeko:~ # echo "PermitRootLogin No" > /etc/ssh/sshd_config.d/permit-root.conf
geeko:~ # cat /etc/ssh/sshd_config.d/permit-root.conf
PermitRootLogin No
geeko:~ # systemctl reload sshd.service
geeko:~ # ssh localhost
(root@localhost) Password:
(root@localhost) Password:
(root@localhost) Password:
root@localhost's password:
Permission denied, please try again.
root@localhost's password:
```

*Figure 7.4 – SSH connection as root denied*

You can see that after using the right password three times, we finally get a `Permission denied` message.

In general, password authentication can be a security risk as the keyboard might be intercepted, someone might be looking over your shoulder, a brute-force attack might be used against the accounts, and so on. Due to this, it's common practice to at least disable it for the `root` user, meaning that someone trying to log in to the system should know the username and password, and from there, use the system tools to become `root`.

Let's learn how to log in to remote systems without having to use passwords by using authentication keys.

# Key-based authentication with SSH

One big advantage of SSH connections is that commands can be given to be executed on remote hosts, for example, to grab updated data that can be used for monitoring without requiring a specific agent on the host. This is the same mechanism used by Ansible to automate tasks, using SSH as the connection mechanism.

Having to provide login details on each connection is not something that we could consider an improvement to the user experience, but SSH also allows us to create a **key pair** that can be used for authentication to remote systems, so that no password or credential input is required.

The key pairs contain two parts, also referred to as **keys**: a **public key** that must be added to each host we want to connect to, and a **private key** that must be secured as it will be used to identify us while we're trying to connect to remote hosts. Some services, such as GitHub, request that you upload your public key so you can use it to authenticate and transfer your repository changes. Never upload your private key anywhere; you have to keep it in the least number of places possible, as it is the one thing that identifies you.

First of all, let's create one key pair for authentication.

> It is recommended to have at least one key pair per use case. For example, we can keep several SSH key pairs to be used in different roles, such as personal systems, production systems, lab systems, and so on. Having to specify the key pair for connecting is an extra security measure: we cannot connect to production systems unless we use the production key pair.

To create a key pair, we can use the `ssh-keygen` tool, which has several options for the key we are creating, as shown in the following screenshot:

```
        ssh-keygen -F hostname [-lv] [-f known_hosts_file]
        ssh-keygen -H [-f known_hosts_file]
        ssh-keygen -K [-a rounds] [-w provider]
        ssh-keygen -R hostname [-f known_hosts_file]
        ssh-keygen -r hostname [-g] [-f input_keyfile]
        ssh-keygen -M generate [-O option] output_file
        ssh-keygen -M screen [-f input_file] [-O option] output_file
        ssh-keygen -I certificate_identity -s ca_key [-hU] [-D pkcs11_provider]
                   [-n principals] [-O option] [-V validity_interval]
                   [-z serial_number] file ...
        ssh-keygen -L [-f input_keyfile]
        ssh-keygen -A [-a rounds] [-f prefix_path]
        ssh-keygen -k -f krl_file [-u] [-s ca_public] [-z version_number]
                   file ...
        ssh-keygen -Q [-l] -f krl_file [file ...]
        ssh-keygen -Y find-principals -s signature_file -f allowed_signers_file
        ssh-keygen -Y match-principals -I signer_identity -f allowed_signers_file
        ssh-keygen -Y check-novalidate -n namespace -s signature_file
        ssh-keygen -Y sign -f key_file -n namespace file [-O option] ...
        ssh-keygen -Y verify -f allowed_signers_file -I signer_identity
                   -n namespace -s signature_file [-r krl_file] [-O option]
geeko:~ #
```

*Figure 7.5 – The ssh-keygen options*

When we run `ssh-keygen` with no arguments provided, by default, it will create a key for the current user and ask for a password for the key. Let's do it: use the defaults and provide no values. Then, hit `Enter` when you are requested to provide a password; this will provide a blank one. We will get an output such as the one shown in the following screenshot:

```
geeko:~ # ssh-keygen
Generating public/private ed25519 key pair.
Enter file in which to save the key (/root/.ssh/id_ed25519):
Enter passphrase for "/root/.ssh/id_ed25519" (empty for no passphrase):
Enter same passphrase again:
Your identification has been saved in /root/.ssh/id_ed25519
Your public key has been saved in /root/.ssh/id_ed25519.pub
The key fingerprint is:
SHA256:KbzpLLZB1ycs78O/m/eEr6z2GHvlx1eOx0ZCyjw8QVA root@geeko.suse.test
The key's randomart image is:
+--[ED25519 256]--+
|          .oE    |
|            .    |
|            .    |
|    . o .   . .  |
|   . = S .+ +    |
|  . . * o  B.o o|
|   . o.. . .=.B.|
|    o+ .o .*ooo O|
|  ..oo .+OB+oo+.|
+----[SHA256]-----+
geeko:~ #
```

*Figure 7.6 – ssh-keygen execution creating an RSA key pair under ~/.ssh/{id_ed25519,id_ed25519.pub}*

From this point on, this system has created a key pair for the `root` user, and it has stored the two pieces of it in the same folder, which is `.ssh` in the user's home directory by default:

- The public key contains the `.pub` suffix. In this case, it is `/root/.ssh/id_ed25519.pub`. This is the file we can share and upload to different hosts and services, such as GitHub.
- The private key is the one without a suffix, which, in this case, is `/root/.ssh/id_ed25519`. This is the file we must keep private.

How do we use them? If we look inside the `.ssh` folder in our home directory, we can see several files, including an `authorized_keys` file and a `known_hosts` file, in addition to the key pair we have just created.

The `authorized_keys` file will contain one entry per line. This contains the public keys that can be used to log in to this system for this user.

> The vast range of options that can be used with `authorized_keys` goes further than adding just regular keys – you can also define commands to execute, expiry times for keys, remote hosts that can be used to connect so that only those hosts will be able to use that key successfully, and many more. Again, the `man sshd` command is your friend. So, check out the `AUTHORIZED_KEYS FILE FORMAT` section there to learn about more complex setups.

To simplify how keys are set up on remote systems, we have the `ssh-copy-id` utility, which connects via SSH to the remote host. This will ask for the SSH password and install the available public keys on our system. However, this requires the system to have password authentication enabled.

The alternate method consists of manually appending our public key to that file (`.ssh/authorized_keys`), as shown in the following screenshot:

```
geeko:~ # ssh-copy-id localhost
/usr/bin/ssh-copy-id: INFO: Source of key(s) to be installed: "/root/.ssh/id_ed25519.pub"
/usr/bin/ssh-copy-id: INFO: attempting to log in with the new key(s), to filter out any th
at are already installed
/usr/bin/ssh-copy-id: INFO: 1 key(s) remain to be installed -- if you are prompted now it
is to install the new keys
(root@localhost) Password:

Number of key(s) added: 1

Now try logging into the machine, with: "ssh 'localhost'"
and check to make sure that only the key(s) you wanted were added.

geeko:~ # cat .ssh/authorized_keys

ssh-ed25519 AAAAC3NzaC1lZDI1NTE5AAAAINy8SBjWFwVhqpmRpQKwLG9M6cxGVM3nCOO7ruXJQ8b5 root@geek
o.suse.test
geeko:~ # cat .ssh/id_ed25519.pub
ssh-ed25519 AAAAC3NzaC1lZDI1NTE5AAAAINy8SBjWFwVhqpmRpQKwLG9M6cxGVM3nCOO7ruXJQ8b5 root@geek
o.suse.test
geeko:~ #
```

*Figure 7.7 – ssh-copy-id running and manual check of public key added to authorized keys*

The first command we used is `ssh-copy-id`, which copies the content of `public_key` to the system we want to connect to the `authorized_keys` file. In this case, as we are using `localhost`; it is the same system, which is easier to compare. Finally, we can now connect to `localhost` with SSH and execute a command without having to provide a password.

> The permissions for the `.ssh` folder and the `authorized_keys` file must not be too wide open (for example, everybody can read or write to it). If this is the case, the SSH daemon will refuse to use it, as someone could have appended new keys and tried to gain access without really being a legitimate user of the system.

In the following screenshot, we can see that once we set `PasswordAuthentication` to `No`, the system doesn't ask for the password. It will rely only on key pairs to provide SSH access. As we have already uploaded our public key, we can access the system:

```
geeko:~ # echo "PasswordAuthentication No" > /etc/ssh/sshd_config.d/no-password-auth.conf
geeko:~ # systemctl reload sshd.service
geeko:~ # ssh localhost
Last login: Mon Apr 14 12:21:31 CEST 2025 from ::1 on ssh
Web console: https://geeko.suse.test:9090/ or https://192.168.122.16:9090/

Have a lot of fun...
geeko:~ #
```

*Figure 7.8 – Restricting password access to our system; we can still access it using SSH key pairs*

What just happened opens a new world of automation. Using the keys being exchanged between our system and the remote hosts, we can now connect remotely to them to run commands interactively or to script commands to be executed.

We can check the results in our terminal. Let's consider this simple script for a system load average check, which is available at `https://github.com/PacktPublishing/SUSE-Linux-Enterprise-Server-16-Official-Administration-Guide/tree/main/chapter-07-remote-systems-administration`:

> Key pair authentication and passwordless login are the default ways to function in all major cloud providers. This way, you avoid having an intrusion by someone attacking your system using brute-force password guessing.

```
#!/usr/bin/bash
for system in host1 host2 host3 host4;
do
    echo "${system}: $(ssh ${system} cat /proc/
loadavg)"
done
```

In this example, we're running a loop to connect to four systems and then outputting the name and the load average of that system, as shown in the following screenshot:

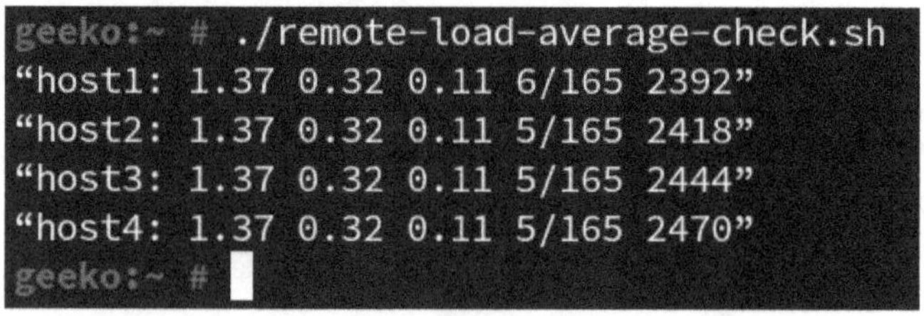


*Figure 7.9 – Passwordless login to four hosts to check their load average*

As we can see, we quickly grabbed the information from four hosts over SSH. If you want to test this in your environment, you might want to put into practice what we learned about creating entries in the `/etc/hosts` file, which points to `127.0.0.1` for the hostnames we want to try, so that the connection goes to your own practice system, as we explained in *Chapter 5, Enabling Network Connectivity*.

Now, think about the different options we have for administering our systems remotely:

- Check IPs for a range of hosts
- Install updates or add/remove one package
- Check the local time in case the system has drifted
- Restart one service after adding a new user to the system

Many more options exist, but these are the ones we have already learned in this book. Keep this in mind when moving forward.

Of course, there are more suitable tools for remotely administering systems and ensuring that errors are detected and handled properly, such as using Ansible. But in this case, for simple tasks, we are good to go.

Previously, we created a key and replied by pressing "Enter" when we were asked for a password, which provided a blank one. What if we had typed one in? We'll look at this in the next section.

# SSH agent

If we decide to create an SSH key with a password to protect it (good choice), we will need to input the password each time we want to use the key. So, in the end, it might be as insecure as having to type in the password, as someone might be checking over our shoulder. To overcome this, we can use a program called `ssh-agent`, which temporarily keeps the password in memory. This is convenient and reduces the chances of someone watching while you type in your key.

When you're using a graphical desktop, such as **GNOME**, as provided by SLES 16, the agent might already be set up to start at session login. If you're using a console (local or remote), the agent must be started manually by executing `ssh-agent`.

When `ssh-agent` is executed, it will output some variables that must be set in our environment so that we can make use of it, as shown in the following screenshot:

```
geeko:~ # ssh-agent
SSH_AUTH_SOCK=/tmp/ssh-XXXXXXy4F4Eb/agent.3887; export SSH_AUTH_SOCK;
SSH_AGENT_PID=3888; export SSH_AGENT_PID;
echo Agent pid 3888;
geeko:~ # echo $SSH_AUTH_SOCK "-" $SSH_AGENT_PID
-
geeko:~ # eval $(ssh-agent)
Agent pid 3890
geeko:~ # echo $SSH_AUTH_SOCK "-" $SSH_AGENT_PID
/tmp/ssh-XXXXXXp1FW6f/agent.3889 - 3890
geeko:~ #
```

*Figure 7.10 – ssh-agent being used to set the required variables*

As shown in the preceding screenshot, before being executed, or just while we're executing the agent, the variables are undefined. However, if we were to execute `eval $(ssh-agent)`, we would accomplish the goal of having the variables defined and ready to use.

The next step is to add the keys to the agent. This can be accomplished with the `ssh-add` command, which can be used without parameters or by specifying the key to be added. If the key requires a password, we will be prompted for it. Once we're done, we might be able to use that key to log in to the systems with the password that's being cached until we exit the session that executed the agent, thus clearing the password from memory.

The following screenshot shows the command that was used to generate a new key pair with a password. Here, we can see that the only difference is that we're storing it in a file named `withpass` rather than what we did earlier in this chapter:

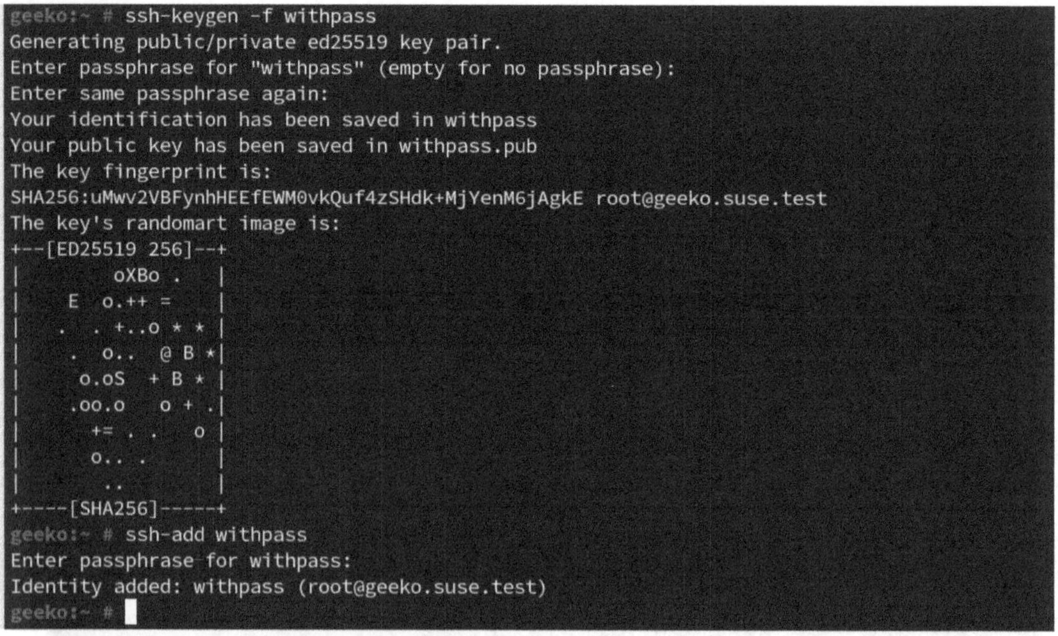


*Figure 7.11 – Creating an additional SSH key pair with a password*

In the next screenshot, you can see how we connect to `localhost`. We added the public key with a password to `.ssh/authorized_keys` and deleted the one without a password to test the connection behavior:

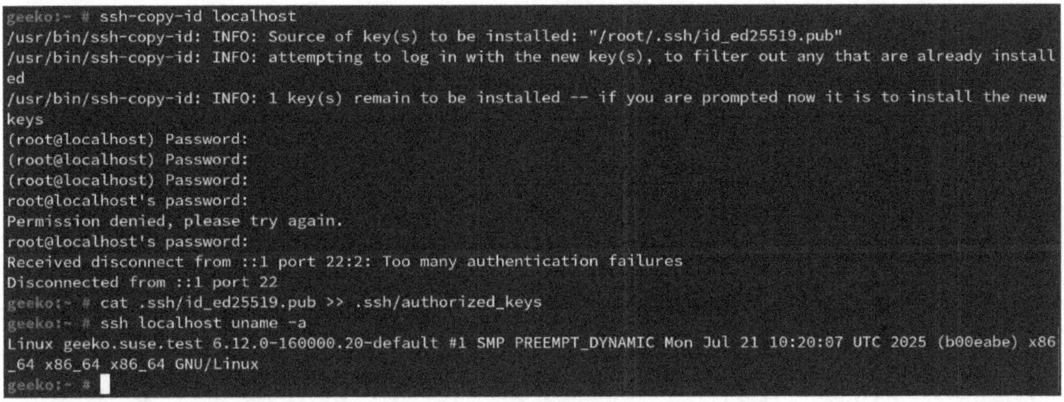


*Figure 7.12 – Using ssh-agent to remember our password*

To make this clearer, let's analyze what's happening:

1. First, we `ssh` to the host. Permission is denied as the default key we used was removed from `authorized_keys`.
2. We `ssh` again, but while defining the identity file (the key pair) to connect to, as we can see, we're asked for the password for the key, not for logging in to the system.
3. Then, we log out, and the connection is closed.
4. Next, we try to add the key, and we get an error because we have not set the environment variables for the agent.
5. As instructed when we introduced the agent, we execute the command for loading the environment variables for the agent in the current shell.
6. When we try to add the key with `ssh-add withpass`, the agent asks for our password.
7. When we finally `ssh` to the host, we can connect without a password as the key is in memory for our key pair.

Here, we have achieved two things: we now have an automated/unattended method to connect to systems and have ensured that only authorized users will know the password to unlock them.

We'll learn how to do remote file management in the next section!

# SCP/rsync – Remote file management

Several services were replaced with SSH on many systems, and one of them was the insecure protocol for file transfer known as **File Transfer Protocol** (**FTP**). It uses a communication that transfers data in plain text, and it was a perfect target for intercepting credentials. FTP is hardly ever used today, and where it is, it is mostly for serving publicly available files on servers that only allow anonymous access.

SSH by default enables two interfaces for copying files: `scp` and `sftp`. The first one is used in a similar way to the regular `cp` command, but here, we're accepting remote hosts as our target or source, while `sftp` uses a client approach similar to the traditional `ftp` command that interacts with FTP servers. Just remember that in both cases, the connection is encrypted and happens over port `22/tcp` on the target host.

We'll dig into `scp` next.

## Transferring files with an OpenSSH secure file copy (scp)

The `scp` command, which is part of the `openssh-clients` package, allows us to copy files between systems using the `ssh` layer for the whole process. This allows us to securely transfer a file's contents, plus all the automation capabilities that were introduced by key pair login, to various systems.

To set up this example, we will use the user created during installation (named `user` in our sample system), which will be used to copy over files using the tools described in this section, as shown in the following screenshot:

```
[miperez@lightning:~]$ ssh-copy-id user@geeko
/usr/bin/ssh-copy-id: INFO: Source of key(s) to be installed: ssh-add -L
/usr/bin/ssh-copy-id: INFO: attempting to log in with the new key(s), to filter out any th
at are already installed
/usr/bin/ssh-copy-id: INFO: 2 key(s) remain to be installed -- if you are prompted now it
is to install the new keys
(user@geeko) Password:

Number of key(s) added: 2

Now try logging into the machine, with: "ssh 'user@geeko'"
and check to make sure that only the key(s) you wanted were added.

[miperez@lightning:~]$ ssh user@geeko
Last login: Mon Apr 14 17:02:48 CEST 2025 from 192.168.122.1 on ssh
Have a lot of fun...
user@geeko:~>
```

*Figure 7.13 – Checking and preparing our system with a user to practice file transfers*

Once our public key has been added to `user@geeko`, we can start testing!

Let's analyze each part of the command using this template:

```
scp origin target
```

In our case, `origin` will be a local file, for example, `/etc/hosts`.

Our target is a remote host. Here, the username is `user`, the host is our test system (geeko), and the folder you should store the files in is the default one, usually the home folder of the user indicated (the one with an empty path after the `:` symbol).

In the following screenshot, we can see the output of the `scp /etc/hosts user@geeko:` command and the validation we can perform later via remote execution:

*Figure 7.14 – Copying SCP files to a remote path and validating the files that have been copied*

In the preceding screenshot, you can also check that the files that were owned by the `root` user are copied. The copied ones are owned by `user`, so the file's contents are the same. But since the creator of the target is `user`, the ownership of these files is also `user`.

We can also make more complex copies by indicating remote files first and the local path as targets so that we download files to our system, or even copy files across remote locations for both the origin and target (unless we specify the `-3` option, they will go directly from `origin` to `target`).

> Time for a reminder! `man scp` will show you all the available options for the `scp` command, but since it is based on SSH, most of the options we use with SSH are available, as well as the host definitions we made in the `.ssh/config` file.

Let's explore the `sftp` client next.

## Transferring files with sftp

Compared to `scp`, which can be scripted in the same way we can script with the regular `cp` command, `sftp` has an interactive client for navigating a remote system. However, it can also automatically retrieve files when a path containing files is specified.

To learn about the different commands that are available, you can invoke the `help` command, which will list the available options, as shown in the following screenshot:

```
geeko:~ # sftp localhost
Connected to localhost.
sftp> help
Available commands:
bye                                Quit sftp
cd path                            Change remote directory to 'path'
chgrp [-h] grp path                Change group of file 'path' to 'grp'
chmod [-h] mode path               Change permissions of file 'path' to 'mode'
chown [-h] own path                Change owner of file 'path' to 'own'
copy oldpath newpath               Copy remote file
cp oldpath newpath                 Copy remote file
df [-hi] [path]                    Display statistics for current directory or
                                   filesystem containing 'path'
exit                               Quit sftp
get [-afpR] remote [local]         Download file
help                               Display this help text
lcd path                           Change local directory to 'path'
lls [ls-options [path]]            Display local directory listing
lmkdir path                        Create local directory
ln [-s] oldpath newpath            Link remote file (-s for symlink)
lpwd                               Print local working directory
ls [-1afhlnrSt] [path]             Display remote directory listing
lumask umask                       Set local umask to 'umask'
```

*Figure 7.15 – Available sftp interactive mode commands*

Let's look at an example of using `sftp` with the help of the following screenshot:

```
geeko:~ # mkdir getfiles
geeko:~ # cd getfiles/
geeko:~/getfiles # sftp localhost
Connected to localhost.
sftp> ls
$MYVIMDIR                        bin                              getfiles
remote-load-average-check.sh     withpass                         withpass.pub
sftp> mget withpass*
Fetching /root/withpass to withpass
withpass                                          100%  464    984.4KB/s   00:00
Fetching /root/withpass.pub to withpass.pub
withpass.pub                                      100%  102    240.4KB/s   00:00
sftp> quit
geeko:~/getfiles # ls -l
total 8
-rw-------. 1 root root 464 Apr 14 17:18 withpass
-rw-r--r--. 1 root root 102 Apr 14 17:18 withpass.pub
geeko:~/getfiles #
```

*Figure 7.16 – Operation with sftp — Interactive transfer*

In this example, we've created a local folder to be our work folder, called `getfiles`. First, we have invoked `sftp localhost`, reaching the default remote path. This starts interactive mode. In this, we can execute several commands, similar to what we can do on a remote shell session. Finally, using the `mget withpass*` command with the `*` wildcard character, we transferred the files to our local system.

In both cases, the files have been transferred from the remote system to our local system, so our goal has been accomplished. However, using `scp` requires knowing the exact path of the files you want to transfer. On the other hand, it might be a bit more user-friendly to navigate the system using the `ls` and `cd` commands within the `sftp` interactive client until we reach the files we want to transfer, if we can't remember them.

Now, let's learn how to quickly transfer files and full directory trees with `rsync`.

# Transferring files with rsync

Although we can use the `-r` option of `scp` to transfer files recursively, `scp` only handles the full copy of the file, which is not ideal if we are just keeping some folders in sync across systems.

In 1996, `rsync` was launched, and many systems implemented it by using a dedicated server that was listening to client connections. This was to allow full directory trees to be synchronized with files. This was done by copying over the differences between the files. Here, we compared parts of the source and destination to see whether there were differences that should be copied over.

With SSH, and with the `rsync` package installed on both the client and the server, we can take advantage of the secure channel that's created by SSH and the faster synchronization provided by `rsync`.

The difference between using the `rsync` daemon and using SSH is the syntax for the source or destination, which either uses the `rsync://` protocol or `::` after the hostname. In other cases, it will use SSH or even the local filesystem.

To get basic help and info on the schema for URLs, we can run the `rsync -help` command.

Now, let's review some of the useful options we can use with `rsync`:

- `-v`: Provides more verbose output during the transfer
- `-r`: Recurses into directories
- `-u`: Updates – only copies files that are newer than the ones at the target
- `-a`: Archive (this includes several options, such as `-rlptgoD`)
- `-X`: Preserves extended attributes

- `-A`: Preserves **Access Control Lists (ACLs)**
- `-S`: Sparse – sequences of nulls will be converted into sparse blocks, which reduces time and bandwidth usage
- `--preallocate`: Claims the space that's required for files before transferring them
- `--delete-during`: Deletes files on the target that are not hosted during the copy
- `--delete-before`: Deletes files on the target that are not hosted before the copy
- `--progress`: Shows progress information on the copy (copied files versus total files)

The `rsync` algorithm breaks the file into chunks and calculates checksums for each that are transmitted to the source, so it can verify that each chunk was transmitted correctly. They are then compared to the ones for local files. `rsync` doesn't check the modification file date and size by default, only the checksum, unless a check is forced for each file candidate to be transferred.

Let's look at a basic example.

`rsync -avr getfiles/ newfolder/` will copy the files in the local `getfiles/` folder to `newfolder/` by showing a progress update, but only for the updated files, as shown in the following screenshot:

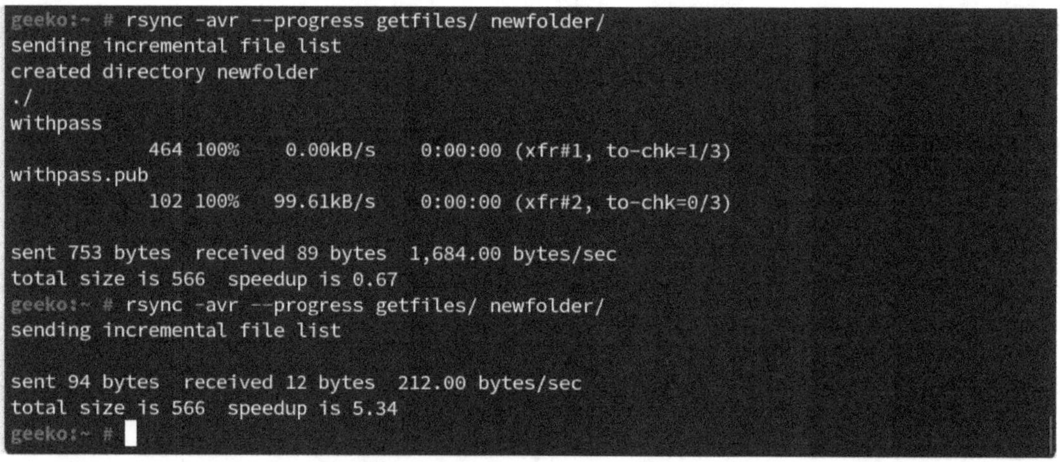


*Figure 7.17 – The rsync operation being used on the same source/destination, repeated to illustrate transfer optimization*

As we can see, the second operation just sent 94 bytes and received 12 bytes. This is because there was a little checksum operation happening internally to validate across the folders, because the files hadn't been changed. The same output can be obtained if we use the remote target approach with `rsync -avr --progress getfiles/ root@localhost:newfolder/`. But in this case, SSH transport will be used.

Let's get some bigger sample files and compare them by checking out a Git repository at some point in time, transferring the files, then updating to the latest version to simulate work on the repository. Then, we will synchronize again.

First, let's install Git if it's not installed and check out a sample repository by executing the following code:

```
geeko:~ # zypper --non-interactive install git
geeko:~ # git clone https://github.com/mmmmmmpc/liberate-formula
geeko:~ # cd liberate-formula
geeko:~/liberate-formula # git reset HEAD~10
geeko:~/liberate-formula # cd ..
```

At this point, we have a folder cloned from a Git repository with the last 10 changes removed; the files are ready for transfer. Once we've done this, we'll execute `git pull` to sync with the latest changes and use `rsync` again to copy the differences. Later, we'll use `--delete` to remove any files that no longer exist on the source.

Let's run `rsync -avr --progress liberate-formula localhost:backup/`. Check out the sequence shown in the following screenshot:

```
             41 100%   40.04kB/s    0:00:00 (xfr#35, to-chk=3/56)
liberate-formula/.git/refs/remotes/
liberate-formula/.git/refs/remotes/origin/
liberate-formula/.git/refs/remotes/origin/HEAD
             30 100%   29.30kB/s    0:00:00 (xfr#36, to-chk=1/56)
liberate-formula/.git/refs/tags/
liberate-formula/liberate/
liberate-formula/liberate/init.sls
          3,972 100%    3.79MB/s    0:00:00 (xfr#37, to-chk=0/56)

sent 132,572 bytes  received 832 bytes  266,808.00 bytes/sec
total size is 129,307  speedup is 0.97
geeko:~ #
```

*Figure 7.18 – Synchronizing the Git folder to a new folder with rsync*

In the preceding screenshot, pay attention to the speedup that's reported in the latest line of the command.

Now, let's execute `cd liberate-formula` and then `git pull` to get the 10 changes we were missing, and repeat `rsync` again. We will get an output similar to the following:

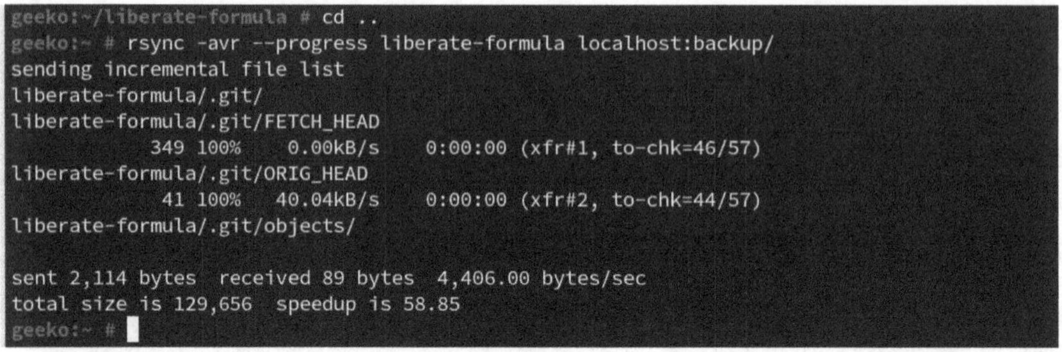


*Figure 7.19 – Using rsync again to copy over the differences*

In the preceding screenshot, pay attention to the speedup reported in the last line so that you can compare it with the previous one.

From this sequence of screenshots, we can check the last numbers for the total bytes that were sent to see the improvement in transfer, along with some of the files that were received (because we added the `-v` modifier to get verbose output and `--progress`).

The biggest advantage comes when a copy is performed over slower network links, and it's performed periodically, for example, as a way to copy to an off-site copy for backup purposes. This is because `rsync` will only copy the changes, update the newer files that have been modified on the source, and allow us to use compression over the `ssh` channel. For example, the Linux kernel at `https://www.kernel.org/` can be mirrored using `rsync`.

In the next section, we will dig into a very interesting feature of SSH to make connecting to servers with no direct access easy.

# Advanced remote management – SSH tunnels and SSH redirections

SSH has two really powerful features: SSH tunnels and SSH redirections. When an SSH connection is established, it can not only be used to send commands to the remote host and let us work on them as if they were our local system, but we can also create tunnels that interconnect our systems.

Let's try to imagine a scenario that is common in many companies, where a VPN is used to reach the internal network with all the services and servers, but with SSH instead of a regular VPN.

So, let's put some context into this imaginary scenario.

We can use a host that gets external traffic for SSH, redirected from our internet router to the SSH service in that system. So, in brief, our router gets connections on port 22 via TCP, and the connection is forwarded to our server. We will be naming this server `bastion` in this exercise.

With this in place, our common sense tells us that we will be able to reach that `bastion` host via SSH, even if we can use other tools or even SSH itself to connect to other systems later.

Can we connect directly to other hosts in the internal network? The answer is yes, because, by default, SSH allows us to use TCP forwarding (the `sshd_config` setting `AllowTcpForwarding`), which empowers us, as remote login users, to create port redirections and even a **SOCKS** proxy to be used for our connections.

For example, we can create a tunnel using that `bastion` host to reach our internal mail server via **Internet Message Access Protocol** (**IMAP**) and **Simple Mail Transfer Protocol** (**SMTP**) by just executing the following code:

```
ssh -L 10993:imap.example.com:993 -L 10025:smtp.example.com:25 user@
bastionhost
```

This command will listen on local ports `10993` and `10025`. All the connections that are performed there will be tunneled until `bastionhost` connects those to `imap.example.com` at port `993` and `smtp.example.com` at port `25`. This allows our local system to configure our email account using those custom ports and use `localhost` as the server, and still be able to reach those services.

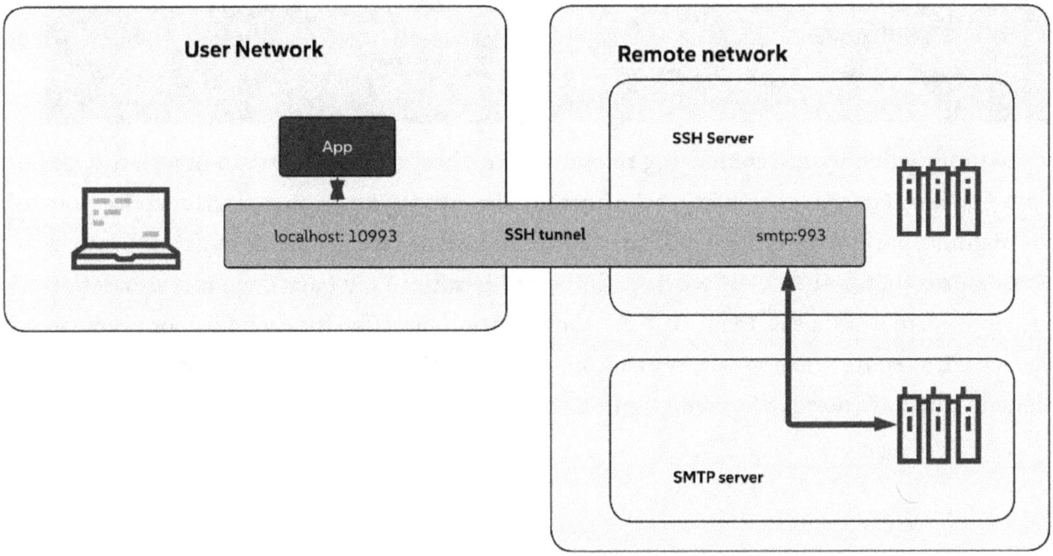


*Figure 7.20 – SSH tunnel diagram redirecting port 10993 to port 993 in a remote server in the same network as the SSH server*

Ports under 1024 are considered privileged ports and, usually, only the `root` user can bind services to those ports. That's why we use them for our redirection ports, `10025` and `10093`, so that those can be used by a regular user instead of requiring the `root` user to perform the SSH connection. Pay attention to SSH messages when you're trying to bind to local ports in case those are in use, as the connections might fail.

Additionally, from the target server's point of view, the connections will appear as if they originated in the `bastion` server, as it's the one effectively performing the connections.

When the list of open ports starts to grow, it is better to go back to what we explained at the beginning of this chapter; the `~/.ssh/config` file can hold the host definition, along with the redirections we want to create, as shown in this example:

```
Host bastion
    ProxyCommand none
    Compression yes
    User myuser
    HostName mybastion.example.com
    Port 330
    LocalForward 2224 mail.example.com:993
    LocalForward 2025 smtp.example.com:25
    LocalForward 2227 ldap.example.com:389
    DynamicForward 9999
```

In this example, when we are connecting to our `bastion` host (via `ssh bastion`), we are automatically enabling `Compression`, setting the host to connect to `mybastion.example.com` at port `330`, and defining port forwarding for our `imap`, `smtp`, and `ldap` servers and one dynamic forward (the SOCKS proxy) at port `9999`. If we have different identities (key pairs), we can also define the one we wish to use via the `IdentityFile` configuration directive for each host, or even use wildcards such as `Host *.example.com` to automatically apply those options to hosts ending in that domain that have no specific configuration stanza.

> Sometimes, while using `ssh`, `scp`, or `sftp`, the goal is to reach a system that is accessible from a `bastion` host. Other port forwarding is not needed here – only reaching those systems is required. In this case, you can use the handy `-J` command-line option (equivalent to defining a `ProxyJump` directive) to use that host as a jump host to the final target you want to reach. For example, `ssh -J bastion mywebsiteserver.example.com` will transparently connect to `bastion` and jump from there to `mywebsiteserver.example.com`.

In the next section, we will learn how to protect ourselves from network issues with our remote connections and get the most out of our remote terminal connections.

# Remote terminals with tmux

`tmux` is a terminal multiplexer, which means that it allows us to open and access several terminals within a single screen. A good similitude would be a window manager in a graphical desktop, which allows us to open several windows so that we can switch context while using only one monitor.

`tmux` also allows us to detach and reattach to the sessions, so it's the perfect tool in case our connection drops. Think, for example, about performing a software upgrade on a server. If, for whatever reason, the connection drops, it will be equivalent to abruptly stopping the upgrade process in whatever status it was at that moment, which can lead to bad consequences. However, if the upgrade was launched inside `tmux`, the command will continue executing, and once the connection is restored, the session can be reattached, and the output will be available to be examined.

First of all, let's install it on our system via `zypper --non-interactive install tmux`. This line will download the package and make the `tmux` command available. Bear in mind that the goal of `tmux` is not to install it on our system (even if this is useful), but for it to be available on the servers we connect to, to get that extra layer of protection in case a disconnection happens. So, it's a good habit to get used to installing it on all the servers we connect to.

In the following screenshot, we can see what `tmux` looks like with the default configuration after executing `tmux` on a command line:

*Figure 7.21 – The tmux default layout after execution*

As shown in the preceding screenshot, the view of our terminal hasn't changed a lot, except for the status bar in the lower part of the window. This shows some information about the host, such as its name, time, date, and the list of open windows, with `0:bash` being the active one, as denoted by the asterisk (*) symbol.

There are lots of combinations for using `tmux`, so let's get familiar with some of them that will cover the initial use case:

- Run `tmux` to create a new session
- Run `tmux at` to attach to a previous session (for example, after reconnecting to a host)
- Run `tmux at -d` to attach to a previous session and detach other connections from it

> In older versions of SLES, the tool that was used for creating virtual multiplexed terminals was `screen`, which has been marked as deprecated; however, it is still available. If you were used to its key bindings (`Ctrl-A + <some key>`), most of them are equivalent in `tmux` via `Ctrl-B + <same key>`.

Once we're inside `tmux`, there is a whole world of commands we can use that are preceded by the *Ctrl + B* keys. Let's view some important ones (remember that *Ctrl + B* must be pressed before you use the next item in the list):

- *?*: Displays inline help about the shortcuts to use
- *c*: Creates a new window
- *n/p*: Goes to the next/previous window
- *d*: Detaches the `tmux` session
- *0–9*: Goes to the window numbered with the pressed number
- *,*: Renames windows
- *"*: Splits the pane horizontally
- *%*: Splits the pane vertically

- *Spacebar*: Switches to the next layout
- *&*: Kills the window
- *pg down/pg up*: Goes higher or lower in the window history
- *Arrow keys*: Select the pane in the direction of the pressed key

Let's look at an example in action in the following screenshot:

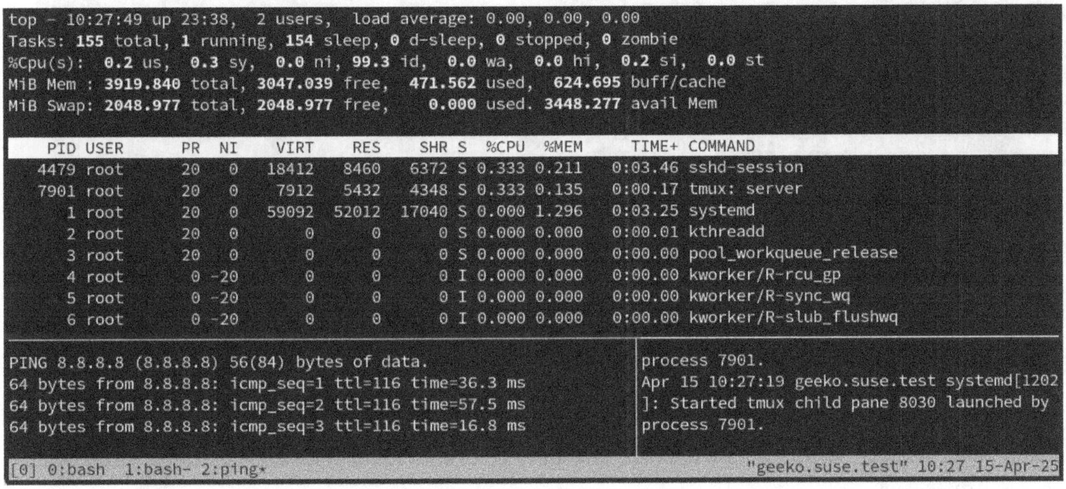


*Figure 7.22 – tmux with three panes running different commands inside the same window*

As we can see, there are several commands running at the same time – `top`, `journalctl -f`, and `ping` - so this is a good way to monitor a system while operations are being performed on it.

Additionally, one of the advantages is that `tmux` can be scripted, so if we are using one layout while administering systems, we can copy that script and execute it as soon as we connect to them, so that we can enjoy the same layout and even the commands being executed.

You can find the following code with extra comments and descriptions at `https://github.com/PacktPublishing/SUSE-Linux-Enterprise-Server-16-Official-Administration-Guide/blob/main/chapter-07-remote-systems-administration/tmux.sh` if you want to try it on your system:

```
#!/bin/bash

SESSION=$USER
tmux -2 new-session -d -s $SESSION # create new session
tmux select-window -t $SESSION:0  # select first window
tmux rename-window -t $SESSION "monitoring" #rename to monitoring
```

```
tmux split-window -h #split horizontally
tmux split-window -v #split vertically
tmux split-window -h # split again horizontally
tmux select-layout tiled #tile panes
tmux selectp -t1 # select pane 1
tmux send-keys "top" C-m #run top by sending the letters + RETURN
tmux selectp -t2 # select pane 2
tmux send-keys "journalctl -f" C-m # run journalctl
tmux selectp -t3 # select pane 3
tmux send-keys "iostat -x" C-m # run iostat
tmux selectp -t0 #select the pane without commands executed
```

Once the session with `tmux` has been set, we can attach the session we've just created and configured by executing `tmux`, which will show a layout similar to the one shown in the preceding screenshot.

# Summary

In this chapter, we covered SSH and how to use it to connect to remote systems, how to use keys to authenticate with or without a password, and how to take advantage of SSH for automation, transferring files, and even making services accessible or reachable via port redirection. With `tmux`, we learned how to make our administration sessions survive network interruptions and, at the same time, show important information at a glance by automating the layouts for it.

In the next chapter, we'll be digging into securing our system network via `firewalld` to only expose the services that are required for operation.

# 8

# Enabling and Using Cockpit

We have seen in previous chapters how to perform common administrative tasks in a system, locally and remotely, such as exchanging **SSH** keys and checking on the average load of the system. However, having an easy-to-use interface to manage a machine is very useful when it comes to performing quick tasks easily and having a nice overview of the system status. **SUSE Linux Enterprise Server (SLES)** used to include a graphical interface called **YaST** (which stands for **Yet another Setup Tool**), which needed to be installed and was not easy to use remotely. SLES 15 SP6 introduced a tool very common in many other Linux distributions: **Cockpit**. This tool is also included in SLES 16 with updates and improvements. In this chapter, we will review how we can make the most of it.

In this chapter, you will learn an easier and faster way to interact with your SLES servers and perform quick tasks on them. We will be covering the following main topics:

- Installing and enabling Cockpit on your system
- Basic Cockpit usage
- Storage, network configuration, and firewall
- Accounts and services
- Other tools

# Technical requirements

You can continue using the virtual machine that we created at the beginning of this book in *Chapter 1, Getting SLES 16 Up and Running (Physical and Cloud)*. Any additional packages that are required will be indicated in the text.

# Installing and enabling Cockpit on your system

**Cockpit** comes included in the default SLES 16 installation as the web administrative interface. We can quickly check that it is installed by simply running the following:

```
user@geeko:~&gt; sudo rpm -qa | grep cockpit
patterns-cockpit-16.0-160000.3.1.x86_64
cockpit-subscriptions-8-160000.1.1.noarch
cockpit-networkmanager-334.1-160000.1.1.noarch
cockpit-repos-3-160000.1.1.noarch
cockpit-system-334.1-160000.1.1.noarch
cockpit-bridge-334.1-160000.1.1.x86_64
cockpit-packagekit-334.1-160000.1.1.noarch
cockpit-selinux-policies-334.1-160000.1.1.x86_64
cockpit-334.1-160000.1.1.x86_64
cockpit-storaged-334.1-160000.1.1.noarch
cockpit-selinux-334.1-160000.1.1.noarch
cockpit-ws-334.1-160000.1.1.x86_64
```

As you can see, a **pattern** package for Cockpit is included in the distribution. What is that? Simply described, it is a package with a set of dependencies to install a full application, as described in *Chapter 6, Adding, Patching, and Managing Software*. As Cockpit is composed of different packages, the recommended way to install it is by installing the pattern as root or by using `sudo`, with the `zypper in -t pattern cockpit` command, as seen in the following screenshot:

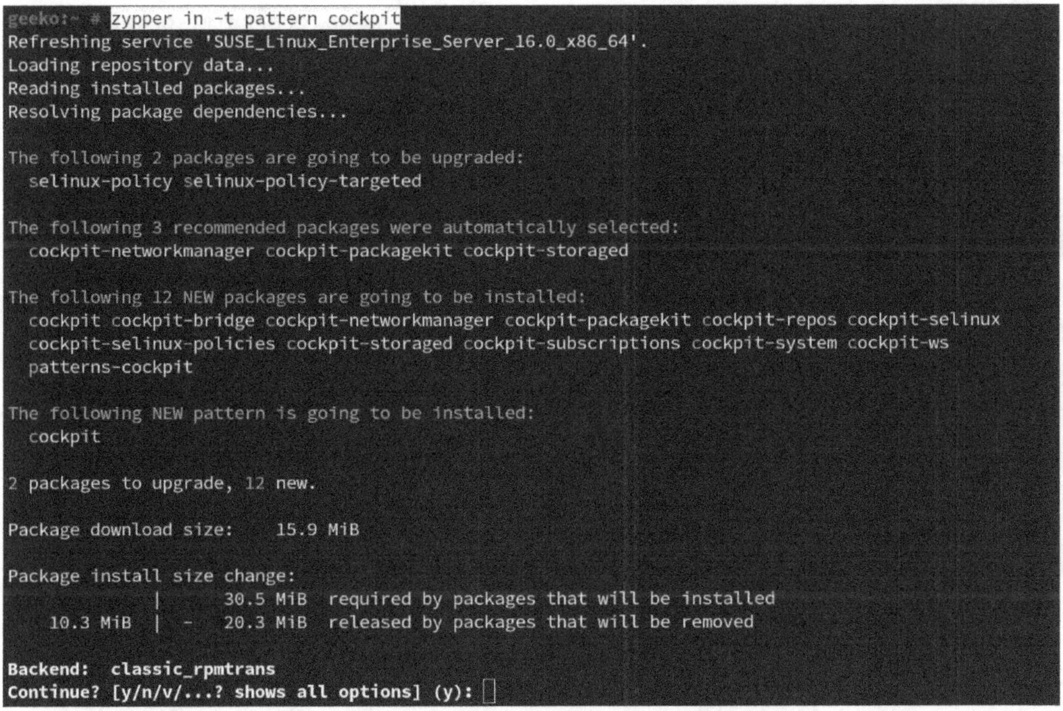


*Figure 8.1 – Installing Cockpit in SLES 16 by using the pattern included in the distro*

After running the command and typing y to accept the installation, all the software will already be available on our system.

However, it will not be running. To run Cockpit, we would need to enable the service. As it is not used continuously, Cockpit applies a nice trick to save resources: it creates a network socket. A network socket is a way to wait for a connection to happen by listening on a port number (in this case, `9090`). When we reach out to this port, the socket automatically starts the service for us.

To enable the socket, we need to run sudo `systemctl enable --now cockpit.socket`. The following screenshots shows the command when is run as `root`::

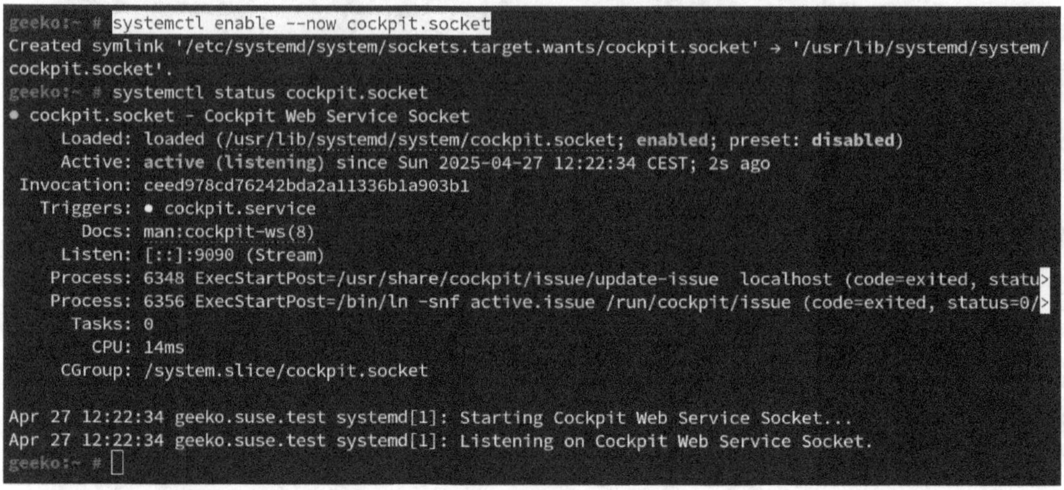


*Figure 8.2 – Enabling the Cockpit socket and checking that it is properly enabled*

Now that we know that the service can be started every time we establish a connection to port `9090`, we need to ensure that the connectivity is possible. In SLES 16, the **firewall** is enabled by default. The firewall will filter all connections to our system. So, we need to verify that the connection to the Cockpit service is allowed. To do so, we shall now check whether the Cockpit service is on the allow list. We can do this by running the following:

```
user@geeko:~&gt; sudo firewall-cmd --list-services
cockpit dhcpv6-client ssh
```

In this case, as we can see, the `cockpit` service is enabled. If that were not the case, the result would be as follows:

```
user@geeko:~&gt; sudo firewall-cmd --list-services
dhcpv6-client ssh
```

There is an additional required step. As you can see, the `cockpit` service is not included in the list of allowed services. We can add it temporarily by running the following command:

```
user@geeko:~&gt; sudo firewall-cmd --add-service cockpit
success
user@geeko:~&gt; sudo firewall-cmd --list-services
cockpit dhcpv6-client http ssh
```

This will immediately enable the service, but it will not survive a reboot. To make it permanent, we shall also run the following:

```
user@geeko:~&gt; sudo firewall-cmd --add-service cockpit --permanent
success
```

Now the access to the Cockpit service is not blocked by our system's firewall and the configuration will be kept after a reboot. Let's start using Cockpit in our SLES system.

# Basic Cockpit usage

We will start with the basics on how to access and use Cockpit from the UI to perform some administrative actions.

## Accessing Cockpit

To access `cockpit`, we need to open a browser and point it to an internal web page, using the `HTTPS` protocol, to the IP address of our machine, specifying to connect to port `9090`.

In the example running in this book, the IP is `192.168.122.16`. So, the address we shall use is `https://192.168.122.16:9090`.

*Figure 8.3 – Pointing our browser to port 9090 and the server IP 192.168.122.16 to access Cockpit*

Once we press the *Enter* key, it will connect to the port, but as we will be using the default self-signed certificate provided, a warning will be raised:

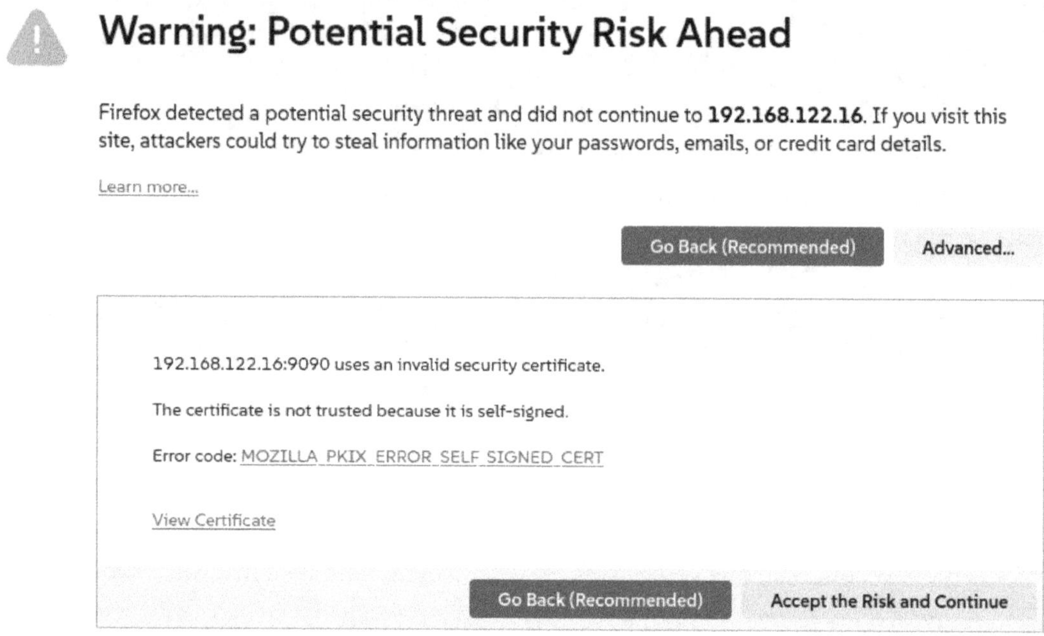


*Figure 8.4 – Certificate warning in the browser accessing the default configuration of Cockpit*

Clicking on **Advanced...** and then **Accept the Risk and Continue** will allow us to access the web UI:

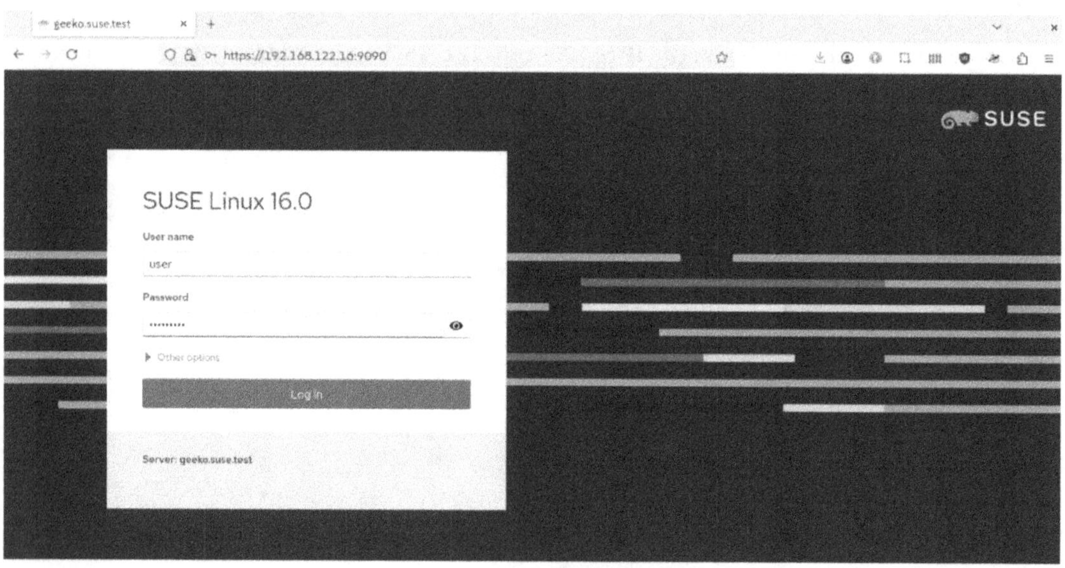


*Figure 8.5 – Cockpit interface login page*

Let's now log in using our system credentials, which means using the username and password we configured during the installation.

## Logging in and enabling administrative tasks

Cockpit uses local authentication to validate your credentials. This means you can log in by typing in the username and password you provided during the installation process, like in a normal terminal. As you can see in the previous screenshot, we are validating using the username and password for `user`. Then, we just need to click on **Log in**, and we'll be able to access the main Cockpit page.

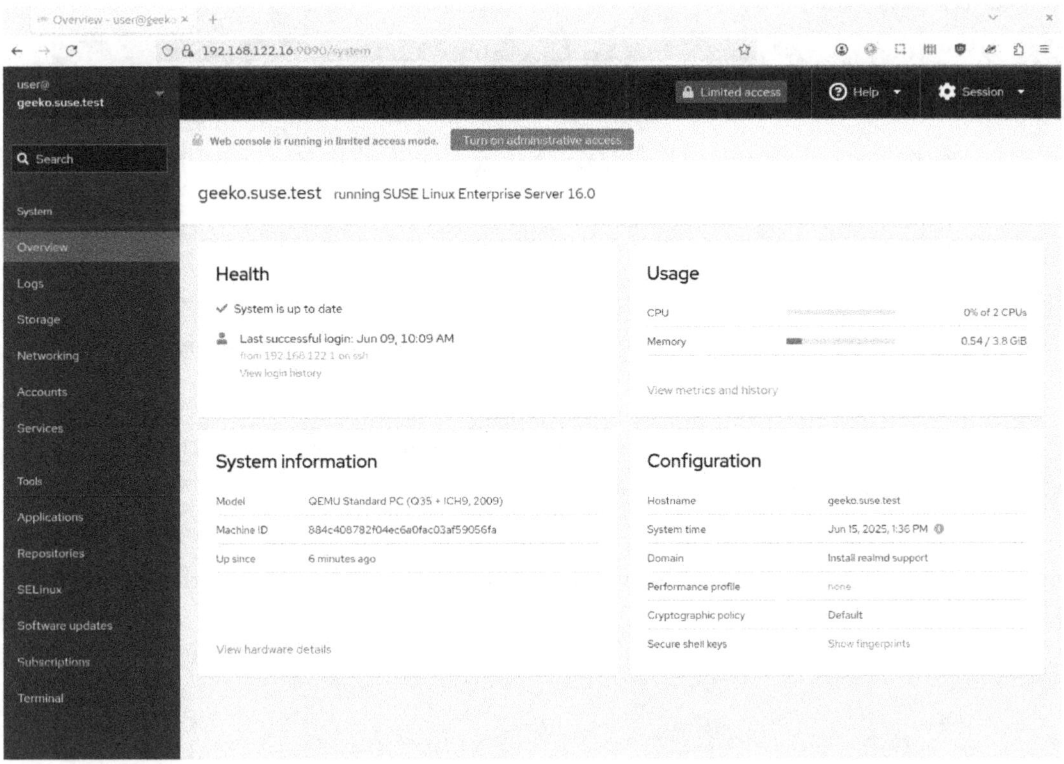


*Figure 8.6 – Cockpit interface | Overview page showing a healthy status. Administrative access is not enabled*

The main Cockpit page, also called **Overview**, is a page to receive basic information on the status of the machine. We will review all of the sections in this chapter.

We can see all of the options available in Cockpit on the left: **Overview**, **Logs**, **Storage**, **Networking**, **Accounts**, **Services**, **Tools**, **Applications**, **Repositories**, **SELinux**, **Software updates**, **Subscriptions**, and **Terminal**. These are the ones that come by default, but there are more extensions that can be installed, such as **VM** and **Container management**.

At the top of the page, we see that we have the possibility of performing administrative tasks and making changes to the system. We just need to click the **Turn on administrative access** button and provide our password.

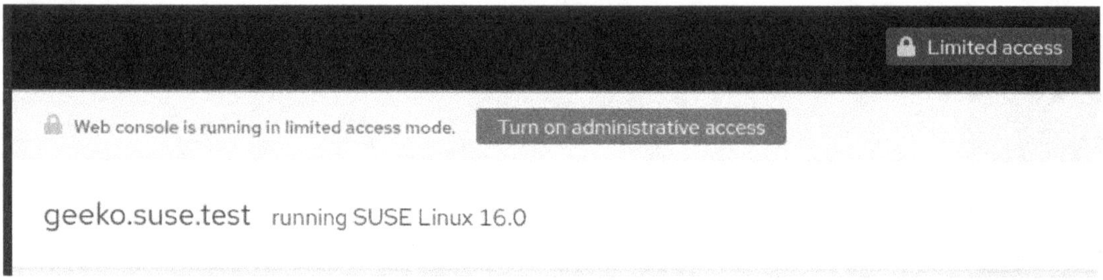


*Figure 8.7 – Turning on administrative access in Cockpit to be able to make changes*

> To have administrative access, you need to be part of the `wheel` group. This can be done as easily as running `usermod -aG wheel username` as root.

When issues are found in the system, some warnings will show up, such as those in the following screenshot:

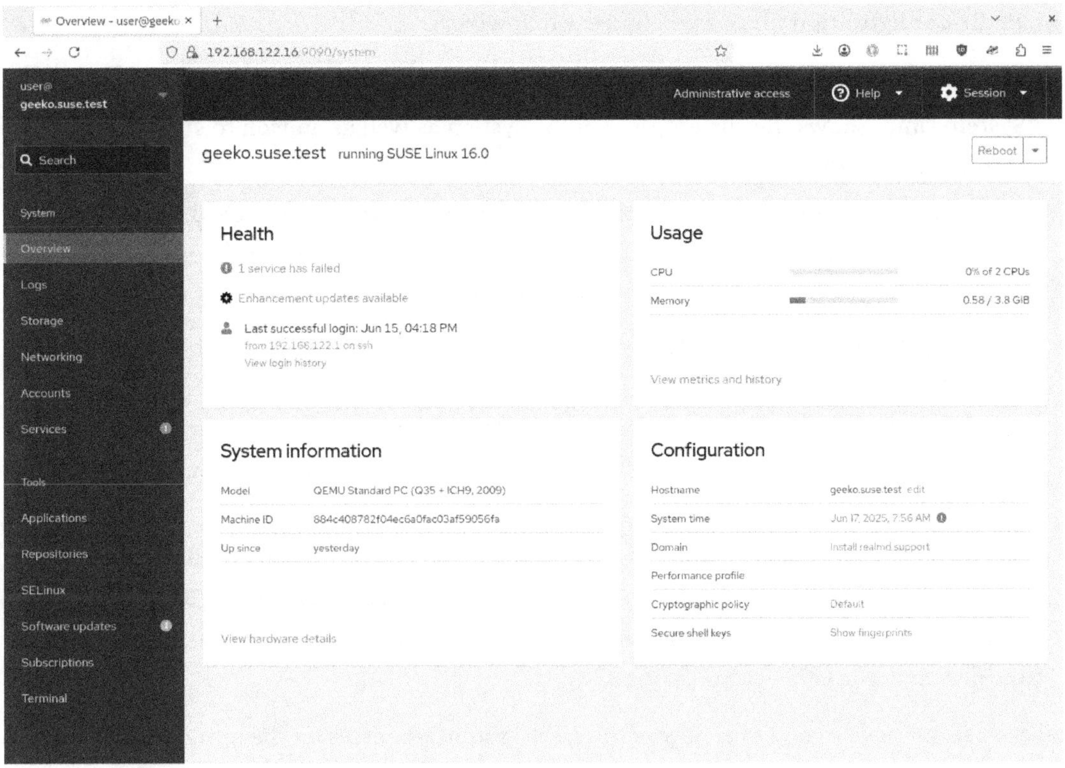


*Figure 8.8 – Cockpit interface | Overview page showing an unhealthy status: patches pending, one service not starting, and time synchronization not working correctly. Administrative access is enabled*

In the **Health** tile (or card), we can see two important bits of information:

- **Software updates**: In *Figure 8.6*, we can see that the system is up to date and that no further updates are required. If there are updates of any kind, such as enhancements or security, they will be shown here, as you can see in *Figure 8.8* If we need to apply updates, the links will will send us to the **Software updates** page.
- **Last login**: The system will show the last successful login and provide access to the login history by sending us to the **Accounts** page.

On the **Usage** card, we can see the current memory and CPU usage, and it provides access to metrics and history, which we will review in the next subsection.

In the **System information** tile, we will be able to see information on the hardware model, the machine ID, and the uptime. Clicking on **View hardware details** will take us to the **Hardware Information** page, which we will also see in a coming subsection.

Finally, in the **Configuration** tile, we will find the following:

- **Hostname**: Shows the system hostname with the possibility to modify it by clicking on **edit**.
- **System time**: Shows the current time of the system as well as an icon to show the synchronization status.
- **Domain**: Shows the Active Directory domain to which the system is attached, or if there is none, the option to install `realmd` to join an Active Directory domain. This is not available in the default installation and requires an extension.
- **Performance profile**: Shows the performance profile if one is selected. This is not available in the default installation.
- **Cryptographic policy**: Shows the policy applied to the system regarding encryption software. By clicking on the policy, in this case, **Default**, we can select a different one. See *Figure 8.9*.
- **Secure shell keys**: The `SSH` protocol enables the machines connecting to identify themselves using a fingerprint to avoid man-in-the-middle attacks. Clicking on **Show fingerprints** will show us the identification that the server is using and that will also be shown the first time you connect to it using SSH.

As you can see, we have a good overview of the main system resources on the initial page, with easy and quick access to modify many of the values. As an example, we can see the different cryptographic policies:

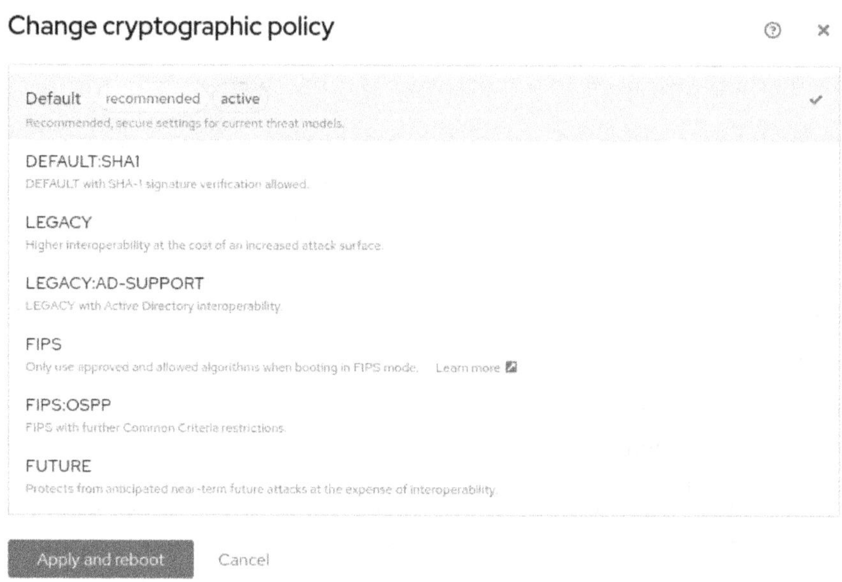


*Figure 8.9 – Different cryptographic profiles available in SLES 16*

Now let's dive into the subsections available from the **Overview** page of Cockpit.

## Metrics and history

The **Overview** page of Cockpit provides access to basic CPU and memory consumption with a link to view metrics and history. Clicking on this link will take us to the **Metrics and history** page, including instant metrics of the system covering the usual concepts of CPU, memory, disk space, and network traffic, as we can see in the following screenshot:

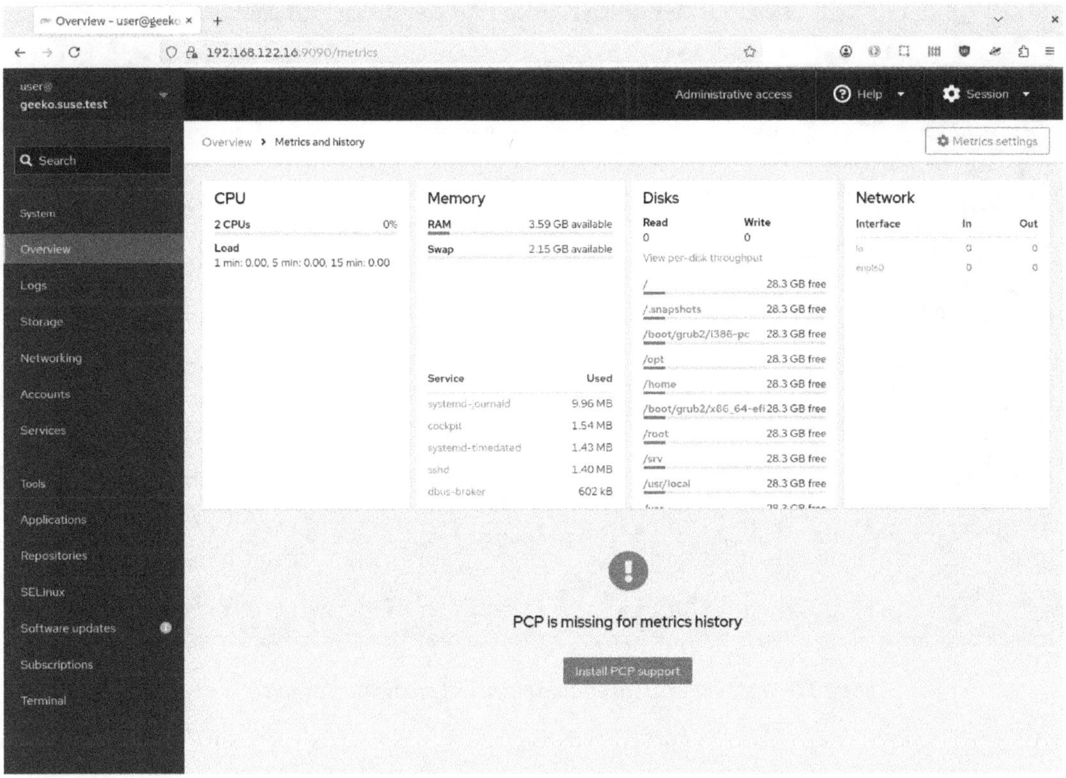

*Figure 8.10 – Metrics and history page in Cockpit without historical data being kept*

Historical data is not kept by default; to have it enabled, we need to install the **Performance Co-Pilot**, or **PCP**. There's an easy way to do this: clicking on the **Install PCP support** button. Then we will see a page overlay with a list of packages to be installed, which can be accepted by clicking on the **Install** button.

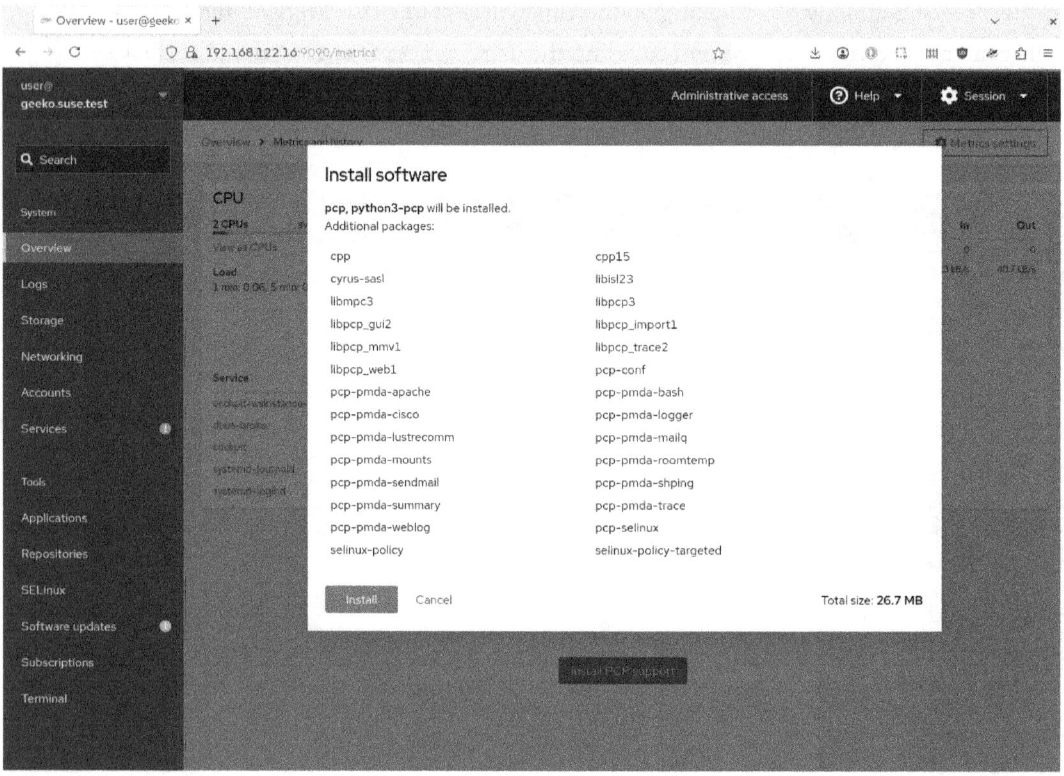


*Figure 8.11 – Installing PCP to enable historical metrics in Cockpit*

Once the packages are installed, we can start gathering and storing data by enabling the `pmlogger` service. This can be done in Cockpit itself by going to the **Services** page, clicking on the **pmlogger** service, and then enabling the toggle to run and activate the service at boot, as can be seen in the following screenshot:

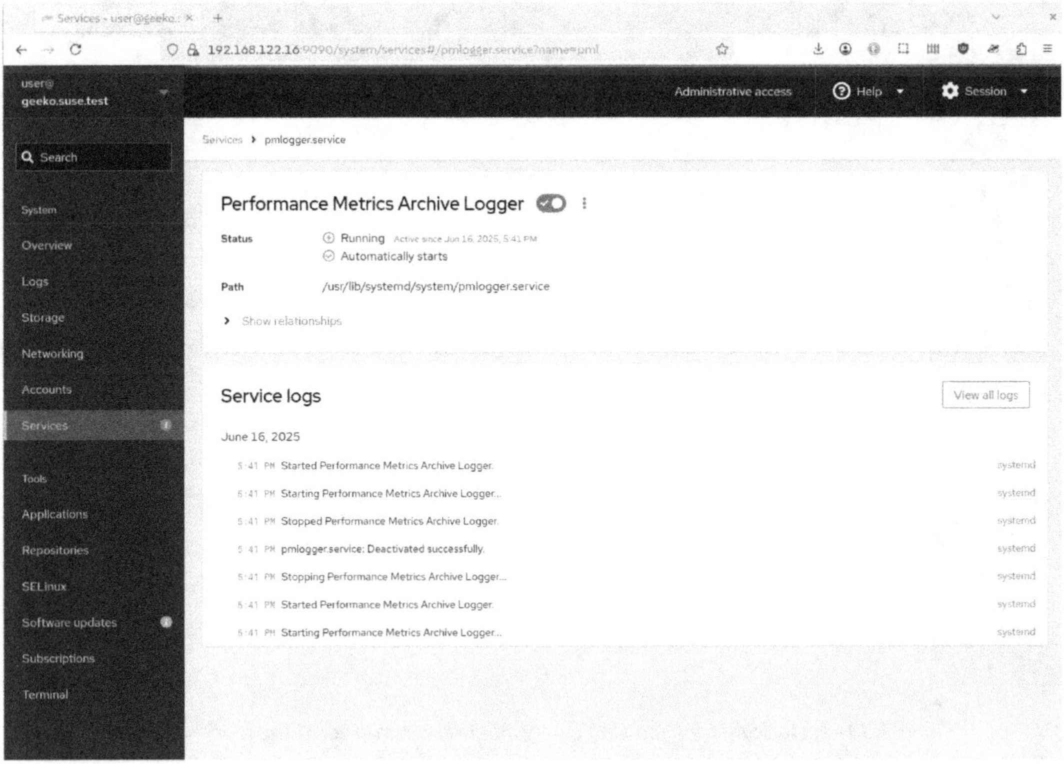


*Figure 8.12 – Enabling the PCP logger service to gather and store metrics data*

Once it is running, we will be able to see the graphs for previous days and even issues found in the metrics, such as network peaks or disk storage running out.

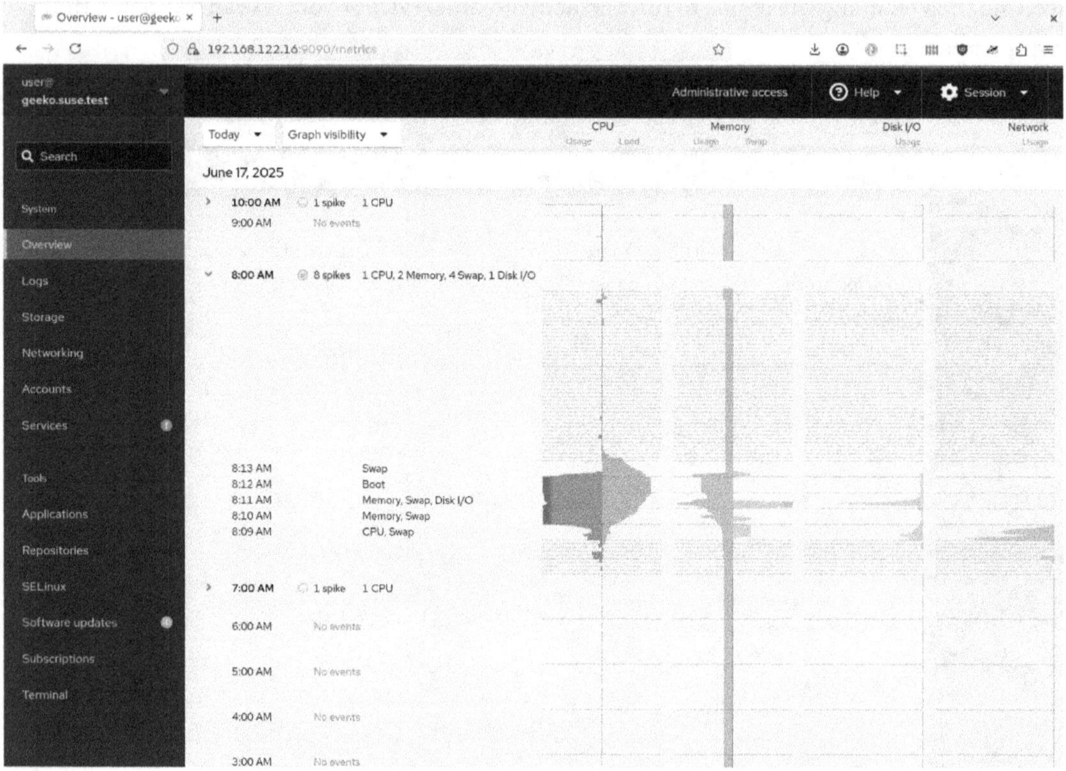

Figure 8.13 – Historic metrics showing a very quiet server with very little load

As we can see, the information is captured and stored. It can be easily retrieved to review the status of the system at any point in time. After reviewing this, let's move to the next section.

# Hardware information and logs

We can review all devices by clicking on the **View hardware information** link in the **System information** tile.

It will display all the basic hardware information in the system, a list of PCI devices, and a list of memory devices:

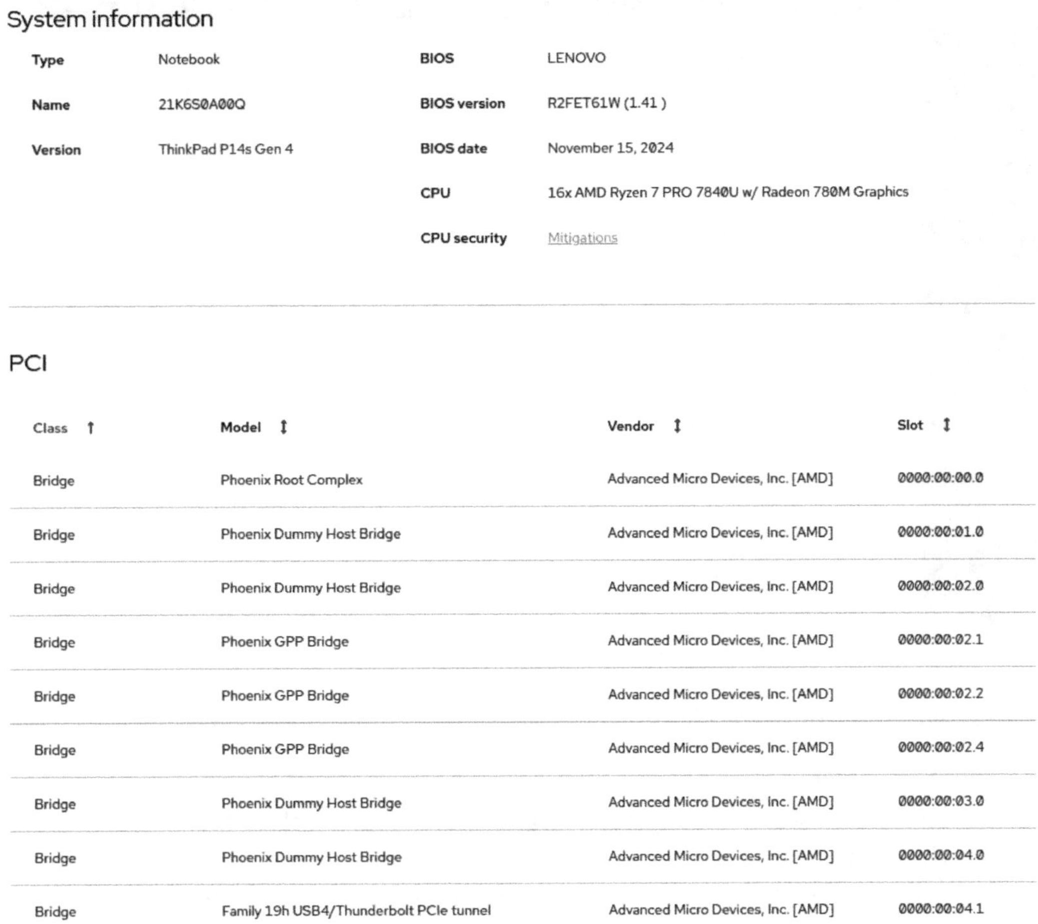


*Figure 8.14 – Example of a hardware information page from Cockpit*

This page is useful for checking all devices connected to the system and reviewing them. One good example is checking the number of memory modules: number, type, size, and speed.

Once we know how to get the basic hardware information, let's move on to checking system logs with Cockpit. To do so, we just need to click on the **Logs** entry on the left bar of the interface. This will take us to the page dedicated to the **journald logs** and **boot logs**, with the possibility of filtering them to obtain useful data.

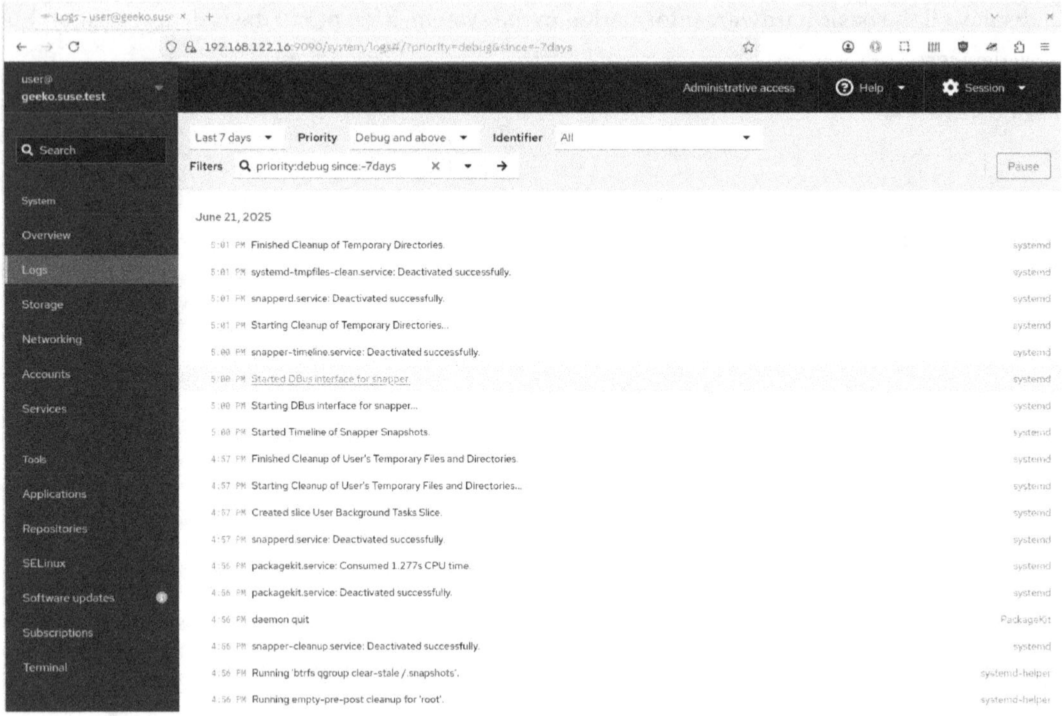

Figure 8.15 – Logs page in Cockpit

On the logs page, there are several filters that will show as drop-down menus to be used:

- **Time/boot**: Situated at the top left of the page, without a label, this enables us to select between the **Last 7 days** and **Last 24 hours** options, referring to the history of the `journald` logs, which is useful to see the status of the services running on the system. We also have the choice to select **Current boot** or **Previous boot** in the menu, which will show the boot sequence of the current process to boot and the previous one, which is useful for checking boot issues.
- **Priority**: This allows us to filter the logs based on their importance. The menu starts with the most important ones and moves to the least important. The first entry, **Only emergency**, will only show the most critical issues happening in the system, and it's usually empty. The coming entries are filtered by level, which are **Alert**, **Critical**, **Error**, **Warning**, **Notice**, **Info**, and **Debug**. The lower the importance, the more logs, as it will include the selected level and above for all the cases.
- **Identifier**: Logs can be filtered by the service that created them, which is the identifier that is shown here. Some examples could be the Cockpit session that we are running, kernel messages, `sudo` actions, or the `auditd` daemon.

It is a really good idea to check the logs of the system when it's running correctly. It will not only help you understand how the system works but also make it easier for you to understand when something is going wrong if you already know what it should look like when it works correctly.

Now that we have learned how to obtain basic information from the system and check the logs, let's move on to other useful information about the storage and network of our system.

# Storage, network configuration, and firewall

Let's move to **storage** and **network**, including the network filtering capabilities that the included firewall provides in SLES 16.

## Storage

The **Storage** section can be accessed in Cockpit by clicking on the **Storage** link in the left bar of the UI. It looks like this:

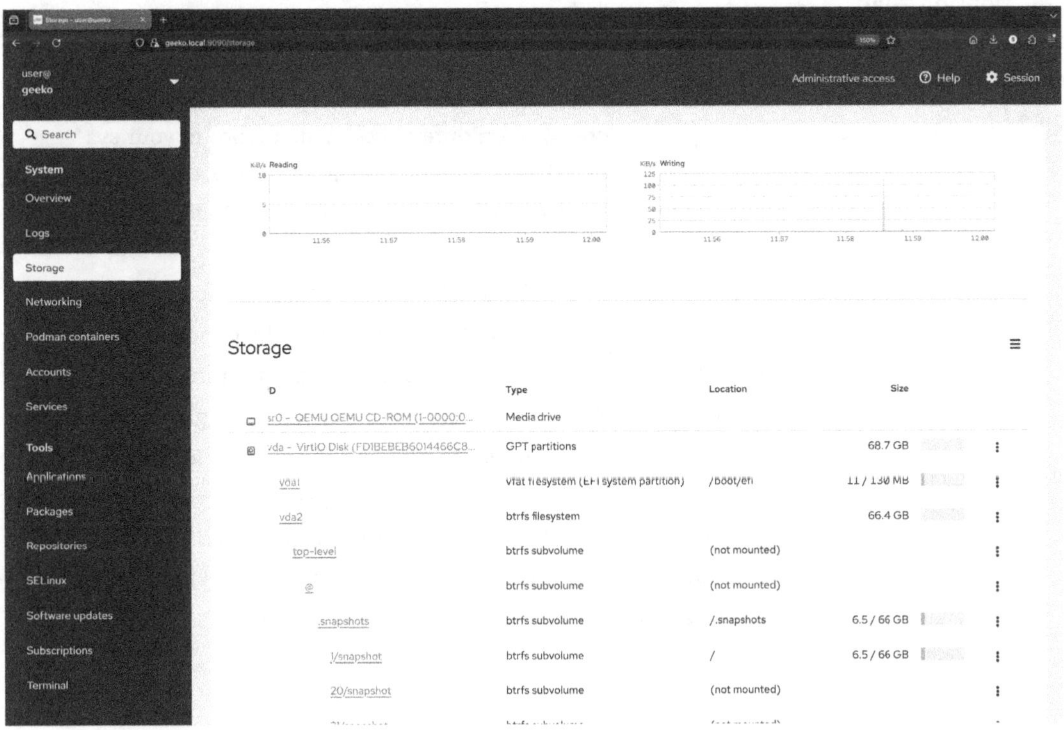


*Figure 8.16 – Storage page in Cockpit*

It has three sections:

- **Performance**: A couple of graphs showing the read and write performance of the storage appear at the top of the page
- **Partitioning**: Labeled as **Storage**, this shows the partitions available in the system, including size and usage
- **Logs**: Labeled as **Storage logs**, this shows all storage-related entries in the log subsystem or `journald`

SUSE Linux Enterprise is, at the time of writing, the only Enterprise Linux distribution that includes BTRFS by default, enabling filesystem snapshots.

As SLES 16 comes with **BTRFS** by default, instead of having different partitions for `/var` or `/opt`, it will use **subvolumes**, which are a more flexible way to redistribute the space available on the disk. One of the main benefits is being able to make **filesystem snapshots**, which allows you to be able to **roll back** to a previous well-known configuration, as well as checking on differences made to files in your system. This is elaborated on in *Chapter 14, Configuring and Using System Snapshots with BTRFS and Snapper*.

Now we have a basic idea of how the Cockpit section for storage works. We will need to better understand the concepts behind storage to be able to use this section of the tool in depth. This understanding will be developed as we go through *Chapter 12, Managing Local Storage and Filesystems*; *Chapter 13, Flexible Storage Management with LVM*; and the already-mentioned *Chapter 14, Configuring and Using System Snapshots with BTRFS and Snapper*. For now, we are good with this basic and graphical introduction to storage. So, we can move on to networking.

# General networking

The **Networking** section can be accessed in Cockpit by clicking on the **Networking** link in the left bar of the UI. It looks like this:

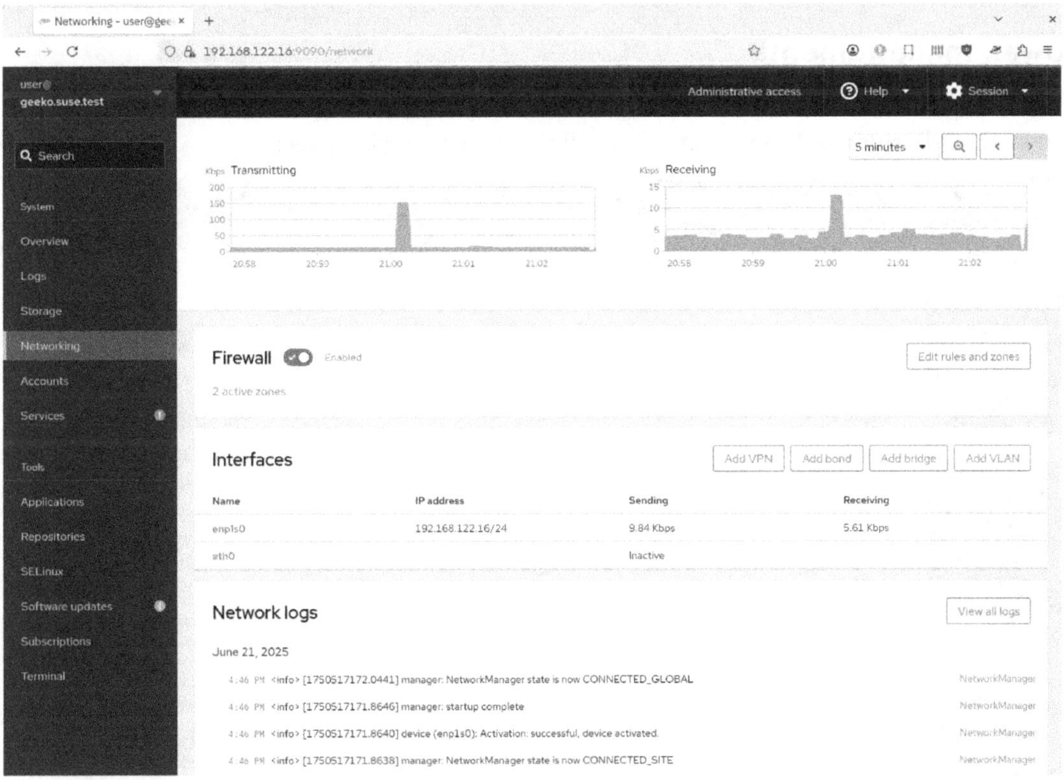


*Figure 8.17 – Networking page in Cockpit*

It has four sections:

- **Performance**: A couple of graphs showing the **Transmitting** and **Receiving** network traffic appear at the top of the page.
- **Firewall:** This shows the number of active zones, which can be edited by clicking on **Edit rules and zones**, as well as on the **2 active zones** text. More details will be covered later in the *Firewall management* section.
- **Interfaces:** This shows the active network interfaces. It enables us to create new ones with **Add VPN**, **Add bond**, **Add bridge**, and **Add VLAN**, as well as editing the current interface by clicking on its name, which in this example is `enp1s0`.
- **Logs:** Labeled as **Network logs**, it will show all network-related entries in the log subsystem or `journald`.

The performance and logs sections are mostly informative, and while you can extend the list of entries in the **Logs** tile or change the timeframe for the metrics, there are no further actions that you perform. Keep an eye on them to ensure they are working correctly and detect issues when they happen. Let's move on to the firewall section.

## Firewall management

The firewall section can be accessed, as we mentioned before, by clicking on the **2 active zones** link or on the **Edit rules and zones** button. It will show the following page:

*Figure 8.18 – Firewall page in Cockpit*

As we can see, we have at the top of the page the main header tile labeled **Firewall**, with the toggle to enable and disable the firewall. There is an **Add new zone** button as well. By clicking on this button, we will be able to add a new managed zone to our firewall, with different restriction/trust levels, and assign it to a network interface in our system.

In the following paragraphs, we will go into details about the different **firewall zones**, which in our example are the **public zone** and **Docker zone**. This is a pretty simple setup with one public network interface, `enp1s0`, and an interface for containers, `docker0`.

**Zones** are the way we associate a set of **filtering rules** with a list of **network interfaces.**

The Docker zone is associated with the `docker0` interface and has the entire subnet allowed, but nothing more. Once we log in to this system, and therefore will be in the same subnet, we will be able to reach out to every container running on it via the `docker0` interface. Once we start running containers in this host, we can consider adding specific rules to this zone.

The public zone is associated with the network interface, `enp1s0`, which itself is connected to public networks and the internet, and it is also associated with the loopback interface, `lo`. So, these rules will also apply to local connections. In this case, we are filtering several services that can be accessed to interact with the system. The services that are *allowed* are as follows:

- `ssh`: The service to allow remote administration, also called Secure Shell
- `dhcpv6-client`: The client for automated configuration for IP version 6 addresses
- `cockpit`: The web administration interface that we are using
- `http`: The web server installed on the system

**Services** are a list of **network ports** and the type of connection, such as **UPD** or **TCP**, associated with providing access to a specific capability in the system.

It will be easy to add another service by clicking on the **Add services** button and selecting the service we want to add, or even adding our own custom ports, as we can see in the following screenshot:

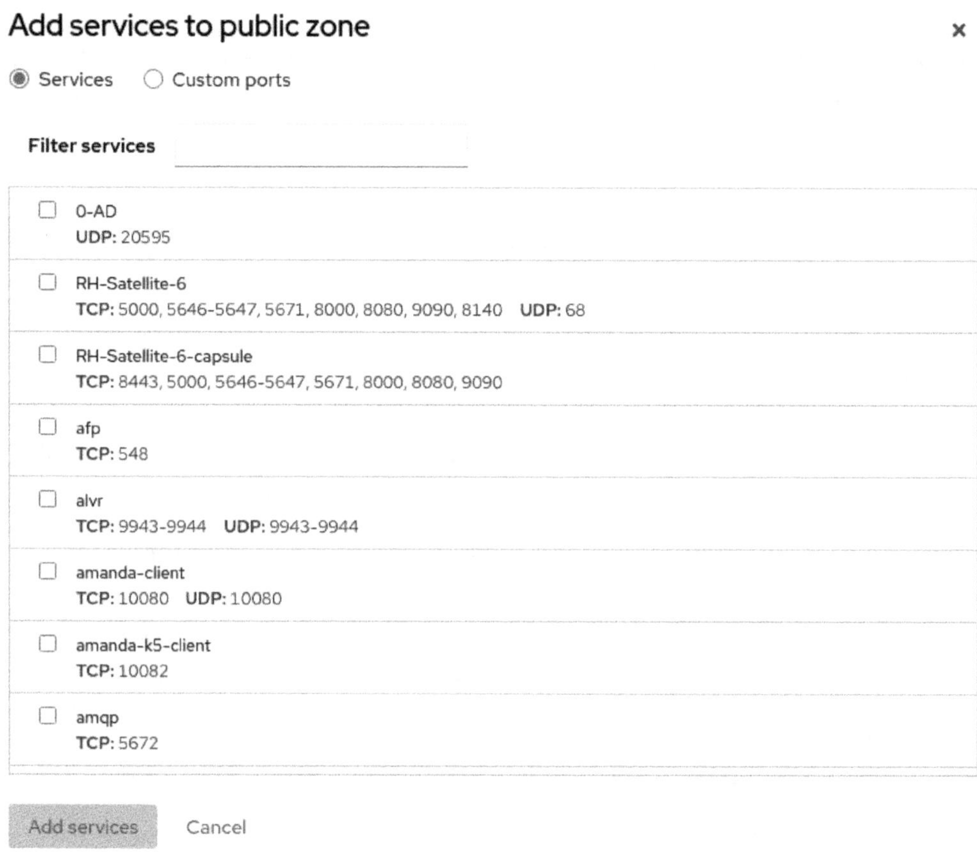


*Figure 8.19 – Firewall page in Cockpit. Section opened to allow a new service in the public zone*

Now we know how to handle rules to allow services to be accessed from other networks. Let's go down one level and see how we can modify the interface we have in the system.

## Network interface management

The interfaces section enables us to add special interfaces and configure the current ones.

To configure the network interface, we just have to click on its name. For example, let's click on the interface we created in *Chapter 5, Enabling Network Connectivity*, which we called `eth0`. Let's look at it in the Cockpit interface:

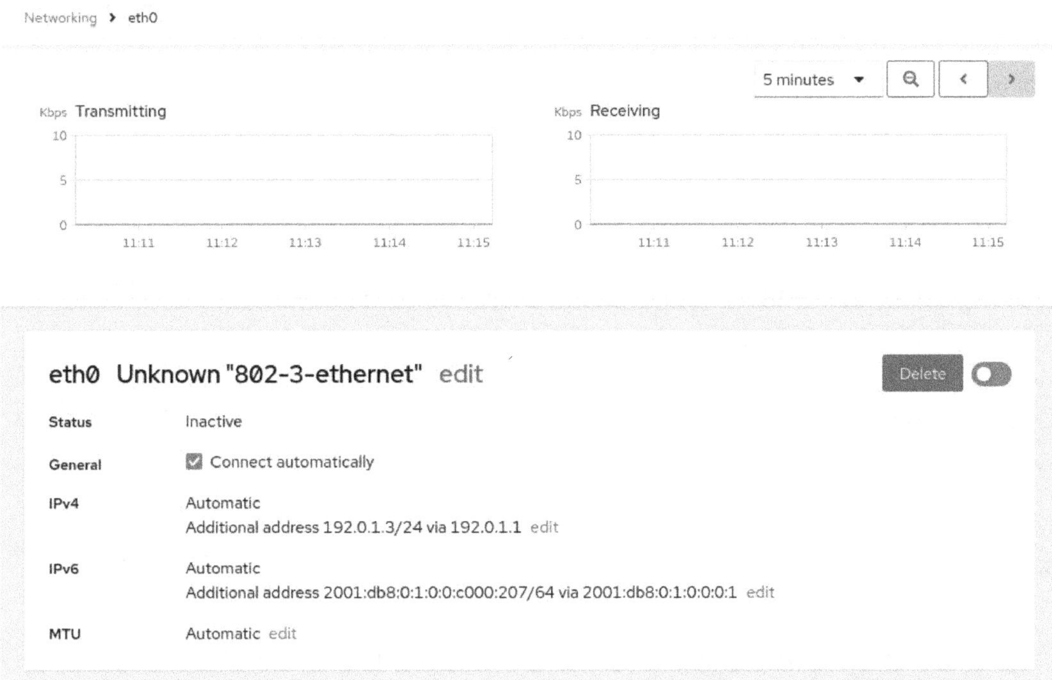


*Figure 8.20 – Interface page in Cockpit. Section to manage the eth0 network device configuration*

As you can see in this screenshot, looking at the metrics at the top of the section, there is no traffic coming through this interface. In the tile below, we can see that the toggle to enable the interface is not enabled. We can enable the interface, modify the IPv4 and IPv6 addressing, and establish the **Maximum Transmission Unit** (**MTU**) for the packages to be delivered through it.

Let's play with it and finally delete it by clicking on the **Delete** button.

Taking a look at the `enp1s0` interface, the one that connects this system to the rest of the networks and the one we are using to connect to the Cockpit web interface, we can see it has traffic, is enabled, and has manual IPv4 addressing configured as we did in the installation. We can see it in the following screenshot:

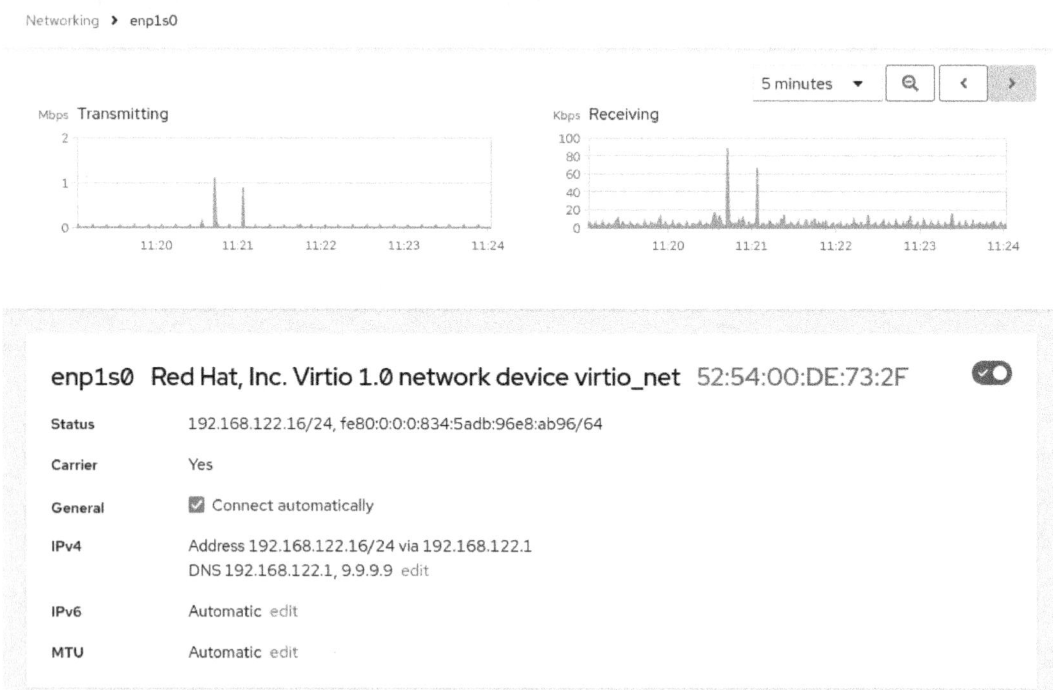


*Figure 8.21 – Interface page in Cockpit. Section to manage the enp1s0 network device configuration*

We could play around with this configuration; however, we have to take into consideration that we might block ourselves from accessing our system. In many production systems, we will have an admin interface to modify the system, which will be the one we will use to access Cockpit. Then, we will have a service interface to provide services, which we will modify from Cockpit without locking ourselves out of the system.

We are ready to modify anything required to access the system through the network. Let's move on to managing user accounts and services.

# Accounts and services

In this section of the chapter, we will take a look at managing user accounts as explained in *Chapter 4, Securing the System with Users, Groups, and Permissions*, and system services, as we learned in *Chapter 3, Managing Regular Operations with Tools*, but we will be doing so from the Cockpit web interface.

## Accounts

We can start this section by going to the **Accounts** page. We will do so by clicking on the **Accounts** link in the left-side bar. The page will look like this:

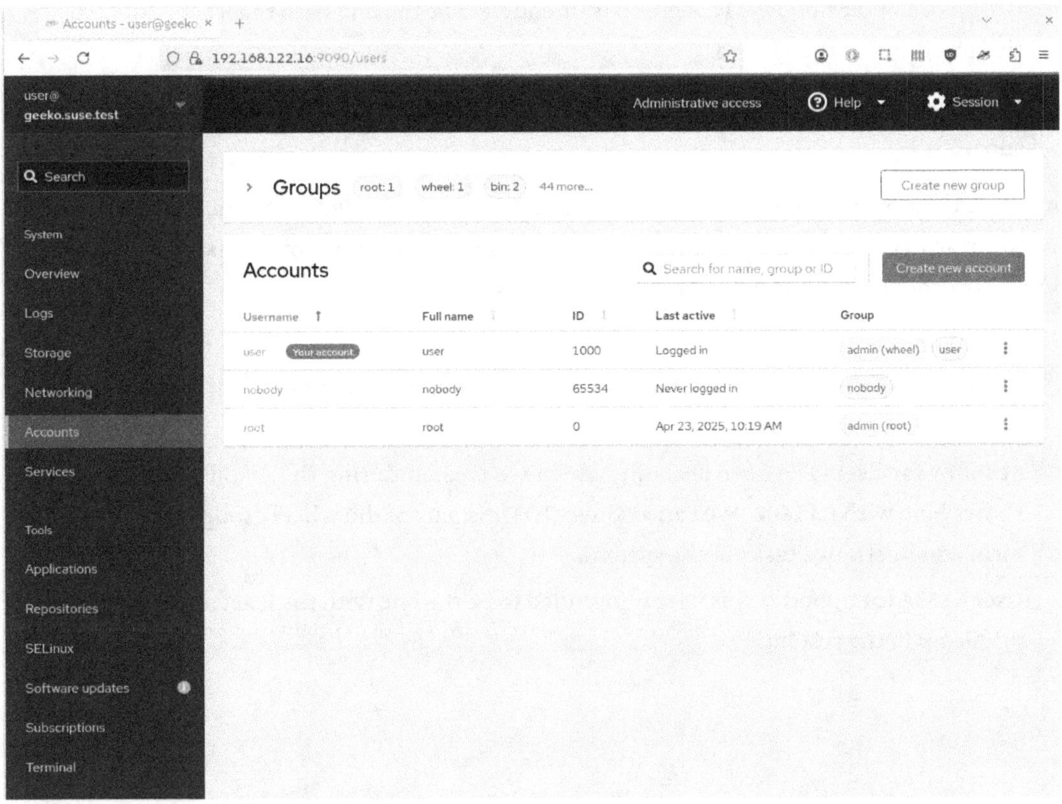


*Figure 8.22 – Accounts page in Cockpit. Section to manage user accounts and groups*

We can see two sections in it:

- **Groups**: The section to manage user and system groups.
- **Accounts**: The section to manage user accounts. System accounts are filtered.

The **Groups** section can help us create a new group, using IDs below `1000` for system groups and IDs equal to or above `1000` for user groups. We have three special system groups:

- **Group 0, for root**: Group assigned to the overall system administrator, the root user.
- **Group wheel**: Group assigned to users who will have administrative access to the system. In our case, it is a group with ID 497.
- **Group 65534 for nobody**: This group is intended to be the one with the least administrative privileges in the system.

In this **Groups** section or tile, you will be able to create a new group easily to be assigned to users and resources.

The **Accounts** section can help us manage users. The section is not oriented to managing system accounts; so, any account with a user ID below `1000` will be filtered out of the list, with one exception for the root user. Let's check the entries in the section:

- **User 0, for root**: User assigned to the overall system administrator, the root user. It always has ID `0`. As in some configurations, we will allow logging as root. If the root login is allowed, it is displayed here.
- **Account for user**: The `user` account, which we created during the installation process, shows here with ID `1000`. We can also see that it is part of the wheel group, so it can perform administrative tasks in the system.
- **User 65534 for nobody**: This user is intended to be the one with the least administrative privileges in the system.

Clicking on the three verticalv points next to any user will show a menu to perform the following actions:

- **Edit user**: To edit values in the account.
- **Log user out**: To close sessions opened by a user in the system.
- **Lock account**: To prevent the user from being able to create new sessions in the system. It will not finish the existing ones.
- **Delete account**: To permanently remove the account from the system.

The **Edit user** page is especially useful, allowing us to perform a nice list of actions. Let's take a look at it:

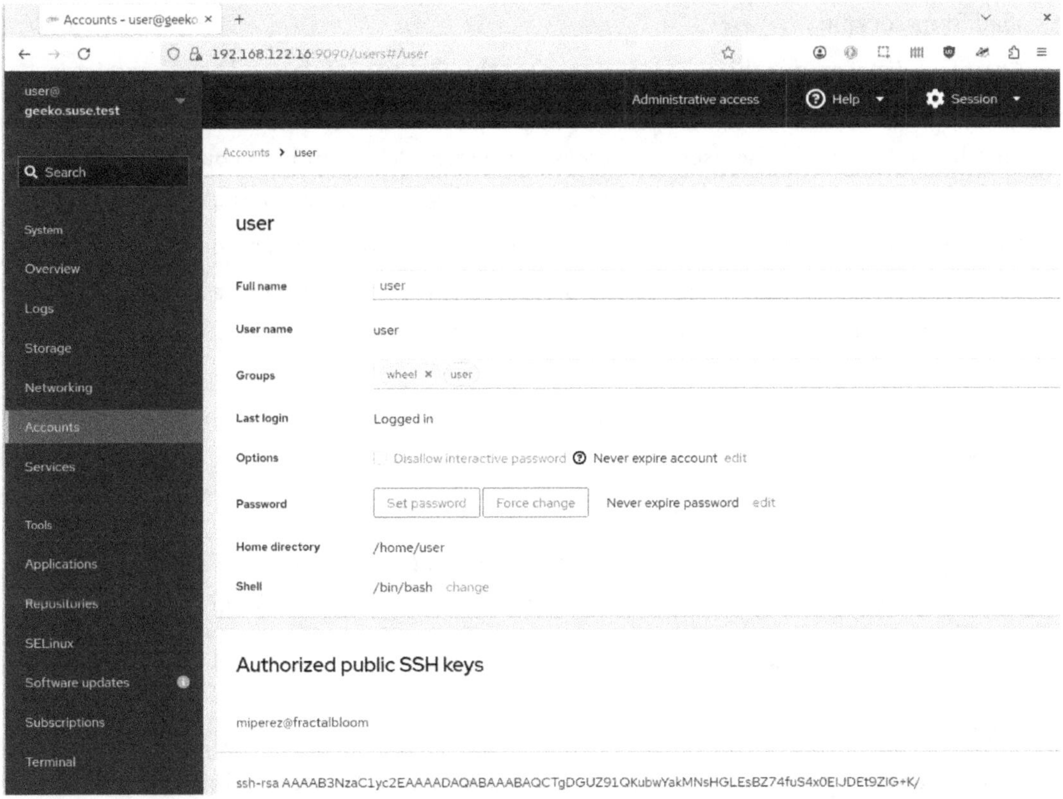


*Figure 8.23 – Accounts page in Cockpit. Section to manage user accounts and groups*

There are three sections on this page:

- **user**: To modify user characteristics
- **Authorized public SSH keys**: A list of public SSH keys that enable access to the account in the system
- **Login history**: A list of sessions run by the user in the system, including start and end times

Let's take a deeper look at the information we see in the **user** tile and what actions we can take:

- **Full name**: The text to identify the user. It is very common to have the official full name of the person assigned to the account here.
- **User name**: Short text used to identify the account and used to log in. It cannot be modified from Cockpit.
- **Groups**: A list of groups this user is assigned to. This is very useful to add or remove users from different groups in the system.
- **Last login**: When did the user last access the system? This can help you decide if the account has been used recently when you are deciding if you need to remove the account.
- **Options**: Some miscellaneous options related to access methods and account expiration.
- **Password**: A section to manage the user's password. We can set a new password, which is useful when the user forgets it, force the user to change the password on the next login, or set an expiration date for the current password.
- **Home directory**: Default folder for the user's options and files. It cannot be modified from Cockpit.
- **Shell**: The shell that the user will run commands on when logging in.

We saw in *Chapter 4, Securing the System with Users, Groups, and Permissions*, the tasks referred to in the previous list. However, it is a lot easier to handle them from this interface.

Let's move on to the **Services** section.

## Services

We can access the **Services** page by clicking on the **Services** link on the left-hand side menu. The page looks like this:

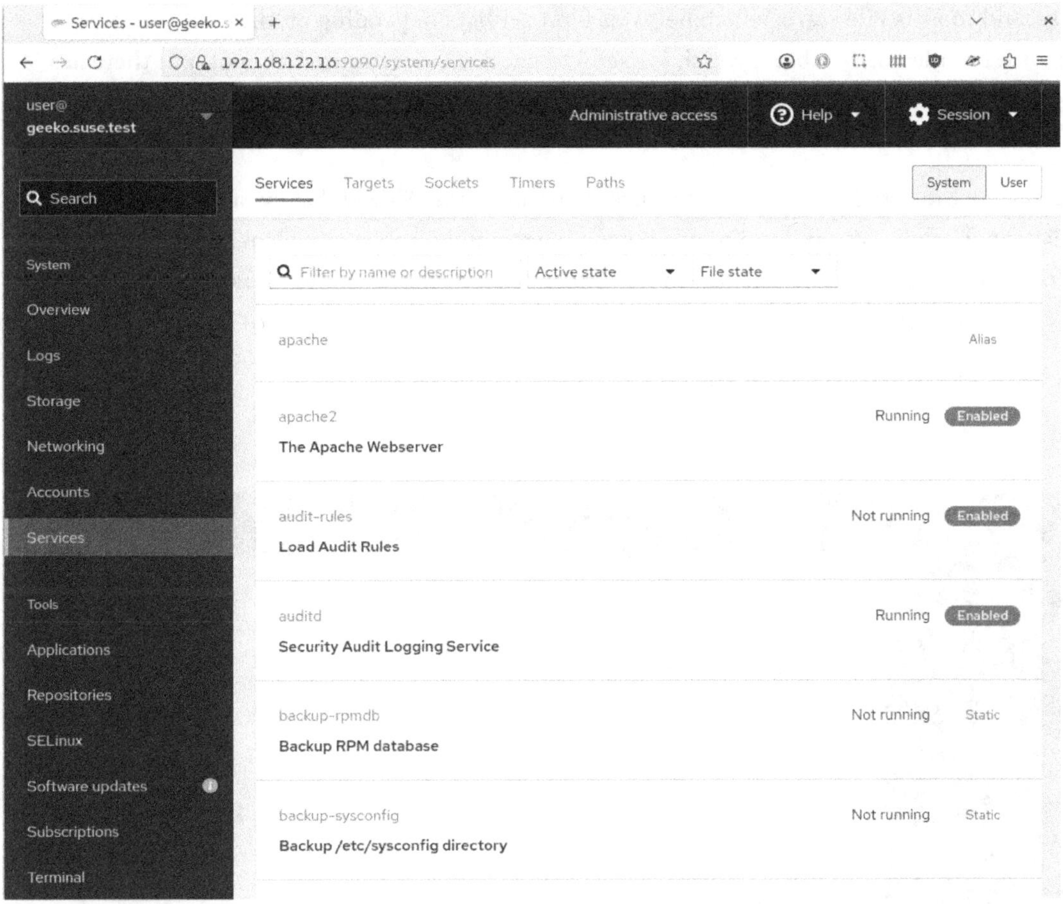


*Figure 8.24 – Services page in Cockpit. Section to manage systemd services and other units*

We can see here the concepts relating to `systemd` that we saw in *Chapter 3, Managing Regular Operations with Tools*.

The top bar has five sections with the main **systemd units: Services, Targets, Sockets, Timers,** and **Paths.** It's very good to go through them and get familiar with the list of units available. To make it easier, on the **Services** page, there are filters at the top of the list that enable us to filter by two different topics.

The first topic is **Active state**, for services that could be running or not running, which is useful for units we want to start temporarily or check whether they were started properly.

The second topic is **File state**, which helps us filter services depending on the behavior during boot with **Enabled** or **Disabled**, which is useful to check services started at boot. But there are other options to filter by the nature of the unit, which helps us know whether they are static units, an alias for another unit, or indirect units.

We can view the details of each unit by clicking on its name. This will show a page that helps us manage the unit. We can see a toggle button to stop and disable, as well as start and enable. There is also a three-point menu, next to the toggle, to easily manage the status of the unit to be able to start, stop, restart, mask, or pin each of them.

Let's take a look at the `chrony` service:

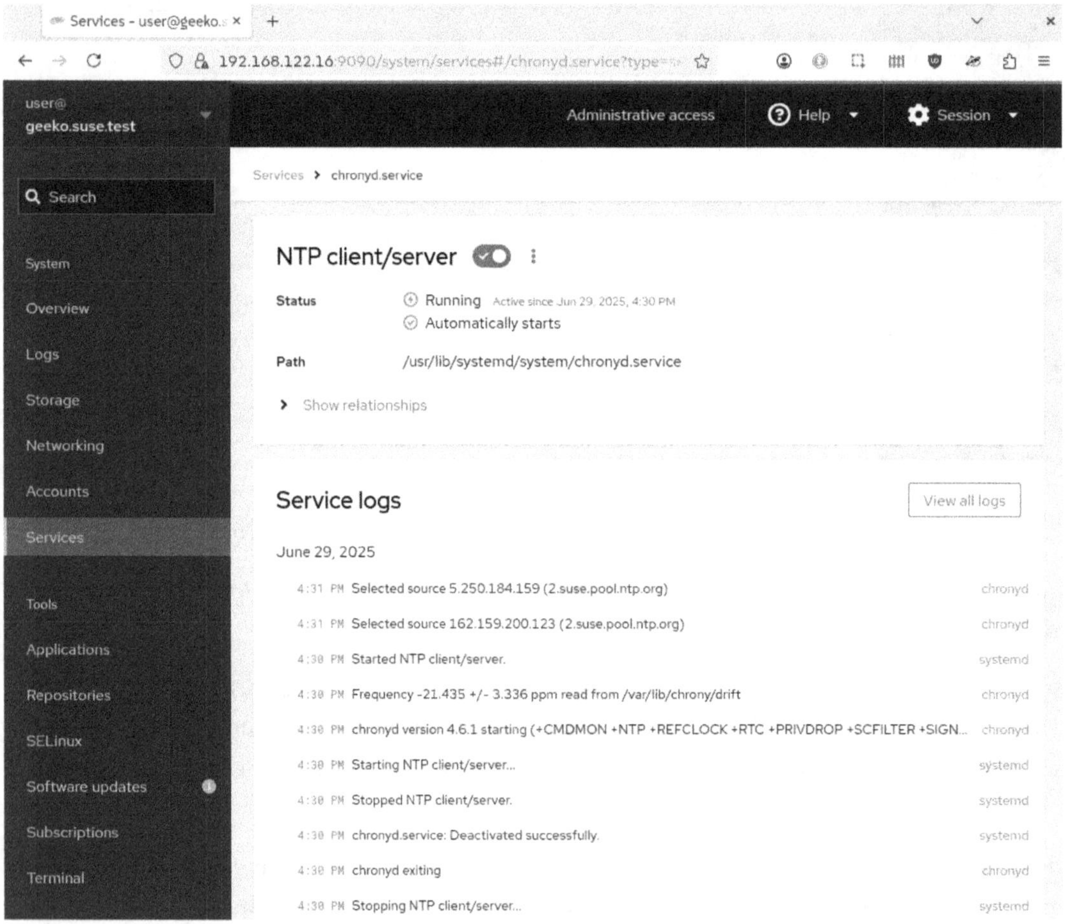


*Figure 8.25 – Unit page in Cockpit, for chronyd.service*

Other sections, such as **Targets**, **Sockets**, and **Paths**, will be explained in depth in *Chapter 15, Understanding the Boot Process*.

The Timers section also has a button, **Create timer,** to help us create a new timer unit, which makes it very easy to schedule repetitive tasks.

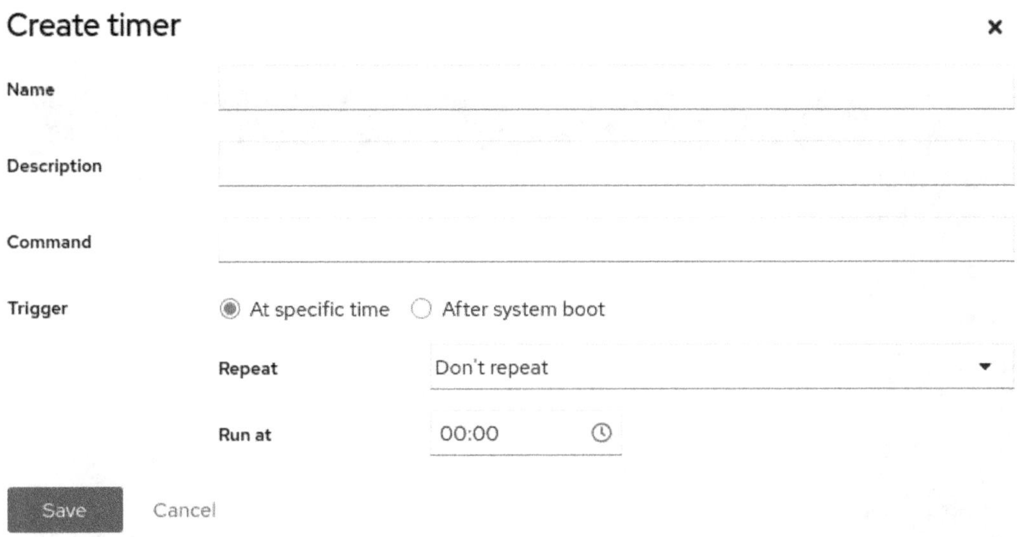


*Figure 8.26 – New timer page in Cockpit*

We can now easily manage the most important resources in the system using Cockpit, from storage to performance and networking to logs. But there are still some more resources we can handle; let's see those in the coming sections.

# Other tools

On the left-hand side menu, we can see two sections: **System** and **Tools**. We have seen all the entries in the first section. Let's move on to the second one, oriented to software management, extensions, SELinux, and other tools.

## Applications

**Applications** provides options to extend the capabilities within Cockpit, not to add or remove software from the system. It only covers extensions that were installed via zypper, so you may see the options grow over time. It looks like this:

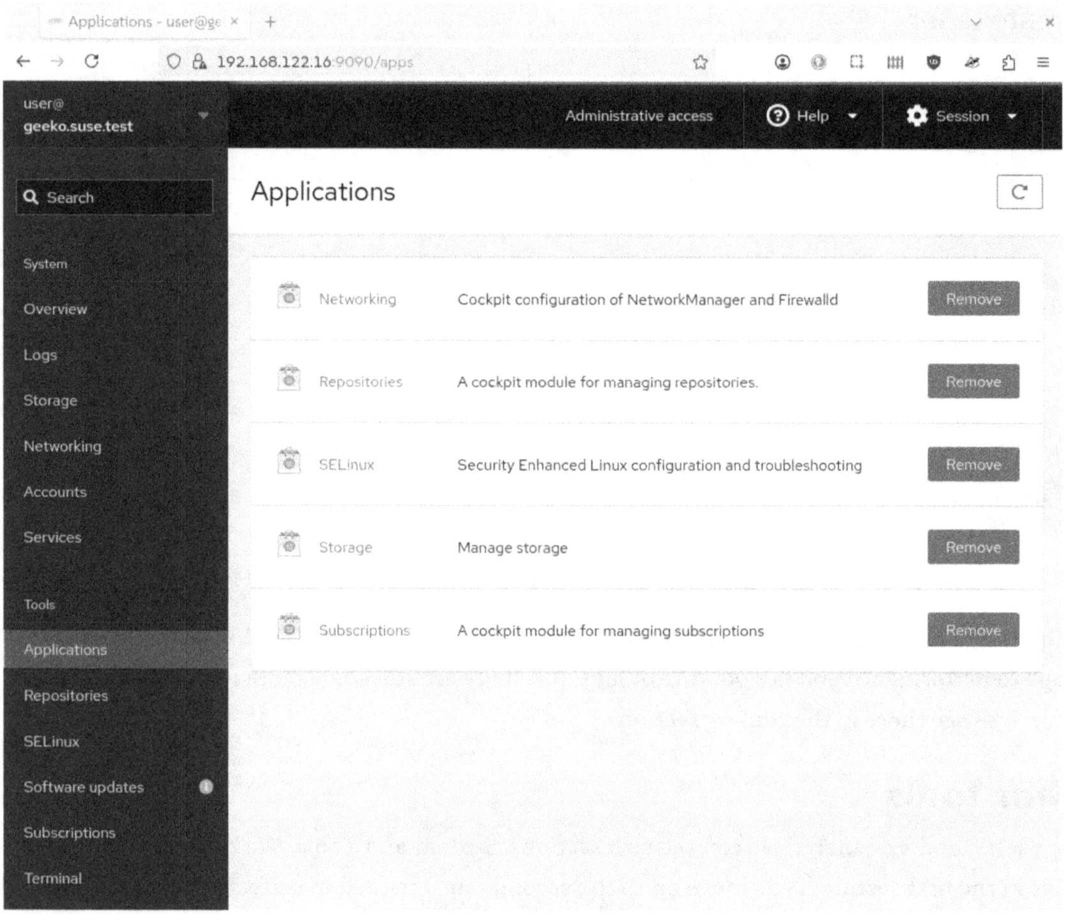


*Figure 8.27 – Applications page in Cockpit*

You can see that we have different extensions already installed by default that cover several sections in Cockpit: **Networking**, **Repositories**, **SELinux**, **Storage**, and **Subscriptions**.

We can click on the **Remove** button next to each of them to eliminate them from the system, but we would need to use zypper to reinstall them.

We could search for extra Cockpit modules by running the `sudo zypper search cockpit` command:

```
user@geeko:~> sudo zypper search cockpit
[sudo] password for user:
Refreshing service 'SUSE_Linux_Enterprise_Server_16.0_x86_64'.
Loading repository data...
Reading installed packages...

S  | Name                     | Summary                                                          | Type
---+--------------------------+------------------------------------------------------------------+--------
i  | cockpit                  | Web Console for Linux servers                                    | package
   | cockpit                  | Pattern for Cockpit, a web based remote system management interface | pattern
i  | cockpit-bridge           | Cockpit bridge server-side component                             | package
   | cockpit-devel            | Development files for for Cockpit                                | package
   | cockpit-doc              | Cockpit deployment and developer guide                           | package
   | cockpit-kdump            | Cockpit user interface for kernel crash dumping                  | package
   | cockpit-machines         | Cockpit user interface for virtual machines                      | package
i  | cockpit-networkmanager   | Cockpit user interface for networking, using NetworkManager      | package
i  | cockpit-packagekit       | Cockpit user interface for packages                              | package
   | cockpit-packages         | A cockpit module for (un)installing packages                     | package
   | cockpit-podman           | Cockpit component for Podman containers                          | package
i  | cockpit-repos            | A Cockpit module for managing system repositories                | package
i  | cockpit-selinux          | Cockpit SELinux package                                          | package
i  | cockpit-selinux-policies | selinux policies required by cockpit                             | package
i+ | cockpit-storaged         | Cockpit user interface for storage, using udisks                 | package
i  | cockpit-subscriptions    | Cockpit module for managing and registering subscriptions        | package
i  | cockpit-system           | Cockpit admin interface package for configuring and troubleshootin-> | package
i  | cockpit-ws               | Cockpit Web Service                                              | package
   | cockpit-ws-selinux       | SELinux security policy for cockpit-ws                           | package
   | patterns-cockpit         | Pattern for Cockpit, a web based remote system management interface | package

  Note: For an extended search including not yet activated remote resources please use 'zypper
```

*Figure 8.28 – List of available Cockpit packages*

Some of the interesting packages available to add are the following:

- `cockpit-kdump`: The module to configure `kdump` options and capture kernel dumps in case of a kernel panic.
- `cockpit-machines`: The module to manage virtual machines on this server. It is very useful for standalone hypervisors and home labs.
- `cockpit-packages`: The module to install and remove available software packages.
- `cockpit-podman`: The module to manage containers running in the system using `podman`.

By installing these packages, you can add more capabilities to your Cockpit interface. This can be done with the `sudo zypper install package-name` command.

## Repositories

The **Repositories** page includes a simple interface to manage the configured repositories in our system that provide `rpm` packages for it. It looks like this:

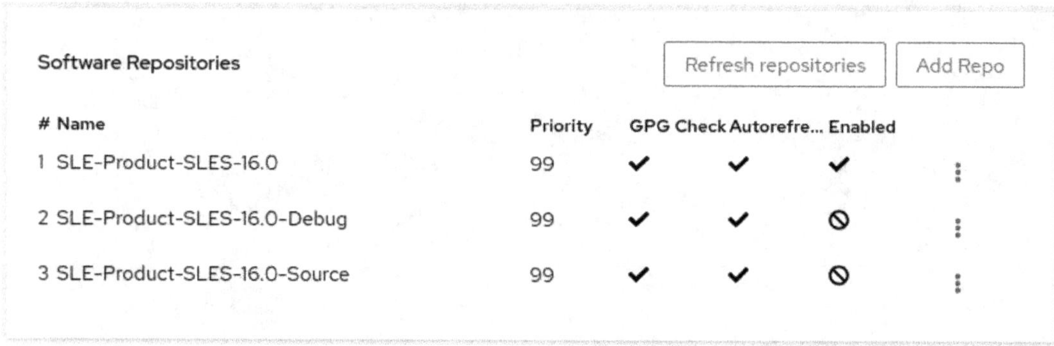


*Figure 8.29 – Cockpit Repositories page*

Two functions are available here. The first one is available through the **Refresh repositories** button to get the latest data from the already-configured repositories. The second one is available through the **Add Repo** button, where you can provide a repository **Uniform Resource Identifier** (**URI**) to add it to the system.

## SELinux

The **SELinux** page includes a basic view to control SELinux. It has three sections, as shown in the following screenshot:

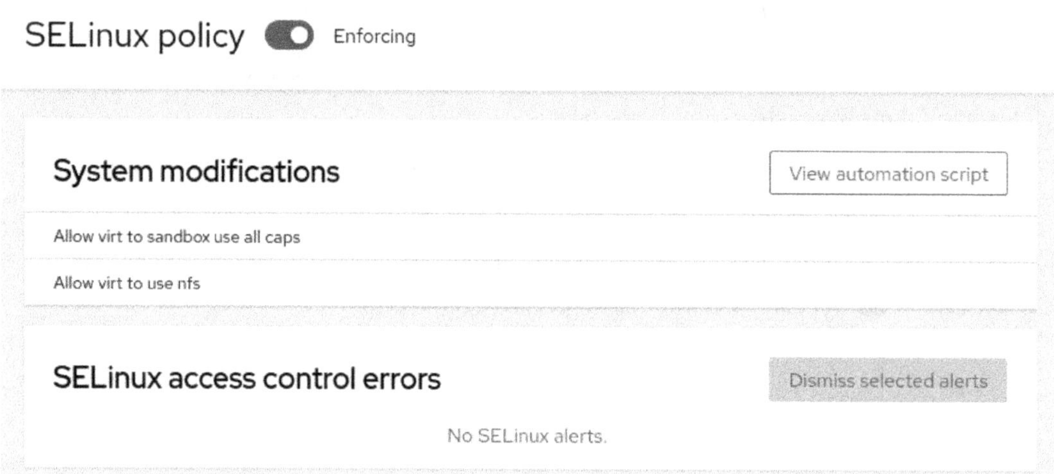


*Figure 8.30 – Cockpit SELinux page*

The first section is the header and allows us to change **SELinux policy** from **Enforcing** mode, which blocks access to different resources, to **Permissive**, which doesn't block anything but will still log what would be blocked by it. It is very useful to check whether something in our system is not working due to SELinux.

The second section, **System modifications**, helps us to make changes to the SELinux behavior by providing some automation to do it. The two common behaviors we can change are **Allow virt to sandbox use all caps**, which allows virtual machines to use all SELinux capabilities, and **Allow virt to use nfs**, which allows virtual machines to access NFS shares.

Finally, the third section, as usual, includes the logs, or in this case, the SELinux alerts.

## Software updates

The **Software updates** page is a simple page to check and apply updates to the system.

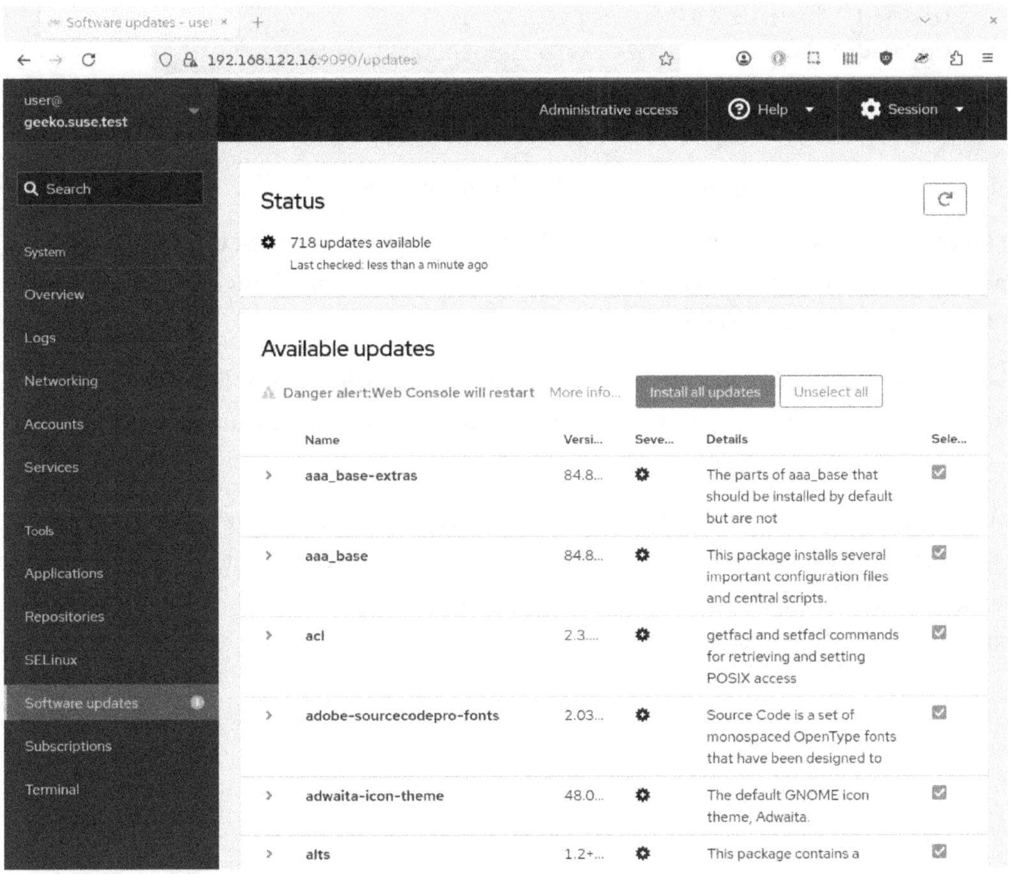


*Figure 8.31 – Cockpit Software updates page*

The header, labeled **Status**, will show if we have any updates available to install. We can refresh the info by clicking on the top-right button with the circle arrow on it.

The section of the page labeled **Available updates** enables us to apply selected updates or all of them. Clicking **Install all updates** will launch the update process with the following interface to track it:

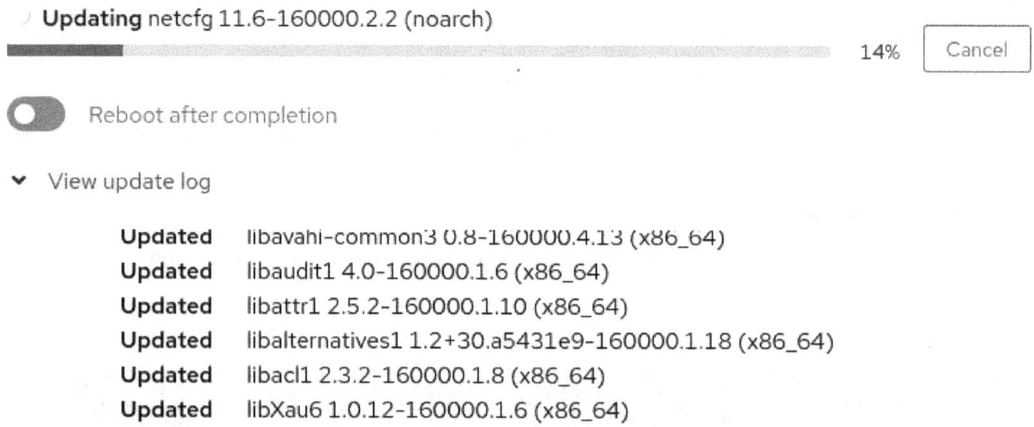


*Figure 8.32 – Cockpit updating the system*

Once it finishes, the system will be up to date. We can even select to reboot the system once it is complete, which is very convenient for non-critical systems to apply changes when updating critical components such as the kernel.

It is good to know that SLES 16 has made the Live Patching extension available to apply patches to the kernel and critical user-space components, so that you can have your system properly updated without having to reboot for up to 12 months.

Also, to handle updates and patches in a distributed fashion, to easily manage a large number of systems and havefine-grained control over what gets installed, you can count on SUSE Multi-Linux Manager. SUSE Multi-Linux Manager is a tool to manage tens to thousands of systems easily and distribute patches and updates to them.

## Subscriptions

The **Subscriptions** page helps register the system to **SUSE Customer Center** (affectionately called **SCC**) and check which subscriptions are assigned, as we can see in the following screenshot:

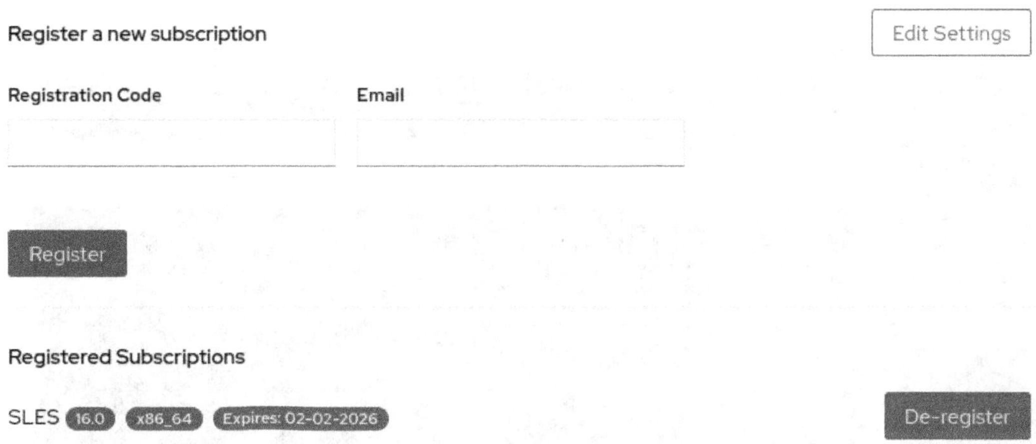


*Figure 8.33 – Cockpit updating the system*

Using your email and registration code, you can register the system in SCC.

As you can see, we have already registered this system in SCC and have assigned a proper subscription to it. Clicking on **De-register** will easily remove the assignment of the subscription to this system. To receive proper support from SUSE, it is very important to have all the systems properly registered.

## Terminal

A very interesting and nice section of Cockpit is **Terminal**. It provides access to the system console, enabling us to launch commands easily, as can be seen in the following screenshot:

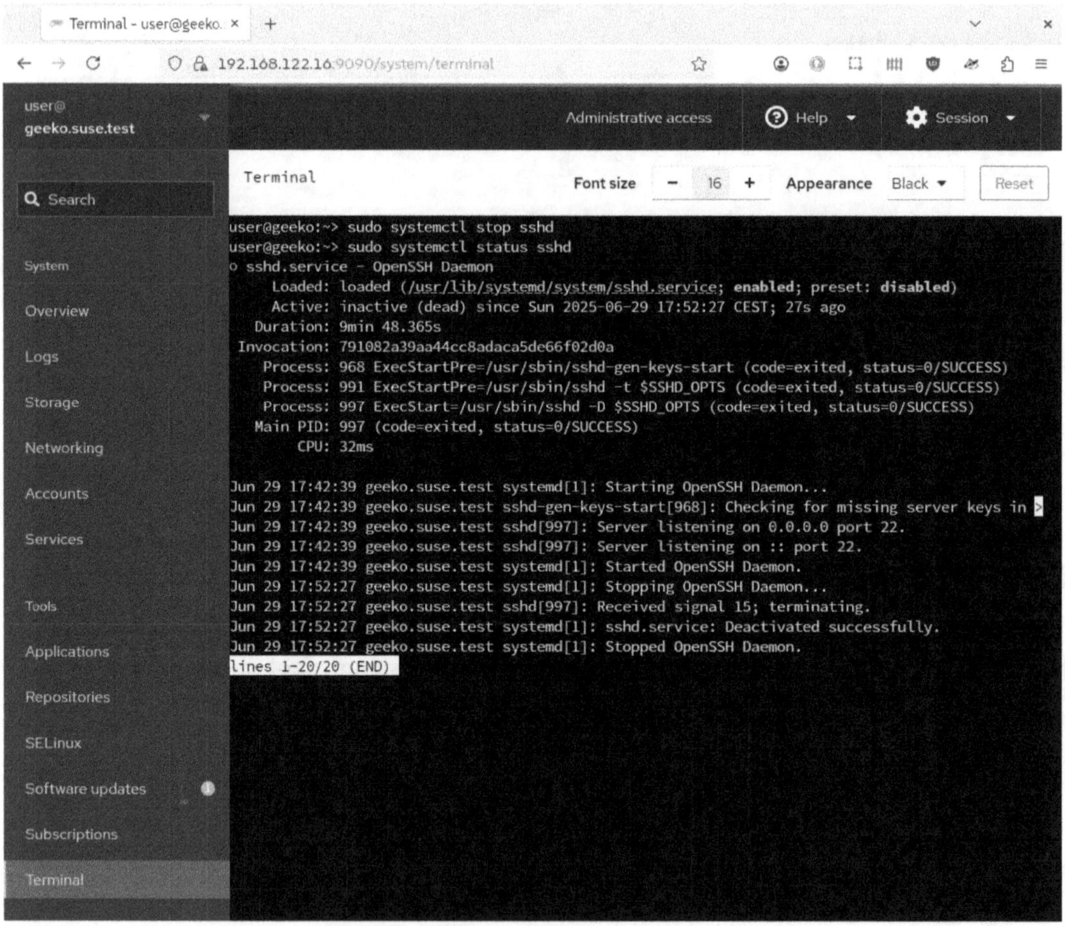


*Figure 8.34 – Cockpit updating the system*

As an add-on, it is nice and comfortable, but it is very interesting to note that it is also a way to fully access the system if you mess up the SSH configuration – another good reason to have it installed on your system.

# Summary

In this chapter, we discovered Cockpit and how to use it for the most common administrative use cases, simplifying many of the tasks we do in our system and providing nice information about what is going on. It is a really good tool for people starting to administrate systems or to simply gather data to troubleshoot issues.

In the next chapter, we'll be digging deeper into securing our system network via **firewalld** to only expose the services that are required for operation. Now that you have gone through this chapter, it will be easier to understand. Let's go!

# 9

# Securing Network Connectivity with firewalld

We have seen legislation that increases liability for CIOs and companies regarding security incidents of software and hardware that is accessible remotely, such as the 2019 Cybersecurity Act of the European Union and the 2024 Cyber Resilience Act, which establishes requirements for products with digital elements connected to the internet or other devices. There are equivalent laws in the United Kingdom (Product Security and Telecommunications Infrastructure Act, 2022) and Australia (Cyber Security Act, 2024), and different laws for government use in the US. Cyber-attacks have become a topic of public interest, and they can cause serious losses of money and reputation for companies due to loss of business, fines, or theft. Even if it is nearly impossible to completely secure a system (unless it is completely disconnected and powered off), it is possible to implement techniques that make it harder for attackers to gain access or privileges.

One of those techniques is to reduce the attack surface using a **firewall**, restricting the possibility of unauthorized remote access while still allowing authorized access, as well as filtering and modifying network packets going in and out. In **SUSE Linux Enterprise Server** (**SLES**) 16, the firewall is configured using an open source package named **firewalld** that supports IPv4 and IPv6 settings, Ethernet bridges, and **network address translation** (**NAT**) operations, and configures the underlying kernel module, **nftables**. It also includes a command-line tool called `firewall-cmd` and a `systemd` service unit to simplify its management.

In this chapter, we will cover the following topics to provide a deep understanding of the firewall usage and configuration:

- Introduction to `firewalld`
- Enabling `firewalld` on the system and reviewing the default zones
- Enabling and managing services and ports
- Creating and using service definitions for `firewalld`

# Technical requirements

We will be using a second server for this chapter, so follow the process in *Chapter 1, Getting SLES 16 Up and Running (Physical and Cloud)* to create a second machine. If you are using **virtual machines (VMs)**, make sure that both VMs are in the same network segment and that they are not isolated so they can reach each other and not just the host.

# Introduction to firewalld

SLES integrates a Linux kernel subsystem to provide filtering and classification of network packages, **nftables**, which replaces the legacy **iptables** component that was present in previous versions. There are two traffic-filtering user-space applications:

- `nft`: This is an advanced tool that provides low-level configuration of the nftables framework.
- `firewalld`: This provides a high-level interface for configuration. It also integrates with other components, such as Podman, libvirt, Docker, and QEMU, to enable their required dynamic configuration.

We will only explain `firewalld` in this chapter. `nft` is only needed for complex configurations beyond the scope of this book, and the examples here should be enough for the normal operation of a server.

> You can use the `nft list ruleset` command to see the current configuration for `nft`. For my test server, the default is a 552-line-long XML file.

## Installing firewalld

`firewalld` is installed by default in SLES 16. You can see that it is installed and running as a service using the following commands. `firewalld` includes a `systemd` service that runs in the background:

```
user@geeko:~> rpm -qa "firewalld*"
firewalld-bash-completion-2.1.2-160000.2.3.noarch
firewalld-2.1.2-160000.2.3.noarch

firewalld-lang-2.1.2-160000.2.3.noarchuser@geeko:~> sudo systemctl status
firewalld
● firewalld.service - firewalld - dynamic firewall daemon
     Loaded: loaded (/usr/lib/systemd/system/firewalld.service; enabled;
preset: enabled)
     Active: active (running) since Fri 2025-07-04 14:00:44 CEST; 1 day
17h ago
Invocation: 2fa28e4b3f3746c5afb2dc2e25028c3a
       Docs: man:firewalld(1)
   Main PID: 842 (firewalld)
      Tasks: 2
        CPU: 214ms
     CGroup: /system.slice/firewalld.service
             └─842 /usr/bin/python3.13 /usr/sbin/firewalld --nofork
--nopid

Jul 04 14:00:43 geeko.suse.test systemd[1]: Starting firewalld - dynamic
firewall daemon...
Jul 04 14:00:44 geeko.suse.test systemd[1]: Started firewalld - dynamic
firewall daemon.
```

If it is not available on the system for any reason, you can install `firewalld` using `zypper`. Once it has been installed, you can use `systemctl` to enable the service if it is not running to make sure it is running when you reboot:

```
user@geeko:~> sudo zypper install firewalld
user@geeko:~> sudo systemctl enable firewalld --now
```

Now that `firewalld` is enabled and running, let's configure it so that it allows the right traffic while filtering out the rest.

# Configuring firewalld

`firewalld` is a stateful, zone-based firewall. Policies and zones are used to organize firewall rules. It maintains separate runtimes and permanent configurations, allowing runtime-only changes, as the runtime configuration does not persist after reboots. Once it is installed and running, there are different ways to configure `firewalld`:

- Use the command-line `firewall-cmd` tool to change configurations in real time
- Add new configuration files under `/etc/firewalld` (as explained later in this chapter in the *Creating and using service definitions for firewalld* section)
- Use **Cockpit**, a web interface that allows you to configure the firewall graphically

We will be focusing on the command line in this chapter, but you can also go to *Chapter 8, Enabling and Using Cockpit*, to find out how to use the graphical interface to configure it.

Let's have a look at the basic concepts for configuration for `firewalld`. The network is logically divided into zones, and policies apply firewall rules to traffic between zones. We will now discuss `firewalld` zones, ports, and services and learn how they affect the rules that are selected and applied.

## Zones

`firewalld` is a zone-based firewall. The network is divided into zones so that traffic ingress takes place through only one zone. Policies are unidirectional too, and, to make it simple, the traffic return path is implicitly allowed, so you don't need to define it in your configuration. The rules can include filtering input and output, forwarding it, or performing NAT.

There are some principles regarding zones:

- Traffic enters one and only one zone
- Traffic exits one and only one zone
- A zone defines a level of trust
- Intra-zone traffic (between the same zone) is allowed by default
- Inter-zone traffic (between different zones) is denied by default

## Ports

The traffic rules take into account the protocol and port that is being filtered, so you can make more granular rules that specify the traffic in more detail. For instance, you can separate rules for traffic using **Transmission Control Protocol** (**TCP**), **User Datagram Protocol** (**UDP**), **Stream Control Transmission Protocol** (**SCTP**), or **Datagram Congestion Control Protocol** (**DCCP**).

A `firewalld` port defines a protocol port number (i.e., `80`) or a port range (`8080-8082`) and a protocol (TCP, UDP, STCP, or DCCP).

## Services

A `firewalld` service is a port or group of ports configured together to allow a system service to work properly. Many applications require more than one port to be open simultaneously, and services allow you to manage them together as a single unit.

> Be aware that a firewall can stop traffic from reaching your application without your application knowing that the connection is happening. There will be no trace left in the application logs. Always check the firewall when you have problems connecting to an application.

Let's now look at the default configuration and learn how we can start and stop the service when we need it.

# Enabling firewalld in the system and reviewing the default zones

We have checked that `firewalld` is enabled by default in the system. However, sometimes the configuration can be hard to test, and you will need to troubleshoot the connection. Let's start looking at how you can manage the system itself, and how you can use `systemctl` to disable, re-enable, start, and stop the firewall. Let's start by learning how to stop the `firewalld` service:

```
user@geeko:~> sudo systemctl stop firewalld.service
user@geeko:~> sudo systemctl status firewalld.service
o firewalld.service - firewalld - dynamic firewall daemon
     Loaded: loaded (/usr/lib/systemd/system/firewalld.service; enabled;
preset: enabled)
     Active: inactive (dead) since Fri 2025-07-11 13:15:25 CEST; 4s ago
   Duration: 9min 4.242s
Invocation: 15d6b2aa17714caba86ede413816d61b
```

```
      Docs: man:firewalld(1)
   Process: 857 ExecStart=/usr/sbin/firewalld --nofork --nopid
$FIREWALLD_ARGS (code=exited, status=0/SUCCESS)
  Main PID: 857 (code=exited, status=0/SUCCESS)
       CPU: 255ms

Jul 11 13:06:20 geeko.suse.test systemd[1]: Starting firewalld - dynamic
firewall daemon...
Jul 11 13:06:21 geeko.suse.test systemd[1]: Started firewalld - dynamic
firewall daemon.
Jul 11 13:15:25 geeko.suse.test systemd[1]: Stopping firewalld - dynamic
firewall daemon...
Jul 11 13:15:25 geeko.suse.test systemd[1]: firewalld.service: Deactivated
successfully.
Jul 11 13:15:25 geeko.suse.test systemd[1]: Stopped firewalld - dynamic
firewall daemon.
```

We stopped the service, and the last line of the log is telling us that the daemon is no longer running. Any traffic in or out of the system won't be modified or filtered, keeping it totally open to the network. We could also have checked the state of `firewalld` using `firewall-cmd --state`:

```
user@geeko:~> sudo firewall-cmd --state
not running
```

This command is a great way to check the state of the firewall in a script. In this case, with the firewall stopped, there are no active rules. Don't worry! We have not lost our previous configuration. `firewalld` differentiates between runtime configuration and permanent configuration, so when we restart the system or the service, the permanent configuration will be copied in memory to become the running configuration so that it can be applied. Remember that the running configuration does not overwrite the permanent one, so this will not apply to the changes in memory.

We can always see the underlying `netfilter` rules by running the `nft list chains` command. You may want to run it before and after stopping the service to see the difference.

Let's restart the service so it is running again and see what happens:

```
user@geeko:~> sudo systemctl start firewalld
user@geeko:~> sudo systemctl status firewalld
• firewalld.service - firewalld - dynamic firewall daemon
     Loaded: loaded (/usr/lib/systemd/system/firewalld.service; enabled;
preset: enabled)
     Active: active (running) since Fri 2025-07-11 13:34:32 CEST; 4s ago
Invocation: 12d6eb4231ee473586067424d8b04ea7
       Docs: man:firewalld(1)
   Main PID: 1573 (firewalld)
      Tasks: 2
        CPU: 197ms
     CGroup: /system.slice/firewalld.service
             └─1573 /usr/bin/python3.13 /usr/sbin/firewalld --nofork
--nopid

Jul 11 13:34:32 geeko.suse.test systemd[1]: Starting firewalld - dynamic
firewall daemon...
Jul 11 13:34:32 geeko.suse.test systemd[1]: Started firewalld - dynamic
firewall daemon.
```

Let's check again whether `firewalld` is running:

```
user@geeko:~> sudo firewall-cmd --state
running
```

If you don't want to run the service when you reboot, you need to disable the service, directing `systemd` not to start it with the next reboot:

```
user@geeko:~> sudo systemctl disable firewalld
Removed '/etc/systemd/system/multi-user.target.wants/firewalld.service'.
Removed '/etc/systemd/system/dbus-org.fedoraproject.FirewallD1.service'.
```

Like every service for `systemd`, disabling the service will not stop it. You can see that the service is still running by running the following commands:

```
user@geeko:~> sudo systemctl  is-active firewalld
active
user@geeko:~> sudo firewall-cmd --state
running
```

You can do more than enabling and disabling services with `systemd` using `systemctl`; you can find more about the different options in *Chapter 8, Enabling and Using Cockpit.*

> If you want to change the configuration now and permanently, you can use the `--now` option. For example, `systemctl disable firewalld --now` will disable and stop the `firewalld` service, and it is possible to enable and start it at the same time using `systemctl enable firewalld --now`. If you prefer, you could also start the service with a second command using `systemctl start firewalld --now`.

Normally, your network will already have a firewall to limit external traffic, but running a system without its own firewall is a bad idea. If an attacker finds access to another server, your production server will immediately be at risk. For that reason, we really want the firewall to be running, and we need to make sure we configure it appropriately. Let's make sure it is enabled and running:

```
user@geeko:~> sudo systemctl enable firewalld --now
Created symlink '/etc/systemd/system/dbus-org.fedoraproject.FirewallD1.
service' → '/usr/lib/systemd/system/firewalld.service'.
Created symlink '/etc/systemd/system/multi-user.target.wants/firewalld.
service' → '/usr/lib/systemd/system/firewalld.service'.
user@geeko:~> sudo firewall-cmd --state
running
```

Now that we know how to start and stop the firewall, let's review the steps required to configure it for both the running and the permanent configuration.

## Reviewing the different configuration items under firewalld

As we discussed before, `firewalld` manages three concepts in its configuration: zones, services, and ports. It also distinguishes between two types of configuration:

- **Running**: The rules that have currently been applied to the system
- **Permanent**: The rules that have been saved and will be loaded when the service starts

> You should think about the running rules as a way to test a new configuration dynamically or for troubleshooting. Once you make everything work as expected, you store them as permanent rules so they get applied on each reboot. Don't forget to check that the rules you want in the system have been saved properly so you don't lose them.

The firewall is configured with a predefined series of zones and rules so it is functional and secure. Let's have a look at them in a new server:

```
user@geeko:~> sudo firewall-cmd --get-zones
block dmz docker drop external home internal nm-shared public trusted work
user@geeko:~> sudo firewall-cmd --get-default-zone
public
```

We have a list of zones defined by default in any new installation. The default zone, `public`, will be assigned to any traffic that can't be associated with another zone, because all the ingress traffic needs to be assigned to one and only one zone. Let's see a description of the default zones and what they are intended for:

| Zone | Enabled services | Other characteristics |
|---|---|---|
| `drop` | `N/A` | Drops all network packages without reply. Only outgoing connections are possible. |
| `block` | `N/A` | Rejects all incoming traffic, answering with an ICMP prohibited message. Only outgoing connections are possible. |
| `public` | `dhcpv6-client, ssh` | For public areas where you don't trust other computers or networks. Only selected incoming connections are accepted. |
| `external` | `ssh` | Accepts incoming traffic related to outgoing connections. Any IP traffic that's forwarded through the interface with this zone assigned will be masqueraded and look as though it originated from this machine. |

| Zone | Enabled services | Other characteristics |
|---|---|---|
| `dmz` | `ssh` | For computers in your demilitarized zone that are publicly accessible and have limited access to your internal network. Only selected incoming connections are accepted. |
| `work` | `ssh` and `dhcpv6-client` | For work areas. You mostly trust the other computers in the network. Accepts incoming traffic related to outgoing connections. |
| `internal` | `ssh`, `mdns`, `samba-client`, and `dhcpv6-client` | You mostly trust the other computers in the network. Accepts incoming traffic related to outgoing connections. |
| `home` | `ssh`, `mdns`, `samba-client`, and `dhcpv6-client` | You mostly trust the other computers in the network. Accepts incoming traffic related to outgoing connections. |
| `docker` | `N/A` | Used for container traffic. Accepts all packages by default. |
| `trusted` | `N/A` | Accepts all incoming traffic. |

*Table 9.1 – Default firewall zones*

You can always access information about these zones, and more, by accessing the `firewalld.zones` manual pages in the system by running `man firewalld.zones`. It is a good idea to review the man page.

If you want, you can get detailed information about a zone with the following command:

```
user@geeko:/bin> sudo firewall-cmd --info-zone home
home
  target: default
  ingress-priority: 0
  egress-priority: 0
  icmp-block-inversion: no
  interfaces:
```

```
  sources:
  services: dhcpv6-client mdns samba-client ssh
  ports:
  protocols:
  forward: yes
  masquerade: no
  forward-ports:
  source-ports:
  icmp-blocks:
  rich rules:
user@geeko:~> sudo firewall-cmd --list-all-zones
<output omitted>
```

The `--info-zone` command and the `--list-all-zones` command provide all the configuration for one or all zones in the system. We will be learning more about what each line means in the rest of the chapter. In this case, we know that the ICMP packages are accepted (block inversion will reject ICMP packages not explicitly allowed by default), that it allows the `dhcpv6-client`, `mdns`, `samba-client`, and `ssh` services, that it allows for free traffic within interfaces in the zone, and that no other rules are configured.

Let's get a better understanding of zones by working with them. We will start by looking at the default zone and then changing it to `home`:

```
user@geeko:~> sudo firewall-cmd --get-active-zones
docker
  interfaces: docker0
public (default)
  interfaces: lo enp0s1
user@geeko:~> sudo firewall-cmd --get-default-zone
public
user@geeko:~> sudo firewall-cmd --set-default-zone=home
success
user@geeko:~> sudo firewall-cmd --get-default-zone
home
```

We have changed the default zone to `home`. Normally, you use more than one zone to have different rules applied to different traffic. You define the zones and rules that select the right zone to be applied to the traffic. For instance, you could apply the `home` zone to your local network (which is safer) while keeping all traffic by default in the `public` zone. Once that is done, it is easy to add filters for each zone so that some services are only available when the traffic is coming from the `home` zone. Let's do that by listing all the interfaces and their IP addresses so that we can apply a filter to use the right zone for all the traffic coming from IPs in the local network subsegment:

```
user@geeko:~> sudo ip -br addr
lo               UNKNOWN        127.0.0.1/8 ::1/128
enp0s1           UP             192.168.68.2/24
fde9:22b8:954e:8aca:94bd:6a29:938a:f2ba/64
fde9:22b8:954e:8aca:e899:2bb5:9de9:8e33/64 fe80::3ea2:e26d:719d:a63e/64
user@geeko:> sudo firewall-cmd --set-default-zone=public
Success
user@geeko:> sudo firewall-cmd --permanent --zone=internal\
--add-source=192.168.68.0/24
Success
user@geeko:~> sudo firewall-cmd --reload
success
```

When you are using the `--permanent` flag, you don't actually change the running configuration. You need to reload the configuration to change those rules and apply the changes.

Let's get active zones for the `docker` zone:

```
user@geeko:~> sudo firewall-cmd --get-active-zones
docker
  interfaces: docker0
internal
  sources: 192.168.68.0/24
public (default)
  interfaces: enp0s1 lo
```

Let's review what we have done. The server had several IP addresses assigned to `enp0s1`. We used the IPv4 range as the source for our `internal` zone, which is identified by the IP range defined. We also have some traffic that is identified because it comes in the `docker0` interface and is assigned to the `docker` zone. Everything else, including local traffic coming with an IPv6 address, is assigned to the `public` zone, the default, because it will be applied by default and specifically to anything coming in the interfaces loopback (`lo`) and `enp0s1`, the only ones in the server.

Remember that, by default, inter-zone traffic is forbidden. If your traffic comes through one zone, it will not be able to communicate with other zones. With this configuration, services in your local network will not be accessible in the public zone (which is the zone for everything else).

You can easily allow all traffic to any service. There is a default zone that allows all traffic to any server. If you want to do that (this is not advisable in production), you need to assign the internal IP network (`192.268.68.0/24`) to the trusted zone so that you will not need to explicitly allow any service. The virtual network that connects your workstation to the server can sometimes be safe enough to be worth the risk in exchange for the convenience. Let's recap the `firewall-cmd` options you will often find:

| **Option** | **Description** |
|---|---|
| `--state` | Checks whether the firewalld daemon is active. |
| `--get-zones` | Lists the zones that have been configured in the system. |
| `--get-default-zone` | Shows the zone that will be used by default. |
| `--set-default-zone=<zone>` | Sets the default zone. This is applied to the running and permanent configuration. |
| `--get-active-zones` | Shows zones in use and interfaces and sources used. |
| `--zone=<zone>` | Used to specify a zone for another option. |
| `--permanent` | Applies the changes to the saved configuration, without updating the running configuration. |
| `--reload` | Reloads the permanent configuration and updates the running firewall rules. Existing connections are kept, but the running configuration that is not stored will be lost. |
| `--add-source=<network>` | Adds a source (network, MAC address, or IP set) to a specified zone. When the zone is not specified, it uses the default one. |
| `--remove-source=<network>` | Moves a source network in CIDR format (i.e., `192.168.1.0/24`) to a specified zone. When the zone is not specified, it uses the default one. |

| Option | Description |
|---|---|
| `--add-interface=<interface>` | Routes traffic from an interface to a zone. When the zone is not specified, it uses the default zone. |
| `--change-interface=<interface>` | Changes the traffic that's being routed to an interface to a zone. When the zone is not specified, it uses the default one. |

*Table 9.2 – firewall-cmd's most common options*

There are many other options available that allow you to create more complex configurations. You can find the complete list on the manual page for `firewall-cmd`. Take some time to go through it, as you will often need it when you're reconfiguring the firewall.

> To view the `firewall-cmd` manual page, simply run `man firewall-cmd`.

To make zones useful, we need to configure the rules that apply to them. Let's learn next how to manage services and ports.

# Enabling and managing services and ports

We defined a **firewalld service** as a port or group of ports configured together to allow a system service to work properly. There are many predefined services in a running SLES system. Some of them are enabled by default in one or more zones, and you can easily add or remove existing services to zones or define your own services. Let's review some of them:

- `ssh`: Allows connections to the **secure shell** (**SSH**) service for remote access, which provides a secure remote console for management. Accepts traffic to port `22` on `TCP`.
- `mdns`: Allows connections to the **multicast DNS** (**MDNS**) service. It provides local name resolution in a local network without a DNS server and is the reason you can find other systems in your network using the `.local` suffix. Opens traffic to port `5353` on multicast address `224.0.0.251` (IPv4) or `ff02::fb` (IPv6) using UDP.
- `samba-client`: This is a file- and print-sharing client that's compatible with Microsoft Windows SMB and Active Directory. It uses ports `137` (`netbios-ns`) and `138` on UDP.
- `dhcpv6-client`: A **Dynamic Host Configuration Protocol** (**DHCP**) for IPv6. Its destination is the special network `fe80::/64`, on `546`, using UDP.
- `cockpit`: The web graphical interface for servers, using port `9090` on TCP. It is enabled by default when Cockpit is installed.

As with the default services for MDNS and Samba, a `firewalld` service can specify more than one port, port range, target address, and even target network.

Now, let's review the predefined services in our firewall and the services enabled in the current zone:

```
user@geeko:~> sudo firewall-cmd --get-services
<output ommited - 245 services aprox.>
user@geeko:~> sudo firewall-cmd --list-services
dhcpv6-client ssh
user@geeko:~> sudo firewall-cmd --list-services --zone=internal
dhcpv6-client mdns samba-client ssh
```

We have used `firewall-cmd` to see the list of all defined services, the ones defined in the default zone, and the ones defined in a specific zone. When you don't specify a zone, you are in fact using the default zone. In this case, without the `--zone=<zone>` option, you get the list of services you would get if you used `--zone=public`. As we have configured more than one zone, access to the server will depend on the zone applied to the traffic, which may be different from the default. Let's check the default zone:

```
user@geeko:~> sudo firewall-cmd --get-default-zone
public
```

Let's configure a different service. We are going to follow the steps to install and enable the Apache `httpd` server and configure the firewall so the system can serve web pages. Let's start by installing the package:

```
user@geeko:~> sudo zypper in apache2
Refreshing service ' SUSE_Linux_Enterprise_Server_16.0_aarch64'.
Loading repository data...
Reading installed packages...
Resolving package dependencies...
The following 2 recommended packages were automatically selected:
 apache2-utils w3m
The following 9 NEW packages are going to be installed:
apache2 apache2-prefork apache2-utils libapr1-0 libapr-util1-0
libbrotlienc1 libgc1 system-user-wwwrun w3m
9 new packages to install.
Package download size: 4.9 MiB
Package install size change:
| 15.7 MiB required by packages that will be installed
```

```
 15.7 MiB   | - 0 B released by packages that will be removed
.... OUTPUT OMITTED
[done]
user@geeko:~>
```

After a couple of pages of information about the different steps required to install the web server, we are back at the command line. The installation of the `apache2` package has an updated list of services available by default. Let's see the definition of the `apache2` service:

```
user@geeko:~> sudo firewall-cmd --info-service=apache2
apache2
  ports: 80/tcp
  protocols:
  source-ports:
  modules:
  destination:
  includes:
  helpers:
```

It is installed but not enabled. Let's enable the `apache2` service in `systemd` so it is running and configured to run after reboots:

```
user@geeko:~> sudo systemctl enable apache2 --now
Created symlink '/etc/systemd/system/httpd.service' → '/usr/lib/systemd/system/apache2.service'.
Created symlink '/etc/systemd/system/apache.service' → '/usr/lib/systemd/system/apache2.service'.
Created symlink '/etc/systemd/system/multi-user.target.wants/apache2.service' → '/usr/lib/systemd/system/apache2.service'.
```

Let's make sure that the service is running before we try to change the configuration of the firewall:

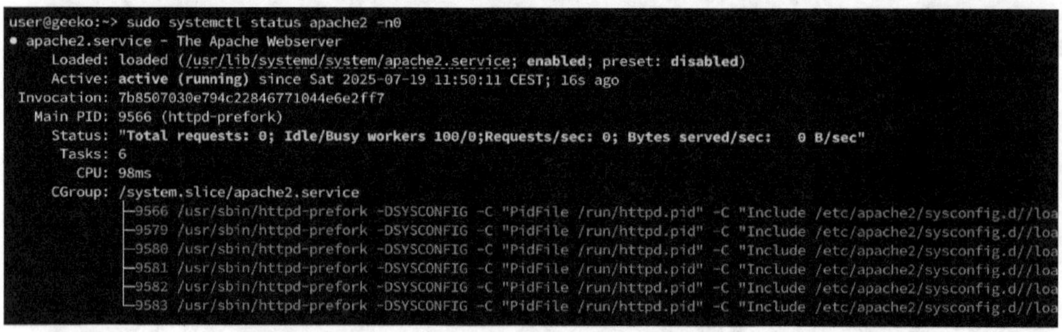


*Figure 9.1 – Output of the systemctl status for apache2*

We can see that the service is enabled and running, and that six parallel threads are waiting for requests. Now, let's check that the web service has been configured by default to listen on all the interfaces. We will use the `ss` command to investigate the socket:

```
user@geeko:~> ss -a -t | grep http
LISTEN    0    4096        *:http            *:*
user@geeko:~> sudo lsof -i :http
COMMAND    PID   USER FD   TYPE DEVICE SIZE/OFF NODE NAME
httpd-pre 1481   root 4u  IPv6  15874      0t0  TCP *:http (LISTEN)
httpd-pre 1495 wwwrun 4u  IPv6  15874      0t0  TCP *:http (LISTEN)
httpd-pre 1496 wwwrun 4u  IPv6  15874      0t0  TCP *:http (LISTEN)
httpd-pre 1497 wwwrun 4u  IPv6  15874      0t0  TCP *:http (LISTEN)
httpd-pre 1498 wwwrun 4u  IPv6  15874      0t0  TCP *:http (LISTEN)
httpd-pre 1499 wwwrun 4u  IPv6  15874      0t0  TCP *:http (LISTEN)
```

The first command tells us that there is a configured socket listening on all addresses on the HTTP port (`80`), while the second one specifies that `httpd-pre` is the listening process.

> When you test your firewall rules, it is important to initiate the requests from the right zone that mimics the actual traffic expected, because what works in one zone can fail in another. Make an effort to simulate the test connections like a customer on an external machine.

Let's use a second machine to test that the firewall is doing its work. We expect the test to fail because the firewall configuration does not allow connections to the HTTP port from that zone. Let's connect to a second VM or server and try to connect to our server using `curl`, a tool for transferring data from a server providing a URL:

```
user@geeko2:~> curl 192.168.70.4:80
curl: (7) Failed to connect to 192.168.70.4 port 80 after 1 ms: Could not
connect to server
```

Connecting from our second server to our web server on the first machine fails. There are many possible reasons, so let's do some quick troubleshooting by installing some tools that will allow us to understand the real issue and rule out a misconfiguration of the firewall.

Let's install `nmap`, a network exploration tool, on our second machine, and use it to see whether we can reach the server:

```
user@geeko2:~> sudo zypper install nmap
[OUTPUT OMITTED]
user@geeko2:~> ping 192.168.70.4
PING 192.168.70.4 (192.168.70.4) 56(84) bytes of data.
64 bytes from 192.168.70.4: icmp_seq=1 ttl=64 time=4.37 ms
^C
--- 192.168.70.4 ping statistics ---
1 packets transmitted, 1 received, 0% packet loss, time 0ms
rtt min/avg/max/mdev = 4.365/4.365/4.365/0.000 ms
user@geeko2:~> sudo nmap 192.168.70.4 -p 80
Starting Nmap 7.92 ( https://nmap.org ) at 2025-07-19 12:14 CEST
Nmap scan report for 192.168.70.4
Host is up (0.00056s latency).

PORT   STATE    SERVICE
80/tcp filtered http
MAC Address: E6:B2:9F:82:5E:75 (Unknown)

Nmap done: 1 IP address (1 host up) scanned in 0.24 seconds
```

`nmap` is reporting that the port is filtered (the packet reaches the port but is being dropped without any reply to inform the client). Let's enable the `http` service on our configured zone in the firewall of the first server to see whether it fixes the issue:

```
user@geeko:~> sudo firewall-cmd --add-service apache2 --zone=internal
--permanent
success
user@geeko:~> sudo firewall-cmd --add-service apache2 --zone=public
--permanent
success
user@geeko:~> sudo firewall-cmd --reload
success
```

We need to reload the configuration because we are only modifying the permanent configuration. If we fail to do so, the running configuration will not be updated:

```
user@geeko:~> sudo firewall-cmd --list-services
--zone=public
apache2 dhcpv6-client ssh
user@geeko:~> sudo firewall-cmd --list-services
--zone=internal
apache2 dhcpv6-client mdns samba-client ssh
```

Let's use nmap again to check the state of the service and firewall to make sure that the web server is now reachable:

```
user@geeko2:~> sudo nmap 192.168.70.4 -p http
Starting Nmap 7.92 ( https://nmap.org ) at 2025-
07-19 12:57 CEST
Nmap scan report for 192.168.70.4
Host is up (0.00050s latency).

PORT     STATE    SERVICE
80/tcp   open     http
8008/tcp filtered http
MAC Address: E6:B2:9F:82:5E:75 (Unknown)
Nmap done: 1 IP address (1 host up) scanned in
0.21 seconds
```

We have fixed the issue! Port 80 is reachable. We can now use curl to download the first lines of the default landing page:

```
user@geeko2:~> curl -s http://192.168.70.4 |
head -n 2
<?xml version="1.0" encoding="UTF-8"?>
<!DOCTYPE html PUBLIC "-//W3C//DTD XHTML 1.0
Strict//EN"
```

> The definitions of the services are stored as independent XML files in the `/usr/lib/firewalld/services` directory. Feel free to check them to learn more about services. The best practice is that you should not modify them directly, but make a copy with a different name in `/etc/firewalld/services` and modify the copy.

Imagine now that we want to restrict the web server to internal users. We thus don't want to allow access from the `public` network, while permitting access from the `internal` zone:

```
user@geeko:~> sudo firewall-cmd --list-services --zone=public
apache2 dhcpv6-client ssh
user@geeko:~> sudo firewall-cmd --remove-service apache2 --zone=public
--permanent
success
user@geeko:~> sudo firewall-cmd --reload
success
user@geeko:~> sudo firewall-cmd --list-services --zone=public
dhcpv6-client ssh
```

We can see that the `public` zone does not include the `apache2` service. Connections from that zone will be rejected again.

You can see that services are really convenient, and predefined services allow us to quickly configure the basic and more common applications, but the list of services can't include every application out there. You can directly open ports without using a service:

```
user@geeko:~> sudo firewall-cmd --list-ports --zone=public
user@geeko:~> sudo firewall-cmd --add-port 80/tcp  --zone=public
--permanent
success
user@geeko:~> sudo firewall-cmd --reload
success
user@geeko:~> sudo firewall-cmd --list-ports --zone=public
80/tcp
```

We have added the port directly, instead of the service. We can see all the configurations in one go. For instance, let's see the full configuration for the `public` zone:

```
user@geeko:~> sudo firewall-cmd --info-zone public
public (default, active)
  target: default
  ingress-priority: 0
  egress-priority: 0
  icmp-block-inversion: no
  interfaces: enp0s1 lo
  sources:
```

```
  services: dhcpv6-client ssh
  ports: 80/tcp
  protocols:
  forward: yes
  masquerade: no
  forward-ports:
  source-ports:
  icmp-blocks:
  rich rules:
```

This is different; we have not opened the service, only the port. But we don't want to open the port to the `public` zone because our server is only intended for internal traffic. We can easily clean up the configuration:

```
user@geeko:~> sudo firewall-cmd --list-ports --zone=public
80/tcp
user@geeko:~> sudo firewall-cmd --remove-port=80/tcp
success
user@geeko:~> sudo firewall-cmd --list-ports --zone=public

user@geeko:~>
```

Now that we know how to use services and ports and review the configuration, let's recap those options for `firewall-cmd` in a table:

| Option | Description |
|---|---|
| `--zone=<zone>` | Used to specify a zone. When no zone is specified, it uses the default zone. |
| `--list-services` | Displays the list of services for the specified zone. |
| `--add-service` | Adds a service to the specified zone. |
| `--remove-service` | Removes a service from the specified zone. |
| `--list-ports` | Lists the ports configured in the specified zone. |
| `--add-port` | Adds a port to the specified zone. |
| `--remove-port` | Removes a port from the specified zone. |
| `--list-all` | Lists everything configured or enabled for the zone. |
| `--info-zone <zone>` | Shows all the information for a zone. |

| Option | Description |
|---|---|
| `--permanent` | Any updates are applied to the permanent configuration, instead of the runtime configuration. Runtime is not updated. |
| `--reload` | Reloads the rules from the saved configuration, discarding the running configuration. |
| `--runtime-to-permanent` | Stores the runtime configuration as the permanent one. |

*Table 9.3 – Options to add services and ports to a zone*

Opening ports is easy and quick, but if your service is complex or you want to share the configuration file between machines, it is better to use a service. Let's see how you can define your own service.

# Creating and using service definitions for firewalld

As we said before, you can find all predefined service definitions for `firewalld` in the `/usr/lib/firewalld/services` folder. Let's start by inspecting a simple service, such as `ssh`. The configuration file is `ssh.xml`:

```
<?xml version="1.0" encoding="utf-8"?>
<service>
  <short>SSH</short>
  <description>Secure Shell (SSH) is a protocol for logging into and
executing commands on remote machines. It provides secure encrypted
communications. If you plan on accessing your machine remotely via SSH
over a firewalled interface, enable this option. You need the openssh-
server package installed for this option to be useful.</description>
  <port protocol="tcp" port="22"/>
</service>
```

A simple XML file with three sections is good enough to define a basic service:

- `short`: A more readable name for a service.
- `description`: What the service does in a longer form so you know how to use it properly.
- `port`: The port or port range in the format `portid-portid`. It can appear more than once if you need it.

Imagine you want to install an Oracle database. The database listens on port `1521` and on TCP. We can create a file called `/etc/firewalld/services/oracledb.xml` to define the service:

```
<?xml version="1.0" encoding="utf-8"?>
<service>
  <short>OracleDB</short>
  <description>Oracle Database service. It
allows connections to the Oracle Database. You
should install the Oracle database with the
standard configuration to make use of it.</
description>
  <port protocol="tcp" port="1521"/>
</service>
```

You must create your configuration file in `/etc/firewalld/services/` and not in `/usr/lib/firewalld/services`. Files in `/etc` will have higher precedence than any in `/usr/lib`.

Now that we have defined the service, we need to make it available, starting by telling the firewall to reload all the configuration so we can use the service. Once we reload the configuration, it will behave like any of the default services. Let's go through the steps:

```
user@geeko:~> sudo firewall-cmd --reload
success
user@geeko:~> sudo firewall-cmd --add-
service=oracledb
success
user@geeko:~> sudo firewall-cmd --list-services
dhcpv6-client oracledb ssh
```

Now that the service is enabled in the runtime configuration, you can add the service to the permanent configuration by writing the commands again for the permanent configuration or by storing the saving the runtime configuration:

```
user@geeko:~> firewall-cmd --add-service
oracledb --permanent
success
user@geeko:~> sudo firewall-cmd --runtime-to-
permanent
success
```

The last command stores all the runtime configuration as the permanent configuration. Be careful because you could modify other configurations if you have updated them in memory.

> On rare occasions, you will need to define more complex services. There are other options that will allow you to create those complex configurations that have not been described here. You can find a better description in the `firewalld.service` manual page with `man firewalld.service`.

Using service definitions simplifies the maintenance of firewall configuration repeatedly. Just copy these files manually or automatically to a new server during installation, and it will be easier to understand and maintain the configuration.

# Summary

Security is a key part of the responsibility of a sysadmin. However, the firewall can create challenges because it can prevent your system from communicating with the outside world, and it needs to be carefully considered. Never disable the firewall on a system, even if you think that the network is secure, because it will expose your server to external threats.

In this chapter, we have seen how easy it is to configure the Linux firewall using `firewalld`, a tool for managing, filtering, and securing the network connections in our system. We used the command line, although you can use Cockpit to configure it with a web interface.

We have learned about key concepts required by `firewalld`. We know how to manage zones and assign them to interfaces. We can adjust zones so that different rules are associated with them, and we can differentiate the runtime config from the permanent one. We used services and ports to configure the zones, and we also learned how to define our own services to simplify configuration.

Now, we are ready to learn more about security in SLES, and specifically about process security. We will see how SELinux enables role-based access control.

# 10

# Keeping the System Hardened with SELinux

In this chapter, we are going to dive deeper into a feature that is new to SLES 16, which is **Security-Enhanced Linux (SELinux)**. Previous versions of SLES used **AppArmor** by default to provide extended security measures for applications. However, to follow technology and market trends, SUSE included SELinux in SLES 15 as an option, without the policies, and the full solution as the default for SUSE Linux Enterprise Micro. SUSE has now applied the lessons learned and made SELinux the default in SLES 16, too.

Let's review the origins of SELinux, including what the default modes and policies are, how it applies to our files, folders, and processes, how to restore them to the system defaults, how to fine-tune the policies using Booleans, and how to troubleshoot common issues with the help of the following sections:

- SELinux usage in `enforcing` and `permissive` modes
- Reviewing SELinux context for files and processes
- The `targeted` policy
- Tweaking the policy with `semanage`
- Restoring changed file contexts to the default policy
- Using SELinux Boolean settings to enable services
- SELinux troubleshooting and common fixes

We will also have extended explanations on how SELinux works to better understand the way it operates, even if using it in reality is a lot simpler. We will also use those examples to illustrate cases where SELinux prevents attacks or misconfigurations.

By the end of this chapter, you will understand how to use SELinux properly and how to benefit from the additional protection that it provides to your system.

Let's get hands-on with SELinux!

# Technical requirements

You can continue using the virtual machine created at the beginning of this book in *Chapter 1, Getting SLES 16 Up and Running (Physical and Cloud)*. Any additional packages required will be indicated in the text. Any additional files required for this chapter can be downloaded from `https://github.com/PacktPublishing/SUSE-Linux-Enterprise-Server-16-Official-Administration-Guide` and will be indicated in the text.

# SELinux usage in enforcing and permissive modes

SELinux was introduced in December 2000 as a project started by the **National Security Agency** (**NSA**) to improve the security of the operating system via **mandatory access control** (**MAC**) and role-based access control (RBAC), as opposed to the traditional **discretionary access control** (**DAC**) (users and permissions) that were already available in the system.

Before SELinux was introduced in the Linux kernel, there was discussion about the proper way to do it. Finally, a kernel framework named **Linux Security Modules** (**LSM**) was introduced, and SELinux was implemented using it so that other approaches could use it, too.

SELinux provides security improvements to Linux, as access to files made by users, processes, or even other resources can be controlled in a very granular way.

Let's look at one example to make it clearer when SELinux comes into play: when a web server is serving pages from users, it reads files from the user's `home` directory (`/home/user`) inside the `public_html` or `www` folder (the most standard ones). Being able to read files from the user's `home` directory could reveal other contents if the web server process is hijacked by an attacker. This is where SELinux comes into play, as it will automatically block access to files that should not be accessible to a web server.

SELinux confines the processes and services to only perform what they are supposed to do, and only over resources that are authorized. This is a really important feature that keeps things under control. Even in the event of software bugs that might lead to access to unexpected files or resources, SELinux will block them if they have not been authorized by the active policy.

> SELinux permissions always come after regular DAC. If a user has no access to a file because of improper file permissions, SELinux has nothing to do with it.

By default, the installation of a system sets the configuration of SELinux to the `enforcing` mode and uses the `targeted` policy. It is possible to check your current system status via the execution of `sestatus`:

```
user@geeko:~> sestatus
SELinux status:                 enabled
SELinuxfs mount:                /sys/fs/selinux
SELinux root directory:         /etc/selinux
Loaded policy name:             targeted
Current mode:                   enforcing
Mode from config file:          enforcing
Policy MLS status:              enabled
Policy deny_unknown status:     allowed
Memory protection checking:     actual (secure)
Max kernel policy version:      33
user@geeko:~>
```

*Figure 10.1 – Output of sestatus for our system*

As we can see, our system has SELinux enabled, using the `targeted` policy, and is currently in `enforcing` mode. Let's learn what that means.

SELinux works by defining a **policy**, that is, a set of predefined rules for granting or denying access to resources. The available ones can be listed via `sudo zypper search selinux-policy` in your system, with `targeted`, `sandbox`, and `minimum` being the most common ones.

We will focus on the `targeted` policy, which is the default one applied to the system.

The mode, listed as `enforcing`, means that the policy is currently being enforced, and all security measures and restrictions are being applied. On the other hand, we have `permissive`, which, even when it is active, will only warn, but not protect.

Why do we have `permissive` instead of just disabling it? This question is a bit tricky, so let's explain a bit more about how this policy works to provide an answer.

SELinux uses **extended attributes** in the filesystem to store the **labels**. Each time a file is created and SELinux is active, a label is assigned based on the policy. This makes `disabled` different from `permissive` because the first one will not create those labels for new files that are created, while the second one will.

Additionally, SELinux in `permissive` mode, while not blocking anything, allows us to see the errors that would be raised if a program has not received a good policy, has bad behavior for it, or if some file has no proper labels.

It is really easy to switch from `enforcing` to `permissive`, and vice versa, via the `setenforce` command, while we can use `getenforce` to retrieve the current status, as we can see in the following figure:

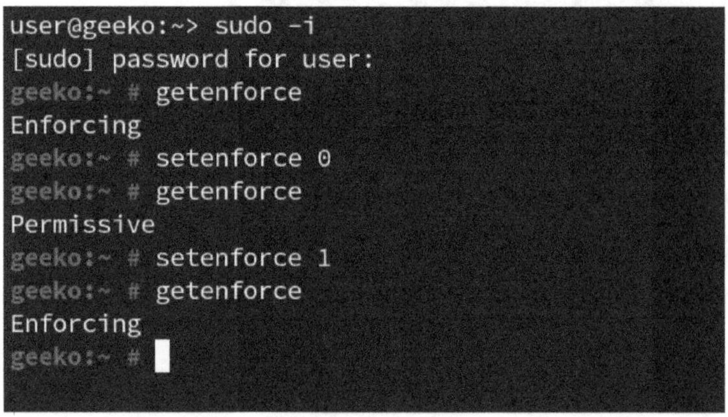


*Figure 10.2 – Changing the SELinux enforcing status*

It might look basic, and it's really as easy as that—a matter of running a command. However, if the status were `disabled`, it would be a completely different story.

The SELinux status is configured by editing the `/etc/selinux/config` file, but changes only take effect after a system reboot. That is, we can switch from `enforcing` to `permissive` at any time or from `permissive` to `enforcing`. However, when changing the policy from `disabled` to `enabled`, or vice versa, SELinux will require us to reboot the system.

The general advice is to leave SELinux in the `enforcing` mode, but if, for whatever reason, it was `disabled`, the recommendation is to switch SELinux to `permissive` as the first step when moving from `disabled`. This will allow us to check that the system actually works without being locked out of it because of the kernel blocking access to files and resources.

> During the reboot after switching from `disabled` to `permissive` or `enforcing`, the system will force a relabeling of the filesystem based on the policy. This is accomplished by the creation of a file in the `root` folder of our filesystem named `/etc/selinux/.autorelabel`, which will trigger the process and reboot afterward.

Why use `disabled` instead of setting it to `permissive`? For example, some software might require setting SELinux to `disabled` even if it can later be reenabled for operations, or there might be other reasons. Bear in mind that SELinux is a security feature that protects your system and should be kept enabled.

SELinux uses **Access Vector Cache** (**AVC**) messages that are logged to the `/var/log/audit/audit.log` file as well as system journals. And yes, it's a cache, so rules are not checked as frequently to speed up the operations.

Let's go back to the idea of the filesystem storing labels, and let's jump into the next section to see how they relate to processes, files, and RBAC, as provided by SELinux.

# Reviewing SELinux context for files and processes

SELinux uses labels, also referred to as a security context attached to each file, and defines several aspects. Let's check one example in our `home` folder with the `ls -l` command, but with a special modifier, `Z`, that will show SELinux attributes as well. We can see these in the following figure:

```
user@geeko:~> ls -lZ
total 0
-rw-r--r--. 1 user user unconfined_u:object_r:user_home_t:s0 0 jul  3 20:11 testfile
user@geeko:~> sudo -i
[sudo] password for user:
geeko:~ # ls -lZ
total 32
drwxr-xr-x. 1 root root unconfined_u:object_r:admin_home_t:s0         0 Mar 28 12:10 $MYVIMDIR
-rw-------. 1 root root unconfined_u:object_r:admin_home_t:s0     15774 Jul  3 20:08 .bash_history
drwx------. 1 root root system_u:object_r:cache_home_t:s0             0 Apr 23 10:15 .cache
drwx------. 1 root root unconfined_u:object_r:config_home_t:s0       12 Mar 31 18:56 .config
drwxr-xr-x. 1 root root unconfined_u:object_r:container_home_t:s0    22 Mar 31 10:25 .docker
drwx------. 1 root root system_u:object_r:gpg_secret_t:s0             0 Jan 28 10:26 .gnupg
-rw-------. 1 root root unconfined_u:object_r:admin_home_t:s0        66 May 17 19:13 .lesshst
drwx------. 1 root root system_u:object_r:ssh_home_t:s0              82 Apr  9 10:05 .ssh
-rw-------. 1 root root unconfined_u:object_r:admin_home_t:s0     11693 Jul  3 20:05 .viminfo
drwxr-xr-x. 1 root root system_u:object_r:bin_t:s0                    0 Jan 28 10:26 bin
geeko:~ #
```

*Figure 10.3 – File listing showing SELinux attributes*

Let's focus on the output for one of the files:

```
-rw-------. 1 root root unconfined_u:object_r:admin_home_t:s0 15774 Jul 3
20:08 .bash_history
```

The SELinux attributes are the ones listed as `unconfined_u:object_r:admin_home_t:s0`. Let's understand the attributes:

- The first part is the user mapping: `unconfined_u`
- The second part is the role: `object_r`
- The third part is the type: `admin_home_t`
- The fourth part is used for the level: `s0` in the multi-level and multi-category security

Something similar happens with processes, and similarly, we can append `Z` to many of the common commands to get the contexts, for example, with `ps Z`, as we can see in the next figure:

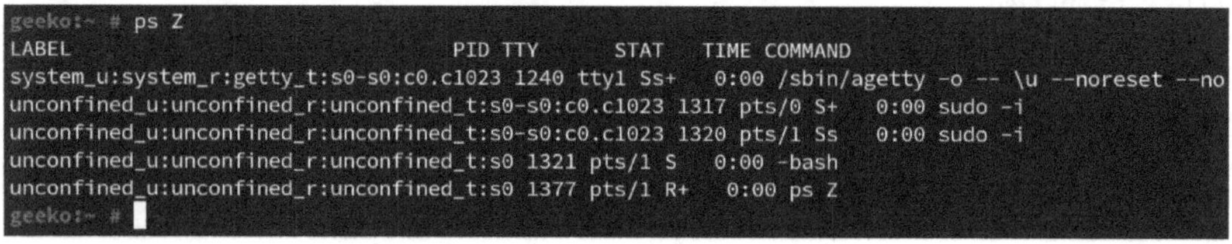


*Figure 10.4 – The ps output with SELinux contexts*

Again, let's examine one of the lines:

```
unconfined_u:unconfined_r:unconfined_t:s0 1321 pts/1 S 0:00 -bash
```

Again, we can see the same approach: user, role, type, and level for multi-level and multi-category security.

Now that we've introduced what it does look like, let's focus on how it works in the `targeted` policy.

# The targeted policy

The `targeted` policy allows everything to run as if SELinux were not enabled in the system, except for the specific services that are targeted by it. This makes a good compromise between security and usability.

During the development of the policy, new services are added, and others are refined, and many of the most common services have policies written for protecting them.

SELinux also features something named **transitions**. A transition allows one process started by a user with a binary with some specific role to transition via the execution into some other role, which is used later to define the permissions for it.

As you might imagine, our user also has a SELinux context, and similarly, we can use the `id -Z` command to check it:

```
unconfined_u:unconfined_r:unconfined_t:s0-s0:c0.c1023
```

So, going back to one example, Apache HTTP Server is provided by the apache2 package, which can be installed via `zypper install apache2`. Once it is installed, let's start it with `systemctl start apache2` and enable it with `systemctl enable apache2`. Then, open the firewall with `firewall-cmd --add-service=http` and `firewall-cmd --add-service=https`. Finally, add the rules as permanent with `firewall-cmd --add-service=http --permanent` and `firewall-cmd --add-service=https --permanent`, as we've done with other services in previous chapters.

The aforementioned commands can be found in the script at `https://github.com/PacktPublishing/SUSE-Linux-Enterprise-Server-16-Official-Administration-Guide/blob/main/chapter-10-selinux/install-apache.sh`.

Let's see how all of this comes into play in this figure:

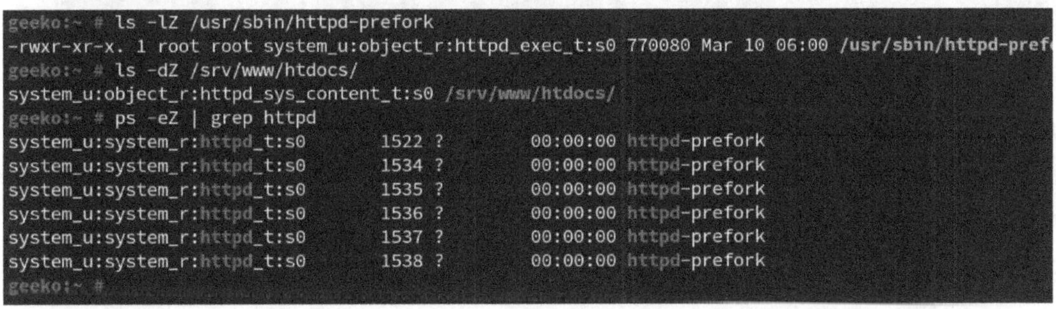


*Figure 10.5 – Web server SELinux contexts*

We can see how the executable on disk, located in `/usr/sbin`, has the `httpd_exec_t` context, the process is `httpd_t`, and the files/folder served by it are `httpd_sys_content_t`, and it works!

Let's now create an `index.html` file in our folder, and let's move it to the Apache web root folder:

```
user@geeko:~> echo '<html><head><title>Our test</title></head><body>This
is our test html</body></html>' > index.html
user@geeko:~> sudo cp index.html /srv/www/htdocs/index1.html
user@geeko:~> sudo mv index.html /srv/www/htdocs/index2.html
```

Let's see what happens when we try to access the files. Look at the following figure:

```
user@geeko:~> echo '<html><head><title>Our test</title></head><body>This is our test html</body>
</html>' > index.html
user@geeko:~> sudo cp index.html /srv/www/htdocs/index1.html
user@geeko:~> sudo mv index.html /srv/www/htdocs/index2.html
user@geeko:~> ls -Z /srv/www/htdocs/*
unconfined_u:object_r:httpd_sys_content_t:s0 /srv/www/htdocs/index1.html
        unconfined_u:object_r:user_home_t:s0 /srv/www/htdocs/index2.html
unconfined_u:object_r:httpd_sys_content_t:s0 /srv/www/htdocs/index.html
user@geeko:~> curl localhost/index1.html
<html><head><title>Our test</title></head><body>This is our test html</body></html>
user@geeko:~> curl localhost/index2.html
<?xml version="1.0" encoding="UTF-8"?>
<!DOCTYPE html PUBLIC "-//W3C//DTD XHTML 1.0 Strict//EN"
  "http://www.w3.org/TR/xhtml1/DTD/xhtml1-strict.dtd">
<html xmlns="http://www.w3.org/1999/xhtml" lang="en" xml:lang="en">
<head>
<title>Access forbidden!</title>
<link rev="made" href="mailto:%5bno%20address%20given%5d" />
<style type="text/css"><!--/*--><![CDATA[/*><!--*/
    body { color: #000000; background-color: #FFFFFF; }
    a:link { color: #0000CC; }
    p, address {margin-left: 3em;}
    span {font-size: smaller;}
/*]]>*/--></style>
</head>

<body>
<h1>Access forbidden!</h1>
<p>
```

*Figure 10.6 – Apache httpd service behavior with the generated files*

As we can see, one file has one SELinux context and the other has a different one. On top of that, Apache is denying access to the one we moved (`index2.html`), but showing the contents for the one we copied (`index1.html`).

What has happened here? We copied one file and moved the other out of the same source, but they have two different SELinux contexts.

We can retry by disabling SELinux temporarily and setting it to the `permissive` mode, and then checking what happens. It will be as shown in this figure:

```
user@geeko:~> setenforce 0
-bash: setenforce: command not found
user@geeko:~> sudo setenforce 0
user@geeko:~> curl localhost/index2.html
<html><head><title>Our test</title></head><body>This is our test html</body></html>
```

*Figure 10.7 – Retrying with SELinux in permissive mode*

As we can see in the figure, we are now able to access the file contents, so one could say, "*What is wrong with SELinux that does not allow my site to work?*", but the right way to express it would be "*Look how SELinux has protected us from disclosing personal files on a website.*"

If, instead of directly moving a file into Apache's `DocumentRoot` directory (`/srv/www/htdocs`), an attacker were trying to reach our home folder files, SELinux would have denied access to those, as, by default, the `httpd_t` process cannot access the `user_home_t` context.

A similar thing happens when we try to get Apache, or any other service under the `targeted` policy, to listen on a port that is not the one configured by default. The best way to get familiar with what we can or cannot do is to learn about the `semanage` utility.

Using `semanage`, we can list, edit, add, and delete the different values in the SELinux policy, and even export and import our customizations. So, let's use it to learn a bit more about it using our example with `httpd`.

Let's learn about `semanage` in the following section.

# Tweaking the policy with semanage

As we introduced earlier, the `targeted` policy contains some configurations that are enforced for the services it has defined, allowing the protection of those services while not interfering with the ones it does not know about. The Apache `httpd` server is one of the services with the best-defined SELinux policy.

Still, there are times when we need to adjust certain settings—for example, allowing the `http` or `ssh` daemon to listen on alternate ports, or granting access to specific file types—without losing the extra layer of protection that SELinux provides. These are uncommon or unexpected behaviors, but sometimes necessary. First, let's ensure that `policycoreutils`, `policycoreutils-python`, and `policycoreutils-python-utils` are installed in our system with `sudo zypper install policycoreutils policycoreutils-python policycoreutils-python-utils`, as they provide the tools we will use in this and the next sections of this chapter.

Let's learn from an example. Let's see which ports `httpd_t` can access with `semanage port -l | grep http`:

```
user@geeko:~> sudo semanage port -l | grep http
http_cache_port_t  tcp 8080, 8118, 8123, 10001-10010
http_cache_port_t  udp 3130
http_port_t                tcp 80, 81, 443, 488, 8008, 8009, 8443, 9000
http_port_t                udp 80, 443
```

```
pegasus_http_port_t        tcp 5988
pegasus_https_port_t       tcp 5989
```

As we can see, the `http_port_t` used by the Apache daemon, by default, is allowed to use ports `80`, `81`, `443`, `488`, `8008`, `9009`, `8443`, and `9000` via `tcp`.

That means that if we want to run Apache on any of those ports, no changes to the policy will be required.

If we repeat the command but for `ssh`, we only see port 22 opened (executing `sudo semanage port -l | grep ssh`):

```
ssh_port_t                     tcp      22
```

We might want to add another port, let's say 2222, to the list of possible ports, so that we hide the standard one being tested by port scanners. We will be able to do it via `sudo semanage port -a -p tcp -t ssh_port_t 2222` and then validate it with the prior `sudo semanage port -l | grep ssh` command, which now shows the following:

```
ssh_port_t                     tcp      2222, 22
```

As we can see, port 2222 has been added to the list of available ports for the `ssh_port_t` type, which enables the `ssh` daemon to start listening on it (this, of course, requires additional configuration for the `ssh` daemon configuration and the firewall before we get a working service).

In the same way, some web services require writing to specific folders, for example, for storing configuration. By default, the context on `/srv/www/htdocs` is `httpd_sys_content_t`. This will mean that SELinux will not allow the Apache `httpd` server to write to disk in the aforementioned folder, because of the way it is labeled.

We can check the available file contexts with `sudo semanage fcontext -l` in a similar way to what we did with the ports, but the list of files is huge, as a web server might use common locations such as `logs` and `cgi-bin`, as well as filesystem files for certificates, configuration, home directories, extensions such as `php`, and so on. When you check the context with the preceding command, pay attention to the different types that are available and what the structure is for one listing, as in this example:

```
user@geeko:~> sudo semanage fcontext -l | grep ^/srv/ | grep www
/srv/([^/]/)?www(/.)? all files system_u:object_r:httpd_sys_content_t:s0
/srv/([^/]/)?www/logs(/.)? all files system_u:object_r:httpd_log_t:s0
```

As we can see, there is a regular expression that matches the files in the `www` folder inside the `/srv/www/` path, applying to all files and setting `httpd_sys_rw_content_t`, which allows read-write access. There are folders here that can be used by the popular blog software WordPress. So, the policy is already prepared for covering some of the most popular service folders' requirements without requiring system administrators to write them ad hoc.

When invoking `semanage`, it will output that it has some subcommands we can use, as follows:

- `import`: Allows importing local modifications
- `export`: Allows exporting the local changes
- `login`: Allows managing the login and SELinux user associations
- `user`: Manages SELinux users with roles and levels
- `port`: Manages port definitions and types
- `ibpkey`: Manages InfiniBand definitions
- `ibendport`: Manages end port InfiniBand definitions
- `interface`: Defines network interface definitions
- `module`: Manages policy modules for SELinux
- `node`: Manages the definition of network nodes
- `fcontext`: Manages file context definitions
- `boolean`: Manages Booleans for tweaking policies
- `permissive`: Manages the `enforcing` mode
- `dontaudit`: Manages the `dontaudit` rules in the policy

For each one of the aforementioned subcommands, we can use the `-h` argument to list help and to learn about the extra arguments that can be used for each one.

For the day-to-day use case, most of the time, we'll be using `port` and `fcontext`, as these will cover extending or tuning the available services that come with SUSE Linux Enterprise Server, like the example we have showcased with `ssh` listening on an additional port.

> Traditionally, **SUSE Certified Administrator (SCA)** or **SUSE Certified Engineer (SCE)** exams had a reboot for validation. This means that for each service that was installed and started, it was also mandatory to remember to enable it to be active on the next reboot. A similar thing happens with SELinux; if we are adding a piece of software that will stay in our system, the best approach is to define, via `semanage`, the `regexp` for the path that will be used. So, if the filesystem is relabeled or restored, the contexts, as we will see in the next section, will still allow the application to continue to work.

Let's see how to manually set the context for files and how to restore the defaults in the next section.

# Restoring changed file contexts to the default policy

In the previous section, we mentioned that `semanage` enables us to perform changes to the policy, which is the recommended way to perform changes and to persist them for future files and folders, but that is not the only way we can perform operations.

From the command line, we can use the `chcon` utility to change the context for a file. It will allow us to define the user, the role, and the type for the file we want to alter, and similar to other filesystem utilities such as `chmod` or `chown`, we can also affect files recursively, so it's easy to set a full folder hierarchy to the desired context.

One feature that we always found very interesting is the ability to use `--reference` to copy the full context of an existing file, so that the same context as the referenced file is applied to the target one.

When we were introducing the example of Apache `httpd` earlier in this chapter, we did a test with two files, `index1.html` and `index2.html`, which were copied and moved to the `/srv/www/htdocs` folder. To go deeper into this example, we will make additional copies of `index1.html` to demonstrate, in the next figure, the usage of `chcon`. Bear in mind that creating the files directly in the `/srv/www/htdocs` folder will set the files to have the proper context. So, we need to create them in our `home` folder, `/home/user`, and then move to the target folder as we did in previous examples.

For example, let's generate `index3.html` in our `home` folder and move it to the `htdocs` folder, then we can fix the SELinux context with `chcon`, using `index1.html` as the reference, as in this screenshot:

```
user@geeko:~> echo '<html><head><title>Our test</title></head><body>This is our test html</body>
</html>' > index3.html
user@geeko:~> sudo mv index3.html /srv/www/htdocs/
user@geeko:~> ls -lZ /srv/www/htdocs/
total 12
-rw-r--r--. 1 root root unconfined_u:object_r:httpd_sys_content_t:s0 84 jul 20 15:08 index1.html
-rw-r--r--. 1 user user unconfined_u:object_r:user_home_t:s0         84 jul 20 15:08 index2.html
-rw-r--r--. 1 user user unconfined_u:object_r:user_home_t:s0         84 jul 20 15:53 index3.html
user@geeko:~> sudo chcon --reference=/srv/www/htdocs/index1.html /srv/www/htdocs/index3.html
user@geeko:~> ls -lZ /srv/www/htdocs/
total 12
-rw-r--r--. 1 root root unconfined_u:object_r:httpd_sys_content_t:s0 84 jul 20 15:08 index1.html
-rw-r--r--. 1 user user unconfined_u:object_r:user_home_t:s0         84 jul 20 15:08 index2.html
-rw-r--r--. 1 user user unconfined_u:object_r:httpd_sys_content_t:s0 84 jul 20 15:53 index3.html
user@geeko:~>
```

*Figure 10.8 – Demonstrating chcon usage*

As we can see, both `index1.html` and `index3.html` now have the proper context—in the first case, using the reference, and in the second, defining the type to use.

Of course, this is not the only method. As we indicated earlier, the recommended way for setting context for applications is to define the path's regular expressions via `semanage`, or better, use the ones already defined by default. This empowers us to use the `restorecon` command to apply the right context to the files, according to the configuration. Let's check how it operates in the next figure:

```
user@geeko:~> ls -lZ /srv/www/htdocs/
total 12
-rw-r--r--. 1 root root unconfined_u:object_r:httpd_sys_content_t:s0 84 jul 20 15:08 index1.html
-rw-r--r--. 1 user user unconfined_u:object_r:user_home_t:s0         84 jul 20 15:08 index2.html
-rw-r--r--. 1 user user unconfined_u:object_r:httpd_sys_content_t:s0 84 jul 20 15:53 index3.html
user@geeko:~> sudo restorecon -vR /srv/www/htdocs/
Relabeled /srv/www/htdocs/index2.html from unconfined_u:object_r:user_home_t:s0 to unconfined_u:
object_r:httpd_sys_content_t:s0
user@geeko:~> ls -lZ /srv/www/htdocs/
total 12
-rw-r--r--. 1 root root unconfined_u:object_r:httpd_sys_content_t:s0 84 jul 20 15:08 index1.html
-rw-r--r--. 1 user user unconfined_u:object_r:httpd_sys_content_t:s0 84 jul 20 15:08 index2.html
-rw-r--r--. 1 user user unconfined_u:object_r:httpd_sys_content_t:s0 84 jul 20 15:53 index3.html
user@geeko:~>
```

*Figure 10.9 – Using restorecon to restore context*

As we can see, we used `restorecon -vR /srv/www/htdocs/` and it automatically changed the `index2.html` file into the `httpd_sys_content_t` that is defined for that folder, as we saw when we were testing `semanage` to list the contexts.

The arguments used, `v` and `R`, make the utility report the changes (verbose) and work recursively on the paths provided.

Let's say we have messed up the system by running `chcon` over the root filesystem. What would be the way to fix it? In this case, as we mentioned earlier, we should follow these steps:

1. Set the operation mode to `permissive` to not block further accesses via `setenforce 0`.
2. Put the marker to have the filesystem relabeled via `touch /etc/selinux/.autorelabel`.
3. Modify the `/etc/selinux/config` file to set the boot mode to `permissive`.
4. Reboot the system to let the relabeling happen.
5. Once the system reboots, edit the `/etc/selinux/config` file again to define the operation mode as `enforcing`.

By operating in this way, instead of just running `restorecon -R /`, we are making sure that the system is operational and will continue to operate after reboot, and that a full relabel is applied to the filesystem, so it is left ready to re-enable the `enforcing` mode safely.

Let's see the next section on how to tune the policy within itself, using the Booleans to tune how it works.

# Using SELinux Boolean settings to enable services

Many services have a wide range of configuration options for many common cases, but not always the same ones. For example, an HTTP server should not access user files, but at the same time, it's a common way of operation to enable personal websites out of the `www` or `public_html` folder in each user's `home` directory.

To overcome that use case and, at the same time, provide enhanced security, the SELinux policy makes use of **Booleans**.

A Boolean is a tunable that can be set by the administrator and can enable or disable conditionals in the policy code. For example, let's get a list of available Booleans for `httpd` by executing `sudo getsebool -a|grep ^http` (list reduced):

```
user@geeko:~> sudo getsebool -a | grep ^http
httpd_can_network_connect --> off
httpd_can_network_connect_db --> off
httpd_can_sendmail --> off
httpd_enable_homedirs --> off
httpd_use_nfs --> off
```

This list is a reduced subset of the available Booleans, but it gives us an idea of what can be accomplished. For example, by default, `http` cannot use the network to connect to other hosts, or send email (usually done in PHP scripts), and it can't even access the `home` folder for users.

If we want to enable users in a system to publish their personal web pages from the `www` folder in their `home` directory (that is, `/home/user/www/`), we will have to enable the `httpd_enable_homedirs` Boolean by running the following:

```
user@geeko:~> sudo setsebool -P httpd_enable_
homedirs=1
```

> The `-P` parameter after `setseebol` is required to make the change permanent. That means writing the change so that it persists even after reboots; without it, the change will be lost once we restart our server.

This will tweak the policy to enable `http` to access the user's `home` directory to serve the pages there. If, additionally, the servers will be stored on an NFS or CIFS mount, additional Booleans will be required. We're still using the same `targeted` policy, but we've enabled the internal conditionals to permit access so that it is not blocked by SELinux.

As we've seen, `getsebool` and `setsebool`, respectively, allow us to query and set the values for the Booleans that tune the policy; `semanage boolean` can also help here, as we can see in the next figure:

```
user@geeko:~> sudo setsebool -P httpd_enable_homedirs=1
user@geeko:~> sudo semanage boolean -E
boolean -m -1 httpd_enable_homedirs
boolean -m -1 virt_sandbox_use_all_caps
boolean -m -1 virt_use_nfs
user@geeko:~>
```

*Figure 10.10 – Using semanage to manage Booleans*

In *Figure 10.10*, we can see the Boolean we edited using `setsebool`.

One of the benefits is that `semanage`, as we introduced, allows us to export and import the local changes to the policy, so any customization made can be exported and imported on another system to ease the setup of similar server profiles.

All the possible Booleans in the policy can be checked with `sudo semanage boolean -l`, as we did to list the binding ports for applications in our HTTP example.

We have learned about using Booleans to tune how the policy adapts to some specific but pretty common cases. Next, we will explore what is probably the most used part for administrators—troubleshooting, but focusing on SELinux.

# SELinux troubleshooting and common fixes

One of the main problems getting used to SELinux is that many people who are not familiar with it blame it for things not working. However, this argument is getting a bit outdated: SELinux was introduced back in 2005.

Most of the time, issues with SELinux and our system are related to changed file contexts, changing ports for services, and, less frequently, issues with the policy itself.

First of all, there are several places where we can check for errors, such as the audit log or the system messages. The first ones, for example, are the `/var/log/audit/audit.log` file we introduced earlier in this chapter.

Bear in mind that SELinux MAC only plays once we have cleared access from regular DAC. That is, if we've no permission to check a file (for example, mode `400` and our user not being the owner), it's highly unlikely that SELinux is blocking the access.

Most of the time, our system will have installed the `setroubleshoot-server` and `setroubleshoot-plugins` packages, which provide several tools such as `sealert` to query the received SELinux messages and, many times, also suggest changes.

Let's cover some of the basics that we should always validate:

- Review that all other controls (user and group ownership and permissions) are properly set
- Do not disable SELinux
- If a program is not working properly and it was shipped with the OS, it might be a bug and should be reported via the SUSE Customer Center, opening a service request, or via Bugzilla
- If a program is not working properly, it might be made to run unconfined, but leaving all remaining system services protected via the `targeted` policy

- Think about what was done before the error happened, if this was an existing program:
    - Files moved instead of copied or created on the destination
    - Changed ports or folders for the software

Having arrived at this point, we should check `audit.log` for relevant messages. For the example we mentioned about wrong context with the files in `/srv/www/htdocs/`, an example audit entry could be the following:

```
type=AVC msg=audit(1753017038.500:148): avc: denied { read } for
pid=1149 comm="httpd-prefork" name="index2.html" dev="vda2" ino=263
scontext=system_u:system_r:httpd_t:s0 tcontext=unconfined_u:object_r:user_
home_t:s0 tclass=file permissive=0
```

It looks strange, but if we check the parameters, we see the path of the affected file, the PID, the source context (`scontext`), and the target context (`tcontext`). So, in brief, we can see that `httpd_t` tried to access (get attributes) for a target context (`user_home_t`) and that was denied.

We can use the `ausearch` and `audit2allow` tools to generate a custom policy and enable this behavior using two commands:

```
user@geeko:~> sudo ausearch -c 'httpd' --raw | audit2allow -M my-httpd
******************** IMPORTANT *********************** To make this policy
package active, execute:
semodule -i my-httpd.pp
user@geeko:~> sudo semodule -X 300 -i my-httpd.pp
```

However, this kind of recommendation should be taken with knowledge of what is being done. That means that the preceding commands will fix `httpd_t` getting access to the `user_admin_t` file. We can learn about what would be done by only running the first command, together with the `audit2allow` pipe.

Running `ausearch -c 'httpd' --raw | audit2allow -M my-httpd` creates several files named `my-httpd` in the current folder, one named `my-httpd.te` and another named `my-httpd.pp`. The second command, `semodule`, which we will not use in production servers, installs the modified policy. But please, don't ever do that until you understand what's going on, as we will see in the following lines.

The interesting file for us is now the `my-httpd.te` file (`te: type enforcement`):

```
module my-httpd 1.0;
require {
type httpd_t;
type unconfined_service_t;
type user_home_t;
class process signull;
class file { open read };
}
#============= httpd_t ============== allow
httpd_t unconfined_service_t:process signull;
#!!!! This avc can be allowed using the boolean
'httpd_read_user_content' allow httpd_t user_
home_t:file { open read };
```

Not sure how many times we should reinstate this, but before acting on a system, think twice, act once. SELinux is a protection mechanism for increasing the safety of your system. Do not disable it; do not blindly accept `audit2allow`-created policies without some initial investigation and understanding of what the issue might be and what the proposed resolution does, as it might be almost equivalent to disabling SELinux.

From there, we can see that it uses a requirements session for the types involved, and later, the rule itself, which allows `httpd_t` access to `user_home_t` files for using the `getattr` function—nothing more, nothing less.

Will this fix our file access issue? It will effectively make `httpd_t` get access to the `index2.html` file, so there will no longer be errors, but this will come at a big cost. From that point, `httpd_t` could also read `home` directory files without any restriction.

If, at this point, we have installed the module created by us with `ausearch`, we can use `semodule` to do the following:

- List: `semodule -l`
- Install: `semodule -i $MODULE_NAME`
- Remove: `semodule -r $MODULE_NAME`

With the preceding commands, we can check or alter the status of the policy-loaded modules.

Going back to reviewing system logs, it might happen that we realize that something fails long after it really started failing. So, using `ausearch` or passing the full logs to `audit2allow` should be used carefully.

In the case of new software being deployed that has no SELinux support, we can do the checks the other way around, in a test system:

- Set SELinux to `permissive` mode
- Deploy the software
- Analyze all the alerts received to see whether there are expected things
- Contact vendors for the software and open a support case with SUSE to work on a policy

If we're getting locked out of our system because SELinux is in `enforcing` mode and we have really messed up the labels very badly, such as by running a bad `chcon` command recursively against our `root` folder (for example, scripting a context change depending on a variable and that variable being empty), we still have ways to get out of trouble:

- Use `setenforce 0` to put SELinux in `permissive` mode
- Run `touch /etc/selinux/.autorelabel`
- Reboot the host so that, at the next boot, SELinux restores the appropriate labels

If we are in a really bad situation, and we cannot use `setenforce 0` or the system cannot even boot or perform the relabeling correctly, there's still hope, but with some extra steps.

When a system is rebooting, we can see the list of installed kernels at the `grub` prompt and use it to edit the kernel boot parameters.

Using the `selinux=0` parameter, we completely disable SELinux, and it's something we don't want, but we can use `enforcing=0` to accomplish having SELinux enabled but in `permissive` mode.

Once we have our system booting into `permissive` mode, we can repeat the previous procedure to get back to the previous behavior and continue debugging the situation within the system itself with the prior indications given (checking system logs, etc.).

# Summary

This chapter introduced SELinux, including how it works, how to check the processes, files, and ports, and how to tune them either by adding new options or using Booleans, and some initial troubleshooting skills that we should explore further to gain extra knowledge and experience.

In the next chapter, we will learn about a new feature included in SLES 16, Agentic AI with mcphost, that allows users to query AI to understand and manage their server state.

# Part 3

# Implementing Agentic AI with mcphost

**Model Context Protocol** (**MCP**) is a standard to connect different services and/or systems to **large language models** (**LLMs**) that power **artificial intelligence** (**AI**). SLES 16 comes with an implementation of MCP called `mcphost`, which enables connecting your operating system to any AI that supports the protocol, such as Google Gemini, ChatGPT, or even a local LLM. Enabling system administrators to use this capability is key to increasing operational efficiency and providing a means to learn more about the system and how to use it.

This part has the following chapter:

- *Chapter 11, Agentic AI with mcphost*

# 11

# Agentic AI with mcphost

SUSE aims to provide the latest technology, and at the time that **SUSE Linux Enterprise Server (SLES)** 16 was launched, **Artificial Intelligence** (**AI**) was pervasive. **Agentic AI** capabilities have been added to SLES 16 in an optional, opt-in, secure manner, so you can use it with confidence and where you want, on your terms.

AI is well-known thanks to tools such as **ChatGPT** and Google's **Gemini**. These are what we call **Large Language Models** (**LLMs**). You provide a question in natural language (i.e., "What is slowing down my system?"). Then, it will parse the information available and provide an answer.

Also, and very importantly, AI has been added in a standard way. The **Model Context Protocol** (**MCP**) has been added, which is the standard used to integrate existing services with AI. This standard enables you to connect your system, in this case SLES, to the LLM of your choice, such as Gemini.

We will keep this simple, as the topic could be the subject of its own book. We will restrict this chapter to discussing the following topics:

- Understanding agentic AI and MCP
- Installing and configuring `mcphost`
- Using `mcphost`

Again, in this chapter, we will continue to use the VM we installed in the first chapter, so there are no further technical requirements to continue.

## Understanding agentic AI and MCP

The field of AI has had a dramatic transformation in recent years (as of the time of writing this book). It was around 2022 that ChatGPT and other chatbots captured the world's attention. However, the underlying theoretical/mathematical and technological foundation is far older. It traces its roots back to 1943, when Warren McCulloch and Walter Pitts created the first mathematical model of a neuron using Boolean logic. It was later on, when large computing power started to become available, that **neural networks** (technically referred to as convolutional and recurrent neural networks in case you want to search for more info) started to blossom in the 1980s and 90s. These breakthroughs paved the way for **pattern recognition** (i.e., image recognition) and, later on, LLMs, which started becoming common in research fields by the early 2000s and started to be widely used in the 2010s. However, the computing power needed to implement natural language interpretation was not there yet.

> The mechanism to build packages in SUSE and openSUSE, the Open Build Service, enables the community and the company adopt quickly new technologies.

How do LLMs work? Well, let's consider it as if it were an advanced statistics problem. We can explain it by using image recognition first. We can provide a large dataset of images of, let's say, apples to a neural network and train it to detect apples. For that, we have to provide sample images of real apples, to be recognized as such, and things that are not apples, to be recognized as something that is not an apple. In other words, we can give the model a new apple image that it hasn't seen before, and it will be able to tell, with some level of certainty, whether the image shows an apple, even if it didn't have that exact image in the training data.

> Wikipedia is a great resource to learn more about any of these topics. We recommend the following page to learn more about the basics of neural networks and how they are trained: `https://en.wikipedia.org/wiki/Neural_network_(machine_learning)`.

This is how modern cameras detect faces, and how your phone can even unlock itself with the camera trained on your face.

The existence of vast amounts of data on the World Wide Web provided huge samples to train these models. If we extend this training to recognizing letters, then recognizing words, sentences, and even paragraphs, we develop what are called LLMs. These LLMs use the idea of a **token**, which is the fundamental unit of text. For simplicity, we can say that a token is almost the equivalent of a word. The more tokens an LLM can process, the larger the context it can work with.

Current LLMs used by Gemini and ChatGPT can handle 1 million tokens in each request, in each conversation. For comparison, the text of a novel such as *Don Quijote de la Mancha* would comprise fewer than 500,000 tokens. This means that we can start asking questions about managing operating systems and beyond, getting more and more accurate results each time.

So, now we have a set of processing engines for words that allow us to use natural language (even in different languages), such as ChatGPT, Gemini, Ollama, Claude, and DeepSeek. (By the time this book is published, there will probably be many new ones that are not in this list.) Many can be run on our own machines, but many others are available as a service. It is likely that the company you work for has sanctioned one or two for your use.

> Once again, Wikipedia is a great resource. A list of LLMs can be found at the following page: `https://en.wikipedia.org/wiki/List_of_large_language_models`.

The question now is, how can we leverage this power with our systems and services?

To do so, an open standard was created and introduced by Anthropic in November 2024 called **Model Context Protocol (MCP)**, together with an open source framework. What it does is it connects your system or service to an LLM engine. It provides an interface for reading files, executing different functions, and processing prompts to make requests. The standard was quickly adopted, and many of the main providers have implemented it (Google, OpenAI, and DeepMind already support it).

> Wikipedia never disappoints. It also has a nice page on MCP right here: `https://en.wikipedia.org/wiki/Model_Context_Protocol`.

> In SUSE, we prioritize choice and openness for users and customers. Hence the use of open standards in our implementations.

In SLES 16, a tech preview of an implementation of MCP is provided, so you can connect your system to an LLM and leverage the capabilities it provides. When using AI to power your machine, as well as running tasks in it, we refer to it as **agentic AI**. Let's get started on using Agentic AI in the next section.

# Installing and configuring mcphost

The way to install software in our SLES system is using `zypper`. The implementation of MCP in SLES is called `mcphost`, and to install it, we can simply run the following command:

```
user@geeko:~> sudo zypper install mcphost
Refreshing service 'SUSE_Linux_Enterprise_
Server_16.0_x86_64'.
Loading repository data... Reading installed
packages...
```

```
Resolving package dependencies...

The following NEW package is going to be installed:
  mcphost
1 new package to install.
Package download size: 10,6 MiB
Package install size change:
    | 41,7 MiB required by packages that will be installed 41,7 MiB | - 0
B released by packages that will be removed
Backend: classic_rpmtrans Continue?
[y/n/v/...? shows all options] (y): y
Preloading: mcphost-0.31.1-160000.4.1.x86_64.rpm [done] Preload finished.
[success (15,5 KiB/s) ] ..........[done] Retrieving: mcphost-0.31.1-
160000.4.1.x86_64 (SLE-Product-SLES-16.0) (1/1), 10,6 MiB
Checking for file conflicts: ......................[done] (1/1)
Installing: mcphost-0.31.1-160000.4.1.x86_64 ..[done] Running post-
transaction scripts ...................[done]
```

In its default configuration, `mcphost` will not access any LLM or anything in our system. We need to configure it. The configuration file is located in the user's home directory. We will use `/home/user` or the ~ shortcut to refer to this home directory. We can provide configurations in two formats:

- **Yet Another Markup Language** (**YAML**)
- **JavaScript Object Notation** (**JSON**)

In this example, we will use Google Gemini as our LLM of choice. We will need to create a **Google Gemini API key** to provide access to it. To do so, we can go to **Google AI Studio** and select **API Keys**, which can be done by entering the following address in our browser: `https://aistudio.google.com/app/api-keys`.

If it is your first time doing this, you will be greeted by the following warning:

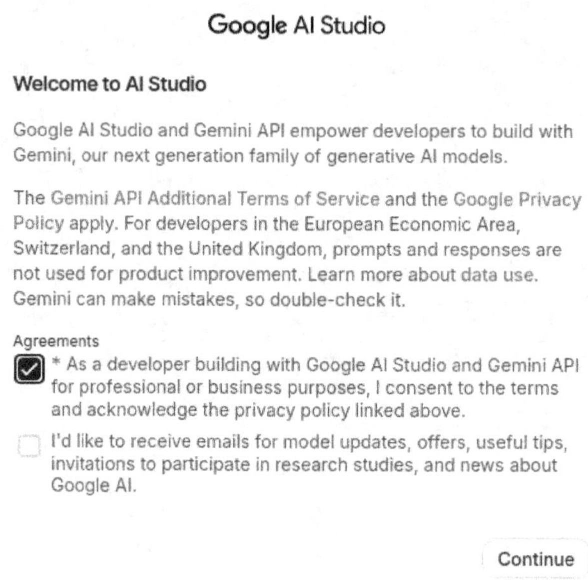


*Figure 11.1 – Google AI Studio warning*

We can proceed by accepting the terms and privacy policy. This will take us to the main page, which looks like the following:

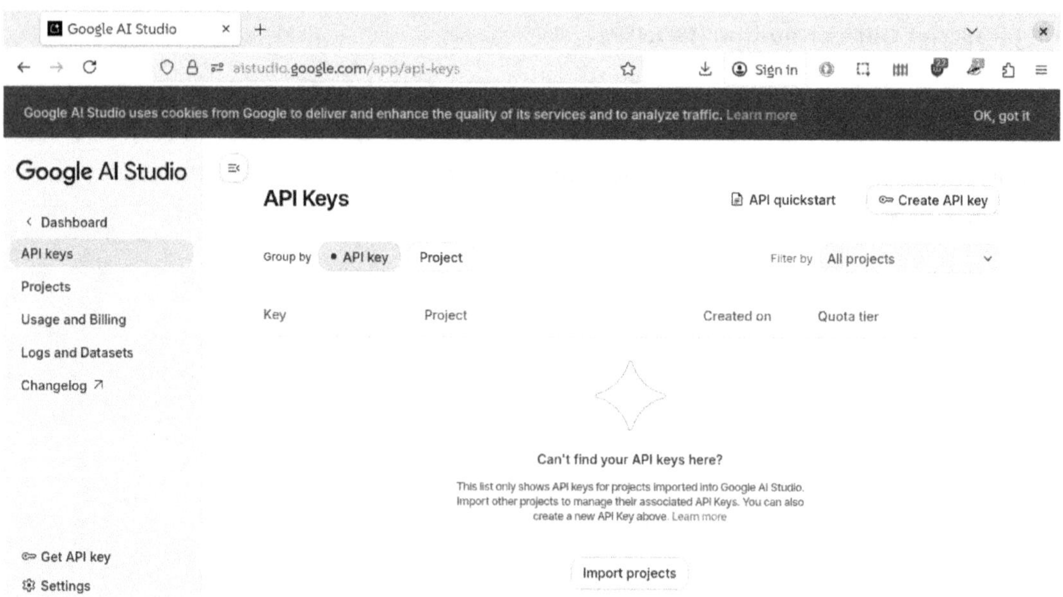


*Figure 11.2 – Google AI Studio*

Once there, we can click on the **Create API key** button in the top-right corner of the page. We will just have to give a name to the key and select a project. In this example, the key name will be `MCP Host` and the project name will be `Default Gemini Project`. We can see this in the following screenshot:

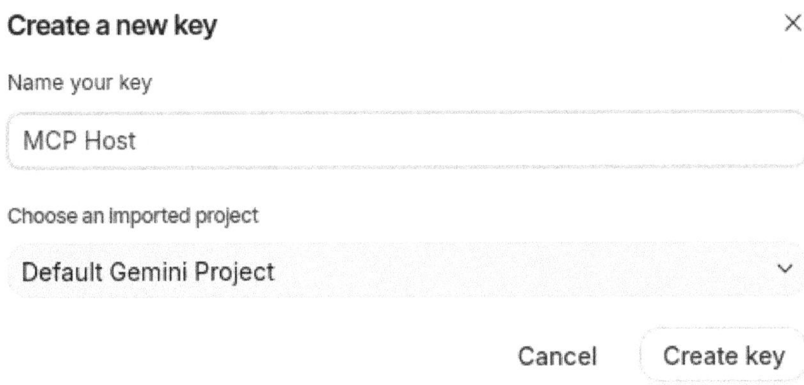


*Figure 11.3 – Google AI Studio: New key creation*

Clicking on **Create key** in the dialog will take us to the main page with the new key available. We can see it here:

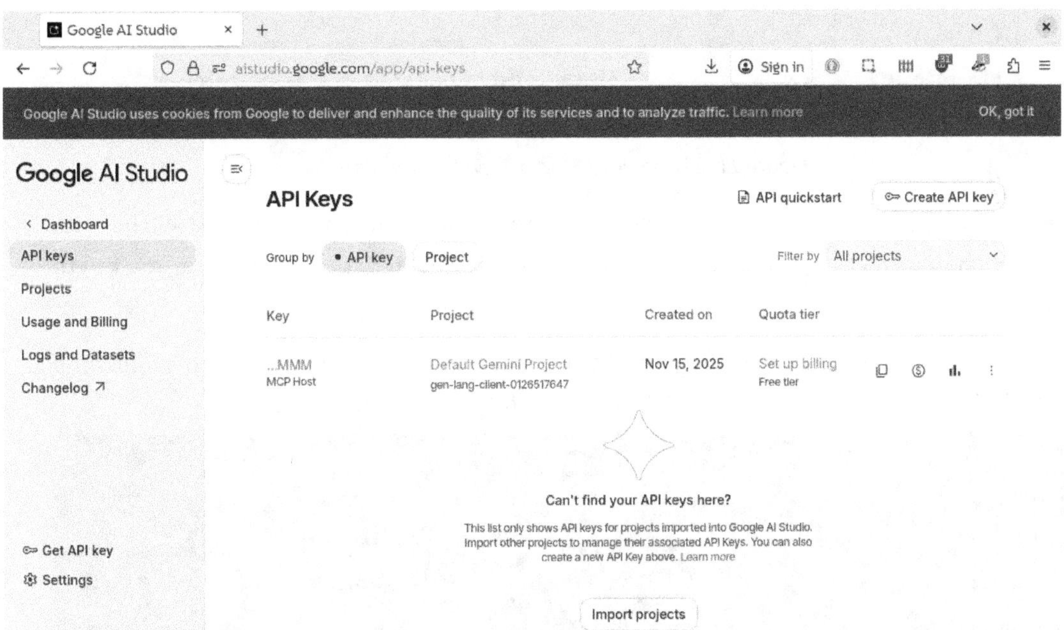


*Figure 11.4 – Google AI Studio: Main page with new key*

On the Google AI Studio main page, seen in the preceding figure, we can find the API key we just created. We will need to open it by clicking on the key name, which in the figure is shown as **...MMM**. Your page will show whatever the name of your key is. Opening it will show the following dialog:

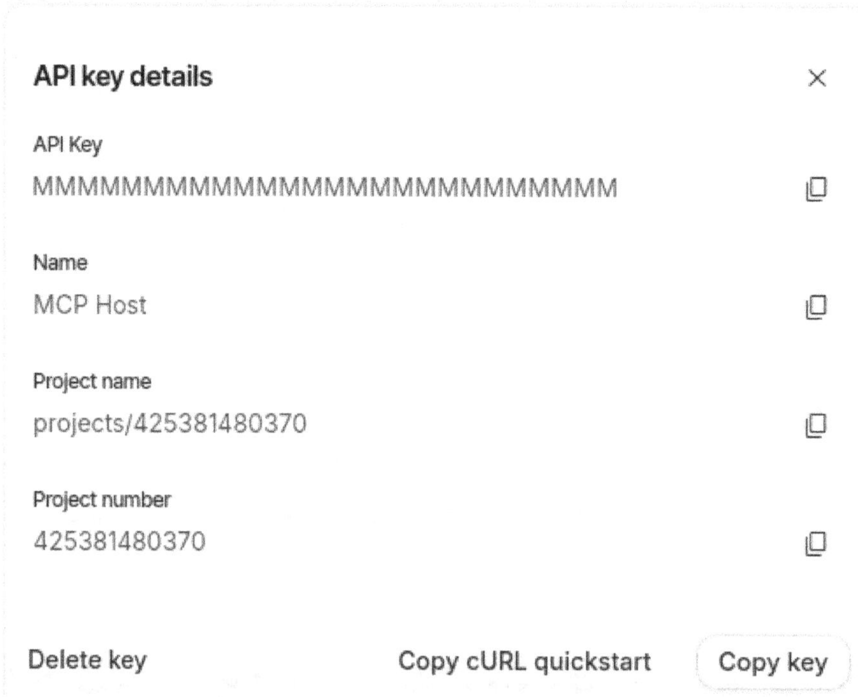


*Figure 11.5 – Google AI Studio: New key details*

In the previous figure, we have changed the API key to a set of `MMM...MMM`. Your key will have its own list of characters. Copy it. Clicking on the two-squares icon next to it will copy the key to your clipboard.

Let's create our first configuration file for `mcphost` in our home directory, which in the following example is `/home/user/.mcphost.yml`. We'll add the following content to it:

```
# MCPHost Configuration File
# Application settings
model: "google:gemini-2.5-pro"
max-steps: 20
debug: true
```

```
# API Configuration
provider-api-key: "MMMMMMMMMMMMMMMMMMMMMMMMMMMMMMMMMMMMMMMMMMMMMMM"
```

Of course, remember to substitute the `MMM...MMM` API key with your own. Now we can run `mcphost`:

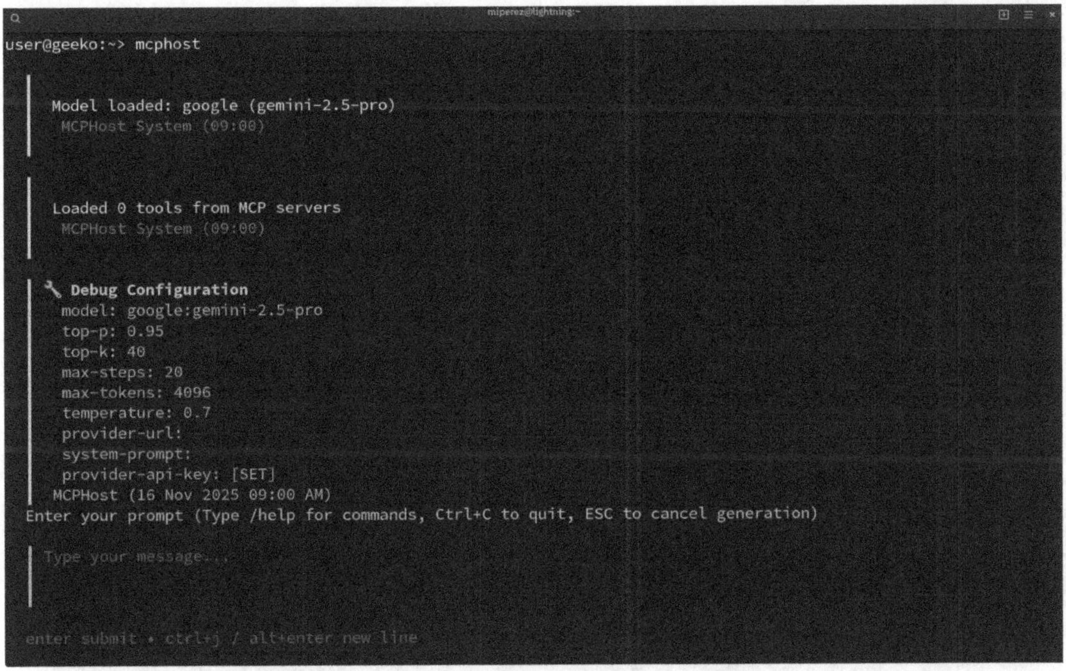


*Figure 11.6 – mcphost running on SLES 16*

> You can download example content for the configuration file from `https://github.com/PacktPublishing/SUSE-Linux-Enterprise-Server-16-Official-Administration-Guide/tree/main/chapter-11-agentic-ai-with-mcphost`.

This is the most basic configuration, but we can already start asking questions. The current configuration required for us to use our Google account to connect to Gemini is now created. Let's see how to use it in the next section.

# Using mcphost

Once we have installed `mcphost` on our machine with SLES 16, obtained an API key to access Google Gemini, and configured `mcphost` to use it, we are ready to start.

The current configuration is the most restrictive one, with no access to the filesystem, logs, or anything else on our system, and a single simple connection to Google Gemini. However, we can start doing interesting things with it.

As you know, there is a mechanism in the SLES 16 command line, called `bash`, that enables us to pass the content generated by another command to our current execution. We use `$(command)` to pass it. For example, if we wanted to create a message that includes the current date, we would run the following:

```
user@geeko:~> echo "Today is $(date). Have a great day."
Today is dom 16 nov 2025 09:55:16 CET. Have a great day.
```

Also, `mcphost` can accept text directly from the command line using the `-p` option, as in the following example:

```
user@geeko:~> mcphost -p "How do I list files in a directory in SLES 16"
```

The output will start with something similar to the following:

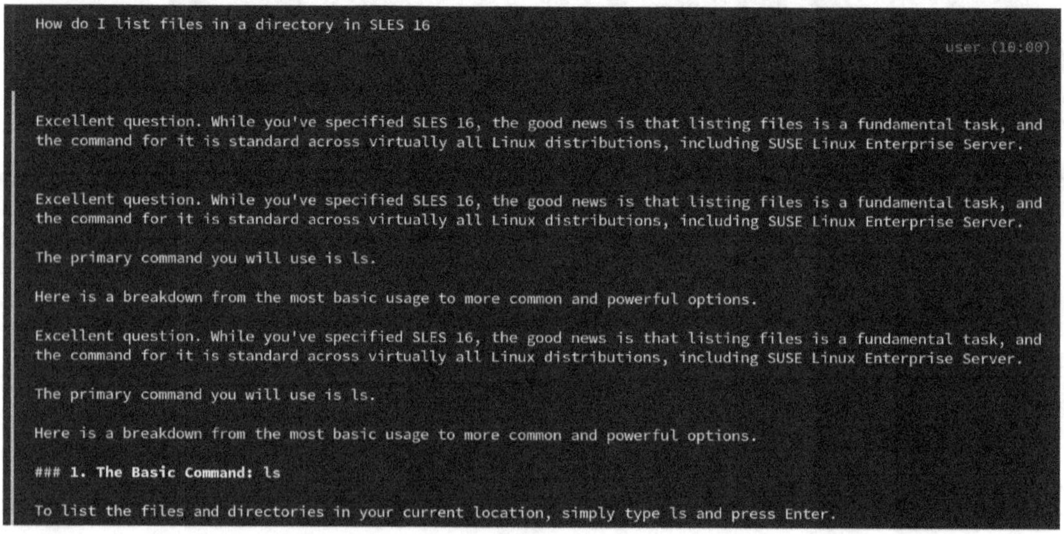


*Figure 11.7 – mcphost output explaining how to list files in a directory*

This provides a really detailed output about using `ls`.

Now, if we combine the two previous actions, passing content to `mcphost -p` using `$(command)`, we can ask our AI to review the last 100 log lines by running the following:

```
user@geeko:~> mcphost -p "What can you tell me about the following logs:
$(journalctl -n 100)"
```

The result will look something similar to this:

```
Of course. This is an excellent set of logs that tells a clear story about
user activity on a Linux system. Here is a detailed breakdown of what
these logs mean, from a high-level summary to a chronological analysis.
### High-Level Summary
These logs show the activity of a user named user on a SUSE Linux test
machine (geeko.suse.test) over several days (Nov 10, 13, 15, 16). The logs
cover three distinct sessions, separated by system reboots.
The user's primary activity involves:
1. Logging into the system, which starts a systemd user session.
2. Using the sudo command to gain root (administrator) privileges.
3. Using the zypper package manager to install, a package named mcphost.
4. Logging out of the system, which cleanly terminates the systemd user
session.
[snip]---8<---8<---8<---[snip]
```

In the same way, we can pass the process list with the following command:

```
user@geeko:~> mcphost -p "Give me a brief summary about the following
processes: $(ps -efa)"
```

This will generate output similar to the following (note that in this case, I'm leaving the full response in as it is very interesting to see how the AI explains everything running on our machine):

```
Of course. This process list shows a snapshot of a running Linux system.
Here is a brief summary broken down into key areas:
This output displays a typical Linux server environment, likely running
as a virtual machine. The processes can be grouped into three main
categories:

### 1. Kernel Threads (Processes in [brackets])
These are low-level tasks managed directly by the Linux kernel, not
standard user programs. They handle core system functions.
• [kthreadd] (PID 2): The parent process for all other kernel threads.
• [kworker/...]: Generic worker threads that perform background tasks for
the kernel, such as handling I/O, timers, and filesystem operations.
• [kswapd0], [kcompactd0]: Manage system memory, swapping pages to disk
when RAM is low and keeping memory contiguous.
• [btrfs-...]: Specific tasks related to the Btrfs filesystem, which is in
use on this system.
```

```
• [irq/...]: Handle hardware interrupts from devices.

### 2. System Services / Daemons (Children of PID 1)
These are the essential background services that make the system
functional. They are all started and managed by systemd (PID 1), the main
init process.
• systemd-journald, rsyslogd: Manage system logging.
• NetworkManager, firewalld: Control network connections and the firewall.
• sshd: The Secure Shell daemon, allowing remote logins.
• httpd-prefork: An Apache web server. The main process (PID 1143) has
spawned several child processes (owned by the wwwrun user) to handle
incoming web requests.
• qemu-ga: The QEMU Guest Agent, which strongly indicates this system is
running as a virtual machine.

### 3. User Session
This section shows a user actively logged into the system.
• A user named user has logged in via SSH (as seen by the sshd-session
processes).
• This login created a shell session (-bash on pts/0).
• The final process, ps -efa, is the very command that was run to generate
this list.
```

> Please take into account that when doing this, we are sharing the information on processes and logs with our AI of choice. In this example, it is Google Gemini. Do not share this information unless your company has given you approval to do so.

We can improve the output of `mcphost` by providing a default system prompt. It will be a prompt to guide all the responses in the future. To do so, we can create the `/home/user/system-prompt.txt` file with the following content:

```
You are an experienced sysadmin, expert in SUSE Linux, that has a profound
focus on security, always interested in keeping your systems running at
its best performance while keeping everything resilient and secure. You
provide clear brief answers to questions with hints on how to improve
the security, resiliency, and performance of the system. You resort to
official SUSE documentation when possible and provide references to it.
You are running a SUSE Linux Enterprise Server 16, please adapt your
responses to this version where possible.
```

Then, add to following lines to our configuration file, `~/.mcphost.yml`:

```
#System Prompt
system-prompt: /home/user/system-prompt.txt
```

It's likely that by now, our model will be overloaded, and we will get a response like the following:

```
Generate content failed: Error 503, Message: The model is overloaded.
Please try again later., Status: UNAVAILABLE,
  Details: [].
```

If you get that message, it's time to let your AI take a break and come back to it later. As an exercise, try running the previous examples after adding the default system prompt.

It's now time to facilitate our `mcphost` to use system resources directly. To do so, we will create an `mcpserver`, which in this case means only modifying the configuration file. We can edit our `~/.mcphost.yml` file and add the following lines:

```
#MCP Servers
mcpServers:
  filesystem_tmp_rw:
    type: builtin
    name: fs
    options:
      allowed_directories:
        - "/tmp"
      allowedTools:
        - "read_file"
        - "write_file"
        - "list_directory"
```

What do those lines mean? Let's go through it line by line:

- `#MCP Servers`: This is a comment to make the block visible in our config file.
- `mcpServers:`: We tell the system that we are adding an MCP server. This means we are adding an "extension" to our `mcphost` to interact with our system.
- `filesystem_tmp_rw:`: This is how we name our server. We can use any name we want, but we have to make it descriptive. We named this one to reflect that we are providing read and write access to `/tmp`.

- `type: builtin`: This is the type of server. As this one comes with the implementation of `mcphost`, we simply say `builtin`.
- `name: fs`: Even though this says `name`, we are specifying the type of server, which in this case is a filesystem. We use the label `fs` for it.
- `options:`: Here, we start specifying how the server will interact with the system
- `allowed_directories:`: We provide access to a set of directories
- `- "/tmp"`: The directory we are providing access to is `/tmp`.
- `allowedTools:`: This is where we define the type of access we want to provide.
- `- "read_file"`: This defines the permission to read files in the directory.
- `- "write_file"`: This defines the permission to write files in the directory.
- `- "list_directory"`: This defines the permission to list files in the directory.

With this, we have provided read and write access to `/tmp` to our `mcphost`. Let's use it. This time, we can simply run `mcphost` and work within it. As we have debugging enabled in our configuration, it will show that the MCP server, `filesystem_tmp_rw`, is active. We can see it in the following figure:

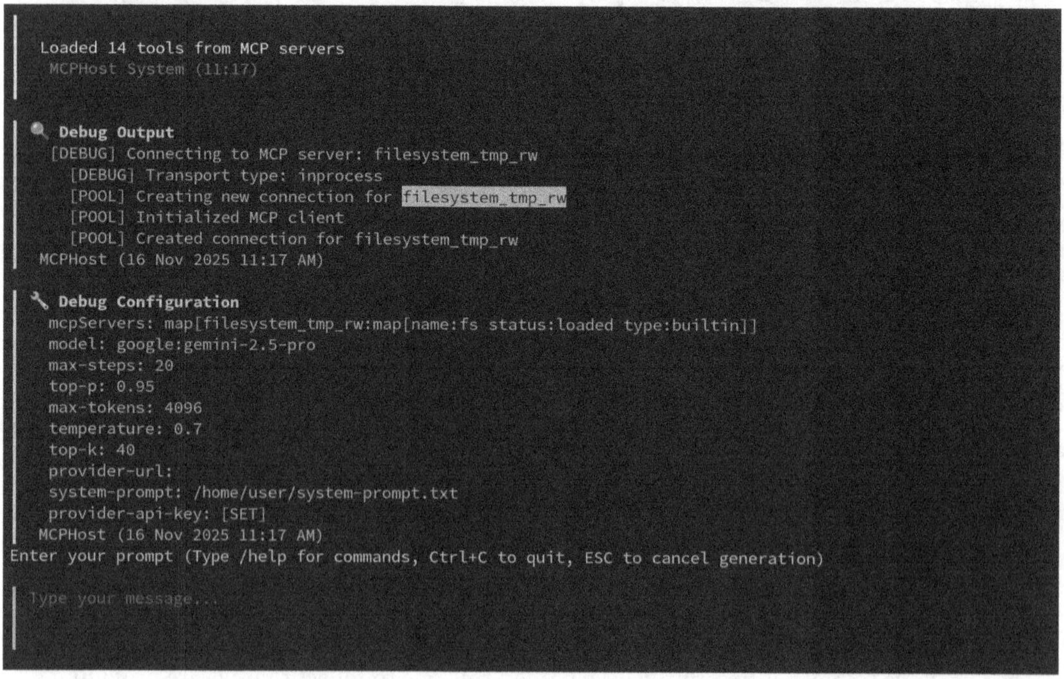


*Figure 11.8 – MCPHost showing Fixed we have added an MCP server to it called filesystem_tmp_rw*

Now we can type the following message into the prompt:

```
Please write an ansible playbook to open port 8888. Put the content in /
tmp/port-8888.yaml
```

Once we hit *Enter*, it will provide us with hints (as stated in the system prompt) on security and performance, as shown in the following screenshot:

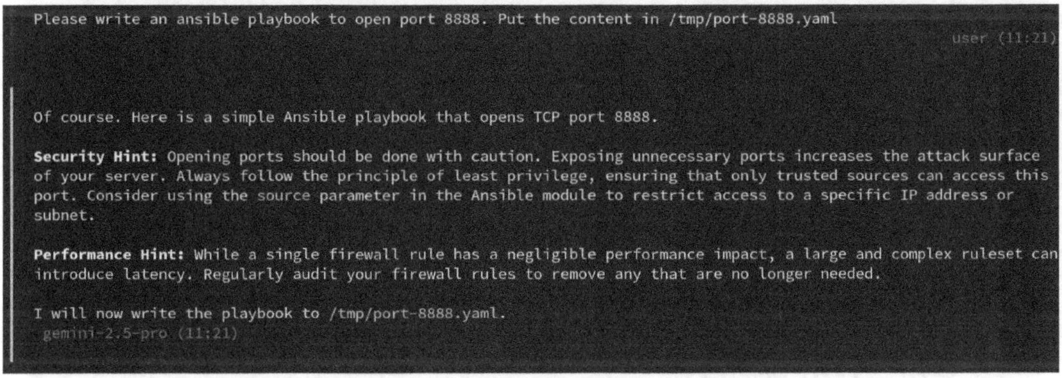


*Figure 11.9 – MCPHost showing hints regarding opening port 8888*

It will notify us that the playbook has been written, as in the following screenshot:

*Figure 11.10 – MCPHost showing playbook was written*

Finally, it will provide us with guidance on how to execute it, as in the following figure:

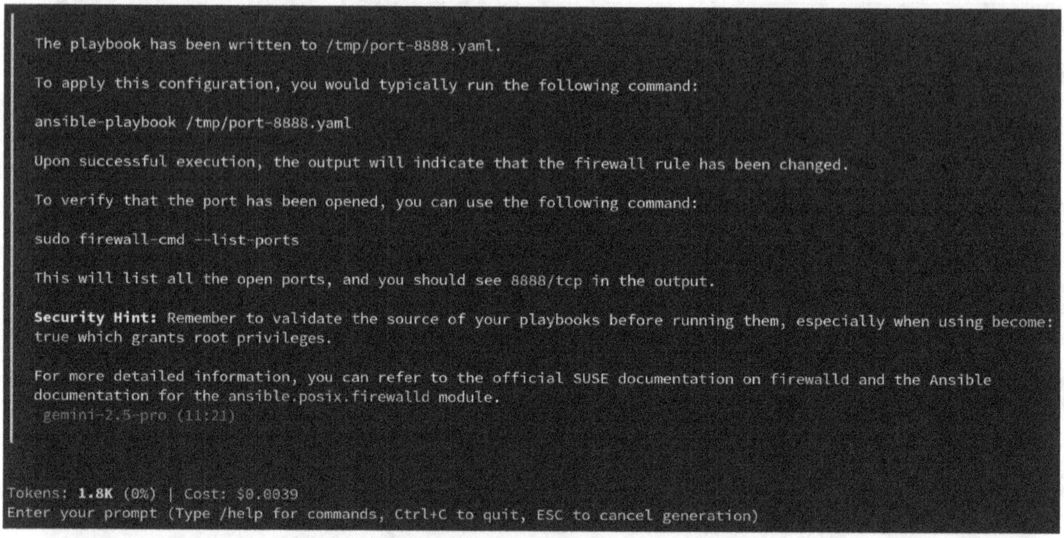


*Figure 11.11 – MCPHost providing guidance on how to use the playbook*

Now we can quit `mcphost` and check that the playbook was created:

```
user@geeko:~> cat /tmp/port-8888.yaml
---
- hosts: all
  become: true
  tasks:
    - name: Ensure port 8888 is open
      ansible.posix.firewalld:
        port: 8888/tcp
        permanent: true
        state: enabled
        immediate: true
```

Now, to execute the playbook on our own machine, we can run the following command (note that we need to be explicit with the connection type and the inventory):

```
user@geeko:~> sudo ansible-playbook --connection=local
--inventory=127.0.0.1, /tmp/port-8888.yaml
```

The resulting output will be as follows:

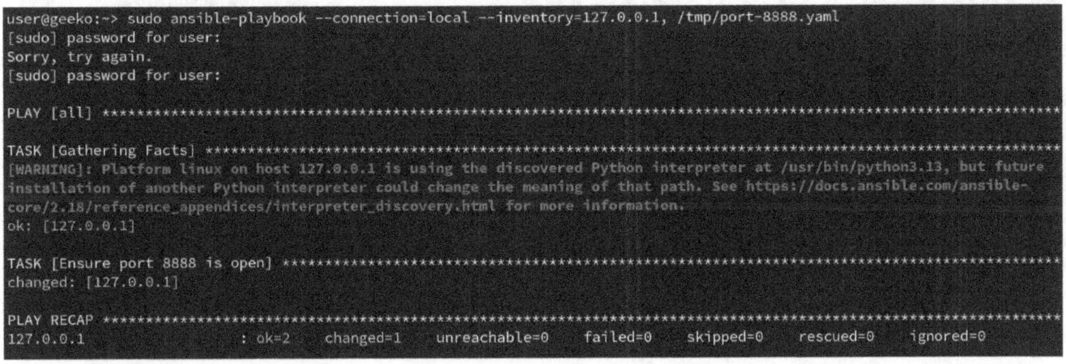


*Figure 11.12 – Ansible playbook running complete*

We can finally check that the port was opened:

```
user@geeko:~> sudo firewall-cmd --list-ports
8888/tcp
```

And with this, we complete our introduction to `mcphost`.

# Summary

By learning the basics of agentic AI with `mcphost`, we have seen that we can analyze our systems and even act on them by providing the proper permissions for what can be accessed.

This way, we can use the LLM of our choice as a sidekick to help us go through all the info in our systems at great speed. It provides hints and even files to be able to act on our systems.

As `mcphost` is in tech-preview, more extensions will come out during the life cycle of the operating system, including new features and capabilities. It is a good idea to stay tuned as it will update frequently.

Let's move on to learn more about how to manage local storage and filesystems.

# Part 4

# Resource Administration: Storage, Boot Process, Tuning, and Containers

In order to maintain the performance and usability of servers, you need to manage the machines running SLES following best practices. Understanding the storage, tuning performance (including the configuration required to make it permanent in the boot process), and automating tasks for long-term maintainability are key capabilities for a system administrator. Containers can help maintain a cleaner environment, isolating processes and assigning resources more efficiently, which are areas in which a system administrator will be involved during their daily work.

This part has the following chapters:


- *Chapter 12, Managing Local Storage and Filesystems*
- *Chapter 13, Flexible Storage Management with LVM*
- *Chapter 14, Configuring and Using System Snapshots with BTRFS and Snapper*
- *Chapter 15, Understanding the Boot Process*
- *Chapter 16, Automating with System Roles*
- *Chapter 17, Managing Containers with Podman*
- *Chapter 18, Introduction to SLES 4 SAP*

# 12

# Managing Local Storage and Filesystems

In the previous chapters, we learned about security and system administration. In this chapter, we will focus on the administration of resources, specifically, storage administration.

Storage administration is an important part of keeping a system running: the system logs can eat into storage space and new applications might require additional storage set up for them (even on separate disks to improve performance), and such issues may require our action to solve them.

In this chapter, we will learn about the following main topics:

- A bit of history on disks and partitions
- Partitioning disks (MBR and GPT disks)
- Formatting and mounting filesystems
- Setting default mounts and options in `fstab`
- Using network filesystems with **Network File System** (**NFS**)

This will provide us with basic knowledge to improve our storage administration skills to keep our systems running.

Let's get hands-on!

# Technical requirements

You can continue the practice of using the **virtual machine** (**VM**) created at the beginning of this book in *Chapter 1, Getting SLES 16 Up and Running (Physical and Cloud)*. Any additional packages required for this chapter will be indicated alongside the text. You will also need partitioning disks (MBR and GPT disks).

# A bit of history on disks and partitions

Before we begin, it's imperative to start with a definition of partition. **Partitioning** is the logical division of a storage device, used to distribute the available storage of a device (usually a disk) into smaller pieces, known as partitions.

To better understand partitioning, let's learn a bit about the origins of storage.

Let's start by explaining a bit about the history of **personal computers** (**PCs**), the software that allows them to boot—**Basic Input/Output System** (**BIOS**)—and how that influenced storage formats, use, and administration.

It might sound a bit strange, but initial storage needs, in the 80s when PCs were created, were just a small amount of **kilobytes** (**KB**). For the first hard drives in PCs, storage was just a few **megabytes** (**MB**). PCs also came with a limitation: they had to be compatible, which meant that subsequent models had to be compatible with the initial **International Business Machines** (**IBM**) PC design.

Traditional disk partitioning uses a space at the beginning of disks after the **Master Boot Record** (**MBR**) that allows four partition registers (all of which have the following characteristics: start, end, size, partition type, active flag), called **primary partitions**.

> MBR is a logical structure for disks that was introduced in PC-DOS in 1983 to enable PCs to load, or boot, the **Operating System** (**OS**) from it and also distribute the disk space into four partitions.

When a PC is booting, BIOS will check the partition table of the disk by running a small program in the MBR, and then it will load the boot area of the active partition and execute it to get the OS booting.

IBM PCs that contained a **Disk Operating System** (**DOS**) or compatible version (such as PC-DOS, MS-DOS, DR-DOS, and FreeDOS) also used a filesystem named a **File Allocation Table** (**FAT**). The FAT contained several structures based on its evolution, known as the cluster addressing size (as well as some other features).

> A filesystem is a logical structure that allows users to write files in a partition. The initial filesystem for PCs was FAT, which was becoming widely popular in the 80s. Linux supports other filesystems, such as EXT4 and XFS. SUSE Linux Enterprise Server uses the BTRFS filesystem, which allows filesystem snapshots.

With a limit on the number of clusters, having bigger disks meant having bigger blocks, so if a file was using a limited amount of space, the remaining blocks couldn't be used by other files. Thus, it became more or less normal to break large hard drives into small logical partitions so that small files would not consume the available space because of limits.

Some of those limitations were reduced by subsequent versions of FAT sizing, which increased the maximum supported disk size. Of course, other OSs introduced their own filesystems, but they used the same partitioning schema (MBR).

Later, to be able to overcome the limit of four partitions per disk, a new partition type was created for the MBR disks: the **extended partition**. This used one of the four **primary partition** slots and allowed extra partitions to be defined inside it, enabling users to create **logical partitions** to be assigned as needed. Additionally, having several primary partitions also allowed the installation, on the same computer, of different OSs with their own dedicated space that was completely independent of other OSs.

So, partitions allowed computers to have different OSs, have a better usage of the available storage, or even logically sort the data by keeping it in different areas, such as keeping OS space separate from user data so that if a user filled the available space, it would not affect the computer's operation.

As we have said, many of those designs came with the compatibility restriction of the original IBM PC. So, when new computers using the **Extensible Firmware Interface** (**EFI**) appeared to overcome the limitations of traditional BIOS, a new partition table format called **Globally Unique Identifier** (**GUID**) **Partition Table** (**GPT**) arrived.

Systems using GPT use 32-bit and 64-bit support rather than the 16-bit support used by BIOS (inherited from IBM PC compatibility). So, bigger addressing can be used for the disks, as well as extra features such as extended controller loading.

Now, let's learn about disk partitioning in the next section.

# Partitioning disks (MBR and GPT disks)

As mentioned, using disk partitions allows us to more efficiently use the space available on our computers and servers.

Let's dig into disk partitioning by first identifying the disk to act on.

> Once we have learned about what caused disks to be partitioned and the limitations of this, we should follow one schema or another based on our system specifications, but bear in mind that *EFI requires GPT*, and *BIOS requires MBR*. So, a system supporting UEFI but containing a disk partitioned with MBR will have to boot the system using BIOS compatibility mode.

Linux uses different notation for disks based on the way they are connected to the system. So, for example, you can see disks marked as `hda` or `sda` or `mmbclk0` depending on the connection being used. Traditionally, disks connected using the **Integrated Drive Electronics** (**IDE**) interface have disks named `hda`, `hdb`, and so on, while disks using the **Small Computer System Interface** (**SCSI**) have disks named `sda`, `sdb`, and so on. Also, virtual devices using VirtIO drivers have names like `vda`, `vdb`, and so on.

We can list the available devices with `sudo fdisk -l` or `lsblk`, as we can see in the following screenshot:

```
user@geeko:~> sudo lsblk
NAME   MAJ:MIN RM  SIZE RO TYPE MOUNTPOINTS
sr0     11:0    1  9,3G  0 rom
vda    254:0    0   32G  0 disk
├─vda1 254:1    0    8M  0 part
├─vda2 254:2    0   30G  0 part /usr/local
│                                /var
│                                /srv
│                                /root
│                                /home
│                                /boot/grub2/x86_64-efi
│                                /opt
│                                /boot/grub2/i386-pc
│                                /.snapshots
│                                /
└─vda3 254:3    0    2G  0 part [SWAP]
user@geeko:~> sudo fdisk -l
Disk /dev/vda: 32 GiB, 34359738368 bytes, 67108864 sectors
Units: sectors of 1 * 512 = 512 bytes
Sector size (logical/physical): 512 bytes / 512 bytes
I/O size (minimum/optimal): 512 bytes / 512 bytes
Disklabel type: gpt
Disk identifier: 3D719288-4531-4B6C-8A62-F580079F3D59

Device        Start      End  Sectors Size Type
/dev/vda1      2048    18431    16384   8M BIOS boot
/dev/vda2     18432 62912511 62894080  30G Linux filesystem
/dev/vda3  62912512 67108830  4196319   2G Linux swap
```

*Figure 12.1 – lsblk and fdisk -l output*

As we can see, our disk named `/dev/vda` has three partitions: `vda1`, `vda2`, and `vda3`, with `vda2` being formatted with a BTRFS filesystem that allows volumes to be created in it.

To demonstrate disk partitioning in a safe way and to make it easier for those of you using a VM for testing, we will create a fake **virtual hard drive** (**VHD**) for testing. However, everything we do to this disk could also be done to any other disk. In doing so, we will use the tool `truncate`, which comes with the `coreutil` package, and the `losetup` utility, which comes with the `util-linux` package.

To create a VHD, we will execute the following sequence of commands as they appear in *Figure 12.2*:

1. `truncate --s 5G myharddrive.hdd`, which will create an empty file with the size we request

> This command creates a 5 GB file, but this will be an empty file, which means that the file is not really using 5 GB on our disk, just showing that size. Unless we use it, it will not consume more disk space. This is called a **sparse file.**

2. `losetup -f`, which will find the next available device
3. `losetup /dev/loop0 myharddrive.hdd`, which will associate `loop0` with the file created
4. `lsblk -fp`, which will validate the newly looped disk
5. `fdisk -l /dev/loop0`, which will list the available space in the new disk

The following screenshot shows the output of the preceding sequential commands:

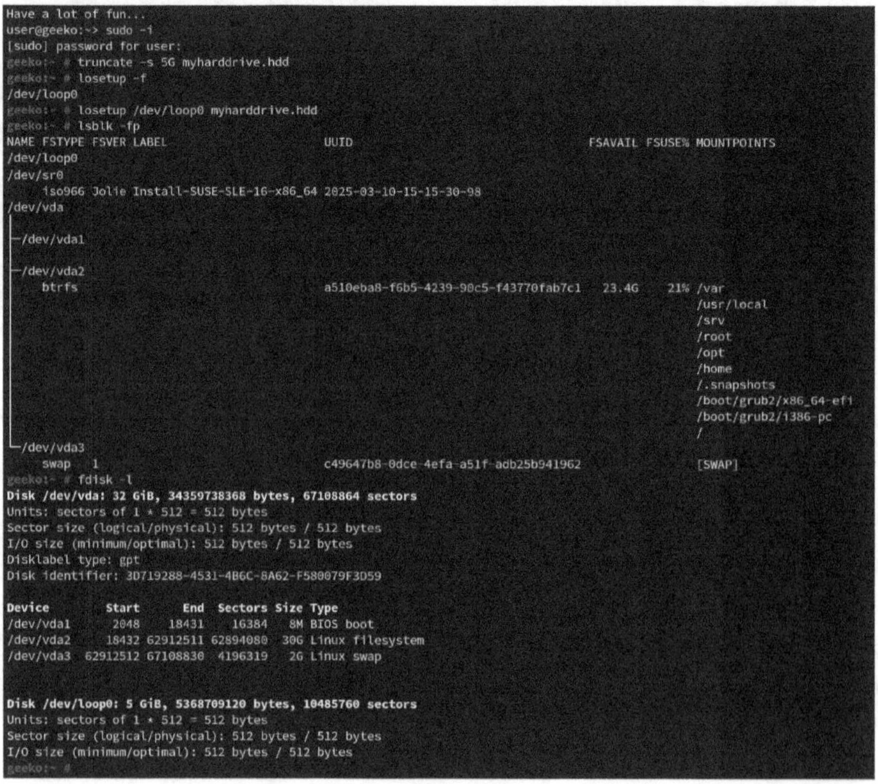


*Figure 12.2 – Execution of the indicated commands for creating a fake hard drive*

The `losetup -f` command finds the next available loopback device, which is a device used for looping back accesses to a backing file. It allows us to use a file as a storage device. This is often used for mounting *ISO* files locally, or for accessing a backup of a disk with `dd`, for example.

With the third command, we use the previously available loopback device to set up a loop connection between the `loop0` device and the file we created with the first command.

As we can see, in the remaining commands, the device now appears when running the same commands we executed in *Figure 12.1*, showing that we have a 5 GB disk available.

> Partitioning operations on disks can be dangerous and can render a system unusable and in need of restoration or reinstallation. To reduce that chance, the examples in this chapter will use the device `/dev/loop0`, which is a fake disk. This way, we will only be interacting with this fake disk, ensuring we cause no harm to the rest of the system. Pay attention when performing portioning operations on real volumes or disks.

Let's start creating partitions by executing `fdisk /dev/loop0` on our newly created device, as shown in the following screenshot:

```
geeko:~ # fdisk /dev/loop0

Welcome to fdisk (util-linux 2.40.4).
Changes will remain in memory only, until you decide to write them.
Be careful before using the write command.

Device does not contain a recognized partition table.
Created a new DOS (MBR) disklabel with disk identifier 0x316da897.

Command (m for help):
```

*Figure 12.3 – fdisk execution on /dev/loop0*

As we can see in *Figure 12.3*, the just-created disk doesn't contain a recognized partition table. So, when running `fdisk` on it, a new DOS partition disk label is created, but the changes only remain in memory until they are written back to the disk.

Inside the `fdisk` command, we can use several options to create a partition. The first one we should be aware of is `m`, as indicated in *Figure 12.3*, which shows the help functionality and the available commands.

The first thing to take into consideration is our previous explanation about UEFI, BIOS, and so on. By default, `fdisk` creates a DOS partition, but as we can see inside the manual (`m`), we can create a GPT partition by running the g command inside `fdisk`.

One important command to remember is `p`, which prints the current disk layout and partition, as shown in the next screenshot:

```
Device does not contain a recognized partition table.
Created a new DOS (MBR) disklabel with disk identifier 0x316da897.

Command (m for help): p
Disk /dev/loop0: 5 GiB, 5368709120 bytes, 10485760 sectors
Units: sectors of 1 * 512 = 512 bytes
Sector size (logical/physical): 512 bytes / 512 bytes
I/O size (minimum/optimal): 512 bytes / 512 bytes
Disklabel type: dos
Disk identifier: 0x316da897

Command (m for help): g
Created a new GPT disklabel (GUID: 7CE13749-796B-4C3F-B8A8-4AB68B193584).

Command (m for help): p
Disk /dev/loop0: 5 GiB, 5368709120 bytes, 10485760 sectors
Units: sectors of 1 * 512 = 512 bytes
Sector size (logical/physical): 512 bytes / 512 bytes
I/O size (minimum/optimal): 512 bytes / 512 bytes
Disklabel type: gpt
Disk identifier: 7CE13749-796B-4C3F-B8A8-4AB68B193584

Command (m for help):
```

*Figure 12.4 – fdisk creating a new partition table*

As we can see, the initial `disklabel` type was `dos` and now is `gpt`, which is compatible with EFI/UEFI.

Let's review some of the basic commands we can use:

- `n`: Creates a new partition
- `d`: Deletes a partition
- `m`: Shows the manual page (help)
- `p`: Prints the current layout
- `x`: Enters advanced mode (extra functionality intended for experts)

- q: Quits without saving
- w: Writes changes to disk and exits
- g: Creates a new GPT disk label
- o: Creates a DOS disk label
- a: In DOS mode, sets the bootable flag to one of the primary partitions

Now, the question is, "What is the sequence for creating a new traditional disk partition layout with a bootable partition for the OS and another one for the user data, with half the disk size each?"

This is the sequence of commands (they are also shown in *Figure 12.5*):

1. Type o and press *Enter* to create a new DOS disk label.
2. Type n and press *Enter* to create a new partition.
3. Press *Enter* to accept a primary partition type.
4. Press *Enter* to confirm use of the first partition (1).
5. Press *Enter* to accept the initial sector.
6. Type +1G and press *Enter* to indicate 1 GB in size from the first sector.
7. Type n and press *Enter* to create a second new partition.
8. Press *Enter* to accept it as a primary partition type.
9. Press *Enter* to accept the partition number (2).
10. Press *Enter* to accept the first sector as the default proposed by `fdisk`.
11. Press *Enter* to accept the end sector as the default proposed by `fdisk`.
12. Type a and press *Enter* to mark a partition as bootable.
13. Type 1 and press *Enter* to mark the first partition.

As you can see, most of the options accept the defaults; the only change was to specify a partition size of +1G, meaning it should be 1 GB (the disk is 5 GB), and then start with the second partition with the n command, now not specifying the size as we want to use all the remaining disk space. The last step is to mark the first partition as active for booting.

Of course, remember that unless we execute the `w` command, the changes are not written to disk. Also, we can use `p` to review them, as shown in the following screenshot:

```
Created a new partition 1 of type 'Linux' and of size 1 GiB.

Command (m for help): n
Partition type
   p   primary (1 primary, 0 extended, 3 free)
   e   extended (container for logical partitions)
Select (default p):

Using default response p.
Partition number (2-4, default 2):
First sector (2099200-10485759, default 2099200):
Last sector, +/-sectors or +/-size{K,M,G,T,P} (2099200-10485759, default 10485759):

Created a new partition 2 of type 'Linux' and of size 4 GiB.

Command (m for help): a
Partition number (1,2, default 2): 1

The bootable flag on partition 1 is enabled now.

Command (m for help): p
Disk /dev/loop0: 5 GiB, 5368709120 bytes, 10485760 sectors
Units: sectors of 1 * 512 = 512 bytes
Sector size (logical/physical): 512 bytes / 512 bytes
I/O size (minimum/optimal): 512 bytes / 512 bytes
Disklabel type: dos
Disk identifier: 0xd1d167d5

Device       Boot   Start      End Sectors Size Id Type
/dev/loop0p1 *       2048  2099199 2097152   1G 83 Linux
/dev/loop0p2      2099200 10485759 8386560   4G 83 Linux

Command (m for help):
```

*Figure 12.5 – Disk partition layout creation and verification before writing it back to disk*

To conclude this section, let's write the changes to disk with the `w` command, and let's move on to discuss filesystems in the next section.

Before that, however, let's execute `partprobe /dev/loop0` to make the kernel update its internal view on the disk and find the two new partitions. Without this, the special `/dev/loop0p1` and `/dev/loop0p2` files might not be created and will not be usable.

Note that some partition modifications will not be updated even after a `partprobe` execution and might require the system to be rebooted. This is, for example, happening on disks that have partitions in use, such as the one holding the root filesystem on our computer.

# Formatting and mounting filesystems

In the previous section, we learned how to logically divide our disk. But that disk is still not usable for storing data. In order to enable this to do so, we need to define a **filesystem** on it as the first step to make it available to our system.

A filesystem is a logical structure that defines how files, folders, and more are stored. Different filesystems provide different sets of features.

The number and types of filesystems supported depend on the OS version because, during its evolution, new filesystems might be added, removed, and so on.

In SLES, the default root filesystem is set to BTRFS to enable filesystem-level snapshots, which will help you roll back to a well-known state if you encounter an issue, as described in *Chapter 14, Configuring and Using System Snapshots with BTRFS and Snapper*. For data partitions, SUSE recommends using the **eXtended File System (XFS)**, but you can see a list of suitable filesystems in the SLES documentation at `https://documentation.suse.com/en-us/sles/15-SP7/html/SLES-all/cha-filesystems.html` (an updated version of the link was not available when writing this book; however, this one still applies), and of course, others such as **Fourth Extended Filesystem (EXT4)** can be used.

> Remember that **SLES** focuses on stability, so there are strict controls about which features are added or phased out for new releases. The advanced testing and build capabilities of **OpenQA** (`https://openqa.opensuse.org/`) and **Open Build Service** (`https://openbuildservice.org/`) enable SUSE to perform component updates, maintaining compatibility during the whole major release, in this case version 16.

The choice of the filesystem depends on several factors, such as usage intention and the types of file that are going to be used, because different filesystems might have performance implications.

For example, both EXT4 and XFS are journaled filesystems that provide more protection against power failures, but the maximum filesystem size differs because of other aspects, such as the likelihood of becoming fragmented.

Before choosing a filesystem, it is a good practice to get an idea of the kinds of file being deployed and their usage pattern because choosing the wrong one might affect system performance.

As we explained in the previous section, with two partitions on our VHD, we can try to create both XFS and EXT4 filesystems. Again, however, be very careful when performing operations because filesystem creation is a destructive operation that writes new structures back to the disk, and when operating as the root user of the system, which is required, selecting the wrong disk can destroy the available data we have on our system within seconds.

> Remember to check the man page for the commands being used in order to get familiar with the different recommendations and the options available for each one. For example, we can run `man 5 btrfs` to learn about the filesystem or `man 8 btrfs` to learn more about the tools included for the filesystem. We can also run `man xfs` or `man ext4`.

Let's use the two partitions we created to test with two filesystems, XFS and EXT4, by using the `mkfs.xfs` and `mkfs.ext4` commands against each one of the partitions created in our fake virtual disk device. We will create an XFS filesystem on *partition one* of the *loop0* device, which is `/dev/loop0p1`, then an EXT4 filesystem on *partition two* of the *loop0* device, which is `/dev/loop0p2`, respectively, as follows:

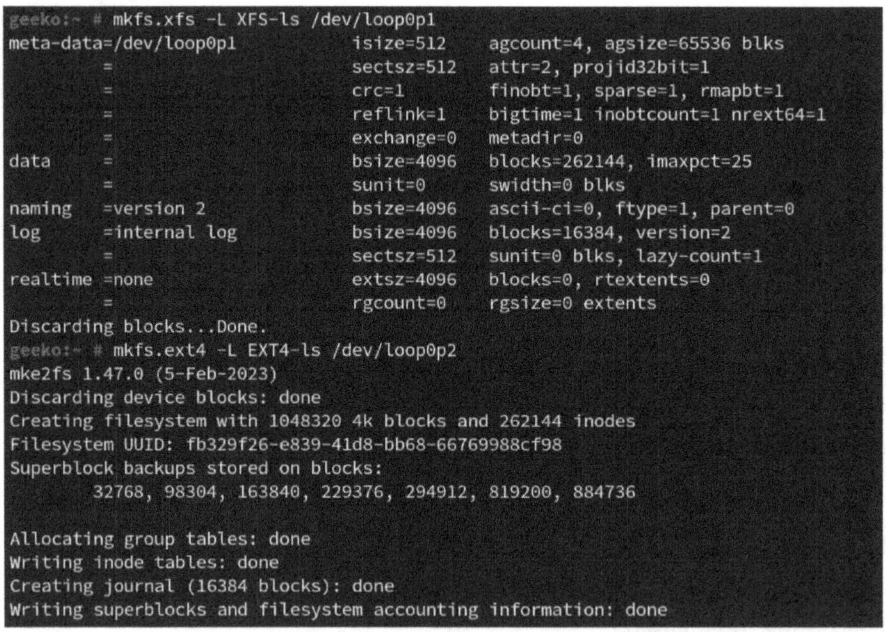


*Figure 12.6 – Filesystem creation on the two partitions of the fake virtual hard drive*

Note that we have specified the different loop device partition, and we have also specified one `-L` parameter for each command. We will look at this again later.

Now that the filesystem has been created, we can run `lsblk -fp` to verify this, and we can see both devices, indicating that the filesystem is in use, as well as `LABEL` and `UUID` values (the ones shown when we created the filesystem with `mkfs`), as we can see in the following screenshot:

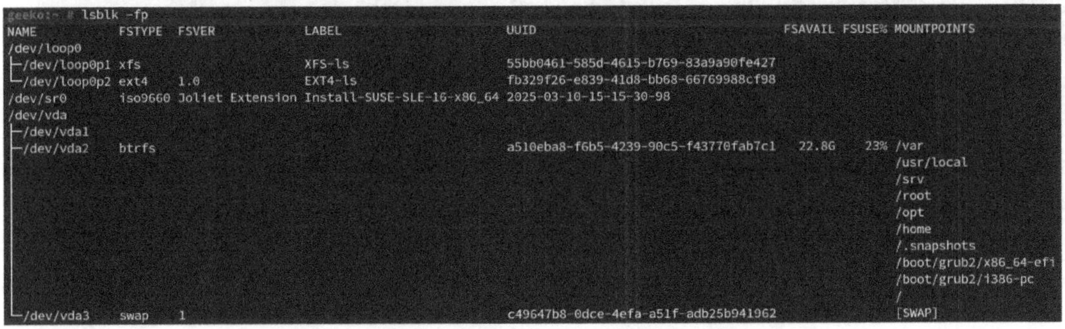


*Figure 12.7 – Output of lsblk -fp after creating the filesystems*

In the preceding output, it's important to pay attention to the `UUID` and `LABEL` values (if you remember, the value listed is the one we specified in the `mkfs` command with the `-L` option), as we will be using them later in this chapter.

Now that the filesystems have been created, in order to use them, we need to mount them. This means making the filesystem available on a path (or directory, or folder) in our system so that every time we store any file inside that path, we will be using that device.

Mounting a filesystem can be done in several ways, but the simplest way is to use **autodetection** and specify the device to mount and the local path to mount it at. But more complex mounting options that allow several options to be defined can be found when checking the `man mount` help page.

> Mounting and unmounting filesystems require root privileges, so they can be done using `sudo`, or switching to a new shell as `root`, which can be done by running `sudo -i`.

To mount our two created filesystems, we will create two folders and then proceed to mount each device by executing the following commands as `root`:

```
geeko:~ # cd
geeko:~ # mkdir first-dir second-dir
geeko:~ # mount /dev/loop0p1 /root/first-dir/
geeko:~ # mount /dev/loop0p2 /root/second-dir/
geeko:~ # mount | grep loop
/dev/loop0p1 on /root/first-dir type xfs
(rw,relatime,seclabel,attr2,inode64,logbufs=8,logbsize=32k,noquota)
/dev/loop0p2 on /root/second-dir type ext4 (rw,relatime,seclabel)
```

At this point, the two filesystems will be available in our home folder (the `root` user) in the subfolders named `first-dir` and `second-dir`.

The kernel automatically detects which filesystem is used for each device. It then loads the appropriate controller for that filesystem. This process usually works without any manual intervention. However, sometimes we may want to specify particular options ourselves. For instance, we can force the filesystem type manually. This was often done in the past when `ext2` and `ext3` were common filesystems—to enable or disable journaling. We can also define options to disable certain built-in features, such as updating file or directory access times. Doing this helps to reduce disk I/O and can improve overall performance.

All options specified on the command line or filesystems mounted will not be available once the system is rebooted, as they are only runtime changes. Let's move on to the next section, which explains how to define default options and filesystem mounts when the system is being started.

# Setting default mounts and options in fstab

In the previous section, we explained how disks and partitions can be mounted so that our services and users can use them. In this section, we will learn how to make those filesystems available in a persistent way.

The `/etc/fstab` file contains the filesystem definitions for our system. It also has a dedicated manual page, which can be accessed with the `man fstab` command. This manual provides useful information about the file's formatting, fields, and ordering. All these details must be carefully followed because this file is critical for the smooth operation of the system. We can take a quick look at it by running `cat /etc/fstab`.

The file format is defined by several fields separated by tabs or spaces, with lines starting with a # considered as comments.

For example, we will use this line to look at each field description:

```
UUID=XXXX-XXXX-XXXX  /  btrfs  defaults  0 0
```

The first field is device identification, which can be a special block device, a remote filesystem, or—as we can see in the example above—a selector made up of `LABEL`, `UUID`, the device name (such as `/dev/vda1`), or, for GPT systems, also `PARTUUID` or `PARTLABEL`. The man page for `mount`, `blkid`, and `lsblk` provides more information about device identifiers. As the name suggests, they are used to identify which device, and partition/subvolume in it, we want to use.

BTRFS includes a way to distribute storage at the filesystem level by using a logical concept called **subvolumes**, making it easier to partition devices.

The second field is the mount point for the filesystem, which is where to make the contents of that filesystem available based on our system directory hierarchy. Some special devices/partitions, such as swap areas, have this defined as `none`, because the contents are effectively not made available via the filesystem.

The third field is the filesystem type, as supported by the `mount` command or `swap`, for swap partitions.

The fourth field is the mount options supported by the `mount` or `swapon` commands (check their `man` pages for more details), being at its default setting an alias for the most common options (read/write, allow devices, allow execution, automount on boot, async access, and so on). Other common options are as follows:

- `noauto`, which defines the filesystem but doesn't mount at boot (often used with removable devices)
- `user`, which allows users to mount and unmount it
- `_netdev`, which defines remote paths that require networking to be up before attempting the mount

The fifth field is used by the `dump` backup utility to determine which filesystems should be used during backups by it—its value defaults to `0`.

The sixth field is used by `fsck` to determine the order for filesystems to be checked on boot. The default is `0`, not `fsck`. Checks, if needed, are performed in parallel to speed up the booting process. Note that with filesystems that have a journal, the filesystem itself can perform a fast validation instead of a full one.

The following screenshot shows how it looks in our system with the output of `cat /etc/fstab`:

```
geeko:~ # cat /etc/fstab
UUID=a510eba8-f6b5-4239-90c5-f43770fab7c1  /                      btrfs  defaults                          0  0
UUID=a510eba8-f6b5-4239-90c5-f43770fab7c1  /var                   btrfs  subvol=/@/var                     0  0
UUID=a510eba8-f6b5-4239-90c5-f43770fab7c1  /usr/local             btrfs  subvol=/@/usr/local               0  0
UUID=a510eba8-f6b5-4239-90c5-f43770fab7c1  /srv                   btrfs  subvol=/@/srv                     0  0
UUID=a510eba8-f6b5-4239-90c5-f43770fab7c1  /root                  btrfs  subvol=/@/root                    0  0
UUID=a510eba8-f6b5-4239-90c5-f43770fab7c1  /opt                   btrfs  subvol=/@/opt                     0  0
UUID=a510eba8-f6b5-4239-90c5-f43770fab7c1  /home                  btrfs  subvol=/@/home                    0  0
UUID=a510eba8-f6b5-4239-90c5-f43770fab7c1  /boot/grub2/x86_64-efi btrfs  subvol=/@/boot/grub2/x86_64-efi  0  0
UUID=a510eba8-f6b5-4239-90c5-f43770fab7c1  /boot/grub2/i386-pc    btrfs  subvol=/@/boot/grub2/i386-pc     0  0
UUID=c49647b8-0dce-4efa-a51f-adb25b941962  swap                   swap   defaults                          0  0
UUID=a510eba8-f6b5-4239-90c5-f43770fab7c1  /.snapshots            btrfs  subvol=/@/.snapshots              0  0
```

*Figure 12.8 – fstab example from our system*

So, why should we use `UUID` or `LABEL` instead of devices such as `/dev/sda1`?

Disk ordering might change when a system is booting because some kernels might introduce differences in the way the devices are accessed, for example, causing changes in the enumeration of the devices. This happens not only for removable devices such as **Universal Serial Bus** (**USB**) devices, but also to internal devices such as network interfaces or hard drives.

When, instead of specifying the devices, we use `UUID` or `LABEL`, even in the event of a device re-ordering, the system will still be able to find the right device to use and boot from it. This was especially important when systems used to have IDE and **Serial Advanced Technology Attachment** (**SATA**) drives or SATA and SCSI drives, or even today, when **Internet SCSI** (**iSCSI**) devices might be connected in a different order than expected, resulting in device name changes and failures when reaching them.

Using `UUID` or `LABEL` allows us to install SLES on a USB drive or an external disk.

Remember to use the `blkid` or `lsblk -fp` commands to check the filesystems' labels and **universally unique identifiers** (**UUIDs**) that could be used when referring to them.

> When editing the `/etc/fstab` file, be extremely careful: altering the mount points used by the system might render your system unusable. If in doubt, double-check for any change and be sure to familiarize yourself with system recovery methods and have rescue media available in case this is needed.

Let's learn about mounting a remote NFS in the next section.

# Using network filesystems with NFS

Mounting a remote NFS is not much different than mounting local devices, but instead of specifying a local device as we did in the previous section with our `/dev/loop0p1` file, we provide `server:export` as a device.

We can find a range of options by checking out the manual page via `man mount`, and this will show us several of the options and the way the devices in our system look.

When an NFS mount is going to be used, the administrator will need to use the host and the export name to mount that device—for example, based on the following data about the NFS export:

- **Server:** `server.suse.test`
- **Export:** `/isos`
- **Mount point:** `/mnt/nfs`

With the preceding data, it's easy to construct the `mount` command, which will look like this:

```
mount -t nfs server.suse.test:/isos /mnt/nfs
```

If we analyze the preceding command, it specifies the type of filesystem to be mounted as `nfs`. The `nfs` service is provided by a server with the hostname `server.suse.test`. It uses the `/isos` NFS export from that server. Locally, this export will be mounted and made available in the `/mnt/nfs` folder.

If we want to define this filesystem as available at boot, we should add an entry in `/etc/fstab`. But how should we indicate this?

Based on the settings explained during this chapter, the constructed entry would look something like this:

```
server.suse.test:/isos /mnt/nfs nfs defaults,_netdev 0 0
```

The preceding line of code includes the same parameters we specified on the command line. It also indicates that this resource requires network access before it can be mounted. This is necessary because the system must establish a network connection to reach the NFS server. The same requirement applies to other types of network-based storage, such as Samba or Windows Share mounts, iSCSI, and similar technologies.

> Reinstating the idea of keeping our system bootable, once we make modifications to the `/etc/fstab` configuration file, it is recommended to execute `mount -a` so that the validation is performed from a running system. If, after the execution, the new filesystems are available and shown when executing, for example, `df`, and no error appears, it should be safe.

# Summary

In this chapter, we've learned about how a disk is divided logically for optimal use of storage and how to later create a filesystem on that disk division so that it can be used to actually store data.

Once the filesystem was created, we learned how to make it accessible in our system and how to ensure that it will be available after the next system restart via modification of the `/etc/fstab` configuration file.

Finally, we also learned about using a remote filesystem with NFS, based on the data that was provided for us, and how to add it to our `fstab` file to make it persistent.

In the next chapter, we will learn how to make storage even more useful via logical volume management, which empowers the definition of different logical units that can be resized, combined to provide data redundancy, and more.

# 13

# Flexible Storage Management with LVM

In the previous chapter, we learned how to manage local storage, but we were constrained by hardware limitations, such as the size of available disks. Linux provides an alternative and flexible logical volume management that creates an abstraction layer on top of the physical storage. The **Logical Volume Manager (LVM)** provides advanced configuration of drives, allowing the use of more than one disk in the same logical volume (the LVM equivalent of a partition), the replication of data to multiple disks, or taking snapshots of a volume to store copies of the content, all while the system is running.

In this chapter, we are going to go through the basic usage and configuration of LVM, starting with the core concepts required to understand how it works. We will prepare disks so they can be used with LVM and aggregate them into a pool to get additional space. We will then distribute that aggregated disk space into volumes that will act as dynamic partitions. To do so, we will go through the following topics:

- Understanding LVM
- Creating, moving, and removing physical volumes
- Combining physical volumes into volume groups
- Creating and extending logical volumes
- Adding new disks to a volume group and extending a logical volume
- Removing logical volumes, volume groups, and physical volumes
- Reviewing LVM commands

# Technical requirements

We will need two additional disks added to the working machine for this chapter. Depending on your infrastructure, you have different options:

- On a physical machine, you can add a couple of USB drives
- On a local VM, you will need to add two new virtual drives
- If you are using a cloud instance, you will need to add two new block devices

For example, we can add two new hard drives to a VM. In many cases, the VM definition would have to be edited, and this will only be possible when the machine is powered off. Edit the characteristics of the VM and add additional drives:

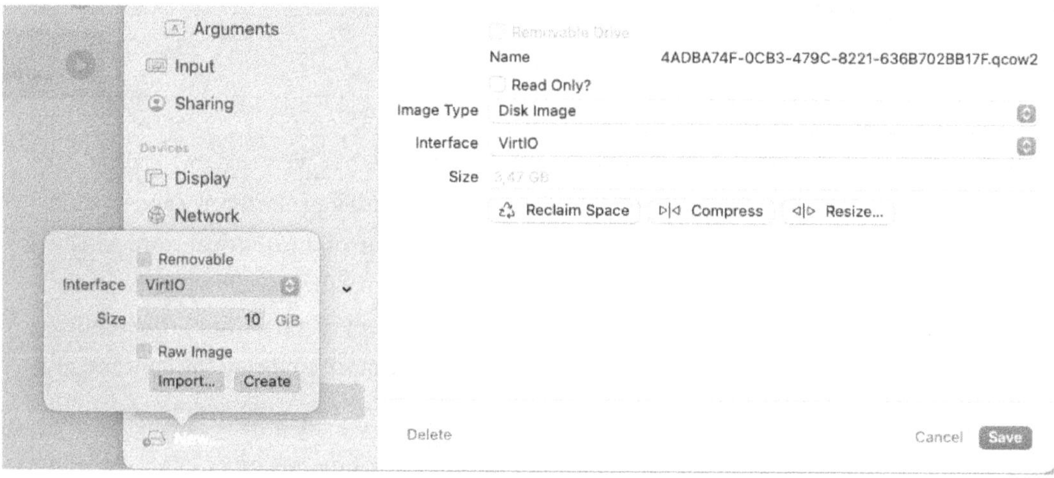


*Figure 13.1 – Editing VM properties*

> Check the documentation of your virtualization platform to find out how to add new hardware, as there are slight differences between hypervisors and versions. **Don't forget to save the changes!**

We are going to create two virtual drives for the VM. Let's add two drives of 2 GiB each. Once you have finished, you should see at least three virtual drives—the original one with the operating system and the two new ones we have created:

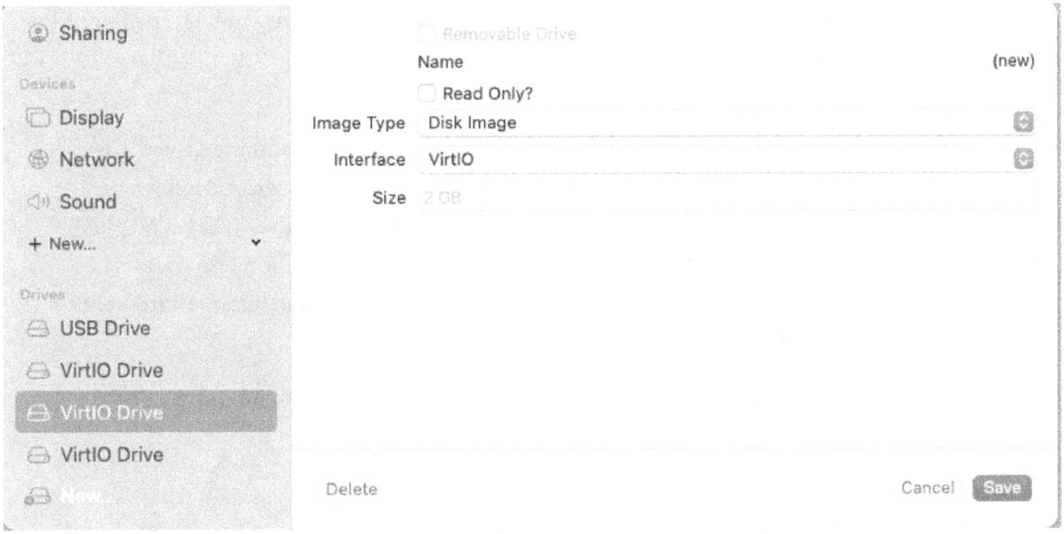


*Figure 13.2 – The original drive and the two new ones added to the VM*

Let's power on the VM and find out how the drives are displayed inside the VM:

```
user@geeko:~> lsblk
NAME   MAJ:MIN RM  SIZE RO TYPE MOUNTPOINTS
sr0     11:0    1 1024M  0 rom
vda    254:0    0   64G  0 disk
├─vda1 254:1    0  128M  0 part /boot/efi
├─vda2 254:2    0 61.9G  0 part /var
│                               /usr/local
│                               /srv
│                               /root
│                               /opt
│                               /boot/grub2/arm64-efi
│                               /home
│                               /.snapshots
│                               /
└─vda3 254:3    0    2G  0 part [SWAP]
vdb    254:16   0    2G  0 disk
vdc    254:32   0    2G  0 disk
```

The new drives are called `vdb` and `vdc`, and their type is `disk`. However, they are not yet configured like the system disk on `vda`. Let's put the new disks to use.

> There is a relationship between the names of devices in Linux and the drivers they use. Devices attached via SATA or SCSI will get a name that starts with `sd` followed by a letter in order of appearance, such as `sda` or `sdb`. On the IDE, they will get `hd` plus the letter, such as `hda` or `hdb`. On VirtIO paravirtualized drivers, the name starts with `vd` and a letter, for example, `vda` or `vdb`. If you frequently add and remove hardware, you can avoid name updates using labels or UUID.
>
> You can check out the rules in the `/usr/lib/udev/rules.d/60-persistent-storage.rules` file.

# Understanding LVM

One of the complexities of a new installation of Linux is understanding how to partition the disk drive. Estimates are hard to get right, and systems that are working for months or years can require more space in some partitions with new versions of the software, or to make room for logs and metrics. In some cases, users just put all the data into a large partition to avoid the problem, even if that could lead to other problems in production.

LVM provides three abstractions to create virtual block devices from physical devices that can have more advanced characteristics than the physical devices themselves:

- **Physical volumes (PVs)**: The base layer of LVM, the actual storage device. A PV can be either a partition on a disk, or the full raw disk itself, or anything that looks like a hard disk, such as a hardware RAID (Redundant Array of Inexpensive Devices) array or a **Logical Unit Number (LUN)**.
- **Volume groups (VGs)**: Aggregations of physical volumes. They create logical pools of space from physical volumes. One PV can only be part of a single VG.
- **Logical volumes (LVs)**: The third layer of LVM. They distribute the space that the VGs aggregate.

> You can't use an unpartitioned disk as the boot partition or where the operating system is installed. An unpartitioned disk appears unused at the system level and can be easily overwritten or misused.

We are going to use our two new disks to create LVs, as shown in the following diagram:

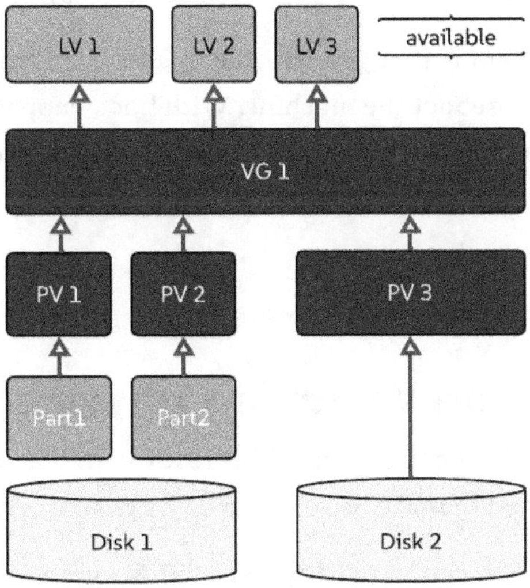


*Figure 13.3 – LVM example using two disks*

Let's go through the different components of the diagram:

- We have two disks, *Disk 1* and *Disk 2*. These are the two virtual disks we added to the VM at the beginning.
- *Disk 1* has two logical partitions: *Part1* and *Part2*.
- *Disk 2* is a raw drive with no partitions.
- We are going to create a PV on each one. A PV makes the physical device recognizable by LVM. We are going to name them *PV#*:
    - *PV 1*, created on the *Part1* partition of *Disk 1*
    - *PV 2*, created on the *Part2* partition of *Disk 1*
    - *PV 3*, created directly on *Disk 2*
- We are going to create one single VG, *VG 1*, that aggregates all three physical volumes *PV 1*, *PV 2*, and *PV 3*. With that, we will consolidate the storage into a single, large unit of space, which will be available to create LVs.
- To distribute the space, we are going to create three LVs – *LV 1*, *LV 2*, and *LV 3*. The LVs do not use all the space available in the VG, allowing us to create new ones or add space if some of the LVs run out of space.

In this chapter, we will keep to the basics, but LVM can do much more. For instance, it is possible to configure LVM drives for **thin provisioning**, **striping** (similar to RAID 0), or for creating **snapshots**.

One of the advantages of using LVM is that you are able to add extra space to any VG without having to unmount the volume or reboot the machine. With hot swappable hardware, you can even add new disks. If the filesystem that is using the LV allows it, it is even possible to resize it without rebooting. This is one of the reasons why LVM is recommended for servers, with very limited exceptions.

Now that we know the concepts, let's put them to work.

# Creating, moving, and removing physical volumes

In the *Technical requirements* section, we left our machine ready with two new disks, `vdb` and `vdc`. We are now going to configure LVM to make use of them as we described in *Figure 13.3*.

Our first step is to partition `vdb` so it can be used by LVM. We are going to use `parted`, a tool included in SLES to manipulate disk partitions, which supports multiple partition tables:

```
user@geeko:~> sudo parted /dev/vdb print
Error: /dev/vdb: unrecognised disk label
Model: Virtio Block Device (virtblk)
Disk /dev/vdb: 2147MB
Sector size (logical/physical): 512B/512B
Partition Table: unknown
Disk Flags:
```

We get an error message because the disk is completely unpartitioned (`unrecognised disk label`). As explained in *Chapter 12, Managing Local Storage and Filesystems*, there are two styles of partition tables that can be used:

- `gpt`: The default partition style for systems using the **Unified Extensible Firmware Interface (UEFI)** firmware for booting
- `msdos` (also **MBR**): The only one supported in systems with legacy **Basic Input Output System (BIOS)**, which supports only four primary partitions for disks up to 2 TB, and is required by older operating systems

Unless you have a defined use case, you should be using `gpt`. In `parted`, partition tables are called **labels**. Let's create one on our disk:

```
user@geeko:~> sudo parted /dev/vdb mklabel gpt
```

You may need to update `/etc/fstab`:

```
user@geeko:~> sudo parted /dev/vdb print
Model: Virtio Block Device (virtblk)
Disk /dev/vdb: 2147MB
Sector size (logical/physical): 512B/512B
Partition Table: gpt
Disk Flags:

Number  Start  End  Size  File system  Name  Flags
```

> Select a different label if you want to use another partition table. `parted` supports several alternatives, including `bsd` and `loop` (for raw disk access). For instance, the command to use MBR is `parted /dev/vdb mklabel msdos`.

Specifying a label does not create partitions but prepares the disk so we can create them. We wanted two partitions on the disk, so let's use `parted` in interactive mode to create the first one:

```
user@geeko:~> sudo parted /dev/vdb mkpart
```

Enter a partition name, such as `mypart0`:

```
Partition name?  []? mypart0
```

The filesystem type is optional, so let's go with the default `ext2`:

```
File system type?  [ext2]? ext2
```

We need to define a start and an endpoint for the partition. We will use the standard first sector, which is `2048s`:

```
Start? 2048s
```

> The GPT table is stored at the beginning of the disk, so you can't create partitions in sector 0. Defining the first sector as `2048s` is a safe way to make sure that the partition is aligned with the physical layout of the hard drive, increasing performance. You can check the sector size using `fdisk -l /dev/vdb`.

The final step is setting the endpoint, which can be described as the size of the partition we want to make (in most systems, the `2048s` sector is 1 MB):

```
End? 256MB
```

The `fdisk` command is complete with the following warning, to remind us that we still have some steps to take to have the partition available for our system:

```
Information: You may need to update /etc/fstab.
```

In scripts, when you need to be sure that the partition table is updated before continuing to make changes, you can wait until the device is generated in `/dev` with the following command:

```
user@geeko:~> sudo udevadm settle
```

> The full command to run in non-interactive mode is `parted /dev/vdb mkpart mypart0 btrfs 2048s 256MB`.

We can see the new partition:

```
user@geeko:~> sudo parted /dev/vdb print
Model: Virtio Block Device (virtblk)
Disk /dev/vdb: 2147MB
Sector size (logical/physical): 512B/512B
Partition Table: gpt
Disk Flags:

Number  Start   End    Size   File system  Name     Flags
1       1049kB  256MB  255MB               mypart0
```

To host LVM PVs, we need to change the partition type, which we can do using the `set` subcommand. We need to update the new partition (partition 1), set up its type to the new one (`lvm`), and activate it so it is visible to the operating system (`on`):

```
user@geeko:~> sudo parted /dev/vdb set 1 lvm on
Information: You may need to update /etc/fstab.

user@geeko:~> sudo parted /dev/vdb print
Model: Virtio Block Device (virtblk)
Disk /dev/vdb: 2147MB
```

```
Sector size (logical/physical): 512B/512B
Partition Table: gpt
Disk Flags:

Number  Start   End    Size   File system  Name     Flags
1       1049kB  256MB  255MB               mypart0  lvm
```

The flags have been updated to include `lvm`.

Let's add a second partition using the rest of the space, `mypart1`:

```
user@geeko:~> sudo parted /dev/vdb mkpart mypart1 xfs \
256MB 100%
Information: You may need to update /etc/fstab.

user@geeko:~> sudo parted /dev/vdb set 2 lvm on
Information: You may need to update /etc/fstab.

user@geeko:~> sudo parted /dev/vdb print
Model: Virtio Block Device (virtblk)
Disk /dev/vdb: 2147MB
Sector size (logical/physical): 512B/512B
Partition Table: gpt
Disk Flags:

Number  Start   End     Size    File system  Name     Flags
1       1049kB  256MB   255MB                mypart0  lvm
2       256MB   2146MB  1891MB               mypart1  lvm
```

We are halfway there. The first disk has two partitions that use the full disk. Our storage now looks like this:

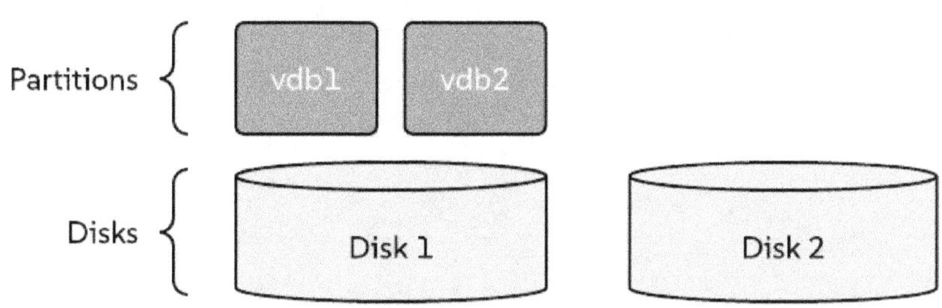


*Figure 13.4 – Partitions created in our two new disks*

parted is not the only tool for manipulating disk partition tables. By default, SLES also includes fdisk. You might find it easier for you, so give it a try.

The next step is to create LVM PVs. We will use the new partitions for that.

First, we will check the available PVs with the pvs command:

```
user@geeko:~> sudo pvs
```

The default filesystem used in SLES is BTRFS, which includes many of the features of LVM, such as snapshots, in the filesystem itself. Using LVM and BTRFS together is not normally needed or recommended.

The next step is to create the PVs with pvcreate:

```
user@geeko:~> sudo pvcreate /dev/vdb1
  Physical volume "/dev/vdb1" successfully
created.
  Creating devices file /etc/lvm/devices/system.
devices
user@geeko:~> sudo pvcreate /dev/vdb2
  Physical volume "/dev/vdb2" successfully
created.
```

Now, the pvs option shows new data:

```
user@geeko:~> sudo pvs
  PV         VG Fmt  Attr PSize   PFree
  /dev/vdb1     lvm2 ---  243.00m 243.00m
  /dev/vdb2     lvm2 ---    1.76g   1.76g
```

Notice that PVs do not have their own names, but they inherit the name of the partition or device:

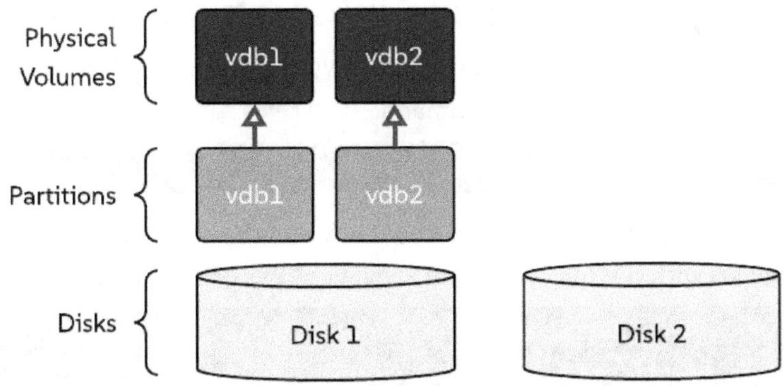


*Figure 13.5 – PVs created in the two new partitions*

You can also create PVs on a raw disk device, such as vdc. It will only be possible if the disk has not been partitioned:

```
user@geeko:~> sudo pvcreate /dev/vdc
[sudo] password for user:
  Physical volume "/dev/vdc" successfully created.
user@geeko:~> sudo pvs
  PV         VG Fmt  Attr PSize   PFree
  /dev/vdb1     lvm2 ---  243.00m 243.00m
  /dev/vdb2     lvm2 ---    1.76g   1.76g
  /dev/vdc      lvm2 ---    2.00g   2.00g
```

The result is the following:

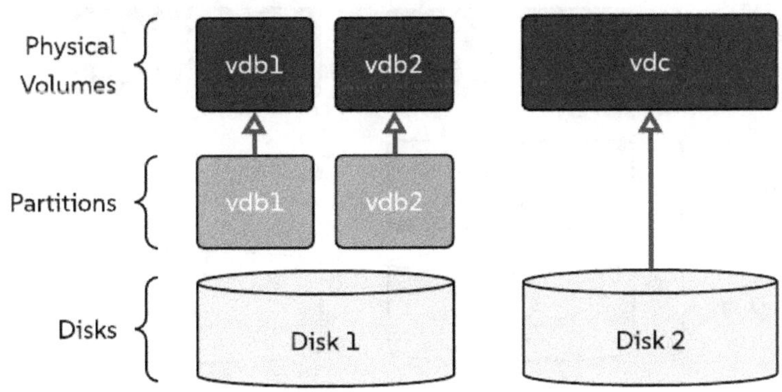


*Figure 13.6 – PVs created in the two new partitions and the new disk device*

Now that wehave the PVs, let's group them using VGs in the next section.

# Combining physical volumes into volume groups

Now that all the space is assigned to PV, we can create a VG for them. As before, we are going to check what VGs are available with the vgs command:

```
user@geeko:~> sudo vgs
```

Again, as the root filesystem is BTRFS, it does not use LVM, and the list is empty. We are going to create a new storage VG with the /dev/vdb1 and /dev/vdb2 PVs using the vgcreate command:

```
user@geeko:~> sudo vgcreate storage /dev/vdb1 /dev/vdc
  Volume group "storage" successfully created
user@geeko:~> sudo pvs
  PV         VG      Fmt  Attr PSize   PFree
  /dev/vdb1  storage lvm2 a--  240.00m 240.00m
  /dev/vdb2          lvm2 ---    1.76g   1.76g
  /dev/vdc   storage lvm2 a--    2.00g   2.00g
user@geeko:~> sudo vgs
  VG      #PV #LV #SN Attr   VSize VFree
  storage   2   0   0 wz--n- 2.23g 2.23g
```

We now have a new VG on top of vdb1 and vdc. The VG's storage space is the sum of vdb1 and vdc, even if they belong to different disks, and they are part of the storage VG:

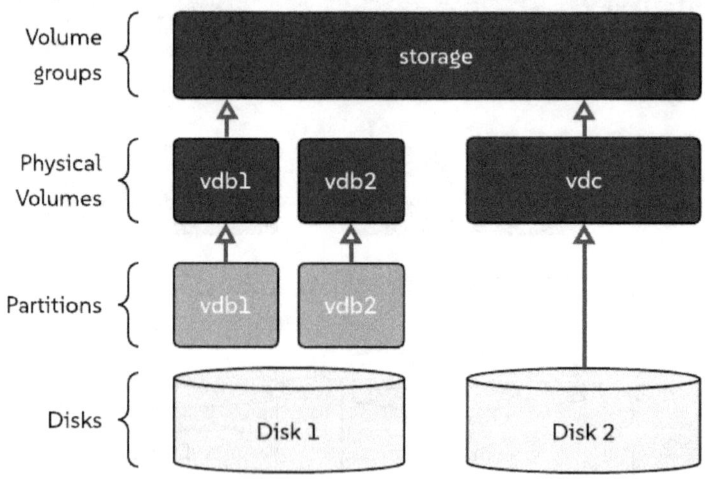


*Figure 13.7 – First VG created with two PVs*

It is time to create LVs and the filesystems on them. We have partitioned the disks and created partitions and PVs, and aggregated them all into a VG that acts as a pool of storage. We are ready to distribute the space.

# Creating and extending logical volumes

> Advanced management of storage, such as striping or mirroring, is configured at the LV level. Consider VG a very thin layer that allows you to group PVs so you don't need to list all of them every time you do something.

As we haven't created any LVs, there are none, but we will be fixing this next. Let's move to the next layers and check the LVs with the `lvs` command:

```
user@geeko:~> sudo lvs
```

We had a 2.23 GB VG. Let's use a 512 MB LV called `data`, 200 MB in size, on the `storage` VG:

```
user@geeko:~> sudo lvcreate --name data --size 512MB \ storage
  Logical volume "data" created.
user@geeko:~> sudo lvs
  LV   VG      Attr       LSize   Pool Origin Data%  Meta%  Move Log
Cpy%Sync Convert
  data storage -wi-a----- 512.00m
```

Our storage looks like this now:

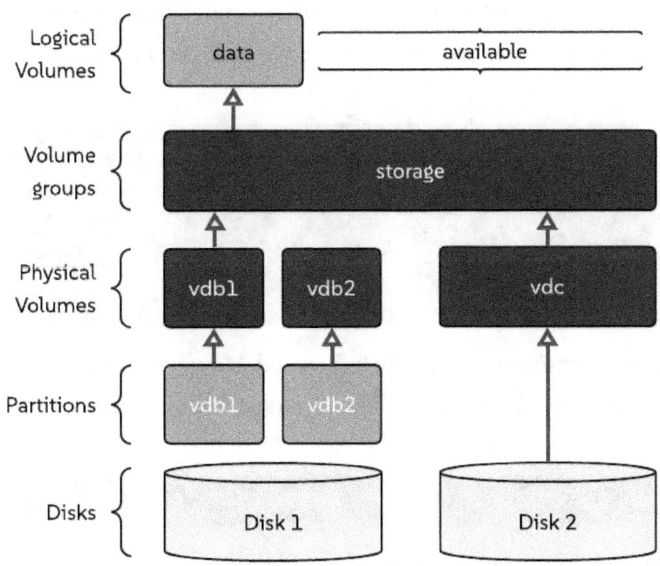


*Figure 13.8 – First LV created on a VG*

The LV behaves like a partition on a block device. In order to be used, we need to format it with a filesystem. As we are using LVM, let's format it using `xfs`:

```
user@geeko:~> sudo mkfs.xfs /dev/storage/data
[sudo] password for user:
meta-data=/dev/storage/data      isize=512    agcount=4, agsize=32768 blks
         =                       sectsz=512   attr=2, projid32bit=1
         =                       crc=1        finobt=1, sparse=1, rmapbt=1
         =                       reflink=1    bigtime=1 inobtcount=1
nrext64=1
         =                       exchange=0   metadir=0
data     =                       bsize=4096   blocks=131072, imaxpct=25
         =                       sunit=0      swidth=0 blks
naming   =version 2              bsize=4096   ascii-ci=0, ftype=1,
parent=0
log      =internal log           bsize=4096   blocks=16384, version=2
         =                       sectsz=512   sunit=0 blks, lazy-count=1
realtime =none                   extsz=4096   blocks=0, rtextents=0
         =                       rgcount=0    rgsize=0 extents
Discarding blocks...Done.
```

We are no longer using autogenerated names for partitions, but the ones we used to create the VG and LV. The LV is ready to be mounted. For instance, we could create the `/srv/data` directory and mount it:

```
user@geeko:~> sudo mkdir /srv/data
user@geeko:~> sudo mount -t xfs /dev/storage/data /srv/data
user@geeko:~> df -h /srv/data
Filesystem                 Size  Used Avail Use% Mounted on
/dev/mapper/storage-data  448M   35M  414M   8% /srv/data
```

The LV is mounted on `/srv/data`, and it is ready to be used. However, if you power off or reboot the system, the configuration will be lost. To make it persistent, you need to add a line to the `/etc/fstab` file:

```
/dev/storage/data   /srv/data    xfs    defaults        0 0
```

To test that the line has been correctly written, we can run the following commands. First, dismount the filesystem:

```
user@geeko:~> sudo mount -a
```

Checking the space again will show that we are now using a different partition:

```
user@geeko:~> df -h /srv/data
Filesystem      Size  Used Avail Use% Mounted on
/dev/vda2        62G  2.8G   58G   5% /srv
```

The output of the `df` (which stands for *disk free*) command shows that the space in the `/srv/data/` directory is the same as the partition mounted on `/srv`. Once we mount it again, the space will reflect that of the underlying LV. We can refresh and mount all systems in `fstab` using the `mount` command:

```
user@geeko:~> sudo mount -a
```

With this command, the system will try to mount all filesystems mentioned in `/etc/fstab`. Errors will be shown if there is a problem mounting them (such as a typo in `/etc/fstab`). Let's check that it is mounted:

```
user@geeko:~> sudo df -h /srv/data
Filesystem                Size  Used Avail Use% Mounted on
/dev/mapper/storage-data  448M   35M  414M   8% /srv/data
```

The `/dev/storage/data` and `/dev/mapper/storage-data` devices link to a device generated by the **device mapper**. They are completely interchangeable.

The filesystem is available, properly mounted, and ready to be used, and will be automatically mounted at each reboot. Let's move on now to more advanced tasks.

## Adding new disks to a volume group and extending a logical volume

LVM allows us to do things that are not possible with traditional partitions. We can easily extend our VG by adding new space, for instance, if a new hard drive is available. Let's add the `/dev/vdb2` partition to the `storage` VG:

```
user@geeko:~> sudo pvs
[sudo] password for user:
  PV         VG      Fmt  Attr PSize   PFree
  /dev/vdb1  storage lvm2 a--  240.00m 240.00m
  /dev/vdb2          lvm2 ---    1.76g   1.76g
```

```
  /dev/vdc    storage lvm2 a--    2.00g   1.50g
user@geeko:~> sudo vgs
  VG       #PV #LV #SN Attr   VSize VFree
  storage   2   1   0 wz--n- 2.23g 1.73g
user@geeko:~> sudo vgextend storage /dev/vdb2
  Volume group "storage" successfully extended
user@geeko:~> sudo vga
sudo: vga: command not found
user@geeko:~> sudo vgs
  VG       #PV #LV #SN Attr   VSize VFree
  storage   3   1   0 wz--n- 3.99g 3.49g
```

We are now using all the storage we added in a single VG that is larger than any of the original disks:

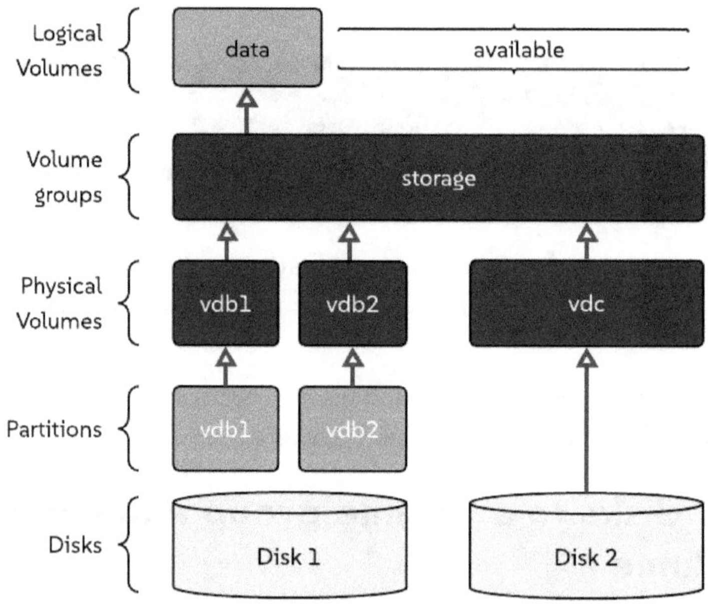


*Figure 13.9 – Extended VG with three PVs*

Let's now extend the `data` LV by adding 200 MB to it:

```
user@geeko:~> sudo lvs
  LV   VG      Attr       LSize   Pool Origin Data%  Meta%  Move Log
Cpy%Sync Convert
  data storage -wi-ao---- 512.00m
user@geeko:~> sudo lvextend --size +600MB /dev/storage/data
```

```
  Size of logical volume storage/data changed from 512.00 MiB (128
extents) to 1.09 GiB (278 extents).
  Logical volume storage/data successfully resized.
user@geeko:~> sudo lvs
  LV   VG      Attr       LSize Pool Origin Data%  Meta%  Move Log
Cpy%Sync Convert
  data storage -wi-ao---- 1.09g
```

We now have an LV with 1.09 GB of space. However, the filesystem is not aware of the change and is still showing the old availability:

```
user@geeko:~> sudo df -h /srv/data
Filesystem                 Size  Used Avail Use% Mounted on
/dev/mapper/storage-data  448M   35M  414M   8% /srv/data
```

Extending the filesystem depends on the tools available for that specific filesystem. In the case of `xfs`, the tool for extending it is `xfs_growfs`. Let's do that now:

```
user@geeko:~> sudo xfs_growfs /dev/storage/data
meta-data=/dev/mapper/storage-data isize=512    agcount=4, agsize=32768
blks
         =                       sectsz=512   attr=2, projid32bit=1
         =                       crc=1        finobt=1, sparse=1, rmapbt=1
         =                       reflink=1    bigtime=1 inobtcount=1
nrext64=1
         =                       exchange=0   metadir=0
data     =                       bsize=4096   blocks=131072, imaxpct=25
         =                       sunit=0      swidth=0 blks
naming   =version 2              bsize=4096   ascii-ci=0, ftype=1,
parent=0
log      =internal log           bsize=4096   blocks=16384, version=2
         =                       sectsz=512   sunit=0 blks, lazy-count=1
realtime =none                   extsz=4096   blocks=0, rtextents=0
         =                       rgcount=0    rgsize=0 extents
data blocks changed from 131072 to 284672
user@geeko:~> df -h /srv/data
Filesystem                 Size  Used Avail Use% Mounted on
/dev/mapper/storage-data  1.1G   47M 1002M   5% /srv/data
```

As you can see, the filesystem now shows the added space. This can be handy if you run out of space on an LV, for instance, because you created an LV to store your logs and they have grown beyond your expectations on the production system. To fix this, you need to have some extra room available or just add new disks when you need them.

> In production, it is typical to need the system to keep running without reboots. Suppose that we have resized the filesystem while it was mounted and used by the system, without the need to reboot. When doing this task, the LV can be mounted and used by the system. Not all filesystems allow this, and only BTRFS allows shrinking online.

Let's now create a second LV on the same VG:

```
user@geeko:~> sudo lvcreate --size 300MB --name img storage
  Logical volume "img" created.
user@geeko:~> sudo lvs
  LV   VG      Attr       LSize   Pool Origin Data%  Meta%  Move Log
Cpy%Sync Convert
  data storage -wi-ao----   1.09g
  img  storage -wi-a----- 300.00m

user@geeko:~> sudo mkfs.xfs /dev/storage/img
meta-data=/dev/storage/img       isize=512    agcount=4, agsize=19200 blks
         =                       sectsz=512   attr=2, projid32bit=1
         =                       crc=1        finobt=1, sparse=1, rmapbt=1
         =                       reflink=1    bigtime=1 inobtcount=1
nrext64=1
         =                       exchange=0   metadir=0
data     =                       bsize=4096   blocks=76800, imaxpct=25
         =                       sunit=0      swidth=0 blks
naming   =version 2              bsize=4096   ascii-ci=0, ftype=1,
parent=0
log      =internal log           bsize=4096   blocks=16384, version=2
         =                       sectsz=512   sunit=0 blks, lazy-count=1
realtime =none                   extsz=4096   blocks=0, rtextents=0
         =                       rgcount=0    rgsize=0 extents
```

```
Discarding blocks...Done.
user@geeko:~> sudo mkdir /srv/img
user@geeko:~> sudo mount -t xfs /dev/storage/img /srv/img user@geeko:~>
sudo df /srv/img
Filesystem                 1K-blocks  Used Available Use% Mounted on
/dev/mapper/storage-img      241664 20304    221360   9% /srv/img
```

LVM internally splits the physical and logical space into chunks of data of the same size, which can vary from 1 KB to 16 GB in powers of 2 (normally 4 KB). They are called **physical extents** (for PV) and **logical extents** (for LV). Having a large number of extents will slow down the tools, but will have no impact on the I/O performance.

The `--size` and `--extents` options for the `lvcreate` command have several options that can be used to define the space to be consumed:

- **Human readable:** We can define the size in human-readable units, such as gigabytes (`GB`), or megabytes (`MB`), for example: `--size 3GB`
- **Extents:** We can use extents as a unit with `--extents`, for example: `--extents 125`)

The `--size` and `--extents` options also apply to the `lvextend` command. We can use the options for `lvcreate` to define the new size of a logical volume. We can also define increments of space:

- **Adding space:** If we provide the + symbol before the size, `lvextend` will increase the size by the amount provided (that is, `--size +1GB` adds one extra gigabyte to the current LV)
- **Percentage of free space:** We can also provide the percentage of free space to create or extend using `-extents` and the percentage of free space to be used, followed by `%FREE` (to extend an LV to 10% of the free space use `--extents 10%FREE`)

Let's extend `img` to use all the available space in the VG:

```
user@geeko:~> sudo lvextend --extents 100%FREE storage/img
  Size of logical volume storage/img changed from 300.00 MiB (75 extents)
to 2.51 GiB (643 extents).
  Logical volume storage/img successfully resized.
user@geeko:~> sudo xfs_growfs /dev/storage/img
meta-data=/dev/mapper/storage-img isize=512    agcount=4, agsize=19200
```

```
blks
         =                        sectsz=512   attr=2, projid32bit=1
         =                        crc=1        finobt=1, sparse=1, rmapbt=1
         =                        reflink=1    bigtime=1 inobtcount=1
nrext64=1
         =                        exchange=0   metadir=0
data     =                        bsize=4096   blocks=76800, imaxpct=25
         =                        sunit=0      swidth=0 blks
naming   =version 2               bsize=4096   ascii-ci=0, ftype=1,
parent=0
log      =internal log            bsize=4096   blocks=16384, version=2
         =                        sectsz=512   sunit=0 blks, lazy-count=1
realtime =none                    extsz=4096   blocks=0, rtextents=0
         =                        rgcount=0    rgsize=0 extents
data blocks changed from 76800 to 658432
```

It is a good practice to run `man lvcreate` and `man lvextend` to get familiar with the syntax for these tools and see other options available.

LVM allows more advanced use cases. For instance, you can specify the data to be distributed among different PVs using stripes. An LV that uses stripes can improve reading and writing performance (such as RAID 0). You can also create LVs that are thinly provisioned, where some of the space reserved can be used by an arbitrary number of thin volumes, which will be expanded dynamically when needed. You can also create LVs with several mirrors, ensuring that data is mirrored into different PVs, with the data being synchronized automatically. Check the manual pages to find out more about these options.

To make the changes persistent across reboots, you need to add the new partitions to `/etc/fstab`.

Our disk space distribution now looks like this:

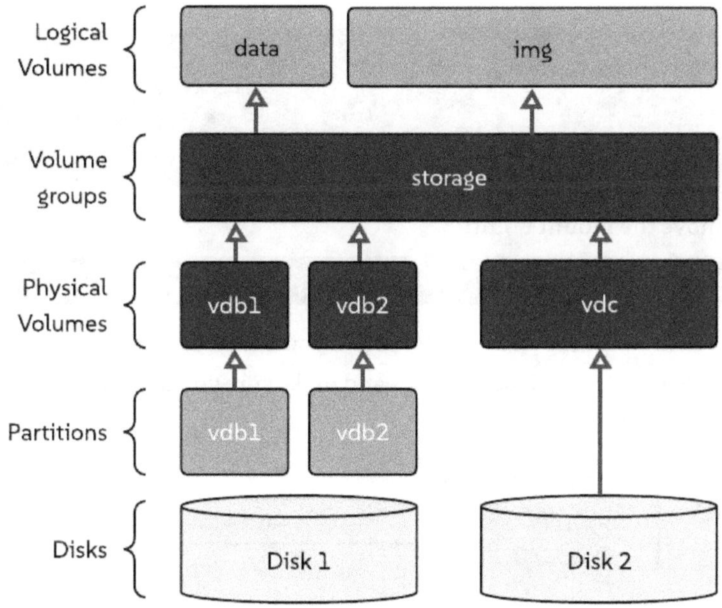


*Figure 13.10 – Extended VG with three PVs*

We have gone through the process of creating LVs with filesystems on them, independently of the distribution of the physical drives. Let's learn how to adjust sizing by removing some of the pieces.

# Removing logical volumes, volume groups, and physical volumes

We won't be able to remove components while they are being used by other layers, so we need to follow the steps in order. Let's start by checking whether `img` is mounted:

```
user@geeko:~> mount | grep img
/dev/mapper/storage-img on /srv/img type xfs
(rw,relatime,seclabel,attr2,inode64,logbufs=8,logbsize=32k, noquota)
```

Let's unmount it so it is not in use:

```
user@geeko:~> sudo umount /srv/img
user@geeko:~> mount | grep img
```

We can't find a mount point that includes `img`, so we know that it is no longer mounted. We can now delete the LV:

```
user@geeko:~> sudo lvremove /dev/storage/img
Do you really want to remove and DISCARD active logical volume storage/
img? [y/n]: y
  Logical volume "img" successfully removed.
```

Now, we can also remove the mount point:

```
user@geeko:~> sudo rmdir /srv/img
```

Don't forget to delete the configuration in `/etc/fstab` if you added the mount point and the LV is gone. This process is not reversible, so be cautious and make sure you don't misspell any storage. We are back to our previous state:

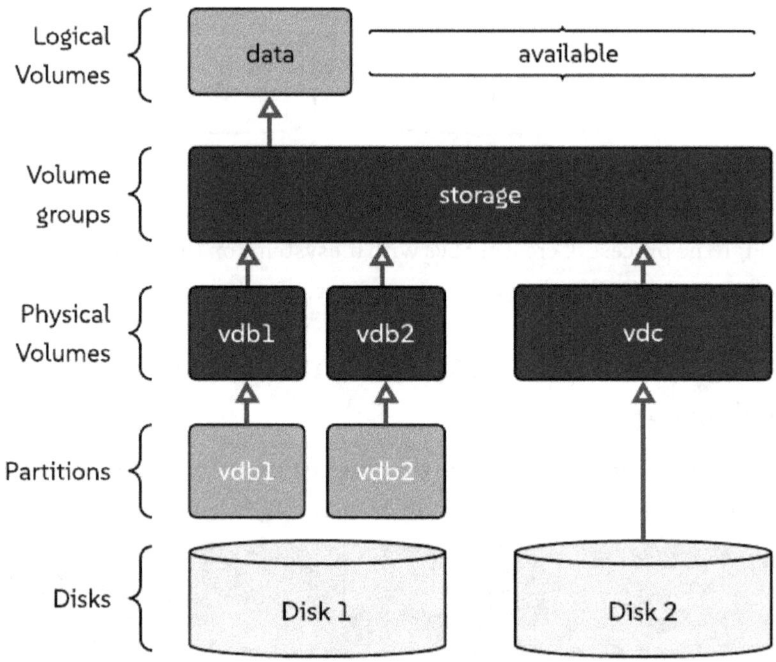


*Figure 13.11 – Our VG with the LV removed*

The next step is more complicated. We want to remove a PV from a VG. As VGs can expand into more than one PV and be spread among different disks, you will need to be careful and make sure you are not losing any data.

Let's copy some data into `data` to see how it is done:

```
user@geeko:~> cd /srv/data/
[user@geeko:/srv/data> sudo curl https://doc.opensuse.org/documentation/
leap/reference/book-reference_en.pdf --output book-reference_en.pdf
  % Total    % Received % Xferd  Average Speed   Time    Time     Time
Current
                                 Dload  Upload   Total   Spent    Left
Speed
100 5905k  100 5905k    0     0  9299k      0 --:--:-- --:--:-- --:--:--
9315k

user@geeko:/srv/data> ll
total 5908
-rw-r--r--. 1 root root 6047632 Jul 28 17:09 book-reference_en.pdf
user@geeko:/srv/data> sudo pvscan
  PV /dev/vdb1   VG storage   lvm2 [240.00 MiB / 240.00 MiB free]
  PV /dev/vdc    VG storage   lvm2 [2.00 GiB / 832.00 MiB free]
  PV /dev/vdb2   VG storage   lvm2 [1.76 GiB / 1.76 GiB free]
  Total: 3 [3.99 GiB] / in use: 3 [3.99 GiB] / in no VG: 0 [0   ]
```

Let's evacuate the data from `/dev/vdc` using the `pvmove` command so it is safe to remove it:

```
user@geeko:/srv/data> sudo pvmove /dev/vdc
  /dev/vdc: Moved: 53.47%
  /dev/vdc: Moved: 100.00%
```

It is possible that the extents allocated belong to a different PV, in which case you may receive a message stating `no data to move for storage`. You can use `pvmove` with other devices if that is the case.

Now, there is no data stored in `/dev/vdc`, and it can be safely removed from the VG. We can do so by using the `vgreduce` command:

```
user@geeko:/srv/data> sudo vgreduce storage /dev/vdc
  Removed "/dev/vdc" from volume group "storage"
```

The `storage` VG now has much less available space:

```
user@geeko:/srv/data> sudo vgs
  VG      #PV #LV #SN Attr   VSize VFree
  storage   2   1   0 wz--n- 1.99g 828.00m
user@geeko:/srv/data> sudo vgdisplay storage
  --- Volume group ---
  VG Name               storage
  System ID
  Format                lvm2
  Metadata Areas        2
  Metadata Sequence No  13
  VG Access             read/write
  VG Status             resizable
  MAX LV                0
  Cur LV                1
  Open LV               1
  Max PV                0
  Cur PV                2
  Act PV                2
  VG Size               1.99 GiB
  PE Size               4.00 MiB
  Total PE              510
  Alloc PE / Size       303 / 1.18 GiB
  Free  PE / Size       207 / 828.00 MiB
  VG UUID               dv8d0i-oNdI-QZcW-Qmgr-AFqb-Jpfy-MqX4kT
```

We can also see that the `/dev/vdc` PV is not attached to any VG:

```
user@geeko:/srv/data> sudo pvs
  PV         VG      Fmt  Attr PSize   PFree
  /dev/vdb1  storage lvm2 a--  240.00m 240.00m
  /dev/vdb2  storage lvm2 a--    1.76g 588.00m
  /dev/vdc           lvm2 ---    2.00g   2.00g
user@geeko:/srv/data> sudo pvdisplay /dev/vdc
  "/dev/vdc" is a new physical volume of "2.00 GiB"
  --- NEW Physical volume ---
```

```
PV Name               /dev/vdc
VG Name
PV Size               2.00 GiB
Allocatable           NO
PE Size               0
Total PE              0
Free PE               0
Allocated PE          0
PV UUID               4ghcr5-YYtk-d11p-Nb88-OfwF-XnJA-88EIDY
```

You can use the `vgdisplay`, `pvdisplay`, and `lvdisplay` commands to show detailed information on VG, PV, or LV.

We have not needed to stop or reboot the system to make these changes available in production. Our disk now looks like this:

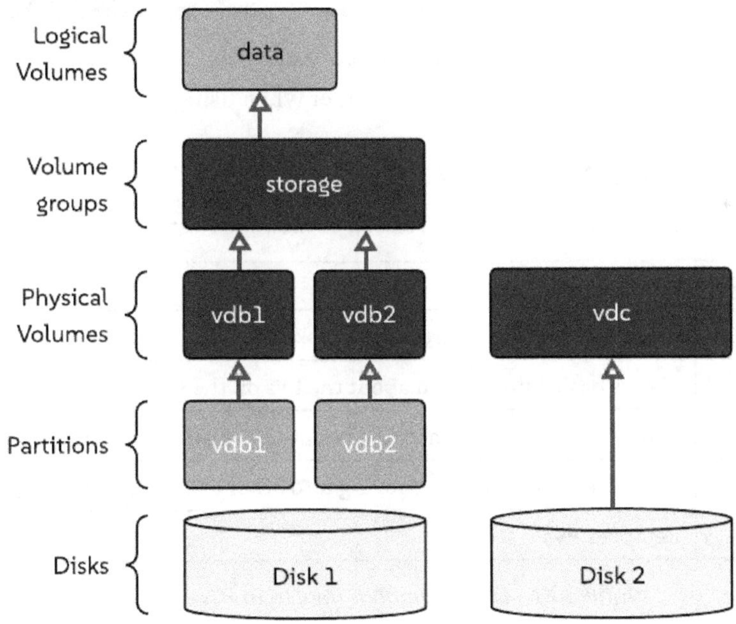


*Figure 13.12 – Our VG with PVs removed*

We can continue removing components. In order to delete the VG, we need to remove anything that is using it, and we now have only one LV left. Let's remove /dev/storage/data, using the --yes option so we aren't asked for confirmation (this is especially important if the command is run in a script):

```
user@geeko:~> sudo umount /dev/storage/data
user@geeko:~> sudo lvremove --yes /dev/storage/data
  Logical volume "data" successfully removed.
```

Now that storage is no longer in use, we can delete it:

```
user@geeko:~> sudo vgremove storage
  Volume group "storage" successfully removed
```

The final step is to clean the PVs:

```
user@geeko:~> sudo pvremove /dev/vdb1 /dev/vdb2 /dev/vdc
  Labels on physical volume "/dev/vdb1" successfully wiped.
  Labels on physical volume "/dev/vdb2" successfully wiped.
  Labels on physical volume "/dev/vdc" successfully wiped.
```

The drives are clean, and we can do whatever we need with them. In the next section, we will review alternative commands that you should remember when using LVM.

# Reviewing LVM commands

The following table contains commands that are used to manage PVs:

| Command | Usage |
|---|---|
| pvcreate | Initializes a PV on a partition or disk |
| pvs | Shows basic information about the PVs on the system |
| pvdisplay | Shows extended information about the PVs on the system |
| pvmove | Evacuates data from PV, moving it to other available PVs |
| pvremove | Removes PVs |

*Table 13.1 – LVM commands related to PVs*

Now, let's review the commands used to manage VGs:

| Command | Usage |
|---|---|
| `vgcreate` | Creates a VG that aggregates different PVs |
| `vgs` | Shows basic information about the VGs on the system |
| `vgdisplay` | Shows extended information about the VGs on the system |
| `vgextend` | Extends an existing VG by adding new PVs to it |
| `vgreduce` | Removes PVs from a VG |
| `vgremove` | Removes a VG |

*Table 13.2 – LVM commands related to VGs*

And finally, let's review the commands used to manage LVs:

| Command | Usage |
|---|---|
| `lvcreate` | Creates an LV on a VG, preparing it to be formatted with a filesystem |
| `lvs` | Shows basic information about the LVs on the system |
| `lvdisplay` | Shows extended information about the LVs on the system |
| `lvextend` | Extends an existing LV by adding available space from the VG to it |
| `lvremove` | Removes an LV |

*Table 13.3 – LVM commands related to LVs*

> The web administration interface, `cockpit`, has a user interface for managing storage. It can be installed with the following command: `zypper install cockpit-storaged`. You can learn more about LVM by navigating through the storage interface in `cockpit`.

# Summary

LVM provides advanced capabilities on top of disks, enhancing the flexibility of the solutions in a live system. Although it is not recommended on BTRFS, the default filesystem, it is highly recommended on other filesystems, such as XFS, which is widely used in production. LVM generates pools of storage from physical devices and is capable of using them to manage, reallocate, distribute, and assign disk space online, without unmounting them or rebooting the system. Managing storage is a key tool in the system administration toolkit, and enables other capabilities such as shared storage via iSCSI.

It is important to be sure of what you are doing when interacting with storage, as data loss can be extremely difficult or impossible to recover. LVM will allow you to modify your system without rebooting, but it cannot protect you from your mistakes.

In this chapter, we have gone through the basic concepts and tasks related to LVM. We have learned about PVs, VGs, and LVs. We have learned to create and manage them and their relationships. We have practiced creating, extending, and removing LVs, VGs, and PVs, and configured filesystems that use them.

In the next chapter, we will learn how to configure and use Snapper to create snapshots of your BTRFS filesystems.

# 14

# Configuring and Using System Snapshots with BTRFS and Snapper

*Chapter 14* already! We have learned a lot about disks, partitions, filesystems, the boot process, and even logical volumes. Now, it's time to learn about a capability that makes **SUSE Linux Enterprise Server (SLES)** pretty special, which is filesystem-level snapshots.

You have probably seen and used other volume/disk-level and even **virtual machine (VM)**-level snapshots, which can be very useful. In this case, having a snapshot capability that works independently of the system type provides a major advantage. It provides extended functionality and useful options for your day-to-day administration tasks.

In this chapter, we will cover the following main topics:

- BTRFS' and Snapper's origins
- Reviewing BTRFS basics, creating filesystems, reviewing status, and mounting
- BTRFS snapshots, how they work, and how to use them
- Snapper, the snapshot management tool

This will help make our systems more resilient and ensure they run correctly, even during major changes. It also allows us to make those changes with confidence. It's time to start rolling!

# Technical requirements

As in previous chapters, you can continue the practice of using the VM created at the beginning of this book in *Chapter 1, Getting SLES 16 Up and Running (Physical and Cloud)*. Any additional packages required for this chapter will be indicated alongside the text.

# BTRFS' and Snapper's origins

Several filesystems are supported in SLES 16, but the one selected to handle the operating system itself is **BTRFS**. This filesystem combines two technologies that already exist in other parts of the ecosystem. On one side, we use **copy-on-write** (**CoW**), which enables different programs to share pieces of data until one of them makes changes to it. This saves resources and makes the filesystem very efficient, as no private copies are created for each program accessing the data. This technique comes from memory management and was later applied to filesystems. On the other hand, we have **logical volume management**—not **Logical Volume Manager** (**LVM**), as we saw in the previous chapter, but a similar capability built into the filesystem rather than the block device or disk space.

This combination of techniques allows BTRFS to carry out snapshots, data scrubbing and deduplication, integrity checking, and data compression, among other things.

It is very important to note that BTRFS has been part of the mainline Linux Kernel since 2009, which means it is maintained and patched as part of it, unlike filesystems such as Reiser or OpenZFS.

At SUSE, BTRFS was adopted as the default operating system filesystem in 2015 for SLES 12 after extensive testing. It has been the default filesystem for SLES since then, so it has already had more than 10 years of production battle testing in this operating system.

To support BTRFS, there is a set of tools for the filesystem that, as with any other filesystem, helps you create, check, fix, extend, and perform many other operations. You can, as usual, learn more about it by reading the manual pages by running `man 5 btrfs` to review topics about the filesystem or `man 8 btrfs` to check on the utilities included to manage it.

An added set of tools is included in SLES 16 to manage the filesystem snapshots in a reliable and easy way. The main tool is called **Snapper**. As with the filesystem, we can learn more about it by running `man snapper`. Whenever you want to do operations with filesystem snapshots, we recommend that you always use Snapper.

> As usual, it's great to go to Wikipedia and check out the article on the technology we are using to extend your knowledge about it. Take a look at `https://en.wikipedia.org/wiki/Btrfs`.

Let's start working with it now.

# Reviewing BTRFS basics, creating filesystems, reviewing status, and mounting

Our first step will be to create a **BTRFS filesystem**. To do so, we can reuse the virtual disk drive that we created in *Chapter 12, Managing Local Storage and Filesystems*, or recreate it if you have deleted it.

Let's do it step by step:

1. Become root using sudo:

```
user@geeko:~> sudo -i
geeko:~ #
```

2. Create a virtual hard disk drive:

```
geeko:~ # truncate -s 5G myharddrive.hdd
```

3. Associate the virtual hard disk drive with a loop device:

```
geeko:~ # losetup -f
/dev/loop0
geeko:~ # losetup /dev/loop0 myharddrive.hdd
```

4. Check that the device has been created:

```
geeko:~ # lsblk -fp
NAME   FSTYPE FSVER  LABEL  UUID  FSAVAIL FSUSE% MOUNTPOINTS
/dev/loop0
/dev/vda
|                                                            ├─/dev/
vda1
├─/dev/vda2
|   btrfs a510eba8-f6b5-4239-90c5-f43770fab7c1  22.2G  25%
|         /var
|         /usr/local
|         /srv
```

```
|         /root
|         /opt
|         /home
|         /boot/grub2/x86_64-efi
|         /boot/grub2/i386-pc
|         /.snapshots
|         /
└─/dev/vda3
     swap  1 c49647b8-0dce-4efa-a51f-adb25b941962  [SWAP]
```

5. Create a partition:

```
geeko:~ # fdisk /dev/loop0

Welcome to fdisk (util-linux 2.41.1).
Changes will remain in memory only, until you decide to write them.
Be careful before using the write command.

Device does not contain a recognized partition table.
Created a new DOS (MBR) disklabel with disk identifier 0x8586f93a.

Command (m for help): n
Partition type
   p   primary (0 primary, 0 extended, 4 free)
   e   extended (container for logical partitions)
Select (default p): p
Partition number (1-4, default 1): 1
First sector (2048-10485759, default 2048):
Last sector, +/-sectors or +/-size{K,M,G,T,P} (2048-10485759,
default 10485759):

Created a new partition 1 of type 'Linux' and of size 5 GiB.

Command (m for help): w
The partition table has been altered.
Calling ioctl() to re-read partition table.
Re-reading the partition table failed.: Invalid argument
```

```
The kernel still uses the old table. The new table will be used at
the next reboot or after you run partprobe(8) or partx(8).
```

6. Refresh the partition table for the kernel:

```
geeko:~ # partprobe /dev/loop0
```

7. Create a BTRFS filesystem in the partition we just created:

```
geeko:~ # mkfs.btrfs /dev/loop0p1
btrfs-progs v6.14
See https://btrfs.readthedocs.io for more information.

Performing full device TRIM /dev/loop0p1 (5.00GiB) ...
NOTE: several default settings have changed in version 5.15, please
make sure
      this does not affect your deployments:
      - DUP for metadata (-m dup)
      - enabled no-holes (-O no-holes)
      - enabled free-space-tree (-R free-space-tree)

Label:              (null)
UUID:               ccb3e628-b894-4d68-a127-31392eaf91d4
Node size:          16384
Sector size:        4096    (CPU page size: 4096)
Filesystem size:    5.00GiB
Block group profiles:
  Data:             single            8.00MiB
  Metadata:         DUP             256.00MiB
  System:           DUP               8.00MiB
SSD detected:       yes
Zoned device:       no
Features:           extref, skinny-metadata, no-holes, free-space-
tree
Checksum:           crc32c
Number of devices:  1
Devices:
   ID        SIZE  PATH
    1     5.00GiB  /dev/loop0p1
```

8. Mount the new BTRFS filesystem to access it:

```
geeko:~ # mount /dev/loop0p1 /mnt/
geeko:~ # df -h /mnt/
Filesystem      Size  Used Avail Use% Mounted on
/dev/loop0p1    5.0G  5.8M  4.5G   1% /mnt
```

As you can see, there is nothing special involved in creating a regular BTRFS. However, there is a set of features that could be interesting for us to use. One of those features, which is used in the default partitioning for SLES 16, is **subvolumes**.

Within BTRFS, we can create different subvolumes that will consume the same disk space in the filesystem; they will have their own set of files and can be mounted in different directories. They behave as if they are independent filesystems, but they use the same space pool. Let's create a couple of subvolumes in our filesystem:

```
geeko:~ # cd /mnt/
geeko:/mnt # btrfs subvolume create vol0
Create subvolume './vol0'
geeko:/mnt # btrfs subvolume create vol1
Create subvolume './vol1'
geeko:/mnt # btrfs subvolume list .
ID 257 gen 12 top level 5 path vol0
ID 258 gen 12 top level 5 path vol1
```

Let's now mount `vol0` in a different directory:

```
geeko:/mnt # mkdir vol0-mnt
geeko:/mnt # mount -o subvol=vol0 /dev/loop0p1 /mnt/vol0-mnt/
geeko:/mnt # mount  | grep mnt
/dev/loop0p1 on /mnt type btrfs
(rw,relatime,seclabel,ssd,discard=async,space_
cache=v2,subvolid=5,subvol=/)
/dev/loop0p1 on /mnt/vol0-mnt type btrfs
(rw,relatime,seclabel,ssd,discard=async,space_
cache=v2,subvolid=257,subvol=/vol0)
geeko:/mnt # df -h *
Filesystem      Size  Used Avail Use% Mounted on
/dev/loop0p1    5.0G  5.9M  4.5G   1% /mnt/vol0-mnt
/dev/loop0p1    5.0G  5.9M  4.5G   1% /mnt/vol0-mnt
-               5.0G  5.9M  4.5G   1% /mnt/vol1
```

This same structure is used to mount the different volumes in our operating system. Now that we have learned how to create and mount a BTRFS, we can unmount and discard the virtual disk we have created and continue with the main disk of the VM where we installed SLES 16.

In this situation, we can list the subvolumes in the root filesystem of our SLES to see how they are distributed:

```
geeko:/ # btrfs subvolume list /
ID 256 gen 19 top level 5 path @
ID 257 gen 3754 top level 256 path @/boot/grub2/x86_64-efi
ID 258 gen 5115 top level 256 path @/boot/grub2/i386-pc
ID 259 gen 6093 top level 256 path @/var
ID 260 gen 6065 top level 256 path @/usr/local
ID 261 gen 5052 top level 256 path @/srv
ID 262 gen 6093 top level 256 path @/root
ID 263 gen 3754 top level 256 path @/opt
ID 264 gen 6035 top level 256 path @/home
ID 301 gen 6024 top level 259 path @/var/lib/machines
ID 265 gen 6043 top level 256 path @/.snapshots
ID 266 gen 6086 top level 265 path @/.snapshots/1/snapshot
ID 285 gen 2051 top level 265 path @/.snapshots/20/snapshot
ID 286 gen 2092 top level 265 path @/.snapshots/21/snapshot
D 287 gen 2248 top level 265 path @/.snapshots/22/snapshot
```

We can see here that mountpoints that used to have their own filesystem, such as `/opt`, `/var`, and `/srv`, are now mounted as subvolumes. We can also see that the filesystem snapshots also appear as subvolumes, which means that you can mount them (it is recommended that they are read-only) and access the data as it was on the system when the snapshot was created. More about that in the following section.

# BTRFS snapshots, how they work, and how to use them

The BRTFS filesystem is built with CoW as its core principle. Other filesystems overwrite blocks as soon as they are available. However, BTRFS tries to avoid modifying existing data blocks. It works at the filesystem level, which means that when a file is modified, instead of overwriting the content with changes, it pushes the changes to unused blocks. File metadata is then modified to point to these new blocks. This simple but powerful concept is the magic that makes filesystem snapshots work.

Let's look at each part of this process:

- **Shared data blocks**: When we create a snapshot, BTRFS doesn't duplicate the data but uses the same data with multiple references, one in each snapshot. This means that the unchanged parts are used by both snapshots and do not need extra space on the disk.
- **Copy-on-write**: When we modify a file, before the changes are written, BTRFS checks whether the data blocks are being used by any of the snapshots. If they are being used, then they remain untouched. Then, it writes the modifications to an unused location on the disk and updates the metadata of the file in the snapshot to point to the newly created blocks.
- **Keeping the past**: The previous snapshot metadata is kept pointing to unchanged data blocks, preserving the previous state of the file when the snapshot was created. This can be cleaned, if required, by deleting the snapshot.
- **Using minimum space**: The total amount of space consumed is the space of the original files plus the changes stored in each of the kept snapshots. This makes the mechanism very efficient.

You may be wondering, "If I have disk-level snapshots in VMware, AWS, Azure, and Google Cloud, what makes BTRFS snapshots special?" Let's see:

- **File versus block**: As we have seen, BTRFS snapshots are file based, meaning that they work within the logical filesystem structure, whereas other block-based snapshots (and these include LVM) work at the raw disk level. The BTRFS approach provides more granularity, uses less space, and allows direct access to the content in the snapshots for the user.
- **Efficient and close to processes**: As BTRFS snapshots do not need to copy data, they are very fast to create. Also, being able to execute at the file/operating system level facilitates performing other tasks before making the snapshot (such as checking the status of a process or freezing it before taking action).
- **A snapshot is a kind of subvolume**: It's important to understand that a snapshot is just a special type of subvolume. This means you can mount it or browse it like any other directory. You can compare files in different snapshots to check what changed easily.

Now, to perform many of the tasks to manage snapshots, let's look at Snapper, a tool that comes with BTRFS in SLES 16.

# Snapper, the snapshot management tool

**Snapper** is the main management tool included in SLES to handle all the management tasks related to BTRFS snapshots.

It is included in the default installation, but if you did a very minimal installation or you are adding it for any other reason, you can install it by running this command:

```
user@geeko:~> sudo zypper install snapper
```

Once Snapper has been installed, we can take a look at the snapshots in the system by running `sudo snapper list`, and we will get an output like the following:

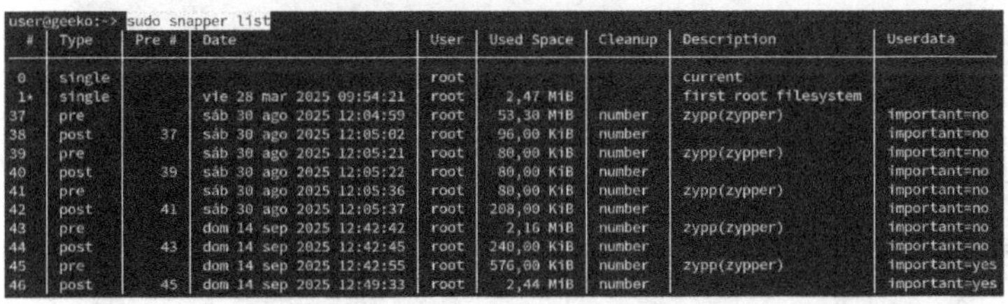
user@geeko:~> sudo snapper list

| # | Type | Pre # | Date | User | Used Space | Cleanup | Description | Userdata |
|---|---|---|---|---|---|---|---|---|
| 0 | single | | | root | | | current | |
| 1* | single | | vie 28 mar 2025 09:54:21 | root | 2,47 MiB | | first root filesystem | |
| 37 | pre | | sáb 30 ago 2025 12:04:59 | root | 53,30 MiB | number | zypp(zypper) | important=no |
| 38 | post | 37 | sáb 30 ago 2025 12:05:02 | root | 96,00 KiB | number | | important=no |
| 39 | pre | | sáb 30 ago 2025 12:05:21 | root | 80,00 KiB | number | zypp(zypper) | important=no |
| 40 | post | 39 | sáb 30 ago 2025 12:05:22 | root | 80,00 KiB | number | | important=no |
| 41 | pre | | sáb 30 ago 2025 12:05:36 | root | 80,00 KiB | number | zypp(zypper) | important=no |
| 42 | post | 41 | sáb 30 ago 2025 12:05:37 | root | 208,00 KiB | number | | important=no |
| 43 | pre | | dom 14 sep 2025 12:42:42 | root | 2,16 MiB | number | zypp(zypper) | important=no |
| 44 | post | 43 | dom 14 sep 2025 12:42:45 | root | 240,00 KiB | number | | important=no |
| 45 | pre | | dom 14 sep 2025 12:42:55 | root | 576,00 KiB | number | zypp(zypper) | important=yes |
| 46 | post | 45 | dom 14 sep 2025 12:49:33 | root | 2,44 MiB | number | | important=yes |

*Figure 14.1 – List of system snapshots*

> As usual, every system utility comes with a manual that can be accessed using the `man` command. In this case, we can see all the options for Snapper by running `man snapper`.

As you can see in the previous screenshot, the system, after some updates using Zypper, has a list of snapshots that have been created.

One of the benefits of having an operating system/filesystem-level snapshot is that it can be integrated with other operating system tools. In this case, the software management tool is Zypper. The default configuration of Snapper is preconfigured with Zypper integration. It also generates a snapshot every time you update the system. This way, every change made during upgrades can be easily rolled back.

> The integration of Snapper and Zypper is performed by the `snapper-zypp-plugin` package that comes installed and preconfigured by default in SLES. It also comes with a man page that you can access by running `man snapper-zypp-plugin`.

As we can also see in the previous screenshot, there are three different types of snapshot:

- **pre**: This is a snapshot that was created *before* an important task that might modify the system. It comes coupled with a *post* snapshot.
- **post**: This is a snapshot that was created *after* an important task. It comes coupled with a *post* snapshot.
- **single**: This is a standalone snapshot that is not related to any other snapshot on the system.

We can create a new snapshot by running `snapper create`. When this is run without options, it will simply create a `single` snapshot with no description associated with it.

Let's see how this snapshot was created in the following screenshot:

```
user@geeko:/etc/zypp> sudo snapper create
user@geeko:/etc/zypp> sudo snapper list
  # | Type   | Pre # | Date                          | User | Used Space | Cleanup | Description           | Userdata
----+--------+-------+-------------------------------+------+------------+---------+-----------------------+--------------
 0  | single |       |                               | root |            |         | current               |
 1* | single |       | vie 28 mar 2025 09:54:21 | root |  16,00 KiB |         | first root filesystem |
37  | pre    |       | sáb 30 ago 2025 12:04:59 | root |  53,30 MiB | number  | zypp(zypper)          | important=no
38  | post   |    37 | sáb 30 ago 2025 12:05:02 | root |  96,00 KiB | number  |                       | important=no
39  | pre    |       | sáb 30 ago 2025 12:05:21 | root |  80,00 KiB | number  | zypp(zypper)          | important=no
40  | post   |    39 | sáb 30 ago 2025 12:05:22 | root |  80,00 KiB | number  |                       | important=no
41  | pre    |       | sáb 30 ago 2025 12:05:36 | root |  80,00 KiB | number  | zypp(zypper)          | important=no
42  | post   |    41 | sáb 30 ago 2025 12:05:37 | root | 208,00 KiB | number  |                       | important=no
43  | pre    |       | dom 14 sep 2025 12:42:42 | root |   2,16 MiB | number  | zypp(zypper)          | important=no
44  | post   |    43 | dom 14 sep 2025 12:42:45 | root | 240,00 KiB | number  |                       | important=no
45  | pre    |       | dom 14 sep 2025 12:42:55 | root | 576,00 KiB | number  | zypp(zypper)          | important=yes
46  | post   |    45 | dom 14 sep 2025 12:49:33 | root |   2,89 MiB | number  |                       | important=yes
47  | single |       | dom 14 sep 2025 20:24:19 | root |  16,00 KiB |         |                       |
```

*Figure 14.2 – List of system snapshots, with snapshot number 47, which is new*

It is recommended to add a description to the snapshot that provides some information about why it was created and what function it performs.

Let's delete the snapshot:

```
user@geeko:~> sudo snapper delete 47
```

Now, let's create a new snapshot with a proper description:

```
user@geeko:~> sudo snapper create --type single --description "Snapshot to learn with Packt"
```

This way, we have a snapshot and we know what it was created for. To avoid consuming more storage space than needed, we can assign an automated cleanup action. As you can see in the previous screenshots, there is a column for this stating the default policy for automatically created snapshots, which is `number`.

This means that only a certain number of this kind of snapshot will be kept, and the oldest ones will be removed. As you can see in the previous screenshot, snapshot `1`, created during the installation, is kept even after several system updates in which other `pre/post` snapshots were created.

> Snapshot `0` is a special one. It refers to the snapshot currently in use and mounted. Therefore, it cannot be deleted. You can find more information by reading the man page by running `man snapper`.

So, what is happening now? Well, the automatically created snapshots will be removed when new ones are created. However, the manually created ones will be kept until we manually clean them up. This way, we do not risk filling up the disk with snapshots, even when their size is minimal.

Let's see how else we can use these snapshots in ways that facilitate tasks that, with VM/disk-level snapshots, would be very difficult, if not impossible.

## Using Snapper to show changes made to files between snapshots

One of the most important things we can do with Snapper is to check differences between snapshots. Remember that in BTRFS, a snapshot is a subvolume. So, we could start mounting them and checking the differences between them with regular Linux tools. However, Snapper provides some functionality that makes this task a lot easier.

First, let's check which files were changed between snapshots. To do that, we use the `snapper status` command (as root/administrator or using `sudo`). We select two snapshots to compare and use their number ID to compare them. You can use `sudo snapper list` to find your snapshot numbers. I've chosen, for example, two snapshots that were created before (`pre`) and after (`post`) running a `zypper update` command, which are 43 and 44. This is the command that I will run:

```
user@geeko:~> sudo snapper status 43..44
c..... /usr/lib/sysimage/rpm/Index.db
c..... /usr/lib/sysimage/rpm/Packages.db
```

As you can see, we have a list of files with a character before each of them. The characters have the following meanings:

- +: The file was added (it exists in the new snapshot but not in the old one)
- -: The file was removed (it exists in the old snapshot but not in the new one)
- c: The file was changed (content has been modified between snapshots)
- t: The file's type changed (e.g., from file to directory, symlink to file, etc.)
- p: The file's permissions have changed
- u: The file's user ownership has changed
- g: The file's group ownership has changed
- x: The file's extended attribute information has changed
- a: The file's **access control list** (**ACL**) has changed
- .: The file has not changed

In our example, we can see that the content of two files has been changed (the rpm package index and package list) but no files have been added or removed.

As the installation created snapshot 1, we can check the differences since the system was installed by running the following:

```
user@geeko:~> sudo snapper status 1..43
-..... /boot/config-6.12.0-160000.4-default
c..... /boot/grub2/grub.cfg
c..... /boot/initrd
c..... /boot/initrd-6.12.0-160000.11-default
c..... /boot/initrd-6.12.0-160000.16-default
[snip] ---8<---8<---[snip]
c..... /usr/share/qemu/vgabios-virtio.bin
c..... /usr/share/qemu/vgabios-vmware.bin
c..... /usr/share/selinux/packages/container.pp.bz2
c..... /usr/share/selinux/targeted/modules.lst
c..... /usr/share/selinux/targeted/nonbasemodules.lst
```

It's time to find some interesting files for changes. We can filter the output of the previous list by grabbing only the files that have /etc/ in their path, as this is where the system-wide configuration customization is kept:

```
user@geeko:~> sudo snapper status 1..43 | grep "/etc/"
....x. /etc/default/grub.old
```

```
c..... /etc/selinux/targeted/contexts/files/file_contexts
c..... /etc/selinux/targeted/contexts/files/file_contexts.bin
c..... /etc/selinux/targeted/contexts/files/file_contexts.subs_dist
c..... /etc/selinux/targeted/policy/policy.34
c..... /etc/selinux/targeted/.policy.sha512 +..... /etc/ssl/fips_local.cnf
c..... /etc/sysconfig/kdump
c..... /etc/zypp/services.d/SUSE_Linux_Enterprise_Server_16.0_x86_64.
service
```

To see the changes in a file, we need to specify two things: the snapshots to be compared and the names of the files in which we want to see the changes. We have to use the `snapper diff` command to see the changes in files, which will be provided in `diff` format. Here, we can see the changes made to `/etc/selinux/targeted/contexts/files/file_contexts` between snapshots 1 and 43:

> You can find more information about diff running the command and its format if you run `man diff`

```
user@geeko:~> sudo snapper diff 1..43 /etc/selinux/targeted/contexts/
files/file_contexts
--- /.snapshots/1/snapshot/etc/selinux/targeted/contexts/files/file_
contexts 2025-09-14 12:49:27.840224430 +0200
+++ /.snapshots/43/snapshot/etc/selinux/targeted/contexts/files/file_
contexts 2025-08-25 17:38:30.758486774 +0200 @@ -3431,7 +3431,6 @@
 /usr/share/gitolite3/commands(/.)? -- system_u:object_r:bin_t:s0 /var/
lib/buildkit/containerd-.(/.?) system_u:object_r:container_ro_file_t:s0
 /usr/lib/libjavascriptcoregtk[^/].so. -- system_u:object_r:textrel_
shlib_t:s0
-/usr/libexec/salt/salt-minion(-[0-9._-]+)? -- system_u:object_r:salt_
exec_t:s0
 /usr/lib/systemd/user/plasma-..(service|target) -- system_u:object_r:xdm_
unit_file_t:s0
/etc/hotplug.d/default/default. system_u:object_r:bin_t:s0
/usr/lib/systemd/generator/lvm. system_u:object_r:lvm_unit_file_t:s0
```

During the writing of this book, we were using beta versions, and we can see how the SELinux policies have been polished, improved, and updated in this example. Several paths have changed their policies to improve execution and security.

We have seen the utility that BTRFS provides to track changes in our systems. Now it's time to use the equivalent of *Ctrl + Z* in SLES 16.

## Using Snapper to roll back to a previous configuration status

Let's try the rollback mechanism using Snapper. Please take into account that there are other ways to start a system in a different snapshot than the current one, such as using GRUB during boot. In this case, however, we will focus on using Snapper on a running system.

As you have seen, multiple `pre/post` snapshots have been created and cleaned up by the integration of Zypper with Snapper. We could use them, but we are going to use the one we created before as a `single` snapshot.

First, we will find the number of the snapshot we created. To do this, we list all snapshots and find the one we created by searching for a term we used in the description:

```
user@geeko:~> sudo snapper list | grep Packt
47  | single |       | dom 14 sep 2025 20:32:29 | root | 224,00 KiB |
| Snapshot to learn with Packt |
```

So, our created snapshot is number 47. Now you can see how useful it is to create a useful description for the snapshot. Now we are going to modify the current system by creating a file in `/etc`:

```
user@geeko:~> sudo touch /etc/test_snapshot
```

Next, we will undo all changes by invoking the rollback using `snapper rollback`:

```
user@geeko:~> sudo snapper rollback 47
Ambit is classic.
Creating read-only snapshot of current system. (Snapshot 54.)
Creating read-write snapshot of snapshot 47. (Snapshot 55.)
Setting default subvolume to snapshot 55.
```

What has happened is that Snapper first creates a snapshot of the *current state*, snapshot 54. Then, it reuses the content of snapshot 47, the one we issued to have a rollback point, to create a *new snapshot* with that content, in this case, snapshot 55. However, the changes have not yet been applied, as we can see:

```
user@geeko:~> ls /etc/test_snapshot
/etc/test_snapshot
```

We will reboot the system to apply the changes:

```
user@geeko:~> sudo reboot
```

The result is that now our system is in the same status as when we created the snapshot:

```
user@geeko:~> ls /etc/test_snapshot
ls: cannot access '/etc/test_snapshot': No such file or directory
```

This can be useful when you are making low-level changes and they suddenly don't behave the way you expected, or when an update didn't go as planned (which is very unusual in SLES). Having a way to undo changes easily always provides a good and easy way to keep systems running.

This mechanism is used by small and also very large companies, such as Meta, saving them millions of dollars, as you can see in the following article: `https://www.phoronix.com/news/Btrfs-Saves-Meta-Billions`.

Now that we have learned about the main functionality of Snapper and BTRFS, let's check briefly on other options available in the tool.

## Other Snapper functions

Snapper provides options to support the core capabilities that we have seen so far. The most important one is `Modify`, which can be used to change the description, cleanup algorithm, or user data of an existing snapshot.

With this option, we can change the characteristics of the current snapshot. We could, for example, take an automatically created snapshot from the cleanup list that we want to keep by running the following:

```
user@geeko:~> sudo snapper modify -c """ 45
```

To access the content of a snapshot at any time, you can use the automated mount point in `/.snapshots`, which is preconfigured by default in SLES 16:

```
user@geeko:~> sudo ls /.snapshots/45
filelist-44.txt.gz  grub-snapshot.cfg  info.xml  snapshot
user@geeko:~> sudo ls /.snapshots/45/snapshot
bin  boot  dev    etc  home  lib lib64  mnt  opt  proc  root  run  sbin
srv  sys  tmp  usr  var
```

Snapper comes with the `mount` and `umount` commands, but having this default configuration makes them unnecessary.

We have several options to apply, modify, or remove Snapper configurations:

- `list-configs`: List all Snapper configurations on the system
- `create-config`: Create a new Snapper configuration (e.g., for another subvolume)
- `delete-config`: Remove an existing Snapper configuration

We can check the default configuration on the system by running the following:

```
user@geeko:~> sudo snapper list-configs
Config | Subvolume
───────┼──────────
root   | /
```

> There is an `/etc/sysconfig/snapper` file with the `SNAPPER_CONFIGS` variable. This variable must be in sync with the content of `/etc/snapper/configs`. So, if you remove or add configs, the `sysconfig` file needs to be adjusted. It is not recommended to create or modify configs manually.

Each Snapper configuration is located in `/etc/snapper/configs/` and can be edited, copied, or removed easily by using the previous command.

Finally, if you want to establish a limit for the amount of space that snapshots/subvolumes consume, you can use `setup-quota`, which allows you to enable or disable BTRFS quota groups for a configuration.

In the default configuration of SLES 16 for the operating system filesystem, the mechanism is preconfigured, which we can check:

```
user@geeko:~> sudo snapper setup-quota
Quota error (qgroup already set).
```

Now we can limit the space to be consumed by snapshots to 2 GB:

```
user@geeko:~> sudo snapper -c root set-config
SPACE_LIMIT=2G
```

We can also use a percentage, such as `SPACE_LIMIT=0.2` for 20% of the total disk space.

# Summary

We now know how to use filesystem-level snapshots for the most common use cases in SLES 16, which can help us make delicate changes with confidence, roll back to a well-known configuration, and even find and analyze the changes made in our systems quickly and easily.

We now have another important tool in our toolbox to work on our systems, in this case something very similar to pressing *Ctrl* + *Z* on a keyboard in a word processor.

It's time to move on to better understanding a critical part of the running process of a system, the **boot process**, which is explained in the following chapter.

# 15

# Understanding the Boot Process

The boot process begins when the machine is powered on. It continues until the system is fully initialized and ready for operation. The server needs to prepare everything and load the operating system into memory. It consists of four stages: the hardware initialization (**UEFI** or **BIOS**), the bootloader program, the Linux kernel initialization, and the systemd initialization.

In this chapter, we will review these stages and provide you with some tips and tricks that will help you fix a failing system.

We will be covering the following topics:

- Understanding the boot process – UEFI booting and legacy BIOS
- Working with GRUB, the bootloader, and `initrd` system images
- Managing the boot sequence with `systemd`
- Updating the root password by modifying the boot process

Even though you won't usually be making changes in the initial stages of the boot process, it is helpful to understand the process, specifically to solve issues with new hardware and drivers. You will find it handy when you are trying to understand why the system is misbehaving in emergencies, when you're conducting forensic examinations, or when dealing with major failures.

The last stage, managed by **systemd**, provides more room for actions and changes to alter which services will be running by default in the system. Many of the tasks have already been discussed in previous chapters, but we will be providing a comprehensive review of what can be done with them.

Let's get started with the first stage.

# Understanding the boot process – UEFI booting and legacy BIOS

Every computer has a motherboard, where you can find different hardware components, such as the CPU and the memory chips. One of the components is a software program included in non-volatile memory called the system firmware. The system firmware is traditionally known as **Basic Input Output System** (**BIOS**), even though most x86 computers use a new version called **Unified Extensible Firmware Interface** (**UEFI**). This **firmware** detects and initializes hardware and devices such as the memory, keyboard, screen, and other peripherals attached to the system, and stores which hardware features are enabled (such as **pre-boot network execution** (**PXE**)).

The boot process is quite dependent on the hardware architecture in its first stages, so we are going to focus only on the default boot process on a PC (or x86). SLES 16 uses UEFI by default, and we will be discussing it in more detail. Support for BIOS is deprecated, but it is still available in some specific circumstances, such as when upgrading from a SLES 15 system. SUSE recommends using UEFI for all new installations. You should only avoid it if you have a strong reason to do so. This recommendation is also meant to prepare for the eventual removal of BIOS support in the future. Additionally, some versions of SLES, such as SUSE Linux Micro, already only support UEFI.

You won't notice big differences between booting on a system that uses UEFI and one that uses BIOS, but they are significant. One of them is that UEFI can perform the boot of the operating system directly instead of requiring a multiple-stage boot process. For the sysadmin, the main difference in the boot sequence is that UEFI understands disk partitions directly and that it can provide capabilities such as **Secure Boot**. The system boot process follows this workflow:

1. When the machine is powered on, the UEFI firmware is loaded and verified.
2. The firmware finds and initializes devices, including memory, CPU, buses, and peripherals such as keyboard, mouse, and local and remote storage.
3. UEFI looks for a bootable EFI partition on storage devices and selects the one with the highest priority. The list of bootable entries is stored in **Non-Volatile Random-Access Memory** (**NVRAM**) as a list of specific entries and utilities.
4. Once the storage device is selected, the partitions on it are read from the **GUID Partition Table** (**GPT**). UEFI looks for an **EFI System Partition** (**ESP**), which includes bootloader files. The EFI bootloader in SLES resides in a dedicated partition, which is mounted at `/boot/efi`. From there, the EFI bootloader proceeds to load the **GRUB** bootloader. Specific drivers are used, defined in `.efi` files, that are only used until the operating system is ready with its own optimized drivers.

5. GRUB selects and loads the **operating system kernel**. In SLES, different kernel versions are stored in files named Image-<kernel-version>-default. The default kernel is represented by a symbolic link called Image. Each kernel version also has a corresponding initial RAM filesystem, stored in a file named initrd-<kernel-version>-default. There is also a symbolic link for the default one, called initrd. All these files are located in the /boot directory.

> GRUB is the default bootloader for SLES 16. It is a stable and feature-rich bootloader that is used in many distributions, but that overlaps in some capabilities with the features provided by UEFI.

> initramfs solves a chicken-and-egg problem. The kernel needs tools and kernel modules to access all the hardware, but those files are stored in hardware that needs to be accessed, so the drivers are not accessible. initrd is a CPIO archive that does not need drivers to be loaded into RAM and acts as a temporary root filesystem until the real filesystem can be accessed. You need a new initramfs archive every time drivers are updated, something that is normally done automatically when the new package is installed.

6. Now, the kernel can load and start the first process of the system, named init. This process is responsible for completing the boot sequence by loading all other services. In SLES, the init process is systemd.
7. systemd loads the rest of the operating system.

UEFI has several advantages over BIOS, enabling new types of hardware, more complete pre-boot environments, access to graphics, and other capabilities, such as Secure Boot and GPT partitions, that can go beyond the 2 TB of **master boot record (MBR)** partitions.

We have been discussing `/boot` and `UEFI` partitions that hold the kernel and `initrd`, and the UEFI binaries. The SLES 16 installer is the one creating the partitions and providing the content needed for the boot process.

The part of pre-boot that needs to be known for the SUSE Certified System Administrator certification is how to load the operating system loader from it. Through BIOS or UEFI, we can select from which storage device the operating system will load and move to the next phase.

When using BIOS, the process has more steps:

1. The machine is powered on, and BIOS firmware is loaded.
2. The firmware initializes devices such as the keyboard, mouse, storage, and other peripherals.
3. The firmware reads the configuration in non-volatile memory, including the boot order, specifying which storage device is the one to continue the boot process with.
4. Once the storage device is selected, BIOS will load the MBR on it, reading and loading the first 512 bytes on the boot disk, which is just enough to read the core operating system loader. And that includes enough filesystem drivers to read the `/boot` folder that contains the rest of the drivers needed by **GRUB 2** and the kernel and the `initramfs` image.
5. GRUB loads the configuration and the operating system kernel and initial RAM disk in the `/boot` partition.
6. The initial boot image will then load `systemd`.
7. `systemd` loads the rest of the operating system.

There are some hardware limitations in the BIOS process. The disk must have an MBR partition table, the MBR needs to be present in the first sector, and the partition assigned to `/boot` must be marked as bootable.

> The MBR partition table format is very limited, allowing only four primary partitions and using extensions such as extended partitions to reach beyond this limit. Don't use it unless you have a very valid reason to do so.

Now that we know the basics of the process used to boot, let's go deeper into the details of how it is implemented in SLES.

# Working with GRUB, the bootloader, and initrd system images

Once the pre-boot execution is completed, the system will be running the GRUB 2 bootloader. SUSE implements the **shim** loader, whose job is to load GRUB 2 and verify it.

In secure implementations, the loader will make sure that only kernels signed by a SUSE key will run. That means that additional steps are required to run custom kernels or drivers that do not come with SLES if Secure Boot is enabled.

UEFI has its own list of entries that are stored in non-volatile memory. You can see the list of entries using the `efibootmgr` command:

```
user@geeko:~> sudo efibootmgr
BootCurrent: 0005
Timeout: 3 seconds
BootOrder: 0001,0005,0003,0000,0002,0004
Boot0000* UiApp FvVol(64074afe-340a-4be6-94ba-91b5b4d0f71e)/FvFile(462caa21-7614-4503-836e-8ab6f4662331)
Boot0001* UEFI QEMU QEMU USB HARDDRIVE 1-0000:00:04.0-4.1 PciRoot(0x0)/Pci(0x4,0x0)/USB(7,0)/USB(0,0){auto_created_boot_option}
Boot0002* UEFI Misc Device VenHw(93e34c7e-b50e-11df-9223-2443dfd72085,00){auto_created_boot_option}
Boot0003* UEFI Misc Device 2 PciRoot(0x0)/Pci(0x6,0x0){auto_created_boot_option}
Boot0004* EFI Internal Shell FvVol(64074afe-340a-4be6-94ba-91b5b4d0f71e)/FvFile(7c04a583-9e3e-4f1c-ad65-e05268d0b4d1)
Boot0005* sles-secureboot HD(1,GPT,ac15b
```

The output of the command tells us the following:

- Entry `0005` is selected as the default
- UEFI waits three seconds to boot
- The default order for the entries is `0001,0005,0003,0000,0002,0004`
- Active entries are labeled with an asterisk, *, after the name

> Your `grub-install` must point to the disk used to boot the system, the one that you configured in the BIOS/UEFI to boot from.

Normally, you should not need to change your configuration unless you are trying to perform some advanced tasks. But sometimes something goes wrong, and you need to fix things manually.

GRUB files are stored in `/boot/grub2`. The main configuration file is `/boot/grub2/grub.cfg`. Anyway, read the file and you will see a header warning you about modifying the file directly:

```
user@geeko:~> sudo head -n 6 /boot/grub2/grub.
cfg
#
# DO NOT EDIT THIS FILE
#
# It is automatically generated by grub2-
mkconfig using templates
# from /etc/grub.d and settings from /etc/
default/grub
#
```

> In SLES, when there is a new version of the kernel, the previous one is not deleted. The new kernel is installed alongside the previous one, adding a new entry to GRUB. Due to this, you will always have an easy way to boot with a previous working kernel. New versions of `initrd` are generated as needed during the installation of the new kernel.

The message lets us know that the file is automatically generated and that you should not edit it manually. How do we implement the changes, then? We will do it by following the instructions mentioned in the `grub.cfg` file. This means editing the `/etc/default/grub` file and/or the contents in the `/etc/grub.d/` directory and then regenerating the GRUB configuration by running `grub2-mkconfig`.

Let's take a look at the current kernel configuration with `grub2-setenv list`. The `-saved_entry` line specifies the default boot entry:

```
geeko:~ # grub2-editenv list
env_block=512+1
saved_entry=SLES 16.0
```

You can list all the available options using `grub2-once --list`:

```
geeko:~ # grub2-once --list
     0 SLES 16.0
     1 Advanced options for SLES 16.0>SLES 16.0, with Linux
6.12.0-160000.5-default
     2 Advanced options for SLES 16.0>SLES 16.0, with Linux
6.12.0-160000.5-default (recovery mode)
     3 Start bootloader from a read-only snapshot> SLES16-SP0
(,2025-09-25T09:31,post,zypp(zypper))
     4 Start bootloader from a read-only snapshot> SLES16-SP0
(,2025-09-25T09:31,pre,zypp(zypper))
     5 Start bootloader from a read-only snapshot> SLES16-SP0
(,2025-09-25T09:30,post,zypp(zypper))
     6 Start bootloader from a read-only snapshot> SLES16-SP0
(,2025-09-25T09:30,pre,zypp(zypper))
```

You can find more information about it by opening the `/boot/grub2/grub.cfg` file and looking for your entry:

```
geeko:/boot/grub2 # grep "menuentry 'SLES 16.0'" -A10 \ grub.cfg
menuentry 'SLES 16.0' --class sles --class gnu-linux --class gnu --class
os $menuentry_id_option 'gnulinux-simple-27d5b027-155f-4622-8baa-
9954252e3bd2' {
     load_video
     set gfxpayload=keep
     insmod gzio
     insmod part_gpt
     insmod btrfs
     search --no-floppy --fs-uuid --set=root 27d5b027-155f-4622-8baa-
9954252e3bd2
     echo 'Loading Linux 6.12.0-160000.5-default ...'
     linux /boot/Image-6.12.0-160000.5-default root=UUID=27d5b027-
155f-4622-8baa-9954252e3bd2 ${extra_cmdline} mitigations=auto quiet
security=selinux selinux=1
     echo 'Loading initial ramdisk ...'
     initrd /boot/initrd-6.12.0-160000.5-default
```

You can see the options used in the entry:

- `linux`: The kernel to boot
- `root`: The partition or logical volume that will be assigned to the root / directory and mounted
- `initrd`: The file containing the RAM disk used at the first phase of the boot process
- `title`: A descriptive title to be shown to the user during the boot process
- `$menuetry_id_option`: The identifier of the boot entry

In a normal boot, you won't be able to see the log messages as they will pass too fast, and because of that, the output is limited. To review boot messages, you can use the `dmesg` command after booting, whose output will be as follows:

```
[    0.000000] [      T0] Booting Linux on physical CPU 0x0000000000 [0x610f0000
]
[    0.000000] [      T0] Linux version 6.12.0-160000.5-default (geeko@buildhost
) (gcc-13 (SUSE Linux) 13.4.0, GNU ld (GNU Binutils; SUSE Linux 16) 2.43.1.20241
209-160000.2) #1 SMP PREEMPT_DYNAMIC Wed Sep 10 15:26:25 UTC 2025 (3545bbd)
[    0.000000] [      T0] KASLR enabled
[    0.000000] [      T0] efi: EFI v2.7 by EDK II
[    0.000000] [      T0] efi: SMBIOS 3.0=0x13f810000 MEMATTR=0x13e802118 ACPI 2
.0=0x13c150018 MOKvar=0x13c080000 RNG=0x13c15fe18 MEMRESERVE=0x13c482e98
[    0.000000] [      T0] random: crng init done
[    0.000000] [      T0] ACPI: Early table checksum verification disabled
[    0.000000] [      T0] ACPI: RSDP 0x000000013C150018 000024 (v02 BOCHS )
[    0.000000] [      T0] ACPI: XSDT 0x000000013C15FE98 00006C (v01 BOCHS  BXPC
    00000001      01000013)
[    0.000000] [      T0] ACPI: FACP 0x000000013C15FA98 000114 (v06 BOCHS  BXPC
    00000001 BXPC 00000001)
[    0.000000] [      T0] ACPI: DSDT 0x000000013C157518 001516 (v02 BOCHS  BXPC
    00000001 BXPC 00000001)
[    0.000000] [      T0] ACPI: APIC 0x000000013C15D898 0002DC (v04 BOCHS  BXPC
    00000001 BXPC 00000001)
[    0.000000] [      T0] ACPI: PPTT 0x000000013C15E718 0000D8 (v02 BOCHS  BXPC
    00000001 BXPC 00000001)
[    0.000000] [      T0] ACPI: GTDT 0x000000013C15E818 000068 (v03 BOCHS  BXPC
    00000001 BXPC 00000001)
[    0.000000] [      T0] ACPI: MCFG 0x000000013C15E918 00003C (v01 BOCHS  BXPC
    00000001 BXPC 00000001)
[    0.000000] [      T0] ACPI: SPCR 0x000000013C15FF98 000050 (v02 BOCHS  BXPC
    00000001 BXPC 00000001)
[    0.000000] [      T0] ACPI: DBG2 0x000000013C15FC18 000057 (v00 BOCHS  BXPC
    00000001 BXPC 00000001)
[    0.000000] [      T0] ACPI: IORT 0x000000013C15FC98 000080 (v03 BOCHS  BXPC
```

*Figure 15.1 – Output of the dmesg command*

> You can modify kernel parameters by modifying the `GRUB_CMDLINE_LINUX_DEFAULT` variable in the `/etc/default/grub` file. Don't forget to run `sudo grub2-mkconfig -o /boot/grub2/grub.cfg` to regenerate the configuration once it is done.

Let's move to the next section of the boot process, `initrd`.

The `initrd` file, or the **initial RAM disk**, contains a minimal system that is loaded in memory and holds the drivers and tools required to access the filesystems where the actual operating system is stored. We found it as a symbolic link in `/boot/initrd`, pointing to `initrd-6.12.0-160000.5-default`. When you need to have new drivers, you can use the `dracut` command to generate a new one. Let's see an example of how to rebuild the current `initrd` file:

```
geeko:~ # dracut --force --verbose
dracut[I]: Executing: /usr/bin/dracut --force --verbose
dracut[I]: Module 'systemd-networkd' will not be installed, because
command 'networkctl' could not be found!
dracut[I]: Module 'systemd-networkd' will not be installed, because
command '/usr/lib/systemd/systemd-networkd' could not be found!
dracut[I]: Module 'systemd-networkd' will not be installed, because
command '/usr/lib/systemd/systemd-networkd-wait-online' could not be
found!
dracut[I]: Module 'systemd-pcrphase' will not be installed, because
command '/usr/lib/systemd/systemd-pcrextend' could not be found[snip]---
8<---8<---8<---[snip]
```

We can see in the previous output the selection of kernel modules and files that are included in the `initrd` file, because they are required for early access. This step can also be useful in the case of a corrupted `initrd` file or when you are restoring a system from a backup into different hardware that requires different storage drivers.

So far, we have learned the basics of the early stages of the boot process so that we can troubleshoot some boot issues. There is a lot more to learn, and we could fill a full book on this topic, but there are very limited cases in which you need to do this in your normal day-to-day activities. For cloud environments, in many cases, troubleshooting is done by rip-and-replace, where a new machine is created from scratch instead of fixing the one that is running, as the workloads are supposed to be ephemeral. In any case, the last chapters of the book will include some exercises about fixing these issues. Let's move on to the next topic, on how services are managed in SLES with `systemd`.

# Managing the boot sequence with systemd

We have learned how the firmware takes care of pointing at a disk to run the operating system loader, which in SLES is GRUB. After GRUB loads the kernel and initial RAMdisk to prepare the system to start, it will start the first process of the system, process 1 or PID 1 (**PID** stands for **process identifier**). This process must take care of loading all the required components of the system efficiently. In SLES, PID 1 is a program called `systemd`, a system and service manager that is responsible for starting the rest of the processes.

We described services and targets in *Chapter 3, Managing Regular Operations with Tools*. In this chapter, we will focus on the boot sequence.

Linux systems are known for being capable of running for years without rebooting, but the first two things we need to learn are how to make `systemd` reboot the system and how it is used to power off. We need to use `systemctl` for that:

```
geeko:/boot # systemctl reboot
```

The system will immediately stop all services in order and reboot. You can use the `uptime` command to see how long the system has been running since the last reboot:

```
user@geeko:~> uptime
08:41:06  up   0:01,  1 user,  load average: 0.15, 0.09, 0.03
```

You can completely stop the system using `systemctl poweroff`:

> Be sure to check that you have a way of powering on the machine again after using `poweroff`. For a VM or cloud instance, it is easy, but you can run into trouble if you are using a remote server in a lab away from your location.

```
user@geeko:~> sudo systemctl poweroff
Broadcast message from root@geeko on pts/1 (Fri 2025-09-26 08:41:34 CEST):
The system will power off now!
```

Power on the machine again to be able to continue.

There is a command that will stop the system, but it will do so without sending the signal to power the machine off. That command is `systemctl halt`. You will rarely need to use it, as you will need to manually switch off the system, but it is good to know that it is there.

> The previously shown commands can be abbreviated to `reboot`, `poweroff`, and `shutdown`. If you check out the `/usr/sbin/reboot` and `/usr/sbin/poweroff` files, you will see that they are symbolic links to `systemctl`.

Earlier, we also reviewed how to set a default `systemd target` with `systemctl`. However, we can override the default configuration during boot time by passing the `systemd.unit` parameter to the kernel. We can do that by interrupting the boot process while in the initial screen, as shown in the following screenshot:

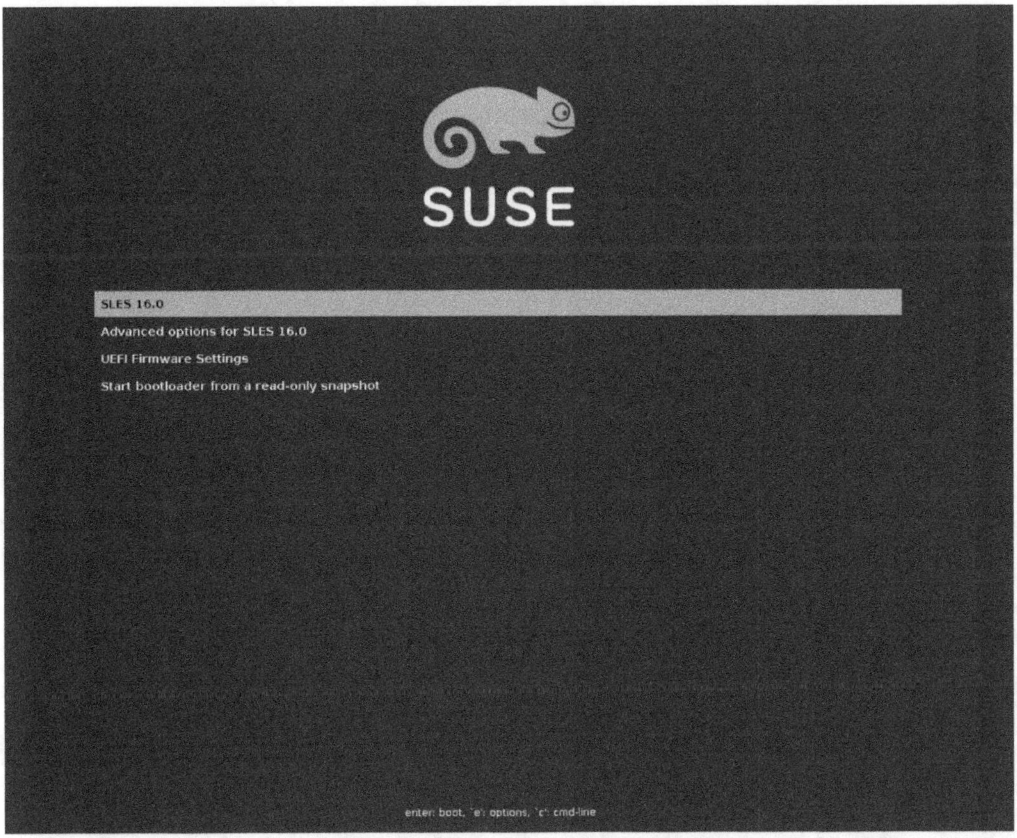


*Figure 15.2 – The GRUB boot menu on SLES 16*

Let's explore the options in the menu in *Figure 15.2*:

- **SLES 16.0**: This is the default boot.
- **Advanced options for SLES 16.0**: This contains a list of installed kernels, including the default. Each one of them is followed by a version that boots in single-user mode, which is named **recovery mode**.
- **UEFI Firmware Settings**: If the firmware allows it, this option will allow you to change some UEFI firmware settings.
- **Start bootloader from a read-only snapshot**: This option allows you to boot into one of the snapshots provided by Snapper instead of the last one. You can see it in the following screenshot:

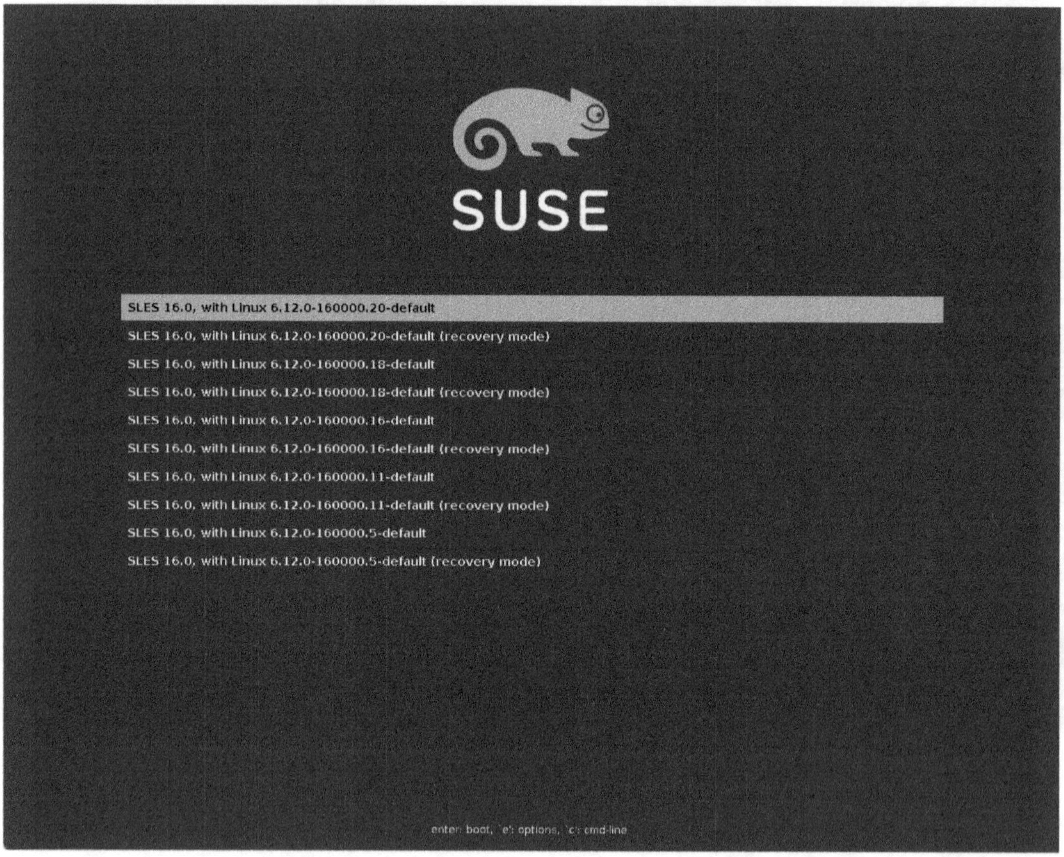


*Figure 15.3 – Advanced options for SLES 16 menu*

Select the line with the kernel version you want to boot and press `e`. The configuration is shown and can be edited. Proceed to edit the kernel line (the one that starts with `linux`) to add `systemd.unit=rescue.target` or `systemd.unit=emergency.target` at the end.

> The difference between `rescue` and `emergency` is the number of services that run. `rescue` will mount only local storage and will start some important services, but it won't start normal services such as the network. If the system fails to start even in that mode, `emergency` will load the root filesystem in read-only mode and will activate only essential services.

In the following screenshot, we can see how to edit an entry in the bootloader to boot to the rescue target:

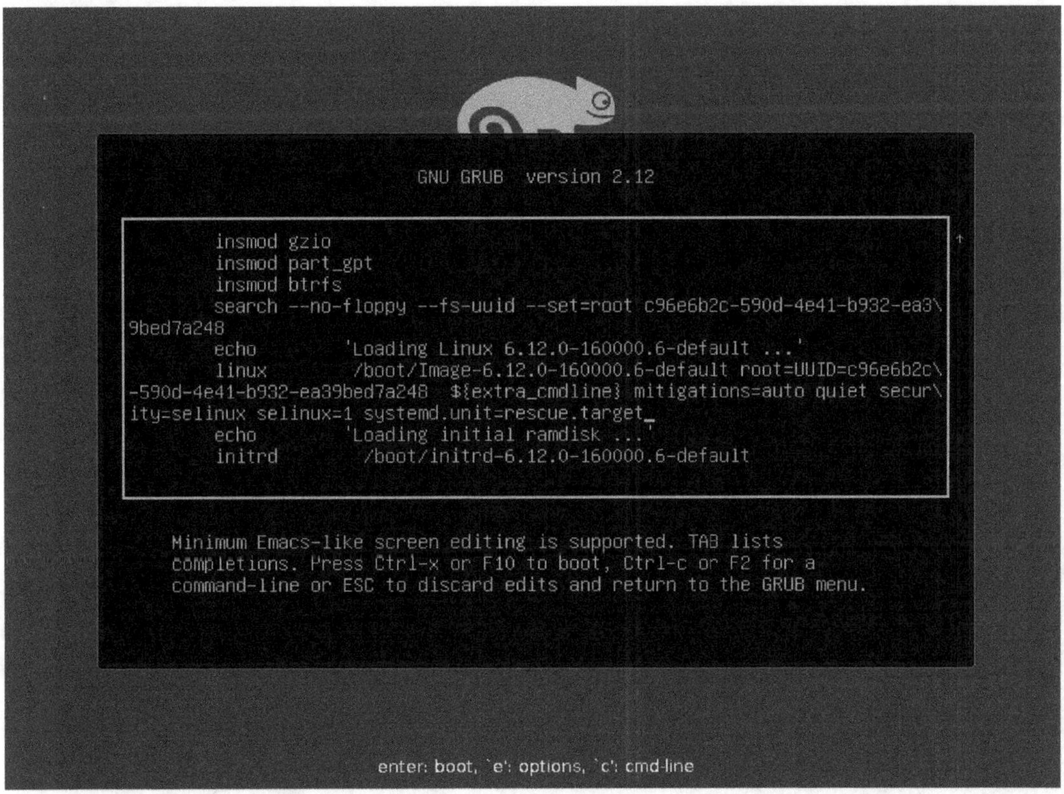


*Figure 15.4 – Editing the menu item*

The system will continue to boot into the target when you press *Ctrl* + *X*. GRUB will pass the target to the kernel, which will pass it over to `systemd`, which in turn will ignore the default configuration and load the services required for the **rescue target**.

When it finishes booting, the system will be in emergency mode and will prompt for the root password to give you control:

```
You are in emergency mode. After logging in, type "journalctl -xb" to view
system logs, "systemctl reboot" to reboot, "systemctl default" or "exit"
to boot into default mode.
Give root password for maintenance
(or press Control-D to continue): _
```

*Figure 15.5 – SLES system booted in emergency mode*

Emergency mode provides a very limited and controlled environment. It is designed to help you diagnose and fix problems without interference. In this mode, no other users or services are active. The root filesystem is mounted as read-only. The `network` service is not running. The only available services are `login`, `bash`, and `system journal`.

You can use this mode to check whether a filesystem is broken. Let's try it with the command for checking the filesystem, which is `brtfs` for BTRFS filesystems:

```
geeko:~ # btrfs check --force /dev/vda2
Opening filesystem to check...
WARNING: filesystem mounted, continuing because of --force
Checking filesystem on /dev/vda2
UUID: 0cfd9b4c-3d83-48b1-9b79-6ee59ebce2f0
[1/8] checking log
[2/8] checking root items
[3/8] checking extents
[4/8] checking free space tree
[5/8] checking fs roots
[6/8] checking only csums items (without verifying data)
[7/8] checking root refs
[8/8] checking quota groups
found 7925678080 bytes used, no error found
total csum bytes: 6945416
total tree bytes: 437895168
```

```
total fs tree bytes: 414695424
total extent tree bytes: 13352960
btree space waste bytes: 105018095
file data blocks allocated: 33607614464
referenced 25567031296
```

The filesystem is fine, but we could run `btrfs rescue` if the system needed help. We could also boot from an old snapshot if we know a point in time when the filesystem was fine. `--force` is needed because the system is mounted, and the command would fail without it.

`rescue` mounts the root filesystem as read-write, but you can find yourself with a read-only root if you are using a snapshot or if there are errors. You can remount it as read-write easily:

```
geeko:~ # mount -o remount -o rw /
```

Remember, you can access the manual pages for the command by running `man mount`. Now, our root filesystem is mounted in / as read-write. Take into account that in SLES, `/boot` is a folder in `/`. Now, we can do some administrative tasks, such as rebuilding `initrd` if a new hardware driver is needed and rebuilding the GRUB message.

> There is an `emergency.target` that loads even fewer services in those cases where rescue does not work. It does not provide anything in `sysinit.target`. A good exercise would be to repeat the previous sequence with `rescue.target`.

In the coming section, we will see how to make a change to boot to a different target. We can make it a permanent change or a one-time boot only. It can also be done easily during the GRUB boot sequence.

# Updating the root password by modifying the boot process

The previous options to rescue or modify the system require you to know the root password to access the system. Sometimes, more often than you expect, you've forgotten or lost the password to the root user, and you still need access to the system.

The boot sequence must not have any disk encrypted for it to work, or you will need the password for the encrypted volumes.

You can gain access to the system by passing some parameters to the kernel. To do so, boot the system, and once the GRUB menu is shown, press any key. GRUB by default waits for a few seconds before booting the default entry, so you can stop the count if you need to by pressing an arrow key. The GRUB menu is shown in the following screenshot so you can easily recognize it:

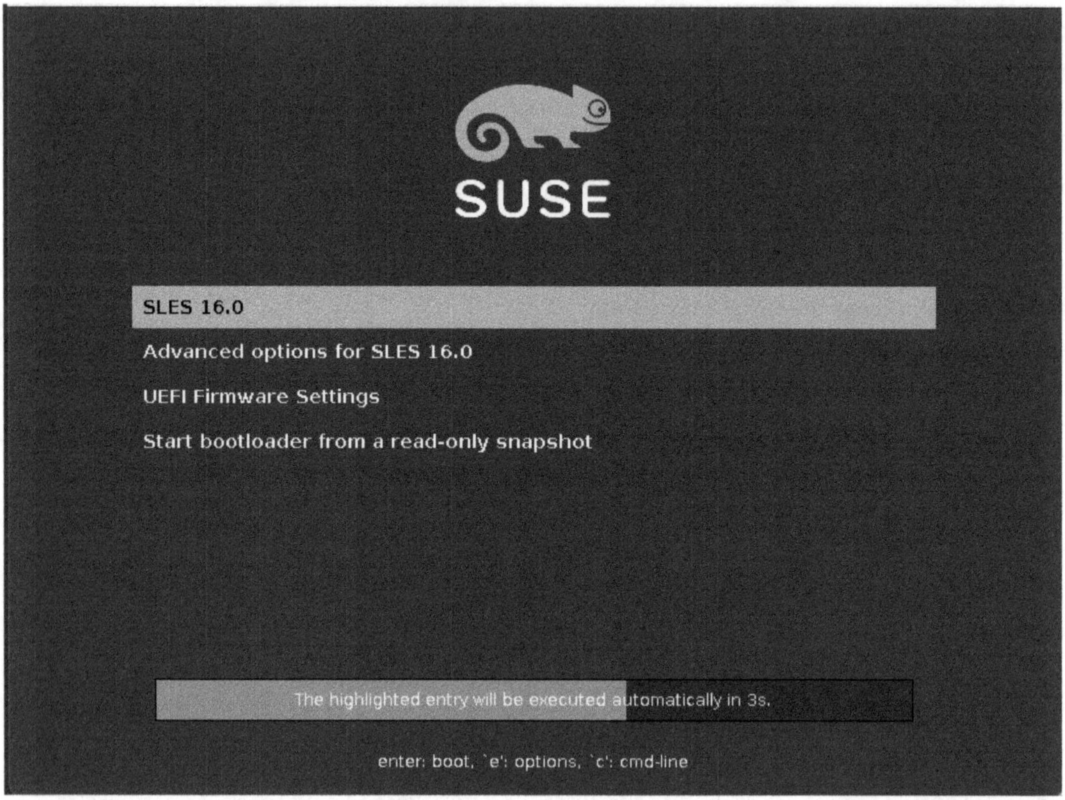


*Figure 15.6 – GRUB menu to select the kernel*

Use the arrow keys to select the first entry and follow the instructions after pressing e. Once you have done that, the following screen will appear:

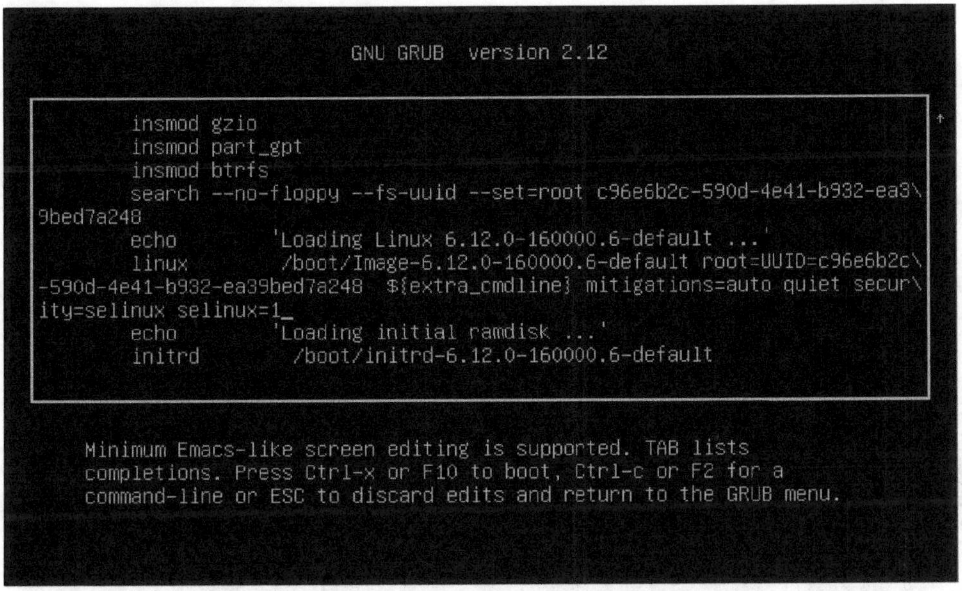


*Figure 15.7 – GRUB menu to select the kernel*

The first lines with `load_video`, `set gfx_payload=keep`, `insmod gzio`, `insmod part_gpt`, and `insmod btrfs` set options for GRUB. The next two options are the ones that are important. Let's review them:

- `linux`: Defines the kernel to be loaded and the parameters that will be passed to it, such as the root partition to use to boot
- `initrd`: Defines where to load the initial RAMdisk and its options

> Please note that the `linux` line is so long that it is wrapped, as we can see by the \ symbols, which mean that the line continues below.

We shall now go to the end of the `linux` line and add the `init=/bin/bash` option, as shown in the following screenshot:

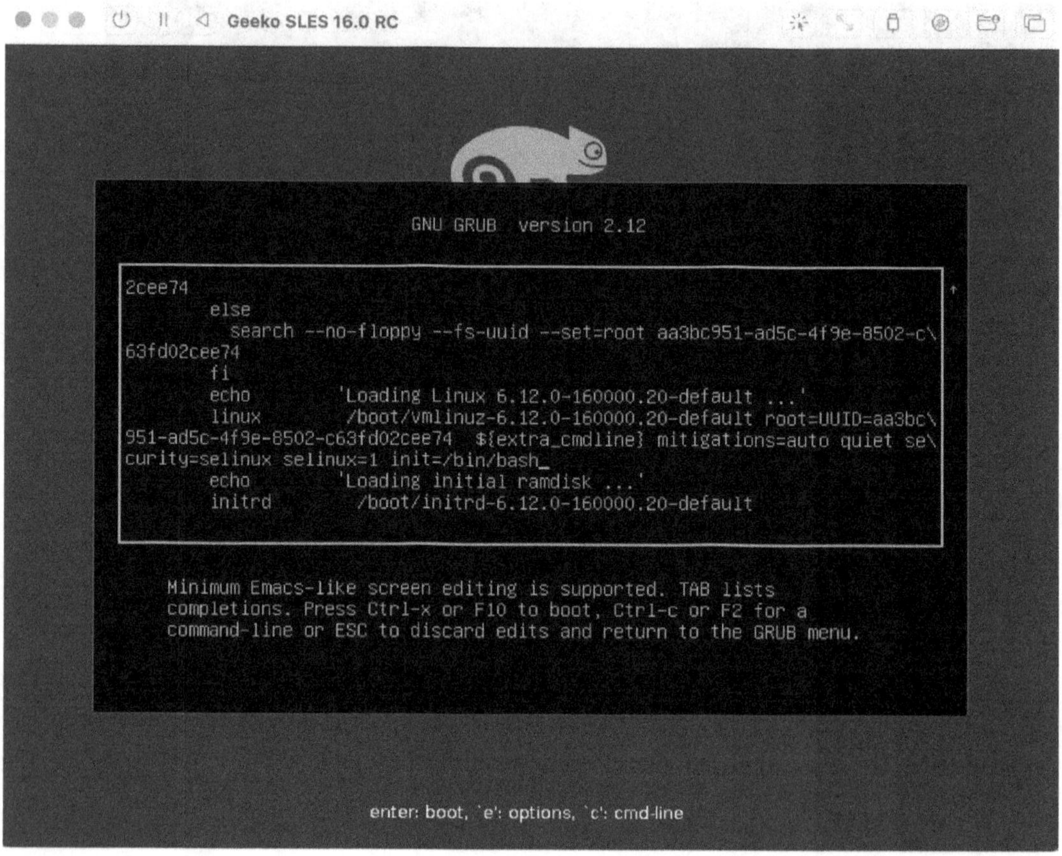


*Figure 15.8 – linux kernel line edited with the rd.break option*

Follow the instructions to boot the edited line, pressing *Ctrl* + *X*. We have booted into the Bash shell, but we don't have the `init` process running; there is no `systemd`. That also means that there is no SELinux running, and any change in files could mess up the labels. This is how the boot to a Bash shell looks when it's complete:

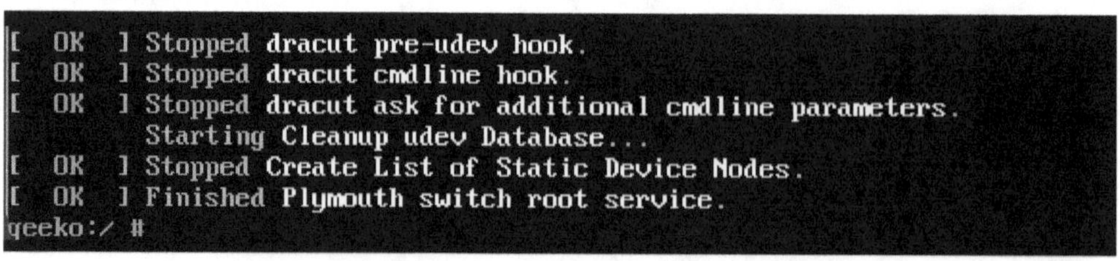


*Figure 15.9 – System booting into a Bash shell directly*

So, what is the status now? Let's review:

- The system directly boots into a single shell
- The root filesystem, /, is mounted as read-only
- No other filesystems are mounted
- SELinux is not loaded

Now, we need to make the filesystem for root, which is /, writeable. We can do it by running the following command:

```
geeko:/ # mount -o remount,rw /
```

Our root filesystem is now mounted read-write and can be modified. Now, we need to change the root user password with the `passwd` command:

```
geeko:/ # passwd
New password:
Retype new password:
passwd: all authentication tokens updated successfully
```

The password for the root user has now been changed, and the `/etc/shadow` file has been updated. However, it was modified, but SELinux was not running, and therefore the file could have access problems during the next boot. We can avoid the issue by asking SELinux to fix the labels during the next boot. You can do that by creating a hidden file in the root folder, `/etc/selinux/.autorelabel`, and then rebooting the system:

```
geeko:/# touch /etc/selinux/.autorelabel
```

Once the file has been created, reboot the system and use the new password. SELinux contexts will be used to relabel all files with the proper SELinux labels. You won't be able to use `reboot` or `shutdown`; you will need to physically power the system off and on. During the next boot, we will see the SELinux autorelabel happening:

```
[    8.892523] [      T1] systemd[1]: Successfully loaded SELinux policy in 247.084ms.
[    8.944773] [      T1] systemd[1]: Relabeled /dev/, /dev/shm/, /run/ in 11.612ms.
```

*Figure 15.10 – SELinux autorelabel during boot*

Now, we can log in with the root user and its new password.

# Summary

In this chapter, we have reviewed with some level of detail the boot process for a UEFI system. Understanding the boot process is important, as failure to boot will make a system unusable, something that can be quite problematic if you don't have a way of connecting to the console remotely. We have learned about GRUB, the different options for a normal system start, and how to modify the sequence if you need to do so. We now have some knowledge of the main files required to book, such as the kernel and the RAM disk.

We also learned how to start in rescue mode and how to modify the root password properly if you have lost it.

We barely scraped the surface. There is still a lot of information about the boot process, UEFI, and `systemd`, including alternative boot systems that could possibly be added to future versions of SLES 16, such as `systemd-boot`. But now, it is time to dive deeper and learn about kernel tuning and performance profiles in the next chapter.

# 16

# Automating with System Roles

Automation has been a critical topic in system management since the early years of Unix. With the need to handle a greater number of systems and be able to make the tasks repeatable, new ways of automation have arisen.

In SUSE, we want to provide choice, and to do so, we have the traditional **shell scripting** in the operating system with **Bash** as the default implementation, which was mentioned in *Chapter 2, Running Basic Commands and Simple Shell Scripts*. Then, we have **SUSE Multi-Linux Manager**, which includes **Salt**, for performing system automation and management at scale (up to 100,000 systems being managed in production). Finally, we can also use **Ansible** in several shapes and forms: one of them is integrating it with SUSE Multi-Linux Manager for distributed management, and another one, which we will cover here, is the use of **system roles**.

System roles can be used to configure specific parts of a system using Ansible playbooks locally.

In this chapter, we will cover the following topics:

- What are system roles?
- Installing system roles
- Using system roles

This knowledge will help use **system roles** as provided by **SUSE Linux Enterprise Server (SLES)** to facilitate running administrative tasks in a predictable way, reducing the possibility of making mistakes. When managing critical systems and/or a large system base, predictability is key, and system roles increase predictability. Let's go.

# Technical requirements

As in the previous chapters, you can continue the practice of using the **virtual machine** (**VM**) created at the beginning of this book in *Chapter 1, Getting SLES 16 Up and Running (Physical and Cloud)*. Any additional packages required for this chapter will be indicated.

# What are system roles?

**System roles** are a simple way to automate the configuration of different components within a system. They can set up the firewall, time synchronization, or even a database. They are built using a very common automation technology called **Ansible**. Therefore, system roles need Ansible to run.

Ansible is an automation engine that helps to configure and run tasks in all kinds of systems. It is very popular due to the fact that it is very easy to get started with it. In Ansible, we create **playbooks** to perform tasks such as enabling services or deploying configuration files. For tasks that are common and recurring, we create a **role**, for example, to configure time synchronization. This way we can reuse roles for our systems and reduce the time needed to automate a task, as well as ensuring consistency and predictability for its execution.

In SLES 16, both Ansible and Python (the programming language that Ansible is built and based on) are included with the operating system, although they are not installed by default. With them, a set of roles built to configure the system is also available. We call these system roles. They can enable consistent configuration of common parts of the operating system, such as setting certificates or even a high-availability cluster. They are very important for SAP deployments.

Like in previous versions of SLES with YaST, we can quickly set up services in SLES in a repeatable way. With the launch of the new SLES 16 version, a set of them has been included, but more will be developed during its life cycle.

Let's look at how to install system roles.

# Installing system roles

To use system roles, we will need Ansible. Since it isn't included in the default packages in SLES 16, let's start by installing it using zypper:

```
user@geeko:~> sudo zypper install ansible
Refreshing service 'SUSE_Linux_Enterprise_Server_16.0_x86_64'.
Loading repository data...
Reading installed packages...
Resolving package dependencies...
```

```
The following recommended package was automatically selected: python313-
Babel
The following 9 NEW packages are going to be installed: ansible ansible-
core python313-Babel python313-Jinja2 python313-MarkupSafe python313-
packaging python313-PyYAML python313-resolvelib python313-tzdata
[snip] ---8<---8<--- [snip]
```

System roles are also not installed by default in SLES 16. To install them, we can use `zypper` by simply running the following:

```
user@geeko:~> sudo zypper install ansible-linux-system-roles
Refreshing service 'SUSE_Linux_Enterprise_Server_16.0_x86_64'. Loading
repository data... Reading installed packages... Resolving package
dependencies...
The following NEW package is going to be installed: ansible-linux-system-
roles
1 new package to install.
[snip] ---8<---8<--- [snip]
```

These two steps will install system roles, Ansible, and the Python extensions needed to run them on your system.

There is one important path for system roles. It is the standardized location for them, which is `/usr/share/ansible/roles/`. Here, we will find a set of symbolic links pointing to the roles installed in the system.

> A symbolic link, or symlink for short, is a type of file that serves as a pointer or shortcut to another file or directory.

To see the roles available for our system, we can run the following command:

```
user@geeko:~> ls /usr/share/ansible/roles/ | grep ^linux-system-roles
linux-system-roles.aide
linux-system-roles.certificate
linux-system-roles.cockpit
linux-system-roles.crypto_policies
linux-system-roles.firewall
linux-system-roles.ha_cluster
linux-system-roles.journald
```

At SUSE, we have packaged many upstream system roles intended to be used for other Linux versions, so you can take a look at and learn about them. They can also be found in `/usr/share/ansible/roles/`. The system roles you can use in SLES are the ones that have the prefix `linux-system-roles`.

```
linux-system-roles.mssql
linux-system-roles.podman
linux-system-roles.selinux
linux-system-roles.ssh
linux-system-roles.suseconnect
linux-system-roles.systemd
linux-system-roles.timesync
```

As you can see from the names, these roles help us use pre-crafted automation to configure several parts of our system.

Now that we have both system roles and Ansible installed on our system, we are ready to use them. Let's see how to do that in the next section.

# Using system roles

Let's start by using the `linux-system-roles.timesync` system role on our system.

To do this, we need to create an Ansible playbook file that includes the mentioned role. In this example, we will use the filename `timesync_config.yml`. This file is the one that we will use from now on to configure time synchronization on our system. In order for it to use the system role, as we said, its contents are as follows:

```
---
- name: Configure time synchronization on SLES
servers
  hosts: localhost
  become: yes
  vars:
    timesync_ntp_servers:
      # Use a list of NTP servers hostnames or
IP addresses
      - hostname: 0.suse.pool.ntp.org
        iburst: true # Recommended for faster
initial sync
      - hostname: 1.suse.pool.ntp.org
```

```
          iburst: true
        - hostname: 2.suse.pool.ntp.org
          iburst: true
      # Optional: Force chrony as the provider
      timesync_ntp_provider: chrony
    roles:
      - name: linux-system-roles.timesync
```

Let's delve deeper into the sections of this playbook. There are three important parts:

- Part one. This is the header:
    - `---`: The header for all YAML files.
    - `- name`: A trailing dash to indicate a new block, then the name to identify the playbook.
    - `hosts: localhost`: We are selecting the host to connect to. In system roles, the logical value is `localhost`, as they will run locally.
    - `become: yes`: This directive is to explain that if we run it as a regular user, it will use `sudo` to run the tasks.
- Part two. These are the values we will pass to the system role:
    - `timesync_ntp_servers`: This starts the section to include the values for NTP servers.
    - `- hostname: 0.suse.pool.ntp.org`: This starts the block for each server to be configured. Please note the dash (`-`) at the beginning of it.
    - `iburst: true`: This is an option that needs to be added to the server in this block. This option forces synchronization on start.
    - `timesync_ntp_provider: chrony`: This is an optional section to indicate the name of the provider (or RPM package in this case) to install.

  All these variables will help us to configure the service properly.
- Part three. This part indicates which system role to use:
    - `roles`: The section that specifies the roles to use
    - `- name: linux-system-roles.timesync`: This is the block that specifies the name of the role to be used

You can find the file at https://github.com/PacktPublishing/SUSE-Linux-Enterprise-Server-16-Official-Administration-Guide/tree/main/chapter-16-automating-with-system-roles, where you can check the spacing and structure.

To find out which variable to use, we will look at the README.md file for each role:

```
user@geeko:~> less /usr/share/ansible/roles/fedora.linux_system_roles.
timesync/README.md
```

We can see here that we are using YAML format, as it is common in Ansible playbooks.

**Yet Another Markup Language**, also known as **YAML**, is a very common format for storing machine-parseable data that is also human-readable. To learn more about it, you can read this Wikipedia article: https://en.wikipedia.org/wiki/YAML.

The extended, yet unsupported, software repository PackageHub contains a package that you can use to check whether you have created the YAML file, called python3-yamllint, correctly. Let's use it.

First, we need to add PackageHub to our system:

```
user@geeko:~> sudo SUSEConnect --product PackageHub/16.0/x86_64
Registering system to SUSE Customer Center
 Updating system details on https://scc.suse.com ...
 Activating PackageHub 16.0 x86_64 ...
-> Adding service to system ...
-> Installing release package ...
 Successfully registered system
```

Then, we can install the python3-yamllint package by running the following:

```
user@geeko:~> sudo zypper in python3-yamllint
[snip]---8<---8<---8<---[snip]
The following 2 NEW packages are going to be installed:
  python313-pathspec python313-yamllint

2 new packages to install.
Package download size:   175,2 KiB
Package install size change:
```

```
     584,2 KiB  required by packages that will be installed
584,2 KiB| 0 B    released by packages that will be removed
[snip]---8<---8<---8<---[snip]
(1/2) Installing: python313-pathspec-0.12.1-160000.2.2.noarch
...................[done]
(2/2) Installing: python313-yamllint-1.36.2-160000.2.2.noarch
...................[done]
Running post-transaction scripts....................[done]
```

Then, it is time to run a check on our file with `yamllint`:

```
user@geeko:~> yamllint --no-warnings timesync_config.yml
timesync_config.yml
  1:4       error    trailing spaces  (trailing-spaces)
  2:55      error    trailing spaces  (trailing-spaces)
  3:19      error    trailing spaces  (trailing-spaces)
  4:14      error    trailing spaces  (trailing-spaces)
  5:8       error    trailing spaces  (trailing-spaces)
  6:26      error    trailing spaces  (trailing-spaces)
  7:60      error    trailing spaces  (trailing-spaces)
  8:38      error    trailing spaces  (trailing-spaces)
  9:59      error    trailing spaces  (trailing-spaces)
  10:38     error    trailing spaces  (trailing-spaces)
  11:21     error    trailing spaces  (trailing-spaces)
  12:38     error    trailing spaces  (trailing-spaces)
  13:21     error    trailing spaces  (trailing-spaces)
  14:45     error    trailing spaces  (trailing-spaces)
  15:34     error    trailing spaces  (trailing-spaces)
  16:9      error    trailing spaces  (trailing-spaces)
  17:40     error    trailing spaces  (trailing-spaces)
```

Since YAML is strict, it should be written using tabs instead of spaces. That's why we get the previous errors. Spaces are commonly accepted. So, if the only error we have here is this one, we are good to continue.

Let's use what we learned in *Chapter 14, Configuring and Using System Snapshots with BTRFS and Snapper*, and create a snapshot before running the system role (using the just-created playbook):

```
user@geeko:~> sudo snapper create --type single --description "Pre-
Playbook"
```

Let's check that the playbook has been properly configured:

```
user@geeko:~> sudo ansible-playbook timesync_config.yml --check
[WARNING]: No inventory was parsed, only implicit localhost is available
[WARNING]: provided hosts list is empty, only localhost is available. Note
that the implicit localhost does not match 'all'
PLAY [Configure time synchronization on SLES servers] ********************
******************************
[snip]---8<---8<---8<---[snip]
RUNNING HANDLER [linux-system-roles.timesync : Restart chronyd] **********
**************************************** changed: [localhost]
PLAY RECAP ************************************************ localhost :
ok=17 changed=3 unreachable=0 failed=0 skipped=30 rescued=0 ignored=0
```

The result here is clear: 17 tasks have run, there were 3 changes, and 30 were skipped (as they were not needed).

It will be useful to see whether the service is running as before:

```
user@geeko:~> sudo systemctl status chronyd.service
Unit chrony.service could not be found.
```

It's not running. It's not even been found! That's because running the playbook with the `--check` option shows all actions to be done but makes no changes. We are now ready to run the playbook and make the changes:

```
user@geeko:~> sudo ansible-playbook timesync_config.yml
[WARNING]: No inventory was parsed, only implicit localhost is available
[WARNING]: provided hosts list is empty, only localhost is available. Note
that the implicit localhost does not match 'all'
PLAY [Configure time synchronization on SLES servers] ********************
******************************
[snip]---8<---8<---8<---[snip]
RUNNING HANDLER [linux-system-roles.timesync : Restart chronyd] **********
**************************************** changed: [localhost]
PLAY RECAP ************************************************ localhost :
ok=17 changed=3 unreachable=0 failed=0 skipped=30 rescued=0 ignored=0
```

The results are the same as in the test we did before. But now, the changes have been applied. It's time to verify it:

```
user@geeko:~> sudo systemctl status chronyd.service
● chronyd.service - NTP client/server
     Loaded: loaded (/usr/lib/systemd/system/chronyd.service; enabled;
preset: enabled)
     Active: active (running) since Sat 2025-09-27 18:49:54 CEST; 3min 33s
ago
[snip]---8<---8<---8<---[snip]
user@geeko:~> cat /etc/chrony.conf | grep -v ^# | grep .
server 0.suse.pool.ntp.org iburst
server 1.suse.pool.ntp.org iburst
server 2.suse.pool.ntp.org iburst
makestep 1.0 3
rtcsync
driftfile /var/lib/chrony/drift
ntsdumpdir /var/lib/chrony
```

We can see that the service is running and the configuration file is using all the servers we have included in the configuration file.

It might be interesting to create another snapshot and look at the differences in the system before and after running the system role:

```
user@geeko:~> sudo snapper create --type single --description "Post-
Playbook"
user@geeko:~> sudo snapper list
```

Find the last two snapshots in the list. In my case, the last two snapshots were the numbers 69 and 70. Please check the numbers of your last two snapshots. Let's proceed with 69 and 70 in the example, but please replace these numbers with the ones you found:

```
user@geeko:~> sudo snapper diff 69..70
--- /.snapshots/69/snapshot/etc/chrony.conf     2025-03-31
18:44:48.552436808 +0200
+++ /.snapshots/70/snapshot/etc/chrony.conf     2025-09-27
18:49:53.176485538 +0200
@@ -1,55 +1,22 @@
-# Use public servers from the pool.ntp.org project.
-# Please consider joining the pool (https://www.pool.ntp.org/join.html).
```

```
-! pool pool.ntp.org iburst
+#
+# Ansible managed
+#
+# system_role:timesync
```

Now, we can combine the knowledge we have acquired in different chapters to perform repeatable actions easily and then review the impact of those actions in the system, and even be able to do a rollback on them.

# Summary

This chapter discussed the automation that is included with SLES 16: system roles. Now, we can use pre-built automation to configure common options and services in our system in an easy, fast, and consistent way. We also learned some of the basics of using Ansible so that we can create playbooks, run them in check mode to verify actions, and finally, apply them. Extending your knowledge of automation is very much encouraged. Please check out other Packt materials, such as the book *Learn Ansible* by Russ McKendrick or the course *Dive Into Ansible – From Beginner to Expert in Ansible* by James Spurin. We can now go a step further in our journey to learn and master SLES 16 and start learning how to use containers with **Podman** in the coming chapter.

# 17

# Managing Containers with Podman

Containers are presented as an alternative to virtualization, but they are more than just that. They underpin Kubernetes, the latest trend in IT and the second most popular open source project in the world based on the number of stars on GitHub, and are one of the key technologies leveraged by many of the best practices in the industry, such as cloud-native, DevOps, and GitOps. Containers provide lightweight isolation of applications without simulating hardware, providing higher density and agility for workloads. Podman is the default container management tool in SUSE Linux Enterprise Server 16.

This chapter covers the fundamentals of working with containers, starting with an introduction to what containers are and how they work. It compares Podman and Docker to help you understand their differences and use cases, and explains the role of registries in storing and distributing container images. You will also learn how to run containers, share data with them, manage and delete containers and images, inspect container logs, and finally, create your own containers.

We will be covering the following main topics:

- What to expect from containers
- Installing Podman
- Working with registries

Understanding containers is a key requirement for both developers and sysadmins. Many applications are designed to run as containers in isolation or orchestrated by Kubernetes, and having a clear understanding of how to use them and perform basic troubleshooting is a necessity, especially when some workloads are delivered as containers, and some operating systems add immutable versions that are designed to run containers up to the point that parts of the operating system are containers themselves.

SLES does provide a solution specifically designed to run virtualized or containerized workloads, named **SUSE Linux Micro**. SLES 16.1 is expected to provide a transactional mode that will be equivalent to SL Micro, and that will be selectable at installation time.

# Technical requirements

It is possible to continue the practice of using the virtual machine created at the beginning of this book, in *Chapter 1, Getting SLES 16 Up and Running (Physical and Cloud)*. Any additional packages required will be indicated in the text. You will also need a connection to the internet to download content from the SUSE registry or configure your own.

# What to expect from containers

Containers are everywhere. **Kubernetes**, an orchestrator for containers, is one of the three most successful open source projects, with around 4,000 contributors at the time of writing just in the main repository, and more than 200 projects associated with it. It defines the future of IT today, and it is important for you to know how to work with containers and understand their limitations.

So, how can we describe containers?

Containers can be seen as two different things:

- A standard unit of software that packages up code and all its dependencies
- A way of isolating applications running on a host, so that they behave as if they are the only application running on the system

Containers solve some problems that cause a lot of headaches to developers and sysadmins, such as the fact that applications could only "run on my machine," but due to dependencies or manual configuration steps, run with errors in production, errors that are hard to replicate, or the fact that some applications become unstable when a dependency gets updated.

Containers are not a new thing. As in many open source technologies, what we use today is the result of participation from companies such as Google, Virtuozzo, and IBM, interested in improving how Linux works with processes.

Containers are based on two major additions to the kernel:

- **Control groups (cgroups)**: A functionality that allows the kernel to limit and prioritize the amount of resources (CPU, memory, network, I/O) used by a group of processes
- **Namespace isolation**: A technology that allows the kernel to isolate applications, providing them with an environment that looks like the application is running as the only application in the system

A different company, Docker, used all of that to provide an opinionated developer-friendly container environment designed to run microservices, and that has a user experience that is easy and powerful. Docker containers come with a configuration format, the Dockerfile, that allows you to automate and simplify container builds.

> **Linux Containers (LXC)** is another container technology included in the Linux kernel that precedes Docker. It provides more flexible customization and is closer to a virtual machine, but it is also harder to use and requires deeper knowledge of Linux and how to use it. One of the good things about Docker containers is that you can use them without too much experience with Linux.

SUSE Linux Enterprise Server recommends the use of **Podman** as the container runtime for Linux, as a drop-in alternative to Docker, although both can also be installed if you are more comfortable doing so. Podman has many advantages, such as the fact that it runs as your user and not as a privileged daemon, enhancing the security and reliability of your system, as it does not need to have privileged user access.

You can substitute any Docker command with the equivalent Podman command and it will continue to work. You can even do `alias docker=podman` so you don't need to remember to change it when you are following some tutorial, or install the `podman-docker` package, which will create the link for you, and other things, such as linking the man pages.

# Installing Podman

Installing **Podman** is easy, just install the `podman` package, and it will install the necessary components and requirements, including upgrades to the networking components and `dns` to support containers and a new interface in Cockpit.

```
user@geeko:~> sudo zypper in podman Refreshing service 'SUSE_Linux_
Enterprise_Server_16.0_aarch64'. Loading repository data... Reading
installed packages... Resolving package dependencies...
The following 13 NEW packages are going to be installed: aardvark-
dns catatonit cockpit-podman conmon fuse-overlayfs libcontainers-
common libcontainers-default-policy netavark passt passt-selinux podman
registries-conf-suse runc
13 new packages to install.
Package download size: 26.9 MiB
Package install size change: | 98.7 MiB required by packages that will be
installed 98.7 MiB | - 0 B released by packages that will be removed
Backend: classic_rpmtrans Continue? [y/n/v/...? shows all options]
[--- EDITED ---]
 (y): Preloading: conmon-2-common-20250409-160000.2.2.noarch
......[done] (12/13) Installing: podman-5.4.2-160000.2.2.aarch64
.....................[done] (13/13) Installing: cockpit-podman-107-
160000.2.2.noarch ................[done] %posttrans(passt-selinux-
20250415.2340bbf-160000.2.2.noarch) script output: ++ SELINUX=enforcing ++
SELINUXTYPE=targeted Running post-transaction scripts ..................
....................[done] user@geeko:~>
```

Now let's test that podman has been properly installed:

```
user@geeko:~> podman info
host:
  arch: arm64
  buildahVersion: 1.39.4
  cgroupControllers:
  - pids
  cgroupManager: systemd
  cgroupVersion: v2
  conmon:
    package: conmon-2.1.13-160000.2.2.aarch64
    path: /usr/bin/conmon
    version: 'conmon version 2.1.13, commit: unknown'
  cpuUtilization:
    idlePercent: 99.77
    systemPercent: 0.14
    userPercent: 0.09
  cpus: 4
  databaseBackend: sqlite
  distribution:
    distribution: sles
    variant: server
    version: "16.0"
  eventLogger: journald
  freeLocks: 2048
  hostname: geeko
  idMappings:
```

*Figure 17.1 – First lines of the output of podman info*

We can see a lot of information, perhaps more than what we need, such as the architecture of the host, the number of CPUs, the OS type, and information about the version.

> SLES supports **rootless containers** by default. Rootless containers are never run as root, even if the container application inside is running with PID 1. To be able to run applications with multiple UIDs and GIDs, subuid is used to map ranges of user IDs from its namespace into child namespaces.

To check if `podman` is installed, it is enough to look at the reported version. We can also find out if the user can run rootless containers with a couple of commands:

```
user@geeko:~> podman --version
podman version 5.4.2
user@geeko:~> cat /etc/subuid
user:100000:65536
user@geeko:~> cat /etc/subgid
user:100000:65536
```

The user with ID `user` (you could also use a numeric ID) can use up to `65536` subordinate UIDs and a GID starting with `100000`. You can add `subuids` and `subgids` if that is not the case with a simple command:

```
user@geeko:~>  sudo usermod --add-subuids
100000-165535 --add-subgids 100000-165535 $(id
-nu)
```

> You can configure Podman to search by default in other registries like docker.io, modifying the `/etc/containers/registry.conf` file and adding the new registries to the section unqualified-search-registries like this:
>
> `unqualified-search-registries = ["registry.suse.com", "docker.io"]`.

In the next section, we will see how to configure registries and how they are used to find and download images.

## Working with registries

In order to create a container, you need a container image that will be used as the basis. A **container image** stores all the binaries, configuration, and dependencies required to run your application, ideally with the minimal selection of packages possible. You can create your images from scratch, but in most cases, it is more practical to use an existing base image instead. Images are stored in **container registries**, and downloading an image from a registry is called a **pull**. SLES, by default, is configured to use only `registry.suse.com`, a secure registry that includes tested, updated, and certified SLE Base Container Images. All images in the SUSE Registry undergo a maintenance process and contain the latest available updates and fixes.

> Many tutorials about the use of containers download containers stored in docker.io. The quality and security of the images stored there are not guaranteed and there are some limits on its use. You should be very careful about using them, but it is a big source of content.

Let's visit the web interface to `registry.suse.com` to find a container image to use:

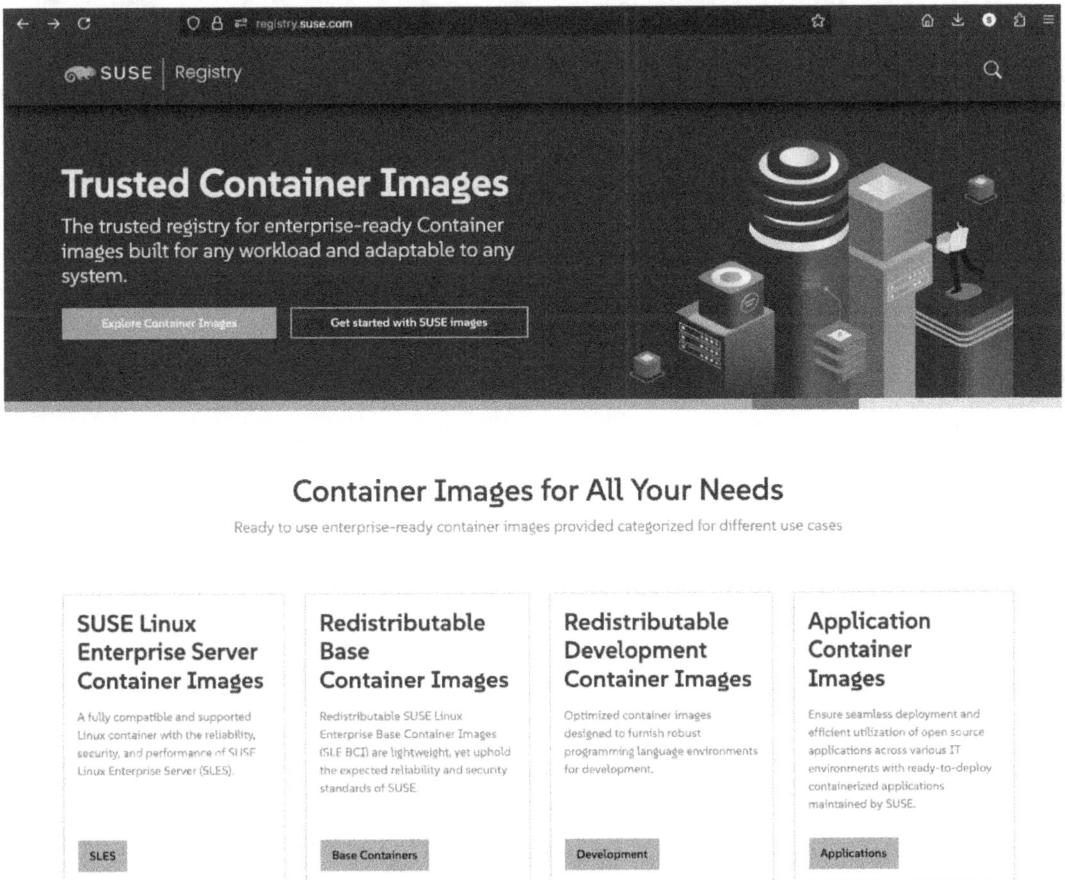


*Figure 17.2 – Web page interface to the SUSE container registry*

There are different types of container images available at `registry.suse.com`:

- **SLE Base Container Images:** Minimal SLES-based images that you can use to develop, deploy, and share applications
- **Redistributable Base Container Images:** Used for building custom container images and for deploying applications
- **Redistributable Development Container Images:** Minimal environments for developing and deploying applications in specific programming languages
- **Application Container Images:** SLE Base container images that include specific applications, such as the PostgreSQL database and the Performance Co-Pilot system-level performance analysis tool

Let's install and run one application. We are going to create a web server using Nginx.

Go to `registry.suse.com` and search for PostgreSQL 17:

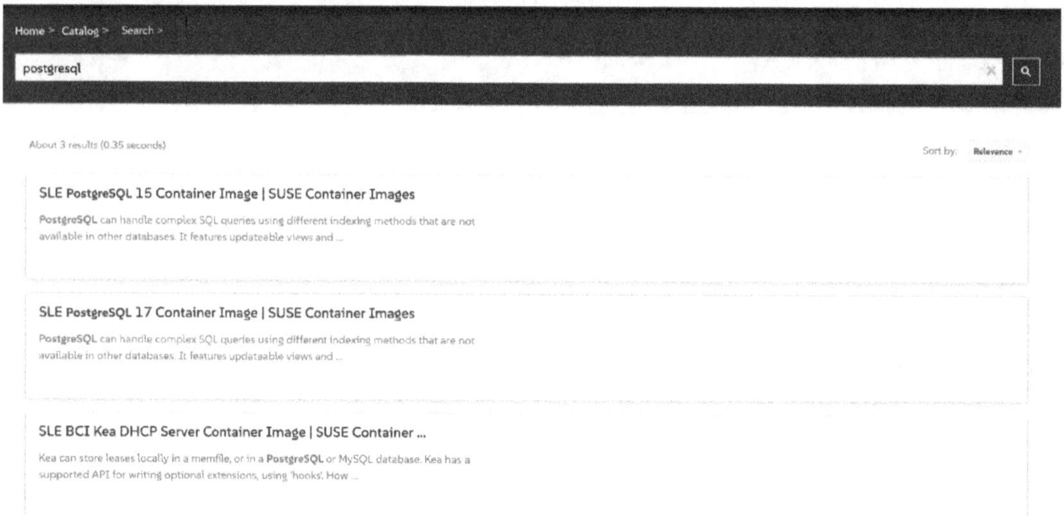


*Figure 17.3 – Search results for postgresql*

Click on the **PostgreSQL 17** link (you can also use another version if you prefer to do so):

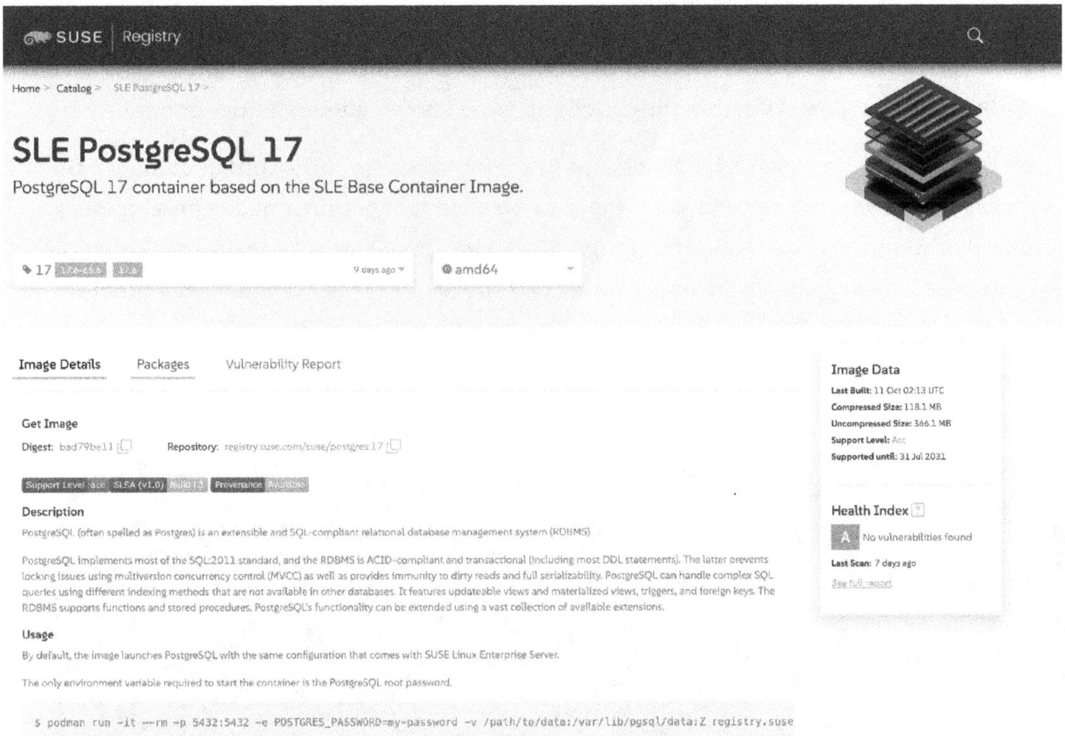


*Figure 17.4 – The web page describing SLE PostgreSQL 17 and its usage*

As you can see, selecting one version will show you additional information about the container (other registries will have a different interface). Let's see what information is available for us:

There are some things we need to know:

- **Labels and architecture**: Each repository contains different versions of the images, identified by a **digest** and one or more **labels**. You can download any of them. Traditionally, repositories will include the *latest* tag, which will be updated every time a newer image is published.

> Using the *latest* tag is never recommended, as it creates a problem: it is not reproducible, so it is possible that what was working in one system does not work in another because the actual image downloaded is different. To avoid these problems, use digests or labels when you can.

- **Image data:** Information about the date, size, and support levels of the image.
- **Image details:** Information about the image and how to use it.
- **Packages:** All the RPMs that are included in the image, with their version and license.
- **Vulnerability report:** Whether the image has some known vulnerabilities or not.

Let's now run a web server. Search for Nginx and go to the web page of the container image. Go to the packages, and you will see why containers are so good for container native development. At the time of writing, the image contained roughly 160 packages, from `tar` to `perl` or `libsqlite`, all required to run open source Nginx appropriately. It does not matter if you need a different version of any of those packages, or if you have already installed them in another container; it will work as expected if you follow some rules when you create the images or run them.

Let's follow the instructions to run it:

```
user@geeko:> mkdir psql_data
user@geeko:> podman run -it --rm -p 5432:5432 -e POSTGRES_
PASSWORD=securepassword -v $PWD/psql_data:/var/lib/pgsql/data:Z registry.
suse.com/suse/postgres:17

Trying to pull registry.suse.com/suse/postgres:17...
Getting image source signatures
Checking if image destination supports signatures
Copying blob db15866adcbe done   |
Copying blob d7259433dcae done   |
Copying config af957f769c done   |
Writing manifest to image destination
Storing signatures
The files belonging to this database system will be owned by user
"postgres". This user must also own the server process.
The database cluster will be initialized with locale "en_US.utf8". The
default database encoding has accordingly been set to "UTF8". The default
text search configuration will be set to "english".
Data page checksums are disabled.
fixing permissions on existing directory /var/lib/pgsql/data ...
ok creating subdirectories ... ok selecting dynamic shared memory
implementation ... posix selecting default "max_connections" ... 100
selecting default "shared_buffers" ... 128MB selecting default time zone
... Etc/UTC creating configuration files ... ok running bootstrap script
... ok performing post-bootstrap initialization ... ok syncing data to
```

```
disk ... ok
initdb: warning: enabling "trust" authentication for local connections
initdb: hint: You can change this by editing pg_hba.conf or using the
option -A, or --auth-local and --auth-host, the next time you run initdb.
Success. You can now start the database server using:
pg_ctl -D /var/lib/pgsql/data -l logfile start

waiting for server to start....2025-10-20 13:46:31.344 UTC [46]
LOG: redirecting log output to logging collector process 2025-10-20
13:46:31.344 UTC [46]HINT: Future log output will appear in directory
"log". done server started
/usr/local/bin/docker-entrypoint.sh: ignoring /docker-entrypoint-
initdb.d/*
waiting for server to shut down.... done server stopped
PostgreSQL init process complete; ready for start up.
2025-10-20 13:46:31.567 UTC [1]LOG: redirecting -t log output to logging
collector process 2025-10-20 13:46:31.567 UTC [1]HINT: Future log output
will appear in directory "log".
user@geeko:~> ls -ld psql_data/
drwx------. 1 100498 user 522 Oct 20 15:51 psql_data/
```

The command will try to run the container from a local copy, and as it is not available, it will download it from the registry. The container does go through several steps. First, it checks if the image can be found locally and downloads it if it is not. The image is stored in reusable layers, so only those layers not present will be transmitted. Then it creates a new read-write layer on top and runs it. Your changes will be implemented in the new layer, without affecting the other layers.

Let's look at the commands we used for `podman run`:

- `--tty, -t`: Connects a terminal so you can interact with the container.
- `--interactive, -i`: Makes `stdin` available to the container, enabling input.
- `-e, --env`: Allows you to define environment variables in the container. In this case, instead of specifying a default password, the container requires the password as the value of the `POSTGRES_PASSWORD` environment variable. If an environment variable is specified without a value, Podman checks the host environment for a value and sets the variable only if it is set on the host.

We are stuck in the command line, in interactive mode, and with the terminal connected, so we won't be able to go back until we stop it with *Ctrl* + *C*. However, we want to run the container as a daemon; for that, we need to substitute `-i` and `-t` for `-d`:

```
user@geeko:~> podman run -d --rm -p 5432:5432 -e
POSTGRES_PASSWORD=securepassword -v $PWD/psql_data:/
var/lib/pgsql/data:Z registry.suse.com/suse/postgres:17
449d17709a4f50e677c13105ad5689db6b264ba8569150afff9d2e286e06b29a
```

The command returns immediately with the identifier for the container. We will use that identifier to be able to troubleshoot it later.

**Defining multiple environmental variables at the same time**

As a special case, if an environment variable ending in * is specified without a value, Podman searches the host environment for variables starting with the prefix and adds those variables to the container.

You can always specify multiple variables, repeating the parameter several times.

- `--volume, -v=[[SOURCE-VOLUME|HOST-DIR:]CONTAINER-DIR[:OPTIONS]]`: Allows you to specify a mount point from your system inside the container. In this case, we are specifying that the `psql_data` directory in the current folder will be seen inside the container as `/var/lib/pgsql/data`.
- `--publish, -p=[[ip:][hostPort]:]containerPort[/protocol]`: Makes a port inside the container available in the host. Without this, you would find the database running, expecting connections on port `5432`, but it would be impossible to access it from outside.

We ran a couple of containers, downloading them from a registry when it was necessary. In the next part, we will see more advanced ways of using registries.

## Using registries

Images need to be stored locally to be used in a container. Downloading and storing an image locally is called a **pull**. Although the image was downloaded automatically before, you can decide to do it beforehand to speed up the process. `docker pull` is used to pull an image from a registry onto the local machine, and `digest` is used to check the image version.

> Images are stored in layers. Changes are not written directly in the image, but on a new layer on top. Images are normally split into several layers, which are stored only once in registries (including your local copy). Layering makes containers efficient, avoiding unnecessary data duplication.

Let's start by downloading a base SLES image from `registry.suse.com`:

```
user@geeko:~> podman pull registry.suse.com/bci/bci-base:15.7
Trying to pull registry.suse.com/bci/bci-base:15.7...
Getting image source signatures
Checking if image destination supports signatures
Copying blob 07355880ecdf [==>-------------------------] 4.5MiB / 45.4MiB
| 322.0 KiB/s
user@geeko:~> podman pull registry.suse.com/bci/bci-base:15.7
Trying to pull registry.suse.com/bci/bci-base:15.7...
Getting image source signatures
Checking if image destination supports signatures
Copying blob 07355880ecdf done   |
Copying config 4d0f7d7dc2 done   |
Writing manifest to image destination
Storing signatures
4d0f7d7dc2bbcd133cb9d9a05c4b80e9a46f69b01040ec42a72f8320ab2c0f9d
```

We haven't created any containers yet, but we have stored the image locally. We can easily list local images:

```
user@geeko:~> podman images
REPOSITORY                        TAG         IMAGE ID      CREATED
SIZE
registry.suse.com/suse/postgres   17          af957f769cad  10 days ago
411 MB
registry.suse.com/bci/bci-base    15.7        4d0f7d7dc2bb  10 days ago
138 MB
```

We have two images locally. The one we use to run PostgreSQL, with the tag 17, which was downloaded automatically, and the new one with the tag 15.7.

Let's use a different method to create a container, the **Dockerfile**. A Dockerfile is a set of instructions to build a container from a base image in a file. Dockerfiles can be easily stored in a content management system such as Git and are perfect for replicable generations of images. A Dockerfile is a text file, so open your preferred text editor and write the following inside a Dockerfile text file in a new folder:

> The container image comes from the free SLE_BCI repository, a repository that contains a subset of all packages from SUSE Linux Enterprise. These containers and the packages included are available free of charge, and they can be redistributed freely. However, they are provided without support, so it is likely that you will need a supported version in production. Check the SUSE web to see the terms and conditions of these images and what alternatives are available

```
FROM registry.suse.com/bci/python:3.10
RUN zypper -n in python3-tools;
EXPOSE 8000
CMD ["python3",  "-m", "http.server"]
```

The **Containerfile** defines a set of steps to create a custom image with automation. Dockerfiles are consistent and reproducible and can be stored in a source control system (such as Git) along with your application code.

This Containerfile is quite simple. It defines a base container to modify (BCI Python 3.10 container), runs a command inside the container that installs a package, exposes port `8000` (where the Python HTTP server will be listening inside the container, a port that needs to be mapped to a host port to be usable), and defines the command that will be used by default.

You can use Podman to build it:

```
user@geeko:~/simple_python> podman build -t my_
image:latest .
STEP 1/4: FROM registry.suse.com/bci/python:3.10
STEP 2/4: RUN zypper -n in python3-tools;
Refreshing service 'container-suseconnect-zypp'.
Retrieving repository 'SLE_BCI' metadata [.....
Warning: The gpg key signing file 'repomd.xml'
has expired.
 Repository: SLE_BCI
 Key Fingerprint: FEAB 5025 39D8 46DB 2C09 61CA
70AF 9E81 39DB 7C82
 Key Name: SuSE Package
 Signing Key build@suse.de
```

```
 Key Algorithm: RSA 2048
 Key Created: Mon Sep 21 08:21:47 2020
 Key Expires: Fri Sep 20 08:21:47 2024 (EXPIRED)
 Rpm Name: gpg-pubkey-39db7c82-5f68629b ......done]
Building repository 'SLE_BCI' cache [....done]
Loading repository data...
Reading installed packages...
Resolving package dependencies...
The following 3 NEW packages are going to be installed:
libpython3_6m1_0 python3-base python3-tools
The following 3 packages are not supported by their vendor:
libpython3_6m1_0 python3-base python3-tools
3 new packages to install.
Overall download size: 8.8 MiB. Already cached: 0 B. After the operation,
additional 37.4 MiB will be used.
Continue? [y/n/v/...? shows all options] (y): y
Retrieving: libpython3_6m1_0-3.6.15-150300.10.51.1.aarch64 (SLE_BCI)
(1/3), 851.1 KiB
 Retrieving: libpython3_6m1_0-3.6.15-150300.10.51.1.aarch64.rpm [....done
(159.1 KiB/s)]
Retrieving: python3-base-3.6.15-150300.10.51.1.aarch64 (SLE_BCI) (2/3),
7.5 MiB
Retrieving: python3-base-3.6.15-150300.10.51.1.aarch64.rpm [.......done
(6.4 MiB/s)]
Retrieving: python3-tools-3.6.15-150300.10.51.1.aarch64 (SLE_BCI) (3/3),
498.0 KiB
Retrieving: python3-tools-3.6.15-150300.10.51.1.aarch64.rpm [...done
(223.1 KiB/s)]
Checking for file conflicts: [..done] (1/3) Installing: libpython3_6m1_0-
3.6.15-150300.10.51.1.aarch64 [..done]
(2/3) Installing: python3-base-3.6.15-150300.10.51.1.aarch64 [.......done]
(3/3) Installing: python3-tools-3.6.15-150300.10.51.1.aarch64 [..done] -->
c5f75614d6f5 STEP 3/4: EXPOSE 8000
 --> 628412a31877 STEP 4/4: CMD ["python3", "-m", "http.server"]
COMMIT my_image:latest
 --> 260367012214
Successfully tagged localhost/my_image:latest
260367012214e1b50b93dd26c8a860817893f22b6e7469e7832755173e0d50fa
```

Remember to specify all commands in the Dockerfile in non-interactive mode, as you won't be able to input data during the build. Our new image is ready and stored locally, and we have labeled it `my_image:latest`. Running images is easy, but we need to remember to publish the exposed port so it can be accessed.

```
user@geeko:~/simple_python> podman run -p 8000:8000 localhost/my_
image:latest
```

If you want to see the output of the command inside the container, you need to attach the STDIN and run the command with the `-t` flag:

```
user@geeko:~/simple_python> podman run -t -p 8000:8000 localhost/my_
image:latest Serving HTTP on 0.0.0.0 port 8000 (http://0.0.0.0:8000/) ...
```

We can use `wget` to see that it is running and accessible on port `8000`:

```
user@geeko:> podman ps
CONTAINER ID IMAGE COMMAND CREATED STATUS PORTS NAMES 1132e415d2de
localhost/my_image:latest python3 -m http.s... About a minute ago Up About
a minute 0.0.0.0:8000->8000/tcp lucid_swirles
user@geeko:> wget localhost:8000
 Prepended http:// to 'localhost:8000'
--2025-10-25 11:44:57-- http://localhost:8000/
Resolving localhost (localhost)... ::1, 127.0.0.1
Connecting to localhost (localhost)|::1|:8000... connected.
HTTP request sent, awaiting response... Read error (Connection reset by
peer) in headers.
Retrying.
```

Even if our Python simple web server is available on port `8000` of our localhost, outside of the container, it is not properly configured, and it does not have content to serve, so it returns an error. We are not going to configure it, as the steps would be similar to running your application on a normal server, but remember that you can do the same with your application, with as many steps as required in the Dockerfile, which can be easily reproduced. Describing Dockerfiles, their syntax, and best practices for their usage is beyond the scope of this book, but can be found in the documentation for SLES.

Next, let's see how to connect to a running container to find information about what is happening in it.

## Connecting to a running container

Sometimes it is necessary to navigate the application inside the container to understand what is going on. For instance, your container could be failing because your application is not working properly or because you forgot to expose the proper port. We can connect to a running container to understand what is going on and test actions using podman exec. In this case, we will flag it as interactive (-i) and connected to a terminal (-t) because we want to send commands to the container to be interpreted.

We will use podman ps first to see what containers are running and connect to the right one:

```
user@geeko:~> podman ps
CONTAINER ID IMAGE COMMAND CREATED STATUS PORTS NAMES
 1132e415d2de localhost/my_image:latest python3 -m http.s... 6 minutes ago
Up 6 minutes 0.0.0.0:8000->8000/tcp lucid_swirles
user@geeko:~> podman exec -it lucid_swirles bash
1132e415d2de:/ # ps aux
USER         PID %CPU %MEM    VSZ   RSS TTY      STAT START   TIME COMMAND
root           1  0.0  0.3  27424 15852 pts/0    Ss+  09:42   0:00 python3
-m http.serve
root           7  0.0  0.0   4784  3816 pts/1    Ss   09:50   0:00 bash
root          36  100  0.0   7724  3272 pts/1    R+   09:51   0:00 ps aux
```

We run bash as *root* inside the container. This root user is different because it is only root inside the container, not in the machine, but for our purposes, it is what we wanted. We can see that Python is running as root with PID 1, and there is no systemd running. We can look around, find the problem if there is one, and update our Dockerfile to reflect the changes until we get it right.

**Cloud-native applications**

In order to run inside a container, many applications need to be updated. For instance, if you hardcode the IP address during compile time, you will always get the IP address of the host where you created the container – something that happened to the author a few years ago – making it impossible to run your application. Be prepared to adapt your application so it can be killed at any time, and make intensive use of environment variables to make the container flexible enough.

Let's kill the container and clean up a little:

```
user@geeko:~> podman kill lucid_swirles
lucid_swirles
user@geeko:~> podman ps
CONTAINER ID  IMAGE       COMMAND     CREATED     STATUS      PORTS
NAMES
```

Let's return to our web server container and see how it is working. We can use the first digits of the identifier, and if there is no conflict, Podman will know which container we are referring to. Let's use it to see the logs:

```
user@geeko:~> podman logs 449d177
 PostgreSQL Database directory appears to contain a database; Skipping
initialization
 2025-11-27 17:20:22.690 UTC   [1]LOG:  redirecting log output to logging
collector process
2025-11-27 17:20:22.690 UTC   [1]HINT:  Future log output will appear in
directory "log".
```

We can also connect with a terminal to investigate inside the container:

```
user@geeko:~> podman exec -it  377018c bash
bash-4.4# ls -ld .
dr-xr-xr-x. 1 root root 26 Nov 27 17:25 .
bash-4.4# pg_isready
/run/postgresql:5432 - accepting connections
bash-4.4# exit
exit
user@geeko:~>
```

Take into account that the container is normally a minimal version of the operating system. In this container, for instance, you won't find `ps`, `curl`, or `zypper`, only the binaries installed with the application, but it is quite important for troubleshooting.

Containers and container images take up space, even if you are not using them. Let's find out next how to liberate that space by deleting the images and containers.

## Deleting containers and images

There is no container running, but containers are not normally deleted when they stop. You can see the list of all the containers using the -a flag:

```
user@geeko:~> podman ps -a
CONTAINER ID  IMAGE                            COMMAND               CREATED
STATUS                      PORTS                     NAMES
88c3cf087115 localhost/my_image:latest python3 -m httpd.... About an hour
ago Exited (1) About an hour ago 0.0.0.0:8000->8000/tcp unruffled_hamilton
035ab7f060b8 localhost/my_image:latest bash About an hour ago Exited (0)
About an hour ago 0.0.0.0:8000->8000/tcp quirky_kirch
d8fe5bd30f68 localhost/my_image:latest python3 -m http.s... 17 minutes ago
Exited (0) 14 minutes ago 0.0.0.0:8000->8000/tcp suspicious_gagarin
1132e415d2de localhost/my_image:latest python3 -m http.s... 14 minutes ago
Exited (137) 2 minutes ago 0.0.0.0:8000->8000/tcp lucid_swirles
```

Because containers are built using layers, only the changes are stored. Let's see those layers and any layers that we have downloaded:

```
user@geeko:~> podman images
REPOSITORY                       TAG          IMAGE ID      CREATED
SIZE
localhost/my_image               latest       260367012214  35 minutes ago
309 MB
<none>                           <none>       338b908d309b  About an hour
ago  253 MB
<none>                           <none>       7e71f69c41a5  About an hour
ago  253 MB
registry.suse.com/bci/bci-base  16.0         eb1bf692b245  11 days ago
105 MB
registry.suse.com/bci/bci-base  15.7         4d0f7d7dc2bb  2 weeks ago
138 MB
registry.suse.com/bci/bci-init  16.0         356a6fd6b214  5 weeks ago
155 MB
registry.suse.com/bci/python    3.10         cd38d8c88797  22 months ago
253 MB
```

The layers without a name have been created from our steps in the Dockerfile.

Deleting the containers is easy; you just need to specify one container with its name or digest to the `podman rm` command:

```
user@geeko:~> podman ps -a --format "{{.Names}}"
unruffled_hamilton
quirky_kirch
agitated_matsumoto
compassionate_jang
hopeful_hermann
beautiful_vaughan
thirsty_sammet
adoring_gauss
sweet_boyd
suspicious_gagarin
lucid_swirles
user@geeko:~> podman rm sweet_boyd
sweet_boyd
```

Let's now delete all remaining containers, as we don't need them anymore. We can always use the image to create a new one.

```
user@geeko:~> podman rm -a
42c3f4d028f4a967b46d930303cd5e45ded66dc84fecf04cbb8c0239d963e735
d8fe5bd30f68e2198f44c872ac397245b4e7af5fff14baf659b7b78d44ce00d1
a5db8cc983a6ece0849d2118e7235fbac6285719a0e182912901569e4311caf2
2133fbd1cc86c62dfda50356f9e89b3fb1ce28dc84642f80b67498f3157d44b8
035ab7f060b8c58377744ef1345f2e2055f8bc1b84e186214410d445e665a9d0
0da9f8d6f09a356f0497be2611d66c8d871704d52c63e8b1b89b56fd1b6de8fe
1132e415d2de4b5d481f0cb5e5a435de65da7b177fa42b4c6b60616fe56205aa
cd373b31878f0b1c670908b6bc7b303f75428547d0bff9be93b89689a2242fb4
9c801b3508fdfda67d0228db3e5535e9a2de05588c3b65b11b741d476d36af2d
88c3cf087115e07f64d929bdd0acc2cc17352756aa11b8bf2b44006754d958d3
```

We have not deleted the images yet, not even the images we created, so they are stored locally to be reused. Let's delete the ones we are not using:

```
user@geeko:~> podman images --all
REPOSITORY                       TAG         IMAGE ID      CREATED
SIZE
<none>                           <none>      628412a31877  2 days ago
309 MB
localhost/my_image               latest      260367012214  2 days ago
309 MB
<none>                           <none>      c5f75614d6f5  2 days ago
309 MB
<none>                           <none>      338b908d309b  2 days ago
253 MB
<none>                           <none>      143dd2b3ccfa  2 days ago
253 MB
<none>                           <none>      7e71f69c41a5  2 days ago
253 MB
registry.suse.com/bci/bci-base  16.0        eb1bf692b245  2 weeks ago
105 MB
registry.suse.com/bci/bci-base  15.7        4d0f7d7dc2bb  2 weeks ago
138 MB
registry.suse.com/bci/bci-init  16.0        356a6fd6b214  5 weeks ago
155 MB
registry.suse.com/bci/python    3.10        cd38d8c88797  22 months ago
253 MB
```

To delete an image, we use the `podman rmi` command:

```
user@geeko:~> podman rmi registry.suse.com/bci/bci-base:15.7
Untagged: registry.suse.com/bci/bci-base:15.7
Deleted: 4d0f7d7dc2bbcd133cb9d9a05c4b80e9a46f69b01040ec42a72f8320ab2c0f9d
user@geeko:~> podman rmi localhost/my_image:latest
Untagged: localhost/my_image:latest
Deleted: 260367012214e1b50b93dd26c8a860817893f22b6e7469e7832755173e0d50fa
Deleted: 628412a31877fcd9e3cb0ba27bb353d8825e7da4e83e2c51ce4b7930c434810d
Deleted: c5f75614d6f5c118349d45f1f5c23479db252709231c9c9fa486ef98bd79f132
```

We can see now that the images have been deleted:

```
user@geeko:~> podman images --all
REPOSITORY                       TAG         IMAGE ID      CREATED
SIZE
<none>                           <none>      338b908d309b  2 days ago
253 MB
<none>                           <none>      143dd2b3ccfa  2 days ago
253 MB
<none>                           <none>      7e71f69c41a5  2 days ago
253 MB
registry.suse.com/bci/bci-base  16.0        eb1bf692b245  2 weeks ago
105 MB
registry.suse.com/bci/bci-init  16.0        356a6fd6b214  5 weeks ago
155 MB
registry.suse.com/bci/python    3.10        cd38d8c88797  22 months ago
253 MB
```

Let's now remove all remaining images. We will use a longer command that is equivalent to `podman rmi`. To delete all images, we use the `-a` flag:

```
user@geeko:~> podman image rm -a
Untagged: registry.suse.com/bci/bci-base:16.0
Untagged: registry.suse.com/bci/bci-init:16.0
Untagged: registry.suse.com/bci/python:3.10
Deleted: eb1bf692b245784f0418fcd8d38caf4b5264577dfebbcbd470eb1f5f201e5c59
Deleted: 356a6fd6b2146484fc0df27ca9f738bbf055c353415b02e248e39e74578c2435
Deleted: 7e71f69c41a564de9eff39f99b4f1937b3b29fb0af6e6eeb99ebef8c712cc812
Deleted: 338b908d309b664578fd999cd4e79601a0745951b0e4781de5d8efd8c4523da9
user@geeko:~> podman image ls -a
REPOSITORY  TAG         IMAGE ID    CREATED     SIZE
```

You can run containers using `podman run -rm`, and the containers will be deleted automatically when they are no longer running. However, you won't be able to see logs or investigate anything in the container once it is deleted.

With this, you have a working understanding of containers and Podman. If you want to learn more about containers, try to go beyond the tutorials that you can find and package your own application, with configuration and a database. Use Dockerfiles to reproduce the steps, as you will find that you will have to modify the code and the container many times until it works as expected.

# Summary

In this chapter, we reviewed what containers are and the basic use of Podman. You can find and download images and create containers from them. You learned how to create a Dockerfile to automate the creation of images, and you went through the steps required to delete images and containers when you no longer needed.

Containers are a very interesting topic that requires more space and time. Feel free to investigate further and even start using SUSE Rancher for a full Kubernetes cluster.

In the next chapter, we will learn about SLES for SAP applications, a version of SLES 16 specifically created to run SAP in production.

# 18

# Introduction to SLES for SAP Applications

We are in the final chapters of the book. Until now, we have learned how to install and maintain a Linux system based on **SUSE Linux Enterprise Server (SLES)** 16. Perhaps you are wondering why you should choose one version of Linux over the other, or why you should choose Linux at all.

The answer is complex and depends on whether you want to run Linux on your laptop or want to install it on a server. For enterprise distributions, the choice is about uptime, security, and support life cycles.

**Enterprise resource planning** (ERP) is a kind of business software and technology that allows companies to automate and computerize their business processes. Organizations can use it to collect, store, manage, and interpret data from business activities. Many ERP systems also help to implement best practices and streamline compliance with legal and regulatory requirements, making them indispensable for big companies that need to collect and process greater amounts of data, consolidating the results of sales, orders, purchases, and revenues to provide unique insights into the business performance. For big companies, an ERP tool integrated into all systems is a requirement.

If one of your workloads uses an ERP tool, it is quite likely that you are using or will use SAP, and that you are running it on top of **SLES for SAP Applications**, a version of SLES that is optimized for SAP workloads. Let's see the difference between the standard SLES and SLES for SAP Applications to understand the improvements for specific workloads. The additional features will also give some ideas on how to choose the proper Linux distribution for your workloads.

**SAP©** was one of the first companies in the world to offer standard software for business solutions, specifically in the area of ERP. Many of the world's largest corporations use SAP products to manage their day-to-day operations and help with strategic planning, in finance, sales, human resources, or product planning.

SAP applications handle business-critical data, which is extremely sensitive and important for their customers' businesses, requiring fine-tuning and hardening to achieve adequate levels of performance and availability required by businesses today. SAP applications consolidate business and customer data into a single database, enabling advanced use cases but increasing the requirements on the full production stack, starting with the **operating system (OS)**.

The latest version of the SAP suite for business, SAP S/4HANA, requires the use of the SAP HANA database and a Linux OS.

You can find more information about SAP and SAP S/4HANA at their website: `https://www.sap.com/`.

SAP is likely the most common workload when using SLES, specifically because it is the gold standard for deploying SAP workloads. The tight integration between engineer teams and additional tools differentiates it from any other distribution, and the tools included will make your life as an administrator much easier.

We will be covering the following main topics in this chapter:

- SLES for SAP Applications
- Trento
- Tuning SLES for SAP
- Converting a SLES system to SLES for SAP Applications

Let's get started!

# Technical requirements

SLES for SAP Applications and its management are part of a different certification and require a separate license. Don't worry; this chapter is merely informative, and you won't need anything to go through it.

# SLES for SAP Applications

As the leading Linux platform for SAP NetWeaver, SAP HANA, and SAP S/4HANA, SLES for SAP Applications delivers reduced downtime, optimized performance, and faster SAP landscape deployments. This solution combines SLES and SUSE Linux Enterprise High Availability with additional software specifically designed to simplify the management and running of SAP applications. It includes features that secure SAP HANA systems and help systems administrators ease the transition to SAP S/4HANA.

Additionally, SLES for SAP Applications includes Live Patching, which ensures your systems have more time online without unplanned downtime by allowing you to update the Linux kernel without having to restart applications or reboot any server. This section provides an overview of important product updates, as well as the high-level general features, capabilities, and limitations of SLES for SAP Applications. You can learn more at the following link: `https://www.suse.com/products/sles-for-sap/`.

It also includes SUSE Multi-Linux Manager, an infrastructure management solution that automates patch and configuration management, reducing the risk of errors, as well as SUSE Linux Enterprise High Availability and SUSE Linux Enterprise Live Patching.

For highly regulated environments, SLES for SAP Applications inherits the security certifications of SLES to provide the only Linux OS certified for Common Criteria EAL4+ and FIPS 140-2, as a testimony of SUSE software supply chain security.

The SLES for SAP Applications life cycle and capabilities have been designed with real use cases in mind for your SAP workloads. Thus, it includes the extensions and capabilities you need by default. For instance, by knowing that changes in the OS need to be carefully tested and verified to follow SAP requirements, it allows you to stay longer in a defined version of SLES, as it includes long-term support, so you can keep your system updated and secure without requiring a migration to the newer minor version. Let's find out what the other capabilities are.

## Long-term support

Customers purchasing subscriptions directly from SUSE or SUSE partners can initiate support requests through regular SAP escalation channels, with SAP contacting SUSE if the request involves the OS. Each version of SLES for SAP Applications comes with 24x7 support, comprising 1.5 years of full support plus limited support for the remaining 3 years. This coverage eliminates the need for additional long-term support options and provides the stability required for SAP deployments, where upgrades require careful planning.

## Workload Memory Protection

One method to increase application availability is running it on more than one server, though this brings its own problems and limitations because data needs to be synchronized between machines. You can achieve high availability if you configure systems for real-time availability of SAP data using **Workload Memory Protection**. This shields SAP transactional and analytics data from Linux kernel memory management, ensuring the data remains in memory and is not written down into the cache, so it is never slowed down.

SUSE High Availability provides flexible, policy-driven clustering to your Linux data center, using open source technologies such as Pacemaker and Corosync to monitor services and restart or migrate them when necessary. SUSE High Availability also includes features for simplified management and data duplication, integrated in Trento.

The following figure shows the architecture of a High Availability deployment using these technologies:

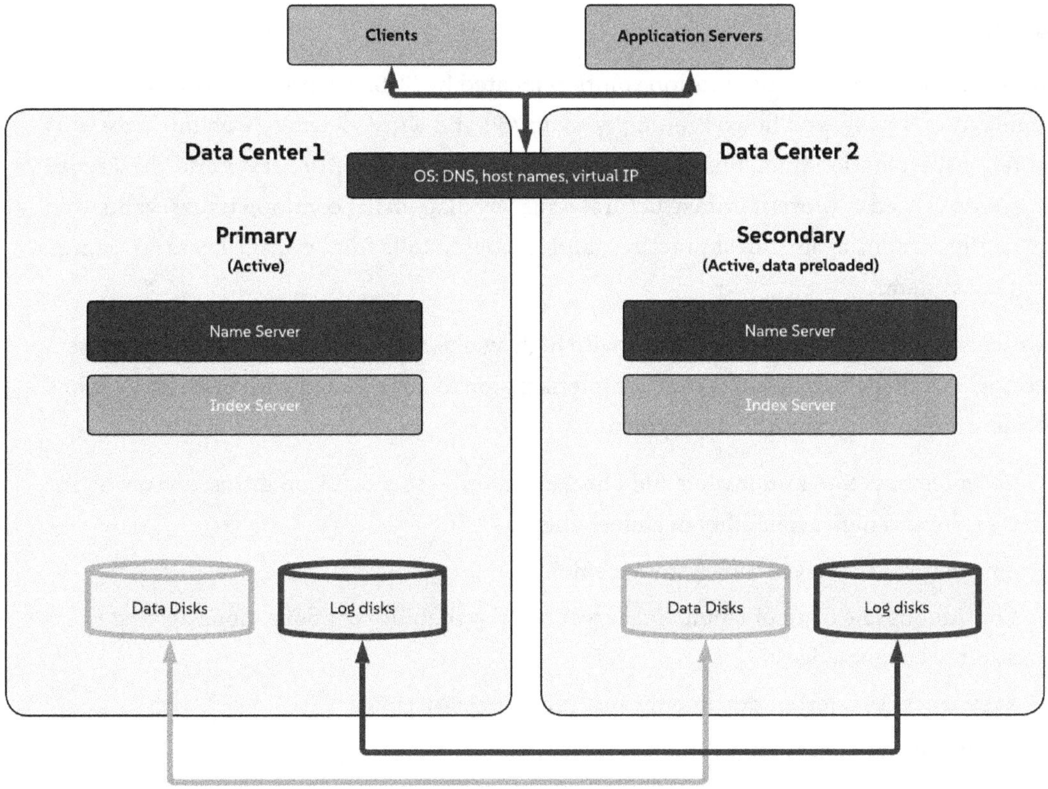


*Figure 18.1 – SLES for SAP Applications High Availability solution*

Let's find out how SLES for SAP Applications helps to increase uptime.

## SUSE Linux Enterprise Live Patching

Another way to increase availability is to reduce the downtime. But if you can't reboot the system, it is not possible to update some core libraries and the kernel, increasing the chances of running your systems in production with versions of packages that have known bugs and vulnerabilities.

Included with SLES 16 in all versions, Live Patching allows you to apply critical updates to the kernel and user-space libraries at runtime with no reboots or restarts. It eliminates the need for system reboots and application restarts, increasing service availability and allowing you to decide when you want to reboot.

Support for required features is important, but SLES for SAP Applications is more than documentation or the possibility to open a support case. Next, we will see tools that help maintain day-2 operations of SAP workloads.

## Trento

**Trento** is the SAP system administration solution created by SUSE to provide advanced discovery, tuning, monitoring, and housekeeping with an API and a user-friendly web interface. It is a comprehensive solution that consists of two components: the **Trento Server** and the **Trento Agent**. Trento is used to prevent infrastructural issues by diagnosing common issues, validating system configurations against best practices, and removing tolls from routine OS tasks on mission-critical systems.

Trento excels at identifying and fixing errors with high availability configurations and SAP system monitoring. It provides capabilities that complement the tools included with SAP Applications to provide a full view of your SAP deployment:

- Complements SAP monitoring and checking tools with a focus on infrastructure at the OS level and high availability of cluster checks
- Automatic discovery of SAP system elements
- Continuous checking of cloud and server high availability configurations against documented best practices
- Easy access to relevant documentation, including SAP Notes
- Recommended fixes
- Monitoring and alerting

The Trento Server is an independent, distributed system designed to run on a Kubernetes cluster or as a `systemd` service. It provides a web frontend for the application and consists of the following components:

- The control plane, a web component that renders the UI and is responsible for internal and external communications
- The checks engine (Wanda), which orchestrates the execution of configuration checks
- A PostgreSQL database
- The RabbitMQ message broker for communications
- A Prometheus instance for metric analysis

The Trento Server does not work on its own. In each server, a small application runs to provide a heartbeat and discovery of information about the target host. The Trento Agent is a `systemd` daemon on each monitored host of the SAP infrastructure that communicates with the Trento Server. Whenever your system stops reporting and updating, it will make sense to check the daemon log to ensure that it is working properly.

You can find more information about Trento on its GitHub page: `https://github.com/trento-project`.

The following picture shows the Trento architecture and components:

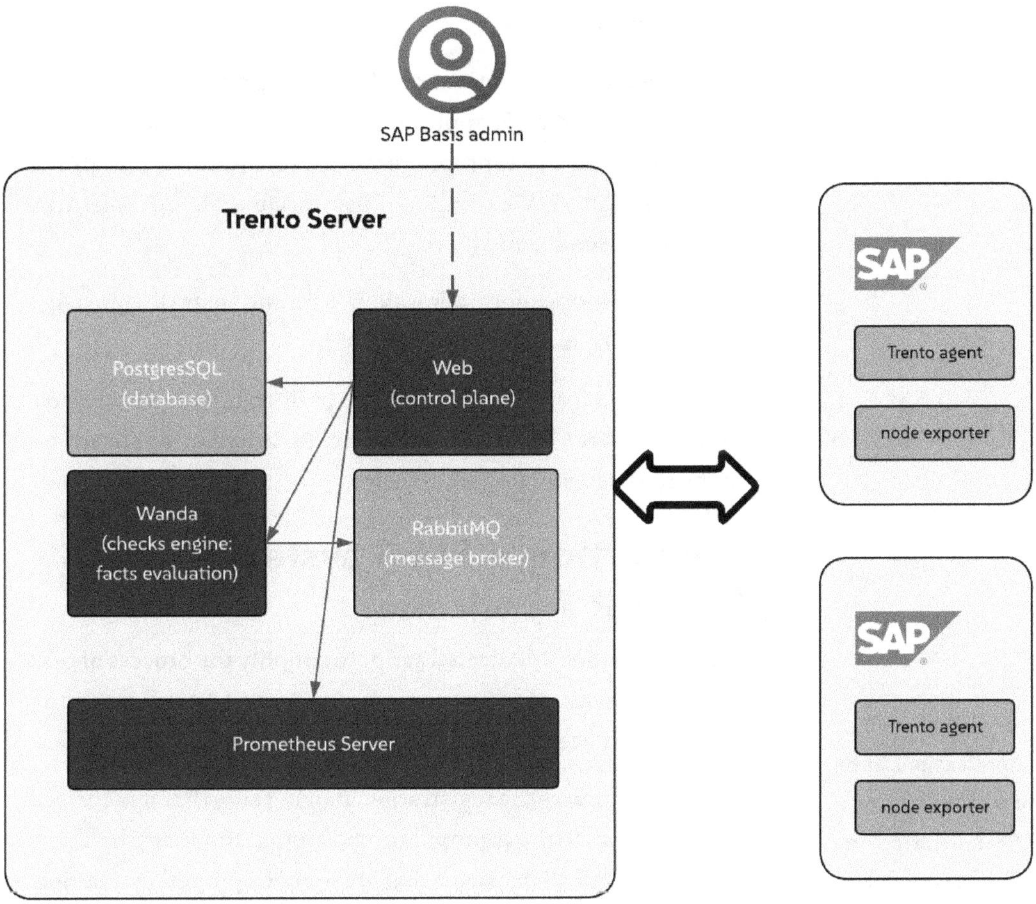


*Figure 18.2 – Trento architecture*

In the next section, we will learn about the tools included in SLES for SAP Applications to get the maximum performance of your server and application.

# Tuning SLES for SAP

Making SAP Applications work properly requires tuning to make sure that the OS can behave with the high level of performance and stability required to run SAP workloads.

SLES for SAP Applications includes **Saptune** to tune the OS to the specific requirements for running SAP workloads. System tuning is a mandatory step described in various SAP notes. Saptune groups those notes and offers solutions that address them, ensuring that no parameter is missed.

There are different solutions available that provide different tuning profiles. Tuning is application-dependent, so you can tune your system for the appropriate workload, including SAP HANA database, SAP NetWeaver, SAP BusinessObjects, SAP S/4HANA Application Server, and more.

You can find more information about Saptune on its GitHub page: `https://github.com/SUSE/saptune`.

Because SLES for SAP Applications is built on top of SAP, it is possible to convert a base SLES system into SLES for SAP Applications. In the next section, we will see how.

## Converting a SLES system to SLES for SAP Applications

SLES 16 includes a dedicated script to simplify the process of converting an existing SLES system into SLES for SAP Applications. It is called `Migrate_SLES_to_SLES-for-SAP.sh`.

> Remember that the SLES for SAP Applications subscription is different from your SLES subscription. You will need to purchase a new subscription to make the transition.

The script updates the registration, making sure that it is correct, and subscribes to the appropriate repositories. However, the script does not install all packages that are part of a proper installation (you can install them yourself by installing the `patterns-server-enterprise-sap_server` pattern). Be careful with pay-as-you-go instances in public clouds, as this script migrates the repositories, but it does not affect the way the system is identified by the cloud provider, so it can be ineffective.

# Summary

SLES for SAP Applications is a SAP-endorsed app, a proven solution to complement and extend SAP products that delivers value quickly, easily, and with support from SAP. Most of the SAP applications running on Linux run on SUSE, as SLES for SAP Applications includes extensions that improve performance, availability, and security.

SLES for SAP Applications includes entitlements and solutions to simplify your SAP deployments' day 0, 1, and 2 operations, from configuration checks to active monitoring and automated deployment. It includes Trento, along with Live Patching and High Availability extensions, and an extended life cycle that allows you to confidently deploy and maintain your SAP environment on-premises or in the cloud.

In the next two chapters, we will finish the book with practice exercises that will put everything we have learned so far into practice. Make sure to go through them so that you are confident that you are ready for your test.

# Part 5

# Practice Exercises

This part comprises practical exercises to review what was learned in the previous parts. It contains an intermediate practice exercise and a more advanced one, letting you assess your status.

This part has the following chapters:


- *Chapter 19, Practice Exercises – 1*
- *Chapter 20, Practice Exercises – 2*

# 19

# Practice Exercises – 1

In this chapter, we will go through a set of exercises to check the knowledge you've acquired through this book. Unlike in the main chapters, not all steps will be indicated, and it's left to you to perform the steps required to accomplish the goals. It is recommended not to check the relevant chapters for guidance and instead to try to use your memory or the tools available on the system. This experience will be a key factor when attempting the official SUSE Certified Architect exams.

It is strongly advised to start this exercise with a timer to keep track of the time it takes to complete it. Execution speed will be key to passing the exam and obtaining the certification.

## Technical requirements

All the practice exercises in this chapter require a **virtual machine** (**VM**) running SUSE Linux Enterprise Server 16 installed with the base installation, as described in *Chapter 1, Getting SLES 16 Up and Running (Physical and Cloud)*. Additionally, new virtual drives will be required for storage operations.

The exercises assume you have the following:

- SUSE Linux Enterprise Server 16 installed with **Minimal Install** selected
- Access to the SUSE Customer Center (`https://scc.suse.com`) with an active subscription (i.e., a trial subscription)
- The VM must be expendable; that is, actions performed on it might render it unusable and it will need to be reinstalled or rolled back to an earlier snapshot

# Tips for the exercise

This is a list of general recommendations for any test. They are mostly common sense, but it's always useful to have them in our minds before taking a test:

- Read all the questions carefully before starting. Specific words have specific meanings that give hints about the requirements or ways to accomplish the goals; that's why reading everything carefully first is important.
- Make yourself comfortable, install your favorite editor (such as Vim), and define your keyboard layout. Install and learn the basics of `tmux` so that you can open new tabs and name them without requiring extra windows.
- Locate dependencies between requests. Some goals depend on others for completion. Find those dependencies to see how you can build up the solution without having to come back and redo some steps because of having taken the wrong path.
- Use a timer. It's important to get an idea of which parts of the exercise took longer to complete to see what can be improved.
- Don't remember specific command lines; learn how to use the documentation available in the system via `man`, `/usr/share/doc/packages` arguments such as `--help` for the commands, and so on.
- Ensure that changes persist and are still active after a reboot. Some changes might be active while you run them, but they must be persisted, such as firewall rules and services to start at boot.
- Remember that you can use `zypper search --provides "*/COMMAND"` to find packages that provide a file that you might be missing.
- Visit `https://www.suse.com/training/exam/sca-sles-16/` for the official **SUSE Certified Administrator** (**SCA**) exam objectives.

# Practice exercise 1

> By design, in the following exercise, there will be no styles on commands, packages, and so on. Remember what you've learned so far to detect the keywords to see what needs to be done.

Don't jump into completing the exercise too early. Try to think and remember what was covered.

Here are the steps of this exercise:

1. Configure the time zone to GMT.
2. Allow passwordless login to the root user using SSH.
3. Create a user named tux that can connect to the machine without a password.
4. The user tux should change their password every week, with two days' warning and one day of usage once the password has expired.
5. The root user must be able to SSH as tux without a password.
6. tux should be able to become root without a password and execute commands without a password too.
7. When a user tries to log in over SSH, display a message about not allowing unauthorized access to our system.
8. Make a pre snapshot named pre-ssh.
9. SSH must listen on port 2222 instead of the default (22) one.
10. Make a post snapshot named post-ssh associated with the snapshot named pre-ssh. Then, check the files that have changed and add them to /root/ssh-files-changed.txt. Finally, note the differences and save them to /root/ssh-changes.txt.
11. Create a group named devel.
12. Make tux a member of devel.
13. Store user membership to a file called userids in the home folder for tux.
14. tux should be able to connect to localhost via SSH without specifying the port and use compression by default for the connection.
15. Find, as tux, all man page names in the system and put the names into a file named man-pages.txt in your home directory.
16. As root, store usernames for users without login permissions to the system in a file called /root/nologin.txt.
17. Monitor available system resources every five minutes. Do not use cron. Save output as /root/resources.log.
18. Create a script to report the available percentage of free disk space and store it in /root/freespace.log so that it shows the filesystem and free space.
19. Configure the system to only leave three days of logs.
20. Configure the log rotation for /root/freespace.log and /root/resources.log.

21. Configure time synchronization against pool.ntp.org with fast sync.
22. Provide NTP server services for subnet 192.168.122.1/24.
23. Configure system stats collection every minute.
24. Configure the password length in the system for users to be 12 characters.
25. Create a bot user called privacy that has files that are only visible to it by default.
26. Create a folder called /shared that can be accessed by all users and, by default, allows all new files and directories to still be accessible to users of the devel group.
27. Configure a network connection with IPv4 and IPv6 addressing named mynic using the following data:
    - Ip6: 2001:db8:0:1::c000:207/64 g
    - gateway 2001:db8:0:1::1
    - Ipv4 192.0.1.3/24
    - gateway 192.0.1.1
28. Allow the host to use the google hostname to reach `www.google.com` and the suse hostname to reach `www.suse.com`.
29. Report the files that are different from what the vendor distributed and store them in /root/altered.txt.
30. Make our system installation media packages available via HTTP at /mirror for other systems to use it as a mirror, configure the repository in our system, and remove the kernel packages from that mirror so that other systems (even ours) can't find new kernels. Ignore the glibc packages from installation from this repository without removing them.
31. Check whether our system conforms to the PCI-DSS standard.
32. Add a second hard drive with 30 GB of space with LVM to the system, but use only 15 GB to move the mirror to it, making it available at boot in /mirror/mirror.
33. Create a second copy of the mirror in /mirror/mytailormirror, removing all packages starting with the letter k.
34. Create a new volume in the remaining space of the added hard drive (15 GB) and use it to extend the mirror filesystem.

In the next section, we'll list the goals and provide an explanation below each of them using proper syntax styles and explanations.

# Exercise 1 solution

## 1. Configure the time zone to GMT

We can check the current system date by executing `date` as the very last part of the printed line, which will show the time zone. To configure it, we can use the `timedatectl` command or alter the `/etc/localtime` symbolic link.

So, to complete this task, we can use either of the following:

- `timedatectl set-timezone GMT`
- `rm -fv /etc/localtime; ln -s /usr/share/zoneinfo/GMT /etc/localtime`

Now, `date` should report the correct time zone.

## 2. Allow passwordless login to the root user using SSH

This short goal has several requirements:

- SSH must be installed and available (that means installed and started)
- The `root` user should have an SSH key generated and added to the list of authorized keys

First, let's tackle SSH:

```
sudo zypper install openssh-server;
sudo systemctl enable --now sshd
```

Now, let's generate an SSH key by pressing *Enter* to accept all of the defaults:

```
ssh-keygen
```

Now, let's add the generated key (`/root/.ssh/id_rsa`) to the authorized keys:

```
sudo -i
cd /root/.ssh
cat id_rsa.pub >> authorized_keys
chmod 600 authorized_keys
```

To validate this, we can execute `ssh localhost date`, and we will be able to get the current system date and time without providing a password.

## 3. Create a user named tux that can connect to the machine without a password

This requires creating a user and an SSH key that is added to authorized keys, similar to what we did with the root user. The next options will also be relevant to a user but, for the purpose of demonstration, we will tackle them as separate tasks. Let's start by creating the tux user and impersonating it:

```
sudo -i
useradd tux
su - tux
```

Now, let's generate an SSH key by typing the following and pressing *Enter* to accept all defaults:

```
ssh-keygen
```

Now, let's add the generated key to the authorized keys:

```
cd ~/.ssh
cat id_ed255219.pub >> authorized_keys
chmod 600 authorized_keys
```

To validate this, we can execute `ssh tux@localhost whoami`, and we will be able to get the current system date and time without providing a password.

You should enter `logout` to return to our `root` user.

## 4. The user tux should change their password every week, with two days' warning and one day of usage once the password has expired

This requires us to tune the user restrictions:

```
chage -W 2 tux
chage -I 1 tux
chage -M 7 tux
```

## 5. The root user must be able to SSH as tux without a password

This requires two steps: enabling `user` with `root's` authorized key and tuning the `sshd` daemon:

```
cat /home/tux/id_ed25519.pub >> /root/.ssh/authorized_keys
```

## 6. tux should be able to become root without a password and execute commands without a password too

This means creating a file called `/etc/sudoers.d/tux` and adding this line:

```
tux ALL=(ALL) NOPASSWD:ALL
```

## 7. When a user tries to log in over SSH, display a message about not allowing unauthorized access to our system

Create a file, for example, `/etc/ssh/banner`, with the message to display, such as `Unauthorized access forbidden. Get out of here`. Then create a file called `/etc/ssh/sshd_config.d/banner.conf` with the following content:

```
Banner /etc/ssh/banner
```

Then, restart the `sshd` daemon with `systemctl restart sshd`.

## 8. Make a pre snapshot named pre-ssh

This is a very simple one. We can become `root`, the administrative account, by running `sudo -i`.

Then, we just run `snapper create -t pre -d "pre-ssh"`.

We can then run `snapper list` to verify that the snapshot has been created properly.

## 9. SSH must listen on port 2222 instead of the default (22) one

This is a tricky one. The first task is to create `/etc/ssh/sshd_config.d/new-port.conf` and define port 2222. To do that, the content of the file should be as follows:

```
Port 2222
```

Once you've done this, restart `sshd` with the following command:

```
systemctl restart sshd
```

Let's check that it's listening on the right port:

```
lsof -i -n -P
```

This, of course, is not enough to be able to connect to `ssh` via port 2222. Why?

The firewall must be configured:

```
firewall-cmd --add-port=2222/tcp --permanent
firewall-cmd --add-port=2222/tcp
```

SELinux must also be configured:

```
semanage port -a -t ssh_port_t -p tcp 2222
```

Now, `sshd` can be restarted:

```
systemctl restart sshd
```

## 10. Make a post snapshot named post-ssh associated with the snapshot named pre-ssh. Then, check the files that have changed and add them to /root/ssh-files-changed.txt. Finally, note the differences and save them to /root/ssh-changes.txt

As `root`, we can create the snapshot easily by running `snapper create`. But first, we need to run `snapper list` to get the `pre` snapshot. In this example, the `pre` snapshot is `81`:

```
geeko:~ # snapper list | grep pre-ssh
81 | pre | Sun Oct 19 16:28:46 2025 | root | 304.00 KiB | pre-ssh
```

Now, we can create the snapshot with the following command:

```
geeko:~ # snapper create -d "post-ssh" -t post --pre-number 81
```

We can verify the creation by running `snapper list`. In this example, the new snapshot is number 82.

Now it's time to check the differences. We can do this with `snapper status` and send the output to the requested file, `/root/ssh-files-changed.txt`:

```
geeko:~ # snapper status 81..82 > /root/ssh-files-changed.txt
```

To see the differences in content, we use `snapper diff`:

```
geeko:~ # snapper diff 81..82 > /root/ssh-changes.txt
```

And we are done!

## 11. Create a group named devel

We only need to use groupadd to create this group:

```
groupadd devel
```

## 12. Make tux a member of devel

To make a user a member of a group, we use usermod. Note the -a option, which adds a group and keeps the rest of the groups assigned to the user as they are. The final command is as follows:

```
usermod -aG devel tux
```

## 13. Store user membership to a file called userids in the home folder for tux

To get user membership, we use the id command, redirecting the output to a file named userids in the home directory with the following command:

```
id tux > /home/tux/userids
```

## 14. tux should be able to connect to localhost via SSH without specifying the port and compression by default for the connection

We altered the default SSH port to be 2222.

Create a file named .ssh/config for the tux user with the following contents including the new port and the option Compression set to yes to activate compression by default to the connection:

```
Host localhost
Port 2222
    Compression yes
```

## 15. Find, as tux, all man page names in the system and put the names into a file named manpages.txt in your home directory

Become tux if you are root:

```
su - tux
```

Man pages are stored in `/usr/share/man`; so to list all the man pages, we have to run the `find` command. Then we redirect the output to the required file as follows:

```
find  /usr/share/man/ -type f > /home/tux/manpages.txt
```

## 16. As root, store usernames for users without login permissions to the system in a file called /root/nologin.txt

We can run a search using `grep` and create a file with the changes. This can be done with the following command:

```
grep nologin /etc/passwd > /root/nologin
```

The preceding command builds a list of users in the system with the `nologin` shell.

We can clean up the unneeded information using `cut`:

```
grep nologin /etc/passwd | cut -d: -f 1 > /root/nologin
```

In the preceding command, we use `-d` to select the delimiter and `-f` to select the field to keep.

## 17. Monitor available system resources every five minutes. Do not use cron. Store as /root/resources.log

An ideal way to monitor something is to use `cron`, but we're told not to use it, so this leaves us with `systemd` timers (you can check out the files tested at `https://github.com/PacktPublishing/SUSE-Linux-Enterprise-Server-16-Official-Administration-Guide/tree/main/chapter-19-exercises/exercise-17`).

Create `/etc/systemd/system/monitorresources.service` with the following contents:

```
[Unit]
Description=Monitor system resources

[Service]
Type=oneshot
ExecStart=/root/myresources.sh
```

Create `/etc/systemd/system/monitorresources.timer` with the following contents:

```
[Unit]
Description=Monitor system resources

[Timer]
```

```
OnCalendar=*:0/5
Persistent=true

[Install]
WantedBy=timers.target
```

Create `/root/myresources.sh` with the following contents:

```
#!/bin/bash
df -h > /root/resources.log
```

Enable the new timer:

```
systemctl daemon-reload
systemctl enable  monitorresources.timer
```

Does it work? No... `journalctl -f` will give us some details: SELinux prevents executing a root file; let's label it as a binary type and let's mark it executable too:

```
chcon -t bin_t /root/myresources.sh
chmod +x /root/myresources.sh
```

# 18. Create a script to report the available percentage of free disk space and store it in /root/freespace.log so that it shows the filesystem and free space

`df` reports used disk space and available space, so we need to do some math.

This command will report the mounted location, size, used space, and available space with `;` as the separator:

```
df|awk '{print $6";"$2";"$3";"$4}'
```

Bash allows us to do some math operations, but without fractional parts. We will need to do a trick.

We will be looping over the mounted partitions/subvolumes:

```
for each in $(df|awk '{print $6";"$2";"$3";"$4}'|grep -v "Mounted")
do
    FREE=$(echo $each|cut -d ";" -f 4)
    TOTAL=$(echo $each|cut -d ";" -f 2)
    echo "$each has $((FREE*100/TOTAL)) free"
done
```

The `for` loop will check all the available data and grab some specific fields, separate them with `;`, and run the loop for each line that contains the list of partitions/subvolumes, stored in the `$each` variable.

We cut the output and we get the fourth field, which is the available space.

We cut the output and we get the second field, which is the total blocks.

As Bash can do integer division, we multiply by 100 and then divide to get the percentage and add a string as part of the output.

Alternatively, but not as illustrative, we could have discounted to 100 the percentage of used already given by using the `df` command.

We also need to store that output in a file, so we can either wrap the whole loop in a redirection or add it to the `echo` line so that it is appended to a file.

Create a `/root/myfreespace.sh` script with the following contents:

```
for each in $(df|awk '{print $6";"$2";"$3";"$4}'|grep -v "Mounted")
do
    FREE=$(echo $each|cut -d ";" -f 4)
    TOTAL=$(echo $each|cut -d ";" -f 2)
    echo "$each has $((FREE*100/TOTAL)) free"
done
```

Then, run `chmod 755 /root/myfreespace.sh` to make it executable.

## 19. Configure the system to only leave three days of logs

Create a file called `/etc/logrotate.d/three-days` and add the following contents:

```
daily
rotate 3
```

## 20. Configure the log rotation for /root/freespace.log and /root/resources.log

Create a file called `/etc/logrotate.d/rotateroot` with the following contents:

```
/root/freespace.log {
    missingok
    notifempty
    sharedscripts
```

```
    copytruncate
}
/root/resources.log {
    missingok
    notifempty
    sharedscripts
    copytruncate
}
```

## 21. Configure time synchronization against pool.ntp.org with fast sync

Edit `/etc/chrony.d/pool.conf` and add the following line:

```
pool pool.ntp.org iburst
```

Then, run the following:

```
systemctl restart chronyd
```

## 22. Provide NTP server services for subnet 192.168.122.1/24

Edit `/etc/chrony.d/subnet.conf` and add the following line:

```
Allow 192.168.122.1/24
```

Then, run the following:

```
systemctl restart chronyd
```

## 23. Configure system stats collection every minute

Start by installing `sysstat`:

```
zypper install sysstat
```

We now need to modify `/usr/lib/systemd/system/sysstat-collect.timer`, so let's create an override.

Edit in `/etc/systemd/system/sysstat-collect.timer.d/` the file `override.conf` with the following content:

```
[Timer]
OnCalendar=*:00/1
```

You can also use `systemctl edit sysstat-collect.timer` to modify the behavior.

Then, reload units with this command:

```
systemctl daemon-reload
```

## 24. Configure the password length in the system for users to be 12 characters

Create `/etc/login.defs.d/99-pass-min-len.conf` with the following content:

```
PASS_MIN_LEN 12
```

## 25. Create a bot user called privacy that has files that are only visible to it by default

```
useradd privacy
su - privacy
echo "umask 0077" >> .bashrc
```

This solution uses `umask` to remove permissions from others on all newly created files.

## 26. Create a folder called /shared that can be accessed by all users and, by default, allows new files and directories to still be accessible to users of the devel group

This is a pretty simple one. We start by creating the folder, then change the owner group and permissions, and finally add the sticky bit to change the default behavior. The commands are as follows:

```
mkdir /shared
chown root:devel /shared
chmod 777 /shared
chmod +s /shared
```

# 27. Configure a network connection with IPv4 and IPv6 addressing named mynic using the given data

Let's use `nmcli` for this. We will need to check all the options in the man page and then we will run the following command:

```
nmcli con add con-name mynic type ethernet ifname eth0 ipv6.address
2001:db8:0:1::c000:207/64 ipv6.gateway 2001:db8:0:1::1 ipv4.address
192.0.1.3/24 ipv4.gateway 192.0.1.1
```

Of course, you can also use `nmtui` or Cockpit.

# 28. Allow the host to use the google hostname to reach www.google.com and the suse hostname to reach www.suse.com

Run the following commands and record the IPs obtained:

```
ping www.google.com
ping www.suse.com
```

Then, edit `/etc/hosts` by adding the following:

```
IPFORGOOGLE google
IPFORSUSE suse
```

Save and exit.

As an example, my results were as follows:

```
172.64.155.66  suse
142.250.185.4  google
```

## 29. Report the files that are different from what the vendor distributed and store them in /root/altered.txt

Checking the options for `rpm` in the man page will take us to the following command:

```
rpm -Va > /root/altered.txt
```

## 30. Make our system installation media packages available via HTTP at /mirror for other systems to use it as a mirror, configure the repository in our system, and remove the kernel packages from that mirror so that other systems (even ours) can't find new kernels. Ignore the glibc packages from installation from this repository without removing them

This is a complex one, so let's analyze the request.

Install `httpd` and enable it:

```
zypper install httpd
firewall-cmd  --add-service=http --permanent
firewall-cmd  --add-service=http
systemctl start apache2
systemctl enable apache2
```

Create a folder under `/mirror`, copy the source media packages, and make the mentioned folder available over HTTP:

```
mkdir /mirror /srv/www/htdocs/mirror
mount /dev/cdrom /mnt
rsync -avr -progress /mnt/ /mirror/
mount -o bind /mirror /srv/www/htdocs/mirror
chcon  -R -t httpd_sys_content_t /srv/www/htdocs/mirror/
```

Remove the kernel packages:

```
find /mirror -name kernel* -exec rm '{}' \;
```

Create the repository files' metadata:

```
zypper in createrepo
cd /mirror
createrepo .
```

Now we need to create a repofile using the repository we created and set it up in our system, ignoring `glibc*` packages from it.

Edit `/etc/zypp/repos.d/mymirror.repo` with the following contents:

```
[mymirror]
name=My SLES16 Mirror
baseurl=http://localhost/mirror/
enabled=1
gpgcheck=0
exclude=glibc*
```

## 31. Check whether our system conforms to the PCI-DSS standard

We can check this with `openscap`. We will need at least 16 GB of RAM. It can be done with the following commands:

```
zypper install openscap  scap-security-guide openscap-utils
oscap xccdf eval --fetch-remote-resources --report pci-dss-report.html
--profile pci-dss-4 /usr/share/xml/scap/ssg/content/ssg-sle15-ds.xml
```

## 32. Add a second hard drive with 30 GB of space with LVM to the system, but use only 15 GB to move the mirror to it, making it available at boot in /mirror/mirror

We need to move the mirror we currently have to a new disk and copy all the content from the old mirror to the newly created space.

We also need a new drive. You can add it in the VM manager or follow the instructions in *Chapter 12, Managing Local Storage and Filesystems.*

If we've the installed media, we can choose to copy it over and repeat the kernel removal or transfer. To do this, first let's create the `newmirror` volume in a partition in our new hard drive (`sdb`):

```
fdisk /dev/sdb
n <enter>
p <enter>
1 <enter>
<enter>
+15G <enter>
w <enter>
```

This will create a partition of 15 GB from the start. Let's create LVM objects on it:

```
pvcreate /dev/sdb1
vgcreate newmirror /dev/sdb1
lvcreate -L 15G -n myvol newmirror
mkfs.xfs /dev/newmirror/myvol
# Let's umount cdrom if it was still mounted
umount /mnt
# Mount newmirror under /mnt and copy files over
mount /dev/newmirror/myvol /mnt
rsync -avr -progress /mirror/ /mnt/mirror/
# Delete the original mirror once copy has finished
rm -Rfv /mirror
umount /mnt
mount /dev/newmirror/myvol /mirror
```

At this point, the old mirror was copied into a folder called `mirror` on the VDO volume, which is mounted in `/mirror`, so we have the original mirror in `/mirror/mirror` as requested. We might need to do the following:

- Bind mount `/mirror` to `/var/www/html/mirror/` to make the file available
- Restore SELinux context to allow `httpd` access to files in `/var/www/html/mirror/`

Adjust the repofile we created to point to the new path.

# 33. Create a second copy of the mirror in /mirror/mytailormirror, removing all packages starting with the letter k

We can run synchronization and then clean up. Finally, create indexes. This can be done with the following commands:

```
rsync -avr -progress /mirror/mirror/ /mirror/mytailormirror/
find /mirror/mytailormirror/ -name "k*" -type f -exec rm '{}' \;
cd /mirror/mytailormirror/
createrepo .
```

## 34. Create a new volume in the remaining space of the added hard drive (15 GB) and use it to extend the mirror filesystem

Let's create the partitions and use the LVM commands to extend the disk:

```
fdisk /dev/sdb
n <enter>
p <enter>
<enter>
<enter>
w <enter>
pvcreate /dev/sdb2
# run vgscan to find out the volume name to use
vgextend newmirror /dev/sdb2
# run lvscan to find out the LV storing the root filesystem and pvscan to
find the maximum available space
lvresize -L +15G /dev/newmirror/myvol
```

That's it! Let's move on to some more exercises in the next chapter.

# 20

# Practice Exercises – 2

In this second practice exercise chapter, we will go through an exercise to check the knowledge you have acquired through this book. Unlike in the main chapters, not all steps will be indicated, and it's left to you to perform the steps required to accomplish the goals. It is recommended not to check the relevant chapters for guidance and instead try to use your memory or the tools available in the system. This experience will be a key factor when attempting the official SUSE Certified Architect exams.

It is strongly advised to start this exercise with a timer to keep track of the time used to complete it. Execution speed will be key to passing the exam and obtaining the certification.

## Technical requirements

The exercise in this chapter requires a **virtual machine** (**VM**) running SUSE Linux Enterprise Server 16 installed with the base installation, as described in *Chapter 1, Getting SLES 16 Up and Running (Physical and Cloud)*. Additionally, new virtual drives will be required for storage operations.

The exercises assume you have the following:

- SUSE Linux Enterprise Server 16 installed with **Minimal Install** selected
- Access to the SUSE Customer Center (`https://scc.suse.com`) with an active subscription (i.e., a trial subscription)
- The VM must be expendable; that is, actions performed on it might render it unusable and should be reinstalled or rolled back to an earlier snapshot

## Tips for the exercise

This is a list of general recommendations for any test. They are mostly common sense, but it's always useful to have them in our minds before taking a test:

- Read all the questions carefully before starting. Specific words have specific meanings that give hints about the requirements or ways to accomplish the goals; that's why reading everything carefully first is important.
- Make yourself comfortable, install your favorite editor (such as Vim), and define your keyboard layout. Install and learn the basics of how to use `tmux` so that you can open new tabs and name them without requiring extra windows.
- Locate dependencies between requests. Some goals depend on others for completion. Find those dependencies to see how you can build up the solution without having to come back and redo some steps because of having taken the wrong path.
- Use a timer. It's important to get an idea of which part of the exercises took longer to complete to see what can be improved.
- Don't memorize specific command lines. Learn how to use the documentation available in the system via `man`, `/usr/share/doc/packages` arguments such as `--help` for the commands, and so on.
- Ensure that changes persist and are still active after a reboot. Some changes might be active while you run them, but they must be persisted: firewall rules, services to start at boot, and so on.
- Remember that you can use `zypper search --provides "*/COMMAND"` to find packages that provide that file that you might be missing.
- Check out `https://www.suse.com/training/exam/sca-sles-16/` for the official SCA exam objectives.

## Practice exercise 2

> By design, in the following exercises, there will be no styles on commands, packages, and so on. Remember what you've learned so far to detect the keywords to see what needs to be done.

Don't jump into completing the exercise too early. Try to think and remember what was covered.

Here are the steps of this exercise:

1. Download the file from the repository.
2. Use the users.txt file to generate users in the system automatically using the values provided in the following order: username, placeholder, uid, gid, name, home, shell.
3. Create a group named susers and add it as the primary group for all users, leaving their own groups, named for each user, as secondary groups.
4. Change the home folders for the users so that they are group-owned.
5. Set up an HTTP server and enable a web page for each user with a small introduction text for each one that is different for each user.
6. Allow all users in the susers group to become root without a password.
7. Create SSH keys for each user and add each key to root and to the other users so that each user can SSH as the other users without a password.
8. Disable password access to the system with SSH.
9. Set each user with a different password using /dev/random and store the passwords in the second field of the users.txt file.
10. If the number of letters in the username is a multiple of 2, add that fact to each user description web page.
11. Create a container that runs the yq Python package as the entry point.
12. Configure password ageing for users whose user id is not a multiple of 2 to expiring.
13. Configure daily compressed log rotation for a month of logs using date-named files.
14. Save all the logs generated during the current day in /root/errors.log.
15. Install all available updates for system libraries.
16. Repair the broken rpm binary using a previously downloaded package available in the /root folder.
17. Make all processes in execution by user miguel run with a low priority, and the processes executed by sonia run with a higher priority (+/- 5).
18. Make the system run with the highest throughput and performance.
19. Change the system network interface to use one higher IP address than it was using. Add an additional IPv6 address to the same interface.
20. Create and add /opt/mysystem/bin/ to the system path for all users.
21. Create a firewall zone, assign it to an interface, and make it the default zone.
22. Add a repository hosted at https://myserver.com/repo/ with a GPG key at `https://myserver.com/mygpg.key` to the system.

# Exercise 2 solution

In this section, we'll discuss each step and provide an explanation using the correct styles and explanations.

## 1. Download the file from the repository

This is the repository: `https://raw.githubusercontent.com/PacktPublishing/SUSE-Linux-Enterprise-Server-16-Official-Administration-Guide/refs/heads/main/chapter-20-exercises/exercise-2/users.txt`.

You can download the file using `wget`, as shown in the following command:

```
wget https://raw.githubusercontent.com/PacktPublishing/SUSE-Linux-
Enterprise-Server-16-Official-Administration-Guide/refs/heads/main/
chapter-20-exercises/exercise-2/users.txt
```

## 2. Use the users.txt file to generate users in the system automatically using the values provided in the following order: username, placeholder, uid, gid, name, home, shell

First, let's examine the `users.txt` file:

```
geeko:~ # cat users.txt
sonia;x;1000;1000; Sonia;/home/sonia1; /bin/false
matilde ;x ;1001 ;1001; Mati; /home/mati ;/bin/false
miguel ;x ;1001 ;1001; Miguel; /home/mig ; /bin/csh
sergio ;x ;1011 ;1011; Sergio Jones; /home/sjones ; /bin/rsh
pilgrim ;x ;2011 ;2011; Scott Pilgrim; /home/spilgrim ; /bin/rsh
laverne; x ; 2020;2020; LaVerne;/home/LaVerne;/bin/bash
```

As described in the request, the fields in that file are `username`, `placeholder`, `uid`, `gid`, `name`, `home`, and `shell`. The `placeholder` is not requested when creating a user (the only field that is usually requested is the password), so we can work with the other data and ignore that.

As we can also see, each field is separated by at least a ; symbol, but some have extra spaces before or after it. As we have names with surnames, we can't just remove all spaces; we need to remove them only before and after the actual text we want.

Let's use `cut` with the field separator of ; to do the work. But first, we need to read it line by line.

We can achieve that with the built-in read Bash function:

```
cat users.txt|while read -r line; do echo ${line};done
```

Using this as a base, we can then start building up everything we're going to need to create the users. Let's start by working on the individual steps and later build up the full command line.

For each line we have, we need to define the fields and remove the ending/starting spaces:

```
NEWUSERNAME=$(echo ${line}|cut -d ";" -f 1)
NEWUID=$(echo ${line}|cut -d ";" -f 3)
NEWNAME=$(echo ${line}|cut -d ";" -f 5)
NEWSHELL=$(echo ${line}|cut -d ";" -f 6)
```

In these examples, we're echoing each line and cutting on the field specified with -f using a field delimiter of ; so that we can select the field containing the data we're looking for. To make it easier, we store each snippet in a variable so that it's easier for us to reuse that snippet of code and still have a clear understanding of what each script will be doing.

The preceding code will work, *but* it will fail with the spaces, so we need to extend it to capture the text without the spaces. Let's use xargs for that:

```
NEWUSERNAME=$(echo ${line}|cut -d ";" -f 1|xargs)
NEWUID=$(echo ${line}|cut -d ";" -f 3|xargs)
NEWNAME=$(echo ${line}|cut -d ";" -f 5|xargs)
NEWHOME=$(echo ${line}|cut -d ";" -f 6|xargs)
NEWSHELL=$(echo ${line}|cut -d ";" -f 7|xargs)
```

The next step is to build the command line for adding a user:

```
useradd -d "${NEWHOME}" -m -s "${NEWSHELL}" -u "${NEWUID}" -U -c
"${NEWNAME}" "${NEWUSERNAME}"
```

Great! We're ready; let's build the solution:

```
cat users.txt| while read -r line ; do
NEWUSERNAME=$(echo ${line}|cut -d ";" -f 1|xargs)
NEWUID=$(echo ${line}|cut -d ";" -f 3|xargs)
NEWNAME=$(echo ${line}|cut -d ";" -f 5|xargs)
NEWHOME=$(echo ${line}|cut -d ";" -f 6|xargs)
NEWSHELL=$(echo ${line}|cut -d ";" -f 7|xargs)
useradd -d "${NEWHOME}" -m -s "${NEWSHELL}" -u "${NEWUID}" -U -c
"${NEWNAME}" "${NEWUSERNAME}"
done
```

We run this directly in the command line, but we can also create a script named `autouseradd.sh` with the `#!/bin/bash` header and run it from there (do not forget to make it executable with `chmod +x`).

To make the previous exercise work, you will need to install the `tcsh` and `fish` packages to have the shells used by users.

An example of the solution can be found here: `https://github.com/PacktPublishing/SUSE-Linux-Enterprise-Server-16-Official-Administration-Guide/blob/main/chapter-20-exercises/exercise-2/autouseradd.sh`.

## 3. Create a group named susers and add it as the primary group for all users, leaving their own groups, named for each user, as secondary groups

In this case, we need to create the groups that we didn't create in the previous step, so we will loop over the users once the new group has been created, create new groups for each one, and then modify each user to join the `susers` group and add their own group as a secondary group:

```
groupadd susers
cat users.txt| while read -r line ; do
NEWUSERNAME=$(echo ${line}|cut -d ";" -f 1|xargs)
usermod -g susers -G ${NEWUSERNAME} ${NEWUSERNAME}
done
```

## 4. Change the home folders for the users so that they are group-owned

Let's parse the file users using a `while` loop, then capture variables, and finally, execute `chown`:

```
cat users.txt| while read -r line ; do
NEWUSERNAME=$(echo ${line}|cut -d ";" -f 1|xargs)
NEWHOME=$(echo ${line}|cut -d ";" -f 6|xargs)
chown -R ${NEWUSERNAME}:susers ${NEWHOME}/
done
```

## 5. Set up an HTTP server and enable a web page for each user with a small introduction text for each one that is different for each user

We start by installing the required software:

```
zypper install apache2
```

Check with `firewall-cmd -list services` to see whether `http` was added. If not, run the following:

```
firewall-cmd --add-service=http --permanent
firewall-cmd --reload
```

Enable the `apache2` service:

```
systemctl enable --now apache2
```

Now, let's create the user folders for `apache2`:

```
cat users.txt| while read -r line ; do
NEWNAME=$(echo ${line}|cut -d ";" -f 5|xargs)
NEWHOME=$(echo ${line}|cut -d ";" -f 6|xargs)
mkdir -p ${NEWHOME}/public_html/
chmod 701 ${NEWHOME}
chmod 755 ${NEWHOME}/public_html/
echo "Hello, my name is ${NEWNAME} and I'm a user of this system" >
${NEWHOME}/public_html/index.html
chmod 644 ${NEWHOME}/public_html/index.html
done
```

SELinux needs a change to a boolean value in its configuration to enable `homedirs`:

```
setsebool -P httpd_enable_homedirs 1
```

Finally, we'll need to check that `homedirs` is enabled by examining `/etc/apache2/mod_userdir.conf` and finding the `UserDir disabled root` line. It is usually configured by default.

To test this, we can access the name of the machine or IP by adding a ~ and the username to the URL. In my case, it becomes `http://192.168.122.16/~sonia/`.

## 6. Allow all users in the susers group to become root without a password

This can be done in several ways, but since we have all users in the susers group, we can add that group to the users with full admin capabilities in sudo:

```
echo "%susers ALL=(ALL) NOPASSWD: ALL" >> /etc/sudoers.d/susers
```

## 7. Create SSH keys for each user and add each key to root and to the other users so that each user can SSH as the other users without a password

First, let's create the keys for each user and add the keys to root:

```
cat users.txt| while read -r line ; do
NEWHOME=$(echo ${line}|cut -d ";" -f 6|xargs)
NEWUSERNAME=$(echo ${line}|cut -d ";" -f 1|xargs)
mkdir -p ${NEWHOME}/.ssh/
chown ${NEWUSERNAME}:susers ${NEWHOME}/.ssh
chmod 700 ${NEWHOME}/.ssh
ssh-keygen -N '' -f ${NEWHOME}/.ssh/id_ed25519
cat ${NEWHOME}/.ssh/id_ed25519.pub >> /root/.ssh/authorized_keys
done
```

Now, let's copy the authorized keys for each user:

```
cat users.txt| while read -r line ; do
NEWUSERNAME=$(echo ${line}|cut -d ";" -f 1|xargs)
NEWHOME=$(echo ${line}|cut -d ";" -f 6|xargs)
cp /root/.ssh/authorized_keys  ${NEWHOME}/.ssh/
chown -R ${NEWUSERNAME}:users ${NEWHOME}/.ssh/
done
```

Validate that the user laverne can SSH as any other user:

```
geeko:~ # su - laverne
laverne@geeko:~> ssh laverne@localhost
The authenticity of host 'localhost (::1)' can't be established.
ED25519 key fingerprint is
SHA256:PQdyVY2iiHkf0G0Dr6kjRfAp1+mnyj1BZrlgjgqsMwY.
This key is not known by any other names.
```

```
Are you sure you want to continue connecting (yes/no/[fingerprint])? yes
Have a lot of fun...
laverne@geeko:~>
```

The preceding command should work for all the users because we copied `authorized_keys`, right? Well, no, as some users have their shell disabled.

## 8. Disable password access to the system with SSH

Edit `/etc/ssh/sshd_config.d/no-password-auth.conf` and replace any value of `PasswordAuthentication` with no:

```
echo "PasswordAuthentication no" > /etc/ssh/sshd_config.d/no-password-
auth.conf
```

Then, restart `sshd`:

```
systemctl restart sshd
```

## 9. Set each user with a different password using /dev/random and store the password in the second field of the users.txt file

From `/dev/random`, we can get random data, but it's binary, so it's probably not valid if we want to use it for logging in later. We can use a hash function on the data received and use that as the password.

```
MYPASS=$(dd if=/dev/urandom count=1024 2>&1|md5sum|awk '{print $1}')
```

This will be the password without being encrypted.

With `passwd`, we can define a password from its encrypted seed. So, we will be combining both, generating a random password and passing it on to the `passwd` command.

Additionally, we're told to store the generated password in the `users.txt` the generated password. To do that, we will need to edit the file.

But there's a problem. Editing a specific field in the `.txt` file might not be easy, but we can just rewrite it completely:

```
cat users.txt| while read -r line ; do
MYPASS=$(dd if=/dev/random count=12>&1|md5sum|awk '{print $1}')
NEWUSERNAME=$(echo ${line}|cut -d ";" -f 1|xargs)
```

```
NEWUID=$(echo ${line}|cut -d ";" -f 3|xargs)
NEWGID=$(echo ${line}|cut -d ";" -f 4|xargs)
NEWNAME=$(echo ${line}|cut -d ";" -f 5|xargs)
NEWHOME=$(echo ${line}|cut -d ";" -f 6|xargs)
NEWSHELL=$(echo ${line}|cut -d ";" -f 7|xargs)
echo  "${NEWUSERNAME};${MYPASS};${NEWUID};${NEWGID};${NEWNAME};${NEWHOME};
${NEWSHELL}" >> newusers.txt
echo ${MYPASS} | passwd ${NEWUSERNAME} --stdin
done
cp newusers.txt users.txt
```

In this way, we've rewritten the `users.txt` file to a new file by adding all the fields we had, and we have overwritten `users.txt` with our new copy.

The last command in the loop reads the password from the variable and feeds it to the `passwd` file, which will encrypt and store it properly, reading it from `stdin`.

## 10. If the number of letters in the user name is a multiple of 2, add that fact to each user description web page

Let's continue from the previous solution and iterate over the `users.txt` file. This time, we will generate index files for personal web pages:

```
cat users.txt| while read -r line ; do
NEWUSERNAME=$(echo ${line}|cut -d ";" -f 1|xargs)
NEWHOME=$(echo ${line}|cut -d ";" -f 6|xargs)
LETTERSINNAME=$(( $(echo ${NEWUSERNAME}|wc -m) - 1 ))
if [ "$((${LETTERSINNAME} % 2 ))" == "0" ]; then
echo "My name is multiple of 2" >> ${NEWHOME}/public_html/index.htm
fi
done
```

In this solution, we repeat the same field calculation, but we add the `wc` command to get the number of characters and remove one to adjust to the number of letters.

In the comparison, we evaluate the remainder when dividing by 2. So, when there's no remainder, it means that our number of letters is a multiple of 2.

## 11. Create a container that runs the yq Python package

When we read "Python package", we should think about pip. It is not recommended to use pip on systems directly because it might alter the system-provided Python libraries. It's better to use a virtual environment for it or, alternatively, use a container that will keep it isolated.

As described in *Chapter 17, Managing Containers with Podman*, the easiest way to build a container image is by creating a file that defines the container creation steps.

For containers, it will also be required to install the `podman` package and the required container-tools modules if you don't have them in your system.

As this file is a Python package, we require a container that already has Python in it, for example, `https://registry.suse.com/repositories/bci-python313`.

So, let's create a `Containerfile` with the following contents (available at `https://github.com/PacktPublishing/SUSE-Linux-Enterprise-Server-16-Official-Administration-Guide/blob/main/chapter-20-exercises/exercise-11/ContainerFile`):

```
FROM registry.suse.com/bci/python:3.13
WORKDIR /app MAINTAINER SLES16 Student student@suse.test
LABEL name="yq image"
maintainer="student AT suse.test"
vendor="Risu"
version="1.0.0"
release="1"
summary="yq execution container"
description="Runs yq"
ENV USER_NAME=risu
USER_UID=10001
LC_ALL=en_US.utf8
RUN pip install --upgrade pip --no-cache-dir &&
pip install --upgrade yq --no-cache-dir
USER 10001
VOLUME /data
ENTRYPOINT ["/usr/local/bin/yq"]
CMD ["-h"]
```

Then, run this:

```
podman build -t yq -f ContainerFile .
```

This command will pull the **SUSE Base Container Image** (bci) with Python so that we can just run the pip install command to install yq, which will then be assigned as the entrypoint.

For example, if we define an invalid entrypoint (because we might not know where the program is installed), we can use podman run -it --entrypoint /bin/bash <podmanid>. We can get the Podman ID by running podman images and checking the generation date for each of the images in our system.

The created container can be tested with podman run -it <podmanid>, where it will output the information about what the yq command does.

Note that yq, as expressed in the project's repository at https://github.com/kislyuk/yq, requires the jq command to be installed. We have left it out on purpose to just demonstrate container creation.

## 12. Configure password ageing for users whose user id is not a multiple of 2 to expiring

We can reuse the previous examples to loop over users to make the task easier. We can do one more loop over the list of users and use chage to apply changes:

```
cat users.txt| while read -r line ; do
NEWUSERNAME=$(echo ${line}|cut -d ";" -f 1|xargs)
NEWHOME=$(echo ${line}|cut -d ";" -f 6|xargs)
LETTERSINNAME=$(( $(echo ${NEWUSERNAME}|wc -m) - 1 ))
if [ "$((${LETTERSINNAME} % 2 ))" != "0" ]; then
chage -M 30 ${NEWUSERNAME}
fi
done
```

Here, we've reused the loop from question 10 but inverted the condition, and as we have no specific requirement about the kind of password ageing, we just define that the maximum number of days before a password change is required to be 30.

## 13. Configure daily compressed log rotation for a month of logs using date-named files

First, we need to make sure that logrotate is installed:

```
zypper install logrotate
```

Once it has been installed, create and edit the `/etc/logrotate.d/monthly` file so that it contains the following:

```
rotate 30
daily
compress
dateext
```

We need to ensure that no other periodicity is defined (monthly, weekly, and so on).

## 14. Save all the logs generated during the current day in /root/errors.log

This has a catch; some programs will log to the journal, and some of them log to `*.log` files.

The date for today can be obtained with `date +%Y-%m-%d`. This uses the year-month-day format commonly used in program logs:

```
grep "$(date '+%Y-%m-%d')" -Ri /var/log/*.log|grep -i error >  /root/
errors.log
journalctl -perr --since "$(date '+%Y-%m-%d')" >> /root/errors.log
```

In this way, we combine both outputs. We could, of course, try to sort the entries by date so that they correlate. But bear in mind that the first `grep` does a recursive search, so the filename is being prepended, making it harder to sort.

## 15. Install all available updates for system libraries

Usually, system libraries start with the `lib` substring. So, the update should be a matter of running the following:

```
zypper update $(rpm -qa | grep ^lib)
```

The `rpm -qa` command lists all packages in the system, and `grep ^lib` filters the ones starting with `lib`.

We then need to update the most important system library, `glibc`:

```
zypper update glibc
```

As these two commands will ask for confirmation, review the listed packages to be updated to make sure that no error was made.

# 16. Repair the broken rpm binary using a previously downloaded package available in the /root folder

This is tricky, yet it is useful to check your knowledge.

First, let's make sure we've the `rpm` package available:

```
zypper download rpm
cp /var/cache/zypp/packages/*/*/rpm*.rpm .
```

Verify that the file we wanted to download exists with the following command:

```
ls -l rpm*.rpm
```

Check the file to make sure we have a way to go back (also, we can use `snapper` if we have an issue):

```
rpm -qip rpm*.rpm
```

Let's get to the destructive action that will help us validate that we are actually solving the issue:

```
rm -fv /usr/bin/rpm
```

From here, it's like *look ma, no hands...* we have no RPM available to install the `rpm*.rpm` package, but we still need to install it to fix the issue. We can run `rpm` in the command line to verify that it's not working:

```
geeko:~ # rpm
bash: /usr/bin/rpm: No such file or directory
```

`rpm` packages are compressed `cpio` archives, so what we can do is as follows:

```
rpm2cpio rpm*.rpm |cpio -idmv
```

This will extract the compressed `rpm` contents without running any scripts.

Move the uncompressed `rpm` back into `/usr/bin`:

```
mv  usr/bin/rpm /usr/bin/rpm
```

Verify the `rpm` installation and operation:

```
rpm -V rpm
```

It might complain, saying that the date has changed, but additionally, it might have updated sizes and `md5sum` if the downloaded file was newer than the one we had in the system (and we deleted).

Move the system to a sane state by reinstalling the rpm package:

```
rpm -i rpm*.rpm
```

It will complain because the package has already been installed (saying that it will overwrite rpm, rpm2archive, rpm2cpio, rpmdb, rpmkeys, and more).

If the rpm version differs from the one we had in the system (which we deleted), we can just upgrade it with the following:

```
rpm -Uvh rpm*.rpm
```

And then, verify again with the following:

```
rpm -V rpm
```

Nothing should be reported as changed compared to what the database contains. If we cannot upgrade, we can then run the installation with the --force argument to tell rpm that it's OK to continue and overwrite the files.

Another approach is to scp the rpm binary from a similar system or to use rescue media.

## 17. Make all processes in execution by user miguel run with a low priority, and the processes executed by sonia run with a higher priority (+/- 5)

We have no way to make this the default, but we can run it once:

```
pgrep -u sonia|xargs renice -5
pgrep -u miguel|xargs renice +5
```

This will use pgrep for all the PIDs for users sonia and miguel and feed it via xargs to the renice process.

Alternatively, we could use something like this as an alternative to the xargs command:

```
renice +5 $(pgrep -u miguel)
```

To make it the default for all processes, pam_limits (nice in limits.conf) could do the trick.

## 18. Make the system run with the highest throughput and performance

tuned is a system daemon we can install to automatically apply some well-known parameters for our system that can later become the base for our optimizations:

```
zypper  install tuned
systemctl enable --now tuned
tuned-adm profile throughput-performance
```

## 19. Change the system network interface to use one higher IP address than it was using. Add an additional IPv6 address to the same interface

Using `nmcli`, check the current system IP address:

```
nmcli con show
```

The output is as follows:

```
geeko:~ # nmcli con show
NAME                UUID                                  TYPE      DEVICE
Wired connection 1  68e1cf09-b890-39cc-b523-92afeaa6c911  ethernet  enp1s0
lo                  ab4e6500-db51-434e-8fcb-85093902e810  loopback  lo
eth0                f382846c-8be7-4218-9dfe-610ebc04e1e9  ethernet  --
mynic               5959e8b0-c96a-4ec2-891a-602693edd222  ethernet  --
```

*Figure 20.1 – Output of nmcli con show*

With this, we can find what system interface is being used and connected. Let's say it's `enp1s0` connected on a connection named `Wired connection 1`.

Let's use `nmcli con show "Wired connection 1"|grep address` to find current addresses.

If our address is, for example, `192.168.122.16`, we'll use the following:

```
nmcli con mod "Wired connection 1" ipv4.addresses 192.168.122.17
nmcli con mod "Wired connection 1" ipv6.addresses 2001:db8:0:1::c000:207
```

Verify it with the following:

```
nmcli con show "Wired Connection"|grep address
```

## 20. Create and add /opt/mysystem/bin/ to the system path for all users

Edit the `/etc/profile.d/mysystempath.sh` file by adding the following:

```
export PATH=${PATH}:/opt/mysystem/bin
```

To validate, create the folder with this:

```
mkdir -p /opt/mysystem/bin
```

Logging in again with the user should show the new path when executing the following:

```
echo ${PATH}
```

## 21. Create a firewall zone, assign it to an interface, and make it the default zone

This is tricky. However, we've explained how to query zones in the book and how to change the default zone, and even shown screenshots of using Cockpit to manage the firewall, so now, as an experienced user, it shouldn't be hard.

The first thing to do when we don't know how to do something is check the manual page:

```
man firewall-cmd
```

It doesn't show a lot of interesting information, but, toward the end of the man pages, there's a section called *SEE ALSO*, where we can find `firewalld.zones(5)`, which means that we need to go to *Section 5* of the manual for `firewalld.zones`.

We don't usually specify the section because there might not be duplicates, so we can just run the following:

```
man firewalld.zones
```

It instructs us to check the default zones in `/usr/lib/firewalld/zones` and `/etc/firewalld/zones`. So, let's go ahead:

```
cp /usr/lib/firewalld/zones/public.xml /etc/firewalld/zones/dazone.xml
```

Now, let's edit the new copied file, `/etc/firewalld/zones/dazone.xml`, change the name from `Public` to `dazone`, and then reload the firewall:

```
firewall-cmd --reload
```

Let's validate that the new zone is there:

```
firewall-cmd --get-zones
```

Let's make it the default zone:

```
firewall-cmd --set-default-zone=dazone
```

Add the default interface (`enp1s0`) in our case:

```
firewall-cmd --add-interface=ens3 --zone=dazone
```

It will fail, as expected, as `enp1s0` is already assigned to a zone (`public`). So, let's run the following:

```
firewall-cmd --remove-interface=ens3 --zone=public
firewall-cmd --add-interface=ens3 --zone=dazone
```

As you can see, even without prior knowledge about creating new zones, we've been able to use our system knowledge about finding information to successfully accomplish this goal.

## 22. Add a repository hosted at https://myserver.com/repo/ with a GPG key at https://myserver.com/mygpg.key to the system

If we don't remember the syntax for adding a repository, we can use one of the examples available on the system, so go to `/etc/zypp/repos.d/myserver.repo`, list the available files, and pick one that we'll be using to create our `myserver.repo` file with these contents:

```
[myserver]
name=My server repository
baseurl=https://myserver.com/repo/
enabled=1
gpgcheck=1
gpgkey=https://myserver.com/mygpg.key
```

We're done with the steps!

We hope you have enjoyed this book and gained enough knowledge about SLES 16 to get started and obtain the SUSE Certified Administrator certification. As we say at SUSE, have a lot of fun!

# 21

# Unlock Your Exclusive Benefits

Your copy of this book includes the following exclusive benefits:

- Next-gen Packt Reader
- DRM-free PDF/ePub downloads

Follow the guide below to unlock them. The process takes only a few minutes and needs to be completed once.

## Unlock this Book's Free Benefits in 3 Easy Steps

### Step 1

Keep your purchase invoice ready for *Step 3*. If you have a physical copy, scan it using your phone and save it as a PDF, JPG, or PNG.

For more help on finding your invoice, visit `https://www.packtpub.com/unlock-benefits/help`.

> **Note:** If you bought this book directly from Packt, no invoice is required. After *Step 2*, you can access your exclusive content right away.

**Step 2**

Scan the QR code or go to `packtpub.com/unlock`.

On the page that opens (similar to *Figure 21.1* on desktop), search for this book by name and select the correct edition.

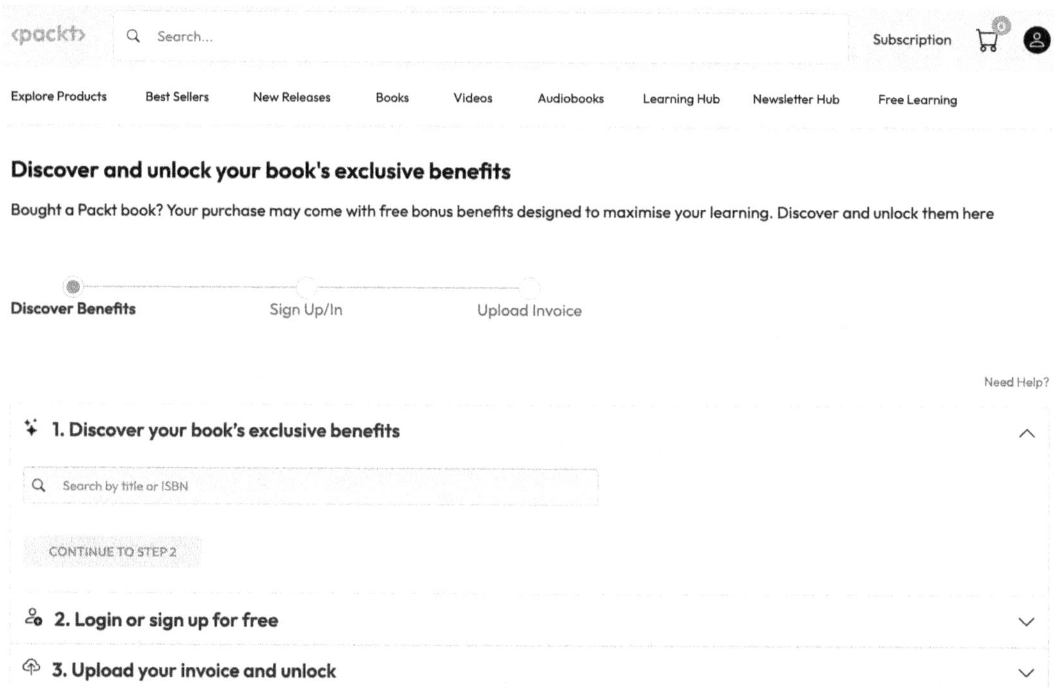


*Figure 21.1 – Packt unlock landing page on desktop*

## Step 3

After selecting your book, sign in to your Packt account or create one for free. Then upload your invoice (PDF, PNG, or JPG, up to 10 MB). Follow the on-screen instructions to finish the process.

### Need help?

If you get stuck and need help, visit `https://www.packtpub.com/unlock-benefits/help` for a detailed FAQ on how to find your invoices and more. This QR code will take you to the help page.

**Note:** If you are still facing issues, reach out to `customercare@packt.com`.

# Other Books You May Enjoy

If you enjoyed this book, you may be interested in these other books by Packt:

**Red Hat Enterprise Linux 9 Administration**

Pablo Iranzo Gómez, Pedro Ibañez Requena, Miguel Pérez Colino, Scott McCarty

ISBN: 978-1-80324-754-0

- Become well versed with the fundamentals of RHEL9—from system deployment to user management
- Secure a system by using SELinux policies and configuring firewall rules
- Understand LVM to manage volumes and maintain VDO deduplication
- Manage a system remotely using SSH and public key authentication
- Get the hang of the boot process and kernel tunable to adjust your systems
- Automate simple tasks using scripts or Ansible Playbooks

**Ansible for Real-Life Automation**

Gineesh Madapparambath

ISBN: 978-1-80323-862-3

- Explore real-life IT automation use cases and employ Ansible for automation
- Develop playbooks with best practices for production environments
- Approach different automation use cases with the most suitable methods
- Use Ansible for infrastructure management and automate VMWare, AWS, and GCP
- Integrate Ansible with Terraform, Jenkins, OpenShift, and Kubernetes
- Manage container platforms such as Kubernetes and OpenShift with Ansible
- Get to know the Red Hat Ansible Automation Platform and its capabilities

## Packt is searching for authors like you

If you're interested in becoming an author for Packt, please visit `authors.packt.com` and apply today. We have worked with thousands of developers and tech professionals, just like you, to help them share their insight with the global tech community. You can make a general application, apply for a specific hot topic that we are recruiting an author for, or submit your own idea.

## Share your thoughts

Now you've finished *SUSE Linux Enterprise Server 16 Official Administration Guide*, we'd love to hear your thoughts! Scan the QR code below to go straight to the Amazon review page for this book and share your feedback or leave a review on the site that you purchased it from.

`https://packt.link/r/1806021595`

Your review is important to us and the tech community and will help us make sure we're delivering excellent quality content.

# Index


## A

absolute path 63
Access Control Lists (ACLs) 239
Access Vector Cache (AVC) 317
Accounts page, Cockpit 273-276
Agama installer 20
agentic AI 336-338
AMD 64 / Intel 64 8
Ansible 439, 440
Apache HTTPD service 209
AppArmor 313
Application Container Images 456
Applications page, Cockpit 280, 281
apropos command 97
assignments
  reviewing 141
autocompletion 69
autodetection 367
awk 81, 82

## B

base repos 207
Bash 439
Bash autocomplete 69, 70
Basic Input Output System (BIOS) 356, 378, 419, 420
basic shell scripts
  creating 91, 92
BIOS/UEFI configuration 10
Boolean 326
boot logs 263
boot process 419-422
boot sequence
  managing, with systemd 428-433
boot targets
  managing 111-113
BTRFS 266, 402
  basics, reviewing 403
  filesystem, creating 403-406
  mounting 406, 407
  reference link 403
  snapshots 407, 408
  status, reviewing 403-407

## C

Carrier-Grade Network Address Translation (CGNAT) 172
cgroups 109, 451
ChatGPT 337
checksums 10
chrony NTP client 117-120
chrony NTP server 120, 121
Classless Inter-Domain Routing (CIDR) notation 175
Claude 337

**clients 167**

**cloud**

SLES, running on 40-48

**cloud-init software 40**

**Cockpit 109, 249, 250, 292**

accessing 253, 254

Accounts page 273-276

administrative tasks, enabling 255-258

Applications page 280, 281

enabling 251, 252

hardware information and logs 262-264

installing 250

logging in 255-258

Metrics and history page 259-262

Networking section 267, 268

Overview page 259

pattern package 250

Repositories page 282

SELinux page 282, 283

Services page 276-278

Software updates page 283, 284

Storage section 265, 266

Subscriptions page 285

Terminal 286

Timers section 279

**command line 67**

**command prompt 54, 56**

**configuration files 168**

**console 54**

**Containerfile 462**

**container images 454**

Application Container Images 456

Redistributable Base Container Images 456

Redistributable Development Container Images 456

SLE Base Container Images 456

**container registries 454**

**containers 449-451**

deleting 467-470

running container, connecting 465, 466

**copy-on-write (CoW) 402, 408**

**coreutil package 359**

**cp command 84**

**CPU 124, 125**

# D

**daemons 60, 105**

**Datagram Congestion Control Protocol (DCCP) 293**

**debug repo 207**

**DeepSeek 337**

**device mapper 387**

**df tool 122**

**diff command 99**

**directories 63, 64, 82**

/ 72, 74

absolute path 63

/bin 72

/boot 72, 74

/dev 72

/etc 72, 74

/home 72, 74

/media 72

/mnt 72

/opt 72

/proc 72

relative path 63

/root 73, 74

/run 73, 74

shortcuts 64

/srv 73
/sys 73
/tmp 73
/usr 74
/usr/bin 73
/usr/etc 73
/usr/lib 73
/usr/local 73
/usr/sbin 73
/var 73, 74

**directory-related commands**
mkdir 84
mkdir -p 84
rm 84
rmdir 84
rm -r 84

**directory tree 63**

**discretionary access control (DAC) 314**

**Disk Operating System (DOS) 357**

**disks 59, 121**
history 356-358
partitioning 358-364

**disk space 122, 123**

**Docker 451**

**Docker CLI 452**

**Dockerfile 451, 462**

**docker.io 455**

**Docker zone 269**

**Domain Name Service (DNS) 167**
configuring 179-182

**Dynamic Host Configuration Protocol (DHCP) 302**

# E

**echo command 68**

**efibootmgr command 423**

**EFI System Partition (ESP) 420**

**Elixir 199, 201**
installing 202
searching 199

**Emacs 91**

**Emacs Doctor 91**

**enterprise resource planning (ERP) 473**

**env command 69**

**environment variables 58, 68**
EDITOR 68
HOME 68
HOSTNAME 68
LANG 68
PATH 68
PS1 68
PWD 69
SHELL 69
USER 69

**Erlang 201**

**exit code 96**

**eXtended File System (XFS) 365**

**extended partition 357**

**Extended Service Set Identification (ESSID) 167**

**Extensible Firmware Interface (EFI) 358**

**extensions 197**

# F


**fdisk command 380**

**File Allocation Table (FAT) 357**

**file permissions 64-67**

checking 152

modifying 154-159

reviewing 152, 153

**file-related commands**

cp 86

cp -r 86

mv 87

rm 86

touch 86

**files 63**

copying 84

moving 85

transferring, with OpenSSH secure file copy (scp) 236, 237

transferring, with rsync 239-242

transferring, with sftp 238, 239

**filesystem hierarchy 71, 72**

**Filesystem Hierarchy Standard (FHS) 71**

**filesystems 357, 365**

formatting 366-368

mounting 366-368

**filesystem snapshots 266**

**File Transfer Protocol (FTP) 236**

**filtering rules 269**

**firewall 183, 252**

configuring 183-185

**firewalld 290**

configuring 292

default zones, reviewing 293-296

enabling, in system 293-296

installing 291

ports 293

ports, enabling 302

ports, managing 302-310

ports, reviewing 296-302

service definitions, using 310-312

services 293

services, enabling 302

services, managing 302-310

services, reviewing 296-302

zones 292

zones, reviewing 296-302

**firewall management 268-270**

**firewall zones 269**

**for loop 93**

syntax 93

**Fourth Extended Filesystem (EXT4) 365**

**free command 121**

**fstab**

default mounts and options, setting 368-370

**Full Disk Encryption (FDE) 33**


# G


**gateway 167**

**Gemini 337**

**Globally Unique Identifier (GUID) 358**

**Global Positioning System (GPS) 116**

**globbing 84**

**GNOME 233**

**Gnu Privacy Guard (GPG) 205**

**Google Cloud 41**

**gpgtar 98**

**grep command 78-82**

**group ID (GID) 60**

groups 59-62
managing 141
primary group 62
private group 62
supplementary group 62
GRUB 2 422
GRUB bootloader 420-426
GUID Partition Table (GPT) 420
gunzip 90
gzip tool 89

## H

hard links 87
creating 87
Hardware Abstraction Layer (HAL) 168
hardware information and logs, Cockpit 262-264
High Availability extension 197
history command 70
home directory 56, 68
hostname
configuring 179-182

## I

if statement 94, 95
syntax 94
images
deleting 467-470
Impression tool 12
InfiniBand 166
info pages 99, 100
INI files 108
initramfs 421
initrd 421, 427
installed system
registering 195-198
Integrated Drive Electronics (IDE) 358
International Business Machines (IBM) 356
Internet Control Message Protocol (ICMP) 186
Internet Message Access Protocol (IMAP) 243
Internet Protocol (IP) 171
Internet SCSI (iSCSI) 370
Internet Service Providers (ISPs) 172
interpreter 67
I/O redirection
in command line 75-78
IP address 166
ip command 126
iptables 290
IPv4 171
IPv6 167, 171
iSCSI 32

## J

journalctl 129, 130
journald logs 263

## K

kernel 104
key-based authentication
with SSH 228-233
key pair 228
keys 228
kilobytes (KB) 65, 356
Kubernetes 450

## L


labels 378

Large Language Models (LLMs)
  working 336

latest tag 457

LDAP server 181

LEAP 13

leap second
  reference link 120

lease time 174

libeconf 71

link-related commands
  ln 88
  ln -s 88

links 66, 87
  hard links 87
  symbolic links 87

Linux, Apache, MariaDB, Perl (LAMP) stack 209

Linux Containers (LXC) 451

Linux Foundation 71

Linux Security Modules (LSM) 314

ln command 87

load average 125

Local Area Network (LAN) 166

logical extents 391

logical partitions 357

Logical Unit Number (LUN) 376

logical volume management 402

Logical Volume Manager (LVM) 31, 373, 376-378
  commands, reviewing 398, 399

logical volumes (LVs) 376
  creating 385, 386
  extending 387-393
  removing 393-398

login process 54, 55

logrotate package 132

log rotation 131-133

logs 129

losetup utility 359

lvcreate command 399

lvdisplay command 399

lvextend command 399

lvremove command 399

lvs command 399


## M


MAC address 167

macOS 223

man command 97

mandatory access control (MAC) 314

manual pages 96-99

Master Boot Record (MBR) 356, 421, 422

Maximum Transmission Unit (MTU) 271

mcphost
  configuring 339-342
  installing 338
  using 343-351

megabytes (MB) 356

memory 121, 122

Metrics and history page, Cockpit 259-262

mkdir command 82

Model Context Protocol (MCP) 338
  implementation 338

modules 198
monitoring tools 126-128
multicast DNS (MDNS) service 302
multi-user system 57
Multi Writer tool 12
mv command 85

## N

namespace isolation 451
Nano 91
National Security Agency (NSA) 314
NetBIOS Extended User Interface (NetBEUI) 166
netfilter 183
netmask 167
Network Address Translation (NAT) 172
Network Basic Input/Output System (NetBIOS) 166
network configuration
  in SLES 166, 167
network connectivity
  testing 186
Network File System (NFS)
  network filesystems, using with 371, 372
Networking section, Cockpit 267, 268
  firewall management 268-270
  network interface management 271, 272
Network Interface Card (NIC) 167
network interface management 271
network interfaces 269
  configuring, with IPv4 and IPv6 170, 171
  configuring, with nmcli 175-177
  configuring, with nmtui 172-174
  configuring, with text files 178, 179
NetworkManager 168-170
network ports 269
Network Time Protocol (NTP) 116
neural networks 336
nftables 183, 290
nmcli 175
  network interfaces, configuring with 175-177
nmtui 172
  network interfaces, configuring with 172-174
Non-Volatile Random-Access Memory (NVRAM) 420

## O

Ollama 337
OOM-Killer 122
Open Build Service
  URL 365
OpenQA
  URL 365
OpenSSH 223
  options 223, 224
  URL 222
OpenSSH client 225, 226
openssh-clients package 222
OpenSSH secure file copy (scp)
  files, transferring 236, 237
openssh-server package 222
openSUSE 195
openSUSE Leap 10, 195

Open Systems Interconnection (OSI) layer definition
  reference link 166
operating system kernel 421
Operating System (OS) 356, 474

## P

package 191, 208
Package Hub 197, 198
package management 190
package managers 191
partitioning 356
partitions
  history 356-358
Partition Table (GPT) 358
partners, public cloud marketplaces
  URL 192
password hashes 141
password policies
  adjusting 141-147
patch 208
pattern recognition 336
patterns 33, 208
  installing 208-210
Performance Co-Pilot 126, 260
permissions 59
personal computers (PCs) 356
physical extents 391
physical volumes (PVs) 376
  combining, into volume groups (VGs) 384
  creating 378-383
  moving 378-383
  removing 378-398
pipe operator 75
pipes 78
playbooks 440
Podman 449, 451
  installing 452-454
Podman CLI 452
policy
  file contexts, restoring to default 324-326
  tweaking, with message 321-323
Portable Operating System Interface (POSIX)
  reference link 59
pre-boot network execution (PXE) 420
Pretty Good Privacy (PGP) 205
previous commands
  restoring 70, 71
primary group 62
primary partitions 356, 357
private group 62
private key 228
process 59
process identifier (PID) 428
product 208
Program identifier (PID) 130
program temporary fixes (PTFs) 208
ps command 124
public key 228
public zone 269
pvcreate command 398
pvdisplay command 398
pvmove command 398
pvremove command 398
pvs command 398

## R


**RAM disk** 104

**recovery mode** 430

**redirect and add operator** 75

**redirect operator** 75

**redirect STDERR operator** 76

**redirect STDOUT operator** 76

**redirect to STDERR operator** 76

**redirect to STDOUT operator** 76

**Redistributable Base Container Images** 456

**Redistributable Development Container Images** 456

**registries**
- using 460-464
- working with 455-460

**regular expressions** 78-82

**regular users** 60

**relative path** 63

**Remote Direct Memory Access (RDMA)** 166

**remote systems**
- accessing, with SSH 226, 227

**remote terminals**
- with tmux 245-247

**repositories** 192, 199
- clean-up options, for Zypper 216
- managing, with Zypper 204-207
- software installation issues, resolving ways 199
- uninstalling 214, 215

**Repositories page, Cockpit** 282

**rescue target** 432

**reverse redirect operator** 75

**rm command** 83

**rmdir command** 82, 83

**role** 440

**roll back** 266

**root account** 55, 56

**root password**
- updating, to modify boot process 433-437

**rpm command** 216

**RPM Package Manager** 216, 217

**rsync**
- files, transferring 239-242

**runlevels** 112
- graphical 112
- halt mode 112
- multi-user mode 112
- networked multi-user 112
- reboot 112
- single-user mode 112


## S


**Salt** 439

**SAP** 474
- URL 474

**SAP©** 474

**SAP S/4HANA** 474

**Saptune** 480
- reference link 480

**scp command** 236

**Secure Boot** 420

**Secure Shell Host (SSH)** 222, 223, 302
- key-based authentication 228-233
- remote systems, accessing 226, 227

**Security-Enhanced Linux (SELinux) 154, 313**
- reviewing, for files and processes 317, 318
- troubleshooting 328-331
- usage, in enforcing and permissive modes 314-317

**SELinux Boolean settings**
- used, for enabling services 326, 327

**SELinux page, Cockpit 282, 283**

**Serial Advanced Technology Attachment (SATA) 370**

**servers 167**

**service definitions**
- creating, for firewalld 310
- using, for firewalld 310, 311

**services 269**
- managing 110, 111

**Services page, Cockpit 276-278**

**sftp**
- files, transferring 238, 239

**sha256 checksums 10**

**shared data blocks 408**

**shared libraries 190**

**shell 67**

**shell script 91, 439**

**shim loader 423**

**signatures**
- managing, with Zypper 204-206

**Simple Mail Transfer Protocol (SMTP) 243**

**SLE Base Container Images 456**

**SLES 16 Agama installer**
- authentication 35-39
- hostname 22
- language and keyboard shortcut access 21
- localization 25
- network 27-29
- Overview page 21
- registration 23, 24
- software 33, 34
- storage 30-33

**SLES 16 installation 10**
- physical server installation 10-12
- virtual server installation 13-17

**SLES 16 ISO image 9**

**SLES Downloads page**
- URL 193

**SLES for SAP Applications 474, 475, 480**
- long-term support 476
- reference link 475
- Workload Memory Protection 476

**SLES installation**
- best practices 49, 50
- booting, from USB thumb drive 12, 13
- running 18, 19
- type 19, 20

**SLES software**
- obtaining 4-9

**SLES system**
- converting, to SLES for SAP Applications 480

**Small Computer System Interface (SCSI) 358**

**Small Office-Home Office (SOHO) network 174**

**smart devices 172**

**Snapper 402, 409**
- functions 415, 416
- used, for showing file changes 411-413
- using 409, 410
- using, to roll back to previous configuration status 414

**snapshots** 378

**SOCKS proxy** 243

**software**
  uninstalling 214, 215

**Software updates page, Cockpit** 283, 284

**source repo** 207

**sparse file** 360

**special permissions**
  set-GID, applying 161, 162
  set-UID, applying 160, 161
  sticky bit, using 162, 163
  using 160

**SSH agent** 233-235

**SSH keys** 249

**SSH redirections** 242-244

**SSH tunnels** 242-244

**static linking** 190

**STDERR (standard error)** 75

**STDIN (standard input)** 75

**STDOUT (standard output)** 75

**sticky bit** 66, 153
  using 162, 163

**Storage section, Cockpit** 265, 266

**Stream Control Transmission Protocol (SCTP)** 293

**subscription** 195

**Subscriptions page, Cockpit** 285

**substitute user** 57

**subvolumes** 266, 369

**su command**
  users, changing 57, 58

**sudo** 147
  configuring, for administrative tasks 147
  custom configuration 149
  default configuration 147-149
  used, for running admin commands 149, 150

**sudoers**
  configuring 151, 152

**superuser** 60

**supplementary group** 62

**SUSE Certified Administrator (SCA) certifications** 222

**SUSE Certified Administrator (SCA) exam** 99, 324

**SUSE Certified Engineer (SCE) exam** 324

**SUSEConnect** 196

**SUSE Customer Center (SCC)** 23, 189, 285
  subscriptions 192-195
  URL 192

**SUSE Linux Enterprise Live Patching** 477

**SUSE Linux Enterprise Server (SLES)** 3, 53, 165, 223, 249, 365, 439
  network configuration 166, 167
  running, on cloud 40-48

**SUSE Linux Micro** 450

**SUSE Multi-Linux Manager** 128, 439, 475

**SUSE Package Hub** 24, 25

**SUSE Shop**
  URL 192

**SUSE subscription** 4
  obtaining 5-9

**symbolic links** 87, 441

**sysstat package** 126

**system administrator (sysadmin)** 91

**systemd 71, 104-106, 419**
boot sequence, managing 428-433
unit file structure 107-109
URL 104
**system documentation 96**
**system documentation, resources**
info pages 99, 100
man pages 96-99
**systemd timers 114, 115**
**systemd units 277**
**system roles 439, 440**
installing 440-442
using 442-447
**system services 104**
**system users 60**

## T

**tar command 89, 90**
**targeted policy 318-321**
**terminal 54**
**Terminal, Cockpit 286**
**text editor 91**
**text files**
network interfaces, configuring with 178, 179
**timers 114**
**Timers section, Cockpit 279**
**time synchronization 116**
**tmux 245**
remote terminals 245-247
**token 337**
**transition 319**
**Transmission Control Protocol/Internet Protocol (TCP/IP) 166**
**Transmission Control Protocol (TCP) 269, 293**
**Trento 478**
architecture 479
reference link 479
**Trento Agent 478**
**Trento Server 478**
**truncate tool 359**

## U

**UAPI Group 71**
**UNetbootin tool 12**
**Unified Extensible Firmware Interface (UEFI) 378, 419, 420, 423**
**Uniform Resource Identifier (URI) 282**
**universally unique identifiers (UUIDs) 370**
**Universal Serial Bus (USB) 370**
**Universal Time Clock (UTC) 120**
**USB thumb drive**
SLES installation, booting from 12, 13
**user accounts 136**
creating 136-138
deleting 139, 140
modifying 138
**User Datagram Protocol (UDP) 116, 269, 293**
**user ID (UID) 60**
**users 60, 61**
changing, with su command 57, 58
regular users 60
superuser 60
system users 60

## V


**vgcreate command** 399

**vgdisplay command** 399

**vgextend command** 399

**vgreduce command** 399

**vgremove command** 399

**vgs command** 399

**Vi** 91

**Vim** 91

**virtual console** 54

**virtual hard drive (VHD)** 359

**Virtual Local Area Network (VLAN)** 167

**Virtual Private Network (VPN)** 167

**virtual server** 13

**volume groups (VGs)** 376
- new disks, adding to 387-393
- physical volumes (PVs), combining into 384
- removing 393-398


## W


**whoami command** 57, 60

**Wicked** 168

**working directory** 63

**Workload Memory Protection** 476


## Y


**Yet Another Markup Language (YAML)**
- reference link 444

**Yet another Setup Tool (YaST)** 249


## Z


**zones** 269

**Zypper** 189, 216, 409
- repositories, managing 204-207
- repository clean-up options 216
- repository-related options 207
- signatures, managing 204-206
- software installation 199-202
- software maintenance options 213
- software, updating 203-212

www.ingramcontent.com/pod-product-compliance
Lightning Source LLC
LaVergne TN
LVHW060013210926
848481LV00013B/3701
*9781806021598*